# WINDOWS 2000
# ADMINISTRATION
# IN A NUTSHELL

*A Desktop Quick Reference*

# WINDOWS 2000
# ADMINISTRATION
## IN A NUTSHELL

*A Desktop Quick Reference*

*Mitch Tulloch*

**O'REILLY**®

*Beijing • Cambridge • Farnham • Köln • Paris • Sebastopol • Taipei • Tokyo*

## Windows 2000 Administration in a Nutshell
by Mitch Tulloch

Copyright © 2001 O'Reilly & Associates, Inc. All rights reserved.
Printed in the United States of America.

Published by O'Reilly & Associates, Inc., 1005 Gravenstein Highway North,
Sebastopol, CA 95472.

**Editor:** Robert Denn

**Production Editor:** Jeffrey Holcomb

**Cover Designer:** Ellie Volckhausen

**Printing History:**

February 2001:     First Edition.

ISBN: 1-56592-713-3
[M]                                                                    [5/03]

# Table of Contents

*Preface* ................................................................................................ *vii*

## Part I: The Lay of the Land

*Chapter 1—Overview* ...................................................................... *3*
  Windows 2000 Flavors ............................................................... 3
  Windows 2000 Kudos .................................................................. 7
  Windows 2000 Gripes ................................................................ 9

*Chapter 2—Quick Start* ................................................................ *17*
  New Tools, Old Tasks .............................................................. 17
  Potpourri ..................................................................................... 22

## Part II: Alphabetical Reference

*Chapter 3—Concepts* ..................................................................... *39*
  Alphabetical List of Concepts ............................................... 40

*Chapter 4—Tasks* ........................................................................... *262*
  Alphabetical List of Tasks .................................................... 264

*Chapter 5—Consoles* ........................................................... *492*

    The Microsoft Management Console ............................... 492

    Alphabetical List of Consoles ........................................ 516

*Chapter 6—Utilities* ............................................................ *572*

    Alphabetical Reference of Utilities ............................... 572

*Chapter 7—Commands* ...................................................... *622*

    Alphabetical List of Commands ..................................... 623

    General Commands ......................................................... 623

    Net Commands ................................................................ 644

    Netshell Commands ....................................................... 679

    TCP/IP Commands .......................................................... 707

    Miscellaneous Utilities .................................................... 744

*Index* .................................................................................. *751*

# *Preface*

For system administrators already familiar with Windows NT, becoming familiar with Windows 2000 can be an awkward process: while the GUI looks very much the same, there are subtle differences, which can easily trip you up, and a whole new set of administrative tools, some of which are obvious at first glance and some of which are bizarre.

This book is designed to be a desktop reference guide that can help advanced administrators move quickly from Windows NT to Windows 2000. It is not a series of tutorials for beginners but a tool to help experienced administrators find information quickly on concepts, tasks, tools, utilities, and commands they need to know to get the job done.

The focus here is on administration of Windows 2000–based networks. Therefore, Windows 2000 Server is emphasized, while coverage of Windows 2000 Professional is limited to how it differs from Server and how it can be installed and managed.

You won't find every detail of Windows 2000 covered here—consider, for example, that the Windows 2000 Server Resource Kit (which is the real Windows 2000 Server manual, as opposed to what's found in online Help) is almost 8,000 pages long! So I've selected those topics, tasks, and tools most likely to be of help to administrators in their day-to-day system and network operations, but even then this book has ballooned to one Very Big Nut indeed!

## *Organization of the Book*

This book is divided into two parts, as follows:

### Part I, *The Lay of the Land*

This part contains two chapters that give you the big picture behind Windows 2000 administration, and are especially useful for administrators familiar with Windows NT. The two chapters here are as follows.

Chapter 1, *Overview*, outlines the new features incorporated into the four flavors of Windows 2000 (Professional, Server, Advanced Server, and Datacenter Server) and then lists my personal kudos and gripes over what I like and don't like about the new operating system.

Chapter 2, *Quick Start*, begins by looking at how administrative tools, utilities, and features differ between Windows NT and Windows 2000 and finishes with a potpourri of suggestions and tips to help administrators make the transition to administering Windows 2000.

## Part II, *Alphabetical Reference*

This part contains the real meat of the book, consisting of five chapters with topics listed in alphabetical order for easy lookup. Cross-references are included in each article to articles in different chapters in Part II: for example, the article *disks* in Chapter 3 refers you to the similarly titled article in Chapter 4, where specific procedures for performing administrative tasks related to disks are described. The five chapters here are as follows:

Chapter 3, *Concepts*, provides background information on key aspects of Windows 2000 administration, as well as some shorter definitions that are cross-referenced to the longer articles in the chapter.

Chapter 4, *Tasks*, lists various administrative tasks you can perform on Windows 2000. The tasks are organized first by concept and then by action. For example, if you want to learn how to publish a resource in Active Directory, you would look up the article *Active Directory* and then find the subheading "Publish a Resource in Active Directory."

Chapter 5, *Consoles*, starts with a brief tutorial on how to create your own custom administrative tools (MMC consoles) and then moves on to cover the most important Windows 2000 administrative tools and snap-ins for the MMC.

Chapter 6, *Utilities*, deals with other GUI tools and user-interface elements, such as the Control Panel utilities, various tools in the Accessories program group, and certain desktop icons that administrators may need to use or at least should be familiar with to get the most out of Windows 2000.

Chapter 7, *Commands*, lists the various commands that can be used for command-line administration of different aspects of Windows 2000.

## *Conventions Used in This Book*

The following typographical conventions are used in this book:

Constant width
> Indicates command-line examples, code examples, and commands.

*Italic*
> Introduces new terms and indicates URLs, directories, UNC and absolute paths, domain names, file extensions, filenames, and cross-references to other topics in the book.

*Constant width italic*

Indicates variables or user-defined elements such as *username*, which would be replaced by the user's logon name in a command example.

**Constant width bold**

Indicates user input, or text that the user should type, in a commmand example.

*(parentheses)*

Indicates the chapter in which a cross-reference can be found; for example, *disks(4)* refers to the *disks* article in Chapter 4.

<brackets>

Indicates variables or user-defined elements such as <username>, which would be replaced by the user's logon name in a pathname, for example.

## Gestalt Menus

In various places (particularly in Chapter 4), I use what I call "gestalt menus" to outline the step-by-step procedures needed to perform a specific task. These are quite easy to understand if you are sitting in front of a Windows 2000 computer while reading them (which is the logical place for you to be, since a quick desktop reference like this book should be sitting on your desk in plain view all the time!)

Here's a simple example of a gestalt menu for sharing a printer:

Start → Settings → Printers → right-click on a printer → Properties → Sharing → Shared As → specify share name

You can see how easy it is to understand these menus when you are sitting at the computer. At each step in the menu, you either click a button, open a property sheet, select a tab, type a value, or perform some other action whose nature is obvious if you are working with the product.

## Request for Comments

I've tried to make this book as accurate and helpful as possible, but if you find any errors or spot anything that is in need of improvement, don't hesitate to send your comments to the publisher:

O'Reilly & Associates, Inc.
1005 Gravenstein Highway North
Sebastopol, CA 95472
(800) 998-9938 (in the United States or Canada)
(707) 829-0515 (international/local)
(707) 829-0104 (fax)

There is a web page for this book, which lists errata, examples, or any additional information. You can access this page at:

*http://www.oreilly.com/catalog/win2000nut/*

To comment or ask technical questions about this book, send email to:

*bookquestions@oreilly.com*

You can also contact me (the author) directly at:

*info@mtit.com*

For more information about books, conferences, software, Resource Centers, and the O'Reilly Network, see the O'Reilly web site at:

*http://www.oreilly.com*

## Acknowledgments

Thanks to Ingrid, my wife, for very patiently putting up with her stressed-out husband during the writing of this book. Once this is in print, I think we need a vacation (or several!)

I would like to acknowledge Eric Pearce, the author of *Windows NT in a Nutshell*, as the spiritual predecessor of my book; I hope I did my job as well as he did. Thanks also to Robert Denn, my editor at O'Reilly. He has been more than helpful on this project, just as he was on my last book with O'Reilly & Associates, *Microsoft Exchange Server in a Nutshell*. Thanks, Robert, for your assistance in finally getting this big baby into print.

I'd also like to thank the following people who took time out from their busy schedules to review the manuscript for this book: Tony Ansley, Ezra Berkenwald, and Jon Forrest.

Thanks to my agent, David Rogelberg, of StudioB Productions (*http://www.studiob.com*). He deserves my gratitude for getting me connected with a great publishing house like O'Reilly & Associates in the first place.

Thanks to MTS Communications, Inc. (*http://www.mts.mb.ca*) for graciously providing me with Internet services, including hosting my business web site, MTIT Enterprises (*http://www.mtit.com*).

Finally, thanks to the readers of my columns on Swynk (*http://www.swynk.com*), a popular site for administrators who work with Microsoft BackOffice products. I currently manage both the Windows NT/2000 and Exchange Server sections on Swynk, and you can find my columns there at *http://www.swynk.com/mitch/*.

—Mitch Tulloch, MCT, MCSE
Winnipeg, Canada

# PART I

# *The Lay of the Land*

# CHAPTER 1

# *Overview*

This chapter begins with a quick overview of the features of the Windows 2000 operating system in each of its four flavors: Professional, Server, Advanced Server, and Datacenter Server. It finishes with my personal offerings of kudos and gripes over how Windows 2000 has been implemented.

## *Windows 2000 Flavors*

Quarks come in six flavors (Up, Down, Strange, Charmed, Top, and Bottom), but so far, Windows 2000 only comes in four. Let's look at the features of these different flavors, starting with the lightweight Professional (which corresponds to the Up and has a mass of only .005 GeV/c2) and moving upwards to the heavyweight Datacenter Server (not yet detected, but estimated to have a mass comparable to the Top quark, or about 180 GeV/c2).

## *Windows 2000 Professional*

Designed to replace the earlier Windows NT Workstation 4.0 and Windows 95/98 platforms on corporate desktop computers, Windows 2000 Professional is pretty much a blend of the best features of these two earlier operating systems. Professional takes the security and stability of Windows NT and combines it with the Advanced Configuration and Power Interface (ACPI) power management and Plug and Play hardware support of Windows 95/98 to provide administrators with real reasons for tossing out their last remaining souped-up 486s and buying all new Pentium IIIs. You can use the following features to justify the purchase to your boss:

*Enhanced installation methods*
> In addition to standard manual installations using local media or downloads from a network distribution server, Windows 2000 includes the Setup Manager Wizard (on the Windows 2000 Server compact disc in the \*Support*\ *Tools*\*Deploy.cab* folder) to simplify creating and configuring answer files for

unattended installation. Windows 2000 also includes the System Preparation Tool (also in the *\Support\Tools\Deploy.cab* folder), which can prepare a configured Windows 2000 Professional system for cloning using third-party disk-duplication software. A third option—if your desktop systems support the NetPC specification or a network adapter with a Pre-Boot Execution Environment (PXE) boot ROM and supporting BIOS—is to perform automated remote installations of Professional clients using the Remote Installation Services (RIS) running on Windows 2000 Server.

*Improved hardware support*

The Plug and Play capability of Windows 2000 makes it easier to install devices and update drivers than in NT. In addition, Windows 2000 supports the ACPI standard. If you are planning a new deployment, you should ensure that your systems support ACPI in order to get the full benefit of Plug and Play and power management in Windows 2000.

*Better mobile access support*

For laptop users there are many benefits to upgrading to Professional, if your laptop hardware supports it. These include:

— Support for offline folders to allow users to transparently access resources when disconnected from the network

— Support for IPSec and virtual private network (VPN) dial-up connections, using PPTP or L2TP as a tunneling protocol, which lets remote users dial in and securely access the corporate network as if they are directly connected

— Better power management with ACPI to get more out of your laptop's batteries

*Improved filesystem support*

The new version of NT File System (NTFS) on Windows 2000 supports advanced features, such as disk quotas, data encryption, and getting past the old 24-drive limit for mapped network drives by creating volume mount points.

*Enhanced printing support*

Like NT, Windows 2000 can print to local or networked printers and can print to NetWare, Unix, and Macintosh print servers using optional components you can install. It also supports Internet printing using the Internet Printing Protocol (IPP), which lets you print to a URL over the Internet or a corporate intranet. For color laser printers and scanners, Windows 2000 includes Image Color Management 2.0 to create and manage color profiles.

*Integrated administration tools*

Windows 2000 administrative tools are implemented using a standard framework called the Microsoft Management Console (MMC). An existing suite of consoles is included in the Administrative Tools program group, but you can also create and customize your own consoles by adding various snap-ins. By installing the Windows 2000 Administration Tools (found on the Windows 2000 Server CD as *\I386\Adminpak.msi*), you can fully manage all aspects of Windows 2000 servers (including both domain controllers and member servers) from a single remote Windows 2000 Professional workstation.

*Easier troubleshooting*

Windows 2000 includes advanced startup options for starting a computer in Safe mode or other modes to troubleshoot hardware problems that could prevent the computer from booting successfully. As with NT, you can create an Emergency Repair Disk (ERD) or boot using Last Known Good Configuration as additional ways to troubleshoot boot problems. An optional Recovery Console can be installed; it provides a minimal, command-line version of Windows 2000 that can be used to manually copy new versions of system files to an NTFS volume, thus replacing missing or corrupted files that are preventing a successful boot. Improved Troubleshooters in online Help provide a question-and-answer approach to helping users troubleshoot problems when tech support can't make it to Help.

## Windows 2000 Server

Professional's big brother is Windows 2000 Server, which supports all the features described above and a whole lot more. Windows 2000 Server is intended to replace the earlier Windows NT 4.0 Server operating system and builds upon the strengths of this system by providing additional functionality, such as:

*Integrated directory services*

Active Directory is an LDAP-compatible directory service that replaces the earlier and not very scalable Windows NT Directory Service (NTDS), which despite its name was not really a directory service at all. With Active Directory, Microsoft steps into the heavyweight ring to slug it out with Novell's NDS and other directory products, but who will win is anyone's guess. Active Directory lets you replace your old system of Windows NT master domains, resource domains, and one-way trusts with a much more scalable (and understandable) system of forests, trees, domains, and two-way transitive trusts for building enterprise networks. This allows users in any location to easily find and access resources anywhere else in the enterprise. Active Directory is not something you just jump into, however: it takes skill and planning to implement it successfully, and implementing it requires a thorough understanding of the Domain Name System (DNS)—the naming and locator service used by Active Directory. See O'Reilly's *Windows 2000 Active Directory* by Alistair Lowe-Norris for a good introduction to the subject.

*Mixed-mode support*

Of course, not everyone will migrate their NT servers to Windows 2000 Server right away (now that's an understatement!) because of the cost and complexity involved. So Microsoft included support for mixed-mode networking environments where newer Windows 2000 domain controllers and legacy Windows NT domain controllers can interoperate transparently with one another until the next budget windfall comes through.

*Group Policy*

Windows NT included an administrative tool called System Policy Editor, which could be used rather awkwardly to lock down user desktops so users could not change the configuration of their systems (since users usually end up breaking things when they try to fix them and then calling technical support to come to the rescue). Windows 2000 goes much further than this with Group Policy, a powerful tool for controlling the behavior of servers, workstations, applications, and data across an enterprise. Group Policy is complex, but it is well worth the effort to learn if you administer a network of more than a few dozen computers.

### Enhanced TCP/IP services

Windows 2000 Server supports enhanced TCP/IP networking services, including:

— Dynamic DNS (DDNS) for allowing clients to update their resource records directly (or other clients to update records indirectly using DHCP) on a Windows 2000 DNS server

— Dynamic Host Configuration Protocol (DHCP) for central management and configuration of IP addresses, including support for Internet Connection Sharing (ICS) and Automatic Private IP Addressing (APIPA) to simplify TCP/IP configuration and Internet access on small SOHO-style networks

— Windows Internet Name Service (WINS) for backward support of legacy Windows clients in mixed-mode environments

### Other networking services

Windows 2000 Server also includes:

— Internet Information Services (IIS) for publishing information using web and FTP sites.

— Distributed File System (Dfs) to make it simpler for users to access shared resources across an enterprise.

— Removable Storage for tracking and managing removable media, such as tapes and optical disks.

— Routing and Remote Access for policy-based control of remote-access servers and the use of multihomed machines as software routers.

— Terminal Services for remotely accessing the Windows 2000 desktop on a central terminal server, something that can extend the life of older hardware that can't run Windows 2000 Professional natively. Terminal Services can also be used for remote administration of Windows 2000 servers.

— Gateway (and Client) Services for NetWare, Services for Macintosh, and Services for Unix to provide interoperability in a heterogeneous networking environment.

There are additional specialized services, such as Telephony, Fax, Certificate, Component, Internet Authentication, Windows Management Instrumentation, QoS Admission, Connection Manager, and IPSec, that you might implement in specialized situations in the enterprise.

### Windows 2000 Advanced Server

Just a step up from Windows 2000 Server is Advanced Server, which has all the functionality of Server, plus:

* Eight-way symmetric multiprocessing (SMP) support
* Memory architecture that supports up to 8 GB of RAM
* Windows clustering for two-node failover clusters
* Network load balancing for up to 32 nodes

### Windows 2000 Datacenter Server

Datacenter Server includes support for:

* 32-way symmetric multiprocessing (SMP)
* 64 GB of memory
* Four-node clustering

## Windows 2000 Kudos

Let's move on now to what's really important in this chapter: my opinion (grin). What follows is my personal expression of things I really like about Windows 2000 and why I like them. (My gripes follow in the next section, which is somewhat longer than this one.)

### MMC Rules

I must confess I like the Microsoft Management Console (MMC) and consider it a big improvement over the old Windows NT administration tools. I can add all the snap-ins I want to a single console and manage virtually anything on any machine in the network. This is cool. In addition, I can customize the console with task-pads and different views, and I would do so if I only had the time (see the beginning of Chapter 5, *Consoles*, for a brief walk-through on how to customize MMC consoles). The one thing Windows 2000 hasn't done for me yet is provide me with more hours in the day.

### Terminal Server

I love the idea that I can remotely administer Windows 2000 servers from a 486 running Windows 95 with the Terminal Services Client installed. I was ready to toss out my old hardware or donate it to the Linux community until I found out I could breathe new life into old hardware by running Terminal Services on my network. Now if only I could run it from my Palm Pilot using a wireless modem while flying at 28,000 feet to the Bahamas . . .

### Active Directory (at Last)

Finally, a real directory service for Microsoft Windows! NT just didn't cut it with its one-way trusts and flat domain namespace. Active Directory lets you build real enterprise-level networks with hierarchical structure that facilitates distributed management through delegation and Group Policy. And it's simple to install and get going, although any real implementation requires careful planning so you won't have to trash it later and start from scratch.

## ADSI

Active Directory Service Interface (ADSI) is a standard set of interfaces for accessing and manipulating information in a directory, as in Active Directory. Using ASDI, you can write scripts to automatically manage users, groups, computers, services, shares, print queues, and just about anything else on Windows 2000. Great stuff!

## Group Policies

One of my favorite Windows 2000 Server features is Group Policy, a powerful tool for performing tasks such as managing and locking down user and computer configuration settings on desktop machines; remotely installing software packages; controlling security settings across sites, domains, and organizational units in the enterprise; redirecting users' work folders to network file servers for easy backup and management; configuring how startup, shutdown, logon, and logoff scripts will run; and so on. And all this can be managed from any Professional machine on which the Windows 2000 administration tools have been installed!

## Disk Quotas

Something that really should have been included in NT (and could have been, since the underlying filesystem architecture was built to support it) is disk quotas. Disk quotas let you manage how much disk space users can use on an NTFS volume.

## EFS

I always used to worry that a lost laptop meant data falling into the wrong hands. But not with Windows 2000 (as long as the user doesn't have a blank password configured!) The Encrypting File System can encrypt data in selected folders on NTFS volumes so that it cannot be accessed and understood by anyone except the logged-on user (or a designated administrator). This feature, together with Windows 2000's support for Plug and Play ACPI power management, makes Windows 2000 a laptop user's dream (and a dream for administrators whose users use laptops).

## Recovery Console

On Windows NT, third-party vendors supplied much needed tools for accessing NTFS partitions from a command prompt. Windows 2000 goes one better by including an optional Recovery Console you can install and use if any of your critical system files become corrupt or go missing and prevent you from booting to the GUI. If this happens, you can use the Recovery Console to copy system files from the Windows 2000 CD or a distribution server and fix your system so it can boot properly. Good stuff!

## The Command Line

Microsoft has powerfully enhanced the Windows command set with new commands, including the powerful Netshell (netsh) command, which you can use to do automated or batch administration of DHCP, WINS, and remote-access servers. The new Secondary Logon feature lets you perform administrative tasks while logged on to a workstation with an ordinary domain user account. A new auto-completion feature lets you enter the start of a file or folder name and have Windows 2000 guess the rest and complete it for you. All in all, you can do a lot more administration (including remote administration) from the command line than you could using Windows NT.

## Those Little Touches

I love the two accessibility features, Magnifier and On-Screen Keyboard. They're implemented wonderfully and are fun to play with. (I don't have any serious disabilities myself, except my sense of humor.) On the other hand, Narrator definitely needs some work, as I can't understand a word it says.

Internet printing is a great new feature, allowing you to print to a print device on the Internet or a corporate intranet using a URL. Very cool.

Right-click on My Computer and select Manage, and the Computer Management administrative console opens up. This is a nice touch, but it would be nice to see it elsewhere, like right-click on My Network Places and select Configure to set up your network, or right-click on My Documents and select Redirect to change the target location for the folder to a network share, or right-click on a folder in Windows Explorer and select Security to open the property sheet for the folder with the focus on the security tab (they did this for Sharing, right?), and so on.

Speaking of right-clicking, try opening the Start menu and, while you're pointing to some Start menu item (like Imaging in the Accessories program group), right-click on the item and select Properties. This is a fast way of determining the executable file associated with an item on the Start menu, so you can run the file from the command line in the future. Or you can select Sort by Name to rearrange the order of items in your Start menu (this should be done automatically though).

And speaking of the command-line, right-click on the taskbar at the bottom of the screen, and select Toolbars → Address to put an Address bar right on the taskbar (you can also drag it off and have it float). Type anything into this Address bar to run or open it; for example, type My Computer, Control Panel, *C:*, *C:\Winnt*, a UNC path, a URL, or a command. If you type something Windows doesn't recognize, it assumes you have entered a URL and opens Internet Explorer to find the item on the Internet.

Enough! I'm happy with the product. It's time to voice a few gripes, though.

# Windows 2000 Gripes

As we've seen above, Windows 2000 has many new features that make it useful for system administrators. But it's not perfect, and this section gives me a chance to voice a few complaints—and use my sense of humor a bit!

## Group Gripes

Groups in Windows NT were confusing: global groups were supposed to be used for organizing users together, whereas local groups were intended for managing the access users had to resources such as shared folders and printers. You could circumvent this however by assigning permissions directly to global groups or even individual users if you liked. Though local groups could contain global groups, they couldn't contain other local groups, and global groups could contain neither local nor global groups.

Have groups been simplified in Windows 2000? Just the opposite. There are now three types of groups that can be used to manage domain users and control their access to resources:

*Domain local groups*
  Similar to but not quite the same as local groups in Windows NT

*Global groups*
  Similar to but not quite the same as global groups in Windows NT

*Universal groups*
  Something entirely new to Windows 2000

With more groups come more rules for using them. The membership and nesting rules for groups in Windows 2000 are complex and differ depending on whether you are running in native mode (domain controllers are all running Windows 2000) or mixed mode (support for downlevel Windows NT domain controllers).

What's really interesting in Windows 2000 are universal groups, which have the following attractive features:

*Scalability*
  The members of a universal group can be from any domain in the forest. (A forest is a collection of domains that trust each other.)

*Flexibility*
  The universal group's members can be domain user accounts, global groups, or even other universal groups, and can be nested to any degree.

*Usability*
  Universal groups can be assigned permissions to grant users access to any resources in the forest.

Universal groups sound really terrific. It appears we can scrap the other types of groups (global and domain local) and instead use only universal groups. And since they can be nested to any degree and can be used to control access to resources in any domain for accounts in any domain, one has a great deal of flexibility in implementing them.

The downside is that universal groups can be used only when running in native mode, which means that you must first upgrade all your Windows NT domain controllers to Windows 2000 before implementing them. There is also a performance issue associated with universal groups: when you make a change to the membership of a universal group, not just the changes you made but the group itself plus its entire membership must be replicated to all global catalog servers throughout the enterprise (global catalog servers help find things in a Windows 2000 enterprise). The result is that if changes are made frequently to the membership of universal groups, the resulting replication traffic may eat up valuable network bandwidth, especially when slow WAN links are involved.

My gripe is that instead of making groups simpler, they've made them more complicated, and while universal groups look attractive on paper, they are limited to situations where group membership is relatively static.

## More Is Less

Another basic area of network administration is using permissions to control access to shared resources. In Windows NT, permissions were fairly simple to understand: you secured a folder by assigning different NTFS permissions on the folder to different users and groups. (This was usually done by assigning each user or group one of the seven standard NTFS folder permissions, though occasionally some custom combination of the six special NTFS folder permissions was used instead for more granular control over the folder.) Then you shared the folder and left the shared-folder permissions set to Full Control for Everyone (that way you didn't have to worry about figuring out the effective permissions resulting when different NTFS permissions and shared-folder permissions were combined).

In Windows 2000, permissions still work basically the same way, but with a wrinkle: the naming, complexity, and method of assignment of NTFS permissions have changed. Specifically:

- The NTFS standard permission called Change in Windows NT is now called Modify in Windows 2000. Why change something when everyone is just getting used to it? And are they really the same?

- In Windows NT there were seven standard folder permissions, but in Windows 2000 there are only six. It sounds like they tried to simplify permissions in Windows 2000, but see my next point.

- In Windows NT you selected one of the standard permissions and assigned it to the user or group to control their access to the resource. In Windows 2000, however, you can specifically Allow or Deny any of the standard permissions. Even more confusing, when you do this, whole groups of checkmarks change in the Permissions list box on the Security tab. This can be really confusing! For example, if you Allow the Modify permission, then the four permissions below it (Read & Execute, List Folder Contents, Read, and Write) all automatically become Allowed as well. If you then Deny the Read & Execute permission, all the Allowed permissions become unchecked *except* Write permission, which remains allowed. Now I suppose this makes sense when you think about it, but the problem is *that* you have to think about it!

- In the above example, when you Deny the Read & Execute permission, a message is displayed below the Permissions box saying "Additional permissions are present but not viewable here. Press Advanced to see them." If you then select the Advanced button, you see a list of Allow and Deny items for different users and groups you have assigned permissions. Select one of these items and click View/Edit, and a list of 13 (!) raw NTFS folder permissions appears, each of which you can individually Allow or Deny.

Do we really need such complexity for such a simple and basic thing as controlling resource access through permissions? Of course, this gives administrators great flexibility and granularity in managing resource access, but isn't it more likely to cause frustrating problems in tracking permissions problems if these advanced permissions are used? Perhaps they should take a lesson from Unix, whose permissions structure is much simpler to understand and implement.

## Divide but Don't Conquer

The Windows 2000 administrative tools are for the most part implemented as MMC consoles, and these consoles typically display a hierarchical tree of resources in the left pane of their window (the hierarchy is referred to as the console tree). So Windows 2000 networks are therefore managed hierarchically, right? In some ways, yes, but the implementation could have been better in my opinion.

To illustrate my gripe, let's say I have a domain tree with several domains, each containing a number of Windows 2000 Server computers, and I want to manage users and computers in different domains simultaneously. Here is how I might do it:

1. Open the Active Directory Domains and Trusts console from the Administrative Tools program group. This console hierarchically displays the various trees of domains in my forest.

2. Select a domain that contains users I want to manage.

3. Right-click on the domain node and select Manage from the shortcut menu. This opens the Active Directory Users and Computers console for the domain I selected, allowing me to manage users, groups, computers, and other published resources of the selected domain.

4. In the Active Directory Users and Computers window for the domain I selected, open the Computers container (or an organizational unit that contains computers I want to manage), right-click on a computer, and select Manage. This opens a Computer Management console for the selected computer, letting me manage various resources on the computer.

5. Repeat steps 2 through 5 until I can manage all the users and computers that I want to manage in the various domains.

What I have now are dozens and dozens of windows open all over my desktop. My gripe is that the Manage option is a good idea, but it's more of an afterthought from poor planning when these tools were designed. In other words, Microsoft's console-based management tools are simply not as integrated or hierarchical as they could have been. Instead of flipping between windows for Active Directory Domains and Trusts, Active Directory Users and Computers, Computer Management, and so on, why not have just *one* snap-in for all these functions that displays a single console tree? Managing a computer would then be as simple as:

1. Open the Active Directory Do Everything Dream Tool console (or whatever you want to call it).

2. Expand the console tree to select the node for the domain whose users and computers you want to manage.

3. Expand the node for the domain, and select the Users container to display the users and groups you want to manage, or select the Computers container to display the computers you want to manage.

4. Expand a node for a computer, and select the appropriate management tool in the System Tools, Storage, or Services and Applications container under the computer node. Select a specific tool to manage the computer.

5. Expand a node for a group to display the users that belong to the group in the console tree under it. Select a user to display further nodes under it, corresponding to the different tabs on the user's property sheet. Select a node for a specific tab to display the settings for the tab in the right-hand pane of the console.

My dream tool would thus allow me to scroll down a single, hierarchical console tree for the entire enterprise and manage selected users and computers without opening any annoying property sheets (I hate property sheets!) or displaying any irritating messages like "Close all property sheets before closing this tool."

## Drag Me and Drop Me

Speaking of the MMC, I have another complaint that I'll illustrate using the Active Directory Users and Computers console from the Administrative Tools program group. In this console you can organize your users, groups, computers, and other published resources (directory objects) by grouping them into containers you create called organizational units (OUs). Now this is very cool, since you can create a hierarchy of OUs to reflect the areas of administrative responsibility in your company and then delegate authority over different OUs to trusted users or apply Group Policy to OUs to control the configuration of objects in them. All this gives you a lot of flexibility in how you implement Active Directory, and I have no complaint about this.

But if you later change your mind and want to rearrange objects in your directory, you can do this by right-clicking on the object and selecting Move from the shortcut menu. What I don't understand is why you can't simply drag and drop objects from the right-hand console pane into any OU in the console tree at the left. This is annoying, and as you start to work with the Microsoft Management Console, you soon discover that drag and drop doesn't work with *any* MMC consoles. As Ratbert says, "Now *that's* an eye-opener!"

## Where's the Browser?

Still on this topic of administrative tools, it's pretty cool that Windows 2000 lets me administer printers from any computer anywhere on the network, as long as it is running a simple web browser. This includes Macintosh and Unix machines. Browser-based administration of printers is a great idea and is superior in many ways to the traditional Printers folder (opened by Start → Settings → Printers), but why didn't Microsoft extend this type of administration to all aspects of Active Directory?

If web-based network management is such a hot thing, then Windows 2000 should let me perform *any* administrative task involving Active Directory from *any* remote computer using only a simple web browser. I should be able to create users and groups, configure shares and permissions, set policies, view logs, run backups, and perform any other administrative tasks from any computer regardless of the operating system it is running, as long as it has a web browser installed.

So why did Microsoft not choose to proceed this way with Windows 2000 and instead create the Microsoft Management Console with its vast and confusing array of different snap-ins? I don't know, but I expect third-party vendors to supply the need here in the near future. And if some vendor does this and does it well, we might soon be kissing MMC goodbye.

## Musical Chairs

Speaking of changing things (recall my discussion of NTFS permissions earlier), it's surprising that many aspects of Windows NT that we have grown comfortable with and did not really need improvement have been significantly changed in Windows 2000. For example:

- Network Neighborhood is now called My Network Places. My guess is that this is part of the My paradigm that seems to be popular with the Me generation, of which I myself am naturally a member.

- Right-clicking on Network Neighborhood used to display your network identification. Now you display your network identification by right-clicking on My Computer instead.

- You used to configure your network protocols by right-clicking on Network Neighborhood and selecting the Protocols tab. Now you right-click on My Network Places to open the Network and Dial-up Connections folder and then right-click on Local Area Connection.

- Windows NT Explorer used to be under Programs in the Start menu. Now it's called Windows Explorer and is found in the Accessories program group.

- Command Prompt used to be under Programs in the Start menu. Now it's in Accessories as well.

- The ODBC configuration utility used to be in the Control Panel. Now it's in the Administrative Tools program group, and it's called Data Sources (ODBC) instead.

- Folder Options used to be available under Settings in the Start menu. Now it's hidden away in the Control Panel.

I could go on and on. Have any of these changes made life simpler for the administrator?

## Read the Manual

Online help is fine and dandy, but I've always been willing to shell out a few extra bucks for the hard-copy version of manuals for Microsoft products so I could take them on the bus and read them. I remember being annoyed when I was writing one of my earlier books (*Microsoft Exchange Server in a Nutshell* from O'Reilly) because when I phoned Microsoft to order the print versions of the Exchange manuals, they said they could send them this time but were planning on discontinuing printed manuals at the end of the year. I thought that was pretty heavy-handed at the time.

I was wrong: Microsoft hasn't discontinued product manuals at all; they've simply renamed them Resource Kits. I've got the *Windows 2000 Server Resource Kit* on my bookshelf, and believe me, this is the manual for the product, not the Help file that comes with the product. Regardless of what books on Windows 2000 you buy, you should shell out some bucks and buy the 8,000-page-long Resource Kit as well, as at some point or another you're going to need it. No handy pocket-sized book can possibly cover in depth all aspects of this behemoth, so the Resource Kit is an essential reference when you need more information. But don't expect either to start reading it from the beginning and learn how Windows 2000 works, as it is divided up into various volumes with lots of interdependency between them in terms of understanding. This is not your light bathroom reading!

## Minor Annoyances

In Event Viewer, which is under System Tools in Computer Management, you still have to double-click on an event to display the detailed information about the event. Sure, you can use the up and down arrow buttons on an event's property sheet to scroll between events, but this is a pain (and the up and down arrow cursor keys won't work here; you have to click the up and down arrow buttons instead). At least this is better than the Previous and Next buttons in Windows NT, where I could never remember if Previous meant the next item up in the list or the next item down. But it would have been nice if there were three panes in the Event Viewer console window instead of two, and if by using the up and down arrow keys, you could scroll the event list and immediately read the detailed description for each event.

In Shared Folders, which is also under System Tools in Computer Management, you can create and manage shares easily, but you cannot display the contents of a share. This is frustrating if you want to manage a share but you can't quite remember which share it is you need to manage, and if you could just take a peek inside . . .

Device Manager (which is again under System Tools in Computer Management) is limited to managing hardware settings on the local computer—you can connect to a remote computer using Computer Management, but in this case Device Manager works in Read-only mode. It would be nice if Device Manager could be used to manage hardware settings on remote machines instead of just locally—but perhaps this is too much to ask, as it depends on not just the capabilities of the operating system but also on the design of the Intel architecture and PC hardware standards as well. Of course, if the remote machine is a Windows 2000 server, you could install Terminal Services on it and run Device Manager from a workstation running Terminal Services Client, but managing hardware settings on remote Windows 2000 workstations is what I am referring to here.

If you install Windows 2000 on a computer and configure it to use DHCP, but the DHCP server is not present on the network when your computer first boots up, you're probably in trouble. This is because the Automatic Private IP Addressing (APIPA) kicks in and assigns the client a temporary IP address from the reserved Class B network 169.254.0.0. The trouble is that this all happens automatically with no warning, and since there were no error messages, you assume that your computer is now up and running on the network. Then you try to log on and browse network resources, but you can't and wonder what's gone wrong. The solution is to disable APIPA manually on Windows 2000 computers using the Registry Editor, but my complaint is why couldn't it have been disabled by default?

Windows 2000 includes a Telnet server now, which is great since it allows you to perform remote administration from the command line. But the handy Telnet client that was included with previous versions has been replaced by a command-line version of the utility. I prefer the old client because you can log a telnet session simply by selecting Terminal → Start Logging from the menu.

Finally, I hate the new personalized Start menu, which only displays shortcuts you have used recently and hides the rest. You can turn this annoying feature off by selecting Start → Settings → Taskbar & Start menu → General → deselect Use Personalized Menus.

# CHAPTER 2

# *Quick Start*

Although this book is intended not as a tutorial but as a quick desktop reference, I've included a brief chapter here to help existing Windows NT administrators quickly orient themselves to working with Windows 2000. We're all in a hurry these days—especially those of us who manage computer networks—and I want to provide you with some suggestions and tips to get you going quickly. More information on the concepts, tasks, tools, and utilities discussed here can be found in the chapters of Part II, *Alphabetical Reference*, of this book.

## *New Tools, Old Tasks*

If you are familiar with the Windows NT administrative tools, you may be thrown off base initially by the Windows 2000 administrative tools, which are almost entirely new tools with very few holdovers. Tables 2-1 through 2-3 help you bridge the gap between the old platform and the new. The correspondence between tools and utilities on the two platforms is unfortunately not one-to-one, so notes are added where necessary to indicate differences. The base Windows NT platform used here includes Service Pack 4 with Internet Explorer 4 installed and Active Desktop enabled. The reference point here for the Windows 2000 tools list is Start → Programs, Start → Settings, or Start → Programs → Administrative Tools, depending on the program.

Table 2-1 lists the Windows NT administrative tools, which you may already be familiar with, and their new Windows 2000 counterparts.

*Table 2-1: Administrative Tools in Windows NT and Windows 2000*

| Windows NT Tool | Windows 2000 Tool(s) |
| --- | --- |
| Administrative Wizards | No real counterpart, but Administrative Tools → Configure Your Server lets you perform some high-level administration tasks |
| Backup | Accessories → System Tools → Backup |
| Disk Administrator | Computer Management → Storage → Disk Management |

*Table 2-1: Administrative Tools in Windows NT and Windows 2000 (continued)*

| Windows NT Tool | Windows 2000 Tool(s) |
|---|---|
| DHCP Manager | Computer Management → Services and Applications → DHCP<br>or: DHCP |
| DNS Manager | Computer Management → Services and Applications → DNS<br>or: DNS |
| Event Viewer | Computer Management → System Tools → Disk Management<br>or: Event Viewer |
| Internet Service Manager | Computer Management → Services and Applications → Internet Information Services<br>or: Internet Services Manager |
| License Manager | Licensing |
| Migration Tool for NetWare | Not included |
| Network Client Administrator | No real counterpart, though you can install Windows 2000 Server administration tools on a Windows 2000 Professional client using \*I386\Adminpak.msi* on the Windows 2000 Server compact disc |
| Network Monitor | Network Monitor |
| Performance Monitor | Performance → System Monitor (note that Computer Management → System Tools → Performance Logs and Alerts can be used to create logs but not to display them) |
| Remote Access Admin | Routing and Remote Access |
| Server Manager | Computer Management → System Tools → Shared Folders (to create and manage network shares, and to send a message to users connected to the server)<br>or: Active Directory Users and Computers (to add a computer to a domain)<br>or: Active Directory Sites and Services (to manually force directory replication between domain controllers) |
| System Policy Editor | Use the Group Policy snap-in (much more powerful) |
| User Manager | Computer Management → System Tools → Local Users and Groups (to manage local users and groups on standalone servers or workstations)<br>or: Local Security Policy (to configure password, account lockout, and audit policies and user rights on standalone servers and workstations) |
| User Manager for Domains | Active Directory Users and Computers (to manage users and groups, and to configure password, account lockout, and audit policies and user rights by opening and editing Group Policy Objects)<br>or: Active Directory Domains and Trusts (to manage explicit trusts) |
| Windows NT Diagnostics | Computer Management → System Tools → System Information<br>or: Accessories → System Tools → System Information |
| WINS Manager | Computer Management → Services and Applications → WINS<br>or: WINS |

Table 2-2 lists selected Windows NT folders and utilities and their Windows 2000 counterparts.

*Table 2-2: Folders and Utilities in Windows NT and Windows 2000*

| Windows NT Folder or Utility | Windows 2000 Counterpart |
|---|---|
| *C:\Winnt\Profiles* (location where local user profiles are stored) | *C:\Documents and Settings* (unless an upgrade from NT was performed, in which case it will remain in its original location) |
| The default location where applications save their files varies in Windows NT | My Documents folder for compliant applications designed for Windows 2000 and Windows 9x (unless an upgrade from NT was performed, in which case it will remain in its original location) |
| Network Neighborhood | My Network Places |
| Find | Search |
| Windows NT Explorer | Accessories → Windows Explorer |
| Command Prompt | Accessories → Command Prompt |
| Internet Explorer → Connection Wizard | Accessories → Communications → Internet Connection Wizard |
| Settings → Folder Options | Control Panel → Folder Options |
| Settings → Active Desktop | Right-click on Desktop → Active Desktop |
| Accessories → Dial-up Networking | Settings → Network and Dial-up Connections (much more powerful) |
| Accessories → Telnet | `telnet` command |
| Accessories → HyperTerminal | Accessories → Communications → HyperTerminal |
| Accessories → Multimedia | Accessories → Entertainment |
| Control Panel → Console | Accessories → Command Prompt → Control Menu → Defaults |
| Control Panel → Devices | Computer Management → System Tools → Device Manager |
| Control Panel → Internet | Control Panel → Internet Options |
| Control Panel → Modems | Control Panel → Phone and Modem Options |
| Control Panel → Multimedia | Control Panel → Sounds and Multimedia |
| Control Panel → Network | Control Panel → Network and Dial-up Connections |
| Control Panel → Network → Identification | Control Panel → Network and Dial-up Connections → Advanced → Network Identification<br>or: Control Panel → System → Network Identification tab |
| Control Panel → Network → {Services \| Protocols \| Adapters} | Control Panel → Network and Dial-up Connections → Local Area Connection → Properties |
| Control Panel → Network → Bindings | Control Panel → Network and Dial-up Connections → Advanced Settings |
| Control Panel → ODBC | Administrative Tools → Data Sources (PDBC) |
| Control Panel → Ports | Computer Management → System Tools → Device Manager |
| Control Panel → Regional Settings | Control Panel → Regional Options |
| Control Panel → SCSI Adapters | Computer Management → System Tools → Device Manager |
| Control Panel → Server | Computer Management → System Tools → Shared Folders |
| Control Panel → Services | Computer Management → Services and Applications → Services<br>or: Services |

*Table 2-2: Folders and Utilities in Windows NT and Windows 2000 (continued)*

| Windows NT Folder or Utility | Windows 2000 Counterpart |
|---|---|
| Control Panel → Sounds | Control Panel → Sounds and Multimedia |
| Control Panel → System → [General | User Profiles] | Unchanged |
| Control Panel → System → Performance | Control Panel → System → Advanced → Performance Options |
| Control Panel → System → Environment | Control Panel → System → Advanced → Environment Variables |
| Control Panel → System → Startup/Shutdown | Control Panel → System → Advanced → Startup and Recovery |
| Control Panel → System → Hardware Profiles | Control Panel → System → Hardware → Hardware Profiles |
| Control Panel → Tape Devices | Computer Management → System Tools → Device Manager |
| Control Panel → Telephony | Control Panel → Phone and Modem Options → Dialing Rules |
| Control Panel → UPS | Control Panel → Power Options → UPS |

Table 2-3 is a quick list of things you commonly administer and the tools you use to administer them in both Windows NT and Windows 2000.

*Table 2-3: Items to Administer in Windows NT and Windows 2000*

| Item to Administer | Windows NT Tool | Windows 2000 Tool(s) |
|---|---|---|
| Account policy | User Manager for Domains | Group Policy snap-in (for domains) Local Security Policy (for workgroups) Default Domain Policy (for domain controllers) |
| Active Directory | Not applicable | Active Directory Domains and Trusts Active Directory Sites and Services Active Directory Users and Computers |
| Adding computers to a domain | User Manager for Domains | Active Directory Users and Computers |
| Advanced startup options | Not applicable | Press F8 during startup |
| Audit policy | User Manager for Domains | Group Policy snap-in (for domains) Local Security Policy (for workgroups) |
| Backup and restore | Backup | Accessories → System Tools → Backup |
| Bindings | Control Panel → Network | Control Panel → Network and Dial-up Connections → Advanced → Advanced Settings |
| Computer names | Control Panel → Network → Identification | Control Panel → System → Network Identification |
| Devices | Control Panel → Devices | Computer Management → System Tools → Device Manager |
| Dial-up connection | Dial-up Networking | Network and Dial-up Connections |
| Directory replication | User Manager for Domains Registry Editor | Active Directory Sites and Services |

| Item to Administer | Windows NT Tool | Windows 2000 Tool(s) |
|---|---|---|
| Disk fragmentation | Third-party utility | Computer Management → Storage → Disk Defragmenter |
| Disk quotas | Third-party utility | Windows Explorer |
| Disks | Disk Administrator | Computer Management → Storage → Disk Management |
| Domain controllers | User Manager for Domains | Active Directory Sites and Services<br>Active Directory Users and Computers |
| Domains | User Manager for Domains | Active Directory Domains and Trusts<br>Active Directory Users and Computers |
| Emergency Repair Disk | `rdisk` command | Accessories → System Tools → Backup |
| Event logs | Event Viewer | Event Viewer |
| Forests | Not applicable | Active Directory Domains and Trusts |
| Global users | User Manager for Domains | Active Directory Users and Computers |
| Group Policy | Not applicable (though System Policy Editor is a weak equivalent) | Active Directory Sites and Services<br>Active Directory Users and Computers<br>Group Policy snap-in |
| Groups | User Manager for Domains | Active Directory Users and Computers |
| Kill a process | Right-click on taskbar → Task Manager | Same |
| Licenses | License Manager | Licensing |
| Local users | User Manager | Local Users and Groups |
| Pagefile | Control Panel → System → Performance → Change | Control Panel → System → Advanced → Performance Options → Change |
| Performance logs | Performance Monitor | Performance Logs and Alerts |
| Permissions | Windows Explorer | Same |
| Printers | Settings → Printers | Same (or *http://<servername>/printers/* if IIS is installed) |
| Protocols | Control Panel → Network → Protocols | Control Panel → Network and Dial-up Connections → Local Area Connection → Properties |
| RAID | Disk Administrator | Computer Management → Storage → Disk Management |
| Registry | *regedt32.exe*<br>*regedit.exe* | Same |
| Remote access | Remote Access Admin | Routing and Remote Access (most functions)<br>Active Directory Users and Computers (to grant users remote-access permission) |
| Rights | User Manager for Domains | Group Policy snap-in (for domains)<br>Local Security Policy (for workgroups) |
| Scheduling tasks | `at` command | Control Panel → Scheduled Tasks |

*Quick Start*

*Table 2-3: Items to Administer in Windows NT and Windows 2000 (continued)*

| Item to Administer | Windows NT Tool | Windows 2000 Tool(s) |
|---|---|---|
| Sending messages to connected users | Server Manager | Computer Management |
| Services | Control Panel → Services | Computer Management → Services and Applications → Services |
| Shared folders | Server Manager | Shared Folders (in Computer Management) |
| Sites | *regedt32.exe* *regedit.exe* | Active Directory Sites and Services |
| Trees | Not applicable | Active Directory Domains and Trusts |
| Trusts | User Manager for Domains | Active Directory Domains and Trusts |
| UPS | Control Panel → UPS | Control Panel → Power Options |

# Potpourri

Chapters 3 through 7 of this book form a quick desktop reference that lets you look up a concept, task, console or snap-in, utility, or command and quickly find what you're looking for. Nevertheless, for readers who are either brilliant, impatient, or have nothing better to do, the remainder of this chapter contains a potpourri of things about Windows 2000 that advanced administrators will want to know to get the most out of it and avoid the pitfalls. Wherever possible, I've drawn comparisons to similar aspects of Windows NT administration and included cross-references to Chapter 3, *Concepts*, and Chapter 4, *Tasks*, in Part II of this book. I've also arranged the sections below in alphabetical order according to topic to help you find useful information more quickly.

## Account Policy

Setting account policy—such as password and account lockout restrictions—was easy in Windows NT using the User Manager for Domains administrative tool. In Windows 2000 you must use Group Policy (or the Domain Security Policy located in Administrative Tools on a domain controller) if you are in a domain environment, and you must configure the appropriate settings of a domain GPO for your domain. See *Group Policy* in Chapters 3 and 4 for more information.

## Active Directory

For many companies Active Directory is the raison d'être for migrating their Windows NT networks to Windows 2000, but implementing it successfully takes careful planning and training of IT staff. For information on planning and implementation, see the following articles in Chapter 3: *Active Directory*, *domain*, *domain controller*, *forest*, *global catalog*, and *tree*. Don't forget that to use Active Directory means you must use TCP/IP and implement DNS servers on your network. See *DNS* and *TCP/IP* in Chapter 3 for more information.

## Administrative Tools

If you're just starting out with Windows 2000, these are the two most important administrative tools to get familiar with:

*Computer Management*
> This lets you connect to a local or remote computer and manage disks, shares, event logs, performance logs, services, and applications, as well as display information about devices and system resources. Computer Management actually integrates over a dozen other snap-ins into a single MMC console, so get familiar with this tool. You can administer most of these things on either a local or remote computer using Computer Management. You can't use this tool on remote computers to change device drivers or uninstall devices on remote machines using the Device Manager node of the tool. (For remote computers, Device Manager operates in Read-only mode so you can't change resource settings like IRQ, I/O, and so on.)

*Active Directory Users and Computers*
> This is used for creating and managing domain user accounts and domain local, global, and universal groups on domain controllers in your enterprise. You can also use this tool to create and configure Group Policy Objects (GPOs), which are mechanisms for configuring desktop settings on collections of computers across an enterprise.

For more information on these consoles, see *Computer Management* and *Active Directory Users and Computers* in Chapter 5, *Consoles*. For information on Group Policy Objects and how to configure them, see *Group Policy* in Chapters 3 and 4.

Instead of going to a domain controller to run Active Directory Users and Computers from the local console, install the complete set of Windows 2000 administration tools on a Windows 2000 Professional workstation, and use this as your main administrator workstation. You can install these tools by running *Adminpak.msi*, which is found in the \\*I386* folder on your Windows 2000 Server compact disc.

You can run most administrative tools from the command line while logged on to a workstation using an ordinary domain user (as opposed to an administrator) account. To do this, you use a Windows 2000 feature known as Secondary Logon. Just open a command prompt and type:

```
runas /user:domain\username cmd
```

where **username** is an administrator account in **domain**. You'll be prompted to enter your password, after which a second command-prompt window opens up that lets you execute commands using your administrator credentials. The current directory of this new window is set to *%SystemRoot%\System32*, which is where most administrative tools (MMC consoles saved as *.msc* files) are located. For example, to run Computer Management as administrator, you just type the following in your new command-prompt window:

```
compmgnt.msc
```

Of course, you need to know what the command-line equivalent of a GUI administrative tool is before you can run it this way. You can usually (but not always) find this out by opening the property sheet of the shortcut for the tool in the Start menu. As a help, I've listed these equivalents in Table 5-1 in Chapter 5.

A few things to note: the Runas service must be started in order to do this, and you can specify your administrator credentials in either of the two standard Windows 2000 forms. For example, if your administrator account is *admin987* and the domain is *mtit.com*, then you can specify either *MTIT\admin987* or *admin987@mtit.com* in the runas command. You can also run a tool in different credentials by right-clicking on it in Windows Explorer and selecting Runas from the shortcut menu.

## Audit Policy

Setting an audit policy for a domain was easy in Windows NT using the User Manager for Domains administrative tool. In Windows 2000 you must use Group Policy if you are in a domain environment and configure the appropriate settings of a domain GPO for your domain. See *Group Policy* in Chapter 3 for more information.

## Connection

Remember, by just creating a dial-up or VPN connection, you don't give users access to resources on your network when they connect to your remote-access or VPN server—you still need to assign suitable permissions for the users to access the resources. For information on the different types of connections you can create in Windows 2000, see *connection* in Chapter 3.

## Computer Names

If you expect to have both Windows NT and Windows 2000 coexist for a while on your network, select NetBIOS computer names that will be compatible with both platforms (maximum 15 characters). Also, since Windows 2000 uses DNS by default as its name-resolution service, make sure your computer names are DNS compatible as well (this means no underscores, periods, or spaces—only letters, numbers, and dashes). For more on naming computers, see *computer name* in Chapters 3 and 4.

Speaking of computer names, there is also the issue of shared names to consider. When naming a shared folder or printer, it's a good idea to avoid using spaces or special characters if your network contains a mix of Windows 2000 and other computers (such as downlevel Windows NT machines, Unix machines, and so on). Otherwise, some clients might have difficulty connecting to your Windows 2000 shares.

By the way, if you need to change the name of a domain controller, you first must demote it to a member server, change the name, then promote it to a domain controller again. This sounds simple, but it can cause problems if you have downlevel Windows NT servers on your network and are using WINS for name resolution for these servers. This is because the WINS databases will maintain the former name of your domain controller for a period of time, which can cause name-resolution problems for clients unless the offending records are flushed from the database.

## Delegation

Delegation is a powerful feature of Windows 2000 that helps administrators shuffle off some of their administrative responsibility to other trusted (trustworthy) users before overwork causes them to "shuffle off this mortal coil." For information on how to implement this feature, see *delegation* in Chapters 3 and 4.

## DHCP

If you are going to deploy and manage IP addressing on Windows 2000 using DHCP, you might want to disable the Automatic Private IP Addressing (APIPA) feature on your machines. APIPA causes an IP address to be automatically assigned to a client machine from the reserved address range 169.254.0.1 through 169.254.255.254 when the system is configured for DHCP but is unable to contact a DHCP server when it first starts up. This can be nasty, since no warning message indicates that the system has used APIPA instead of DHCP to obtain its address, resulting in an inability to access other machines on the network because they are on a different subnet.

See the section "Automatic Private IP Addressing (APIPA)" in the article *TCP/IP* in Chapter 3 for information on how to disable APIPA. For further general information on DHCP, see *DHCP* and *DHCP relay agent* in Chapters 3 and 4.

## Disk Quotas

A good tip when implementing disk quotas is to configure global quotas only and not quotas for individual users. Not following this can make quota administration a real headache. For more information see *disk quota* in Chapters 3 and 4.

## Disks

Microsoft has borrowed the concept of mounted volumes from Unix and implemented the ability to mount a FAT or NTFS volume in an empty folder on an NTFS volume in Windows 2000. This feature helps you get beyond the 24-letter limit for mapped drives. See *disks* in Chapters 3 and 4 for details. Note that you can cause problems for yourself with this feature: nothing prevents you from mounting a volume in a folder on a mounted volume, or even mounting a volume in a folder on itself!

## DNS

DNS is used as the name-locator service in Windows 2000. This means you must have DNS servers implemented on your network if you want to connect to resources without specifying their IP address. DNS is also required if you want to use Active Directory on your network. For more information see *Active Directory* and *DNS* in Chapter 3.

NetBIOS is another option for name resolution. NetBIOS over TCP/IP is enabled by default (even in native mode domains) so that downlevel (Windows NT or Windows 98/95) computer names can be resolved if such systems are present. You can disable NetBIOS over TCP/IP by using the Advanced TCP/IP settings box (see *TCP/IP* in Chapter 4). Note that if you disable NetBIOS over TCP/IP, you won't be able to restrict a user's access to specific workstations using the Account tab of the user account's property sheet. This feature requires NetBIOS over TCP/IP in order to work.

 If you manually modify any resource records on a Windows 2000 DNS server, select Update Server Data Files to make sure these changes are propagated to other DNS servers on your network. See *DNS* and *DNS server* in Chapter 4 for more information on how to manage DNS in Windows 2000.

## Domain Controllers

In Windows NT, one domain controller was special within a domain—the primary domain controller (PDC). The PDC was the only domain controller with a writable copy of the domain directory database, and all changes made to user, group, or computer accounts in the domain had to be made on the PDC. (If the PDC was unavailable, then those changes could not be made.) All other domain controllers in the domain were backup domain controllers (BDCs), which contained Read-only versions of the domain directory database.

Windows 2000 promised to be different in that domain controllers are all peers and each domain controller contains a full writable copy of the Active Directory database. Replication between domain controllers follows a method called multi-master replication in which there is no single master domain controller. However, if you look under the surface, you find out that this is not quite the case. There are actually five special domain-controller roles (called operations master roles), which are restricted to certain domain controllers in an enterprise. For information on these special roles, see *domain controller* in Chapters 3 and 4.

Speaking of PDCs and BDCs, the usual way of upgrading a Windows NT domain to Windows 2000 is to upgrade the PDC first, then the BDCs. The hitch is this: make sure the former PDC is available on the network when you are upgrading the BCDs. If it isn't, the first BDC you upgrade will think it's the first domain controller in the domain and will assume some of the operations master roles discussed above. Then when the former PDC comes back online, you will have a serious conflict between them, and the only way to resolve it is to wipe your former BDC and reinstall it from scratch.

By the way, if you have only upgraded some of your downlevel Windows NT BDCs to Windows 2000 domain controllers, you need to make sure each domain has a global catalog server in order for cross-domain authentication to take place successfully in a forest of trees. Native mode domains do not have this restriction, and in a well-connected enterprise (no slow WAN links), you can probably get away with only one global catalog server if it can handle the load.

After promoting a Windows 2000 member server to the role of a domain controller using the Active Directory Installation Wizard (*dcpromo.exe*), be sure to check the *Dcpromo.log* and *Dcpromoui.log* log files that are created in the *%SystemRoot%\debug* folder. These logs will list any problems that occurred during the promotion.

## Domains

Active Directory in Windows 2000 has changed the whole nature of domains and how they connect together using trusts. You no longer need to separate master (account) domains from slave (resource) domains as you did in Windows NT or create trusts manually between domains. Instead, when you promote a Windows 2000 member server to the role of a domain controller, you can either:

- Add it to an existing domain as a peer domain controller

- Make it the first domain controller of a new child domain under an existing parent domain, with a two-way transitive trust created automatically between the parent and child domains

- Make it the first domain controller of a new root domain, creating a new tree in an existing forest, with a two-way transitive trust created automatically between the new root domain and the root domains of existing trees in the forest

- Make it the first domain controller of the root domain of the first tree in a new forest (in other words, this is the very first Windows 2000 domain controller on your network)

The whole thing is done using Active Directory Installation Wizard (*dcpromo.exe*). The hierarchies of domains that result (trees in a forest) are all interconnected by trusts automatically so that any user in any domain can access any resource in any other domain immediately, provided they have suitable permissions. For more information on planning Windows 2000 domains and domain structures, see these articles in Chapter 3: *Active Directory, domain, forest, OU, tree,* and *trust.*

## Dual-Boot

I don't recommend dual-boot configurations except for playing around at home, and you should know that volumes formatted with the version of NTFS on Windows 2000 (called NTFS5) only support dual-boots on Windows NT 4.0 with Service Pack 4 or higher. If you are using an earlier version of NT and want to maintain it on a dual-boot configuration, you will be unable to use advanced features of Windows 2000's NTFS, such as disk quotas and EFS.

By the way, just because you encrypt a file or folder using EFS doesn't mean you can't accidentally delete it!

## Emergency Repair Disk

You no longer use the `rdisk` command to create ERDs; you use Backup, which is in the System Tools subgroup of the Accessories program group. I thought I'd let you know since you are no longer prompted during Setup to create an ERD, but have to do it manually afterwards.

Also, Windows 2000 ERDs do not contain everything Windows NT ERDs used to have. In fact, the only files on a Windows 2000 ERD are *autoexec.nt, config.nt,* and *Setup.log* (the last of which contains system state information and minimal versions of registry hives for the system). When you create an ERD, you can also choose to back up the full registry hives as well to the *%SystemRoot%\repair* directory. For more information see *Emergency Repair Disk (ERD)* in Chapters 3 and 4.

## Event Logs

Event logs are pretty much the same as they were in Windows NT, although an MMC console is used to manage them now (Event Viewer, which is also part of Computer Management). One thing to note is that if you are running a high-security networking environment, you can configure a Windows 2000 system to halt when the event log becomes full. You need to configure a registry setting to do this—see *event logs* in Chapters 3 and 4 for more information.

Also, when you install or upgrade a machine to Windows 2000, configure your event log size and wraparound settings immediately so you won't lose valuable data that might be useful for troubleshooting purposes later on.

## Global Users

What were called global user accounts in Windows NT (user accounts that could be used for logging on to the domain) are called domain user accounts in Windows 2000. These are created and managed using the Active Directory Users and Computers console. For more information see *domain user account* in Chapters 3 and 4 and *Active Directory Users and Computers* in Chapter 5.

## Group Policy

If you are configuring Group Policy for your Windows 2000 network, you may want to test your new Group Policy settings without rebooting machines or waiting for Group Policy to auto-refresh (90 minutes or more). The trick is to use the `secedit` command to force Group Policy to refresh on the local machine. To do this, type the following at the command prompt:

```
secedit /refreshpolicy machine_policy
```

For more information see *Group Policy* in Chapters 3 and 4.

## Groups

A new type of group (universal group) and enhanced functionality of domain local and global groups (nesting, more membership options) are available for Windows 2000 domains running in native mode. These are attractive reasons to switch your domains to native mode instead of leaving them in mixed mode. There are some pitfalls, however, particularly with universal groups. When you change the membership of a universal group, the entire list of group members is replicated to all global catalog servers on the network, and in an enterprise with global catalog servers located at different sites separated by slow WAN links, this can be a problem. The best solution is to restrict the membership of universal groups to other groups only (either global or universal) and exclude individual user accounts from membership in universal groups. Also, you should keep the number of members of a universal group fairly small (preferably in the tens). Finally, select the membership for a universal group such that it is not expected to change frequently. For more information see *group* in Chapters 3 and 4.

## Hardware

Like Windows NT before it, Windows 2000 is forgiving of problems created when you update devices with incorrect or corrupt drivers. Such updates can sometimes prevent the system from booting to the point where you can log on. If this is the case, simply press the F8 function key when the boot-loader menu prompts you to select an operating system to boot. This causes the Advanced Startup Options menu to appear. One of the menu items is the familiar Last Known Good Configuration, which restores the system to the state in which it last booted successfully. If this fails, you can select the Safe Mode option to boot using a minimal set of device drivers. For more information see Table 3-10 in the article *disaster recovery* in Chapter 3.

Speaking of the boot menu, in a normal Windows NT installation this menu displayed two options: normal boot and VGA mode boot. In Windows 2000, however, there is only one boot option: normal boot (there is no VGA mode boot menu option because Safe mode takes care of this). The result is that in a normal Windows 2000 installation (only one operating system installed) the boot menu doesn't appear at all. In this case, to open the Advanced Startup Options menu, just press F8 while it says "Starting Windows" at the bottom of the screen.

If the Recovery Console is installed on a machine, however, the boot menu *does* appear since the Recovery Console is essentially a different operating system (a command-line version of Windows 2000). See *Recovery Console* in Chapters 3 and 4 for details.

## Installing Windows 2000

With Windows NT, some administrators chose to make their boot partition FAT while using NTFS to secure their data partitions. This enabled them to repair missing or corrupt system or driver files by booting from a DOS disk when these missing or corrupt files were preventing them from successfully booting the system. This hack is no longer necessary with Windows 2000 because of two new features:

*Recovery Console*
> Provides a way of booting to a minimal command-line version of Windows 2000 that lets you copy files to NTFS volumes

*Safe mode*
> Lets you boot using a minimal set of device drivers to repair the system, which is useful when a corrupt or missing driver is preventing a successful boot

The bottom line is that you should use only NTFS for your Windows 2000 boot volume, as it is more secure than FAT or FAT32. For more information on the features described earlier, see *Advanced Startup Options* and *Recovery Console* in Chapter 3. Further useful information on troubleshooting boot failures or recovering from them can be found in *disaster recovery* and *Emergency Repair Disk (ERD)* in Chapter 3 and *backup and restore* and *recovery options* in Chapter 4.

A useful tool for performing unattended installations of Windows 2000 is Setup Manager, which is included in the Windows 2000 Server Resource Kit (and is also included in the \Support\Tools folder of the Windows 2000 Server CD). Setup Manager walks you through the process of creating an answer file for unattended installations. For more information on Setup Manager (and other methods for unattended installation of Windows 2000), see *install* in Chapters 3 and 4.

---

 If you're using answer files for unattended installations, the answer file created by Setup Manager is plain text (unencrypted). This is fine, except that if you specified that the system you will install should join a domain, you probably entered your administrator account and password when running Setup Manager, and this information is therefore contained in the answer file in unencrypted form. So carefully protect the disk containing the answer file, or change your administrator account after performing the installation. An alternative is to install your new systems as members of a workgroup and then manually join them to the domain afterwards. See *computer* in Chapter 4 for information on how to do this.

---

## IntelliMirror

Where's the IntelliMirror console in Windows 2000? There ain't no such beast! You see, IntelliMirror is just an umbrella term or buzzword for a series of Windows 2000 features that enable users to access their desktops and data conveniently from any computer on (or off) the network. Specifically, IntelliMirror has four aspects:

*User data management*
> This is just another buzzword for two features of Group Policy:

> *Folder redirection*
>> Lets you redirect users' personal folders such as My Documents to a network file server so they are available to the user from anywhere on the network. For more information see *folder redirection* in Chapters 3 and 4.

> *Offline folders*
>> Lets users who are working offline (on laptops disconnected from the LAN) access shared network resources as if they were still connected to the LAN. Users can synchronize their files once they connect again to the LAN. For more information see *offline files* in Chapters 3 and 4.

*User settings management*
> This is really just another name for roaming profiles, which let users log on to any workstation on the network and have their personal desktops appear. For more information see *user profile* in Chapter 3 and *roaming user profile* in Chapter 4.

*Software Installation and Maintenance*
> This is another feature of Group Policy that lets administrators remotely install software packages and updates on users' workstations. For more information see *Windows Installer* in Chapter 4.

*Remote Installation Services*
> This is an optional Windows 2000 service that can be used for mass deployments of Windows 2000 Professional on corporate networks.

## MMC

The Microsoft Management Console can be used for building customized administrative tools, which can then be distributed by email or by storing them on a network share. See the first part of Chapter 5 for information on the MMC and how to customize it.

## Permissions

Like the earlier Windows NT operating system, Windows 2000 provides you with two sets of permissions for security access to files and folders: NTFS permissions and shared-folder permissions. The basic approach for secure shared resources is the same as in NT, but NTFS permissions will require some relearning in Windows 2000. For more information see *permissions* in Chapter 3 and the articles *offline files* and *shared-folder permissions* in Chapter 4.

## Printers

One terrific feature of Windows 2000 is that you can manage printers remotely across a network (or even over the Internet) using only a web browser. See *printer* in Chapters 3 and 4 for more information about this feature. By the way, to print to a Windows 2000 print server over the Internet, open the printer in your web browser and click Connect. This installs the appropriate drivers on your computer and creates a network printer to let you print to the remote print device.

---

Let Windows 2000 detect Plug and Play printers and install drivers for them automatically. If you install the driver manually and reboot your machine, you may end up with two printers for the same print device!

In addition, specify a location for your printer when you create it using the Add Printer Wizard. Users will then be able to search for printers by location when they search Active Directory using Start → Search → For Printers. This makes life easier for your users.

---

## Remote Access

If you have migrated a Windows NT domain to Windows 2000 but still have Windows NT RAS (or RRAS) servers on your network, there may be a problem: Windows NT RAS servers that are configured as member servers will be unable to communicate with Active Directory to authenticate users trying to initiate RAS sessions. There are two solutions to choose from:

- Upgrade your Windows NT RAS server (member server) to a domain controller. This way, the RAS server doesn't need to contact a different domain controller for authenticating RAS users.

- Weaken RAS permissions for your Windows 2000 domain by adding the Everyone built-in special identity to the local group called Pre–Windows 2000 Compatible Access on a Windows 2000 domain controller. This lets the RAS server use LTLM for authenticating RAS users.

For more information on remote access in Windows 2000, see *remote access* in Chapter 3 and *remote-access server* in Chapter 4.

## Rights

Modifying system rights for a user or group in Windows NT was a relatively straightforward task involving the use of User Manager for Domains. In Windows 2000, however, you must use Group Policy to do this if you are in a domain environment and must configure the appropriate settings of a domain GPO for your domain. See *Group Policy* in Chapters 3 and 4 for more information.

## Scheduling Tasks

Although the Windows NT 4.0 Server Resource Kit included a GUI utility to complement the at command-line utility, Windows 2000 carries this further with Task Scheduler, a wizard for scheduling tasks to be run. For more information see *Task Manager* in Chapter 6, *Utilities*. The at command is still available for batch scripting purposes however, but there are some compatibility issues. For example, if you create a task using the at command and then reconfigure its settings using the GUI Task Scheduler tool, you will then be unable to use the at command to further configure it.

 If a computer's date and time are not set correctly, your task may not run as expected (or at all). With Windows 2000 computers, date and time should be synchronized automatically within a domain, so this shouldn't be a problem.

## Sending Messages to Connected Users

You can use Computer Management to send a console message to users connected to a Windows 2000 computer on the network. This is an advisable practice as it's not nice to disconnect users unexpectedly and have them lose their work. See *Computer Management* in Chapter 5 for more information.

## Service Pack

Service Pack 1 for Windows 2000 addresses a number of operating-system issues regarding system reliability and application compatibility. SP1 also includes a new feature called *integrated installation* that makes an administrator's life simpler: you can apply the service pack to a network distribution point containing the Windows 2000 installation files. By doing this, the source files themselves become updated with the fixes in the service pack so that any future network installations that are performed from the distribution point will cause new systems to apply service pack fixes automatically during Setup. The one downside of integrated installation is that you cannot uninstall SP1 if you simultaneously install Windows 2000 and SP1 on a machine.

Another new feature of SP1 is that you no longer need to reapply the service pack after installing new system components or devices (hooray!)

## Shared Folders

If you have a lot of shared folders scattered across different file servers, there are two ways you can make it simpler for your users to locate the shared resources they need:

* Use the Distributed File System (Dfs) to combine your shared folders into one or more Dfs trees. Users just connect to a Dfs tree and browse the tree for the share they need, and they do not need to know the name of the file server on which the share is located.

* Publish the shares in Active Directory so users can search for them by location and by using friendly names. In this way users do not need to know the names of the file servers hosting the shares. You can also configure permissions on the shared folder object you publish to Active Directory—not to control access to the share but to control who can find and view the information you have published to Active Directory about the share.

For more information see *Dfs* in Chapters 3 and 4 and *Active Directory* in Chapter 4. For general information about how to share folders on local and remote machines, see *shared folder* in Chapters 3 and 4.

## Sites

Managing directory replication between Windows NT domain controllers and sites connected by slow WAN links was a hit-and-miss procedure of juggling various registry entries such as ChangeLogSize, ReplicationGovernor, and so on. Things are simpler in Windows 2000: use Active Directory Sites and Service to create logical sites that map the physical (geographical) topology of your network and map well-connected subnets to each site, and to handle the replication between the sites (or configure the site links manually if desired, by specifying bridgehead servers, replication schedules, and such). See *site* in Chapters 3 and 4 for more information.

In Windows 2000 the term "directory replication" refers to updating Active Directory information among domain controllers; in Windows NT it referred to copying a tree of folders between NT servers using the Directory Replicator service. This service is not needed in Windows 2000 since the Distributed File System service included with it is much more powerful and versatile. See *Dfs* in Chapters 3 and 4 for more information.

## System Policy

If you have a Windows NT 4.0 network with System Policy implemented for locking down client desktops and other features, you should be aware that when you upgrade your network to Windows 2000, these System Policies will not be upgraded to Group Policies. The reason is that Group Policy modifies special areas of the registry rather than the actual registry entries of the settings managed, whereas System Policy directly modifies the registry settings involved.

Likewise, if you migrate a portion of your network to Windows 2000, then be aware that any Group Policies you configure will have no effect on your remaining Windows NT computers. Therefore, you may want to continue using Windows NT's System Policy Editor (*poledit.exe*) to create and manage System Policy on your downlevel machines (place the *Ntconfig.pol* file in the *SYSVOL* folder on your Windows 2000 domain controller for it to be applied). For more information on Group Policy, see *Group Policy* in Chapters 3 and 4.

## Terminal Services Advanced Client (TSAC)

The Service Pack 1 CD for Windows 2000 also includes Terminal Services Advanced Client (TSAC), a Win32 ActiveX control that enables you to run Terminal Services sessions within Internet Explorer (IE). This is a useful feature since it allows administrators to administer Windows 2000 servers remotely over the Internet from any computer on which IE is installed, without the need of installing the standard (full) Terminal Services Client software (*mstsc.exe*) on the computer. TSAC is included on the SP1 CD but is not part of SP1 and is not automatically installed when SP1 is applied. TSAC also includes a Windows Installer (MSI) Setup package for deploying an updated full Terminal Services Client on machines running Windows 2000 Professional (or on earlier versions of 32-bit Windows that have had Windows Installer installed).

## Trusts

Windows 2000 promised to be simpler to manage than Windows NT at the enterprise level because of two-way transitive trusts. In Windows 2000, two-way trusts are automatically established between adjacent parent and child domains in a domain tree and between the root domains of trees in a forest, when you create a new child domain or new tree. However, the fine print is that these trusts are only transitive once you convert your domains to native mode, meaning that you no longer have any Windows NT BDCs in your domains. For more information on domain modes, see *mixed mode* and *native mode* in Chapter 3. For information on changing the mode of a domain, see *domain* in Chapter 4.

Speaking of native mode, it's quite OK to still have Windows NT 4.0 member servers as part of a Windows 2000 domain running in native mode. It's also OK to have Windows NT 4.0 Workstation or Windows 95/98 desktop machines as part of such a domain. Native mode simply means there are no more Windows NT domain controllers present in the domain.

Also, it's OK to have some domains in native mode and others in mixed mode in the same tree of domains. It's OK, but not terrific, as it complicates trusts and authentication (see my next point).

Kerberos authentication is used for authentication across domain boundaries; it can be a complex process that generates significant network traffic when it occurs between domains in different trees of a forest. Kerberos traffic can be limited, however, by establishing an explicit trust between a domain where resources are located and the domain where users who need to access those resources are located. For more information see *trust* in Chapters 3 and 4.

## User Accounts

Besides using the Active Directory Users and Computers console to create and configure new user accounts, you can also use the **csvde** command-line utility to bulk-import account information from a comma-delimited text file (*.csv* file) that has been previously exported from a spreadsheet or database. This is a great way of creating large numbers of user accounts at one shot. See *csvde* in Chapter 7, *Commands*, for more information.

## Windows 2000 Professional

Upgrading your Windows NT servers to Windows 2000 Server has clear advantages for enterprise network management—the most obvious of which is Active Directory. But what about upgrading your desktop machines to Windows 2000 Professional? This is bound to be a costly exercise since hardware on existing machines will have to be beefed up (or replaced entirely) in order to make them compatible with Windows 2000. Is it worth it?

It probably is, for several reasons:

- Remote management of Windows 2000 Professional computers is a breeze using the Computer Management console, and it's bound to reduce your help-desk costs significantly.

- Group Policy adds additional dimensions of enterprise-wide management of desktop settings, software installation, roving desktops, and other useful features.

- Costs for training users will be minimal if users are already familiar with the features of the Windows 95/98 and Windows NT 4.0 Workstation GUI.

I'll stop there lest I sound like an ad for Microsoft, but the fact is that there are compelling reasons why migrating desktop computers to Windows 2000 Professional makes sense.

# PART II

# *Alphabetical Reference*

# CHAPTER 3

# *Concepts*

As described in the Preface, this chapter begins the alphabetical reference portion of the book and covers the underlying terms and concepts relating to Windows 2000 Server and its administration. Before looking up how to perform a particular administrative task in Chapter 4, *Tasks*, you may first want to read the background information on the topic in this chapter.

Concepts are listed here alphabetically and are cross-referenced with articles in this and other chapters where appropriate. I've tried to facilitate learning while avoiding too much repetition; I decided the best way to do this was probably to center explanations of key Windows 2000 concepts in main articles, while briefly defining subsidiary concepts and cross-referencing them to the main articles. For example, *simple volume*, *mirrored volume*, *spanned volume*, and other concepts relating to Windows 2000 disk technologies are defined briefly under their own headings and cross-referenced to the main article *disks* where a detailed explanation of these concepts and how they relate to each other is provided.

Sometimes, however, it seemed better instead for me to reverse this procedure. For example, making the article *user account* cover all types of Windows 2000 user accounts would require too lengthy an article, so instead the article *user account* has only a brief definition of the concept of a user account, along with cross-references to fuller articles like *domain user account*, *local user account*, and *built-in user account*. Another reason for sometimes adopting this approach was because different MMC snap-ins are used to administer local and domain user accounts, and since these topics would therefore need to be separated in Chapter 4 it seemed logical also to do this in this chapter.

Whichever way the information is organized here, cross-references are included to guide the reader through the material. The form of these cross-references is to use a number in parenthesis to indicate the destination chapter; for example, *disks(4)* refers to the article entitled *disks* in Chapter 4.

# Alphabetical List of Concepts

## account lockout

A security feature that prevents a user from logging in for a time interval after a threshold number of failed logon attempts.

**See Also**

*account policy(3)*

## Account Operators

Built-in group for granting users the rights to administer accounts.

**See Also**

*built-in group(3)*

## account policy

A policy used to manage security for user logons.

**Description**

An account policy is the portion of a Group Policy Object (GPO) that specifically deals with password and account lockout settings for users. Account policies can be applied only at the domain level or on a local computer policy for standalone servers and workstations. So if they are configured in a GPO at the site or OU level, they are ignored. The specific portion of a GPO dealing with this function is the container:

> Computer Configuration → Windows Settings → Security Settings → Account Policies

For more information on account policies, see the section "Security" in the article *Group Policy* later in this chapter.

**See Also**

*Group Policy(3)*

## Active Directory

The directory service of Windows 2000.

**Description**

Active Directory is the central repository of information on a Windows 2000–based network. Active Directory stores information about where different resources are located on the network. These resources include user and group accounts, computers, printers, and shared folders. Active Directory can be used to locate these resources quickly so that:

- Ordinary users can access them if they have suitable permissions to do so.

- Administrators can create, delete, configure, and maintain them as needed.

Active Directory gives administrators a great deal of flexibility in how their network resources should be administered. By managing resources from any location in the enterprise, you can centralize IT administration in a few users or a single location. On the other hand, Active Directory allows you to create structure using domains and OUs and then to delegate authority over these portions. This allows for decentralized administration where certain administrative tasks are devolved to various trusted users throughout the enterprise.

Active Directory is managed primarily through the GUI but can also be programmatically accessed through an API called the Active Directory Service Interface (ADSI). By writing scripts that use ADSI, administrators can automate most Active Directory administrative procedures, but this requires a good understanding of VBScript or JScript and is beyond the scope of this book.

The rest of this article provides a general overview of how Active Directory works and how it should be implemented in an enterprise.

## How Active Directory Works

There are various ways of understanding what Active Directory is and how it works. Let's look at these now.

### Logical Structure

Active Directory represents the security framework of your enterprise with an essentially hierarchical structure of various logical objects (see Figure 3-1). These objects include:

*Forest*
> This is the widest and most encompassing of security objects in Active Directory. A forest generally represents everything in your enterprise: users, groups, computers, domains—everything!

*Tree*
> A forest consists of one or more trees, joined at their roots by transitive trusts.

*Domain*
> A tree consists of one or more domains joined in a strict tree-like hierarchy by transitive trusts.

*Organizational unit (OU)*
> OUs are logical containers you can use to group objects in a domain for purposes of security and administration. You can create hierarchical tree-like structures of OUs to reflect your company's geographical, organizational, or administrative structure (this is discussed more later in this section).

*Objects*
> Active Directory objects include computers, users, groups, printers, contacts, and shared folders. Each User object represents an actual user in the enterprise, each Computer object a computer, and so on.

A big part of planning for Active Directory involves planning the logical structure that best meets your administrative and security needs. Figure 3-1 displays the logical structure of Active Directory, with domains represented as black dots connected by two-way transitive trusts, and domain trees marked by closed curves. The entire diagram represents a forest. In addition, domains may also contain a hierarchy of organizational units.

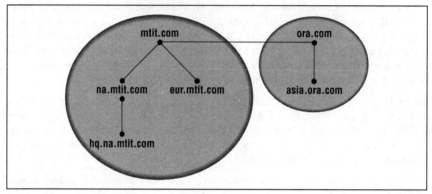

*Figure 3-1: The logical structure of Active Directory*

### Topological Structure

Large computer networks based on IP generally have a mesh-like structure in which smaller networks called subnets are joined together with routers into a single large internetwork. These subnets may be located at different geographical locations, in which case wide-area network (WAN) connections are used to join locations together. This means that certain connections in a large network are generally slower than others. (WAN connections are usually slower than local-area network, or LAN, connections.) To ensure that Active Directory performs optimally over such an arrangement, a topological structure can be created within Active Directory to reflect the actual network connections of the internetwork.

The main elements of such a topology are sites. A site is a grouping of subnets that have high-speed (LAN) connections throughout. Sites are joined to other sites using site links. Sites are important because domain controllers replicate the information contained in Active Directory to one another; this replication traffic can be controlled using sites so that it doesn't swamp the available bandwidth of slow WAN connections between different locations. See *site* in this chapter for more information on this.

### Physical Structure

A third way of looking at Active Directory is the actual structure and location of the directory database itself. From this point of view, Active Directory resides on computers called domain controllers that are running Windows 2000 Server. Domain controllers authenticate users and provide them with access to directory services for locating and accessing resources on the network.

Every domain controller within a given domain contains an identical copy of Active Directory, and this synchronization is maintained by a process called *multimaster replication*. This essentially means that there is no master domain controller in a domain; you can update an object or attribute value on any domain controller, and the update will then be replicated to every domain controller within the domain. This is different from the Windows NT model where one master domain controller (the PDC) in a domain contained the only writable copy of the database of user, group, and computer accounts for the domain. All other domain controllers (BDCs) in the domain replicated with the master domain controller to obtain Read-only copies of the database.

If there is more than one domain in the forest, the entire Active Directory is not replicated between all domain controllers in the forest, as this would make the directory database on each domain controller unmanageably large and too slow to respond to queries. Instead, a subset of Active Directory information called the global catalog is maintained in each domain to speed up queries and facilitate pass-through authentication and cross-domain logons. See *domain controller* and *global catalog* in this chapter for more information.

### Object Naming Conventions

Objects within Active Directory are uniquely identified within the directory database using several different naming conventions:

*Distinguished name (DN)*
This is an LDAP naming convention that uniquely identifies an object within the directory. For example, the DN for a user object named Bob that is located within a top-level OU called Sales within the Windows 2000 domain called *mtit.com* would be:

> *CN=Bob,OU=Sales,DC=mtit,DC=com*

These abbreviations are the three different kinds used in DNs, namely:

— CN stands for common name

— OU stands for organizational unit

— DC stands for domain component

*Canonical name*
This is just the DN written in reverse order (except that the full DNS domain name is written in its normal sense), omitting the abbreviations and using slashes as separators. In the above example the canonical name for the object Bob would be:

> *mtit.com/Sales/Bob*

---

 The canonical name is the form displayed on the Security tab of an object's property sheet in Active Directory Users and Computers.

---

### Relative distinguished name (RDN)

This is another LDAP naming convention and is the portion of the DN that identifies the object within its parent container. In the above example the RDN for the object Bob would be simply:

*CN=Bob*

### GUID

This stands for globally unique identifier, a 128-bit unique number that is assigned to each object in the directory when the object is created. While the DN, RDN, or canonical name for an object may change (for example, if the object is moved to a different OU in the domain), the GUID for an object never changes. GUIDs are used internally by Active Directory when the directory service needs to search the directory database for objects and for directory replication purposes.

### User principal name (UPN)

This type of name is used only for user accounts and consists of the user's logon name with an @ symbol and the user object's domain appended to it. For example, the UPN for Bob would be:

*bob@mtit.com*

---

 User, Group, and Computer objects are referred to as security principals because they are assigned security identifiers (SIDs), which they can use to log on to the network and be authenticated for resource access.

---

### Partitions

Active Directory is divided into several partitions that each store different kinds of information:

### Schema

This partition stores information defining the various classes of objects and types of attributes that Active Directory supports, including which attributes are supported by each type of object. This information replicates to all domain controllers in a forest. In other words, you only have one schema per forest.

### Configuration

This partition stores information about the structure of your forest and the trees within it, and it replicates to all domain controllers in the forest.

### Domain

This partition stores all the objects created in the domain (users, groups, computers, printers, and so on) and the values of their attributes. The information in this partition replicates only with domain controllers in the local domain, and not with those in other domains. However, a portion of this information (selected attributes for all objects) replicates to global catalog servers in other domains in the forest.

### Directories and Files

The Active Directory database and log files are created by default in the directory *%SystemRoot%\NTDS*. This location can be changed when the Active Directory Installation Wizard is run to promote a standalone or member server to the role of a domain controller. These files must be located on an NTFS partition.

The main directory database file (also called the datastore) is the file *NTDS.dit* and uses the same Jet database engine used in Microsoft Exchange Server 5.5, namely the Extensible Storage Engine (ESE). The database can grow to a maximum size of 16 terabytes and can contain more than 10 million objects. The database defragments and repairs itself automatically, but it can also be taken offline and manually defragmented using the *Ntdsutil.exe* tool if its performance is poor or it needs to be repaired due to corruption.

For best performance the log files should be placed on a separate physical disk. The log files record transactions written to the datastore and can be used to help restore a system if the datastore volume is lost. This can be done when the Active Directory Installation Wizard is run on the machine. A good configuration might be:

— Windows 2000 operating system on a mirrored volume

— Datastore file on a RAID-5 volume (at least 4 GB is recommended to accommodate future datastore growth)

— Database log files on a mirrored volume

Make sure you also back up the database regularly (see *backup and restore* in Chapter 4).

The datastore file *NTDS.dit* contains three main tables:

*Schema table*
Stores the Active Directory schema information

*Link table*
Stores the links between objects and their attributes

*Data table*
The bulk of the datastore; stores the instantiated objects and the values of their attributes

### Sysvol

Active Directory also creates and shares the default directory:

*%SystemRoot%\SYSVOL*

and shares the subdirectory:

*%SystemRoot%\SYSVOL\sysvol*

using the share name Sysvol. The Sysvol share contains domain security policies, logon scripts, and other important files that are replicated to all domain controllers in the domain. Other than placing your logon scripts into the correct subdirectory of Sysvol, you should not fool around with any of the files stored there. For more information on the Sysvol share, see *Group Policy* in this chapter. Note that *%systemroot%\sysvol\scripts* uses the share name NETLOGON and contains the logon scripts for domain users.

### Active Directory Permissions

Objects and their attributes are secured against unauthorized access with Active Directory permissions. These permissions are similar to NTFS permissions in many ways (see *permissions* in this chapter for more information). Users cannot access or perform actions on objects in Active Directory unless they have suitable permissions assigned to them. In most cases, however, the default permissions assigned when objects are created in Active Directory will suffice.

You can manually configure permissions on objects in Active Directory using the Active Directory Users and Computers console. You must first use View → Advanced Features to make the Security tab visible on the property sheets for objects. See *Active Directory* in Chapter 4 for more information.

---

 Be careful when modifying permissions on an object in Active Directory! Always make sure there is at least one user that has Full Control permission over the object. If this is not the case, the object may become inaccessible even to administrators.

---

When setting permissions on objects in Active Directory, the following should be considered:

- The kinds of permissions that can be set for objects in Active Directory differ with the type or class of object involved. For example, the permission Reset Password can be set for a User object but not for a Printer object since printers do not use passwords to control access.

- Permissions can be either allowed or denied on an object. If you deny a permission for a user but allow it for a group to which the user belongs, the following rule applies: denied permissions override allowed ones.

- In most cases, use standard permissions instead of special permissions when managing access to objects in Active Directory. Standard permissions consist of common groupings of different special permissions, which are the raw permissions under the hood that can be assigned. Table 3-1 lists some of the more commonly assigned standard permissions used to secure objects in Active Directory. (There are many more types of standard permissions that are only available for specific types of objects, however.) There are times when you will have to use special permissions to give more granular delegated rights. When not using standard permissions, be sure to document it.

*Table 3-1: Some Common Active Directory Standard Permissions*

| Permission | Description |
|---|---|
| Full Control | Lets you take ownership, change permissions, and do anything else with the object |
| Write | Lets you change any of the attributes of an object |
| Read | Lets you view objects and their attributes, view the owner of the object, and view the permissions set on the object |
| Create All Child Objects | Lets you add any type of object to an OU |
| Delete All Child Objects | Lets you remove any type of object from an OU |

- Inheritance can be used to simplify the administration of permissions on hierarchies of objects in Active Directory. By default, permissions assigned to an OU are inherited by child objects within the OU.

- However, you can prevent inheritable permissions from propagating to an object from its parent OU, thus breaking the chain of inheritance. When you do this, you can either:

  — Copy the previously inherited permissions from the parent to the child.

  — Remove the previously inherited permissions entirely.

  In either case, you can then explicitly configure or modify the permissions on the child as desired.

Special permissions allow you a whole host of different options on how inheritance occurs between parent and child. Special permissions are exceedingly complex, however, with Computer objects having 25 special permissions you can allow or deny. I strongly recommend that you only use standard permissions when manually configuring permissions on objects in Active Directory, and that you manually configure these permissions only when absolutely necessary.

 An easy way of assigning Active Directory permissions for objects to specific users is to use the Delegation of Control Wizard (see *delegation* in this chapter for more information).

### Planning an Active Directory Implementation

This is the most important thing to remember when planning implementation of Active Directory in your enterprise: *Keep it simple!* For example, if you can get by using only a single Windows 2000 domain (as Microsoft suggests most companies will be able to do), then do this. Having said that, the next most important thing is to *test, test, test!* Set up a test model of your planned implementation and get thoroughly familiar with Active Directory and how it works before you start implementing it in your real-world network.

Let's look at some specific planning issues related to implementing Active Directory in your enterprise.

### DNS Namespace

Since Active Directory requires DNS to be used on your network, you need to carefully plan your DNS namespace and how it will be mapped to Windows 2000 domains before you begin to implement Active Directory in your enterprise. The most important choice here is to decide on your DNS root name, which is the name of the root domain of your forest. You should generally select a root name that reflects the largest scope of your entire organization, taking into account all of its branch offices, subsidiaries, partners, and even planned acquisitions and mergers. For example, MTIT Enterprises (my own company) has the DNS domain name *mtit.com*, which is suitable for the name of my Windows 2000 root domain as well. From this root name I can name my branch offices (if I had any), such as *namerica.mtit.com* and *europe.mtit.com*.

Another reason it's important to plan your DNS namespace carefully is that it is not easily changed. Most importantly, you need to decide on your root name from the start because *you can't change it afterwards!* Furthermore, once you create a structure of domains and OUs in Active Directory, you don't want to restructure it later, as this can be difficult or impossible without reinstalling Active Directory. You should therefore choose a root name that is:

• Recognizable as being associated with the widest extent of your company's holdings

• Stable and not likely to change for at least three to five years (a long time in today's e-business economy!)

• Unique in DNS namespace if you plan to connect your business to the Internet (a given nowadays)

• Compliant with all DNS naming guidelines from ICANN to ensure easy intercommunication between your private network and the Internet

Determining your DNS namespace is only one issue associated with planning the structure of Active Directory—there are other issues such as delegation that are important as well (see *delegation* in this chapter for more information). See *DNS* in this chapter for more information on implementing DNS with Windows 2000. Also, for more information on naming Windows 2000 domains, see *domain*, *tree*, and *forest* in this chapter.

Related to the usefulness of implementing DNS is the question of whether your company has (or plans to have) a presence on the Internet. If so, your DNS implementation will need to account for this. For example, you may already have BIND name servers running on your network. Do you want to keep them or migrate entirely to Windows 2000 DNS servers? (See the "Planning a Windows 2000 DNS Implementation" section at the end of the article *DNS* in this chapter and also the section "BIND and Windows 2000" in that article.) Remember, if you plan to have some or all of your network resources exposed to the Internet, you will need to register a DNS domain name with ICANN or some other name registration authority (new ones are probably on the way soon).

### Schema

The schema is the portion of Active Directory that defines what classes of objects the directory can contain and what attributes these objects can have. Active Directory comes with a default schema that may be suitable for most companies, but the schema is also extensible for companies that need to create new object types and attributes for their directory. See *schema* in this chapter for more information on this topic.

### Hierarchy of Domains and OUs

Active Directory has a hierarchical structure, and two of its most important objects are domains and OUs. A domain is a security boundary for a Windows 2000 network. A domain is also a datastore partition since the domain is the boundary for domain object replication. Only a partial set of attributes gets replicated outside the domain. Objects within a domain share common security characteristics, such as logon rights and domain controller replication. OUs are more flexible containers that can be created as desired to contain other Active Directory objects, such as users, computers, groups, printers, or even more OUs. The typical way of creating structure in Active Directory is first to create your domains (arranged in one or more domain trees that are grouped together into a forest) and then to create OUs within your domains to create more granular structure that facilitates administration and delegation. The key thing here is that the domains and upper-level OUs you create should be stable and unchanging to simplify administration, delegation of permissions, and application of Group Policy. Lower-level OUs can then be created and modified as your IT needs change and evolve. OUs are typically created for delegation of rights, applying group policies, and organizing or hiding objects in the directory.

There are several common models for how IT responsibilities and functions are organized in an enterprise; they have various strengths and weaknesses as far as modeling your Active Directory structure after them is concerned. I'll classify these models by naming their main distinguishing criteria:

### By location

In a company that is spread out geographically across different cities, states, countries, or continents, IT functions can be either centralized in one location or decentralized across multiple locations. In either case, you generally have at least one network administrator at each location to handle installation, maintenance, and troubleshooting issues, even if much of the overall administration is handled at headquarters.

With Active Directory you could implement a location-based model two different ways (and these are not mutually exclusive):

### Hierarchy of domains

In a less centralized model where branch-office administrators assume more responsibility, you could create a tree of domains with the root domain at headquarters. For example, if headquarters for MTIT Enterprises is in Seattle while the branch offices are in Tampa and Cincinnati, you could use the domain names *mtit.com* for headquarters while *tampa.mtit.com* and *cincinnati.mtit.com* would be the subdomains for the branch offices.

*Concepts
A*

### Hierarchy of OUs

In a more centralized model where branch office administrators need to be delegated only limited administrative privileges, you could use a single domain for the entire company and create a tree of OUs within the domain to represent the various locations. You could create a top-level OU called Seattle and beneath it two child OUs called Tampa and Cincinnati. Seattle administrators could have full control over the hierarchy of OUs and delegate limited administrative powers for each child OU to suitable trusted users at each branch office.

Either method will work well, with the single-domain model being inherently simpler to administer and the multiple-domain model perhaps more familiar and comfortable to Windows NT administrators. The model is also quite flexible: if a new branch office is opened, a new domain or OU can be added to Active Directory.

## By business model

If separate divisions or departments of your company each have relatively autonomous IT divisions, you could base your Active Directory structure upon your business model. For example, if MTIT Enterprises had separate Manufacturing and R&D divisions (whether at the same location or across multiple locations), you could create a domain tree with the Executive division as the *mtit.com* domain while the Manufacturing and R&D divisions are the *mfg.mtit.com* and *rd.mtit.com* subdomains, respectively. If R&D itself is subdivided into Programming and Engineering departments, you could create a hierarchy of OUs in the R&D domain to represent this, with an R&D OU as the top-level OU for general administrative functions and Prog and Eng child OUs beneath it. Limited administrative powers could be delegated by the R&D administrator to trusted users in the Programming and Engineering departments.

The downside of implementing this model is that if your company restructures itself (a common thing nowadays), you may need to make considerable changes to your Active Directory structure to accommodate the changes. Furthermore, if divisions span multiple locations connected by slow WAN links, directory replication may impact network traffic significantly.

## By function

If you have a smaller enterprise with decentralized IT administration, you could implement Active Directory quite simply according to function. In this case you would typically create a single domain for the company and then create a hierarchy of OUs representing different IT department functions. Your top-level OUs might be called Network Management, Customer Support, and Development. Network Management might have child OUs called File Servers, Printers, Web Servers, and Routers. Web Servers might have child OUs called Corporate and Public, and so on. The advantage of this structure is that if locations change or departments are reorganized, the same basic Active Directory structure can be maintained—you may simply need to move groups to different OUs to accommodate the changes. One negative aspect is that it is easy for the hierarchy of OUs to grow several levels deep, and this can create complexities when Group Policies are implemented at various OU levels.

Based on these three basic models for Active Directory structure, there are several ways in which they can be combined into more complex or hybrid models. These models are particularly relevant for large enterprises:

*By location then by business model*
> Create a domain tree with corporate headquarters as the root domain and subsidiaries in different locations as subdomains. Then create a hierarchy of OUs in each domain representing the different IT departments for each division of the subsidiary. Alternatively, create a forest of domain trees if your company has several regional headquarters and no real worldwide headquarters (decentralized administration), then create the OUs within each domain. Still another alternative in a decentralized model is to create a root domain that contains only an Enterprise Admins group and nothing else, then create every other domain as a child domain of that root domain, followed by the OUs in each domain. Active Directory gives you a lot of flexibility in the way you can do things, and at this point in the product's history, it's often hard to say which implementation methods work the best (time will tell).

*By location then by function*
> Create a domain tree with headquarters at the root and subsidiaries in different locations as subdomains. Then create a hierarchy of OUs in each domain according to different IT administrative functions. This approach only works well if administration is decentralized in your company and not concentrated at headquarters. Alternatively, create a forest of domain trees or use a dummy root domain, as in the previous example.

*By business model then by location*
> Create a domain tree with the managerial or executive division in the root domain and different business groups as subdomains. Then create a hierarchy of OUs in each domain to represent different locations, with headquarters as the top-level OU.

The list goes on and on. No one model is necessarily best for any given organization, and no single model fits the needs of every enterprise.

---

 The needs and goals of your business will have a direct impact on how you design your Active Directory. Will you be upgrading your entire enterprise to support Active Directory? Does this include subsidiaries and business partners? Are there any acquisitions planned in the near future? Are you planning a merger with another company soon? These are important questions as they relate to how you will implement your domain structure—that is, whether you will use a single domain, a domain tree, a forest of trees, or several forests. See *domain*, *tree*, and *forest* in this chapter for more information on these entities and planning issues related to implementing them.

---

### Sites

If your enterprise network spans multiple locations connected by relatively slow WAN links, you can create sites within Active Directory to represent these different locations. Sites allow you to control and schedule Active Directory replication traffic between different parts of your network to optimize bandwidth usage over slow WAN links. Sites are different from domains: sites represent the physical topology of your network, whereas domains represent the different security boundaries for administrative purposes. For more information see *site* later in this chapter.

### Delegation

Whether you choose to partition your directory based on domains, OUs, or a combination of the two, you can use delegation to give limited administrative powers to trusted users in your enterprise. It is important to plan your domain/OU hierarchy to facilitate delegation, not to make it more difficult. See *delegation* in this chapter for more information on how to do this.

### Group Policy

Your Active Directory design should also take into account how you want to use and apply Group Policy within your enterprise. Group Policy is a powerful management feature of Windows 2000 that can be applied at the site, domain, and OU levels in Active Directory, so you need to plan your site topology and hierarchy of domains and OUs to facilitate this. See *Group Policy* in this chapter for more information.

### See Also

*Active Directory(4), backup and restore(4), delegation(3,4), domain(3,4), domain controller(3), forest(3), global catalog(3), Group Policy(3), OU(3,4), permissions(3), schema(3,4), site(3,4), tree(3), trust(3,4)*

---

# administrative share

A volume or folder shared by the operating system for administrative purposes.

### Description

Windows 2000 Server automatically shares certain volumes and folders to support remote administration and to enable access to network printers. Many of these administrative shares are hidden shares. As a result, they are not visible in My Computer, My Network Places, or Windows Explorer, but they are visible in the Computer Management console under Shared Folders.

Table 3-2 lists common administrative shares and their function. Depending on the configuration of your machine, not all of these shares may exist on your machine. For example, the Sysvol share is present only on domain controllers.

---

## *Active Directory Client*

Although Windows 2000 Server and Professional have built-in client software for accessing Active Directory, older versions of Microsoft Windows do not. However, Microsoft has supplied Active Directory client software for Windows 95/98 in the \\*Clients* folder on the Windows 2000 Server compact disc as an installation package called Directory Services Client (*Dsclient.exe*).

When you install *Dsclient.exe* on a Windows 9x client computer, it can query the global catalog using DNS to locate any Windows 2000 domain controller so that you can log on to the network. In addition, the client computer can search the global catalog using LDAP for published information about different users, groups, computers, and printers. Without *Dsclient.exe* installed, Windows 9x computers can connect only to the special Windows 2000 domain controller called the PDC emulator, since this domain controller emulates the functionality of a Windows NT 4.0 primary domain controller (PDC) for legacy clients like Windows 9x. Windows NT 4.0 Server and Workstation computers do not have a directory-services client and so should be upgraded to Windows 2000 Server and Professional to take advantage of the power of Active Directory.

Before you install an Active Directory client on a Windows 9x computer, you need to ensure that:

- Internet Explorer 4.01 or higher is installed
- Active Desktop is enabled

If you do install *Dsclient.exe* on a Windows 9x computer but the computer cannot locate a domain controller to log on to the network with, the domain controller running the operations master role called PDC emulator for your domain may not be operational. Downlevel Windows clients specifically require the PDC emulator to be available in order to log on using Active Directory. See *domain controller* in this chapter for more information about operations masters.

*Table 3-2: Administrative Shares*

| Administrative Share | Function |
| --- | --- |
| *<drive_letter>$* | For example, *C$*, *D$*, and so on; allows Administrators or Server Operators to connect to a drive's root directory on a remote machine for administration purposes. |
| *ADMIN$* | Share name for the \\*Winnt* system directory; used to allow remote administration of Windows 2000 machines. |
| *IPC$* | Share used for communication between machines using named pipes; an interprocess communication (IPC) method supported by Microsoft Windows operating systems. |

*Table 3-2: Administrative Shares (continued)*

| Administrative Share | Function |
|---|---|
| NETLOGON | Share name for the directory \ *Winnt*\*SYSVOL*\*sysvol*\*<domain_name>*\*scripts* on domain controllers, where *<domain_name>* is the DNS name of the Windows 2000 domain (e.g., *mtit.com*). This share is used for processing domain logon requests and contains domain policies and logon scripts. If a network default user profile is configured, it should be stored here as well. Note that this administrative share is not a hidden share. |
| print$ | Share name for \ *Winnt*\*System32*\*Spool*\*Drivers*; the location of the printer drivers; used for administration of network printers by providing a share point where client machines can download printer drivers. |
| SYSVOL | Share name for \ *Winnt*\*SYSVOL*\*sysvol*, which is used for storing the public files for a domain. This share is only present on domain controllers and is not a hidden share. |

### Notes

- You should not stop sharing or otherwise modify these administrative shares. If you do stop sharing one, it will be reshared when you reboot your system or when the Server service is restarted. For security reasons, administrative shares should be removed by editing the registry (this will prevent the shares from reappearing). In most cases, administrators will probably want to create hidden replacement shares with different names.

- If you are an administrator, you can quickly display and access the contents of any drive (for example, *C:* drive) on a remote machine (for example, *Server9*) by Start → Run → \ \ *Server9*\ *C$*.

### See Also

*files and folders(3,4), shared folder(3,4)*

---

## Administrator

Built-in user account with full system rights and permissions on the computer or domain.

### See Also

*built-in user account(3)*

---

## Administrators

Built-in group for granting users full rights and permissions to the computer or domain.

### See Also

*built-in group(3)*

## Advanced Startup Options

Alternative ways of starting Windows 2000, accessed by pressing F8 during the boot process.

### See Also

*disaster recovery(3)*

## attribute

A property of a file or folder that indicates something about its state.

### Description

The attributes you can set for files or folders depends on whether the underlying partition or volume is formatted using FAT, FAT32, or NTFS. Table 3-3 indicates which attributes are available for each filesystem.

*Table 3-3: File and Folder Attributes Available on Different Filesystems*

| Attribute | Filesystem | |
|---|---|---|
| | *FAT/FAT32* | *NTFS* |
| Read-only | ✓ | ✓ |
| Hidden | ✓ | ✓ |
| Archive | ✓ | ✓ |
| Index | | ✓ |
| Compress | | ✓ |
| Encrypt | | ✓ |

Here is a brief description of the different attributes you can set for files and folders on both FAT/FAT32 and NTFS volumes:

*Read-only*
> When applied to a file, this prevents the contents of the file from being modified. If applied to a folder, you can choose to make either the folder alone Read-only or the folder and all its contents (including subfolders) Read-only. Making the folder alone Read-only isn't very useful since new files you create in the folder do not inherit this attribute. By default, operating-system files are always marked Read-only, Hidden, and System.

*Hidden*
> This hides the file or folder from normal view the next time you view the parent folder's contents. To display hidden files, use Tools → Folder Options → View → Show hidden files and folders. By default, operating-system files are marked Read-only and Hidden.

*Archive (or File is ready for archiving)*
> When marked, this indicates that the file or folder should be backed up during the next backup cycle. Once the file or folder has been backed up, the Archive attribute is automatically cleared. When a file or folder is created or its contents are modified, this attribute is automatically set.

*For fast searching, allow Indexing Service to index this file*
> The Indexing Service is a Windows 2000 service that works automatically in the background and builds a catalog of the properties of specified files and folders. This speeds up search queries for files and folders. By default, all files and folders on NTFS volumes have this attribute marked, which is another good reason for using NTFS instead of FAT or FAT32.

*Compress contents to save disk space*
> This stores the file or folder in a compressed state on an NTFS volume. See *compression* in this chapter for more information.

*Encrypt contents to secure data*
> This stores the file or folder in an encrypted state on an NTFS volume. See *EFS* in this chapter for more information.

### Notes

- For information on how to set or clear attributes of files and folders, see *files and folders* in Chapter 4 and *attrib* in Chapter 7, *Commands*.

- There is another type of attribute called System on both FAT/FAT32 and NTFS volumes. Critical operating-system files have their Read-only, Hidden, and System attributes all set by default.

- The term *attribute* has a different meaning in the context of Active Directory. See *Active Directory* in this chapter for more information.

### See Also

*attrib(7), compression(3), EFS(3), files and folders(3,4)*

---

# auditing

Tracking user and operating-system activities.

### Description

Auditing records user and operating-system activities as events (audit entries) in the security log. A typical event records what action was performed, who performed it, whether the action succeeded or failed, what computer the action was initiated on, and so on. Auditing is generally performed for two purposes:

*Security*
> By auditing failures of activities such as logon attempts or attempts to access a restricted share on the network, administrators can detect when unauthorized access is being attempted.

*Resource usage*
> By auditing successful attempts to access shared folders, administrators can track patterns of usage for that resource to help determine upgrade and maintenance procedures.

### Audit Policy

An audit policy is a type of security policy that specifies what kinds of user and system activities will be audited. Before you enable auditing on a computer, you must configure the audit policy. The following types of events can be audited for success or failure:

*Account logon events*
> A user is authenticated by the security database on the local machine (if part of a workgroup) or by Active Directory on a domain controller (if part of a domain).

*Account management*
> An administrator creates, deletes, or modifies a user or group, resets a password, or performs some similar action.

*Directory service access*
> A user attempts to access an object in Active Directory. (This requires further configuration; see "Auditing Files, Folders, Printers, and Active Directory Objects" later in this section.)

*Logon event*
> A user logs on or off from the local computer, or the user creates or terminates a network connection to the local computer. (This event is always recorded on the computer being accessed by the user, whether local or on the network.)

*Object access*
> A user attempts to access a file, folder, or printer. (This requires further configuration; see "Auditing Files, Folders, Printers, and Active Directory Objects" later in this section.)

*Policy change*
> A user changes a security setting, such as password options, user rights, or the audit policy itself.

*Privilege use*
> A user exercises a right to perform an action, such as modifying the system time or taking ownership of a file.

*Process tracking*
> An application performs some specific action (generally useful only to the developer of the application).

*System*
> A user shuts down or restarts the computer, or some other action occurs that impacts security in general on the machine.

For procedures on creating an audit policy, see *auditing* in Chapter 4.

### Auditing Files, Folders, Printers, and Active Directory Objects

You can audit the success or failure of user attempts to access files, folders, printers, and Active Directory objects by configuring this in an audit policy. Once you have done this, however, you then need to specify which files, folders, printers, and Active Directory objects will be audited.

Filesystem objects (files and folders) can be audited only if they reside on NTFS partitions and volumes. For more information on how to audit these different resources, see *auditing* in Chapter 4.

**Viewing the Security Log**

- Audit entries recorded in the security log can be viewed in the Event Viewer console, which is in the Administrative Tools program group. See *Event Viewer* in Chapter 5, *Consoles*, for more information.

- You can configure event log settings using Group Policy. See the section "Security" in the article *Group Policy* in this chapter for more information.

*See Also*

*auditing(4), Event Viewer(5), Group Policy(3,4), Local Security Policy(3,4)*

---

## Authenticated Users

Built-in system group representing all users who have valid user accounts for the computer or domain.

*See Also*

*built-in group(3)*

---

## backup

Process of copying critical system files and data to tape or some other medium.

*See Also*

*backup and restore(4), disaster recovery(3)*

---

## Backup Operators

Built-in group for granting users the rights and permissions to back up and restore computers.

*See Also*

*built-in group(3)*

---

## basic disk

A hard disk that contains partitions and logical drives. A basic disk may also be part of a mirror set, volume set, stripe set, or stripe set with parity.

*See Also*

*disks(3), dynamic disk(3)*

## basic storage

A disk-storage technology used by Windows 2000 and earlier versions of Windows that divides disks into a limited number of partitions and logical drives and supports various advanced disk-storage technologies including mirror sets, volume sets, strip sets, and stripe sets with parity.

### See Also

*disks(3), dynamic storage(3)*

## bindings

Logical connections between network-adapter card drivers, network protocols, and network clients and services.

### Description

Bindings establish a virtual path between different components of a computer's networking subsystem, allowing packets to be passed up and down the various OSI layers as the computer communicates over the network. Windows 2000 allows a network adapter to be bound to one or more protocols, a protocol to be bound to one or more network adapters, and so on, providing great flexibility in how packets are processed as they are received from or prepared for the network.

If multiple protocols are bound to a network adapter, for example, there is a specific order (called a binding order) that determines the way in which the card will attempt to use these protocols to communicate over the network. You can rearrange the binding order to specify which protocol is attempted first, second, and so forth. You can also enable and disable specific bindings on specific network adapters in a multihomed machine, for example, if each card is connected to a different network segment running a different protocol. There is no need to have TCP/IP bound to an adapter if the segment to which the adapter is connected has computers that only run NWLink.

For information on how to configure bindings, see *bindings* in Chapter 4.

### Notes

Network clients and services include components such as:

- Client for Microsoft Networks
- Client for NetWare Networks
- File and Printer Sharing for Microsoft Networks
- Gateway (and Client) Services for NetWare

### See Also

*bindings(4), network protocol(3,4)*

## *boot partition/volume*

The partition or volume on which the Windows 2000 operating-system files are located, such as the *%SystemRoot%* directory and its contents.

### See Also

*disks(3)*

## *built-in domain local group*

Type of built-in group used for granting users the rights to perform system tasks on domain controllers.

### See Also

*built-in group(3)*

## *built-in global group*

Type of built-in group used for grouping users together who have similar needs for accessing network resources in a domain environment.

### See Also

*built-in group(3)*

## *built-in group*

A special group that is created during installation of Windows 2000 Server.

### *Description*

A number of special groups are created during the installation of Windows 2000 Server. These built-in groups have predefined sets of rights that simplify the job of administering user accounts. For example, by adding a user account to the Administrators built-in group, that user gains all the rights and privileges that the special Administrator account has.

Different built-in groups are available depending on whether you are working with member servers or domain controllers, and whether you have implemented your Windows 2000 environment as a workgroup or a domain.

### *Workgroup Setting*

In a workgroup setting, each standalone server running Windows 2000 Server or client computer running Windows 2000 Professional has only one type of built-in group available, namely, built-in local groups. These built-in local groups can be used to simplify the job of administering the computer on which they exist. They control access to resources on the local computer on which they exist as well as grant users the rights to perform system tasks on this computer.

Built-in local groups exist within the Local Security Database on standalone servers or client computers running Windows 2000. They are created within the Users folder of the *Local Users and Groups* console (see Chapter 5). The six basic built-in local groups and their functions are as follows:

*Administrators*
Members can perform any administrative task on the local computer.

*Backup Operators*
Members can back up and restore the local computer.

*Guests*
Members have no rights or permissions on the local computer unless they are specifically assigned.

*Power Users*
Members can administer local user accounts, share folders and printers, and perform other limited administrative tasks on the local computer.

*Replicator*
This special group supports file replication in a domain using Dfs, and it needs no members added to it.

*Users*
Members have the rights and permissions that are normally assigned to ordinary users of the local computer, or other rights and permissions as they are specifically assigned.

Table 3-4 shows the initial membership of these built-in local groups on a standalone server or client computer that is part of a workgroup.

*Table 3-4: Initial Membership of Built-in Local Groups*

| Built-in Local Group | Initial Membership |
| --- | --- |
| Administrators | Administrator |
| Backup Operators | None |
| Guests | Guest |
| Power Users | None |
| Replicator | None |
| Users | None |

## Domain Setting

In a domain setting there are four types of built-in groups available:

Built-in local groups
Built-in global groups
Built-in domain local groups
Built-in system groups

The first type exists in the Local Security Database of member servers or client computers running Windows 2000 and are found within the Groups folder of the *Local Users and Groups* console (see Chapter 5). The remaining three exist within

Active Directory on Windows 2000 domain controllers and are found in the Builtin and Users organizational units of the *Active Directory Users and Computers* console (see Chapter 5). Let's look at each one of these types separately.

### Built-in Local Groups

Built-in local groups are found only on member servers or client computers in the domain; they are used to control access to resources on the local computer on which they exist and to grant users the rights to perform system tasks on this computer. They function essentially the same way in a domain-based network as they do in the workgroup setting described above. The only difference is that when a standalone server or client computer is moved from a workgroup to a domain, the membership of its built-in local groups changes from what is shown in Table 3-4 to that shown in Table 3-5. These changes occur to give administrators, users, and guests in the domain appropriate rights and permissions to the resources on the computer.

*Table 3-5: Initial Membership of Built-in Local Groups on a Member Server or Client Computer That Is Part of a Domain*

| Built-in Local Group | Initial Membership |
|---|---|
| Administrators | Administrator, Domain Admins |
| Backup Operators | None |
| Guests | Guest, Domain Guests |
| Power Users | None |
| Replicator | None |
| Users | Domain Users |

An example might help. When a standalone server running Windows 2000 and belonging to a workgroup joins a domain (and hence becomes a member server in that domain), the built-in global group Domain Admins (which is defined in Active Directory on domain controllers in the domain), becomes a member of the Administrators built-in local on the member server. In this fashion, any users that belong to the Domain Admins global group also belong to the Administrators local group on all member servers in the domain, giving them full administrative rights and permissions on all member servers in the domain. Built-in global groups are discussed later.

An additional built-in local group called Pre–Windows 2000 Compatible Access is created when you promote a member server to a domain controller. This group lets you choose between stronger Windows 2000 security and weaker security that might be needed to continue running legacy applications. If you have problems running legacy applications after promoting a server to a domain controller, add the special group Everyone to this group and reboot your domain controllers.

### Built-in Domain Local Groups

When a member server is promoted to a domain controller, the existing built-in local groups on the machine are changed to built-in domain local groups, and additional ones are created. Built-in domain local groups have predefined rights and permissions on domain controllers to simplify the task of administering domain controllers and the domain in which they reside. They are used to control access to resources on domain controllers and to grant users the rights to perform system tasks on these computers. The standard built-in domain local groups on a Windows 2000 domain controller include:

*Account Operators*
> Members can create, modify, and delete user accounts and groups on domain controllers in the domain.

*Administrators*
> Members can perform any administrative task on domain controllers in the domain.

*Backup Operators*
> Members can bypass file security to back up and restore any files on any domain controllers in the domain.

*Guests*
> Members have no rights or permissions on domain controllers in the domain, unless they are specifically assigned.

*Print Operators*
> Members can administer network printers on domain controllers in the domain.

*Replicator*
> This special built-in domain local group is used to implement file replication in a domain and does not need any members added to it.

*Server Operators*
> Members can share folders and backup domain controllers in the domain.

*Users*
> Members have the rights and permissions that are normally assigned to ordinary users for domain controllers in the domain, or other rights and permissions as they are specifically assigned.

---

 If a domain is changed from mixed mode to native mode, the built-in domain local groups are sometimes just called security groups.

---

Additional built-in domain local groups may also be present, depending on which optional Windows 2000 components are installed. These optional built-in domain local groups include:

*DHCP Users*
> Members have Read-only access to settings on a DHCP server.

*DnsAdmins*
> Members can administer DNS servers.

*RAS and IAS Servers*
   Members are servers that can access remote-access properties of users.

*WINS Users*
   Members have Read-only access to WINS servers.

Table 3-6 shows the initial membership of the standard built-in domain local groups on a member server that has just been promoted to the role of domain controller.

*Table 3-6: Initial Membership of Standard Built-in Domain Local Groups on a Domain Controller*

| Built-in Domain Local Group | Initial Membership |
|---|---|
| Account Operators | None |
| Administrators | Administrator, Domain Admins |
| Backup Operators | None |
| Guests | Guest, Domain Guests |
| Print Operators | None |
| Replicator | None |
| Server Operators | None |
| Users | Domain Users |

Here's another example to make things clear. A domain controller is configured as the print server for a network printer. Sally needs to be granted the necessary rights and permissions to manage the network printer. To do this, simply add Sally's user account to the Print Operators group on any domain controller in the domain.

### Built-in Global Groups

Built-in global groups on domain controllers are used to group together domain users who have similar resource access needs, making it easier to assign permissions to them for shared network resources. Built-in global groups have no predefined rights or permissions; you typically grant them rights and permissions by making them members of domain local groups on domain controllers or local groups on member servers.

The standard built-in global groups on a domain controller are:

*Domain Admins*
   Members are all users who need full administrative rights in the domain.

*Domain Computers*
   Members are all member servers and workstations in the domain.

*Domain Controllers*
   Members are all domain controllers in the domain.

*Domain Guests*
   Members are all users who require only temporary access to resources in the domain.

*Domain Users*
> Members are all ordinary users in the domain.

*Enterprise Admins*
> Members can administer any domain in the forest.

Additional built-in global groups may also be present, depending on which optional Windows 2000 components are installed. These optional built-in global groups include:

*Cert Publishers*
> Members are enterprise certification and renewal agents.

*DnsUpdateProxy*
> Members are DNS clients that are allowed to perform dynamic updates on behalf of other clients (typically DHCP servers).

*Group Policy Creator Owners*
> Members can modify Group Policy for the domain.

*Schema Admins*
> Members can administer the Active Directory schema.

 When the forest root domain is changed from mixed mode to native mode, the scope of the Enterprise Admins and Schema Admins groups becomes universal instead of global. You could call these groups built-in universal groups if you like.

Table 3-7 shows the initial membership of the standard built-in global groups.

*Table 3-7: Initial Membership of Built-in Global Groups*

| *Built-in Global Group* | *Initial Membership* |
| --- | --- |
| Domain Admins | Administrator |
| Domain Computers | Varies |
| Domain Controllers | Varies |
| Domain Guests | Guest |
| Domain Users | None |
| Enterprise Admins | Administrator in the forest root domain |

### Built-in System Groups

Built-in system groups exist on all computers running Windows 2000—whether server or client computers and whether they operate in a workgroup or a domain. Built-in system groups were formerly called special identities in Windows NT.

You cannot modify the membership of a built-in system group. Instead, users temporarily become members of different system groups, depending on what kind of system or network activity they are involved in. In other words, it's not who you are but what you are doing that determines whether you belong to one or more of the built-in system groups on a computer.

For example, if you log on to the local computer using its keyboard and try to access a folder on that computer, you are considered a member of the Interactive system group as far as accessing that resource is considered. If the Interactive group is explicitly denied access to the folder, no one who logs on locally to the computer will be able to access the folder (a rather extreme example).

System groups are not displayed as groups in Local Users and Groups console or the Active Directory Users and Computers console. Instead, they are displayed and can be selected when you are configuring permissions on files and folders on NTFS volumes, on printers, or on objects in Active Directory.

The following are some of the more important built-in system groups on a Windows 2000 computer:

*Authenticated Users*
> All users who have valid user accounts on the computer or domain; this is the same as the Everyone group, except that it does not include anonymous users or guests

*Creator Owner*
> The user who owns the particular local or network resource under consideration

*Everyone*
> All network users, including users with valid user accounts on the computer or domain, users from other domains (trusted or untrusted), and guest users

*Interactive*
> The user who is currently logged on locally at the keyboard of the local computer and is accessing a resource on this computer

*Network*
> All users who are currently logged on to computers on the network and are accessing a resource on the local computer

## Notes

- Members of the Guests built-in group cannot permanently modify the desktop settings on their Windows 2000 computer.

- If additional services like Internet Information Services or Terminal Services are installed on a standalone server, additional built-in user accounts will be created as members of the Guests group. See Table 3-8 in the *built-in user account* article in this chapter for more information.

- You cannot change the scope (domain local, global, or universal) or the type (security or distribution) of a built-in group. This provides an easy way of determining whether a given group is built-in or user defined.

- Strangely enough, built-in groups on domain controllers are located in two different places in Active Directory:
  - The basic built-in domain local groups are located in the Builtin OU.
  - Some additional built-in domain local groups (depending on which additional services are installed), plus all built-in global groups and the Enterprise Admins built-in universal group are located in the Users OU.

- Account Operators cannot make changes to the rights or membership of the following built-in groups:

  Administrators
  Account Operators
  Backup Operators
  Domain Administrators
  Print Operators
  Server Operators

  This places account operators further down on the administrative totem pole from the other built-in administrative groups.

- Don't confuse built-in domain local groups with built-in local groups. See the "Notes" section in the *local group* article in this chapter for more information.

- Built-in system groups are not listed in Active Directory, but you can 'assign permissions to them for shared resources. One useful tip is to assign permissions to the Authenticate Users group instead of the Everyone group to secure your network resources from untrusted users.

- In Active Directory Users and Groups, groups are located by default in the following two containers:

  — Builtin contains the built-in domain local groups.

  — Users contains the built-in global groups and all user-defined groups.

  This makes things a bit messy from the administrative point of view. For example, user accounts and groups are mixed together in the same OU. You have several options:

  — Create a new OU called Groups and store your user-defined groups there. The problem is that you cannot move the built-in groups to another OU, so if you plan to use the built-in groups to simplify administration, you're probably better off leaving things the way they are. On the other hand, if you are working with a really big company, you probably want to create a whole series of new groups for different levels of user access and administrative control, and then you can forget about most of the built-in groups.

  — Select Users OU → Action → View → Filter Options → "Show only groups" lets you display just the groups in the Users OU. The problem here is that filters are applied globally to all OUs, not just the selected one. This is probably the best solution, although it would have been nice if Microsoft had included some default filter buttons on the toolbar, such as Show Users, Show Groups, and so on, instead of simply the default Filter button which opens the Filter Options dialog box.

  Note that both Builtin and Users are containers, not organizational units (OUs). Group Policy can be applied to OUs but not to other types of containers within Active Directory.

- Limit membership in the Domain Admins global group for each domain. Members of this group have powerful privileges, including:

  — The ability to define domain-wide security policies.

  — The ability to take ownership of any object in the domain.

A good strategy is to keep membership in this group small and to delegate limited administrative authority over different OUs in the domain to specific groups of trusted users.

### See Also

*Active Directory Users and Computers(5), built-in user account(3), group(3), local group(3), Local Users and Groups(5)*

---

# built-in local group

Type of built-in group used for granting users the rights to perform system tasks on standalone servers or client computers in a workgroup environment.

### See Also

*built-in group(3)*

---

# built-in system group

Type of built-in group that users temporarily become members of when they are involved in certain kinds of system activity.

### See Also

*built-in group(3)*

---

# built-in user account

A special user account created during installation of Windows 2000 Server.

### Description

Two default user accounts are created during installation of Windows 2000 Server. These accounts are called built-in user accounts, and they can be renamed but not deleted. The accounts are:

*Administrator*
An account that has full administrative rights for the domain or computer.

*Guest*
An account used to grant temporary access to network resources in the domain or computer. This account is disabled by default and should be enabled only when needed.

On a member server or client computer, the Administrator and Guest accounts are local user accounts and are stored in the local security database. For example, the Administrator account on a member server has full administrative rights on that member server (and no rights on any other computer in the network). On a domain controller, however, these accounts are domain user accounts and are stored in Active Directory. The Administrator account on a domain controller thus has full rights on every computer in the domain.

---

Depending on which optional components of Windows 2000 Server are installed, there may be other built-in user accounts. Table 3-8 lists and describes the most common of these accounts.

*Table 3-8: Optional Built-in User Accounts*

| Account | Name | Description |
| --- | --- | --- |
| Internet Guest Account | IUSR_<computername> | Used by Internet Information Services (IIS) to provide anonymous users with access to IIS resources |
| Launch IIS Process Account | IWAM_<computername> | Used by IIS to launch out-of-process web applications |
| TsInternetUser | TsInternetUser | Used by Terminal Services |
| krbtgt | krbtgt | Key Distribution Center service account (disabled by default) |

### Notes

- A good practice is to rename the Administrator account. Make sure you also assign the Administrator account a complex password and protect this password carefully.

- Do not use the Administrator account as your everyday user account if you are a network administrator. Instead, create an ordinary user account for yourself, and use this account to check your email, work on documents, and so on. Use the Administrator account (or any account that belongs to the Domain Admins group) *only* when performing network and system administration tasks that require this level of privilege.

- Review permissions assigned to the Guest account (and Guests group) for shared network resources before enabling this account.

### See Also

*built-in group(3), user account(3)*

---

## compression

A method for reducing the disk space required on NTFS volumes.

### Description

Files and folders stored on NTFS volumes can be compressed to minimize the amount of disk space they occupy. When these files are accessed, the operating system uncompresses them automatically so they can be read or modified; when the modified files are saved or closed, they are automatically compressed again. The whole process is transparent to the user.

Both files and folders can be compressed. If a folder is compressed, the files within it need not be compressed—or some may be and others not.

*Concepts*
*C*

### Notes

- For information on how to compress files and folders, see *files and folders* in Chapter 4.

- Certain file types can be effectively compressed, resulting in significant gains in disk space, while compressing other file types shows little gain in space. For example, a compressed bitmap (*.bmp*) may need only 25% or less of its uncompressed space, while compressing a binary executable program file (*\*.exe*) rarely results in a significant gain in space. You should not try to compress files that are already compressed, such as WinZip (*.zip*) files. This simply results in wasted processing power.

- You must have NTFS write permission on a file or folder in order to compress it.

- In order to compress a file, you need enough free space on the disk to hold the file in both its compressed and uncompressed state.

- When a file is copied from one place to another, it is first uncompressed, copied, and then compressed again. If there is insufficient disk space to hold the uncompressed file, an error message will occur and the copy will fail.

- You cannot both compress and encrypt a file at the same time.

---

 Data that is frequently modified, such as users' work files in their home folders, generally should not be compressed due to the overhead of the compression process. In addition, if you are using disk quotas to manage how much disk space is allocated to users, these disk quotas are calculated on the basis of the uncompressed size of users' files. So it really doesn't make sense to compress frequently accessed files. Instead, compress data that is relatively static in nature—for example, archived financial records stored on disk. This is really the only practical use for compression on NTFS volumes.

---

### See Also

*attribute(3), files and folders(3,4)*

---

## computer name

A name used to identify a Windows 2000 computer on a network.

### Description

Windows 2000 computers have a dual identity on a network:

- A computer name that is based on the Domain Name System (DNS)

- A NetBIOS name that is used for communication with downlevel computers (those running an earlier version of Microsoft Windows, such as Windows NT 4.0)

---

### Example

If the computer name is *MS1* (for Member Server One) and it belongs to the domain *mtit.com*, the full computer name is thus *MS1.mtit.com*.

### See Also

*computer name(4), DNS(3)*

---

## connection

In Windows 2000, a mechanism for connecting your computer to another computer, a remote-access server, a dedicated network access device, or the Internet.

### Description

Connections in Windows 2000 are classified in different ways. For example, you can create:

*LAN connections*
  These are connections to the local network through a network adapter installed in the computer. Unlike other kinds of connections in Windows 2000, LAN connections are created automatically during setup. LAN connections enable a computer to communicate with other computers on the network.

*WAN connections*
  These include both dial-up and dedicated connections to other networks through hardware devices such as modems, ISDN terminal adapters, X.25 pads, and access routers. Windows 2000 supports a broad range of different WAN connectivity options. Another name for these connections are remote-access connections, as they allow a remote client to access resources on a private corporate network.

*Direct computer connections*
  This is a special form of connection between two computers using a serial (RS-232C) or parallel (ECP) file-transfer cable, or an infrared port. It is used only for establishing a connection to transfer files between machines.

In addition, you can classify connections according to whether they are inbound or outbound:

*Outbound connections*
  These connections enable your computer to initiate or establish a connection with a computer on a remote network or the Internet. In an outbound connection your computer assumes the role of a client requesting networking services from a remote-access server or device. Windows 2000 supports different types of outbound connections:

  — Dial-up connections to a remote private network using a modem or ISDN adapter

  — Dial-up connections to the Internet using a modem or ISDN adapter

— Direct connections to another computer using a null-modem cable or other device

— Virtual private network (VPN) connections that securely tunnel through the Internet to a remote private network and use a dial-up or dedicated (LAN) connection to the Internet

*Inbound connections*

These connections enable your computer to listen for and respond to connection attempts by remote clients. In an inbound connection your computer assumes the role of a server and can grant clients access to resources on the local computer or act as a secure gateway to allow them to access resources on the local network. Windows 2000 supports dial-in inbound connections through dial-in connections using a modem, modem pool, ISDN adapter, serial or parallel cable, infrared port, or other hardware.

### Implementing Connections

On Windows 2000 all outbound connections are created using Network and Dial-up Connections. For information on using this tool to create and configure different types of outbound connections, see *dial-up connection, direct computer connection*, and *VPN connection* in Chapter 4.

How inbound connections are implemented in Windows 2000 depends on the role of the computer involved:

- On Windows 2000 Server computers configured as standalone servers and on Windows 2000 Professional computers, use Network and Dial-up Connections to create inbound connections and configure a standalone remote-access server. For more information on how to do this, see *incoming connection* in Chapter 4.

- On Windows 2000 domain controllers and on member servers (belonging to a domain), use the Routing and Remote Access Service console to create inbound connections and configure a domain-based remote-access server. For more information on how to do this, see *remote-access server* in Chapter 4.

Finally, for general information on how remote access works in Windows 2000, see *remote access* in this chapter.

### See Also

*dial-up connection(4), direct computer connection(4), incoming connection(4), local-area connection(4), Network and Dial-up Connections(6), remote access(3), remote-access server(4), Routing and Remote Access(5), VPN connection(4)*

---

# Creator Owner

Built-in system group representing the user who owns the selected resource.

### See Also

*built-in group(3)*

---

# *delegation*

The process of granting limited administrative authority to users over portions of Active Directory.

## *Description*

Delegation allows administrators to give users different levels of control over objects in Active Directory. This distributes the administrative burden of managing Active Directory to trusted users and groups in an enterprise thus easing the workload for administrators. For example, you can delegate the right to change users' passwords to a trusted individual in your network without giving them any other administrative privileges. You can even delegate the right to delegate if you desire. In order for delegation to work properly, however, the structure of domains and OUs in Active Directory must be carefully planned.

For descriptions of the various ways of delegating authority in Active Directory, see *delegation* in Chapter 4.

### *Planning an Active Directory Structure That Facilitates Delegation*

For delegation to work well, you need to model your Active Directory structure after the different categories of administrative tasks performed or the functions that your IT staff have, not after the political or organizational chart for your company. For example, a company's organizational chart might show the CEO as the head or root of the organizational tree, with different departments, such as HR, Sales, IT, and Finance, beneath. These departments might then have subdivisions, such as Accounts and Payroll, under Finance. This is generally not the model you should follow when creating your Active Directory structure of domains and OUs, as it does not reflect how different IT administrative tasks can be delegated. For example, you are hardly likely to delegate Active Directory administrative tasks to the CFO who manages the Finance department, as administering Active Directory is an IT task, not a financial one, and requires a high level of IT expertise.

Instead, you should adopt a model that more closely associates different domains and OUs with specific administrative tasks. Do this by documenting the flow of IT tasks and responsibilities throughout your organization. Determine who is responsible for what in what branch or location, and use this as the basis of planning your Active Directory structure. Ask yourself what the general structure of IT functions is right now in your company. Do you have one centralized IT department with a single user or group in charge? Or is IT spread across several geographical locations, with each location fairly independent of the others (decentralized IT department)? Are some of your IT functions outsourced to other companies, or is everything handled internally? For example, if management of your public web servers is outsourced but they are to be included in Active Directory, you could create a special OU to contain them and then delegate control of the OU and its contents to users from the outsourced companies. Do you have a large number of servers grouped according to department or function? You could create a top-level OU called Servers and then several child OUs beneath it called Manufacturing, Engineering, and Sales. Administrators then can delegate management of department servers to trusted users in that department. You could also put each department's users and groups into the same OUs and delegate management of users to the same or different trusted users.

Try to leave some flexibility in how you design your Active Directory structure, taking into account the growth and evolution of your company. Do this by not getting too heavily into delegation, and not delegating the right of delegation to others.

Unfortunately, there is no single model of Active Directory structure that provides the best support for delegation while simultaneously meeting the needs of every type of company or enterprise. And delegation is not the only criteria (or even the most important criteria) in deciding what hierarchy of domains and OUs you should create in Active Directory. For more information on different models for Active Directory structure and their strengths and weaknesses, see *Active Directory* in this chapter.

### Delegation Strategies

There are different approaches and methods you can use with respect to delegation in Active Directory:

*Assigning permissions*
> Active Directory permissions can be assigned to individual objects (OUs, users, groups, computers, printers, and so on) within the directory, to contiguous branches of objects, to a particular type of object, or to a specific attribute. In general, it's best to assign permissions only to objects, and more particularly, to OUs, so that the objects within the OU will inherit the permission. Assigning permissions at more granular levels of the directory make them hard to track when things don't work as expected. For more information on Active Directory permissions, see *Active Directory* in this chapter.

*Object-based delegation*
> One way of delegating administrative privileges in Active Directory is to assign permissions over specific types of objects contained in sites, domains, or OUs to specific users or groups. These objects can include computers, users, groups, printers, and so on. For example, an administrator could delegate Full Control permission over Computer objects in an OU called Web Servers to a Webmasters global group, giving members of this group full control over the servers in their department.

*Task-based delegation*
> Another way of performing delegation is to delegate the authority to perform a particular task for a site, domain, or OU to specific users or groups. For example, an administrator could delegate authority over a domain to a global group called CompAdmins to perform the task "Add a computer to the domain."

*Delegating the power to delegate*
> By delegating the permission to assign permissions on objects to users and groups, you can empower trusted users to entrust others with limited administrative privileges. This sounds like a good idea, but if not documented properly, you will soon lose track of who can do what on your network.

*Delegating to groups*

Always delegate administrative authority over directory objects to groups, not to users. This simplifies Active Directory administration in the long run as your company grows and reorganizes. Take advantage of the power of nesting groups as well so as to simplify complex administration. See *group* in this chapter for more information.

*Use common permissions*

Avoid using the more granular Active Directory permissions, as these are harder to document and keep track of. Keep your permissions assignments as simple as possible, granting just enough permissions to allow trusted users to do the jobs you want them to.

*Use inheritance*

Delegate authority over the parent OUs so permissions can flow down the hierarchy to child OUs beneath them. Creating an object within an OU automatically results in the object inheriting the permissions of its parent OU. How inheritance is applied depends on how you assign permissions. Specifically, you can have permissions on the parent OU apply to:

— The OU only

— The OU and all its child objects

— Its child objects only

— Specific types of child objects (e.g., Computers)

You also need to know how permissions flow when you are delegating authority over sites, domains, and OUs:

*Sites*

Delegating authority over a site usually (but not always) spans the domains that are within (or overlap) the site.

*Domains*

Delegating authority over a domain automatically delegates this authority over all objects within the domain.

*OUs*

Delegating authority over an OU may affect only the OU and its objects or all child OUs and their objects, depending upon how you decide to go.

 Delegating authority at the OU level is preferable to doing so at the site or domain level. When delegating authority at the OU level, do so at the highest level possible to take advantage of inheritance, which simplifies the assignment of Active Directory permissions. You can also override the permissions that a child object might inherit from its parent object. This is called blocking and prevents future changes to the parent's permissions from flowing to the child. Blocking makes permissions hierarchies more complicated and should be avoided unless absolutely necessary to achieve some purpose. Instead, it's better to move objects you want to block to a different OU and assign suitable permissions to that OU.

### Notes

- After you delegate authority over an object, it may take several minutes until the users or groups will be able to perform the tasks delegated them while Active Directory processes the request.

- Delegation is a good reason why you might choose to adopt a single-domain model with multiple OUs instead of the more complex multiple-domain model. You can delegate authority over domains as well, but there are fewer administrative groups to manage with only one domain.

- Delegation of authority over Group Policy Objects (GPOs) is different from delegation of authority over containers. See *Group Policy* in this chapter for more information.

### See Also

*Active Directory(3), delegation(4), domain(3,4), forest(3), group(3), Group Policy(3), OU(3,4), tree(3)*

---

## Dfs

Stands for Distributed File System, a tool that lets you create a logical tree of shared-disk resources that are physically located on different computers on the network.

### Description

The Dfs simplifies the task of managing shared-disk resources across a network and makes it easier for users to find and access these resources. Dfs does this by letting you create a single logical tree of resources that are physically located at different places on the network.

From users' point of view, the Dfs tree appears to be a single hierarchy of folders located on a single server, whereas in actuality, it may consist of shared folders on many different computers. Users do not need to know the computer on which a shared folder resides in order to access the folder—they simply connect to the Dfs tree and access the folder. For example, documents for the Sales department could be located on three different file servers on the network, but by implementing Dfs, users can access these documents as if they were all stored on the same server.

---

 Dfs does not add any additional access control to the shared folders it manages. If users have suitable permissions to access a shared folder on the network, they can access it through Dfs. However, when administrators add a Dfs root or Dfs link, they can specify who has permission to add new Dfs links to the tree.

---

From the point of view of administrators, Dfs simplifies the task of managing shared resources by centralizing them to a single logical tree. For information on procedures for implementing Dfs, see *Dfs* in Chapter 4.

---

### *Dfs Implementation Methods*

There are two ways in which Dfs can be implemented on a network:

*Standalone Dfs*
> This is the simplest method and stores the configuration information for the Dfs tree on a single Windows 2000 standalone server (not part of a Windows 2000 domain). Users locate and access shared resources by first connecting to the Dfs tree on the standalone Dfs server. Standalone Dfs is relatively simple to implement and configure. If the Dfs server is down, however, users on the network cannot make use of Dfs. Standalone Dfs does not use Active Directory, cannot share Dfs roots, and can have only a single level of Dfs links.

*Domain-based Dfs*
> This method stores the Dfs configuration information in Active Directory and makes this information available on all domain controllers in a domain. It is also known as fault-tolerant Dfs: if a file server fails, the administrator can move the child nodes mapped to shares on that server to shares on a different file server—a process that is completely transparent to the users, who still see the same Dfs tree. Domain-based Dfs can be hosted on either a member server or domain controller running Windows 2000 Server, can share Dfs roots, automatically has its hierarchy published to Active Directory, and according to Online Help can have multiple levels of Dfs links (but this functionality seems to be absent from the release version of Windows 2000 Server). Note that domain-based DFS shares are only accessible via Windows 2000 systems that are part of the domain—workgroup systems cannot access these shares.

### *Dfs Tree*

The Dfs tree (also called the Dfs topology) consists of the following elements:

*Dfs root*
> This is a container for files and Dfs links. The Dfs root for a domain-based Dfs must be created on a Windows 2000 domain controller or a member server within a domain, while the Dfs root for a standalone Dfs must be created on a Windows 2000 standalone server. Another name for the server on which a Dfs root resides is a *host server*. A Dfs root can be replicated to other host servers in the domain by creating a *root share*.

 A Windows 2000 server (whether a standalone server, a member server, or a domain controller) can only host one Dfs root.

*Dfs links*
> These are links from a Dfs root to one or more target shared folders, a shared volume, or another Dfs root. You can attach up to 1,000 Dfs links to a Dfs root. If the target folder of a link has a shared folder on a Windows 2000 computer, it can have subfolders within the tree. If it is not on a Windows 2000 computer, it cannot have subfolders. Each link has a time interval associated

with it. This interval specifies how long a Dfs client that has accessed that link will cache the location of the link before needing to connect to the Dfs root again to find it.

### Dfs shared folders

These are the folders in which files are located—also called *replicas*. A single Dfs link can point to one or more Dfs shared folders, with a maximum of 32 shared folders allowed per link. When you create a link, you add the first shared folder (replica) to the link. The set of all replicas associated with a given Dfs link is called a replicate set. When a client tries to connect to the Dfs link, it tries connecting to the first replica first; if that fails (for example, if the file server where that share resides is unavailable), then the client tries the second replica and so on until it succeeds or fails.

Domain-based Dfs also supports replication of Dfs roots and Dfs shared folders. This provides fault tolerance so users can still access their files if a Dfs host server becomes unavailable.

For example, you can replicate a Dfs root from one host server to another so that if the first host server is unavailable, users can still connect to the Dfs tree using a different host server. The same is true for Dfs shared folders: you can have Dfs store a duplicate copy of the contents of a shared folder in a different location on the network, and then have Dfs set a replication policy to control replication of files between the folders. Replication can be either manual or automatic for domain-based Dfs (standalone Dfs supports only manual replication).

You can also use this technique to provide load balancing for files that are frequently accessed by users. From the users' point of view, these files are stored in a single location on the network, whereas in actuality they are stored in multiple locations.

### Example of a Dfs Tree

Let's say you want to implement Dfs on a file server called Bob, and you have the following file servers and shares on your network:

> \\Bob\sales
> \\Bob\pub
> \\Mary\pub
> \\Mary\support

You could create a new share \\Bob\resources and create a Dfs root that points to this share. (The Resources share will be a container for all shared folders on the network.) Then you could create three Dfs links as follows:

> Sales link points to \\Bob\sales
> Tech link points to \\Mary\Support
> Pub link points to \\Bob\pub

Note that a Dfs link doesn't need to have the same name as the share it points to (e.g., Tech listed previously). Finally, you can add a second Dfs shared folder to the Pub link so that it points to \\Mary\pub as an alternate.

If a user on a computer with a Dfs client installed then connects to \\*Bob*\ *resources* by any standard method (browsing My Network Places or Windows Explorer, using Start → Run → \\*Bob*\*Resources*, or mapping a network drive to \\*Bob*\*resources*), then the window that opens for \\*Bob*\*resources* contains what appears to be three subfolders (they are actually Dfs links): Sales, Tech, and Pub. If the user tries to open the Pub subfolder, Dfs will try first to access \\*Bob*\*pub*, and if this is not available, will then try \\*Mary*\*pub* as an alternate (both are members of the same replica set).

### Dfs Clients

It's not enough to set up Dfs on a server for it to work: the client computers that users use must also support Dfs. Dfs clients are available for the following Microsoft Windows operating systems:

*Windows 2000*
Includes Dfs 5.0 client (fully functional)

*Windows NT 4.0 with Service Pack 3 or higher*
Includes Dfs 4.x/5.0 client (works with standalone Dfs servers only)

*Windows 98*
Includes Dfs 4.x/5.0 client (works with standalone Dfs servers only), but a Dfs 5.0 client can also be downloaded from Microsoft's web site, which supports domain-based Dfs servers as well

*Windows 95*
Allows a downloadable Dfs 4.x/5.0 client (works with standalone Dfs servers only)

---

 A computer running a Dfs client must be a member of the domain where the Dfs root is located. In other words, Dfs is limited to single-domain browsing.

---

To use Dfs, users connect to the root of the tree using any standard method of accessing shared folders (My Network Places, Windows Explorer, Run box, mapped drive) and then browse it to find the child node they want to access. To connect to the Dfs root, the client uses the DNS name of the host server for the root. From the users' point of view, Dfs is like a series of folders located within one shared folder on one file server. In order to connect to a Dfs tree, however, the client computer must be running Dfs client software.

---

 Clients access Dfs roots on standalone Dfs host servers by specifying the UNC path to the root. For example, if the Dfs root named Files points to the shared folder Pub on member server George, then you would access the Dfs root using \\*George*\*Files*. By contrast, for domain-based Dfs, you specify the DNS name of the domain in the UNC, e.g., \\*mtit.com*\*Files*.

---

### Planning and Implementing Dfs

1. Select a Windows 2000 standalone server (for standalone Dfs) or a member server belonging to a domain or a domain controller (for domain-based Dfs) for your host server.

2. Create a Dfs root on your host server and add a root share.

3. Add Dfs links to your root and assign Dfs shared folders to the links.

4. If desired, configure replication of your Dfs root to other host servers.

5. Monitor the status of your Dfs tree using the Dfs console.

6. Add, remove, and reconfigure Dfs links and shared folders as desired.

### Notes

- Windows NT 4.0 with Service Pack 3 includes Dfs server support, but only for standalone Dfs.

- Using Dfs eliminates the need to map network drives on client computers, making accessing network resources simpler for users.

- Dfs replication can be used to replicate:

    — Dfs links that have multiple Dfs shared folders in their replica set

    — Dfs roots that have multiple Dfs root replicas

- Automatic replication is not supported for Dfs shared folders hosted on FAT volumes. If you want to use automatic replication with domain-based Dfs, you must install Dfs on NTFS.

### See Also

*Dfs(4), Distributed File System(5), shared folder(3,4)*

---

# DHCP

Stands for Dynamic Host Configuration Protocol, a TCP/IP client/server protocol used to automatically configure IP addresses and other TCP/IP settings for hosts on the network.

### Description

DHCP simplifies the configuration of host addresses on a TCP/IP network by allowing hosts to automatically obtain their IP address, subnet mask, and other settings from a centrally located DHCP server. This simplifies the assignment, administration, and maintenance of TCP/IP settings and is easier than the alternative—going in person to every host on the network and manually configuring a static IP address (for a third method, see the section "Automatic Private IP Addressing (APIPA)" in the article *TCP/IP* in this chapter).

### How DHCP Works

When a *DHCP client* starts up, it contacts a *DHCP server* (in our case, a Windows 2000 Server computer with the DHCP Server service installed and configured on it) and requests IP addressing information. The DHCP server responds by selecting an

---

available IP address from the range of addresses that it manages (called the server's *scope*). It then leases this address to the DHCP client for a certain period of time (eight days by default) and sends the client, in addition to its IP address, the following information:

- Subnet mask (required)

- Default gateway address (optional)

- Addresses of DNS servers (optional)

- Addresses of WINS servers (optional)

- Other optional TCP/IP settings

Once a *lease* is obtained, the DHCP client has to renew the lease periodically with the DHCP server to maintain its address. If a client shuts down properly, it releases its lease and the server may offer the address to a different client, unless the address has been reserved for that client.

### DHCP Clients

The following Microsoft operating systems can be configured to operate as DHCP clients (different operating systems are configured differently to operate as DHCP clients):

- Windows 2000 (all versions)

- Windows NT (all versions)

- Windows 95 and 98

- Windows for Workgroups 3.11 (must be running TCP/IP-32 add-on)

- MS-DOS (must be running Microsoft Network Client 3.0 for MS-DOS)

In addition, most Unix and Macintosh systems can be configured to operate as DHCP clients.

### DHCP Servers

See *DHCP* in Chapter 4 for the procedure for configuring a Windows 2000 Server computer to operate in the role of a DHCP server.

### DHCP Traffic

If you have Network Monitor (see Chapter 6, *Utilities*) installed or are using a packet sniffer, you can use it to monitor DHCP traffic on your network. To understand this traffic, you need to know more about the DHCP lease and renewal process. There are four basic kinds of DHCP packets:

*DHCPDISCOVER*

This packet is broadcast by the client when it starts up. It contains the MAC address (physical or hardware address) and computer name of the client and essentially says, "If there is a DHCP server out there, please offer me a lease." This is repeated every five minutes until successful.

### DHCPOFFER

This packet is broadcast by a DHCP server in response to a DHCPDISCOVER packet. It contains:

— The MAC address of the DHCP client that sent the DHCPDISCOVER packet

— The IP address and subnet mask being offered to the client

— The duration of the lease being offered

— The IP address of the DHCP server

### DHCPREQUEST

This packet is broadcast by the client in response to the first lease offer it receives. The DHCPREQUEST packet includes the IP address of the DHCP server offering the lease and basically says, "I'll take the lease you are offering me." Other available DHCP servers also hear this message but respond to it by withdrawing their offered leases (no message sent).

### DHCPACK

This packet is broadcast by the server and tells the client, "It's yours for . . . days." At this point the client initializes its TCP/IP stack and can begin communicating over the network.

### Lease Renewal

When 50% of the lease time has expired, the DHCP client sends a DHCPREQUEST packet directly to the DHCP server requesting a renewal. If the server is available, it responds with DHCPACK and the lease clock is reset.

If the server is not available, the client waits until 87.5% of the lease time has expired and then broadcasts a DHCPDISCOVER packet that basically says, "Is there any DHCP server out there that can renew my lease?" A different server can respond with DHCPOFFER if the scope of the server overlaps the scope of the client's original DHCP server.

If 100% of the lease time expires and the client hasn't heard from any DHCP servers, it releases its address and starts broadcasting DHCPDISCOVER packets to begin the lease process anew. In the meantime, it cannot use TCP/IP to communicate on the network.

If a client is shut down properly, it releases its IP address. When it restarts, it tries to renew the same address it had before. If it cannot contact a DHCP server, it continues to use the address until its current lease expires. If the lease expired while the client was offline, the lease process starts from the beginning.

### DHCP Terminology

Here is some more terminology you need to be familiar with if you are planning on using Windows 2000 Server computers as DHCP servers in your network:

### Activation

Once a scope is created on a DHCP server, it must be activated (turned on) before the server can start leasing IP addresses from the scope to clients.

---

*Authorization*

Before a Windows 2000 DHCP server can lease IP addresses to clients, it must be authorized by a user belonging to the Enterprise Admins group. This just gives you an extra level of control over your network to prevent unauthorized DHCP servers from hijacking your clients.

*Reservation*

An IP address is reserved by a particular client that has a specific MAC address. Instead of manually assigning static IP addresses to your network servers, you can create reservations for them so they can obtain their addresses from DHCP servers but will always receive the same addresses from the DHCP servers, so no DNS or WINS confusion results.

*Scope*

A scope is a set of IP addresses that a DHCP server can issue to clients on a particular subnet. A scope is typically a contiguous block of addresses, possibly with certain addresses excluded from it. (You exclude addresses that have already been manually assigned—for example, to servers.) See the sidebar entitled "Types of DHCP Scopes" later in this article for information on multicast scopes and superscopes.

*Scope options*

Additional TCP/IP settings are issued by the DHCP server to its clients. Scope options are specified by number, and the ones commonly used on Microsoft networks are described in Table 3-9.

*Table 3-9: DHCP Scope Options Used in Microsoft Networks*

| Scope Option | Description |
|---|---|
| 003 Router | IP address of default gateway |
| 006 DNS Servers | IP address of a DNS server |
| 015 DNS Domain Name | DNS name of the client's domain |
| 044 WINS/NBNS Servers | IP address of a WINS server |
| 046 WINS/NBT Node Type | Method used by client for NetBIOS over TCP/IP (NetBT) name resolution |
| 047 NetBIOS Scope ID | Local NetBIOS scope ID of client |

Scope options can be configured for application in four different ways:

*Server level*

Options configured for this level are applied to all DHCP clients managed by the DHCP server. An example would be specifying the same WINS server (option 044) for all clients no matter what subnet they reside on. Server-level options are overridden by scope or reserved client-level options.

*Scope level*

Options configured for this level are applied only to clients who lease their address from the particular scope. An example would be specifying a unique default gateway address (option 003) for each subnet/scope. Scope level options are overridden by reserved client-level options.

*Class level*

Options configured for this level are applied only to clients belonging to a specified class. For example, you could assign the address of a DNS server only to the class of client computers running Windows 2000 as their operating system.

*Reserved client level*

Options configured for this level are applied only to the client having the particular reservation.

## Implementing DHCP Servers

To use a Windows 2000 Server computer as a DHCP server, you typically do the following:

- Manually specify a static IP address, subnet mask, and (optionally) a default gateway address for the DHCP server

- Install the DHCP Server service on the system

- Authorize the DHCP server in Active Directory

- Create a scope on the DHCP server, exclude IP addresses as necessary from the scope, and configure any scope options needed

- Create reservations for DHCP clients that must always obtain the same IP address (such as servers whose TCP/IP settings you want to configure using DHCP instead of static addressing)

- Activate the scope

- Configure client computers to obtain an IP address automatically from a DHCP server and then reboot the client computers

For fault tolerance, it's a good idea to have two DHCP servers per subnet, one with 80% of the available addresses and the other with 20%. (This is called the 80/20 rule.)

You usually need at least one DHCP server per subnet, unless you have configured your routers to forward DHCP traffic. DHCP traffic is mostly of the broadcast type, but it's not a very heavy load unless you have a large number of DHCP clients and the lease period is very small. A third alternative is to have one central DHCP server and one DHCP relay agent per subnet. See *DHCP relay agent* later in this chapter for more information.

---

 The DHCP Server service can work together with the DNS Server service to simplify administration of both IP addresses and DNS host-names on the network. See the sidebar "DHCP and DNS" in the article *DHCP* in Chapter 4 for more information.

---

# Types of DHCP Scopes

There are three different kinds of scopes you can create with Windows 2000 DHCP servers:

*Ordinary scope (or just Scope)*
> Specifies a range of IP addresses (with exclusions) that can be leased to DHCP clients on a connected subnet.

*Multicast scope*
> Can issue a multicast address to a group of computers on the network. Multicasting is used for conferencing applications, such as Microsoft Windows Media Technologies, and can be used to "broadcast" information to a specific group of computers.

*Superscopes*
> Consist of two or more scopes grouped together so they can be administered as a single entity. Any scope within a superscope can lease an address to any client on the subnet. Superscopes are useful when:

> — You planned for a certain number of DHCP clients on your network but later discovered you had more clients than you anticipated. You can create an additional scope for the extra clients and then combine this with the original scope to create a superscope without needing to delete your old scope and create a new one.

> — You must replace an existing range of IP addresses with a new one.

For information on creating and configuring these different scope types, see *DHCP* in Chapter 4.

## Notes

- DHCP is generally used only for configuring client computers, not servers. However, it is a good practice to use DHCP to assign reserved, server IP addresses (effectively making them static). It is usually best to manually configure TCP/IP settings for server since IP addresses of servers are included in DNS and WINS databases.

- This DHCP lease and renewal process occurs separately for each network adapter that is configured for automatic TCP/IP addressing. Each adapter in a multihomed computer must have its own, unique IP address to communicate using TCP/IP.

- If a client tries to renew an address already owned by some other computer on the network, the DHCP server responds with a DHCPNACK packet that basically tells the client, "You can't have that address; give it up."

- You can force a client to release its IP address before its lease expires by using the `ipconfig /release` command. You can force a client to attempt to renew a lease with `ipconfig /renew`. See *ipconfig* in Chapter 7 for more information. A typical use for this procedure is when you physically move a computer from one subnet to another in your internetwork.

- If you configure scope option 044, then option 046 is automatically configured as well.

- NetBIOS scope IDs are a method of creating multiple, logical network segments on a single, physical network segment.

- If you want to reserve an IP address for a client but there is more than one DHCP server available to the client, you must configure the same reservation on each DHCP server.

- If no DHCP server is available when a DHCP client starts up, the client may autoconfigure its own IP address using APIPA. See the section "Automatic Private IP Addressing (APIPA)" in the article *TCP/IP* later in this chapter for more information.

- The DHCP Server service is relatively disk-intensive, so take this into account in selecting the hardware for your server. RAID may be an option for DHCP servers that will service a large number of clients.

- Dial-up clients should have leases of short duration, typically three days or less.

- Members of the Administrators, DHCP Users, and DHCP Administrators groups can all connect to a DHCP server, but members of the DHCP Users group cannot modify the configuration of the DHCP server. The DHCP Users and DHCP Administrators groups are domain local groups on the DHCP server.

- If a DHCP server has a network adapter with more than one IP address configured on it, only the first address is used for servicing DHCP clients.

### See Also

*DHCP(4), DHCP relay agent(3,4), ipconfig(7), TCP/IP(3,4)*

---

## DHCP relay agent

An agent that listens for DHCP client requests and forwards such requests to a DHCP server on a different subnet.

### Description

There are three main ways of implementing DHCP servers on an internetwork consisting of multiple physical subnets connected together by routers:

- Locate a DHCP server in each subnet. This is a straightforward solution, but it increases the complexity of the job of administering DHCP.

- Place DHCP servers in a central location and configure the routers to forward DHCP broadcast traffic between subnets. The router must be RFC 1542–compliant to do this; in other words, it must be able to pass broadcast traffic on UDP ports 67 and 68.

- Place a DHCP server in a central location and have one DHCP relay agent on every other subnet (but not on the subnet where the DHCP server is located). This way you don't need to reconfigure routers or allow DHCP broadcast traffic to flood the internetwork unnecessarily.

A DHCP relay agent is an optional service that runs on a Windows 2000 Server and helps a client on one subnet lease and renew its address from a DHCP server on a different subnet.

### How It Works

Let's consider a DHCP client on subnet A requesting a lease from a DHCP server on subnet B via a DHCP relay agent configured on subnet A:

- The client on subnet A broadcasts a DHCPDISCOVER packet on its subnet (see *DHCP* in this chapter for more information about DHCP packets).

- The relay agent on subnet A hears the client's DHCPDISCOVER broadcast, picks up the packet, readdresses it using directed (not broadcast) IP to the DHCP server on subnet B, and sends it off.

- The packet from the relay agent is forwarded by the router from subnet A to subnet B (since routers forward directed traffic but typically block broadcast traffic).

- The DHCP server on subnet B receives the DHCPDISCOVER packet from the relay agent. Instead of responding with a broadcast DHCPOFFER packet, it sends the DHCPOFFER packet directly to the relay agent on subnet A.

- The relay agent on subnet A receives the DHCPOFFER packet from the server, readdresses it as a local subnet broadcast, and broadcasts the packet to subnet A.

- The client on subnet A hears the DHCPOFFER packet broadcast by the relay agent but interprets it as if it were broadcast by a DHCP server on its subnet. (The relay agent thus acts as a proxy for the DHCP server.)

- The client responds by broadcasting a DHCPREQUEST packet and the process continues—with the relay agent acting as a proxy—until the client can lease an address.

For information about how to configure a Windows 2000 Server computer to act as a DHCP relay agent, see *DHCP relay agent* in Chapter 4.

### Notes

- Windows 2000 Server computers can be configured to operate as DHCP relay agents in two different ways:

  - As a server on the subnet (for example, a file/print server) that also functions in the role of a DHCP relay agent

  - As an IP router connecting two or more subnets (the computer must be multihomed) that also functions on one or more network interfaces as a DHCP relay agent

- Many third-party routers can also be configured as DHCP relay agents. You typically configure the agent by specifying the IP Helper Address of the DHCP server to which the agent will forward DHCP client traffic.

### See Also

*DHCP(3,4)*, *DHCP relay agent(4)*

## *disaster recovery*

Recovering from hardware or software failures on Windows 2000 computers.

### *Description*

Windows 2000 includes various features that help administrators recover from hardware or software failures, which are discussed in this article.

### *Windows 2000 Backup and Recovery Tools*

The single most important way to prepare for possible disasters is to ensure that important data is backed up regularly. Windows 2000 includes a utility called Windows 2000 Backup and Recovery Tools (or simply Windows Backup), which lets administrators perform several important disaster recovery functions.

#### *Backup*

Windows Backup lets you back up entire volumes, subtrees of folders, or individual folders to any other backup media where a file can be written to, such as a tape drive, hard disk, removable disk, or writable compact disc. Using Windows Backup, you can perform either or both of the following scopes of backups:

*Local backup*
> Each computer to be backed up requires its own backup media device, and the backup is performed by the user at the local computer. Users can back up their own files and folders and any files they have Read permission on.

*Network backup*
> An administration can back up data from multiple computers on the network to a central server with a backup media device attached. Administrators, Backup Operators, and Server Operators can back up any files on any computer in the domain.

---

 If you are using Windows 2000 Backup, then system-state data for a computer can only be backed up using a local backup. This means that important computers, such as domain controllers, need to be backed up locally. See the sidebar "System-State Data" for more information.

---

The backup process can be configured using either a standard Explorer-like interface or a friendly wizard. You can initiate a backup immediately or schedule a backup job that uses any of the common backup methods including normal, copy, differential, incremental, or daily copy. Backups can be verified as they are performed and compressed to save space on the backup media. For procedures for backing up data using Windows Backup, see *backup and restore* in Chapter 4.

Some Windows Backup terminology for you:

— A *backup job* is a single process of performing a backup.

— A *backup set* is a group of files, folders, and volumes that has been backed up and stored either on a tape or as a *.bkf* file on a hard drive, removable drive, or similar medium.

— A *catalog* is a summary of the files, folders, and volumes that has been saved in a backup set.

— A *backup log* is a text file created while running Windows Backup that records the success or failure of each step of the backup operation.

### Restore

Windows Backup lets you restore files, folders, volumes, or entire backup sets to either the original or an alternate location. The restore process can be configured using either an Explorer-like interface or a wizard. For procedures on restoring data using Windows Backup, see *backup and restore* in Chapter 4.

### Emergency Repair Disk (ERD)

The ERD contains information about your current Windows system settings. It can help start a system when there are specific problems associated with corruption of Windows 2000 system files, the partition boot sector or the system disk, or the configuration settings for multiboot systems, all of which may prevent the system from booting up to the point where you can log on.

Note that the ERD cannot be used to restore a corrupted registry; use the Recovery Console instead to do this. You should use Windows Backup to create a new ERD whenever you make changes to the partitions or operating system on your machine, and you should keep the ERD in a safe place. See *Emergency Repair Disk (ERD)* in Chapter 4 for information on how to use the ERD to repair a system.

### Advanced Startup Options

These are alternate methods for starting Windows 2000, which can be used to troubleshoot various kinds of hardware- and software-related startup problems. They allow you to start up Windows 2000 to the point that you can make repairs so that normal startup can be achieved.

Advanced Startup Options can be selected by pressing the F8 function key at the beginning of the Windows 2000 boot process. The different startup options are shown in Table 3-10.

*Concepts D*

## *System-State Data*

This is information that defines the configuration of the operating system on a Windows 2000 computer. System-state data includes the following:

- Registry
- System startup (boot) files
- Class registration database (for Component services)
- Certificate Services database (if the server is running Certificate Services)
- Active Directory database (domain controllers only)
- Sysvol share (domain controllers only)

You can (and should) back up the system-state data regularly on key servers using Windows Backup. If you plan to restore system-state data, be aware that:

- The restore process will overwrite the existing configuration information on the server, so if you restore from an old backup set, you will lose any configuration changes made since that set was made. You will then have to make these configuration changes manually (hopefully, you documented them).

- To restore system-state data on a domain controller, you must use the Advanced Startup Options to start the computer in Directory Services Restore Mode. See *Active Directory* in this chapter.

*Table 3-10: Advanced Startup Options*

| Option | Description | Purpose |
|--------|-------------|---------|
| Enable Boot Logging | Creates *Ntbtlog.txt* log file in *%SystemRoot%* to record success or failure of initialization of device drivers and system services. | Use this option if you can boot successfully but problems are indicated. Review the log to determine the device or service causing the problem. |
| Safe Mode | Loads only mouse, keyboard, storage, base video drivers, and a limited set of system services. Also creates *Ntbtlog.txt* log file (see previous). | Use this option if an optional device or service is preventing a successful boot. |
| Safe Mode with Networking | Same as Safe Mode except that basic networking drivers and services are enabled. | Use this option if an optional device or service is preventing a successful boot and you need to connect to shared resources to resolve the problem. |
| Safe Mode with Command Prompt | Same as Safe Mode except that a command prompt is opened instead of the GUI. | Use this option if a GUI problem is preventing a successful boot. |
| Enable VGA Mode | Same as a normal boot except that VGA video driver is used. | Use this option if a problem with your video driver is preventing a successful boot or preventing the GUI from appearing. |

*Table 3-10: Advanced Startup Options (continued)*

| Option | Description | Purpose |
|---|---|---|
| Last Known Good Configuration | Same as a normal boot except that the HKLM\System\CurrentControl- Set registry key is replaced with the previous key that enabled a successful boot. | Use this option if you made a configuration change to your system and, upon restarting, the system failed to boot successfully. |
| Directory Services Restore Mode | Lets you start Windows 2000 on a domain controller without starting the Active Directory service. | Use this option if you need to repair or restore Active Directory or the Sysvol share. |
| Debugging Mode | Lets you transmit debugging information through a serial port to a second computer for debugging purposes. | Used only by advanced technicians, such as Microsoft support specialists. |

### Recovery Console

This is a minimal, command-line version of the Windows 2000 operating system, which can be used to start your computer as a last resort when the Advanced Startup Options fail. The Recovery Console can be used to:

- Repair a corrupt master boot record (MBR).

- Format a hard disk.

- Read and write files on NTFS partitions. For example, you could use it to copy system files from the Windows 2000 compact disc.

- Enable or disable services. This can be useful if a specific service is preventing Windows 2000 from starting.

The commands supported by the Recovery Console are:

attrib, batch, cd, chdir, chkdsk, cls, copy, del, delete, dir, disable, diskpart, enable, exit, expand, fixboot, fixmbr, format, help, list of, listsvc, logon, map, md, mkdir, more, ren, rename, rd, rmdir, set, systemroot, and type.

For more information on any of these commands, see Chapter 7.

Note that the Recovery Console should normally be installed before you need to use it! See *Recovery Console* in Chapter 4 for more information.

### Which Tool to Use

If your computer doesn't start, try the following, usually in this order:

1. Safe Mode or Last Known Good Configuration (depending on whether the problem suddenly appeared or occurred after a hardware upgrade)

2. Recovery Console

3. Emergency Repair Disk

If all else fails, you will need to rebuild the server (see *backup and restore* in Chapter 4).

## Notes

- Always check Event Viewer whenever there is a problem, as the information logged there may be useful to you in troubleshooting the problem.

- To avoid trouble, always check the Hardware Compatibility List (HCL) on Microsoft's web site before installing new hardware. Contact your vendor to ensure that you have the latest version of the drivers for your hardware.

- Use a power-conditioning UPS to ensure that surges don't cause write errors to your drives.

- Always keep a printed record of your backup sets and procedures, and keep the Windows 2000 CD handy.

## See Also

*Active Directory(3), backup and restore(4), Emergency Repair Disk (ERD)(4), Recovery Console(4)*

---

# disk quota

A method of managing the amount of disk space that users can utilize.

## Description

New to Windows 2000 Server is the capability of allocating disk space to users in the form of disk quotas. Disk quotas are only available on NTFS partitions and volumes, not those formatted with FAT or FAT32.

Disk quotas can be configured in a number of ways:

- Warnings can be issued when a user is nearing the configured quota limit.

- Quota limits can be either enforced (hard limit) or not (soft limit). If enforced, users who exceed their limits will be denied access.

- An entry can be logged in the event log when a warning is issued, when a limit is exceeded, or both.

Disk quota limits are based on file ownership and not on where the files are located on a quota-enabled NTFS volume; that is, they are established on a *per-user* basis. For example, if a user moves a file from one folder to another on the volume, he still shows the same amount of disk space used in My Computer or Windows Explorer. If a user takes ownership of a file on an NTFS volume, the file is charged against the user's quota.

In addition, disk quotas apply to specific volumes only and not to folders within volumes—that is, on a *per-volume* basis. If a physical disk has several volumes or partitions (or if you have multiple physical disks), each partition or volume may have quotas either enabled or disabled, and those on which quotas are enabled may have different quota limits set (unless it's a spanned volume).

### Types of Quota Limits

Disk quota limits can be one of two types:

*Soft quotas*
> When the user exceeds the limit, an event may be logged to the event log, but the user is not prevented from exceeding the quota.

*Hard quotas*
> When the user exceeds the limit, an event may be logged to the event log, and the user is prevented from using any additional space on the disk.

Once enabled on a volume, disk quota limits are tracked for all users who store files on that volume. However, different quota limits can be set for specific users to override the global settings for all users. Once quota limits have been established on a volume, users are monitored for any action that increases the amount of disk space used. These actions include:

- Copying or moving files to the disk

- Creating (saving) new files on the disk

- Taking ownership of existing files on the disk that belong to other users

User applications may respond differently when users try to create or save files on volumes where a hard quota limit has been exceeded. In general, the application will act as if the volume is full.

### Strategy for Using Disk Quotas

1. Begin by establishing realistic estimates of how much disk space users require on average and how these needs are likely to grow in the immediate future. To do this, you may want to classify users into three different categories, such as heavy users, moderate users, and light users.

2. Next, create partitions, volumes, and logical drives in such a way as to make easy assignment of space to different types of users. Allocate some volumes for heavy users, some for moderate, and some for light. Create home folders or data folders on these drives for each user or group of users, and assign NTFS permissions accordingly to restrict access. Make sure you leave unallocated space on the drives in case you need to increase the quota limits. Consider using dynamic storage so that you can extend simple volumes and create spanned volumes when simple volumes become full.

3. Assign disk quotas to each volume, partition, or logical drive according to the type of user storing data there. Use soft limits initially in case your estimates of user needs are too small.

4. Now share the folders for access over the network. Closely monitor disk quota entries over a period of time to see if realistic limits have been set.

5. Once you have determined that your quota limits are appropriate, make them hard quotas to prevent careless users from over-utilizing disk space.

*Concepts*
*D*

6. Monitor quotas periodically to determine whether they should be increased for all users. Check if specific users might require individual quotas for special projects and so on.

7. If a user no longer needs to store data on a volume, remove the files (or take ownership of them) and then delete the user's quota entry to free up space on the volume.

---

 Make sure you enable quotas on a disk *before* any users have stored files on it. If a user has already stored a file and you then enable quotas and set quota limits, the user's quota limit will be No Limit and you will have to change the quota entry manually for this user. Only new users who later store files on the disk will be assigned the quota limits you expect them to have.

---

### Notes

• Enabling disk quotas on a volume creates a small amount of overhead. As a result, filesystem performance may degrade slightly.

• Disk quotas are useful to set on Windows 2000 Professional client computers when more than one user uses the same computer.

• Generally, you should not set disk quotas on the system partition since problems may result if the operating system runs out of space. This occurs if you try to install new applications while logged on as a user who does *not* have administrative privileges. If you install these applications while logged on as Administrator, however, quota settings are ignored.

• File compression is ignored when disk quotas are calculated. Compressed files are charged to the quota according to their uncompressed size.

### See Also

*disk quota(4)*, *disks(3,4)*, *Disk Management(5)*

---

## disks

Overview of disk storage technologies supported by Windows 2000 Server.

### Description

Windows 2000 Server supports the older disk technologies of previous versions of Microsoft Windows and also includes some new technologies to increase performance and make disk management easier.

### *Types of Disk Storage*

Windows 2000 Server supports two types of disk storage:

*Basic storage*

This storage technology is the same as that of earlier versions of Microsoft Windows, including Windows NT 4.0 and 3.51, Windows 98, and Windows 95. Basic storage divides disks into a limited number of partitions and logical drives and supports advanced features such as volume sets, strip sets, stripe sets with parity, and mirror sets.

*Dynamic storage*

This technology is new to Windows 2000 Server and divides disks into an unlimited number of volumes. Dynamic storage supports advanced features such as spanned volumes, striped volumes, RAID-5 volumes, and mirrored volumes.

In addition, Windows 2000 Server supports certain types of removable storage.

### **Basic Storage**

When Windows 2000 Server is installed on a system, all disks use basic storage. A disk that uses basic storage is called a *basic disk*. Basic disks are similar to disks in Windows NT 4.0 and can consist of either:

- Up to three primary partitions plus one extended partition. The extended partition can have up to 24 logical drives. Each primary partition and logical drive is identified by a unique drive letter from *C* to *Z*.

- Up to four primary partitions and no extended partition or logical drives.

The main disadvantages of a basic disk are:

- There is a limit of 4 primary partitions and 24 logical drives that you can create.

- Configuration information concerning the disk is stored in the registry rather than on the disk itself. If the registry becomes corrupted, the data on the disk becomes unusable.

- Basic disks in Windows 2000 Server cannot be used to create the mirror sets, volume sets, stripe sets, and stripe sets with parity which you can create in Windows NT. In order to use these advanced disk storage features in Windows 2000 Server, you must use dynamic storage instead of basic.

 You can have mirror sets, volume sets, stripe sets, and stripe sets with parity on Windows 2000 Server systems using basic storage, but only if you upgraded the system from an earlier Windows NT Server system that already had these storage technologies in place. To create new mirrored volumes, spanned volumes, striped volumes, or RAID-5 volumes in Windows 2000 Server, you must first upgrade your disks from basic to dynamic storage.

The main advantage of using basic storage is that you can dual-boot between Windows 2000 Server and other operating systems such as Windows NT 4.0 Server or Windows 98—something you are unlikely to want to do, however.

Basic disks in Windows 2000 Server can be formatted using any of the following filesystems: FAT, FAT32, and NTFS. This is different from Windows NT 4.0 Server, which only supported FAT and NTFS.

### Dynamic Storage

Windows 2000 Server also supports a more advanced form of disk storage called dynamic storage. A disk that uses dynamic storage is called a *dynamic disk*. Dynamic disks consist of an unlimited number of volumes. These volumes can be identified by either:

- Associating a volume with a drive letter. However, this can only be used to identify up to 24 different volumes (or 25 if you have no *B:* floppy drive in your system).

- Mounting a drive, which associates a volume with a folder on an existing volume. This method overcomes the drive-letter limitation and also enables friendly names like *My Volume* to be used to identify volumes.

The main advantages of a dynamic disk are:

- There is no limit to the number of volumes you can create from a drive or collection of drives.

- Configuration information concerning the disk is stored on the disk instead of the registry and is replicated to all other dynamic disks in the system for fault tolerance.

- You can extend a simple volume on a dynamic disk by adding unallocated space to it from the same disk. You cannot extend partitions on basic disks.

- Dynamic disks support spanned volumes, mirrored volumes, striped volumes, and RAID-5 volumes.

---

 Actually, the number of volumes you can create on a dynamic disk is limited by the size of the physical drive itself. From a practical point of view, you can create hundreds of volumes from a single large drive. I'm not sure why you would want to do this, however.

---

The main disadvantage of using dynamic disks is that you cannot dual-boot between Windows 2000 Server and some other operating system, such as Windows NT 4.0 Server or Windows 98. Also, once you convert a disk to dynamic storage, you cannot convert it back to basic storage without losing all your data.

Windows 2000 Server using dynamic storage supports similar advanced disk-storage technologies to those supported by Windows NT 4.0 Server; the main difference is that they are named differently. Table 3-11 contrasts the disk terminology used in Windows 2000 and Windows NT Server.

*Table 3-11: Disk Terminology in Windows 2000 Server and Windows NT Server*

| | Windows 2000 | |
| --- | --- | --- |
| Windows NT | Basic Storage | Dynamic Storage |
| Partition | Partition | Simple volume |
| Primary partition | Primary partition | Simple volume |
| Extended partition | Extended partition | N/A |
| Logical drive | Logical drive | Simple volume |
| Mirror set | N/A | Mirrored volume |
| Volume set | N/A | Spanned volume |
| Stripe set | N/A | Striped volume |
| Stripe set with parity | N/A | RAID-5 volume |

Here is a more detailed explanation of Windows 2000 Server disk terminology than is provided by the summary in Table 3-11:

*Volume*
An area of disk storage in a Windows 2000 Server system that is configured for dynamic storage.

*Simple volume*
A volume that occupies contiguous space on a single physical disk. Simple volumes are for dynamic storage what primary partitions and logical drives are for basic storage. Simple volumes can be extended with unallocated space from the same drive as long as they are formatted with NTFS.

*Mirrored volume*
Consists of two, separate simple volumes that are configured to be identical copies of each other and are located on different physical disks. When data is updated on one disk, it is automatically updated on the other as well. (The pair of volumes is identified to the system by a single drive letter or mount point.) If one disk in a mirrored volume fails, you still have the complete data on the other disk. This technology is fault tolerant and is also referred to as RAID 1.

*Spanned volume*
Created from two or more areas of contiguous free space on the same or on different physical disks that are combined together into a single, larger, logical storage area. Spanned volumes can be extended without losing existing data by adding further areas of contiguous free space, up to a maximum of 32 areas on up to 32 different disks. However, once extended they cannot be reduced in size. Data is written to the first area of the volume until it becomes full, whereupon further data is written to the next area. Spanned volumes are not fault tolerant, and if one disk fails, the entire spanned volume is unrecoverable.

*Striped volume*
Created from two or more areas of contiguous free space on different physical disks that are combined together into a single, larger, logical storage area. Like spanned volumes, striped volumes can consist of between 2 and 32 areas of contiguous free space. Unlike spanned volumes, however, each area of a striped volume must be on a different physical disk, all areas must be the same size, and data is written in an interleaved fashion across all areas instead of sequentially area by area. This generally provides better read performance

than a spanned volume. Like spanned volumes, striped volumes are also not fault tolerant. Another name for a striped volume is a RAID-0 volume.

*RAID-5 volume*

Created from three or more areas of contiguous free disk space on different physical disks that are combined together into a single, larger, logical storage area. RAID-5 volumes are similar to striped volumes, except that error-correcting parity information is distributed across the set. The result is a popular fault-tolerant disk-storage technology called RAID 5, which maintains data integrity in the event of failure of a single physical disk belonging to the set. RAID-5 volumes can use between 3 and 32 different disks.

### Converting Disks

If you want to extend volumes or create striped, spanned, or fault-tolerant volumes, you first have to convert your disks from basic to dynamic storage. This process is called upgrading your disks and can be accomplished without rebooting the system (unless the disk contains your system or boot partition or the active paging file).

Basic disks require a minimum of 1 MB of free space in order to successfully convert them to dynamic disks. This free space is used to store the database that contains the configuration information concerning all the dynamic disks in the system. So when you partition a basic disk, make sure you leave at least 1 MB of free (unallocated) space on the disk in case you later want to convert it to dynamic storage.

### Identifying Partitions, Drives, and Volumes

In earlier versions of Microsoft Windows, you identified partitions, logical drives, floppy drives, and CD-ROM drives by assigning them a unique drive letter from *A* to *Z*. *A* and *B* were generally reserved for floppy drives, *C* for the system and boot partition, and the remaining 23 letters for the data partitions and CD-ROM drives in the system.

Windows 2000 Server still supports drive letters, but it also lets you mount a local partition, volume, logical drive, or CD-ROM drive to an empty folder on a local NTFS partition or volume. This has two advantages:

- You can identify more than 24 partitions or volumes on a single system (if you want to).

- You can give partitions or volumes friendly names like *Accounting* and *Human Resources*, which may be more accessible to users than drive letters.

As an example, create a folder in the root of *C:* drive and call it *Data Volumes*. Within this folder create three subfolders called *Accounting*, *Human Resources*, and *Management*. You could then mount three simple volumes on your NTFS drive as follows:

Volume 1 → *C:\Data Volumes\Accounting*
Volume 2 → *C:\Data Volumes\Human Resources*
Volume 3 → *C:\Data Volumes\Management*

These volumes could then be shared using the share names, *Accounting*, *Human Resources*, and *Management*, and assigned suitable permissions.

## Notes

- Disks must be either basic or dynamic; they cannot contain a mixture of partitions and volumes. However, your computer can have a combination of basic and dynamic disks in its disk subsystem.

- Dynamic storage is not supported on portable computers or on removable media. Only primary partitions are allowed on removable media.

- You cannot reinstall Windows 2000 Server in a volume that has been created from unallocated space on a dynamic disk. This is because under the hood there are really two types of volumes:

  — Those that were created from partitions when a basic disk was upgraded to a dynamic disk. This type of volume has a partition table similar to that in a partition of a basic disk, and it cannot be extended.

  — Those that were created after the conversion process from unallocated space on a dynamic disk. This type of volume has no partition table and therefore cannot be recognized by the Setup program of Windows 2000 Server. It can be extended if desired.

- Dynamic disks cannot be accessed by MS-DOS or earlier versions of Microsoft Windows. For example, if you physically move a dynamic disk from a Windows 2000 Server to a Windows NT 4.0 Server computer, the new system will not be able to use it.

- When you add a new hard disk to a Windows 2000 Server computer, it is initially identified as basic.

- The system and boot partitions cannot be part of a volume set, stripe set, or stripe set with parity. They can be part of a mirror set, however, which is a good way of providing fault tolerance for these partitions. However, hardware RAID can be used for system and boot partitions.

- Assigning a drive letter or mounting a folder to a partition or volume does not make the partition or volume available on the network: you still need to share it.

- Drive paths can be assigned to folders on either partitions or volumes, as long as the partition or volume is formatted using NTFS.

- You cannot extend a simple volume formatted with FAT or FAT32; you can only do so with NTFS.

- You cannot mirror a spanned volume that exists on multiple physical disks; you can only do so with a simple volume that exists on a single physical disk.

- You cannot "un-extend" a simple volume once you have extended it, and you similarly cannot do so with spanned and striped volumes.

- You cannot extend a simple volume once you have mirrored it.

- You cannot extend or mirror a RAID-5 volume.

## See Also

*disk quota(3)*, *disks(4)*, *Disk Management(5)*

## distribution group

Type of group used only for grouping email recipients together.

**See Also**

*group(3)*

## DNS

Stands for Domain Name System (DNS), a TCP/IP client/server protocol used as a naming system for network hosts.

### Description

DNS provides both a system for logically naming computers on an IP network and a way of resolving logical hostnames into their associated IP addresses (and vice versa). DNS is intimately associated with Windows 2000's Active Directory and is important for two reasons:

* DNS is the naming system used for naming Windows 2000 domains. In Windows NT, domains had NetBIOS names that had nothing to do with DNS. For example, a Windows NT domain called HEADQUARTERS could have the DNS domain name *mtit.com*. In Windows 2000, the situation is different: *mtit.com* would be both the DNS domain name and the Windows 2000 domain name of *mtit.com*. This simplifies things but also complicates them, for you could easily implement Windows NT domains without regard to DNS. But in Windows 2000 using DNS is not optional.

* DNS is also used by Windows 2000 as its domain-locator service. In other words, Active Directory uses DNS for locating hosts on the network, and especially for locating domain controllers so that clients can log on to a Windows 2000 domain. We could say that DNS is the "service locator" for Active Directory services, since services such as ldap, dcs, and so on are stored in special subdomains that can be searched by Windows 2000 systems.

Let's be clear about the difference between a DNS domain and a Windows 2000 domain:

*DNS domain*
Identifies a managed portion of the DNS namespace, and is associated with resource records within a zone database file located on one or more DNS servers that are authoritative for that zone.

*Windows 2000 domain*
Is a group of computers bounded by a common security framework that controls how users can log on to the network and access shared resources. Windows 2000 domains are associated with objects stored in Active Directory on one or more domain controllers throughout the domain.

Both DNS domains and Windows 2000 domains are named identically in Windows 2000. However, while each Windows 2000 domain requires an associated DNS domain to be created and configured for it, each DNS domain does not require a corresponding Windows 2000 domain. This is because DNS is not restricted to Active Directory–based networks, but applies to the whole of the Internet.

Because of the large number of different administrative tasks associated with DNS on Windows 2000, you can find procedures for administering DNS in three different articles in Chapter 4:

*DNS*

> General tasks such as installing the DNS Server service and configuring DNS clients

*DNS server*

> General tasks associated with DNS servers, such as creating zones, configuring scavenging, clearing the cache, and so on

*zone*

> Specific tasks such as creating and modifying resource records, configuring zone transfers, and so on

---

 This article and the ones in Chapter 4 only cover the basics of DNS plus some features specific to Windows 2000 Server—for more detailed information see Paul Albitz and Cricket Liu's *DNS and BIND* and Paul Albitz, Matt Larson, and Cricket Liu's *DNS on Windows NT,* both books from O'Reilly & Associates.

---

## How DNS Works

DNS is a client/server protocol that is implemented using the following components:

- A hierarchical naming system

- A distributed database of resource records that map a host's name to its IP address

- DNS servers on which the DNS database is stored, and the zones that the servers manage

- DNS clients that can query DNS servers to resolve hostnames into their associated IP addresses

- DNS queries issued by DNS clients to DNS servers and by DNS servers to other DNS servers; this system of queries is an essential part of the process of DNS *name resolution* (using DNS servers to determine what IP address is associated with a particular fully qualified domain name)

Let's consider these various components of DNS in more detail.

# More on the Importance of DNS for Active Directory

DNS is important to Windows 2000 primarily because it is the locator service that clients use to find domain controllers in Active Directory. Clients must be able to locate a domain controller to enable users to log on to the network; they do so by querying a DNS server for the SRV and A records of domain controllers. If you want to use Active Directory on your network, you must have DNS installed as your locator service.

In Windows NT, a computer was identified on the network primarily by its NetBIOS name, a 16-byte string that uniquely identifies a computer or service on the network. (One byte identifies the type of service, while the other 15 bytes specify the name of the host or domain associated with it.) DNS was an optional second method in Windows NT of identifying computers and domains.

In Windows 2000, however, NetBIOS is an option needed only if the network contains a mixture of Windows 2000 and legacy Windows NT or earlier computers; in a pure Windows 2000 network, NetBIOS is not required. For information about using NetBIOS name-resolution methods on mixed Windows NT/2000 networks, see the article *WINS* in this chapter.

In Windows NT, clients that needed to locate a resource on the network would use NetBIOS first (broadcasts or WINS servers), and if that failed, then they would try DNS (if it was configured). Windows 2000 clients always attempt to use DNS first as their primary means for locating network resources.

If you are going to use Active Directory on your network, use the Active Directory Installation Wizard to have Windows 2000 automatically configure DNS when you promote a member server to a domain controller. This is, in fact, the easiest way of configuring DNS on Windows 2000–based networks. When you run the wizard, it tries to locate an existing DNS server that is authoritative over your zone, and if it finds one, it tests if the server supports dynamic updates. If it can't find a DNS server (for example, when you promote your first Windows 2000 member server to the role of domain controller to create the root domain of your enterprise), then the wizard installs the DNS Server service on the server, adding the necessary forward-lookup zone for your host records and configuring the zone to accept dynamic updates. For more information see *DNS* in Chapter 4.

Configuring DNS manually gives you more control over your name servers' configurations and might be a necessary approach if you have to interoperate with legacy Windows NT or third-party name servers, such as Unix machines running BIND. See the section "BIND and Windows 2000" later in this article for more information.

### Hierarchical Naming System

DNS defines a *namespace* (an abstract tree of logical names and rules for creating them), which is hierarchical in structure. The root (top) of the namespace is called the *root domain* and is represented by a period (.). Beneath this root domain are *top-level domains*, which are of two types:

*Functional*
    Examples are *.com*, *.org*, *.edu*, *.gov*, and so on

*Geographical*
    Examples are *.us*, *.ca*, *.uk*, and so on

Beneath each top-level domain are *second-level domains*, commonly just called *domains*. These domains can be registered by individuals, companies, and organizations, with various rules in place for each type of top-level domain and usually involving a fee. An example is *microsoft.com*, which Microsoft Corporation has registered within the *.com* top-level domain.

Organizations that have registered their own domain also have the right to subdivide it any way they like into *third-level domains* (usually called *subdomains*). An example would be *msdn.microsoft.com*, which Microsoft uses as a subdomain for their Microsoft Developer Network site.

---

To register a domain name for yourself or your company, you can go to the web site of Network Solutions (*http://www.networksolutions.com*), the only registrar of domain names in the *.com* and other popular domains. With possible new top-level domains on the horizon, other companies will probably soon be getting into the domain registration act.

You can also try registering through your ISP, or through one of the many companies that "park" unused domain names for users. Domain names typically have to be renewed every two years, and the fee is minimal.

---

An individual *host* (computer, router, printer, or some other TCP/IP-enabled device) is uniquely described within the DNS namespace by its *fully qualified domain name* (FQDN). For example, the computer whose hostname is bob and that is located in the sales subdomain of the *mtit.com* domain (the domain name for my own company) would have *bob.sales.mtit.com* for its FQDN.

In Windows NT, the term *domain* could mean two different things:

* A group of Windows NT computers whose security is managed centrally using domain controllers

* A collection of computers running TCP/IP that have the same domain name according to the Domain Name System

For instance, a Windows NT server named BOB might simultaneously belong to the Windows NT domain called HEADQUARTERS and to the DNS domain called *mtit.com*. This was a source of great confusion to new Windows NT administrators (and students pursuing their MCSE designation).

The situation in Windows 2000 is different: DNS is now the primary naming system for computers (instead of NetBIOS in Windows NT), and a Windows 2000 domain is essentially the same as a DNS domain (both would be called *mtit.com*, for example).

FQDNs can only consist of the letters a–z and A–Z, the numbers 0–9, and the dash (-) symbol if they are to be RFC 1123–compliant (although both letters a–z and A–Z are allowed, FQDNs are in fact case-insensitive). This is particularly important when your Microsoft DNS servers need to interoperate with other name servers such as Unix systems running BIND or legacy Windows NT name servers.

DNS in Windows 2000, however, supports several broader character sets, making it potentially incompatible with existing BIND or Windows NT name servers on the network. The reason for this is that Microsoft wanted to simplify the process of migrating existing Windows NT networks with their NetBIOS-named computers to Windows 2000 with DNS as its locator service. NetBIOS names in Windows NT can contain unicode characters and numbers, white space, and a variety of special symbols. Upgrading these networks to Windows 2000 required either having DNS support such a broad range of characters or requiring hosts to be renamed in order to be compliant with RFC 1123. Microsoft chose the former course, supposedly in the cause of simplicity (while in effect throwing the existing Domain Name System into something of a curve). See the section "BIND and Windows 2000" in this article for more information.

### Distributed Database

The DNS database essentially contains the IP address of each host on the internetwork. If we are talking about DNS on the Internet, we mean millions of FQDN-to-IP address records within the DNS database, while if we are using DNS on a private internetwork, then the number of records may be much smaller.

DNS enables communications on a TCP/IP network without the need of remembering the cumbersome IP addresses of hosts you are trying to communicate with. It's generally easier to remember that you can download tech support documents from the computer called *ftp.tech.mtit.com* than to have to remember that its IP address is 172.16.13.55 (or whatever). The DNS hierarchical naming system thus has several advantages over plain IP addresses:

- FQDNs are easier to remember than IP addresses.

- FQDNs can be arranged hierarchically regardless of the IP addresses used. This makes FQDNs intrinsically easier to search for than IP addresses.

A third advantage of FQDNs is that by organizing them into a series of domains and subdomains, you can distribute the content and management of the entire DNS database to different servers, creating what is called a distributed DNS database. This way, instead of requiring that each DNS server contain and manage the entire DNS database of millions of records (if we're dealing with DNS on the Internet) or thousands of records (in a corporate enterprise setting), DNS servers can be assigned smaller subtrees of the database. This is done through the creation and management of DNS *zones*, which is discussed later in the section "Zones."

### Resource Records

The records in the DNS database are called *resource records* because they are primarily records of the resources (servers, gateways, and so on) located on the network (there are other types of records, too). On a DNS server these resource records can be stored in an ASCII file called the *zone file* (discussed later). The most important types of resource records as far as DNS on Windows 2000 is concerned are the following:

*SOA (Start of Authority) record*
> Each zone file contains only one SOA record, which identifies which DNS server is *authoritative* (is regarded as the authoritative source of DNS database information) for a particular zone and the DNS subdomains within the zone. The SOA record specifies:
>
> — The primary name server that is authoritative over the zone
>
> — The email address of the DNS administrator for the zone
>
> — The minimum time-to-live (TTL) for resolvers to cache records within the zone
>
> — Various internal parameters used for zone replication

*NS (Name Server) record*
> An NS record contains the FQDN and IP address of a DNS server assigned to (authoritative in) the zone. Each primary and secondary name server authoritative in the domain should have an NS record.

*A (Address) record*
> By far the most common type of resource record, an A record is used to resolve the FQDN of a particular TCP/IP host on the network into its associated IP address.

*CNAME (Canonical Name) record*
> A CNAME record contains an alias (alternate name) for a host. For example, if a server functioned as both a web server and an FTP server, its A record could contain the FQDN *www.mtit.com* while the CNAME record defines ftp as an alias for www. You can also use CNAME records to hide the true names of hosts on your internal network from external clients. For example, your FTP server could be named *BOB312.mtit.com* on your internal network, but a CNAME record can enable you to identify it to external clients as *ftp.mtit.com.*

*PTR (Pointer) record*
> The opposite of an A record, a PTR record is used to resolve the IP address of a TCP/IP host into its FQDN.

*SRV (Service) record*
> An SRV record is used by clients to locate a server that is running a particular service—for example, to find a domain controller in ,order to log on.

*MX (Mail Exchange) record*
> An MX record points to one or more computers that will process SMTP mail for an organization or site.

SRV records were not used in DNS on Windows NT. On Windows 2000 they can be used in both standard and Active Directory integrated zones.

There are a number of other less commonly used resource record types, but the ones described here are the ones used in Microsoft Windows networks. One type I didn't mention is the WINS record, used to enable a WINS server to resolve name queries that cannot be resolved using DNS. The WINS record is non-RFC-compliant and was used in Windows NT networks, but is only used in Windows 2000 networks when WINS is configured for interoperability with legacy Windows NT portions of the network.

## DNS Servers

The backbone of the Domain Name System is the DNS servers that contain the distributed DNS database and the DNS administrators who maintain these servers. Another name for a DNS server is a *name server*, since the main job of these servers is to *resolve* FQDNs into IP addresses when requested to do so by DNS clients. In other words, they server out IP addresses when clients submit DNS names to them—hence the term, name server.

On the Internet most DNS servers are Unix machines running software called BIND, which stands for Berkeley Internet Name Domain (BIND). Within most medium- to large-size corporate networks, you will generally find a mixture of Unix servers running BIND and Windows NT servers running Microsoft's DNS Server service (though BIND still predominates). Windows 2000 will probably change things—in order to use Active Directory, you need to install Windows 2000's DNS Server service, and there promises to be lots of sparks as Windows and Unix DNS clash to decide which will be the primary source of DNS services for corporate networks. See the section "BIND and Windows 2000" in this article for more information.

DNS servers can be classified into four types, depending on how they are configured to manage different DNS zones (see the "Zones" section in this article for an explanation of zones):

*Primary name server*
> A DNS server that maintains the (only) writable copy of the zone file for a zone. (Name servers can also hold zone files for domains other than their own.) DNS administrators create, modify, and delete DNS database records on primary name servers. There can and must be only one primary name server for a given zone.

*Secondary name server*
> A DNS server that keeps a Read-only copy of the zone file for a zone. Secondary DNS servers obtain fresh copies of the zone file by replicating it from a master name server using a process called zone transfer. There can be zero, one, or multiple, secondary name servers for a given zone to provide fault tolerance in case the primary server goes down. Secondary servers can

be used to reduce the load on the primary DNS server. They can also be located at remote branch offices to prevent clients there from performing name resolution over slow WAN links with the primary name server at headquarters.

*Master name server*

A DNS server from which secondary name servers download copies of the zone file for a zone. A master name server may be either a primary or secondary name server.

*Caching-only name server*

A DNS server that does not contain any copy of a zone file. These name servers cache the IP addresses of the most frequently requested FQDNs and use them to answer queries by DNS clients.

Caching-only name servers are particularly useful in reducing unwanted WAN traffic. For example, say you have a primary name server located at company headquarters and configure a caching-only name server at a smaller branch office that is connected to headquarters over a slow WAN link. If clients at the branch office use DNS to issue name queries, the caching-only name server receives the requests and uses the WAN link to query the primary name server for the information. When the primary server returns a response, the caching-only server passes it on to the client but caches it in case it is required later by another client. This reduces the WAN traffic that would occur if no name server was located at the branch office.

Similar results could be obtained by placing a secondary name server at the branch office. The difference is that the caching-only server generates no zone-transfer traffic while the secondary server does (albeit not very much since Windows 2000 DNS uses incremental zone transfers instead of full ones). Another difference is that if only headquarters is connected to the Internet so that the branch office connects to the Internet indirectly via the WAN link, there will be a lot of DNS queries at the branch office that a secondary name server cannot resolve. So configuring a caching-only name server there as a *forwarder* (see the section "Using Forwarders" later in this article) is a better solution.

What's confusing about all this to the newcomer to DNS is that:

- A master name server can be either a primary or a secondary name server. In other words, secondary name servers can download their zone file from either a primary name server or another secondary name server.

- A DNS server can be a primary name server for one zone and a secondary name server for a different zone. In other words, each DNS server can service multiple zones and have different roles in different zones.

 Both primary and secondary name servers are authoritative for any zones they administer. In other words, they can give the DNS clients that query them an authoritative answer to their queries. Caching-only name servers are not authoritative for their zones.

## BIND and Windows 2000

Microsoft says that certain versions of BIND are compatible with Active Directory and that you can elect to retain existing BIND name servers if you like when implementing Active Directory. The procedures for implementing BIND with Windows 2000 are not trivial, however. Since Active Directory uses DNS as its name-locator service, your name servers must be properly configured if Windows 2000 clients are to locate domain controllers and log on to the network or to locate and access shared resources on the network or the Internet.

First off, there are several ways you can choose to integrate existing BIND name servers and Windows 2000:

- You could use BIND exclusively. Your DNS administrator may prefer this method. You must use BIND 8.2.1 or later if you plan to keep your BIND servers and not implement Windows 2000 DNS servers, however. This is because BIND 8.2.1 supports Dynamic DNS (DDNS), SRV resource records, incremental zone transfers, and negative caching—all features which Active Directory needs to fully implement Windows 2000 features. Note, however, that BIND does not support WINS and WINS-R records, which may be needed if you also plan to integrate WINS with DNS (for example, if part of your Windows 2000 network will remain Windows NT). Furthermore, BIND does not support the Secure Dynamic Update method used by Windows 2000 DNS servers (though it probably will soon). If you want to implement a BIND name server to support the root domain of Active Directory, you need to create the subdomains *_msdcs.<domainname>*, *_sites.<domainname>*, *_tcp.<domainname>*, and *_udp.<domainname>*, where *<domainname>* is the DNS domain name you registered with ICANN for your company. These special subdomains are used by Active Directory for storing various configuration information on the DNS server. See the *Deployment Planning Guide* of the *Windows 2000 Server Resource Kit* for more information on this.

- You could use Windows 2000 DNS name servers exclusively for both internal and external access. This is the simplest solution from the point of view of Windows 2000, but requires an upheaval of your existing BIND name servers and DNS administration, plus the retraining of your DNS administrators. With the proven stability of BIND, many DNS administrators may be unwilling to go this route until time has shaken out the bugs in Windows 2000's implementation of DNS.

- You could use Windows DNS servers for your internal network and BIND name servers for Internet access. This might be the best solution, and it doesn't even require upgrading BIND. What you might do here is to register a second DNS domain name from ICANN and use this for your Active Directory root domain. You could then leave your BIND server to manage DNS for the portion of your network you don't plan to migrate to Windows 2000 and to manage DNS for your Internet hosts. Then create a secondary zone on your BIND name server for your Windows 2000 domain and a secondary zone on your Windows 2000 DNS server for your BIND server's domain.

- You could use BIND for both the internal and external network and configure your Windows 2000 root domain as a subdomain of your company's existing DNS domain. This might be a good solution if you are planning to migrate some (but not all) of your network to Windows 2000. On the BIND server you then delegate authority for the Windows 2000 subdomain to Active Directory, which manages the delegated portion of DNS namespace for the network. You must be running BIND 8.2.1 or later if you go this route, however. What you need to do is create a delegation record on your BIND name server for the new subdomain and then configure the Windows 2000 DNS server to use the subdomain as the root domain for Active Directory.

Whatever your choice concerning DNS and Windows 2000, the road is sure to be rocky at the start. To help you out, Table 3-12 compares the features supported by Windows 2000 DNS and different versions of BIND.

*Table 3-12: DNS Features Supported by Windows 2000 and BIND*

| DNS Feature Supported | Windows 2000 | BIND 8.2 | BIND 8.1.2 | BIND 4.9.7 |
|---|---|---|---|---|
| SRV records defined by RFC 2782, "A DNS RR for specifying the location of services (DNS SRV)" | Yes | Yes | Yes | Yes |
| Dynamic update of DNS records | Yes | Yes | Yes | No |
| Secure dynamic update using GSS-TSIG algorithm | Yes | No | No | No |
| WINS and WINS-R records | Yes | No | No | No |
| Fast zone transfer | Yes | Yes | Yes | Yes |
| Incremental zone transfer | Yes | Yes | No | No |
| UTF-8 character encoding | Yes | No | No | No |

### Zones

DNS servers manage portions of the DNS namespace called zones. A *zone* is a contiguous (unbroken) subtree of DNS namespace, for example, a domain and several of its subdomains. Zones are defined by a *zone file*, an ASCII file that is stored on a DNS server and contains the records of the hosts that the DNS server manages.

Actually, zones are defined by ASCII zone files only on:

— BIND name servers

— Windows NT servers running the Microsoft DNS Server service

— Windows 2000 member servers running the Microsoft DNS Server service

If you install the DNS Server service on a Windows 2000 domain controller, the zone information is stored in Active Directory instead of a traditional ASCII file. This is discussed further later in this article.

Each zone has one primary name server that is authoritative over that zone and zero, one, or more name servers that are associated with the same zone but are not authoritative. When you create a zone, you choose between three different types:

*Standard primary zone*

Has a writable copy of the zone file for the zone. When you need to add, remove, or modify resource records for a zone, you make changes to the zone file on the name server on which you created the standard primary zone (in other words, on the primary name server for the zone).

*Standard secondary zone*

Has a Read-only copy of the zone file for the zone. Changes made to the zone file for the standard primary zone are replicated to the zone file for the standard secondary zone. Zone files for standard secondary zones are located on secondary name servers, as expected.

---

 If you will be using standard zones instead of Active Directory integrated zones, you must create a primary zone before you create any associated secondary zones. This is because a primary zone *defines* a zone, since it contains the writable copy of the zone file.

---

*Active Directory integrated zone*

Does not have an ASCII zone file containing its resource records—instead its information is stored in Active Directory. The advantages of this over traditional (standard) zones are:

— Zone transfers are subsumed into Active Directory multimaster replication, a process that is more efficient than traditional DNS zone transfers. Also, there is only one replication topology to configure (just Active Directory), not two (AD and DNS).

— All zones are primary zones and can have resource records modified on them, which provides a degree of fault tolerance. (In a traditional scenario, if a primary name server goes down, you have to promote a secondary name server to take its place.)

— Active Directory makes zone information more secure and can prevent unauthorized clients from performing dynamic updates.

— Active Directory integrated zones can interoperate and perform zone transfers with standard zones.

If you're interested, you can view zones stored in Active Directory as follows::

Administrative Tools → Active Directory Users and Computers → View → Advanced Features

This displays several additional OUs and their objects that are normally hidden from day-to-day administration. Expand the console tree as follows:

Root node → domain → System → MicrosoftDNS

You can view but not modify DNS information using this console.

---

The management tasks associated with standard primary and standard secondary zones include:

- Planning and creating zones on name servers (creating a standard primary zone creates its associated zone file as well)

- Adding, deleting, and modifying resource records in the primary zone

- Configuring how zone transfers will occur between primary and secondary zones

Management of zones is much simpler with Active Directory integrated zones since zone transfers are performed automatically and efficiently as part of the Active Directory replication process. The downside of course is that you have to implement Active Directory itself to benefit from these gains, and this is far from trivial to plan and implement, especially in a large enterprise. Using Active Directory integrated zones also has the advantage of providing greater fault tolerance since all DNS servers are in effect "primary" servers (they contain writable copies of the DNS database).

You can only create Active Directory integrated zones on a name server that is configured to use *DNS dynamic updates* (see the section "Dynamic Update" later in this article).

### Zone File

Zone files contain the actual resource records for the zone, including the SOA record that defines the zone. Zone files are typically used for two tasks:

- Resolving FQDNs into IP addresses to enable network communications using DNS naming conventions

- Resolving IP addresses into FQDNs to enable certain DNS troubleshooting tools like *nslookup* to work

These two functions are covered by two kinds of zones:

*Forward-lookup zone*
    Has resource records for resolving FQDNs into IP addresses (mostly A records, but also any records except PTR records). A DNS client uses a *forward-lookup* query to resolve a remote host's FQDN into an IP address. Most DNS queries are forward lookups.

*Reverse-lookup zone*
    Has records for resolving IP addresses into FQDNs (mostly PTR records, but also any records except A records). This kind of query is called a *reverse lookup*. Some DNS troubleshooting tools such as *nslookup* use a reverse-lookup query to resolve an IP address into its associated FQDN. Network security tools that used FQDNs to determine whether clients should be granted or denied access also use reverse lookups. Reverse lookups do not try to search all DNS namespace to resolve their IP address into an FQDN; instead they use a special DNS domain called *in-addr.arpa*, which uses a reverse ordering of the dotted IP address notation for identifying hosts and stores this information in PTR records.

*Concepts D*

## Root Domain

The *root domain* is the top-most domain in DNS namespace. On the Internet, the root domain is managed by *top-level name servers*, of which there are about a dozen. These top-level name servers (or *root name servers*) are authoritative over the *root* (top) of the hierarchical DNS namespace and contain zone files defining the root zone of the Internet's DNS. The zone's resource records are used to locate the Internet's *second-level name servers*, that is, name servers authoritative over top-level domains such as *.com, .org, .net,* and so on.

Root name servers are very important in the DNS system: if a client's local DNS servers are unable to resolve a name into its IP address, a root name server must be contacted and the DNS hierarchy is searched from the top (root) of the tree downward until the name is found.

What if your network is not connected to the Internet, or it's connected through a firewall that uses Network Address Translation (NAT) to hide the internal network's IP addresses from the outside world? In this case you would have to set up your own root name server and configure its root zone. In fact, the first time you open the DNS console, you are prompted whether you wish to create a root zone for your network.

A *root hints file* contains the information needed to resolve FQDNs outside of the domains over which the name server is authoritative. This file is *%SystemRoot%\System32\Dns\Cache.dns* in a Windows 2000 DNS server, and it contains NS and A records for the root name servers. The Configure DNS Server Wizard, which is run when you install the DNS Server service on Windows 2000 Server, tries to determine if your network is connected with the Internet. If it is, it creates a *Cache.dns* file with the Internet's root name servers listed in it. If your network is not connected to the Internet or is hidden behind a firewall, you need to specify your own root name servers to create a custom *Cache.dns* file.

Some name servers support a third kind of name query called an inverse-lookup. An inverse lookup involves trying to resolve an IP address into an FQDN, but the inverse lookup does not use the *in-addr.arpa* domain to accomplish this. Instead, the name server simply checks through all its own zone files and gives an answer based on this information, without any referrals to other name servers. Inverse lookup was needed by legacy versions of nslookup and is supported by Windows 2000 Server.

The terms zone and zone file are sometimes used interchangeably, although the zone file (or zone database file or database file or db file) is the physical expression of the logical zone entity.

If your network is directly connected to the Internet without using NAT, or if your DNS server will be on the far side of the firewall so it is directly connected to the Internet (more likely), then you don't need to create a root zone. Instead, you can use the default root-zone file *cache.dns*, which is located in *%SystemRoot%\System32\ dns* and contains records for the root name servers on the Internet. Make sure this file is up-to-date to ensure name resolution works properly.

### Zone Transfers

Zone transfer is the process of replicating zone files between different name servers. This ensures that all name servers for a zone have identical copies of the zone file, which is necessary to ensure that clients can use any name server in the zone to perform name resolution.

In the earlier implementation of DNS on Windows NT, zone files were updated by a process called *full zone transfer* using an *AXFR request*. This meant that when a DNS administrator updated one or more resource records in the primary zone, the full DNS zone file would be replicated from the primary to all associated secondary zones. This procedure was wasteful of network bandwidth and has been replaced in Windows 2000 with *incremental zone transfer* using an *IXFR request*, in which only changes to the zone files are updated. Incremental zone transfers initiate when one of the following events occurs:

- The master server in a zone notifies all designated, secondary name servers in the zone that records have changed in its zone file and that they need to request an update. The process used by the master name server to notify secondary name servers is called *DNS Notify*. The secondary name servers then contact their master name server requesting the updates for their zone files.

- The DNS Server service on a secondary name server starts up or is restarted. The secondary name server then contacts the designated, master name server for the zone, requesting the updates for its zone file.

- The refresh interval configured on the secondary server expires. The secondary name server then contacts the master name server for the zone, requesting the updates for its zone file.

The advantage of incremental zone transfers is that they generate less DNS zone transfer traffic on the network than full zone tranfsers do. The disadvantage is that name servers configured for IXFR need more disk space, as they need to keep a record of version history for their zone files (a DNS transaction log, in effect).

### Resolvers

In addition to name servers, there's also the client side of DNS. A resolver is software running on a client computer that enables the computer to communicate with name servers to resolve FQDNs into IP addresses. In other words, a name server represents the server side of DNS while a resolver represents the client side. Every version of Microsoft Windows contains a resolver built into its TCP/IP networking component. Resolvers have to be configured to enable them to locate name servers (see *DNS* in Chapter 4).

The Windows 2000 resolver is a caching resolver service—when a name is resolved, the results are cached locally by the client in case it needs to resolve the name again in the immediate future (before the time-to-live—or TTL—of the resolved entry expires). Windows 2000 resolvers also cache negative name-query responses (failure to resolve a name).

 A resolver can be running on a DNS server and not just on users' desktop client computers. In other words, one name server can be a client with respect to another name server.

### DNS Queries

The last ingredient in DNS is the actual messages sent between DNS clients and DNS servers and between servers and other servers. There are essentially two types of DNS queries:

*Iterative query*

> When a DNS client or server issues an iterative query to a DNS server, the server must respond with its best current answer *without* contacting any other servers itself. This best answer is either:

> — The requested information (typically the IP address associated with the FQDN sent in the query). If this response is returned, the client is satisfied because it has what it wants.

> — A time out or error message. If this is the case, the client is satisfied because an authoritative answer was received. However, since the answer was "I don't know," the desired network communications can't take place.

> — A pointer to an authoritative DNS server that is located one level down in the hierarchical DNS namespace. This kind of response is known as a *referral*. If a referral is returned, the client goes on to interactively query the lower-down name server. This process continues until one of the two previous responses is received by the client.

*Recursive query*

> When a client or server issues a recursive query to a DNS server, the server that receives the query takes on full responsibility for finding an answer for the client's request, and does so itself iteratively querying other DNS servers until it has an answer or receives an error or time-out message. Whatever the result of the process is, it is passed on to the client.

Recursive queries are used by:

— DNS clients (resolvers), such as those running on Windows 2000 Professional or other desktop Microsoft Windows operating systems.

— DNS servers that are configured to forward unresolved names to another DNS server. A DNS server that has been configured to perform recursive instead of iterative queries is called a *forwarder* because it forwards queries for resolving FQDNs outside of its domain to a different DNS server.

### Using Forwarders

Forwarders are particularly useful in a scenario such as the following: you have a corporate network with a DNS server and a slow WAN link connecting you to the Internet. The DNS server on your network is authoritative only for your domain (which we'll say is called *mtit.com*), that is, for the computers on your TCP/IP network.

What happens when a client computer on your network tries to connect to a site on the Internet (such as *www.microsoft.com*)? The client has to contact your local DNS server first to resolve the name of the remote Internet host (which is in a different domain than yours) into its IP address in order to communicate with it. However, since your DNS server is only authoritative over your own domain, it must first find a name server that is authoritative over the *microsoft.com* domain (since such a name server would be able to resolve the host *www.microsoft.com* into its IP address). What happens is what I call the "DNS walk-a-thon." Let's look at this in detail:

- A client computer issues a recursive query to a local name server asking to resolve *www.microsoft.com*.

- The local DNS server issues an iterative query to a root name server (authoritative over the "." domain) on the Internet, asking for the IP address of a name server that is authoritative over the *.com* top-level domain.

- The root name server replies to the local name server with the IP address of a name server for the *.com* top-level domain.

- The local name server then issues a second iterative query, this time to the name server for the *.com* domain, asking for the IP address of a name server which is authoritative over the *microsoft.com* second-level domain.

- The name server for the *.com* domain replies to the local name server with the IP address of a name server for the *microsoft.com* domain.

- The local name server then issues a third iterative query, this time to the name server for the *microsoft.com* domain, asking for the IP address of the host *www.microsoft.com*.

- The name server for the *microsoft.com* domain replies to the local name server with the requested IP address (if nothing goes wrong).

- The local name server now replies to the client computer on your network, giving it the IP address for *www.microsoft.com*. The client computer can now contact the remote host.

*Concepts D*

Now you can see that if your network is connected to the Internet over a slow WAN link, then a single name query for a remote domain can lead to a lot of WAN traffic. The solution to this is to use a forwarder. You set up a second DNS server outside your network directly connected to the Internet. This external DNS server is now your forwarder and requires no further configuration. You then configure your original (internal) DNS server to ask the forwarder to send a recursive name query to the forwarder whenever the internal DNS server can't resolve a client's name query. Now the name resolution process works like this:

- The client computer issues recursive query to the internal name server asking to resolve *www.microsoft.com.*

- The internal name server recognizes that it is not authoritative for the *microsoft.com* domain, and sends a recursive query to the external name server (the forwarder), asking it to take on the job of resolving the name.

- The forwarder then contacts a root name server, which replies with the address of a *.com* name server. The forwarder then contacts the *.com* name server, which replies with the address of a *microsoft.com* name server. The forwarder then contacts the *microsoft.com* name server, which replies with the IP address for the host *www.microsoft.com.* All of this communication takes place outside of your network and does not eat up valuable WAN link bandwidth.

- Finally, the forwarder passes the resolved IP address to the internal name server, which passes it on to the client.

What happens if the forwarder cannot resolve the name query submitted to it by the internal name server? It depends on whether the internal name server is configured to use the forwarder in exclusive or nonexclusive mode:

*Exclusive mode*
> The internal name server depends entirely on the forwarder to resolve the name query. If the forwarder returns a query failure response to the internal name server, the internal name server simply passes this response to the client that issued the query. In this configuration the internal name server is commonly called a *slave.*

*Nonexclusive mode*
> If the forwarder returns a query-failure response to the internal name server, the internal name server makes an attempt at resolving the query on its own as best it can and returns its decision to the client.

## Other Features of Windows 2000 DNS

Here are a few other things you can do with DNS on Windows 2000 Server.

### Delegation

You can create subdomains in your DNS domain and then delegate authority over those subdomains to different name servers. This allows you to:

- Distribute the work of maintaining DNS in an enterprise where there are a large number of hosts and more than a couple of name servers.

- Delegate to users in different departments the job of administering DNS for their subdomain.

For example, in the large enterprise *mtit.com* domain, there might be several subdomains such as *ontario.mtit.com, quebec.mtit.com, bc.mtit.com,* and so on. You can have one or more DNS servers to service each geographical location within the enterprise and make them authoritative over their own subdomain.

### Dynamic Update

Dynamic update is a process that enables resolvers to automatically update their associated resource records on their zone's primary name server. This is a big improvement over traditional (static) DNS in which administrators would manually create and update resource records in the zone files. Dynamic DNS can be used with either standard or Active Directory integrated zones. The DNS message used to perform dynamic updates is called an UPDATE message, and it can be used to add or remove resource records.

Dynamic DNS can also be used in conjunction with DHCP to make the DNS administrator's job even easier. Whenever a client releases and renews its IP address, its resource records are updated (if necessary) on the DNS server. What typically happens is:

- The DHCP client itself updates its A record on the DNS server.

- The DHCP server updates the client's PTR record on the DNS server.

### Load Sharing

DNS in Windows NT could use a mechanism known as *round-robin* to load-balance access to multiple servers offering the same services. For example, if you had three web servers hosting mirroring copies of the same site, you create three A records as follows:

```
www.mtit.com          IN   A   172.16.11.55
www.mtit.com          IN   A   172.16.11.56
www.mtit.com          IN   A   172.16.11.57
```

Then when clients contacted the name server to resolve *www.mtit.com* into an IP address, the server returned the IP addresses in round-robin fashion: the first client request receives the response 172.16.11.55, the next request 172.16.11.56, and so on.

This is not how it works in Windows 2000's version of DNS. Instead, Windows 2000 tries to determine which of the three resource records is nearest to the client and uses this record to resolve the name. This is the same kind of load-balancing that is done by BIND 4.9.3 and later.

 You can configure DNS in Windows 2000 to perform the same kind of round-robin load balancing as used in Windows NT. See *DNS* in Chapter 4 for more information.

## Planning a Windows 2000 DNS Implementation

There are basically three ways you can implement a DNS namespace using Active Directory.

### Same Domain Names

Using my existing DNS domain name for my private network and as the name for my Windows 2000 root domain in Active Directory, and using the same DNS domain name for my public servers that are connected directly to the Internet.

For example, if my company MTIT Enterprises already has the registered DNS domain name *mtit.com* and I want to migrate my enterprise to Windows 2000, I could choose *mtit.com* as the name of the first or root Windows 2000 domain I create. The advantage of this solution is that it is the simplest form of namespace I can adopt. The disadvantage is that I need to consider carefully how I can secure my private corporate network from the Internet since both my private and public servers use the same naming system. The solution is to implement a secure firewall or firewall/proxy server combination, with identical DNS zones created on each side (private and public, internal and external network) of the firewall using internal and external DNS servers.

My internal DNS server needs resource records for all the IP hosts on my private network, including special records to support Active Directory. Using a Windows 2000 DNS server is a good choice for my private network, since it fully supports Active Directory's features. My external DNS server needs only those web servers and other hosts that I maintain outside my firewall for public access, and it can be either Microsoft DNS or BIND. I can then configure my internal DNS server to forward client requests for Internet resources to my external DNS server.

The advantages here are:

- Users need only to remember a single DNS domain name when they want to access my company's resources, whether within the private corporate intranet or on my public Internet servers.

- I only need to register one company name with ICANN.

The disadvantages are:

- The additional DNS administration work involved in making sure internal and external DNS servers contain only the records they are supposed to have

- The complexity of reconfiguring my firewall

- The fact that if I maintain some resources on both my internal and external networks, I need to figure out how to keep them synchronized properly

### Different Domain Names

Using my existing DNS domain name for my private network and as the name for my Windows 2000 root domain in Active Directory, and obtaining a second DNS domain name for my public servers that are connected directly to the Internet.

For example, I could use the DNS domain name *mtit.com* for the internal private network of my company and register a new DNS domain name such as *mtitenterprises.com* with ICANN and use this on my external network that is connected directly to the Internet. I configure my internal and external DNS servers separately and configure my external servers as a forwarder from the point of view of the internal one. I still need to configure a firewall and/or proxy server, but this is less complex than the previous case due to the different DNS domain names of my two networks.

The advantages here are:

- I can leave my existing corporate DNS naming hierarchy and zone files (if implemented) intact and simply upgrade DNS servers to Windows 2000.

- The DNS naming hierarchy of my private Windows 2000 domains, trees, and forests is hidden from external users on the Internet.

- The security of my network resources is greater because internal and external resources are clearly distinguished by belonging to different DNS domains.

- If desired, I can configure my firewall/proxy server so that I no longer need to replicate content between my internal and external web servers. Instead, I can allow external clients access to specific resources on my private network.

The disadvantages are:

- I need to register a second DNS domain name for my company with ICANN.

- Some users might be confused by the fact that my company has two DNS domain names. Which one do they use?

### Domain and Subdomain

Using my existing DNS domain name for my public servers that are connected directly to the Internet and for the legacy portion of my internal network that I do not plan to migrate to Windows 2000, and creating a new DNS subdomain for the portion of my private network that I plan to upgrade to Windows 2000 and as the name for my Windows 2000 root domain in Active Directory.

This might be the solution in a heterogeneous network where I will only be migrating a portion of my network to Windows 2000, especially if DNS is already configured on my existing network. For example, my existing network uses the DNS domain name *mtit.com*, and I want to install Active Directory on a portion of my network. In this case I could create a DNS subdomain such as *windows.mtit.com* and make this the name of my new Windows 2000 root domain. (It would be better to use *windows.mtit.com* instead of *win2000.mtit.com* in case I decide to upgrade my network to Windows 2001 next year!) Accomplishing this requires a few special steps:

- Create a DNS zone for *windows.mtit.com*, preferably on a Windows 2000 DNS server since it will be supporting Active Directory.

- Create a delegation record on the existing DNS server that is authoritative for the *mtit.com* domain. The delegation record will indicate that authority for the *windows.mtit.com* subdomain is delegated to my Windows 2000 DNS server.

- Install Active Directory with *windows.mtit.com* as the root domain and root of my forest.

The advantages of doing it this way are:

- It provides a contiguous namespace for Active Directory, which I can easily administer.

- It does not necessitate the upgrade of my existing DNS servers, so I can keep my BIND servers if I like.

- I can leave my firewall pretty much the way it is right now.

The main disadvantage is that it makes my DNS naming structure longer for naming resources on my Windows 2000 network. That's only a minor bother however, unless your domain name is something like *wishicouldthinkofabetterdomainnamethanthis.com*!

---

 Another good DNS naming method is to make the root domain name *corp.net*. This allows a more flexible naming scheme in case of mergers and/or acquisitions.

---

Finally, here are some additional tips relating to planning a DNS implementation for a Windows 2000 Active Directory–based network.

- Use Windows 2000 DNS servers exclusively, if at all possible, as they are designed to fully support Active Directory. If you must use BIND for some or all of your DNS servers, see the section "DNS Servers" earlier in this article for tips on how to do this.

- Choose a DNS name for your Windows 2000 root domain (the first Windows 2000 domain you install in your enterprise) that reflects the full scope of your company's business activities. For more information see *Active Directory* in this chapter.

### Notes

- DNS replaces the *Hosts* file, which was the original method for performing hostname-to-IP address name resolution on a TCP/IP network. However, the *Hosts* file can still be used in smaller Windows 2000 networks instead of DNS if desired, such as in a small intranet with no connection to the Internet.

- Standard zone files are stored in *%SystemRoot%\System32\dns* as a file with a *.dns* extension. For example, the forward-lookup zone for the *mtit.com* domain would, by default, be stored in the zone file *mtit.com.dns*.

- Using Dynamic DNS with Active Directory integrated zones enables resource records on name servers to be automatically updated more securely than when using standard primary and secondary zones. This works because only clients and servers that have been authorized in Active Directory can update their own records on the DNS server.

- Resolvers can query both remote name servers and the local computer if it is running the DNS Server service.

- DNS servers and zones don't map one-to-one. In fact:

  — One DNS server can manage one or more zones for efficiency and delegating administration of subdomains.

  — One zone can be stored on one or more DNS servers for fault tolerance and load balancing.

- It is generally best to have at least one secondary name server per zone. This way if the primary name server for the zone goes offline, clients can still resolve names.

- Windows NT clients only attempted to use DNS for name resolution when the name that needed to be resolved either:

  — Was more than 15 characters long

  — Contained one or more periods (and hence was an FQDN)

  If neither of these was the case, the Windows NT client used NetBIOS name resolution methods instead (e.g., broadcast or WINS server). In Windows 2000 the situation is different: Windows 2000 clients always try to use DNS for name resolution.

- The general format for a resource record is space- or tab-delimited values for the fields, Owner TTL Class Type RDATA, where:

  Owner
  : Name of the host or DNS domain.

  TTL *(optional)*
  : Time-to-live in seconds, which a name server or resolver should cache the response to before discarding. If not specified here, the TTL specified in the SOA record is used by default.

  Class
  : The protocol family, which is now always IN for Internet.

  Type
  : The type of resource record (e.g., A, NS, PTR, and so on).

  RDATA
  : The data for the record. For an A record, this would be the IP address of the Owner host.

### See Also

*Active Directory(3), DNS(4), DNS server(4), WINS(3), zone(4)*

---

## domain

A container in Active Directory that defines a logical boundary for objects sharing common security requirements, administration, and replication.

### Description

Think of a domain as a security boundary. Within the boundary, objects (users, groups, computers, printers, and so on) share common security requirements. For example, all users in a domain can log on to the network using their username, password, and domain name. Domains also have their own security policy (Domain Security Policy), which defines account policies such as password and account lockout settings.

A domain is created when you install the first domain controller for the domain. This can be done either during Windows 2000 Setup or by promoting a stand-alone server to the role of domain controller using the Active Directory Installation Wizard. Domains are also units of replication: all domain controllers in a domain automatically replicate their Active Directory updates to each other. See *domain controller* in this chapter for more information.

Domains share common administration, and members of the Domain Admins group have full rights and permissions for performing any tasks they want on any object in the domain. These administrators can also delegate aspects of domain administration to other trusted users using the Delegation of Control Wizard. Administrators can add further structure to a domain by creating a hierarchy of OUs within the domain. An OU (organizational unit) is a container in Active Directory that can contain other objects (including other OUs). Administrators can delegate authority over OUs to trusted users to allow them to perform specific administrative tasks upon the objects within the OUs. See *delegation* and *OU* in this chapter for more information.

---

 Domains are not the same as *sites*. Domains are logical groupings of users, computers, and other Active Directory objects, while sites are physical divisions between networks based on low-bandwidth connections. One domain can span several sites, and one site can contain several domains. For more information see *site* in this chapter.

---

Domains can exist by themselves, or they can be grouped into multidomain hierarchical structures called trees and forests. A tree consists of a root domain and other domains connected to the root or to each other in a hierarchical fashion. A forest consists of two or more trees joined at the roots. All domains in a tree or forest implicitly trust each other using two-way transitive trusts, allowing users to log on to a client computer anywhere in the enterprise and access shared resources on any server. For more information see *forest*, *tree*, and *trust* in this chapter.

---

 When you are planning an Active Directory implementation, always start by assuming that a single domain will suffice. Use multiple domains only if necessary to separate administrative functions more sharply between business subsidiaries, locations, or departments.

---

### Naming a Domain

Domains in Windows 2000 are named using DNS domain names. For example, the root domain for MTIT Enterprises could have the name *mtit.com*. Domain names can be assigned at will, but if your network will be connected to the Internet, you should register your DNS domain name with ICANN. For more information on naming domains, see *Active Directory* and *DNS* in this chapter.

### Root Domain

The root domain is the first domain you create in Active Directory. Remember, when you begin implementing Windows 2000 on your network and install your first Windows 2000 domain controller, this action creates Active Directory on your network. It also creates the root domain, the first Windows 2000 domain in your enterprise. This root domain will be:

---

- The root of your first tree

- The root of your entire forest (the forest root)

- The parent of any child domains you later add to your first tree

You cannot change the name of your root domain once you create it. (If you want to change it, the only way is to create a new forest.) That's why it's important to choose its name carefully to reflect the widest possible scope of your enterprise. Your root domain should have a name that is permanent, easy to remember, and identifies broadly with your company.

### Domain Mode

Windows 2000 domains can run in one of two modes:

*Mixed mode*
Lets Windows NT BDCs coexist with Windows 2000 domain controllers

*Native mode*
Supports only Windows 2000 domain controllers

For more information see *mixed mode* and *native mode* in this chapter. For information on tasks relating to a domain, see *domain* and *domain controller* in Chapter 4.

### Migrating Windows NT Domains

If you are migrating an existing Windows NT–based enterprise to Windows 2000, the migration strategy you use depends on which of the four, standard, Windows NT domain models you currently employ.

---

 Note that upgrading a Windows NT 4.0 domain to Windows 2000 leaves existing trust relationships in their present state (either one-way or two-way).

---

#### Single Domain Model

If you are currently using the single domain model in your Windows NT network, you simply upgrade the existing Windows NT domain to create a root domain of a new Windows 2000 forest. See *domain controller* in this chapter for information about upgrading Windows NT domain controllers to Windows 2000.

#### Single-Master Domain Model

This model consists of an account domain (the master domain) that is trusted by one or more resource domains (slave domains). You first upgrade the account domain to create the root domain of your new forest, and you then upgrade the resource domains to become child domains of the root domain. This results in a single tree with one or more first-level child domains.

An alternative is to upgrade your account domain to a root domain, create one top-level OU in the root domain for each existing resource domain, and then join the member servers and workstations to the OUs within the root domain, discarding the domain controllers in the resource domains. This leaves you with a single domain to manage.

### Multiple-Master Domain Model

This model consists of two or more account domains (master domains), which trust each other, and one or more resource domains (slave domains), which each trust every account domain. A recommended procedure is first to create a new Windows 2000 domain as the root domain of your forest. This domain is left empty except for administrators belonging to the Enterprise Admins group. Next, you migrate the account domains to become child domains of the empty root domain. Finally, you migrate the resource domains to each become a child domain of the most appropriate, former account domain. The result is a tree with three levels of domains.

Alternatively, you can create OUs in the former account domains and join servers and workstations in the resource domains to these former account domains, placing them in the appropriate OUs. The result is a tree with only two levels instead of three (a process called flattening the domains), which is easier to manage.

### Complete Trust Model

This model consists of two or more Windows NT domains that trust each other. The recommended procedure here is first to create an empty root domain in a new forest, and then migrate every Windows NT domain to become a child domain of the root domain.

### Notes

It's OK to have mixed-mode and native domains in the same forest or tree.

### See Also

*Active Directory(3), delegation(3), DNS(3), domain(4), domain controller(3,4), forest(3), group(3,4), mixed mode(3), native mode(3), site(3,4), tree(3), trust(3,4)*

---

# Domain Admins

Built-in group for logically grouping together all users who need full system rights and permissions on all computers in the domain.

### See Also

*built-in group(3)*

---

# domain controller

A computer on which Active Directory is installed.

### Description

Domain controllers serve several purposes in Windows 2000:

- They enable users to log on to the network.

- They provide pass-through authentication to allow users to access network resources for which they have suitable permissions.

- They allow users to search Active Directory for published information about users, groups, computers, printers, and other directory objects.

---

A domain can have one or more domain controllers, but a minimum of two is recommended for fault tolerance. The number of domain controllers needed in a domain depends mainly on:

- The number of active users in the enterprise who need to log on to the domain or access its resources

- The number of sites that the domain spans and the available bandwidth of the WAN connections between the sites

### User Authentication

When a user on a Windows 2000 network wants to log on to the network from a client computer, the client computer first needs to find a domain controller to authenticate its request. A DNS lookup is used to locate the nearest domain controller that the client can use. The client then contacts this domain controller, and authentication is performed using either:

*Kerberos v5 authentication protocol*
    This is used for clients running Active Directory client software when contacting Windows 2000 domain controllers. This includes Windows 2000 Server and Professional computers, and Windows 95 and Windows 98 computers with the Active Directory client software installed on them.

*NTLM (Challenge/Response) authentication protocol*
    This is used for Windows NT Workstation or Server clients and when contacting downlevel Windows NT BDCs in mixed-mode environments.

---

For more information on Active Directory client software, see the sidebar "Active Directory Client" in the article *Active Directory* in this chapter. For more on Kerberos authentication, see the sidebar "Kerberos Authentication Within a Forest" in the article *forest* in this chapter.

---

### Replication

Unlike the Windows NT model where one domain controller (the PDC) in each domain was the master domain controller (the one containing a writable copy of the domain directory database), Active Directory follows a more fault-tolerant model in which all domain controllers in a domain are peers and contain identical, writable copies of the directory database. Domain controllers within a domain automatically replicate updates made on them to all other domain controllers in the domain. This process is called multimaster replication and requires no configuration unless the domain spans multiple sites (see *site* in this chapter for more information).

Domain controllers in different domains do not fully replicate with each other. Otherwise, the directory database in a large enterprise might grow too large to provide adequate performance for queries issued against it, and replication traffic could swamp other normal network traffic. Instead, Active Directory creates a global catalog that contains a partial replica of the Active Directory information from every domain in the forest (see *global catalog* in this chapter for more information).

### Operations Master Roles

Although most Active Directory functions on domain controllers support multi-master replication where no single domain controller is more important than the others (all domain controllers are peers), there are special domain controller roles that use single master replication instead. Such a domain controller is called an operations master because it is the only domain controller in the domain that can accept requests for a specific type of Active Directory operation. There are five different roles for operations masters in an Active Directory domain. These roles are assigned by Active Directory to one or more specific domain controllers by default. These five roles are:

*Domain naming master*
> This domain controller allows domains to be added or removed from the forest. There must be one and only one domain naming master in the forest.

*Infrastructure master*
> This domain controller is responsible for updating group information when groups are renamed or have their membership changed and allows these changes to take effect domain-wide immediately. There must be one and only one infrastructure master in each domain of the forest.

*PDC emulator*
> When your domain is running in mixed mode (there are Windows NT BDCs present in addition to your Windows 2000 domain controllers) or when there are Windows NT client computers on the network, there must be one Windows 2000 domain controller that acts as a PDC for these legacy computers to perform directory replication and to process password changes. There must be one and only one PDC emulator in each domain of the forest.

*Relative ID master*
> This domain controller ensures that unique security IDs (SIDs) are assigned to newly created objects (users, computers, groups, and so on) in Active Directory. There must be one and only one relative ID master in each domain of the forest.

*Schema master*
> This domain controller accepts modifications and updates them to the Active Directory schema. There must be one and only one schema master in the entire forest. (Otherwise, the schema could become inconsistent by having conflicting modifications made to it on different schema masters.)

How these various roles are assigned by Active Directory depends on the number of domains in your forest and the number of domain controllers in your domains:

*Single domain with one domain controller*
> The domain controller assumes all five operations master roles.

*Single domain with multiple domain controllers*
> The first domain controller installed assumes all five roles. A second domain controller can be assigned the role of standby operations master to assume the various operations master roles in case the first one fails.

*Multiple domains*

The schema master and naming master roles remain in the root domain. Each time a child domain is added to the first tree (or a root domain is added for a new tree), the first domain controller in this new domain is assigned the infrastructure master, PDC emulator, and relative identifier master roles.

### Upgrading Windows NT Domain Controllers

If you are migrating a Windows NT domain to Windows 2000, you start by upgrading the Windows NT PDC to a Windows 2000 domain controller. This action creates the new Windows 2000 domain, which by default runs in mixed mode so that the Windows NT BDCs (if any) can interoperate and synchronize with the new Windows 2000 domain controller.

Once the PDC has been upgraded, the remaining BDCs and member servers can then be upgraded.

---

 An alternative approach is to upgrade your member servers first, then take a year off to learn in detail how Active Directory works, and finally upgrade your PDC followed by your BDCs. A lot of admins seem to favor this approach!

---

### Notes

- Note that an operations master role generally can be moved from one domain controller to another in a domain, which is why they are sometimes called flexible single-master operations.

- If you want to use *movetree.exe* from the Windows 2000 Server Resource Kit to move objects from one domain to another in the forest, you must initiate the move on the relative ID master for the domain where the objects initially exist.

- The PDC emulator also has a role in native-mode domains: it keeps track of password changes so that if users cannot log on to a different domain controller, their logon attempt is forwarded to the PDC emulator as a last resort.

- The global catalog should not be located on the same domain controller as the one hosting the infrastructure master role unless there is only one domain controller in the domain.

- Don't forget to backup your Windows NT PDC before upgrading it to Windows 2000!

### See Also

*Active Directory(3,4), domain(3,4), domain controller(4), forest(3), global catalog(3), member server(3), mixed mode(3), native mode(3), site(3)*

*Concepts D*

## Domain Guests

Built-in group for logically grouping together all users who need only temporary (guest) access to resources in the domain.

### See Also

*built-in group(3)*

## domain local group

Type of group used to grant permissions for users to access resources in a specific domain.

### See Also

*group(3)*

## domain user account

A user account that lets a user log on to a domain and access shared network resources.

### Description

Domain user accounts are user accounts that are domain-wide in scope and stored within Active Directory for that domain. This is in contrast to local user accounts that are valid only on the computer on which they are defined. Domain user accounts are created by administrators on domain controllers.

Authentication of a domain user account works as follows:

- The user provides her credentials to log on to the network and her client computer forwards the credentials to Active Directory on the first available domain controller.

- The domain controller compares the user's credentials with those stored for the user in Active Directory and determines whether to provide the user with access to the network.

- If the user is to be granted access to the network, Active Directory provides an access token that specifies the permissions and rights that the user will have on the network.

### Notes

- Always use domain user accounts for users in domain-based Windows 2000 networks if you want users to have access to shared resources on the network (which is generally the purpose of having a network).

- Domain user accounts are internally identified within Active Directory by their security identifier or SID. If you delete an account and create a new account with the same name, it will have a different SID than the deleted account had.

- Domain user accounts are created by default within the Users organizational unit of the Active Directory Users and Computers console (see Chapter 5), but they can also be created in any OU you choose or in a user-defined OU.

### See Also

*Active Directory Users and Computers(5), domain user account(4), local user account(3,4), net accounts(7)*

---

## Domain Users

Built-in group for logically grouping together all ordinary network users in the domain.

### See Also

*built-in group(3)*

---

## dynamic disk

A hard disk that contains volumes. A dynamic disk may also be part of a mirrored volume, spanned volume, striped volume, or RAID-5 volume.

### See Also

*disks(3), basic disk(3)*

---

## dynamic storage

A disk-storage technology new to Windows 2000 Server that divides disks into an unlimited number of volumes and supports various, advanced disk-storage technologies, including mirrored volumes, spanned volumes, striped volumes, and RAID-5 volumes.

### See Also

*disks(3), basic storage(3)*

---

## EFS

Stands for Encrypting File System, a feature of NTFS on Windows 2000 that supports encryption of files and folders on NTFS volumes.

### Description

NTFS permissions on Windows NT systems provide a way of securing files and folders from unauthorized local access. For example, if two users share the use of a computer, assigning full control for each user to his own files prevents the users from accessing each other's files. Administrators have the right to take ownership of any files on the system, however, but normally users with administrative privileges are considered trustworthy.

A problem could occur if someone illicitly gained access to a user's Windows NT computer and removed the hard drive from the system. The person could then install the NTFS drive in her own computer, log on as the local Administrator for that computer, and take ownership of any files on the stolen drive. NTFS permissions themselves therefore cannot protect data from the theft of the hard drive itself.

Additionally, third-party utilities have been developed for Windows NT that allow users to boot their computer from a floppy disk and access NTFS partitions directly. These utilities, though of some administrative use in troubleshooting situations, nevertheless pose a security risk for sensitive data stored on physically accessible, Windows NT systems.

NTFS on Windows 2000 systems adds the security feature of encryption to NTFS permissions in order to deal with the scenarios described earlier. Files and folders that are stored on NTFS volumes can be encrypted to protect them from unauthorized local access. When these files are accessed by their associated application, the operating system decrypts them automatically so they can be opened for reading or modification. When the modified files are saved or closed, they are automatically encrypted again. The whole process is transparent to the user. Both files and folders can be encrypted or unencrypted. If a folder is encrypted, the files within it don't need to be encrypted, or some may be and others not.

When a user decides to encrypt his own datafiles, only that same user can decrypt the files, and no other user can read them. To share an encrypted file's contents with another user in order to collaborate on work, the user must first decrypt the file so the other user can use it. Members of the Administrators group, however, have the right to decrypt any encrypted files.

---

 Never encrypt files in the system directory where the Windows 2000 Server boot files are located. Since the key for decrypting these files cannot be accessed until the operating system has booted and a user has logged on, Windows 2000 will not be able to start. Of course, Windows 2000 safeguards against this by preventing you from encrypting files that have the System attribute set. But if you have removed the System attribute from these files using the `attrib` command (perhaps while troubleshooting startup problems) and failed to reset this attribute on the files afterwards, the possibility of encrypting them exists.

---

### How EFS Works

EFS is integrated into NTFS and uses private-key cryptography to ensure that data encrypted by users can only be accessed by that user (or by an administrator). For each file that a user encrypts, an associated private key called the file-encryption key is created, which can be used later to decrypt the file. This file-encryption key is itself encrypted in the form of an encryption certificate or EFS certificate, which is encrypted using both the user's public key and the public key of an authorized recovery agent (so the file can be decrypted after disaster recovery has been performed). The Administrator by default is an authorized recovery agent.

---

To decrypt an encrypted file, the file-encryption key for the file must first itself be decrypted. This can be done using either:

- The private key corresponding to the public key that belongs to the user who encrypted the file (in other words, by the user herself)

- The private key of an authorized recovery agent (Administrator)

Once the file-encryption key for the encrypted file has been decrypted, the encrypted file itself can be decrypted.

### Strategies for Using Encryption

Encryption is particularly useful for users with portable computers. Should your laptop be stolen while traveling, encryption provides a way of keeping your data safe from prying eyes.

Otherwise, the decision to employ encryption on file servers throughout your enterprise should be weighed carefully. Since encryption results in additional over-head on file servers, a better solution might be to secure these servers physically in locked rooms.

On a system where you decide that encryption should be implemented, the following folders should be encrypted:

- *My Documents* and any other folders where the user regularly stores work

- *Temp* folders (such as \ *Winnt\ Temp*), so that any temporary files that are created but not deleted by applications are encrypted

You generally should encrypt folders instead of files, since some applications create temporary files in odd locations that may not be encrypted.

In addition to the previous procedure, the user should export the data-recovery certificate, store it in a secure location, and then delete it from the system itself.

### Recovery Policy

By default, when the Administrator logs on to the computer (local Administrator account) or domain (domain Administrator account) for the first time, a recovery policy is created to enable the Administrator to perform the recovery of encrypted data during disaster recovery. Otherwise, encrypted data restored from tape would not be decryptable if the users' private keys and the encryption certificates associated with the files happened to be lost when the disaster occurred.

The recovery policy creates a special encryption certificate and private key that the recovery agent can use to decrypt files that were created and encrypted by domain users. As preparation for disaster recovery, the recovery agent should use the Export command in the Certificates console to make a copy of the recovery certificate and private key on a floppy disk, and keep this in a safe location. After restoring the crashed system, this certificate and key can then be imported into the personal certificate store of the recovery agent, enabling the agent to decrypt the restored files. For information on how to recover encrypted files and folders, see the sidebar "EFS Recovery" in the article *files and folders* in Chapter 4.

### Notes

- For more information on how to encrypt files and folders, see *files and folders* in Chapter 4.

- You cannot encrypt a file or folder that has been compressed, and you cannot compress a file or folder that has been encrypted.

- You cannot encrypt a file that is marked Read-only or System.

- If you copy or move an encrypted file within or between NTFS volumes, it remains encrypted. If you copy or move it to a FAT/FAT32 volume or a floppy disk, it is decrypted.

- Encrypt only datafiles; encrypting program files adds unnecessary system overhead.

- When encrypted files are copied between computers over the network, the data is sent in an unencrypted state. To encrypt data sent over a network, you must use SSL or IPSec.

- Remember, to read an encrypted file, you don't have to decrypt it manually— Windows 2000 does that automatically for you. You only need to decrypt a file when you want to share its contents with other users.

- Folders are actually not encrypted themselves, just marked so. The marker tells the operating system that any files that are later added to the folder should be encrypted, if they are not already so.

- Encrypted files cannot be accessed by Macintosh clients.

- Backups of encrypted files are also encrypted, provided they are on NTFS volumes.

- If you have partitions in a Windows 2000 system that are formatted using NTFS for Windows NT 4.0 or earlier and you attempt to encrypt files on this volume, a chkdsk operation is run and the filesystem is converted to the Windows 2000 version of NTFS.

- Users with roaming user profiles can use the same encryption key with trusted remote systems.

### See Also

*files and folders(3,4)*

---

## Enterprise Admins

Built-in group whose members can administer any domain in the forest.

### See Also

*built-in group(3)*

# environment variable

A string that contains information used to control some aspect of the operating system or applications.

## Description

Environment variables contain information such as the path to an important system file or directory, the number and type of processors on the motherboard, and so on. Windows 2000 Server makes use of two types of environment variables:

*User variables*
> These differ for each user who logs on to the computer, and users can create and modify their own user variables and assign them values. By default, Windows 2000 Server creates the user variables listed in Table 3-13.

*Table 3-13: User Environment Variables*

| Variable | Description | Default Value |
|---|---|---|
| TEMP | Path to the user's temporary directory | %USERPROFILE%\Local Settings\Temp |
| TMP | Path to the user's temporary directory | %USERPROFILE%\Local Settings\Temp |

*System variables*
> These are the same for all users who log on to the computer, and their effect applies to the whole operating system. Only members of the Administrators group can create or modify system variables. The default system variables are listed in Table 3-14.

*Table 3-14: System Environment Variables*

| Variable | Description | Default value |
|---|---|---|
| ComSpec | Path to command interpreter | %SystemRoot%\system32\cmd.exe |
| NUMBER_OF_PROCESSORS | Number of processors on the motherboard | Reflects actual number of processors in system |
| OS | Operating system installed | Windows_NT |
| OS2LibPath | Path to OS/2 library | %SystemRoot%\system32\os2\dll |
| Path | Order in which directories are searched when executing a command | %SystemRoot%\system32; %SystemRoot%; %SystemRoot%\system32\Wbem |
| PATHEXT | Order in which commands are executed when they differ only by extensions | .com; .exe; .bat; .cmd; .vbs; .vbe; .js; .jse; .wsf; .wsh |
| PROCESSOR_ARCHITECTURE | Type of process family | x86 on all Intel platforms at present |
| PROCESSOR_IDENTIFIER | Version of processor | X86 Family 6 Model 5 Stepping 2 Genuine Intel (for example, for a Pentium II 400 MHz) |
| PROCESSOR_REVISION | Firmware revision | 0502 (example) |
| TEMP | Path to operating-system temporary directory | %SystemRoot%\Temp |

*Table 3-14: System Environment Variables (continued)*

| Variable | Description | Default value |
|----------|-------------|---------------|
| TMP | Path to operating-system temporary directory | *%SystemRoot%\Temp* |
| windir | Path to operating-system files | *%SystemRoot%* |

### How Environment Variables Are Defined

System and user variables are defined using System in the Control Panel. Their values are stored in the registry so they are available upon reboot. See *environment variable* in Chapter 4 for procedures on setting and modifying system and user variables.

During the startup process, Windows 2000 sets environments in this order:

1. System environment variables

2. Variables defined in *autoexec.bat* (except for Path variables)

3. User environment variables

4. Path variables defined in *autoexec.bat*

Any variable defined in one step can be overridden in a subsequent step of the process, with the exception of Path settings, which are cumulative.

### Using Environment Variables

System variables may be used in defining paths for logon scripts, home directories, and user profiles. They may also be used within logon scripts or in commands executed at the command prompt. To use an environment variable, enclose it in percent signs. For example, typing the command:

```
C:\>cd %windir%
```

produces the following result:

```
C:\WINNT>
```

You can easily display the value of an environment variable from the command line. For example, to display the name of the installed operating system using the OS system variable, just type:

```
C:\>echo %os%
```

which produces the result:

```
Windows_NT
```

Who says Windows 2000 isn't really just NT5!

### Notes

- Installing new operating-system components or applications may create additional environment variables or modify existing ones such as Path.

- You can also display and set environment variables from the command line using the **set** command.

- There are additional system and user environment variables that are not displayed using System in the Control Panel and so are not listed in Tables 3-13 and 3-14. Examples of these are shown in Tables 3-15 and 3-16. Some of these, such as SystemRoot, are sometimes called replaceable variables instead of environment variables. These additional environment variables can be accessed from the command line. For example, to display the name of the local machine, type the following at the command prompt:

```
C:\>echo %computername%
```

*Table 3-15: Additional Nonmodifiable System Environment Variables*

| Variable | Description | Default Value |
|---|---|---|
| ALLUSERSPROFILE | Path to default local user profile | *C:\Documents and Settings\All Users* |
| CommonProgram-Files | Path to Common Files directory | *C:\Program Files\ Common Files* |
| COMPUTERNAME | Name of the computer | Varies |
| PROCESSOR_LEVEL | Level of processor | 6 (for Pentium II, for example) |
| ProgramFiles | Path to directory where program files are located | *C:\Program Files* |
| PROMPT | Command-line prompt | $P$G |
| SystemDrive | System partition | *C:* |
| SystemRoot | Path to operating-system files | *C:\Winnt* |

*Table 3-16: Additional Nonmodifiable User Environment Variables*

| Variable | Description | Default Value |
|---|---|---|
| APPDATA | Path to Application Data folder for currently logged-on user | *C:\Documents and Settings\<user_name>\ Application Data* |
| HOMEDRIVE | Network drive letter mapped to user's home directory (if assigned) | Varies |
| HOMEPATH | Full path to user's home directory (if assigned) | Varies |
| LOGONSERVER | Domain controller that has authenticated the currently logged-on user | Varies |
| USERDOMAIN | Domain of currently logged-on user | Varies |
| USERDNSDOMAIN | DNS domain of currently logged-on user | Varies |
| USERNAME | Logon name of currently logged-on user | Varies |
| USERPROFILE | Path to local user profile for currently logged-on user | *C:\Documents and Settings\<user_name>* |

**See Also**

*environment variable(4), logon script(3), net(7), System(6)*

## Emergency Repair Disk (ERD)

Stands for Emergency Repair Disk, a floppy disk that contains information used to help repair a server.

### See Also

*disaster recovery(3)*

## event logs

Record activities of the operating system and applications for monitoring and troubleshooting purposes.

### Description

An event is a specific occurrence of some activity of the Windows 2000 operating system, an installed component, or an application. Events are generated automatically and are recorded in event logs, which can then be viewed and analyzed using the Event Viewer console in Administrative tools.

### Default Logs

There are three event logs that are present on every Windows 2000 computer:

*System log*
> This log contains events generated by activities of the operating system. Examples of system events include the activities of services such as the NetLogon service, failures of drivers to initialize properly, changes in the role of a server from member server to domain controller, and so on. System events come in three flavors:

*Information events*
> These events simply describe a normal activity that has occurred, such as the successful startup of the Event Log service itself, the establishment of a remote-access connection, a browser forcing an election on the network, and so on. Some information events also record failures of certain activities that have no real consequence on network operations.

*Warning events*
> These events describe an occurrence that may possibly be a problem, such as failure of dynamic registration of a DNS name due to DNS client misconfiguration, failure of the Windows Time Service to find a domain controller, space running low on a disk, a scope on a DHCP server being 100% leased, and so on. You might be able to get by for a while with a warning, but you should resolve the problem as soon as you can.

*Error events*
> These events describe critical occurrences that could result in loss of data or other significant problems. Error events include the failure of a required service such as Workstation to initialize, the refusal of a dynamic DNS update from a DNS server, the PDC emulator of the forest root domain not having its time synchronized with a member server or clocking device, failure of a device driver, and so on.

*Application log*

> This log contains events generated by applications running on the computer. The vendor must specifically code their applications to generate these events. Application events are usually only of help when you give the information to the vendor to help troubleshoot problems you are encountering. Some Windows 2000 system events are also logged here, however, such as Dr. Watson events for application failures, security events related to Group Policy, violations of export cryptography restrictions for IPSec, IIS activities involving Active Server Pages (ASP) functionality, and so on. Application log events are also either information, warning, or error events.

*Security log*

> This log contains events generated when auditing is configured on the computer. (If auditing is not configured, then the security log is empty.) Security log events are either:

*Success events*

> These indicate that the audited action occurred successfully—for example, a user successfully logged on to the network, successfully accessed a file on a share, or successfully exercised a system right he possesses.

*Failure events*

> These indicate that the audited action failed in its attempt—for example, a user tried to log on but failed because of entering a wrong password, tried to access a mapped drive but couldn't because of permission problems, tried to access a printer object in Active Directory but was refused, and so on.

For more information on auditing, see *auditing* in this chapter.

**Other Logs**

Depending on which optional Windows 2000 components are installed on your computer, there may be other event logs visible in Event Viewer for your machine:

*Directory Service log*

> This log records the activities of Active Directory and is present on Windows 2000 domain controllers. Events are either information, warning, or error type.

*DNS Server log*

> This log records the activities of a Windows 2000 DNS server. Events are either information, warning, or error type.

*File Replication Service log*

> This log records the activities of the File Replication Service (FRS) on a Windows 2000 server on which Dfs is configured. Events are either information, warning, or error type.

**Working with Event Logs**

The key thing is to regularly monitor the event logs on your servers using Event Viewer and to deal with any actions that need to be taken. You can use Event Viewer to search for or filter particular types of events if the log becomes excessively large.

It is also important to configure the size limit and retention period for event logs as soon as you set up a new server. Logs can wrap (newer events start over-writing older ones) once they reach a certain size, but this may cause important information to be lost. It's better to configure a decent chunk of disk space for each log and then archive and clear logs regularly, so that your information is saved but disk space is freed up. For procedures on managing event logs, see *event logs* in Chapter 4.

### Notes

- Critical system events requiring immediate attention are usually displayed in a pop-up alert or warning box on the screen of the server. If the event is signifi-cant but doesn't require immediate attention, the event is logged instead to the System or Application log.

- You can use archived security logs to track resource-usage trends over time to help in planning for hardware and software upgrades on your network.

- Event logs are located in *%SystemRoot%\System32\config*. They can be archived (saved) in one of three formats:

    *Log-file format (.evt file)*
    Can only be opened and viewed again in Event Viewer

    *Comma-delimited text file (.csv file)*
    Can be imported into a spreadsheet or database

    *Text-file (.txt file)*
    Can be cut and pasted into a Word or other document

    Use the *.evt* format if you want to keep the binary information recorded in events, as this information is discarded with the other formats.

### See Also

*auditing(3,4), event logs(4), Event Viewer(5)*

---

## Everyone

Built-in system group representing all current network users, regardless of whether they have valid domain accounts or not.

### See Also

*built-in group(3)*

---

## files and folders

Elements of the hierarchical filesystem used to store data and programs in Windows 2000.

### Description

The basic concept of files and folders is familiar to anyone who has worked with earlier versions of Microsoft Windows, so I will cover it here only briefly. Regard-less of which disk filesystem (FAT, FAT32, or NTFS) is used to format local partitions and volumes, Windows 2000 organizes files by grouping them into folders (also called directories). These folders are themselves grouped hierarchically into a tree of files and folders starting with the root of each partition or volume.

For example, the executable for the game of Solitaire (*sol.exe*) by default is found in the *System32* folder, which is in the \*Winnt* folder, which is in the root of *C:* drive. The location of *sol.exe* can be specified either by its absolute path (*C:\Winnt\System32\sol.exe*) or by the relative path from the current directory (e.g., if the current directory is *C:\Winnt\Help*, then the relative path to *sol.exe* would be ..\*System32\sol.exe*).

The local filesystem can be accessed in many different ways. For example, to display the icon representing *sol.exe*, you could:

- Open Windows Explorer from the Accessories program group and browse the folder hierarchy in the lefthand pane until *C:\Winnt\System32* is selected, and then locate *sol.exe* in the righthand pane. You can then click the Search button on the toolbar to open a lefthand Search pane and use it to find *sol.exe* within *System32*.

- Open My Computer on the Desktop and browse through the *C:* drive until you open the *System32* folder. Again, click the Search button on the toolbar to open a lefthand Search pane, and use it to find *sol.exe* within *System32*.

- Use Start → Run → *C:\Winnt\System32* to open a window showing the *System32* folder and locate *sol.exe*.

- Open a command prompt and type `start C:\Winnt\System32` to open a window showing the *System32* folder.

- Use Start → Search → For Files or Folders, and search for *sol.exe* on the local hard disks.

- Right-click on any folder in Windows Explorer or My Computer, and select Search from the shortcut menu. Search for *sol.exe*, but change the search context from the selected folder to local drives.

- Open the Computer Management console from the Administrative Tools program group, select Disk Management, right-click on *C:* drive, and select Open or Explore.

- Open Internet Explorer, type `C:\Winnt\System32` into the address box, and press Enter. Make the *System32* folder a favorite if you want to access it again easily.

- Right-click on the desktop, select New → Shortcut, type `C:\Winnt\System32`, and click Next and then Finish to create a shortcut on your desktop to the *System32* folder. Double-click on this shortcut to open the folder, and locate *sol.exe*.

- Go to another computer in the same or trusted domain, log on as Administrator, and use:

  Start → Run → \\<*computer_name*>\*C$*\*Winnt*\*System32*

- Go to another computer in the same or trusted domain, log on as Administrator, open Internet Explorer, and type the following into the address bar:

  `\\computer_name\C$\Winnt\System32`

### File and Folder Properties

Whichever method you use to locate the icon for a file or folder, right-click on it and select Properties to open the property sheet for the selected file or folder. Most properties of files and folders are the same regardless of the underlying file-system used, but there are significant differences and enhancements associated with files and folders located on NTFS volumes.

Table 3-17 summarizes the properties associated with folders, and Table 3-18 summarizes those associated with files. Beside each property in parentheses is where you can find additional information on the selected property.

*Table 3-17: Properties of Folders*

| Folder Property | FAT/FAT32 | NTFS |
| --- | --- | --- |
| General properties (size, path, creation date, and so on) | ✓ | ✓ |
| Attributes | Read-only Hidden Archive | Read-only Hidden Archive Index Compress Encrypt |
| Web sharing | ✓ | ✓ |
| Sharing | ✓ | ✓ |
| Security | N/A | ✓ |

*Table 3-18: Properties of Files*

| File Property | FAT/FAT32 | NTFS |
| --- | --- | --- |
| General (size, path, file association, and so on) | ✓ | ✓ |
| Attributes | Read-only Hidden Archive | Read-only Hidden Archive Index Compress Encrypt |
| Security | N/A | ✓ |
| Summary | N/A | ✓ |

### Notes

For a summary of administrative tasks you can perform on files and folders, see *files and folders* in Chapter 4.

### See Also

*attribute(3)*, *compression(3)*, *EFS(3)*, *files and folders(4)*, *permissions(3)*, *shared folder(3)*

## *folder redirection*

A method of changing the storage location of key user folders to a centrally located network share.

### *Description*

A useful feature of Group Policy in Windows 2000 is folder redirection, which allows My Documents, Start menu, Desktop, and Application Data folders for each user be centrally located on a network share instead of each user's local machine. These folders are normally part of a user's profile and are stored locally in the *C:\Documents and Settings\<username>* folder on the client computer that the user uses.

There are several advantages to redirecting folders:

- It makes users' work easier to back up since datafiles are stored in a central location on a network file server.

- The data in these folders can be accessed easily by users no matter which computers they use to log on to the network.

Folder redirection is an alternative to implementing roaming users on your network and has several advantages over implementing roaming users:

- My Documents and other special folders are normally part of a user's roaming profile, and when a roaming user logs on to a computer, her entire roaming profile (including My Documents and its contents) is copied to the local computer. This is done to create a local profile on the machine and can use up a lot of disk space on client computers if users have a lot of files in My Documents and if a lot of users share a single machine. In addition, the bigger the contents of My Documents, the longer it takes for a roaming user to log on to the network. If users make changes to their datafiles during a session and then log off, the changes are copied to the server and slow down the logoff process as well.

- By contrast, files stored in redirected folders are not copied to the local computer when a user logs on, with the result that logon and logoff traffic is minimized. Only when a user tries to access a file in a redirected My Documents folder is network traffic generated.

For procedures to implement folder redirection, see *folder redirection* in Chapter 4. For more information on Group Policy, see *Group Policy* in this chapter.

### *Planning Folder Redirection*

You can choose to redirect all four folders for each user to the same share or to separate shares, and you can redirect some of the folders and not the rest if you choose. Here are some specific reasons why you might want to redirect each folder:

**Concepts**
**F**

*Application Data*

This folder contains user-specific data for applications such as Internet Explorer and should be redirected if users need to use these applications from any client computer.

*Desktop*

This folder contains the shortcuts and files on the user's desktop and should be redirected if you desire users to have standardized desktops.

*My Documents*

This folder contains the work files for the user and is the default location for commands such as Open and Save in Windows 2000–compliant applications. You should redirect this folder if you want users to be able to access their work files from any computer on the network and to centralize user work files for backup purposes.

*Start menu*

This folder contains the user's Start menu shortcuts and folders and should be redirected if you desire users to have a standardized Start menu. (Redirect all users to the same share and assign them NTFS Read permission so they can't alter their common Start menu.)

### See Also

*folder redirection(4), Group Policy(3,4), My Documents(3)*

---

## forest

A collection of trees.

### Description

A forest consists of one or more trees. If more than one, the trees are automatically joined together at their root domains by two-way transitive trusts. When you install the first Windows 2000 domain controller in your enterprise, you automatically create a forest with one tree in it. The first Windows 2000 domain you create is:

- The root domain of your first tree

- The forest root domain of your entire forest

Then when you create additional Windows 2000 domains, you can choose whether to:

- Add the new domain to an existing tree of your forest

- Make the new domain the root domain of a new tree in your forest

- Create an entirely new forest (if you select this option, your new domain controller will not be automatically connected to your other domains using two-way transitive trusts)

For more information on trees, see *tree* in this chapter.

## Namespace

While a tree uses a contiguous DNS namespace, the namespace of a forest is not contiguous. The root domain of each tree in a forest must have its own unique DNS domain name to identify it within the forest. However, the forest itself is uniquely identified with respect to other forests by the DNS domain name of its forest root domain, that is, the DNS name of the first domain created in the forest.

As an example, let's say that the Canadian company MTIT Enterprises (whose DNS domain name is *mtit.com*) decides to start a separate, worldwide operation called MTIT Enterprises Worldwide, whose domain name will be different (e.g., *mtitworld.com*). In this case the forest root domain and the root domain of the first tree could be *mtit.com* with subsidiaries *vancouver.mtit.com* and *toronto.mtit.com*, while the root domain of the other tree would be *mtitworld.com* with subsidiaries *mexico.mtitworld.com*, *france.mtitworld.com*, and so on.

### Using Forests

You would implement a multiple-tree forest in an enterprise if the organization were very large and had multiple public identities. For example, you might create a multiple-tree forest if:

- Your company has one or more distinct subsidiaries in different locations.

- Your company and another company have recently merged, established joint ventures, or formed high-level partnerships.

 If two companies, which have already implemented a multiple-tree forest, merge with each other, you can create explicit trusts between the two forests in order to grant users in one forest access to resources in the other forest. See *trust* in this chapter for more information.

### Notes

- You can join together separate domains in different forests by using explicit trusts (see *trust* in this chapter for more information). Note that domains in separate forests that are joined together through explicitly created external trust relationships do not share a common schema, configuration, or global catalog. Note also that you cannot join forests together; you can only join separate domains in each forest with each other.

- All trees and domains in a forest share a common schema, configuration, and global catalog.

- To chop down a tree in a forest or to clearcut an entire forest, you use the *Chopper.exe* utility, which will soon be available with the next edition of the Windows 2000 Server Resource Kit. The Resource Kit is expected to swell to a staggering 15,000 pages and is slated for release April 1, 2001, unless legal action by Greenpeace blocks it.

### See Also

*Active Directory(3)*, *domain(3,4)*, *tree(3)*, *trust(3,4)*

## Kerberos Authentication Within a Forest

When a user in one domain wants to access resources across a forest, the Kerberos v5 authentication protocol is used. Kerberos is a shared-secret authentication protocol in which both the client requesting access and a trusted intermediary called the Key Distribution Center (KDC) both share knowledge of the user's password. (Passwords are stored in Active Directory.) Kerberos thus makes use of mutual authentication in which both the user and the network services providing authentication must be mutually authenticated with each other to proceed. Every Windows 2000 domain controller is configured to run the Kerberos Key Distribution Center service and is thus a KDC.

Kerberos is the default Windows 2000 authentication service. It is more complex than NTLM (also called Challenge/Response and Windows Integrated) authentication, which is the earlier authentication protocol used by Windows NT and which Windows 2000 uses for authenticating downlevel (Window NT/98/95) clients that do not have the new Directory Services Client software installed on them. NTLM stored password information in the SAM database and authenticated only the client, not the network service providing authentication.

As an example, let's say a user on a client computer in *vancouver.mtit.com* wants to access resources on a server in *mexico.mtitworld.com*, which is part of the same forest. The process by which client authentication occurs happens automatically and is completely transparent to the user. Here is how it works (I've left out a few steps for simplification):

1. The client submits the user's credentials to the KDC in its local domain, *vancouver.mtit.com*, to receive a Kerberos session ticket.

2. The client presents the session ticket to the KDC in the root domain, *mtit.com*, of the local tree, which then grants the client a second session ticket for the root domain, *mtitworld.com*, in the remote tree.

3. The client presents the second session ticket to the KDC in the *mtitworld.com* domain, which then grants the client a third session ticket for the *mexico.mtitworld.com* domain in the remote tree.

4. The client finally presents the third session ticket to the KDC in the *mexico.mtitworld.com* domain, which then grants the client access to the shared resources on the server that the client wants to access.

From this scenario you can see why it's good to try to "flatten" your domains in Windows 2000 and use only a single domain if that is at all possible: the more domains and trees you have in your enterprise, the more network bandwidth will be consumed by Kerberos authentication traffic.

Note also that switching a Windows 2000 domain from mixed mode to native mode automatically disables NTLM authentication and leaves only Kerberos as the default authentication protocol for clients.

# global catalog

A feature of Active Directory designed to speed the process of performing search queries on Active Directory.

## Description

The global catalog contains:

- A full replica (all attributes) of all objects in its own domain
- A partial replica (most commonly searched attributes) of all objects in other domains in the forest

The purpose of the global catalog is to help speed up search queries issued against Active Directory, especially tree- or forest-wide queries. This is because a multidomain query can be resolved by accessing a single domain controller (the global catalog server) instead of accessing a different domain controller in each of the queried domains.

The global catalog also supports the network logon process in native-mode domains by supplying a user's membership information in universal groups to the domain controller the user tries to log on to. If the global catalog is not available in a native-mode environment, users will not be able to log on to the network (they can only log on to their local computers). Because of this, in a multisite environment it is a good idea to have at least one global catalog server in each site, especially when the WAN links between sites are slow or unreliable.

### Global Catalog Server

By default, the first domain in the forest (forest root domain) is designated a global catalog server, and the global catalog is created automatically on this server. Other domain controllers can be configured to host the global catalog, and you can modify the default location of your global catalog to a different domain controller as well. For information on this, see *global catalog* in Chapter 4.

## Notes

- The global catalog is important because query-related traffic on Active Directory–based networks usually much exceeds traffic relating to directory updates and replication.
- Members of the Domain Admins group can log on to the network even when the global catalog is not available in a native-mode environment.
- If you have multiple domain controllers in a domain, do not host the infrastructure master on the same domain controller that hosts the global catalog, or the infrastructure master will not work properly. For more information see "Operations Master Roles" in the article *domain controller* in this chapter.

## See Also

*Active Directory(3)*, *domain controller(3,4)*, *global catalog(4)*

# global group

Type of group used to group users together logically in a given domain if they have similar needs for accessing network resources.

## See Also

*group(3)*

---

# group

A collection of user accounts.

## Description

Groups allow user accounts to be logically grouped together for administrative purposes. For example, instead of granting Read access on a shared folder to three separate user accounts, create a group that contains these accounts and assign Read permission to the group. It may be more initial work to do things this way, but if you later want to change the users' access to Full Control, you can do it in one step by granting this permission to the group instead of granting it for each user individually. Also, if other users need these same permissions in the future, you just make them members of the group since members of a group receive whatever permissions have been assigned to the group (a user can belong to more than one group at a time).

The general strategy that Microsoft recommends for managing resource access by user accounts is called **AGP**: organize user Accounts into Groups to which suitable Permissions are assigned. A good way to begin is to determine which user accounts in your domain require access to the same file, printer, and other network resources. For example, users in the Customer Support department might all need access to the FAQ share, so create a group called Support for this purpose.

However, in Windows 2000 it's a little more complicated than this: there are different types of groups, and these groups can have different scope. In addition, groups can contain not just user accounts but also computers and other groups. In fact, groups can be nested within groups to any degree desired, which can make for some rather complex administration scenarios. Let's take a look at these features one at a time.

## Group Types

There are two basic types of groups in Windows 2000. Both types are stored in Active Directory and, therefore, are accessible from anywhere in the network using applications enabled for Active Directory. These two types are:

*Security groups*
Used primarily for controlling the access that users have to network resources, but can also be used for sending email messages to users. Security groups in Windows 2000 correspond to the concept of groups in the earlier Windows NT operating system.

*Distribution groups*
Used only for sending email messages to users.

In practice, you will almost always use security groups, since they include the capabilities of distribution groups. Microsoft Exchange 2000 Server can use distribution groups instead of distribution lists (DLs) for performing mass mailings. But if you don't have Exchange 2000 deployed, you can pretty much ignore distribution groups, so I'll limit the rest of this discussion to security groups.

### Group Scopes

There are three different scopes that groups in Windows 2000 can have. The scope of a group is essentially a restriction on the membership and use of the group. These three scopes are:

*Global groups*
> These groups can be used to grant access to resources in any domain in the forest and are typically used to organize users who have similar needs for accessing resources. For example, you could create a Marketing global group and make all employees in the Marketing department members of this group, since they all need to access the same file and print resources, web sites, applications, and so on. Global groups are similar to global groups in Windows NT when used in mixed-mode Windows 2000 domains.

*Domain local groups*
> These groups can be used for access to resources in the local domain only. For example, if you want users in the *mtit.com* domain to be able to access the Pub shared folder in the same domain, you can create a domain local group called PublicUsers, make selected users or global groups members of it, and assign suitable permissions to it for accessing the resource. Domain local groups are similar to local groups in Windows NT when used in mixed-mode Windows 2000 domains.

*Universal groups*
> These groups can be used to access resources in any domain in the forest. They differ from global groups in that they are only available in Windows 2000 domains running in native mode, not mixed mode. Also, their membership can be drawn from any domain, whereas global group members can only come from the group's own domain. Universal groups are new to Windows 2000 and have no corresponding type in Windows NT.

---

 Windows 2000 also has a fourth type of group scope called the *local group*. Local groups can be created only on standalone servers running Windows 2000 Server or client computers running Windows 2000 Professional. Local groups are generally not used in Windows 2000 networks since their scope is restricted to the local computer. See *local group* later in this chapter for more information.

---

### Group Membership

The membership that different group scopes are allowed depends on whether the Windows 2000 domain they are created in is running in mixed mode or native mode. See *mixed mode* and *native mode* in this chapter for more information.

### Mixed Mode

This mode allows for interoperability between Windows 2000 domain controllers and Windows NT BDCs with a domain. In mixed mode the rules for group membership are essentially the same as the rules in Windows NT for backward compatibility (allowing for the fact that Windows 2000 trusts are transitive), specifically:

- Domain local groups can contain:
  - Domain user and computer accounts from any domain in the forest
  - Global groups from any domain in the forest
- Global groups can contain only domain user and computer accounts from their own domains.
- Universal groups are not available in mixed mode domains.

### Native Mode

This mode does not support backward compatibility with Windows NT BDCs and should be used only when you have completely migrated your Windows NT network to Windows 2000. In native mode the membership rules for different group scopes are much more complicated, as outlined in Table 3-19. As you can see, the membership restrictions for domain local and universal groups are the same. The difference is that domain local groups can only be used to access resources in the local domain while universal groups can access resources in any domain in the forest.

*Table 3-19: Membership Restrictions for Group Scopes in Native-Mode Domains*

| | Can Contain | |
|---|---|---|
| Scope | From Same Domain | From Other Domains in the Forest |
| Global | Domain users<br>Computers<br>Global groups | None |
| Domain local | Domain users<br>Computers<br>Global groups<br>Universal groups | Domain users<br>Computers<br>Global groups<br>Universal groups |
| Universal | Domain users<br>Computers<br>Global groups<br>Universal groups | Domain users<br>Computers<br>Global groups<br>Universal groups |

### Nesting of Groups

Nesting means making one group a member of another. Nesting lets you reduce the number of times permissions must be assigned in order to grant users access, but it can also make group permissions more hidden and obscure. Nesting groups in a multidomain environment can also have the benefit of reducing replication traffic between domains. Rules for nesting groups also depend on whether the domain is running in mixed or native mode.

### Mixed Mode

The rules for nesting groups in mixed-mode domains are essentially the same as in Windows NT, that is:

- You can nest global groups within domain global groups.
- You cannot nest global groups within each other or domain local groups within each other.

In other words, groups don't really nest at all in mixed mode (or you could say they nest to one level only, and that for global groups within domain local groups only).

### Native Mode

Nesting is a much more powerful feature when domains are running in native mode. Table 3-20 summarizes the various ways in which different group scopes can be nested in native-mode domains. Note especially that:

- Global groups can now be members of global groups. This is different from how global groups worked in Windows NT.
- Domain local groups still cannot be members of other groups.

It is also important to realize that where nesting is allowed, it can be performed to any level. In other words, you could have an Enterprise Managers global group, which contains Branch Managers global groups, which contain Division Managers global groups, which contain Department Managers global groups, and so on.

This flexibility is almost too much of a good thing, and Microsoft recommends that groups be nested no more than one or two levels. Otherwise, permissions assignments may be difficult to track and troubleshoot if problems arise.

*Table 3-20: Allowable Nesting of Groups in Native-Mode Domains*

| | Can Be Nested Within | | |
| --- | --- | --- | --- |
| Scope | Global | Domain Local | Universal |
| Global | ✓ (from the same domain only) | ✓ | ✓ |
| Domain local | | | |
| Universal | | ✓ | ✓ |

### Converting Scopes

Windows 2000 lets you convert one type of group scope into another. This gives you greater flexibility than you had in Windows NT. However, converting groups from one scope to another can be performed only on domains running in native mode (otherwise, it would conflict with what you can do in Windows NT, which is what mixed mode is designed to support).

Table 3-21 shows the various kinds of scope conversions that can be performed on different groups in native-mode domains.

*Table 3-21: Allowable Scope Conversions in Native-Mode Domains*

| Scope | Can Be Converted to | | |
|---|---|---|---|
| | *Global* | *Domain Local* | *Universal* |
| Global | | | ✓ |
| Domain local | | | ✓ |
| Universal | ✓ | ✓ | |

### Using Groups

Careful planning is the key to effective use of the different Windows 2000 group scopes. The key issue is whether your domain is running in mixed mode or in native mode.

### Mixed Mode

The mantra here is **AGDLP**, which means:

1. Create Accounts for your domain users within each domain.

2. Create Global groups within each domain to organize your domain users according to similar resource access needs or job description, and add your domain user accounts to your global groups as desired.

3. Create Domain Local groups in each domain to control access to specific sets of network resources within the domain, and assign appropriate Permissions for these resources to these groups.

4. Add global groups from various domains to domain local groups in each domain in order to grant access to these network resources to users everywhere in the forest.

This procedure is essentially the same as it was for Windows NT–based networks, except that domain local groups were called local groups in NT (and thus the mantra was AGLP instead of AGDLP). Here is an example to illustrate the principles involved:

> Users in the Marketing department need access to the color laser printer to produce their flashy spreadsheets. Other users in other departments may also need access to the printer. To accomplish this, create a global group called Marketing, and make users in the Marketing department members of this group. Create a domain local group called ColorPrinter, and assign Print permission for the shared printer to the ColorPrinter group. Add the Marketing group to the ColorPrinter group.

A tempting shortcut to this procedure is to eliminate either the global group or the domain local group from the process. For example:

> Create a global group called Marketing, and make users in the Marketing department members of this group. Assign Print permission for the shared printer directly to the Marketing group. This strategy may be described as AGP.

Alternatively:

> Create a domain local group called ColorPrinter, and assign Print permission for the shared printer to the ColorPrinter group. Make users in the Marketing department members of this group. This strategy may be described as ADLP.

## *Using Universal Groups*

On the face of it, universal groups seem to make user management extremely simple and provide a good incentive to change your domains to native mode. After all, universal groups:

- Can contain domain user and computer accounts from any domain in the forest

- Can contain other universal groups from any domain in the forest

- Can be used to access resources in any domain in the forest

- Can be nested within themselves to any degree

So why not just change all your domains to native mode and then convert all your existing domain local and global groups to universal groups and be done with all this AGLP and AGDLP stuff? The reason has to do with how these groups are replicated in the global catalog. The global catalog is a domain controller that contains a partial replica of objects in every domain in Active Directory. Instead of containing all attributes of Active Directory objects, the global catalog contains only selected attributes, specifically those attributes that are most commonly used in search queries performed on Active Directory. How group objects participate in the global catalog depends on their scope:

- Domain local groups are not contained in the global catalog since their scope is restricted to a single domain. (Actually, domain local groups in the local domain are contained in the global catalog, while domain local groups in other domains are contained as objects but their attributes are not contained.)

- Global groups are contained in the global catalog, but only selected attributes are present and not a list of their members.

- Universal groups are contained in the global catalog, and both their selected attributes and a list of all their members are contained. (These members can be user accounts, global groups, or other universal groups.)

As a result of this, using universal groups carelessly can result in:

- Excessive global catalog replication traffic each time the membership of a universal group is changed

- Excessively slow logons when universal groups contain many members

The key issue with universal groups is that if you want to use them, you should:

- Define your universal groups so that their membership changes only rarely.

- Place global groups (or other universal groups) within them, but not individual user accounts (which change more frequently than groups).

- Use nesting of groups to reduce the number of objects contained within.

For more information see "Native Mode" under "Using Groups" in this article.

Concepts
G

The problem with the second and third strategies is that they don't scale well if you later decide to add other domains to your enterprise. In the first case, if you want to allow users in a new domain access to the color printer in the local domain, you will have to explicitly assign permissions to the appropriate global group in the new domain instead of simply adding the global group to the Color-Printer group in the local domain. This makes for somewhat more complicated administration. In the second place, if you want to grant permissions for a printer in the new domain to members of your local ColorPrinter group, you will again have to assign these permissions explicitly since domain local groups cannot be members of any other groups.

### Native Mode

In native mode you can modify the AGDLP strategy somewhat since you can also use universal groups whose scope of membership and resource access span all domains in the forest. I call the mantra here **AGUNP**, which means:

1. Create **A**ccounts for your domain users within each domain.

2. Create **G**lobal groups within each domain to organize your domain users according to similar resource access needs or job description, and add your domain user accounts to your global groups as desired.

3. Create **U**niversal groups to organize enterprise-wide users according to similar enterprise-wide resource access needs, and add your global groups from each domain to your universal groups as desired.

4. If you have large numbers of global groups, consider **N**esting universal groups within other universal groups to reduce the number of members in any individual universal group.

5. Assign appropriate **P**ermissions for accessing network resources across the enterprise directly to your highest level of universal groups (or assign permissions to domain local groups, and place universal groups within domain local groups if you want to keep it complicated).

For an explanation of different administrative tasks relating to groups, see *group* in Chapter 4.

### Notes

- If you make a user a member of a group in order to grant the user permissions on network resources, but the user is currently logged on to a computer in the forest, the new permissions will not take effect until the user next logs on to the network.

- You can change both the type and scope of a group after it has been created, which gives administrators a lot of flexibility.

- Use simple and meaningful names for your groups to help other administrators locate them in Active Directory and to minimize the amount of time you spend documenting your arrangement. For example, if the parent domain is *mtit.com*, use Support for the global group used for customer support people in your domain. Child domains, such as *ny.mtit.com* and *sf.mtit.com*, could use Support NY and Support SF for their corresponding global groups in the New York and San Francisco branch offices.

- Domain local, global, and universal groups are created by default within the Users folder of the *Active Directory Users and Computers* console (see Chapter 5), but they can also be created in any organizational unit you choose or in a user-defined OU.

- You must be a member of the Enterprise Admins group to modify the membership of universal groups.

### See Also

*Active Directory Users and Computers(5), group(4), Group Policy(3), local group(3), mixed mode(3), native mode(3), permissions(3,4), user account(3,4)*

---

## Group Policy

A feature of Active Directory that enables centralized policy-based management of a Windows 2000 network.

### Description

Group Policy lets you centrally define various user and computer settings for Windows 2000 computers on your network. These settings are then periodically refreshed to ensure their effect is maintained when changes occur in the objects they apply to. The advantages of using Group Policy on your network include the ability to:

- Centralize all policy settings for your enterprise at the domain or site level to enforce uniformity across administrative and physical locations. Group Policy is defined in Active Directory, the central repository of computer and network configuration information in Windows 2000.

- Manage different sets of users and computers by applying different policies to different sites, domains, and OUs in Active Directory. Administrators can also reduce their own workload by delegating management over different portions of the Active Directory hierarchy to trusted users and groups.

- Manage users' desktop environments on their client computers to make users more productive and to reduce time spent troubleshooting configuration problems. This includes the ability to lock down users' machines to prevent them from making changes to their working environment and the ability to have users' data folders be accessible from any computer on the network.

- Manage the installation, update, repair, and removal of software on users' client computers. This can be used for applications, service packs, operating-system updates, and fixes, and can ensure that the same applications are available to users whatever computer they log on to.

- Manage the security of computers and users in your domain by creating and managing account policies, audit policies, EFS recovery settings, and other security features.

For information on the procedures for implementing Group Policy, see *Group Policy Objects (GPOs)* in Chapter 4.

### Group Policy Objects

Group Policy settings are contained within a Group Policy Object or GPO. There are two different ways of looking at a GPO: logical and physical.

#### Logical Structure

There are two main types of settings within a GPO:

*Computer configuration*
> These settings are applied to any computer affected by the GPO.

*User configuration*
> These settings are applied to any user affected by the GPO.

For more information on the different categories of Group Policy settings available under user and computer configuration, see "Group Policy Settings" later in this article.

#### Physical Structure

The information specified in a GPO is actually stored in two, separate, physical locations on domain controllers:

*Group Policy Container (GCO)*
> This is a container within Active Directory where the attributes and version information of GPOs are stored. The GCO is used for two purposes:
>
> — Domain controllers use it to determine whether they have the most recent version of GPOs. For example, if you update a GPO on one domain controller in a domain, other domain controllers will check the GCO during Active Directory replication and discover that the version they have is an old one, and they will then replicate the new GPO to themselves.
>
> — Client computers use it to locate the Group Policy Template associated with each GPO that is being applied to them.

 The GCO can be displayed in the Active Directory Users and Computers console by first using View → Advanced Features to display the hidden containers in Active Directory. Then expand the System → Policies container, which contains the different GCO containers associated with each GPO. Each GCO is named using the globally unique identifier (GUID) of its associated GPO. You can view this information for interest's sake, but there is nothing for you to administer here.

*Group Policy Template (GPT)*
> This is a hierarchy of folders in the Sysvol share, which is located on domain controllers. Each GPO has an associated GPT folder hierarchy in the Sysvol share, which is also named using the globally unique identifier (GUID) of the GPO. This GPT contains the administrative templates, security settings, scripts, software installation settings, and folder redirection settings associated with the GPO. In order to obtain these settings when a GPO is being applied, the client computer connects with the Sysvol share on a domain controller and downloads the settings.

## Group Policy Settings

There are five different categories of Group Policy settings: administrative templates, folder redirection, scripts, security, and software installation settings. This section will explain these different categories in detail.

### Administrative Templates

These are settings that are used primarily for managing user environments. Administrative templates (and scripts) enable administrators to control the appearance and functionality of user work environments (desktops) and can be used to lock down user and computer settings to prevent desktops from being altered. This is important as ordinary users sometimes try to reconfigure their desktop settings themselves, resulting in extra support calls to the IT department and wasted time and money. Specifically, administrative template settings can be used to:

- Prevent users from accessing certain operating-system functions such as Control Panel or Internet Explorer

- Enforce a standard desktop and Start menu across an enterprise or department

- Prepopulate users' desktops with shortcuts to shared folders and network connections they will need

- Enable users to access their personal desktop settings from any computer on the network

There are seven groups of administrative template settings, with some of these under User Configuration in a GPO, some under Computer Configuration, and some under both, as Table 3-22 shows.

*Table 3-22: Categories of Administrative Template Settings*

| Type | Description | Configuration |
|------|-------------|---------------|
| Control Panel | Lets you hide all or part of the Control Panel and restrict access to Add/Remove Programs, Display, Printers, and Regional Options | User |
| Desktop | Lets you control the appearance of the user desktop, enable or disable Active Desktop, and limit user ability to query Active Directory | User |
| Network | Lets you configure and manage aspects of offline files and network connections | User and Computer |
| Printers | Lets you control web-based printing, the automatic publishing of printers in Active Directory, and other aspects of network printing | Computer |
| Start menu & Taskbar | Lets you control the appearance and functionality of the Start menu and taskbar | User |
| System | Lets you control logon and logoff functionality, set disk quotas, specify a primary DNS suffix, control how Group Policy is applied, disable registry editing tools, disable Autoplay, and configure other aspects of the local system | User and Computer |
| Windows Components | Lets you control the functionally of Internet Explorer, NetMeeting, Task Scheduler, Windows Installer, Windows Explorer, and the Microsoft Management Console | User and Computer |

If a conflicting administrative template setting is found in both the User and Computer Configuration in a GPO, the Computer setting usually overrides the User setting even if these settings are from different GPOs and the one with the Computer setting was applied first.

Administrative templates are implemented as settings that modify the registry on users' machines. These settings are stored in two files, both called *Registry.pol*, which are located within two folders in the GPT of the GPO in the Sysvol share of domain controllers in the domain. Specifically, the path to these two files within the Sysvol share is:

- *Sysvol\\<domain>\Policies\\<GUID_for_GPO>\MACHINE\ Registry.pol*

- *Sysvol\\<domain>\Policies\\<GUID_for_GPO>\USER\ Registry.pol*

When administrative template settings are applied to a client computer (when the GPO is applied), these settings are written to the client computer in two registry locations:

- User configuration templates settings modify the HKEY_CURRENT_USER (HKCU) hive

- Computer configuration template settings modify the HKEY_LOCAL_ MACHINE (HKLM) hive

These settings are saved to two special sections of these hives:

- *\Software\Policies*

- *\Software\Microsoft\Windows\CurrentVersion\Policies*

By saving GPO administrative template settings to these special areas of the registry, the original (default) registry settings are unchanged so that when the GPO settings are removed (for example, by unlinking the GPO from the OU containing the User or Computer object), the default registry settings take effect. This allows you to free up desktops that had previously been locked down by Group Policy.

 If a resultant GPO setting stored in the registry areas described previously conflicts with the default registry setting for that same operating-system function, the GPO setting wins, of course (otherwise, Group Policy could never be applied!) If a resultant GPO setting is Not Configured, then the default registry setting applies for that function.

For information on how to configure administrative template settings, see "Configure Administrative Templates Settings" in the article *Group Policy Objects (GPOs)* in Chapter 4.

### Folder Redirection

These are settings that let administrators redirect the storage location of My Documents and other essential user folders from their local machines to a central, network file server. For more information see *folder redirection* earlier in this chapter.

### Scripts

These are settings that let you automate how scripts (batch files, Windows Scripting Host scripts, or even executable program files) are run on client computers. There are four types of scripts that can be configured to run automatically on using Group Policy:

*Startup scripts*
These run synchronously (one after another, not concurrently) when a client computer is booted up.

*Logon scripts*
These run asynchronously (you can run multiple logon scripts concurrently) when users log on.

*Logoff scripts*
These run asynchronously when the user logs off.

*Shutdown scripts*
These run synchronously when the system is shut down normally.

If a startup or logon script fails to terminate properly, it must time out before another startup script can execute. The default timeout value is 10 minutes, which means that if your startup script has a problem, users are going to be pretty frustrated. You can configure the timeout value using the following GPO setting that applies globally to all scripts:

Computer Configuration → Administrative Templates → System → Logon → Maximum wait time for Group Policy scripts

If multiple startup scripts are configured, they execute in the order in which they are listed on the Script tab of Startup Properties (see "Configure Scripts Settings" in the article *Group Policy Objects (GPOs)* in Chapter 4).

---

 You can also assign a specific logon script to an individual user using the Profile tab of the property sheet in Active Directory Users and Computers (see "Modify Properties of a User Account" in the article *domain user account* in Chapter 4 for more information).

---

For information on configuring scripts settings, see "Configure Scripts Settings" in the article *Group Policy Objects (GPOs)* in Chapter 4.

### Security

These are settings that can be used to secure various aspects of Windows 2000 computers on your network. Security policies may be configured at the site, domain, or OU level, but most commonly at the domain level. Security settings are found in a GPO in:

Computer Configuration → Windows Settings → Security Settings

If you have Certificate Services installed, then User Configuration → Windows Settings → Security Settings is used also for these services.

There are nine groups of security settings available here:

### Account policies

This includes password, account lockout, and Kerberos policies that control the security of the logon process. Password policies include the minimum length, age, history, and complexity of passwords used for users. Note that changing a password setting by using Group Policy has no effect upon current user passwords until users try to change their passwords, so it's a good idea to ensure that users regularly change their passwords if you implement password policies on your network.

Account lockout settings determine how long and after how many attempts users will be locked out when they fail to enter their correct password. Once a lockout policy is configured, it is applied immediately for all users. Kerberos policies are used to configure aspects of Kerberos authentication for cross-domain authentication.

---

 Account policy settings (password and account lockout) apply to all users and work only for a GPO linked to a domain, not to a site or OU. You can configure account policy settings on a GPO linked to a site or OU, but these settings are ignored. Furthermore, account policy settings configured for a domain cannot be blocked by GPOs linked to OUs. You can, however, link one GPO to multiple domains to enforce account policy settings across a domain tree or forest. See *Group Policy Objects (GPOs)* in Chapter 4 for more information about linking and blocking GPOs.

---

### Local policies

This includes audit policies, user rights, and miscellaneous security settings that affect individual computers instead of the domain. For more information see *auditing* and *rights* in this chapter.

### Event log

These are settings that allow you to configure the size and behavior of the system, security, and application logs.

### Restricted group

These are settings for controlling the membership of specified groups using security policies.

*System services*

> These are settings that can be used to configure the startup and security settings of Windows 2000 services running on all computers in a domain or OU.

*Registry*

> These are settings that allow you to configure permissions on subtrees of registry keys on all computers in a domain or OU.

*Filesystem*

> These are settings that allow you to set consistent NTFS permissions on selected files or folders on all computers in a domain or OU.

*Public key policies*

> These are settings that allow you to configure trusted certificate authorities and encrypted data recovery agents.

*IP Security policies on Active Directory*

> These are settings that let you configure IPSec settings on all computers in a domain or OU.

For procedures that implement the above security settings, see *security policy* in Chapter 4.

### Software Installation

Group Policy can also be used in conjunction with Active Directory and Windows Installer to enable administrators to remotely install, upgrade, maintain, and remove software applications on client computers from a central location. The umbrella term for this Windows 2000 feature is *Software Installation and Maintenance*. Windows Installer consists of two components:

*Windows Installer service*

> This is a client-side service on Windows 2000 computers, which allows the installation and configuration of software to be fully automated. The service can install applications either from a CD-ROM or network share (distribution point) directly, or it can be done using Group Policy.

*Windows Installer package*

> This is the packaged application to be installed or upgraded. It consists of a Windows Installer file (an *.msi* file), external source files, package summary information, and a reference to the location of the distribution point where the files reside.

Windows Installer has several benefits over traditional Setup programs for installing applications:

- It automatically fixes an application when one or more of its critical files become corrupt or missing.

- It cleanly removes all files and registry settings when an application is uninstalled.

- It allows software installation, upgrade, maintenance, and removal processes to be fully automated using Group Policy.

You can deploy software in two ways using Software Installation and Maintenance:

*Assigning software*

Assigning software causes the software to be installed automatically when users require it. Software can be assigned either to:

*Users*

This option places shortcuts on the desktop and Start menu of any computer that the user logs on to. When the user double-clicks on the desktop shortcut, selects the Start menu option, or even double-clicks a file that has the specified file association, the application automatically installs on the computer the user is logged on to. The advantage of assigning software is that the software is available on an as-needed basis and does not fill up the hard drives of client computers unnecessarily.

*Computers*

This option causes the software to be installed automatically when the designated computers are booted up. Then when users log on to their machines, the software is already deployed and available.

---

If an application that is deployed with assigning software becomes damaged, it will be reinstalled automatically the next time the user logs on and activates a document associated with the application (Users option) or the next time the computer boots up (Computers option).

---

*Publishing software*

Publishing software creates information in Active Directory telling client computers that the software is available from a network distribution point. When users open Add/Remove Programs in the Control Panel, the application appears as available for installation by the user. Alternatively, if users double-click on a file with the appropriate file association for the application, the client computer automatically contacts Active Directory, finds the published application, locates the distribution point, and begins the installation process.

Other options you can configure using Software Installation and Maintenance include:

*Software modifications*

Also called transform files, these .*mst* files can be used to deploy multiple configurations of an application for different groups in your enterprise.

*Software categories*

This lets you group published applications into different categories, making it easier for users to find and install them using Add/Remove Programs in the Control Panel.

For procedures on how to deploy software using the Software Installation and Maintenance feature of Windows 2000, see *Windows Installer* in Chapter 4.

---

### Using Group Policy

To implement Group Policy, you must do two things:

*Create a GPO*
> If there is an existing GPO that contains the settings you want to configure, you can modify that GPO instead of creating a new one. If you create a new GPO, then by default none of the settings in the GPO are configured.

*Link the GPO*
> This associates the GPO with a container (site, domain, or OU) in Active Directory whose objects (users and computers) you want the GPO applied to. Once a GPO is linked to a container, the GPO settings will be applied to the users and computers in that container. Linking GPOs can be done in different ways:
>
> — You can link one GPO to multiple containers in Active Directory.
>
> — You can link multiple GPOs to a single container.

Once you have linked a GPO to a container in Active Directory, any users and computers in that container will have the GPO's settings applied to them (see "When Group Policy Is Applied" later in this article). In addition, simply moving a user or computer object into the container automatically applies the GPO's settings to it (see *Active Directory* in Chapter 4 for information on how to move objects within Active Directory).

### How Group Policy Is Applied

You must understand the rules that control how GPOs are applied to users and computers, otherwise you may configure a GPO setting and never see it applied! Here are the key things to remember about how Group Policy is processed:

*Order of application*
> GPOs are applied in a specific order:
>
> *Local*
> > Group Policies applied to the local machine are processed first.
>
> *Site*
> > The GPO linked to the site in which the user or computer resides is applied first, if in fact there is a GPO linked to the site. (By default, sites do not have a default GPO linked to them.)
>
> *Domain*
> > The GPO linked to the domain in which the user or computer resides is applied next. This may be the Default Domain Policy or some custom GPO you have created.
>
> *OU*
> > The GPO linked to the OU in which the user or computer resides is then applied, if there is a GPO linked to the OU.

*Conflicting settings*
> All GPO settings in all GPOs are applied in order so as to produce the resultant Group Policy settings for a User or Computer object in Active Directory. The exception is if two or more GPOs in the chain conflict on one or

more settings. If conflicts arise, the setting from the last GPO in the conflict are applied. For example, if a GPO linked to the domain hides the Control Panel for all users in the domain, but the Vancouver OU has a GPO linked to it that displays (unhides) the Control Panel, then users logging on in Vancouver (i.e., User objects in the Vancouver OU) will see the Control Panel in their Start menu.

The exception is that if a User setting and a Computer setting conflict, the Computer setting is usually the winner regardless of the order in which the GPOs are applied.

### Multiple GPOs

A site, domain, or OU may have multiple GPOs linked to it. If this is the case, these GPOs are applied in the order in which they are listed in the Group Policy Object Links list on the Group Policy tab of the property sheet for that container.

### Inheritance

GPO settings are inherited from site to domain to OU. Child containers inherit the settings of parent containers and can have Group Policy applied to them even if no GPO is explicitly linked to them. For example, if the Canada OU contains the Vancouver OU and a GPO is linked to Canada, User and Computer objects in Vancouver will have the GPO settings applied to them as well.

---

 If a GPO is linked to an OU and a parent OU higher up in the Active Directory hierarchy, the GPO inherited from the parent will be applied first, after which the explicitly linked GPO will be applied.

---

### Blocking

You can explicitly prevent Group Policy settings from being inherited from a parent container (OU, domain, or site) by using blocking. Blocking is limited by two factors:

— If a parent container has a forced GPO linked to it, blocking on the child does not stop GPO inheritance from the parent.

— Otherwise, if you enable blocking on a container, it blocks all settings from all GPOs higher up in the Active Directory hierarchy.

### Forcing

You can force GPO inheritance on objects in child containers, regardless of whether the inherited settings conflict with those from GPOs processed—even when blocking is configured on child containers.

### Filtering

You can filter GPO settings to prevent inheritance by specific users, computers, and security groups in the container. This is done by suitably configuring Group Policy permissions on the container.

## When Group Policy Is Applied

When a computer starts, Group Policy settings (if any GPOs are linked to the site, domain, or OU in which the associated Computer object resides in Active Directory) are applied as follows:

- Computer settings are processed.

- Startup scripts (if any) are processed.

When a user logs on to a computer, Group Policy settings (if any GPOs are linked to the site, domain, or OU in which the associated User object resides in Active Directory) are applied as follows:

- User settings are processed.

- Logon scripts (if any) are processed.

 Logon scripts assigned in a GPO are executed before scripts specified in the user's profile.

Once a computer for which Group Policy is assigned is running (whether a user is logged on or not), the Group Policy settings on the computer are refreshed at regular intervals, as follows:

- Domain controllers refresh every 5 minutes. This ensures that domain-controller security settings are always fresh.

- Client computers refresh every 90 minutes, plus a random offset of up to 30 minutes. This ensures that client-computer lockdown settings are maintained.

 Software-installation and folder-redirection policies are processed only during startup and logon and are not refreshed periodically as other policies are.

## Planning for Use of Group Policy

Group Policy can be used to configure and manage computer and user environments to any degree desired. A large enterprise might want to use Group Policy to manage network security, enforce desktop standards, configure offline folders, deploy software, and perform and manage other administrative functions. The site, domain, and OU structure of an organization must be structured carefully in order to optimize the use of Group Policy.

There are considerations you need to be aware of when using Group Policy at each of the site, domain, and OU levels in Active Directory:

*Site level*

A GPO linked to a site is applied to all computers and users that are physically located at that site, but does not affect mobile users from that site that travel to a different site in your organization. If a site spans multiple domains, the site GPO affects all the domains in the site.

A typical use of a site GPO is to prevent software installation from occurring beyond site boundaries since sites are usually joined by slow WAN links.

Do not use a site GPO if your organization has only one site and one domain. Use a domain GPO instead.

*Domain level*

A GPO linked to a domain is applied to all computers and users in the domain. A GPO in a parent domain does not affect a GPO in a child domain of the parent. A domain GPO can only be configured by a domain administrator; it cannot be delegated to someone not in that group.

A typical use of a domain GPO is to specify security settings for the domain (password and account lockout policies).

You can link a GPO to more than one domain, but this is not recommended since it increases interdomain network traffic. Instead, create a separate GPO for each domain. Unfortunately, you cannot copy a GPO from one domain to another.

*OU level*

A GPO linked to an OU is applied to all computers and users in the OU. Group Policy settings are inherited from a parent OU to its child OUs. Administrators can reduce their workload by delegating management of OU GPOs to trusted users in the enterprise (see *delegation* in this chapter).

Some typical uses for OU GPOs are:

— Managing user rights, auditing, event-log settings, and local security settings on OUs containing domain controllers and member servers

— Managing software deployment and local security settings on OUs containing workstations

— Managing desktop lockdown, folder redirection, and EFS policy on OUs containing users

Here are some additional tips on applying Group Policy in your enterprise:

• Design your domain and OU structure to use as few GPOs as possible. The more GPOs you use, the:

— Slower logons may become

— More network traffic will be generated

— Greater the chance of conflict between settings in different GPOs, causing unpredictable results

— More difficult it will be to troubleshoot problems associated with GPOs

- Keep the number of GPOs that are applied to a given user account small (two or three, usually). It is generally better to merge policy settings from several GPOs into a single GPO whenever possible to speed up the process by which GPOs are applied and refreshed.

- Link each GPO you create to only a single site, domain, or OU. GPOs linked to several domains or sites can significantly slow logons, and linked GPOs generally make it difficult to troubleshoot GPO problems when they occur.

- Use blocking when you have a special group of users or computers that needs unique Group Policy settings in your site, domain, or OU.

- Use forcing sparingly, and only then for containers high up in the Active Directory hierarchy and for GPO settings that are critical throughout the enterprise, such as security settings.

- Try not to use GPO filtering, as this makes troubleshooting Group Policy problems complex. Create an additional GPO instead of filtering an existing one.

- Disable the User or Computer Configuration portion of a GPO if it is not needed. This will speed up processing.

- Use the default security templates included in Windows 2000 as a starting point for configuring security settings in domain GPOs.

- Test your Group Policy settings by logging on to workstations using ordinary user accounts, and see if the settings are as you expected.

- Document your GPOs, where they are linked, and what settings have been configured.

- Use the *GPResult.exe* command-line tool from the Windows 2000 Server Resource Kit to determine what Group Policy settings have been applied to a specific computer and to the user currently logged on to the computer. This is a useful tool for troubleshooting Group Policy problems on your network.

### Notes

- Administrators can delegate control to a trusted user over existing GPOs linked to a container. This step is not necessary, however, if the user has already delegated administrative authority over the container itself, as this automatically gives the user the privilege to create and modify GPOs as desired for the container. See *delegation* in this chapter for general information on the subject.

- Only Enterprise Admins can create GPOs at the site level.

### See Also

*Active Directory(4), auditing(3), delegation(3), Domain Controller Security Policy(5), Domain Security Policy(5), domain user account(4), folder redirection(3), Group Policy(3,4,5), Local Security Policy(3,4), rights(3), security policy(3,4), Windows Installer(4)*

## *Guest*

Built-in user account for granting temporary guest access to resources on the computer or domain.

### *See Also*

*built-in user account(3)*

## *Guests*

Built-in group for granting users guest-access resources on the computer or domain.

### *See Also*

*built-in group(3)*

## *hardware*

Any physical device connected to your computer.

### *Description*

Windows 2000 Server supports a much wider range of hardware devices than the earlier Windows NT Server operating system, including support for:

- Plug and Play devices
- Legacy (non–Plug and Play) devices
- USB and IEEE 1394 devices
- Multiple simultaneous monitors

The hardware compatibility list (HCL) lists the devices supported by Windows 2000 Server. This HCL can be found on:

- The Windows 2000 Server CD at *\Support\hcl.txt*
- The Microsoft web site at *http://www.microsoft.com/hwtest/hcl/*

For procedures on how to add, remove, configure, and troubleshoot hardware devices, see *hardware* in Chapter 4.

### *See Also*

*Add/Remove Hardware(6), Computer Management(5), Device Manager(5), hardware(4), System(6)*

# hardware profile

Settings that specify which devices are enabled or disabled when your computer starts up.

### Description

Hardware profiles were used particularly for laptop installations of Windows NT Workstation where you could define one profile for mobile use and another for docked use. With Windows 2000 Server's support for Plug and Play, creating hardware profiles is generally not needed since the laptop can automatically detect whether it is docked and enable or disable devices accordingly. For information on how to create hardware profiles, see *hardware* in Chapter 4.

### See Also

*Device Manager(5), hardware(3,4), hardware profile(4), System(6)*

# hibernation

A power-management option that powers off your display and hard disks, writes the contents of physical memory (RAM) to disk, and powers off your computer. When you restart, your desktop is returned exactly as you left it.

### See Also

*hibernation(4)*

# home folder

A centralized location on a network file server where users can store their personal documents.

### Description

Home folders were a feature of Windows NT that allowed users to store their personal files on network file servers, which could be backed up easily, instead of on their local machines. While Windows 2000 still supports home folders for backward compatibility with legacy applications, the default location for users to store their personal files is now the My Documents folder. By default, this folder is located on a user's local machine and is part of the user's profile.

Instead of configuring home folders on network file servers for your users, you can use Group Policy instead to redirect users' My Documents folders to network shares. See *folder redirection* in this chapter for more information.

The only reason you might consider using home folders instead of My Documents is to provide support for legacy MS-DOS and Windows 3.x/9x/NT applications that cannot recognize My Documents as the default storage location for users' work files. You're really better off migrating your applications to Windows 2000–compatibile versions that support My Documents instead of creating and configuring NT-style home folders for your users.

### Notes

- Make sure you create home folders on an NTFS volume to ensure users' work is secured. Each user will have Full Control permission on his own home folder, and no other user (including Administrators) will have access to his home folder.

- You can assign a single home folder to multiple users if desired. All temporary users might be assigned the same home folder, for example.

- Home folders are mapped to a drive on the client computer. A typical choice is to assign the letter *H:* to a user's home folder. Instructions for users are then as simple as, "Be sure to save all your work in *H:*."

### See Also

*folder redirection(3), home folder(4), user profile(3)*

---

## install

Planning for deployment of Windows 2000 Server.

### Description

There are a number of issues you need to consider as you prepare to deploy Windows 2000 Server in your enterprise. This section deals with these preparatory issues; for detailed information on different installation methods and the procedures involved, see *install* in Chapter 4.

#### Installation Methods

The method you use to install Windows 2000 Server will depend upon several factors:

*Scope of deployment*
It's one thing to upgrade two or three servers from Windows NT to Windows 2000 in a small company; it's another thing entirely when you have to upgrade thousands of servers across multiple locations in a large enterprise. In the first scenario you would probably run Setup directly from the compact disc, but when then number of servers exceeds about a dozen, then network installations performed from distribution servers become a more practical solution.

*Hardware homogeneity*
Having large numbers of servers with identical hardware configurations makes disk imaging a simple and efficient way of installing or upgrading them. If servers are from a multitude of different vendors and have customized hardware configurations, disk imaging is probably not recommended.

*Staff availability*
If only a few staff will be performing the deployment, you need to consider some form of automated installation either using answer files and UDFs or using disk imaging. If the servers to staff ratio is small, however, it may not be cost-effective to spend the time learning how to perform these types of installations. It may simply be better to install or upgrade from the CD or off a network distribution server.

The standard deployment methods for installing or upgrading to Windows 2000 Server include the following:

*CD installation*

Setup is run directly from the Windows 2000 Server compact disc. This method only allows you to install or upgrade one system at a time (unless the CD is shared over the network). You typically use this method when you only have a few servers to deploy in your network. You are limited mainly by the number of CDs you have and the number of staff who are available to respond to the prompts as Setup is run.

*Network installation*

The Windows 2000 Server source files are first copied to a folder on one or more file servers, and these folders are then shared over the network. File servers that share the Windows 2000 Server source files are called distribution servers. The servers to be installed or upgraded then connect to and run Setup from these distribution servers. This method can be used to simulta- neously deploy dozens or even hundreds of servers. You are limited mainly by the speed of the distribution servers, the network bandwidth available, and the number of staff available to respond to the prompts as Setup is run.

---

It's not a good idea simply to insert the Windows 2000 Server com- pact disc into a machine and share it out for network installation. The read-access time of a CD-ROM is much slower than that of the typical hard drive. So while it might take a bit longer than usual to perform a network installation of 10 servers from a shared folder, it will take forever to do the same from a shared CD-ROM!

---

*Automated installation*

Using a tool called Setup Manager, which is part of the Windows 2000 Server Resource Kit (and is also available in part on the Windows 2000 Server CD), you can easily create answer files and UDFs for performing automated instal- lations either over the network or using the Windows 2000 Server CD.

An *answer file* is a specially formatted text file that answers some or all of the prompts during installation. This allows installations and upgrades to be performed without any user interaction other than starting the Setup process.

A *uniqueness database file*, or *UDF*, is a specially formatted text file that supplements or overrides some of the information in the answer file. While the answer file provides responses to general prompts, such as which optional components to install or which domain to join, UDFs are typically used to provide system-specific information, such as the names of computers or their IP address if DHCP is not being used. You would typically have one answer file for a group of servers in the same department or having the same function, and then each installation or upgrade of a server would require its own UDF.

### Disk imaging

Disk imaging (also called disk duplication or disk cloning) is the process of making an exact bitwise duplication of a hard drive. You first create a master image of the system/boot disk of a Windows 2000 Server system and then copy or clone this image to other systems. This can be a very efficient method for deploying a large number of new installations of Windows 2000 Server, but only when the systems you are deploying to have identical or very similar hardware configurations. One of the great advantages of disk imaging is that you can use it to install not just a bare-bones version of Windows 2000 Server but also a fully loaded server with numerous preinstalled applications. However, simply cloning a drive is not enough, since the resulting system will have security identifiers (SIDs) identical to the original system. Since Windows 2000 uses SIDs to internally represent all unique information about computers, users, and so on, simply cloning a system will result in conflicts when the new system is brought online on the network.

Windows 2000 Server unfortunately does not include disk-imaging software (see the sidebar "Disk-Imaging Software" for information on third-party disk-imaging software). However, it does include a utility called the System Preparation Tool (*Sysprep.exe*), which is used to help prepare a system for cloning by ensuring that the cloned systems will have their own unique SIDs. Sysprep works by deleting the SIDS on your existing system, which generates unique SIDs on the target systems when they are restarted after the image has been cloned to them.

 Since Sysprep removes all SIDs (and thus all computer-specific and user-specific information) from the system it is run on, Sysprep should only be run on a test system, not a production system!

You can also use Setup Manager to create a *Sysprep.inf* file. This file allows Sysprep to be run in unattended mode to allow for automatic disk imaging.

Unlike other installation methods, disk imaging cannot be used for upgrading previous systems, only for performing fresh installations. This is because disk imaging wipes out all existing information from the destination disk to which the image is copied, and thus it can make no use of existing hardware- or software-configuration settings on the target system.

### Preinstallation Issues

There are some issues you need to consider and some decisions you have to make prior to installing or upgrading a system to Windows 2000 Server:

### Supported hardware

You must ensure that all of your hardware is fully supported by Windows 2000 Server. The best way to determine this is to consult the Windows 2000 Hardware Compatibility List or HCL, which lists those devices whose drivers have been tested for and comply with Windows 2000 Server. Microsoft only supports hardware that is listed on the HCL, so be sure to comply with this list if you want to be eligible for technical support from them.

## *Disk-Imaging Software*

Several companies currently offer third-party disk-imaging software that can be used to rapidly deploy Microsoft Windows software on large numbers of computers. At the time of writing, however, some of these utilities support Windows 2000 Professional but not Windows 2000 Server (but check their web sites to see if this has changed by the time you read this):

- Server Magic 3.0 from PowerQuest (*http://www.powerquest.com*) includes a utility called Server Image that can currently be used to clone and install images of Windows NT and NetWare, and there are plans for it to support Windows 2000 Server as well. PowerQuest also has another tool called Drive Image Pro 3.0 that supports deployment of Windows 2000 Professional.

- ImageCast IC3 Version 4.0 from Innovative Software (*http://www. innovativesoftware.com*) supports deployment of Windows 2000 Professional.

- RapiDeploy from Codework (*http://www.codework.com*) will support deployment of Windows 2000 Professional in its upcoming version.

- Norton Ghost from Symantec (*http://www.symantec.com*) will support Server and Professional versions.

The HCL can be found on the Windows 2000 Server CD as text file \*Support*\ *HCL.txt*, but this copy may be outdated. It's best to consult the most recent version of HCL on Microsoft's web site at *http:www.microsoft.com/bwtest/bcl/*.

### Hardware requirements

You must also meet the minimum hardware requirements for installing Windows 2000 Server (though experience tells us that we should go well beyond the recommended hardware requirements if we want to see decent performance in a Microsoft product). Table 3-23 lists the minimum and recommended hardware requirements for installing Windows 2000 Server.

*Table 3-23: Hardware Requirements for Windows 2000 Server*

| Component | Minimum Hardware Requirement | Recommended Hardware Requirement (if Any) |
|---|---|---|
| Processor | Pentium 133 MHz | |
| Memory | 128 MB | 256 MB |
| Hard disk | 1.2 GB free space | 2.0 GB free space |
| Video | VGA | SVGA |

### Disk partitioning

Although a 1.2-GB partition will suffice for installing Windows 2000 Server, Microsoft recommends using at least a 2-GB partition to leave room for additional Windows 2000 components you may want to install later. You can create and delete partitions during the text-based initial portion of Setup.

Microsoft recommends that you use Setup only to create the partition on which you plan to install Windows 2000 Server and then use *Disk Management* (see Chapter 5) after the installation is complete to create and format other partitions. Besides quickening Setup, using Disk Management gives you the option of converting your disk subsystem to dynamic storage so you can create extended and fault-tolerant volumes.

### Filesystem

During the text-based portion of Setup, you can specify which filesystem will format the partition on which you will install Windows 2000 Server. You can choose between FAT, FAT32, and NTFS, but the logical choice is NTFS. NTFS provides additional security and manageability through NTFS file and folder permissions, EFS encryption, disk compression, and disk quotas. The only reason you might want to choose FAT or FAT32 is if you want to be able to dual-boot your system, but this is a highly unlikely choice with a production server.

### Licensing mode

Decisions must be made prior to installation of how you want to license your server. There are three aspects of Windows 2000 Licensing:

— One server license is required to license your right to install and run Windows 2000 Server on the computer.

— Multiple client-access licenses (CALs) are required to license client computers with the right to connect to your server and access its services.

— Additional Microsoft BackOffice licenses are required if you have other BackOffice applications installed and running on your server.

In addition to determining the number of CALs you require, you also need to decide whether you will license these CALs in a per-server or per-seat mode. For more information on CALs, see *Licensing* in Chapter 5.

### Security model

You need to decide whether your server will be installed as a standalone server that is part of a *workgroup* or as a member server belonging to a *domain* (for installing domain controllers see the "Results of Installation" section later in this article).

If you plan to join the computer to a domain during Setup, then you will require:

— The name of the domain you plan to join (e.g., *mtit.com*).

— A computer account to be created for your computer in the domain you plan to join. This can be done by creating the computer account ahead of time using Active Directory Users and Computers (see Chapter 5), or you can create the computer account during Setup, provided you have the credentials of an administrator in the domain (member of the Domain Admins group for the domain).

— A domain controller for the domain that is online.

— A DNS server for the domain that is online.

Note that both the domain controller and DNS server may be the same machine.

### Other system preparation issues

If any existing partitions from a previous operating system have been compressed with DriveSpace or DoubleSpace, make sure you uncompress them. If you have a mirror set from a previous operating system, break the mirror prior to upgrading, then re-create the mirror set after the upgrade is complete. Finally, if you are using a UPS, disconnect it before installing Windows 2000 Server on a machine.

### Results of Installation

The result of installing Windows 2000 Server on a system is either:

### Member server

If the server belongs to a domain

### Standalone server

If the server belongs to a workgroup

If instead you want the result to be a *domain controller*, you can:

- Run the dcpromo command afterwards to promote your server to a domain controller.

- Create an answer file for a member server installation using Setup Manager. Then create a second answer file for running *dcpromo*. Finally, create a batch file that performs both of these actions, and run the batch file.

- Use disk-imaging software to duplicate an existing, Windows 2000 domain controller while using *Sysprep.exe* to ensure the resulting system has unique SIDs.

If you are upgrading servers from earlier Windows NT Server instead of performing fresh installations, the result of upgrading a domain controller is a domain controller.

### Post-Installation Issues

If the installation or upgrade to Windows 2000 Server seems to have completed successfully, there are still several things you should do to make sure your server is prepared for production use on your network:

- When you first log on to your newly installed or upgraded system, the utility Configure Your Server runs, prompting you to make further configuration changes for your system. You should generally close this utility and proceed with the remaining post-installation issues first, then later you can run it again using Start → Programs → Administrative Tools → Configure Your Server. For more information see *Configure Your Server* in Chapter 5.

- Check Event Viewer to see if there are any error or warning messages associated with the installation process. Also, configure your event-log settings as desired.

- Use Services in Computer Management to check that all services set to Automatic have started successfully.

- Use Device Manager in Computer Management to ensure that your hardware devices have been detected properly and assigned appropriate resource settings.

- Use System in the Control Panel to configure background/foreground application responsiveness and your paging file settings.

- Use System in the Control Panel to configure your Startup and Recovery settings as desired.

- Use Power Options in the Control Panel to configure your APM power scheme. Servers should generally have their hard drives configured *not* to power down during idle times.

- Use Display in the Control Panel to configure your display for at least 800x600 screen resolution.

- Verify your IP address, DNS, and WINS settings by typing `ipconfig /all` at the command prompt (see Chapter 7 for information on *ipconfig*).

- Try connecting to a shared folder on the network to see if you can access it. (The level of your access depends on the permissions assigned to the resource.)

- Verify the full DNS name of your computer by typing `net config rdr` at the command prompt (see Chapter 7 for information on *net config*), and check this with the information in Active Directory.

- Optimize your server for the role it is going to play on your network. Proceed as follows:

  Start → Settings → Control Panel → right-click on Network and Dial-up Connections → Properties → File and Print Sharing for Microsoft Networks → Properties → select Optimization setting

  See *Network and Dial-up Connections* in Chapter 6 for more information.

- Back up your system once you have verified everything is working properly.

### Notes

- If you join a workgroup during Setup, you can always join a domain later. See *computer* in Chapter 4 for procedures on how to join a computer to a domain. For example, if a domain controller is not available for some reason, then install Windows 2000 Server as a standalone server that is part of a workgroup (any workgroup will do). Then when a domain controller becomes available, you can join the domain to become a member server in that domain.

- If you create a computer account using Active Directory Users and Computers prior to installing Windows 2000 Server on your machine, you need to use the computer name you specified for this account when you are performing the installation, or it will not succeed.

- In addition to the four installation methods described in this article, administrators of enterprise-level networks can also perform simultaneous installations on multiple servers using push technologies such as Microsoft Systems Management Server.

- Note that the Windows 2000 Server service called Remote Installation Services is a tool designed for mass deployment of Windows 2000 Professional desktop machines, *not* for deploying Windows 2000 Server on machines. However, the registry can be edited to allow RIS deployments of Windows 2000 Server.

- Prior to deploying Windows 2000 Server, be sure to read the following important files on the Windows 2000 Server compact disc to make sure you will not be affected by other installation or upgrade issues:

  *Read1st.txt* (in root directory)
  *Readme.doc* (in root directory)
  *Srv1.txt*, *Srv2.txt*, and *Srv3.txt* (in \*Setuptxt*)

  You may find updated versions of these files on Microsoft's web site at *http://support.microsoft.com/support/*.

- If you want to create a dual-boot system by installing Windows 2000 Server into a new *%SystemRoot%* directory on an existing Windows NT 4.0 Server machine, you should:

  — Ensure you have the latest Service Pack for Windows NT 4.0 Server installed in order to maximize filesystem compatibility on NTFS partitions. You must use at least Service Pack 4.

  — Install Windows 2000 Server on a different physical drive or partition than Windows NT 4.0 Server. Unfortunately, this means you will also have to reinstall all your applications a second time!

  — Make sure each operating system has a different computer name assigned to it.

  — Make sure you do not afterwards use Windows 2000 Server to encrypt files on an NTFS partition, as Windows NT 4.0 Server will then be unable to access them.

  Microsoft actually recommends that if you want to dual-boot, first install Windows NT 4.0 on a FAT partition, and then install Windows 2000 Server on a separate NTFS partition. The point is, Microsoft does not really recommend dual-booting between Windows 2000 Server and Windows NT 4.0 Server!

### See Also

*Active Directory Users and Computers(5)*, *computer(4)*, *Configure Your Server(5)*, *Disk Management(5)*, *install(4)*, *ipconfig(7)*, *net config(7)*, *Network and Dial-up Connections(6)*, *upgrade(3,4)*

## Interactive

Built-in system group representing the user who is currently logged on locally and accessing a resource on the local computer.

### See Also

*built-in group(3)*

## Internet Information Services (IIS)

Enables Windows 2000 to run as an Internet server.

### Description

Internet Information Services (IIS) provides server-side support for the most popular, Internet, application-layer protocols including Hypertext Transfer Protocol (HTTP), File Transfer Protocol (FTP), Simple Mail Transfer Protocol (SMTP), and Network News Transfer Protocol (NNTP). The primary use of this service is to enable a Windows 2000 computer to function as a web server.

> The SMTP and NNTP services included in IIS have limited useful-ness. For more powerful versions of these protocols, use Microsoft Exchange Server.

IIS is installed by default on Windows 2000 Server and provides a wealth of config-uration options that would fill half of this book to explain. I recommend my book *Administering IIS5* (McGraw-Hill) for a full treatment of the capabilities of this component of Windows 2000 Server. The discussion here focuses on basic concepts and terminology related to creating and configuring web sites. See *web site* in Chapter 4 for procedures to create and configure a web site on an IIS server.

> In most cases you want to have DNS implemented on your network if you are going to use IIS. Otherwise, users will have to specify the IP address of the IIS server they want to access.

#### IIS Terminology

The following is a sample of some more important IIS terminology:

*Internet Services Manager*
> The shortcut in Administrative Tools that opens the Internet Information Services console.

*Web site*
> A virtual server hosted on the IIS machine and identified by an IP address, a TCP port, an optional host-header name, and the path to the home directory that contains the home page (typically *default.htm* or *default.asp*) for the site.

For example, the URL for the home directory of the web site for MTIT Enterprises (my company) might be *http://www.mtit.com*, which is mapped to the directory *C:\junk* on the IIS server.

*Virtual directory*

A mapping between the path portion of a URL and a physical directory where web content is stored. For example, the URL *http://www.mtit.com/stuff/* might be mapped to the directory *C:\trash* on the IIS server. In this case *stuff* is an alias for *trash*. The location of the mapped directory can be on either the IIS server (local virtual directory) or a shared folder on a network file server (remote virtual directory). The advantage of using remote virtual directories is that it allows you to leave content where it is on network file servers instead of moving it to the IIS server. The downside is that this slows performance somewhat.

*Anonymous access*

If configured for a web site, this allows users to access content (web pages) in the site without needing to specify credentials (username or password). Internally, anonymous access uses a special user account called *IUSR_<server_name>*, which is in the Guests group. Content configured with NTFS Read permission for Everyone or for *IUSR_<server_name>* can be accessed by anonymous users.

*Basic authentication*

If configured for a web site, authenticates users using their username and password before they can access content in the site. Users are prompted for their credentials before they can proceed further. Basic authentication is not very secure since users' passwords are transmitted in clear text across the connection.

*Digest authentication*

This is more secure than Basic authentication since it transmits a hashed value for the password instead of the clear-text version. In order to digest authentication, the IIS server must be part of a domain, not a workgroup. In addition, users' passwords must be available in clear-text form on the server, which necessitates the server being physically secured.

*Integrated Windows authentication*

This is the Challenge/Response authentication method used in Windows NT networks. It is more secure than Basic authentication since the password is not transmitted over the connection. Furthermore, the user is not prompted for credentials since the credentials of the logged-on user are used automatically. If Active Directory is installed on the IIS server, Integrated Windows authentication uses Kerberos authentication instead.

## Notes

- Integrated Windows authentication does not work over a proxy connection.

- The approximate 3,000 pages of IIS Help files are separate from the rest of Windows 2000 Help and can be accessed using Internet Explorer with the URL *http://<IIS_server>/iishelp/iis/misc/default.asp*.

## See Also

*web site(4)*

# *local group*

A collection of local user accounts.

## *Description*

Local groups allow local user accounts to be grouped together for administrative purposes. Local groups are created in the same local security database where local user accounts are created on a machine. Local groups are created within the Groups folder of the *Local Users and Groups* console (see Chapter 5).

Since use of local user accounts is usually confined to standalone servers running Windows 2000 Server or client computers running Windows 2000 Professional, local groups are rarely used in Windows 2000–based networks. One possible use of local groups is for several users to share a single standalone server or client computer, and you can then secure files and folders located on that machine. In this case you can create local groups to group local user accounts together in order to manage permissions more easily. Another use is for you to implement a Windows 2000 network using a workgroup model where each machine manages its own security settings.

Here are the membership rules concerning local groups:

- Local groups can contain:

    — Local user accounts from the computer on which the group resides

    — Global or universal groups from any domain

- Local groups cannot be members of other groups.

One confusing difference between Windows 2000 and Windows NT is in the use of *local groups*. On Windows NT, local groups:

- Are used for assigning permissions to resources in the domain

- Can contain user accounts and global groups from the local domain and trusted domains

- Can be created on domain controllers, member servers, and workstations

However, on Windows 2000, local groups:

- Are not recommended for use in domain-based networks

- Can contain local user accounts from the local machine and global or universal groups from any domain

- Cannot be created on domain controllers

The long and the short of it is, where you used to use local groups in Windows NT, use *domain local groups* in Windows 2000 instead.

## *Notes*

- Use local groups only if your network is configured as a workgroup or if you are using standalone machines that are not networked together.

- Do not create local groups on computers that belong to a domain since local groups can only be used to secure resources located on the computer you create them on. For example, if you had several member servers that were part of a domain, you could secure resources on each member server as follows:

1. Create a local group on a member server.

2. Assign suitable permissions to the local group for the shared resources on the member server.

3. Place appropriate global groups in the local group in order to grant users permission to the resources on the member server.

4. Repeat this procedure for each member server.

This is workable, but step 4 shows that the procedure is unwieldy since it has to be repeated for each member server every time you want to modify who can access the resources on the servers. A better approach would be to:

1. Create a domain local group on a domain controller in the domain.

2. Assign suitable permissions to the domain local group for the shared resources on each of the member servers.

3. Place appropriate global groups in the domain local group in order to grant users permission to the resources on each of the member servers.

- You cannot create local groups on a Windows 2000 domain controller since a domain controller has no local security database.

### See Also

*group(3), local user account(3), Local Users and Groups(5)*

## Local Security Policy

A system policy used for securing the local computer.

### Description

Local Security Policies are used to secure certain aspects of standalone Windows 2000 Server or Professional computers that are configured as part of a workgroup. A local security policy applies only to the machine on which it is configured. For Windows 2000 computers that are part of a domain, use Group Policy instead to implement security for Windows 2000 computers on your network. For procedures on implementing Local Security Policy on a machine, see *Local Security Policy* in Chapter 4.

Although mainly intended for use in workgroup environments, Local Security Policies can have an effect on computers that are configured as part of a domain as well. This is because policy settings are applied in the following order:

1. Local Security Policy

2. Group Policy for the site

3. Group Policy for the domain

4. Group Policy for OUs

If, for example, the Local Security Policy on a computer specifies a minimum password length of 12 characters while none of the Group Policies that are implemented override this setting, the local setting will determine the result even though the computer belongs to a domain instead of a workgroup. For more information on the order of application of Group Policy, see *Group Policy* earlier in this chapter.

### Security Settings

The security settings that can be configured using Local Security Policy are a small subset of those for Group Policy. In particular, Local Security Policy supports the following kinds of settings:

*Account policies*
> This includes password and account lockout policies. For example, you can specify a minimum password length or have the lockout counter reset itself after a specified number of minutes.

*Local policies*
> This includes audit policies, the rights assigned to different users and groups, and various other local security settings.

*Public key policies*
> This contains a certificate declaring the Administrator an EFS recovery agent.

*IP Security policies*
> This includes settings to configure IPSec for secure communications across a virtual private network (VPN).

### Security Templates

Security templates are text files that contain various settings that can be used to configure your computer using Local Security Policy. Windows 2000 includes a number of predefined security templates. There are four different levels of security templates included in the *%SystemRoot%\security\templates* directory on Windows 2000 machines:

*Basic level*
> This template specifies a base-security configuration. For example, the password policy uses a maximum password age of 42 days, but zero passwords are remembered. The template files at this level are:
>
> — *Basicsv.inf* for standalone and member servers
>
> — *Basicdc.inf* for domain controllers
>
> — *Basicwk.inf* for client computers

*Compatible level*
> This template leaves all security settings as undefined (applying this template will thus have no effect on the security settings of the machine). The template file is *Compatws.inf* for both servers and workstations.

*Secure level*
> This template specifies a medium-security configuration. For example, the password policy specifies that 24 passwords are remembered and that it has an account lockout duration of 30 minutes. The template files are *Securews.inf* for member servers and workstations and *Securedc.inf* for domain controllers.

*High level*

This template specifies a high-security configuration. For example, the account lockout duration is permanent (users are locked out until the administrator unlocks their accounts). The template files are *Hisecws.inf* and *Hisecdc.inf.*

You can view the various settings of the different security templates using the Security Configuration and Analysis snap-in (see *Security Configuration and Analysis* in Chapter 5).

### Notes

- Windows 2000 must be installed on an NTFS partition if you want to apply security to the computer using Local Security Policy.

- If you upgrade from Windows NT to Windows 2000, the security settings are maintained.

- You can create your own custom security templates. See *Local Security Policy* in Chapter 4 for more information.

- If you are testing application of Group and Local Security Policies after making changes to them, you may need to force Group Policy propagation to occur in order to see your expected results.

- Windows NT 4.0 system policies (stored in *.pol* files) cannot be migrated to Windows 2000.

### See Also

*Group Policy(3,4), Local Security Policy(4), Security Configuration and Analysis(5)*

---

## local user account

A user account that lets a user log on to a single computer and access resources only on that computer.

### Description

Local user accounts are valid only on the computer on which they are defined. They are stored within the computer's local security database. This is in contrast to domain user accounts, which are valid for any computer in the domain and which are stored within Active Directory for that domain. Local user accounts are created within the Users folder of the *Local Users and Groups* console (see Chapter 5).

Authentication of a local user account works as follows:

- The user provides her credentials to log on the local machine.

- The local machine compares the user's credentials with those stored for the user in the local security database on that machine and determines whether to provide the user with access to the machine.

- If the user is to be granted access to the machine, the local security database provides an access token that specifies the permissions and rights that the user will have on the machine.

### Notes

- Local user accounts can be created only on member servers and client computers; they cannot be created on domain controllers.

- Use local user accounts only for users on standalone computers who have no need to access shared resources on the network. Otherwise, always use domain user accounts for users in Windows 2000 networks.

- Local user accounts are not replicated to Active Directory.

### See Also

*built-in user account(3), domain user account(3), Local Users and Groups(5)*

---

## local user profile

A type of user profile stored on the local machine where the user logs on.

### See Also

*user profile(3)*

---

## logon

The process of having your credentials authenticated so you can gain access to the network or local machine.

### Description

There are two kinds of logons in Windows 2000:

*Logging on to a domain*
If a user has a domain user account defined in Active Directory for a given domain, the user can log on to the domain and access shared resources on the network.

*Logging on locally*
If a user has a local user account defined in the local security database on a Windows 2000 computer, the user can log on only to the local computer and access resources only on that machine.

The usual way is to log on to a domain. Windows 2000 uses a single logon process, which means that users need only one set of credentials to gain access to all resources on the network (provided they have suitable permissions for accessing those resources).

### Logon Names

There are two types of logon names a user can use to log on to a Windows 2000 network:

*Downlevel logon name*
This is the user account name for the user—for example, *msmith* for Mary Smith. The downlevel logon name for a user must be unique within the user's domain. Downlevel logon names are used primarily when logging on to client computers running versions of Microsoft Windows earlier than Windows 2000.

*User logon name*

Also called the user principal name (UPN), this is the standard logon name for a user on a Windows 2000 network. It consists of three strings appended together:

— The user principal name prefix, which is the user account name and must be unique in the entire forest

— An @ symbol

— The user principal name suffix, which by default is the DNS name of the domain where the user account is created

The user logon name for Mary Smith might be *msmith@mtit.com,* for example.

Users on Windows 2000 client computers can use either logon name to log on to the network and be authenticated by a domain controller. Using user logon names is recommended because they are unique within Active Directory and do not change even if a user account is moved to a different domain in the forest.

### Notes

- You can only log on locally to:

— A member server (running Windows 2000 Server)

— A client computer (running Windows 2000 Professional)

— A computer that does not belong to a domain

- You cannot log on locally to a domain controller. (You can log on to the local console on a domain controller, but you must use a domain user account to do so.)

- The user logon name for a user can look like their email address, but it is not the same thing.

- You can configure an additional UPN suffix for a user. This lets users in child domains like *sales.mtit.com* to use the DNS name of their forest root domain (instead of the DNS name of the child domain) as the UPN suffix of their user logon name. See *log on* in Chapter 4 for more information.

### See Also

*log on(4)*

---

# logon script

A file containing a series of commands that runs on the client computer when a user logs on to the network.

### Description

Logon scripts were used extensively in legacy versions of Windows for helping to configure certain aspects of a user's environment, such as:

- Connecting mapped network drives to shared folders on file servers

- Starting background processes or foreground applications on the client computer

- Configuring environment variables such as the location of the temporary directory

- Executing other scripts

Logon scripts are an optional feature still supported by Windows 2000, but this is primarily for support of downlevel client computers running legacy versions of Microsoft Windows. For client computers running Windows 2000 Professional and Windows NT Workstation, user profiles are a better way of configuring users' personal desktop and network settings. However, if you want to administer only minor aspects of users' environments and don't want to go to the trouble of configuring and managing user profiles, logon scripts are a useful alternative.

Logon scripts are generally ASCII files that have the extension *.bat*, a holdover from MS-DOS computing days when batch files were used to run a set of commands without user intervention. A text editor such as Notepad is typically used for creating a logon script. Logon scripts, however, can come in all sorts of other flavors, including:

- ASCII text files in the form of *.cmd* files

- ASCII text files in the form of windows-scripting host files (*.vbs* or *.js*)

- Executable files (*.exe*, *.com*)

- Various third-party scripting languages such as KIXSTART

Table 3-24 shows some of the replaceable variables that can be used in logon scripts. System environment variables can also be used in logon scripts.

*Table 3-24: Replaceable Variables Used in Logon Scripts*

| Variable | Description |
| --- | --- |
| %HOMEDRIVE% | The drive letter on the client computer that is mapped to the user's home directory |
| %HOMEPATH% | The full path to the user's home directory |
| %USERDOMAIN% | The domain in which the user's account resides |
| %USERNAME% | The username |

### Notes

- Logon scripts can be used for creating new network connections on client computers. One limitation of user profiles is that they can only be used for restoring existing network connections that were created during the previous user session, and they cannot be used to create new connections.

- Group policies enable you to configure scripts that run at logon, logoff, startup, and shutdown for the group of users to which the policy is assigned. They also let you assign logon scripts to domains, sites, organizational units (OUs), groups, or individual users, giving administrators a lot of flexibility in how they can configure a user's environment.

- Windows 2000 also supports using Windows Script Host files as logon scripts. These scripts may be written in VBscript or JScript.

### See Also

*environment variable(3), Group Policy(3), user profile(3)*

## mandatory user profile

A roaming user profile that the administrator configures and the user cannot change.

### See Also

*user profile(3)*

## member server

A server on a network that is not a domain controller.

### Description

Member servers are computers that are running Windows 2000 Server and that do not contain a copy of Active Directory. Member servers therefore cannot authenticate users for network logon or resource access the way domain controllers can. Member servers are generally used instead as dedicated file, print, or application servers.

By default, when Windows 2000 Server is installed on a machine, the result is a member server. Member servers can belong to either a workgroup or a domain.

### See Also

*domain controller(3)*

## mirrored volume

Two simple volumes that are exact duplicates of one another and behave as a single volume. Mirrored volumes correspond to mirror sets in Windows NT.

### See Also

*disks(3)*

## mixed mode

A domain mode that supports downlevel Windows NT domain controllers.

### Description

You can create a new Windows 2000 domain by either:

- Installing a fresh copy of Windows 2000 Server on a computer and then promoting it to the role of domain controller using the Active Directory Installation Wizard

- Upgrading an existing Windows NT 4.0 PDC to Windows 2000, which upgrades it to the role of domain controller automatically

Either way you do this, the result is a Windows 2000 domain running in mixed mode. In mixed mode, Windows 2000 domain controllers use NTLM as their protocol for authenticating both clients and servers running either Windows NT or

Windows 2000. This enables users to continue to log on and access network resources during the migration process while there remains a mixture of Windows 2000 and Windows NT domain controllers in the domain.

Once you have fully migrated all your servers and clients from Windows NT to Windows 2000, however, you should change the domain from mixed mode to native mode to make use of the more secure, Kerberos v5 authentication protocol supported by Windows 2000 clients and servers.

### Notes

- NTLM is also used for authentication by Windows 2000 computers that are configured to belong to a workgroup instead of a domain.

- Mixed mode does not support universal groups, nested groups, or transitive trusts between domains.

- Windows 2000 domain controllers configured as remote-access servers and running in mixed-mode domains must have separate remote-access policies created for each type of connection allowed and support more limited dial-in properties than those running in native mode.

### See Also

*domain(3,4), native mode(3)*

---

## My Documents

A special folder that is part of a user profile.

### Description

The *My Documents* folder is the default location for users to store their personal and work files. When you select File → Open from the menu of a "designed for Windows 2000" application, the application looks by default in the *My Documents* folder for the currently logged-on user. Similarly, when a user selects File → Save As to save work, it goes into the *My Documents* folder.

Each user who logs on to a Windows 2000 machine has his own separate *My Documents* folder for storing files. Each user also has an icon on the desktop that allows him easy access to his files.

The *My Documents* folder for a user is contained within the user profile for that particular user. For example, if a user named Bob has his local user profile stored in *C:\Documents and Settings\Bob* on his machine, Bob's personal and work files will be stored in the subfolder *C:\Documents and Settings\Bob\My Documents*.

---

My Documents and other important user profiles can also be redirected to a network share using Group Policy. This ensures that users have their data available no matter which client computer they log on with. See *folder redirection* in this chapter for more information.

---

### Notes

- Legacy (pre–Windows 2000) applications may not be aware of the *My Documents* folders, in which case administrators may need to instruct users how to locate and store their work manually in their *My Documents* folders for these applications.

- If roaming user profiles have been configured for your users, they may experience a delay when they log on or log off the network. This is caused by the contents of the *My Documents* folder being copied to and from the network file server where their roaming profiles are stored. Overall network performance can be degraded for other users as well when many megabytes of files are copied across the network. In a situation like this, implementing *home folders* might be a better way of storing user files on the network.

### See Also

*folder redirection(3)*, *home folder(3)*, *user profile(3)*

---

## native mode

A domain mode that supports only Windows 2000 domain controllers and not downlevel Windows NT ones.

### Description

When you create a new Windows 2000 domain either by installing a fresh copy of Windows 2000 Server on a computer and promoting it to the role of domain controller or by upgrading the PDC of an existing Windows NT domain, the resulting Windows 2000 domain is set by default to operate in mixed mode to support downlevel Windows NT domain controllers. Once your Windows NT domain has fully migrated to Windows 2000, there are several reasons why you should change the domain to native mode—a mode that does not support backward compatibility with Windows NT domain controllers. The main reason is that native mode supports the following features that mixed mode does not:

- Universal groups (mixed mode supports only global and domain local groups)

- Nesting of groups beyond a single level

- Automatic transitive trusts between domains in a tree

- Kerberos v5 as the network authentication protocol, instead of NTLM

---

For information on mixed mode, see *mixed mode* later in this chapter. For information on converting modes, see *domain* in Chapter 4.

---

### Notes

- If a domain is running in native mode, users cannot log on to the network unless a global catalog server is available for them to connect to.
- You can switch a domain from mixed mode to native mode, but not the reverse.
- It's OK to have some domains running in native mode and others in mixed mode during the migration process. Clients will still be able to access network resources as they have been doing it in the mixed-mode domains.

### See Also

*domain(3,4), mixed mode(3)*

---

## NetBEUI

A fast and efficient LAN protocol used for small workgroups.

### Description

NetBEUI is suitable only for use in small workgroups consisting of a few dozen computers. This is because:

- It is not routable and hence cannot be used in an internetwork with many subnetworks connected by routers.
- Active Directory cannot be used on top of NetBEUI, and so you cannot use it to build Windows 2000 domains.
- It cannot be used to connect to the Internet without a suitable gateway to translate between NetBEUI and TCP/IP.
- It relies strongly on broadcasts for its operation, which limits the number of workstations that can effectively communicate with it on a network segment.

As a result, it is generally better to abandon NetBEUI altogether and adopt TCP/IP, the default Windows 2000 networking protocol. If you do want to install it, however, see *network protocol* in Chapter 4.

### Notes

- Once NetBEUI is installed, there is nothing to configure.
- I've heard that Microsoft plans to abandon NetBEUI in Whistler, the next release of Windows 2000—it's about time!

### See Also

*network protocol(3,4), TCP/IP(3,4)*

---

## Network

Built-in system group representing all users who are currently accessing a resource on the local computer from over the network.

### See Also

*built-in group(3)*

---

## network protocol

A protocol used for communication over a network.

### Description

Windows 2000 Server supports four common network protocols:

*NetBEUI*
> A fast, efficient protocol that is nonroutable and, therefore, primarily of use in a small, workgroup setting where machines running older versions of Microsoft Windows need to be supported

*NWLink*
> Microsoft's version of Novell's IPX protocol; used primarily to support legacy Novell NetWare 3.x and 4.x networks

*TCP/IP*
> The widely supported Internet protocol that has become the de facto standard for LANs and WANs today

*AppleTalk*
> Microsoft's version of Apple's legacy protocol for networking Macintosh computers

For more information on any of these protocols, see their associated topic in this chapter. For general information about types of network connections supported by Windows 2000 Server, see *connection* in this chapter. For information on how to install and configure network protocols, see *network protocol* in Chapter 4.

### Notes

If you want to use Active Directory, you must use TCP/IP.

### See Also

*connection(3)*, *NetBEUI(3)*, *Network and Dial-up Connections(6)*, *network protocol(4)*, *NWLink(3)*, *TCP/IP(3)*

---

## NWLink

Microsoft's version of Novell's LAN protocol suite IPX/SPX.

### Description

NWLink is an implementation of Novell's Internet Packet Exchange/Sequential Packet Exchange (IPX/SPX) suite of network protocols used in legacy Novell NetWare Version 3.12 and earlier networks (which exclusively use IPX/SPX) and in NetWare Version 4.1 networks (which support IP encapsulated into IPX/SPX). Novell NetWare Version 5 now supports native IP, making IPX/SPX obsolete.

The NWLink protocol supports two higher-level APIs:

*NetBIOS over IPX*
> To enable NetWare clients running NetBIOS to communicate with Windows 2000 servers

*Winsock*
> To support NetWare applications that use the Sockets API

### NWLink Terminology

To configure NWLink, you need to understand its terminology, which is borrowed from IPX/SPX:

*Network number*
> Also called an external network number, a 4-byte hexadecimal number that uniquely identifies a network segment on a network running IPX. Network numbers are associated with the physical network adapters in the computers. All computers on the same segment that are configured with the same frame type (see later on in this list) must also have the same network number in order to communicate. Each network segment in an IPX internetwork must have its own unique network number.

*Internal network number*
> A 4-byte hexadecimal number that identifies a virtual network within a computer running IPX. Internal network numbers are used for addressing and routing purposes between client and server applications on different computers.

*Frame type*
> IPX supports different types of network frame formats, or different ways of putting the packet and header information on the wire. The supported types are:
>
> > Ethernet 802.2
> > Ethernet 802.3
> > Ethernet II
> > Sub Network Access Protocol (SNAP)
> > Token Ring 802.5

In general, two computers need to use the same frame type to communicate with each other. A computer can be configured to use multiple frame types, each associated with its own unique network number. Table 3-25 shows which frame types are used in different LAN architectures.

*Table 3-25: LAN Architectures and Their Supported IPX/SPX Frame Types*

| Architecture | 802.2 | 802.3 | Ethernet II | SNAP | 802.5 |
|---|---|---|---|---|---|
| Ethernet | ✓ | ✓ | ✓ | Defaults to 802.2 | |
| Token Ring | | | | ✓ | ✓ |
| FDDI | ✓ | ✓ | | | |

### When to Use NWLink

Some of the situations where you might use NWLink are:

- To enable NetWare clients to access Windows 2000 servers running File and Print Services for NetWare (a separate product obtained separately from Microsoft).

- To enable Microsoft Windows client computers to access File and Print Services on a NetWare server using Gateway (or Client) Services for NetWare (discussed elsewhere in this chapter).

See *NWLink* in Chapter 4 for information on installing and configuring the protocol.

### Notes

- NWLink also enables NetWare clients to directly access certain BackOffice components, such as Microsoft SQL Server and Microsoft SNA Server.

- Gateway (and Client) Services for NetWare do not support IP and, therefore, cannot work with NetWare 5 unless it runs IPX/SPX.

- The standard IPX/SPX frame type for NetWare 2.2 and 3.11 on Ethernet networks is 802.3. From NetWare 3.12 on, the default frame type is 802.2.

### See Also

*network protocol(3,4), NWLink(4)*

---

# offline files

A feature that lets users work with files in shared folders even when the network connection is unavailable.

### Description

When users want to work with their files, they typically connect to shared folders on network file servers to retrieve these files. When they modify these files, they save their changes in the shared folders. This procedure has several benefits:

- It allows users to roam between different client computers and still be able to access their files from a central location on the network.

- It centralizes management of users' files, allowing them to be easily backed up by administrators.

The downside is that when the network connection becomes unavailable—due to either a network problem or the file server being down—the users are unable to access their files and can't do their work. The solution is to use the offline-files feature of Windows 2000, which allows files stored in network shares to be cached on the user's local computer so that these files are always available for the user.

Use offline files if users frequently need to work offline with files stored in shared folders on network file servers. If you occasionally need to transfer files between a laptop and a desktop computer using a direct cable connection, Briefcase will suffice.

### How It Works

When offline files are configured, the process of accessing network resources is the same whether the user is connected to the network or not. When the user logs on, the locally cached copies of her files are synchronized with the copies on the network file servers so that both of files are identical. Once synchronization is complete, the user can begin working with her files. The user can access these locally cached files the same way she accesses the copies on the network—for example, by browsing My Network Places or Windows Explorer, entering the UNC path to the share in the Run box from the Start menu, or accessing a mapped network drive. The user works with the remote copy of the file in the shared folder on the network file server, but if the network connection to the file server becomes unavailable, the user is switched transparently to the locally cached version of the file on the user's client computer. The user still thinks she is accessing shared folders on the network, whereas she is actually working from her own offline files cache. A notification can be configured to appear over the system tray to alert the user that she is working offline. When the user logs off, her locally cached files are again synchronized with the copies on the network file server if the connection has been restored.

How the user works on the files depends on how you configure offline files on the server:

- If you specify *manual* caching for documents, then the user must specifically designate remote files or shared folders for offline use. Changes to files not designated for offline use are made only on the file servers. If the network connection fails, the file or folder is automatically taken offline and the user works only with the cached version.

- If you specify *automatic* caching for documents, then any remote files or the shared folders they are in are automatically cached locally for offline use. Any changes they make to the files are made to both the local and network versions of the files.

If the network connection is unavailable at the start of or during a user's session, the user can still work on his files locally. From the user's perspective, the process is the same as working with files stored on a network file server. This is particularly advantageous with computers that are, for the most part, only temporarily connected to the network, such as laptop computers.

If two users modify locally cached copies of the same file and one of them logs off (automatically synchronizing her files), when the second user logs off, a message will appear indicating that someone else on the network has modified the file and providing the user with the option of:

— Saving his version on the network

— Retaining the other version on the network

— Saving both versions on the network

In other words, changes made by two or more users are not merged but are handled intelligently.

### Implementing Offline Files

You must do two things to implement offline files on Windows 2000:

- Configure your file server for offline file operation. Windows 2000 Server computers have offline files enabled by default, but you need to configure how this feature should operate. In addition, you need to configure how offline files will be synchronized.

- Enable local caching of files on the client computer.

Tasks associated with these steps are outlined in *offline files* in Chapter 4.

### Notes

- Offline files lets you make any shared files or folders on a Microsoft network available for offline use, provided the computer supports Server Message Block (SMB) protocol for file sharing. This includes Windows NT 4.0, Windows 98, and Windows 95 computers, but does not include Novell NetWare servers.

- You can make shared folders, specific files within shared folders, or mapped network drives available for offline use on Windows 2000 clients.

- Heavy use of offline files can slow down the logon and logoff process for users. Enable this feature only when needed, such as for laptop computers or when the network connection is unreliable.

### See Also

*offline files(4)*, *shared folder(3,4)*

## OU

Stands for organizational unit, a type of container in Active Directory used to group objects for administrative purposes.

## Description

OUs are a form of container object in Active Directory—that is, they can contain other objects. For example, they can contain users, computers, groups, printers, or even other OUs. OUs are the smallest units in Active Directory to which:

- Permissions and tasks can be delegated (see *delegation* in this chapter)
- Group Policies may be applied (see *Group Policy* in this chapter)

### Using OUs

When Active Directory is installed on a computer (making the computer assume the role of domain controller for a domain), there are a number of default containers (some of them are OUs and some are other types) created within the domain container (see *Active Directory Users and Computers* in Chapter 5 for more information on these). In a small, single-domain implementation of Active Directory, you could simply use these default containers and create no additional ones. But in larger domains or in multidomain enterprises, it is useful to create additional OUs for delegating administration and applying Group Policy to specific collections of users, groups, computers, printers, and other objects.

The general strategy for using OUs within a domain is to create a hierarchical or tree-like structure at least two levels deep consisting of top-level OUs and lower-level OUs. (You can have more than one top-level OU—that is, you can have multiple trees in your structure.) The hierarchy you create should mirror the administrative functions and security needs of IT in your company, not the organizational chart of who is politically responsible to whom.

A different way of hierarchically structuring Active Directory is to create a hierarchy of domains instead of OUs. You should:

- Use a domain hierarchy when different portions of your enterprise need complete administrative control over their local users and resources, as in a decentralized-administration model.
- Use an OU hierarchy within a domain when different portions of your enterprise need only limited administrative control over users and resources, as in a centralized-administration model.

You can of course use both methods and create OU hierarchies within domains that are part of a domain hierarchy. See *Active Directory* in this chapter for more information on planning the structure of Active Directory.

When you're designing this structure, the top-level OUs should be carefully chosen so that they do not need to be changed afterwards unless a major company restructuring occurs. Top-level OUs should reflect some relatively static aspect of your enterprise, such as the different cities, states, countries, or continents in which it has a business presence, or the different kinds of objects you administer in Active Directory, such as users, groups, computers, and printers. If your enterprise is multidomain in scope (as with those with a national or international presence), then consider standardizing top-level OU names for all domains in your forest.

Once you've standardized upon and created your top-level OUs in each domain, you can create child OUs beneath them, which represent more granular levels of administrative authority. You can then delegate authority to different branches of OUs or individual OUs and apply Group Policies to manage them.

 If you create a child OU within a parent OU, the child OU inherits the settings of the parent OU by default.

Here are a few examples to illustrate how you might structure OU hierarchies within a domain or across domains:

- A company that does business both locally and in other countries and that administers these two business functions with relative independence could have two top-level OUs within its domain called National and Foreign. Users, groups, computers, and printers could be placed in the appropriate OU, and authority could be delegated by administrators to trusted users in each business area.

- A similar arrangement could be set up for a company that deals locally with both the private sector (wholesale or retail) and the public sector (government): create two top-level OUs called Private and Public. Within Public you could create two second-level OUs called Wholesale and Retail. Place objects in different OUs; delegate authority and apply Group Policies as desired.

- A company that has several large stores in different locations could have a separate top-level OU representing each store. Within each store OU, you could create second-level OUs for Sales and Support. Within each second-level OU, you could create third-level OUs for Users, Groups, Computers, and Printers. Within the Printers OU, you could have two fourth-level OUs called Standard and Color. You could then delegate administrative authority over the Color OU to a trusted user who knows how to work with color laser printers.

 How deep should you nest OUs when you create structure in your domain? The answer is basically "as deep as you need and no deeper." If nesting is too deep, then the structure can be more confusing than helpful, and application of multiple Group Policies can make permissions problems hard to troubleshoot. If nesting is too shallow, you won't be able to take advantage of delegation for shifting the burden of administration from Domain Admins to other trusted users in your company.

### Notes

- An OU can only contain objects from its own domain, not from other domains.

- Be sure to test your Group Policies and the tasks or permissions you have delegated to OUs as you implement them. This is especially important when there are several levels of OUs involved, as the application of policies can become quite complex.

### See Also

*Active Directory(3), Active Directory Users and Computers(5), delegation(3,4), domain(3,4), forest(3), Group Policy(3,4), OU(3,4), tree(3)*

---

## owner

The user who controls how permissions are set on an object.

### Description

Ownership is an aspect of permissions in Windows 2000. Every file or folder created on an NTFS volume has an owner. When a user creates a file, the user becomes the owner of that file and can set permissions on it to allow others access to the file. And when a user installs a printer, the user becomes the owner of the printer. Objects in Active Directory also have owners and can be assigned permissions as well.

Ownership cannot be given; it can only be taken. In order to assume ownership of a file or other object, a user needs Take Ownership permission. If the owner grants this permission on a file to another user, that user can then take ownership of the first user's file. Administrators, however, have the power to take ownership of any object that they can manage (anything except system objects essentially). For procedures on how to take ownership of an object, see *ownership* in Chapter 4.

### See Also

*ownership(4), permissions(3)*

---

## pagefile

A hidden file that provides virtual memory for applications requiring more memory than the available RAM.

### Description

Windows 2000 Server swaps code between physical memory (RAM) and a hidden file on the hard disk called the pagefile or paging file. This creates the illusion of virtual memory, that is, that the system has much more memory than it actually has (RAM + pagefile = virtual memory). The paging file is called *pagefile.sys* and is located by default on the root of the partition where the operating-system files are installed.

A pagefile that is too small limits the number of applications that can run simultaneously on the computer. More importantly, a small pagefile will cause information to be paged more frequently between RAM and disk, resulting in degraded system performance. On the other hand, a pagefile that is too large simply wastes disk space.

For information on managing the pagefile on Windows 2000 Server, see *pagefile* in Chapter 4.

### Performance and the Pagefile

The initial size of the pagefile should be no less than 1.5 times the RAM in your system. If your pagefile is spread across multiple partitions, then apply this guideline to the total paging file for all drives.

The pagefile grows as it is stressed when multiple applications are used. If it reaches its specified maximum size, it cannot grow any further and starting additional applications will not be possible.

If you have multiple physical disks in your computer, performance can be enhanced by spreading the pagefile across several disks, as long as each disk has its own controller to allow multiple, simultaneous reads/writes to be performed. Note that if you have only one disk with multiple partitions, it does *not* improve performance to spread the pagefile across the partitions. The best solution to improve performance is to buy more RAM and adjust your pagefile accordingly.

Another way to enhance performance is to move the pagefile entirely off the system/boot partition where Windows 2000 Server is installed. By moving the pagefile to a different physical drive on a two-drive system, the operating system and the pagefile will not have to compete with each other for disk access, improving overall system performance. Even better would be to move the pagefile to another physical disk that is on a separate controller from the system OS. However, in order to take advantage of the recovery options of Windows 2000 Server, you must place at least a portion of the pagefile on the boot partition (see *System* in Chapter 6 for more information).

### Notes

- The pagefile never decreases below its specified initial size. When you reboot your system, the pagefile is automatically set to its initial size regardless of how large it has previously grown since the last reboot.
- The minimum size of a pagefile on a partition is 2 MB.

### See Also

*pagefile(4), startup options(4), System(6)*

---

# password

Secret part of a user's credentials.

### Description

Passwords in Windows 2000 can be up to 128 characters long and can contain upper- and lowercase letters, numbers, and nonalphanumeric characters.

Here are some tips on using passwords in a Windows 2000 environment:

- Assign the Administrator account a complex password, and keep it secure. If you are really paranoid (or believe that someone in your enterprise might be running password cracking software), change the password every week or so.

- Let users control their own passwords. This frees administrators from maintaining lists of user passwords and places the onus of responsibility upon the user. It also removes the temptation for administrators to snoop in users' home folders.

- Educate users on how to select a password that is hard to crack. One suggestion is to think of an original and catchy phrase that is easy to memorize and then to form the password from the acronym generated by the phrase. For example, "I always brush my teeth two times per day" generates the password *iabmt2tpd*. Also educate users on what makes a bad password, such as your dog's name, postal code, phone number, and so on.

- Prohibit users from changing their passwords if multiple users share the same user account. For example, do this for temporary employees using a temporary account or the Guest account for network access.

- Required passwords for services or applications should be non-expiring.

### See Also

*user account(3)*

---

## permissions

Used for securing access to resources on the computer or network.

### Description

To grant users access to files and folders on the local computer or network, you assign these users permissions. However, there are two kinds of permissions that can be used to secure access to these resources: NTFS permissions and shared-folder permissions. You need to understand both kinds of permissions and how they work together.

### NTFS Permissions

NTFS is the primary Windows 2000 filesystem (FAT/FAT32 are not recommended for most purposes), and partitions formatted with NTFS can have their files and folders secured using NTFS permissions. These permissions secure the filesystem for *both local and network access*. For example, if user Mary Jones is granted NTFS Read permission on folder *Pub* and its contents (which are stored on her *C:* drive), she can log on to her machine, view the contents of *Pub*, and open any file stored in it. If *Pub* is then shared with the default shared-folder permissions of Full Control for Everyone, she can log on to a different machine and access the *Pub* share and its contents over the network. Whether Mary is trying to access a resource on an NTFS volume locally or over the network, NTFS permissions will apply.

### Special Permissions

The most granular NTFS permissions are called *special permissions*. These permissions give administrators the highest degree of control over how users can access files and folders stored on NTFS volumes. By selecting different sets of special permissions, administrators can create custom permissions for files or folders that need special access control.

The 18 NTFS special permissions are listed and described in Table 3-26.

*Table 3-26: NTFS Special Permissions for Files and Folders*

| Special Permission | Description |
| --- | --- |
| *Folders Only* | |
| Traverse Folder | Lets you drill into the folder to other files and folders, even if you have no permissions on intermediate subfolders |
| List Folder | Lets you view the names of subfolders and files in the folder |
| Create Files | Lets you create files in the folder |
| Create Folders | Lets you create subfolders within the folder |
| *Files Only* | |
| Execute File | Lets you execute the file |
| Read Data | Lets you read the file |
| Write Data | Lets you modify the file |
| Append Data | Lets you append to the file (you cannot modify existing data, only append) |
| *Both Folders and Files* | |
| Read Attributes | Lets you view the attributes of the file or folder (attributes include Read-only, Hidden, System, and Archive) |
| Read Extended Attributes | Lets you view custom attributes that may be defined by certain applications for the file or folder |
| Write Attributes | Lets you modify the attributes of the file or folder |
| Write Extended Attributes | Lets you modify custom attributes that may be defined by certain applications for the file or folder |
| Delete Subfolders and Files | Lets you delete subfolders or files |
| Delete | Lets you delete the file or folder (even if this permission is denied on a file, you can delete it if its parent folder has been granted Delete Subfolders and Files permission) |
| Read Permissions | Lets you view the permissions on the file or folder |
| Change Permissions | Lets you modify the permissions on the file or folder |
| Take Ownership | Lets you take ownership of the file or folder |
| Synchronize | Lets threads in multithreaded programs wait on the file or folder handle and synchronize with another thread that signals it |

### File Permissions Versus Folder Permissions

The NTFS special permissions are really too granular for administrators to use for securing files and folders in day-to-day usage. To make life simpler, Microsoft has grouped these special permissions into two different sets: *folder permissions*, for securing folders and their files and subfolders, and *file permissions*, for securing individual files within folders (and overriding folder permissions). These *standard*

NTFS *permissions* are described generally in Tables 3-27 and 3-28, while Tables 3-29 and 3-30 present a more detailed view by showing how they are created from NTFS special permissions.

*Table 3-27: Standard NTFS File Permissions*

| File Permission | Description |
|---|---|
| Read | Open the file and view its permissions, attributes, and ownership |
| Write | Modify the file, modify its attributes, and view its permissions, attributes, and ownership |
| Read & Execute | Execute the file, plus do everything Read permission allows |
| Modify | Delete the file and do everything Read & Execute and Write permissions allow |
| Full Control | Take ownership, modify permissions, and do everything Modify permission allows |

*Table 3-28: Standard NTFS Folder Permissions*

| Folder Permission | Description |
|---|---|
| Read | View contents of folder and view its permissions, attributes, and ownership |
| Write | Create new files and folders in the folder, modify its attributes, and view its permissions, attributes, and ownership |
| List Folder Contents | View contents of folder only |
| Read & Execute | Traverse subfolders within the folder plus do everything Read and List Folder Contents permissions allow |
| Modify | Delete the folder and do everything Read & Execute and Write permissions allow |
| Full Control | Take ownership, modify permissions, and do everything that Modify permission allows |

*Table 3-29: File Permissions as Combinations of Special Permissions*

| Special Permission | Read | Write | Read & Execute | Modify | Full Control |
|---|---|---|---|---|---|
| Read Data | ✓ | | ✓ | ✓ | ✓ |
| Read Attributes | ✓ | | ✓ | ✓ | ✓ |
| Read Extended Attributes | ✓ | | ✓ | ✓ | ✓ |
| Read Permissions | ✓ | ✓ | ✓ | ✓ | ✓ |
| Synchronize | ✓ | ✓ | ✓ | ✓ | ✓ |
| Write Data | | ✓ | | ✓ | ✓ |
| Append Data | | ✓ | | ✓ | ✓ |
| Write Attributes | | ✓ | | ✓ | ✓ |
| Write Extended Attributes | | ✓ | | ✓ | ✓ |
| Execute File | | | ✓ | ✓ | ✓ |
| Delete | | | | ✓ | ✓ |
| Delete Subfolders and Files | | | | | ✓ |
| Change Permissions | | | | | ✓ |
| Take Ownership | | | | | ✓ |

*Table 3-30: Folder Permissions as Combinations of Special Permissions*

| Special Permission | Read | Write | List Folder Contents | Read & Execute | Modify | Full Control |
|---|---|---|---|---|---|---|
| List Folder | ✓ | | ✓ | ✓ | ✓ | ✓ |
| Read Attributes | ✓ | | ✓ | ✓ | ✓ | ✓ |
| Read Extended Attributes | ✓ | | ✓ | ✓ | ✓ | ✓ |
| Read Permissions | ✓ | ✓ | | ✓ | ✓ | ✓ |
| Synchronize | ✓ | ✓ | ✓ | ✓ | ✓ | ✓ |
| Create Files | | ✓ | | | ✓ | ✓ |
| Create Folders | | ✓ | | | ✓ | ✓ |
| Write Attributes | | ✓ | | | ✓ | ✓ |
| Write Extended Attributes | | ✓ | | | ✓ | ✓ |
| Traverse Folder | | | ✓ | ✓ | ✓ | ✓ |
| Delete | | | | | ✓ | ✓ |
| Delete Subfolders and Files | | | | | | ✓ |
| Change Permissions | | | | | | ✓ |
| Take Ownership | | | | | | ✓ |

### Using NTFS Permissions

In order to configure NTFS permissions on a file, folder, or NTFS volume, at least one of the following must be true:

- You must be a member of the Administrators group.

- You must have Full Control permission for the file, folder, or volume.

- You must be the owner of the file, folder, or volume.

NTFS permissions must be *explicitly* applied to a file or folder in order to grant a user access to it. In other words, if a file has no permissions specified for a particular user or for the groups to which that user belongs, the user has no access to the file.

Having said that, however, when you explicitly assign permissions to a folder, by default all subfolders and files within that parent folder *inherit* the permissions assigned to the parent. Another way of saying this is that permissions automatically *propagate* from the parent to the child. This is done to simplify and speed up the job of assigning permissions.

If you like, you can later change the permissions to any subfolder or file within the parent folder without affecting the permissions assigned to the parent. In other words, you can *prevent* permissions inheritance at a given folder or file within the filesystem hierarchy. You can do this two ways:

- You can *copy* the permissions inherited from the parent folder to the subfolder or file under consideration and then explicitly modify these permissions as desired.

- You can *remove* the permissions inherited from the parent folder to the subfolder or file under consideration and then explicitly assign new ones as desired.

*Concepts
P*

Either way, the subfolder or file under consideration now becomes the new parent from which the subtree of files and folders beneath it inherit their permissions (a file has no subtree beneath it, of course). An example might help here: lets say that folder A contains folder B, which contains folder C, which contains file F. Begin by assigning Read permission to folder A for user Dennis. By default, this permission is automatically propagated to folders B and C and file F. Now prevent permissions inheritance from folder B by copying the permissions from its parent A. All folders and files still have Read permission for Dennis, but folder C and file F now inherit their permissions from folder B instead of A. Change the permissions on B from Read to Full Control. Folder C and file F now inherit Full Control permission from folder B, while folder A remains Read permission, as expected. In general, it simplifies things if you simply let permissions be inherited from their highest parent and don't try to prevent permissions at subfolders in the hierarchy unless absolutely necessary. Use the K.I.S.S. (Keep It Simple, Stupid!) principle when administering NTFS permissions, unless you're really good at keeping things documented. Otherwise, you may find yourself spending unnecessary time troubleshooting resource-access problems.

When you create a *new* file or folder on an NTFS volume, the new file or folder automatically inherits the permissions assigned to its *parent* folder. If the file or folder is created in the root directory of the volume, it inherits the permissions assigned to that root directory. By default, if you create a new NTFS volume by formatting a partition with NTFS, its root directory is assigned the permission Everyone has Full Control, so any new folder or file created in the root will automatically inherit Everyone has Full Control permission.

---

 It's generally a good idea when you create an NTFS volume to change the default Everyone has Full Control permission to Authenticated Users have Full Control before you start creating directories and storing files on the volume. This enhances the security of the volume since the Authenticated Users built-in system group represents all users who have valid domain user accounts on the network, while the Everyone group also includes untrusted users from other connected networks.

What you shouldn't do is try to modify the default permissions of system volumes like the \ *Winnt* folder. These permissions are necessary for the proper functioning of the operating system, so don't change them.

---

If you assign a particular user or group permission on a *folder*, by default the user or group is granted the three permissions—Read & Execute, List Folder Contents, and Read—for the folder. You can then change these permissions to whatever kind of access you want the user or group to have. Similarly, if you assign a user or group permission on a *file*, by default the user or group is granted the two permissions, Read & Execute and Read, for the file. Change these permissions to whatever kind of access you want the user or group to have.

When you assign a particular NTFS permission to a file or folder, you can either explicitly *allow* the permission to grant the user or group access to the object, or you can explicitly *deny* the permission to prevent the user or group from accessing it. Most of the time, you explicitly allow permissions to enable users to access files and folders, but there are certain situations where you might want to explicitly deny a user permission on an object. For example, if Bob has Read permission to the Accounts folder and all its contents, you could deny Bob Read permission to the particular document in Accounts that describes the plans for Bob's upcoming surprise party to prevent him from reading it. Users can have multiple NTFS permissions assigned for the same file or folder. This is because users can belong to groups, and permissions are assigned separately to user accounts and groups. For example, Susan could have Read permission on the *Pub* folder, while the Marketing group to which she belongs has Modify permission on the same folder. In the case of multiple permissions, the *effective permission* for the user is determined by adding them together (logical OR). In this example Susan's cumulative level of access to *Pub* will be Modify. To determine the effective permissions in a given situation, use Tables 3-27 through 3-30.

The exception to this is that a permission *denied* always overrides a similar permission *allowed*. For example, if Susan is denied Read permission to *Pub* while the Marketing group to which she belongs is allowed Read permission, she is effectively denied Read permission on *Pub*.

Permissions for a *file* override those for the *folder* that contains the file. For example, if Susan has Read permission on *Pub* but has Modify permission on the file *Readme.txt* within *Pub*, Susan will be able to make changes to the file and save them.

Once you've explicitly assigned permissions to your parent folders on an NTFS volume and started creating subfolders and files, you need to know what will happen if you try to copy or move these files and folders. This is because the act of copying and moving files and folders can have an effect on the permissions assigned to them. The general rules are as follows:

*Copying files or folders*
> Whether the destination parent folder is on the same or different NTFS volume, the copied file or folder inherits the permissions of the parent folder.

*Moving files or folders*
> If the destination parent folder is on the same NTFS volume, the moved file or folder retains its original permissions. However, if the destination parent folder is on a different NTFS volume, the moved file or folder inherits the permissions of the parent folder (since a move to a different volume is really a copy followed by the delete of the original).

For both copies and moves, if the destination volume is formatted with FAT, all permissions are lost from the copied or moved file or folder. For more information on copying and moving files on NTFS volumes, see *files and folders* in Chapter 4.

### Shared-Folder Permissions

NTFS permissions are the primary means of securing filesystem resources on a computer or network. However, they can only be used on volumes formatted with

NTFS, and not on FAT or FAT32 volumes. Furthermore, assigning NTFS permissions to a folder does not make the contents of that folder available over the network. To do this, we have to *share* the resource, and this means we have to deal with a whole other set of permissions called shared-folder permissions and how these combine with NTFS permissions to secure shared network resources.

Shared-folder permissions are permissions assigned to folders or volumes that have been shared. These folders may be on NTFS, FAT, or FAT32 volumes, and any of these volumes may themselves be shared at their root directory. In fact, shared-folder permissions are the only permissions that can be used to secure resources on FAT and FAT32 volumes. Shared folders only secure resources at the network level, however, and not at the local level. For example, if you share the folder *Pub,* which is located on a FAT volume, you control which users can access the folder over the network and the level of access they can have, but anyone who can log on locally to the machine where the volume is located has unrestricted (full) access to the folder and all its contents. So if you are concerned about securing resources from local access, you must use NTFS instead of FAT or FAT32. Microsoft correctly recommends that all volumes where applications, data, or users' home folders are located should be NTFS.

Another reason for always using NTFS is that shared-folder permissions are not as granular as NTFS permissions for controlling access, as you can see from Table 3-31 (note that there is no equivalent in shared-folder permissions to the highly granular NTFS special permissions). Also, shared-folder permissions apply uniformly to the folder and all its contents; if you want to prevent shared-folder permissions at a subfolder of a shared folder, you must create a new share at the subfolder. Furthermore, shared-folder permissions can only be applied to folders and volumes, while NTFS permissions can also be applied to individual files.

*Table 3-31: Shared-Folder Permissions*

| Permission | Description |
|---|---|
| Read | View contents of folder and traverse subfolders, open files and view their attributes, and run executable files |
| Change | Create new files and folders in the folder, modify and append data to files, modify file attributes, delete folders and files, plus do everything Read permission allows |
| Full Control | Take ownership and modify permissions of files (on NTFS volumes only), plus do everything Change permission allows |

### Using Shared-Folder Permissions

In order to share a folder and configure its permissions, you must be a member of at least one of the following built-in groups:

- Administrators
- Server Operators
- Power Users

In addition, if the folder you want to share is on an NTFS volume, you must have a minimum NTFS permission of Read for the folder in order to share it.

Folders (or volumes) must be shared and permissions *explicitly* assigned in order to grant a user access to the contents over the network. If a folder is shared but no shared-folder permissions are explicitly assigned to it, users will be able to see the share in My Network Places, but they won't be able to access its contents. Sharing a volume simply means sharing the root folder on the volume.

When you assign a particular shared-folder permission from the list in Table 3-31, you can either explicitly *allow* the permission for the folder to grant the user or group access to the contents of the folder, or you can explicitly *deny* the permission to prevent the user or group from accessing it. Most of the time you will explicitly allow permissions instead of denying them.

When you share a folder, the default shared-folder permission assigned to it is Everyone has Full Control. It's usually a good idea to change this to Users have Full Control before you start storing files in the folder. When you assign a particular user or group permissions on a shared folder, by default the user or group is granted only Read permission for the folder. You can then change the permissions to whatever kind of access you want the user or group to have.

Like NTFS permissions, users can have multiple shared-folder permissions for the same folder—for example, when the user account is assigned one permission while a group to which the user account belongs is assigned a different permission. The *effective permission* is determined again by adding the different permissions together (logical OR). Once again, a permission denied always overrides a similar permission allowed. Copying or moving files to other shared folders always gives them the permissions assigned to the destination folder. Copying the shared folder itself leaves the original folder shared but the new folder not shared. Moving a shared folder causes it to stop being shared.

### General Strategy for Assigning Permissions

The general strategy for using permissions to secure shared network resources is to proceed as follows:

1. Format the volume where the shared folder will be created using NTFS instead of FAT or FAT32. Create the folder you are going to share.

2. Assign NTFS permissions to the folder first. Grant your users and groups suitable levels of access to the folder, giving each user and group only as much access as they need. It generally simplifies administration if you only assign permissions to groups and not to individual users. Check your NTFS permissions assignments to make sure they are correct.

3. Now share the folder and leave its shared-folder permission set to the default Everyone has Full Control setting. You're done.

The advantage of doing things this way is that you really only have to deal with configuring one set of permissions, namely NTFS. For comparison, let's say you followed this strategy instead:

1. Format the volume using NTFS. Create the folder you are going to share, and leave its NTFS permissions set to the default Everyone has Full Control setting.

2. Share the folder and grant your users and groups suitable levels of access to the folder using shared-folder permissions.

The problems with this scenario are:

- The folder is secure for network access but not for local access. So if some-one is able to log on locally to the computer where the volume is located, they will have unrestricted access to the folder and its contents.

- Shared-folder permissions are limited to Read, Change, and Full Control, while NTFS folder permissions can be Read, Write, List Folder Contents, Read & Execute, Modify, and Full Control. NTFS permissions thus give you greater granularity in controlling access than shared-folder permissions.

- You can also use NTFS file permissions to control access to individual files or create custom permission lists using NTFS special permissions. You can't do any of these things using shared-folder permissions.

- Shared-folder permissions provide the same level of access for all files and subfolders within the folder, while NTFS permissions allow you to explicitly assign different permissions to subtrees of folders and files within the parent folder.

Let's take a look at one more strategy:

1. Format the volume using NTFS, and create the folder you are going to share.

2. Assign NTFS permissions for the folder to users and groups to grant them different levels of access. For example, assign the Marketing group Read permission for the *Pub* folder.

3. Share the folder and assign shared-folder permissions for the folder to users and groups to grant them different levels of access. For example, assign the Marketing group Change permission for the *Pub* folder.

The problem is, now you've got the administrative headache of managing two separate sets of permissions instead of just one. Also, you must be aware of how NTFS and shared-folder permissions combine. The general rule is: when NTFS and shared-folder permissions combine, the *most restrictive permission* applies. In other words, for the Marketing group:

Read (NTFS) + Change (shared folder) = Read (combined)

What use is this second set of permissions (shared-folder permissions) if our strategy will always be to carefully assign NTFS permissions but leave shared-folder permissions at their default of Everyone has Full Control? Simple: shared-folder permissions are the only permissions that can be used to control resources for data stored on FAT volumes. Why would you want to use FAT instead of NTFS? Possible reasons are:

- When you are setting up a peer-to-peer network using a workgroup model for a small business that can't afford an administrator to manage a domain controller.

- When you want to dual-boot a machine between Windows 2000 and Windows 95/98, which requires that you install Windows 2000 on FAT instead of NTFS.

Neither of these are particularly compelling reasons, however.

## Notes

- Always give users and groups just enough access to meet their needs. For example, don't assign Modify permission to a folder if you only want users to read files in the folder and not change or delete them.

- Never assign Full Control permission to folders used by ordinary users (except their home folder). Otherwise, a user might modify the permissions on the folder and cause difficulties for other users. Use Modify permission instead when you want to give the widest range of access to a folder for ordinary users. Modify will allow them to create, modify, and delete files and subfolders within the folder under consideration, which is pretty well all they ever need to be able to do.

- If you want users to be able to do everything except delete files, assign Read & Execute and Write permissions to the folder instead of Modify.

- By assigning Full Control to Creator Owner, users who create a subfolder or file within the given folder will have Full Control over that subfolder or file and will thus be able to delete it even if the Users group is assigned Read & Execute and Write permissions, as described earlier.

- A suitable NTFS permission for a folder where applications will be stored is Read & Execute. Folders used for storing data shared by different users should have Modify permission (or Read & Execute and Write, as described earlier). Home folders for users should be owned by users, and they should have Full Control.

- Assign the Administrators group Full Control of all folders except users' home folders, where they should have no access.

- Assign permissions to groups not users. To grant a user access to a resource, add the user to the group that has the suitable permissions.

- When you copy a file or folder on an NTFS volume, you become the owner of the copy.

- Denying a permission for a user takes precedence over any allowed permissions assigned to groups to which that user belongs.

- You can deny all access for a user or group to a folder or file by denying Full Control permission for that user or group.

- Always assign NTFS permissions to a folder first before sharing it. If you share the folder first, there is a chance someone might access the share before you have properly secured its contents.

- You can also use the built-in system groups called Network and Interactive to control access to shared resources:

  — Any permissions you assign to the Network group apply to all users who try to access the resource from other machines over the network.

  — Any permissions you assign to the Interactive group apply to all users who try to access the resource from the local machine where the resource is located.

## See Also

*files and folders(4), offline files(4), shared-folder permissions(4)*

## *power scheme*

A collection of settings for managing the power consumption of your system.

### *Description*

Windows 2000 Server includes a number of default power schemes, which are listed in Table 3-32. These power schemes determine how long a period of inactivity is required before your monitor and hard disk power down and before your system goes into standby when running on AC power. You can modify these default schemes or create your own schemes (see *power scheme* in Chapter 4).

*Table 3-32: Default Power Schemes*

| Name | Turn off Monitor After . . . | Turn off Hard Disks After . . . | Go into Standby Mode After . . . |
|---|---|---|---|
| Home/Office Desk | 20 min | Never | Never |
| Portable/Laptop | 15 min | 30 min | 20 min |
| Presentation | Never | Never | Never |
| Always On | Never | Never | Never |
| Minimal Power Management | 15 min | Never | Never |
| Max Battery | 15 min | Never | 20 min |

### *Notes*

- Your system hardware must be able to support power management for power schemes to work.

- On portables, you can specify one scheme for battery use and another for AC use.

### *See Also*

*hibernation(3,4), Power Options(6), power scheme(4), standby(3,4)*

## *Power Users*

Built-in group for granting users limited administrative rights and permissions on a member server, standalone server, or client computer.

### *See Also*

*built-in group(3)*

## *print device*

Hardware used to generate printed documents.

### *See Also*

*printer(3)*

# *printer*

A software interface between the operating system and a print device.

## *Description*

Printing terminology in Microsoft Windows can be confusing for users familiar with other operating-system platforms. You should be familiar with these four main terms:

*Print device*

A piece of hardware that generates printed documents; in common parlance, this is called a "printer."

*Print server*

The computer that is actually responsible for managing the print device. The print server receives print jobs from the client machines, formats them accordingly, and passes them to the print device to generate printed output. You need a print server in order for client computers to use a printer over the network.

 Print servers can be computers or dedicated network devices. If you use a computer running Windows 2000 Professional as a print server, you are limited to 10 simultaneous client connections; Windows 2000 Server has no such limit. To make sure your Windows 2000 print server performs effectively, make sure that it has lots of RAM for document processing and disk space for spooling.

*Printer*

Not a "printer" in the usual sense, but instead a software interface on the client machine that manages the printing process. This is sometimes called a "logical printer" but is usually just referred to as a "printer." A printer must first be created on a client machine for that machine to be able to print documents. Printers are also used to configure print devices by specifying things like print schedule, job priority, who to notify when the job is done, which paper tray to use, what print quality to use, and so on.

*Printer driver*

Software installed on the print server that processes jobs received from client computers and turns them into a series of printer commands, which can be understood by the particular type of print device being used.

## *Types of Printers*

Windows 2000 supports the same two kinds of print devices that were supported by earlier versions of Microsoft Windows:

*Local print device*

A printer directly connected to the print server using a serial, parallel, USB, or other physical port on a print server.

*Network-interface print device*

A printer directly connected to the network using its own network card. The print server manages the print device but is not directly connected to it.

### The Printing Process

The basic process of printing over the network works like this:

1. The user clicks the Print button on an application or performs some other action to print a document.

2. The printer driver on the client computer creates a print job by rendering the document into a series of printer commands, and then it spools (temporarily stores) the job for printing. By default, on Windows 2000 and Windows NT clients, the document is only partially rendered at this point, resulting in an enhanced metafile format (EMF) file. EMF is a kind of universal printer-command format. Typically, non-Windows clients fully render the document into a RAW file consisting of actual machine-specific printer commands. EMF can be disabled in Windows 2000 to use RAW instead, but EMF is preferred because a spooled EMF job typically occupies less disk space than a similar RAW one.

3. The client computer forms a connection with the appropriate print server using Remote Procedure Calls (RPCs) and then forwards the job to the print server.

4. The print server receives the job and spools it for further processing and until a print device becomes available.

5. The print provider (software on the print server) finishes processing the job by converting it from EMF into RAW format (if necessary).

6. When a print device becomes available, the job is despooled to the appropriate print monitor (more software on the print server), which then forwards the rendered document to the print device, which finally turns it into a printed document.

### Notes

- To control who can use a printer or who manages it, use printer permissions.
- You can create multiple printers for a given print device. One reason for doing so is having two different groups with different needs and privileges who are using the same print device. Different permissions, print priority, print times, and so on may be assigned to each group. For example, managers may be allowed to print documents at any time with top priority, while the large jobs submitted by accounts have low priority and can only be run at night.

### See Also

*net print(7), printer(4), print queue(4), print server(4), printer permissions(4)*

---

## printer driver

Software installed on a print server for rendering print jobs into commands understandable to the print device.

### See Also

*printer(3)*

---

# printer permissions

Used for securing access to printers.

## Description

To grant users access to printers attached to the local computer or connected to the network, you assign printer permissions. Permissions can also be used to specify who is allowed to manage printers and their documents. There are three levels of printer permissions:

*Print*
> Used to assign ordinary users permissions for connecting to printers, printing documents, and managing their own documents

*Manage Documents*
> Used to delegate the job of managing all documents to users with limited administrative privileges

*Manage Printers*
> Provides complete administrative control over all aspects of printers and the printing process

Table 3-33 gives more detail concerning the specific privileges conveyed by each of the previous three types of printer permissions. These permissions can be assigned to both users and groups, but assigning them to groups is preferred since it reduces the amount of administration needed. Note that printer permissions are only effective when the printer is shared for use over the network.

*Table 3-33: Printer Permissions*

| | Printer Permission | | |
|---|---|---|---|
| Printing Task | Print | Manage Documents | Manage Printers |
| Connect to a printer | ✓ | ✓ | ✓ |
| Print a document | ✓ | | ✓ |
| Pause, resume, restart or cancel your own document | ✓ | ✓ | ✓ |
| Manage job settings for all documents | | ✓ | ✓ |
| Pause, resume, restart, or cancel any user's documents | | ✓ | ✓ |
| Cancel all documents | | ✓ | ✓ |
| Pause or resume a printer | | | ✓ |
| Take a printer offline | | | ✓ |
| Share a printer | | | ✓ |
| Delete a printer | | | ✓ |
| Modify the properties of a printer | | | ✓ |
| Change the printer permissions | | | ✓ |

### Default Printer Permissions

The printer permissions assigned by default to a newly created printer are shown in Table 3-34. In order to modify these permissions, you must either:

- Be the owner of the printer
- Have the Manage Printers permission

*Table 3-34: Default Printer Permissions*

| Group | Default Printer Permission |
|---|---|
| Administrators | Manage Printers |
| Print Operators | Manage Printers |
| Server Operators | Manage Printers |
| Creator Owner | Manage Documents |
| Everyone | Print |

### Advanced Printer Permissions

The three basic printer permissions described previously are actually comprised of combinations of six advanced printer permissions, as shown in Table 3-35. This is a bit confusing since three of these advanced permissions have the same names as the basic printer permissions. Advanced permissions can be applied either to:

- This printer only
- Documents only
- This printer and documents

Advanced printer permissions can also be selectively modified to provide a group of users with special (custom) printer permissions, if desired. However, it is highly unlikely that you will need (or want) to do this.

*Table 3-35: Advanced Printer Permissions*

| Advanced Printer Permissions | Basic Printer Permissions | | |
|---|---|---|---|
| | Print[a] | Manage Documents[b] | Manage Printers[a] |
| Print | ✓ | | ✓ |
| Manage Printers | | | ✓ |
| Manage Documents | | ✓ | |
| Read Permissions | ✓ | ✓ | ✓ |
| Change Permissions | | ✓ | ✓ |
| Take Ownership | | ✓ | ✓ |

[a] Assigned to this printer only.
[b] Assigned to documents only.

### Planning Printer Permissions

Like access to any other shared resource, access to print devices is controlled by assigning permissions to groups and users. The best way of doing this is to:

1. Create a domain local group for a print device. Give the group a recognizable name such as HP5L Users (using the type or model of the device) or Barney Users (if you give your printers friendly names).

2. Assign the local group Print permission.

3. Put global groups into the local group to give users access to the printer.

Also be sure to assign suitable permissions to Administrators or Print Operators so they can manage the device and its print queues.

### Notes

• Printer permissions may be allowed or denied, and denied permissions override allowed ones. For example, if you deny Print permission to Everyone, then no one will be able to print to the printer.

• All users are allowed to print by default, since Print permission is assigned to Everyone. You may want to remove this permission and assign Print permission to the Users group instead, so that only authorized users who have logged on to the network are allowed to connect to the printer and print to it.

• Alternatively, you may want to limit access for some printers to specific groups of users. For example, you could grant Print permission for using the color laser printer to the Managers group only.

• Printer permissions are most important with print devices used for printing sensitive business information, such as payroll checks. Make sure you restrict permissions accordingly for such devices, and be sure to locate them in secure areas as well.

• Users with Manage Documents permission do not have the privilege of printing documents unless they are also explicitly given Print permission as well. Users with Manage Printers permission do, however, also have the privilege of printing documents.

• If you have Macintosh clients on your network and Print Services for Macintosh is installed on your print server, these clients can print without restriction. In other words, there is no control of printer access for Macintosh clients.

### See Also

*printer(3,4)*

---

## Print Operators

Built-in group for granting users rights and permissions for administering network printers for the computer or domain.

### See Also

*built-in group(3)*

---

## print server

A computer used to manage print jobs sent to a print device.

*See Also*

*printer(3)*

## RAID-5 volume

A volume that spans more than one disk drive, contains parity information to provide fault tolerance, and which is organized in an interleaved fashion. RAID-5 volumes correspond to stripe sets with parity in Windows NT.

*See Also*

*disks(3)*

## Recovery Console

A minimal command-line version of Windows 2000 used to repair a system.

*See Also*

*disaster recovery(3), Recovery Console(4)*

## remote access

Allows remote clients to connect to a server or network using a dial-up connection over a phone line, a VPN connection tunneled through the Internet, or a direct computer connection using a null-modem cable or similar device.

*Description*

Remote access is designed to allow remote clients, such as mobile users with laptops, the ability to connect to their private corporate network and access shared resources on that network. This article covers the basics of the server-side portion of remote access in Windows 2000; for an explanation of the client-side portion of remote access in Windows 2000, see *connection* in this chapter.

*How Remote Access Works*

Apart from LAN connections, which are created automatically by Windows 2000, and direct computer connections, which are temporary connections used to transfer files between two machines, all other forms of connections are used for establishing or providing remote access to computers, networks, or the Internet. Remote access works as follows:

1. A remote-access client attempts to connect to a remote-access server (or remote-access device) using a WAN connection such as a dial-up connection over a phone line using a modem.

2. The remote-access server responds to the connection attempt from the client and negotiates a suitable WAN protocol, such as PPP, that both the client and server can understand. WAN protocols are discussed further later in this article.

3. The client uses the WAN protocol to encapsulate the network-level data packets (usually IP packets). Typically, both client and server need to use the same LAN protocol, unless the server is performing LAN protocol conversion in addition to providing remote access to the client.

4. The server provides the client with access to its own resources only, or it acts as a gateway to allow the client to access resources on the server's connected network, depending on how remote access is configured on the server.

### *Implementing Remote Access*

To implement remote access, you basically need to do two things:

- Configure a remote-access server to receive inbound connections from remote clients.

- Configure client computers with outbound connections for connecting to the remote-access server.

---

 An *inbound* connection is a connection configured on a remote-access server, while an *outbound* connection is a connection configured on a remote-access client. The connection is usually initiated by the remote client dialing in to the server or tunneling through the Internet.

---

In addition, you need to:

- Grant the users of your client computers suitable permission to connect to your remote-access server. This can be allowed or denied on a per-user basis by configuring each user's account, but it can also be managed by creating and implementing a remote-access policy (see "Remote-Access Policies" later in this article).

- Specify whether the clients can access only resources on the remote-access server or also resources on the LAN connected to the server (gateway function of remote-access server).

### *Implementing Server-Side Remote Access*

The rest of this article deals only with implementing the server side of remote access. For further information on the client side of remote access, see *connection* in this chapter.

There are two primary ways of implementing the server side of a remote-access solution using a Windows 2000 computer:

*Standalone remote-access server*
>This is a standalone Windows 2000 Server computer (or a Windows 2000 Professional computer) that has been configured to accept inbound connections from remote clients. Standalone remote-access servers are created and configured using Network and Dial-up Connections. For information on how to configure a standalone remote-access server, see *incoming connection* in Chapter 4.

*Domain-based remote-access server*
>This is a Windows 2000 domain controller or a member server belonging to a domain that has been configured to accept inbound connections from remote clients. Domain-based remote-access servers are created and configured using the Routing and Remote Access Service console in the Administrative Tools program group. For information on how to configure a domain-based remote-access server, see *remote-access server* in Chapter 4.

Both kinds of remote-access servers described earlier can accept dial-up, direct computer, and VPN connections from remote clients. You create and configure outbound connections on Windows 2000 computers using Network and Dial-up Connections. For information on creating and configuring specific types of outbound connections on client computers, see the following articles in Chapter 4:

- *dial-up connection*
- *direct computer connection*
- *VPN connection*

Also see *local-area connection* in Chapter 4 for information about how this type of connection is configured in Windows 2000.

---

 In Windows NT, outbound connections were created using Dial-up Networking in the Accessories program group, while inbound connections were created using the Remote Access Service (RAS).

---

## Remote-Access Terminology

There are a number of buzzwords associated with remote access, and I'll deal with them briefly here under suitable headings.

### LAN Protocols

Windows 2000 Server supports remote-access connectivity for the following LAN protocols:

*AppleTalk*
>Supports remote-access connections to Macintosh file and print servers using the AppleTalk Remote Protocol (ATCP) over dial-up PPP connections

*IPX/SPX*
>Supports remote-access connections to legacy NetWare file and print servers using the IPX Configuration Protocol (IPXPC) over PPP

---

*NetBEUI*

Supports remote-access connections to Windows NT RAS and legacy LAN Manager servers configured as NetBIOS gateways

*TCP/IP*

Supports remote-access connections to private TCP/IP networks and the Internet using TCP/IP over PPP or SLIP

For more information on different LAN protocols, see their associated articles in this chapter.

---

The phrase "TCP/IP over PPP" means:

— TCP/IP is the LAN protocol that both the remote-access client and server understand.

— PPP is the WAN protocol that both the client and server under-stand.

— TCP/IP packets are encapsulated into PPP frames in order to send them over the WAN link between the client and server.

---

**WAN Protocols**

Also called remote-access protocols, the following WAN protocols are supported by Windows 2000 Server:

*SLIP*

Stands for Serial Line Internet Protocol, a legacy WAN protocol that is not used much anymore. Windows 2000 Server can function as a SLIP client but not as a SLIP server. Windows 2000 SLIP clients must use TCP/IP and commu-nicate with SLIP servers via a serial COM port on the client machine.

*PPP*

Stands for Point-to-Point Protocol, the most common WAN protocol in use today. PPP is suitable for establishing WAN connectivity between different platforms such as Microsoft Windows, Unix, or Macintosh. PPP supports several methods for authenticating clients (discussed later) and also supports data encryption and compression. Windows 2000 supports PPP both for inbound and outbound connections and for any LAN protocol.

*Microsoft RAS*

This is a legacy WAN protocol that was used on Windows NT 3.1, Windows for Workgroups 3.11, MS-DOS, and Microsoft LAN Manager. Microsoft RAS protocol requires that these clients use NetBEUI. Windows 2000 Server supports both client and server implementation of Microsoft RAS.

*ARAP*

Stands for AppleTalk Remote Access Protocol. ARAP can be used by Macin-tosh clients to connect to Windows 2000 remote-access servers. Windows 2000 does not include an ARAP client.

### Multilink Connections

A multilink connection consists of multiple, physical connections combined into a single, logical connection. For example, you could use multilink to combine two 56-Kbps dial-up modem connections together into a single 112-Kbps connection to provide increased bandwidth for remote access. Windows 2000 supports two protocols for multilink connections:

*PPP Multilink (PPMP)*
> Allows one or more dial-up PPP connections to be combined into a single, logical connection. PPP Multilink can be used with modems, ISDN adapters, or X.25 cards to provide additional bandwidth for these connections.

*BAP*
> Stands for Bandwidth Allocation Protocol. BAP is a dynamic multilink protocol that allows physical links to be added or dropped as needed. This is particularly useful if service-carrier charges depend on bandwidth utilization by clients.

### Authentication Protocols

WAN connections can use any of several authentication protocols for authenticating remote-access clients that are attempting to connect to a remote-access server. The authentication protocols supported by outbound dial-up connections on Windows 2000 are (in order of increasing security):

*PAP*
> Stands for Password Authentication Protocol, an older scheme that transmits passwords as clear text.

*SPAP*
> Stands for Shiva Password Authentication Protocol, a variant of PAP developed by Shiva corporation that uses two-way (reversible) encryption for securely transmitting passwords. SPAP does not support data encryption, however, only password encryption.

*CHAP*
> Stands for Challenge Handshake Authentication Protocol. It uses the secure one-way hashing scheme, Message Digest 5. CHAP lets the client prove its identity to the server without actually transmitting the password over the WAN link, so it is more secure than the reversible scheme used in SPAP.

*MS-CHAP*
> Stands for Microsoft Challenge Handshake Authentication Protocol, a version of CHAP specifically tailored for Microsoft Windows remote-access clients and servers. A newer version MS-CHAP v2 requires both the client and the server to prove their identities to each other before allowing a connection. MS-CHAP v2 is supported only by Windows 2000, Windows NT 4.0, and Windows 98 clients and servers.

In addition to these authentication protocols, Windows 2000 also supports Extensible Authentication Protocol (EAP), an extension to PPP that supports a wide range of additional security mechanisms including:

* Token cards
* Smart cards

- MD5-CHAP

- TLS/SSL

 Windows 2000 also supports Remote Authentication Dial-in User Service (RADIUS), a client/server authentication protocol widely used by Internet Service Providers. RADIUS is implemented on Windows 2000 using the Internet Authentication Service (IAS) and provides a way of centrally managing user authentication, authorization, and accounting functions.

Table 3-36 summarizes which multilink and authentication protocols are supported by different Microsoft Windows dial-up clients.

*Table 3-36: Microsoft Windows Client Support for PPP Authentication Protocols*

| | Authentication Protocols | | | | | | | |
|---|---|---|---|---|---|---|---|---|
| Client | PAP | SPAP | CHAP | MS-CHAP | MS-CHAPv2 | EAP | PPMP | BAP |
| Windows 2000 | ✓ | ✓ | ✓ | ✓ | ✓ | ✓ | ✓ | ✓ |
| Windows NT 4.0 | ✓ | ✓ | ✓ | ✓ | ✓a | | ✓ | |
| Windows NT 3.5x | ✓ | ✓ | ✓ | ✓ | | | | |
| Windows 98 | ✓ | ✓ | ✓ | ✓ | ✓b | | ✓ | |
| Windows 95 | ✓ | ✓ | ✓ | ✓ | ✓c | | | |

a Requires Service Pack 4 or higher.

b Requires Service Pack 1 or higher.

c With the Windows Dial-Up Networking 1.3 Performance & Security Upgrade for Windows 95 only (supports MS-CHAPv2 over VPN connections but not over dial-up connections).

### Encryption Protocols

In addition to the encrypted authentication protocols described earlier, Windows 2000 supports several protocols for encrypting data transmitted over remote-access connections. These are:

*MPPE*
Stands for Microsoft Point-to-Point Encryption, a data-encryption scheme that uses a 40-, 56-, or 128-bit RSA RC4 encryption algorithm (depending on export requirements for your country).

*IPSec*
Stands for Internet Protocol Security, a scheme that uses a 56-bit DES or 168-bit Triple DES encryption algorithm.

 Be aware that data encryption is not supported for the following authentication protocols: PAP, SPAP, and CHAP.

### Virtual Private Network (VPN)

Windows 2000 supports creating virtual private networks (VPNs), which can be used to provide remote-access services to clients without the need of implementing a remote-access server or purchasing additional hardware such as modems or multiport adapters. Instead, you can utilize existing dedicated WAN or Internet connections, such as T1, lines to provide remote-access services to clients.

VPNs work by encapsulating LAN protocol packets, such as TCP/IP packets, into PPP frames. These PPP frames are then transported using a secure VPN protocol, such as PPTP or L2TP, over the WAN link. A common scenario for implementing a VPN is as follows:

1. Mobile users with laptops running Windows 2000 Professional have an outbound dial-up VPN connection configured on their machines. These users want to securely access their company's intranet using an insecure Internet connection. From a remote location a user dials up a regional Internet Service Provider (ISP) to gain access to the Internet to establish a VPN with their corporate intranet.

2. On the company side, a Windows 2000 Server with a dedicated T1 connection to the Internet has an inbound VPN connection configured on it. This remote-access server will use the insecure Internet for servicing remote clients, rather than using the traditional remote-access solution of using a modem bank (which typically adds the additional expense of leasing a number of additional phone lines for remote-access purposes, and since our company already has a T1 line anyway to provide LAN users with Internet access, then why not make use of it for remote access as well).

3. The client dials up her ISP and connects to the Internet. Once connected, the client uses PPTP or L2TP to establish a secure, encrypted communications session with the VPN server at corporate headquarters. In effect, the client securely becomes part of the corporate LAN by *tunneling* through the unsecure Internet between them.

---

 VPN connections can even be used within a LAN to provide secure network communications between a VPN client and a VPN server.

---

The two WAN protocols supported by Windows 2000 for creating VPNs are:

*PPTP*
　　Stands for Point-to-Point Tunneling Protocol, which is derived from PPP, uses PPP encryption for data, and works only with TCP/IP as the underlying network protocol. PPTP is generally viewed as less secure than L2PT but is easier to implement.

*L2TP*

Stands for Layer 2 Tunneling Protocol, which is derived from the Layer 2 Forwarding (L2F) protocol. L2TP supports both data encryption and tunneled authentication using IPSec and works with TCP/IP, X.25, Frame Relay, ATM, and other point-to-point packet-oriented WAN links (but the Windows 2000 version only supports TCP/IP natively). L2TP also supports header compression for more efficient transfer of data.

## Remote-Access Policies

A remote-access policy is a collection of conditions and connection settings. Remote-access policies simplify the administrative task of managing remote access for users and groups in your enterprise. Using remote-access policies, you can:

- Allow or deny remote access depending on the time or day of the week, the group membership of the remote user, the type of connection (VPN or dial-up), and so on

- Configure remote-access settings to specify authentication protocols and encryption schemes to be used by clients, maximum duration of a remote-access session, and so on

Remote-access policies consist of three parts:

*Conditions*

These are attributes that are compared to the settings of the remote connection to determine whether the connection attempt should be allowed or denied. If there are multiple conditions specified in the policy, they must all match the settings of the client or the connection attempt will be refused. Examples of conditions include the phone number of the remote-access server, date and time restrictions, domain-based groups the user belongs to, and so on.

*Remote-access permission*

If the specified conditions are met, then remote-access permission is either granted or denied, depending on how you configure this setting in the policy. (By default, this is set to Deny when a new policy is created.)

*Profile*

These are settings applied to the connection once it has been authorized (in other words, once remote-access permission has been verified—note that *authorization* is different from *authentication*, which has to do with the user's credentials being accepted at the server end). Profile settings can include maximum session time allowed, whether Multilink is enabled, types of authentication protocols and encryption schemes allowed, and so on. These policy settings must also match the settings of the client, or the connection attempt will finally be denied.

Remote-access policies are configured using the Routing and Remote Access Service console. They are contained within the Remote Access Policies container under the server node in the console tree.

There is a default remote-access policy created when the Routing and Remote Access Service is installed on a computer. This policy is called "Allow access if dial-in permission is enabled" and specifies that users will be denied remote-access permission by the policy if:

- Their user account has its remote access controlled by remote-access policies (the default on a native-mode, domain-based, or standalone Windows 2000 remote-access server).

- Their account logon restrictions allow them to log on anytime (also the default).

In other words, the default remote-access policy denies remote access to all users unless a user account explicitly has remote access allowed for it.

See *remote-access server* in Chapter 4 for procedures on implementing remote-access policies on a remote-access server.

---

 Remote-access policies are stored on their associated remote-access servers in Windows 2000 rather than in Active Directory to facilitate application of these policies to client connections without generating additional network traffic.

---

### How Remote-Access Policies Work

Let's start by considering how remote access by users to a remote-access server can be explicitly controlled without using remote-access policies. You explicitly allow or deny a user remote-access permission by using the Dial-in tab of the property sheet for the user account, using the:

- Local Users and Groups in the Computer Management console on a stand-alone Windows 2000 Server computer (or on a Windows 2000 Professional computer)

- Active Directory Users and Groups console on a Windows 2000 domain controller or a member server that belongs to a domain

If you want to control remote access for users using remote-access policies, however, then instead of selecting Allow or Deny on the Dial-in tab for a user, you specify instead that Windows 2000 should "Control access through Remote-Access Policy." (This setting is configured by default for built-in and new users in Windows 2000 domains configured to run in native mode, and on standalone Windows 2000 remote-access servers.) In this case the permissions setting of the policy will determine whether the user will be allowed to establish a connection with the remote-access server.

If your Windows 2000 domain is running in mixed mode, you do *not* have the option of selecting "Control access through Remote-Access Policy"—this option is grayed out on the user account's property sheet. The reason is that mixed-mode domains may contain both Windows 2000 and Windows NT domain controllers, and Windows NT RAS servers do not support remote-access policies. You should convert your domain from mixed mode to native mode if you want to use remote-access policies on domain-based remote-access servers (standalone Windows 2000 servers do support remote-access policies, however). If you have a domain-based remote-access server running in a mixed-mode domain, you should delete the default remote-access policy if it is present.

By default, all built-in and new user accounts on native-mode domain-based and standalone remote-access servers have "Control access through Remote-Access Policy" selected in their properties (unless their setting was previously changed from Deny to Allow, in which case it becomes Deny). On mixed-mode domain-based servers, all built-in and new user accounts have Deny as their remote-access permission.

Remote-access policies are used to control connection attempts in the following way:

1. The remote client (with the user account set to "Control access through Remote-Access Policy") tries to connect to a remote-access server (here a domain-based server where the domain is running in native mode).

2. The server checks its list of policies:

   — If there is no remote-access policy configured, the connection is refused.

   — If there is only one policy, all conditions in the policy must match the user's connection settings in order to move on to step 3.

   — If there are multiple policies, these are tested in order, one at a time, until one matches and you move on to step 3, or all fail and the connection is refused.

3. If a policy whose conditions match the user is found, the server checks the remote-access permission of the policy. If this is set to Deny, then connection is refused; otherwise, move on to step 4.

4. If remote-access permission has been allowed to the user through a policy, the server checks the profiles associated with the policy. If these profile settings match the user, the connection is established and the user connects to the server; otherwise, no other untried policies are tried and the connection is finally refused.

For information on how to create and configure remote-access policies, see *remote-access server* in Chapter 4.

### See Also

*connection(3), dial-up connection(4), direct computer connection(4), incoming connection(4), local-area connection(4), Network and Dial-up Connections(6), remote-access server(4), Routing and Remote Access(5), VPN connection(4)*

---

## restore

The process of restoring system information or datafiles from backup media.

### See Also

*backup and restore(4), disaster recovery(3)*

---

## *rights*

Privileges to perform different system tasks.

### *Description*

User rights are a kind of privilege granted to users and groups that allow them to perform specific tasks, such as:

- Logging on locally to a computer
- Forcing a system to shut down from a remote console
- Adding workstations to a domain
- Backing up files and directories

By default, the Administrators group is granted the most rights on a system, but other built-in groups have different rights assigned to them as well. You can assign or remove rights from users or groups, but this requires good understanding of how Group Policy works, or the results may be unexpected. For more information see *rights* in Chapter 4.

---

 Rights are different from permissions, which grant users or groups different levels of access to NTFS objects, shared folders and their contents, printers, and objects within Active Directory. For more information see *permissions* earlier in this chapter.

---

### *See Also*

*Group Policy(3,4), Local Security Policy(3,4), permissions(3), rights(4)*

---

## *roaming user profile*

A type of user profile that enables users to access the desktop and personal settings from any machine on the network.

### *See Also*

*user profile(3)*

---

## *schema*

A portion of Active Directory that contains the definitions of all classes of objects that Active Directory can contain and the types of attributes these objects may have.

### *Description*

Active Directory contains a default schema that defines hundreds of different object classes and attribute types, and this may suffice for organizations implementing Active Directory on their network. The Active Directory schema, however,

---

is extensible and allows new classes of objects and types of attributes to be defined. For example, if documenting every user's favorite song is an important issue in your enterprise, you can create a new attribute called Favorite Song and make this a required attributed for all objects of the Users class.

Another way the schema might be modified is by installing a directory-enabled application from some third-party software company. Such an application may be designed to make certain modifications to the schema of Active Directory in order to perform its intended functions.

### Schema Objects

Schema objects are uniquely identified by an object identifier (OID), which is represented by a set of numbers separated by dots. OIDs form a hierarchical namespace that is ultimately administered by the International Standards Organization (ISO). You can apply to the ISO to register a portion of OID space for your company, and once this is approved, you can then create and assign OIDs within your subspace at will without fear that some other vendor's directory-enabled application will try to overwrite your OIDs for its own purposes.

For example, Microsoft has been assigned 1.2.840.113556 as their portion of OID space and can therefore create, organize, and assign any OIDs of the form 1.2.840. 113556.a.b.c . . . as they desire. As an example, Microsoft has organized their subspace as follows:

*1.2.840.113556.1*
A branch called Active Directory for defining and managing the schema

*1.2.840.113556.1.5*
A branch called Classes within the Active Directory schema

*1.2.840.113556.1.5.4*
A branch called Builtin domain within Classes within Active Directory

and so on.

### Modifying the Schema

To directly modify the schema, you can either:

- Create a custom administrative console by adding the Active Directory Schema snap-in to a blank MMC console
- Write a script that uses the Active Directory Service Interface (ADSI) to modify the schema automatically

The primary kinds of modifications supported include:

- Creating a new class
- Creating new attributes and adding them to an existing class

See *schema* in Chapter 4 for an example of how to modify the schema.

### Effects of Modifying the Schema

It's easy to cause havoc within your Active Directory by carelessly modifying its schema. For example, let's say you create a new class of objects and new attributes for it as well. Then you instantiate objects in that class (create objects that belong to the class) and assign values to their attributes. Now you deactivate one of the attribute types used by your new class of objects. The result? All the objects you created for that new class are suddenly invalid.

Another issue you should consider before modifying the schema is replication. Active Directory replicates schema modifications separately from replication of other objects such as users, groups, or computers. Schema modifications are made on a special domain controller in each domain called the schema operations master. Changes are made to this domain controller and are then replicated to all other domain controllers. You should be aware that if you create a new class or attribute in the schema and then mark it for inclusion in the global catalog, the global catalog is automatically generated from scratch again and replicated throughout your enterprise, which can use quite a lot of network bandwidth for a period of time (especially on slow WAN links between sites).

Finally, if you create a new class or attribute in the schema, it may not be displayed correctly (or at all) in the default tools included in Windows 2000 for administering Active Directory—namely, the Active Directory Users and Computers, Active Directory Sites and Services, and Active Directory Domains and Trusts consoles. These tools are specifically designed to support the default schema and may not work with extensions you define.

### Notes

- You cannot delete a class or attribute you have added to the schema; you can only deactivate it.

- You cannot deactivate the default schema objects that Windows 2000 creates when you install Active Directory.

- You cannot modify or deactivate attributes marked system.

- You cannot modify the syntax rules for attributes. For example, you can't create a numeric attribute that requires being specified using a base-5 field format.

- When you create a class, you can specify which attributes it must have and which it may have. Once the class is created you cannot change the "must" list.

- Don't confuse creating schema objects with creating user, computer, group, or other common objects. The latter are by far more important to daily administration of Active Directory, as far as administrators are concerned; modifying the schema should be a rare event (if done ever).

- You must be a member of the Schema Admins group to modify the schema. By default, the Administrator account in a domain is a member of this group.

- Members of the Domain Admins and Enterprise Admins groups have the right to add or remove members from the Schema Admins group, so you should carefully guard membership in the Domain Admins and Enterprise Admins groups.

### See Also

*Active Directory(3), schema(4)*

## security group

Type of group used for controlling access by users to network resources.

### See Also

*group(3)*

## security policy

The part of a Group Policy Object (GPO) that implements security in the domain and on local computers.

### Description

Security polices are used to secure various aspects of Windows 2000 computers. Security polices are implemented using Group Policy and can be identified with the following subset of a GPO:

Computer Configuration → Windows Settings → Security Settings

There may be as many as nine different groups of security policy settings depending on whether you are configuring security at the domain or local-machine level. See the section "Security" in the article *Group Policy* in this chapter for information on these different groups of settings.

#### Default Security Policies

There are three default security policies in Windows 2000 (for more information about each security policy, see their associated articles in Chapter 5):

*Local Security Policy*
This is actually a system policy (not a GPO) that can be configured on stand-alone Windows 2000 computers or on Windows 2000 computers that are part of a workgroup instead of a domain.

 Local Security Policy also exists on computers that are part of a domain, but you should use Group Policy instead to configure security on these computers, as this provides the benefit of centralized management of security settings.

*Domain Security Policy*
This is the Security Settings portion of the Default Domain Policy GPO, which is linked to the domain container in Active Directory Users and Computers.

*Domain Controller Security Policy*
This is the Security Settings portion of the Default Domain Controller Policy GPO, which is linked to the Domain Controllers OU within a domain container in Active Directory Users and Computers.

### Implementing Security Policies

You can implement security policies on Windows 2000 networks either by:

* Editing the default security policies described earlier

* Creating new GPOs linked to site, domain, and OU containers and configuring the Security Settings portions of these GPOs

In addition, you can use the Security Configuration and Analysis tool and the *Secedit.exe* command-line tool to implement and analyze security settings on individual computers or groups of computers.

For more information on implementing security policies, see *security policy* in Chapter 4.

### See Also

*Domain Controller Security Policy(5), Domain Security Policy(5), Group Policy(3,4,5), Local Security Policy(5), security policy(4)*

---

## Server Operators

Built-in group for granting users the rights and permissions for administering servers.

### See Also

*built-in group(3)*

---

## service

A process that runs in the background on a machine to support client requests.

### Description

Services in Windows 2000 Server are the equivalent of daemons on Unix platforms. An example of a service is the World Wide Web (WWW) service, which runs on a server on which Internet Information Services (IIS) is installed. The WWW service runs in the background on the server, waiting to receive Hypertext Transfer Protocol (HTTP) requests from web browsers. When an HTTP request is received, the WWW service responds by sending the requested files or performing the requested action.

Table 3-37 provides a list of services on Windows 2000 Server computers. Note that this list contains both the services installed during a default Typical installation of Windows 2000 member server and domain controller, and also additional services added when optional Windows 2000 Server components are installed. Installing other Microsoft BackOffice applications, such as Microsoft Exchange Server or Microsoft SQL Server, also adds additional services to the list. Also shown in the table are the default startup types for these services, which are explained below and keyed as follows:

A (Automatic)
M (Manual)
D (Disabled)

*Table 3-37: Windows 2000 Server Services*

| Service | Startup Type | Description |
|---|---|---|
| Alerter | A | Notifies selected users and computers of administrative alerts |
| Application Management | M | Provides software installation services, such as Assign, Publish, and Remove |
| Boot Information Negotiation Layer | M | Provides the ability to install Windows 2000 Professional on PXE remote boot-enabled client computers |
| Certificate Services | A | Issues and revokes X.509 certificates for public key–based cryptography technologies |
| ClipBook | M | Supports ClipBook Viewer, which allows pages to be seen by remote ClipBooks |
| COM+ Event System | M | Provides automatic distribution of events to subscribing COM components |
| Computer Browser | A | Maintains an up-to-date list of computers on your network and supplies the list to programs that request it |
| DHCP Client | A | Manages network configuration by registering and updating IP addresses and DNS names |
| DHCP Server | A | Provides dynamic IP address assignment and network configuration for Dynamic Host Configuration Protocol (DHCP) clients |
| Distributed Filesystem | A | Manages logical volumes distributed across a LAN or WAN |
| Distributed Link Tracking Client | A | Sends notifications of files moving between NTFS volumes in a network domain |
| Distributed Link Tracking Server | A | Stores information so that files moved between volumes can be tracked for each volume in the domain |
| Distributed Transaction Coordinator | A | Coordinates transactions that are distributed across two or more databases, message queues, filesystems, or other transaction-protected resource managers |
| DNS Client | A | Resolves and caches DNS names |
| DNS Server | A | Answers query and update requests for DNS names |
| Event Log | A | Logs event messages issued by programs and windows; Event Log reports contain information that can be useful in diagnosing problems; reports are viewed in Event Viewer |
| Fax Service | M | Sends and receives faxes |
| File Replication Service | A | Maintains file synchronization of file-directory contents among multiple servers |
| File Server for Macintosh | A | Enables Macintosh users to store and access files on this Windows server machine |
| FTP Publishing Service | A | Provides FTP connectivity and administration through the Internet Information Services (IIS) snap-in |
| Gateway Service for NetWare | A | Provides access to file and print resources on NetWare networks |
| IIS Admin Service | A | Allows administration of web and FTP services through the Internet Information Services snap-in |
| Indexing Service | M | Indexes contents and properties of files on local and remote computers; provides rapid access to files through flexible querying language |

*Table 3-37: Windows 2000 Server Services (continued)*

| Service | Startup Type | Description |
|---------|--------------|-------------|
| Internet Authentication Service | A | Enables authentication, authorization, and accounting of dial-up and VPN users; IAS supports the RADIUS protocol |
| Internet Connection Sharing | M | Provides Network Address Translation, addressing, and name-resolution services for all computers on your home network through a dial-up connection |
| Intersite Messaging | A | Allows sending and receiving messages between Windows Advanced server sites |
| IPSEC Policy Agent | A | Manages IP Security policy and starts the ISAKMP/Oakley (IKE) and the IP Security driver |
| Kerberos Key Distribution Center | A | Generates session keys and grants service tickets for mutual client/server authentication |
| License Logging Service | A | Manages licenses |
| Logical Disk Manager | A | Logical Disk Manager watchdog service |
| Logical Disk Manager Administrative Service | M | Administrative service for disk-management requests |
| Message Queuing | A | Provides a communications infrastructure for distributed, asynchronous messaging applications |
| Messenger | A | Sends and receives messages transmitted by administrators or by the Alerter service |
| Microsoft Search | A | Manages search functions |
| Net Logon | A | Supports pass-through authentication of account logon events for computers in a domain |
| NetMeeting Remote Desktop Sharing | M | Allows authorized people to remotely access your Windows desktop using NetMeeting |
| Network Connections | M | Manages objects in the Network and Dial-Up Connections folder, in which you can view both local-area network and remote connections |
| Network DDE | M | Provides network transport and security for dynamic data exchange (DDE) |
| Network DDE DSDM | M | Manages shared dynamic data exchange and is used by Network DDE |
| Network News Transport Protocol (NNTP) | A | Transports network news across the network |
| NT LM Security Support Provider | M | Provides security to remote procedure call (RPC) programs that use transports other than named pipes |
| Performance Logs and Alerts | M | Configures performance logs and alerts |
| Plug and Play | A | Manages device installation and configuration and notifies programs of device changes |
| Print Server for Macintosh | A | Enables Macintosh users to send print jobs to a spooler on a server running Windows 2000 |
| Print Spooler | A | Temporarily stores files for later printing |

*Table 3-37: Windows 2000 Server Services (continued)*

| Service | Startup Type | Description |
| --- | --- | --- |
| Protected Storage | A | Provides protected storage for sensitive data, such as private keys, to prevent access by unauthorized services, processes, or users |
| QoS Admission Control (RSVP) | A | Provides network signaling and local, traffic-control, setup functionality for QoS-aware programs and control applets |
| Remote Access Auto Connection Manager | M | Creates a connection to a remote network whenever a program references a remote DNS or NetBIOS name or address |
| Remote Access Connection Manager | M | Creates a network connection |
| Remote Procedure Call (RPC) | A | Provides the endpoint mapper and other miscellaneous RPC services |
| Remote Procedure Call (RPC) Locator | A | Manages the RPC name service database |
| Remote Registry Service | A | Allows remote registry manipulation |
| Remote Storage Engine | A | Coordinates the services and administrative tools used for storing infrequently used data |
| Remote Storage File | A | Manages operations on remotely stored files |
| Remote Storage Media | A | Controls the media used to store data remotely |
| Remote Storage Notification | M | Notifies client about recalled data |
| Removable Storage | A | Manages removable media, drives, and libraries |
| Routing and Remote Access | D | Offers routing services to businesses in LAN and WAN environments |
| RunAs Service | A | Enables starting processes under alternate credentials |
| SAP Agent | A | SAP agent |
| Security Accounts Manager | A | Stores security information for local user accounts |
| Server | A | Provides RPC support and file, print, and name pipe sharing |
| Simple Mail Transport Protocol (SMTP) | A | Transports electronic mail across the network |
| Simple TCP/IP Services | A | Supports the following TCP/IP services: Character Generator, Daytime, Discard, Echo, and Quote of the Day |
| Smart Card | M | Manages and controls access to a smart card inserted into a smart-card reader attached to the computer |
| Smart Card Helper | M | Provides support for legacy smart-card readers attached to the computer |
| SNMP Service | A | Includes agents that monitor the activity in network devices and report to the network console workstation |

*Table 3-37: Windows 2000 Server Services (continued)*

| Service | Startup Type | Description |
|---|---|---|
| SNMP Trap Service | M | Receives trap messages generated by local or remote SNMP agents and forwards the messages to SNMP management programs running on this computer |
| System Event Notification | A | Tracks system events such as Windows logon, network, and power events; notifies COM+ Event System subscribers of these events |
| Task Scheduler | A | Enables a program to run at a designated time |
| TCP/IP NETBIOS Helper Service | A | Enables support for NetBIOS over TCP/IP (NetBT) service and NetBIOS name resolution |
| TCP/IP Print Server | A | Provides a TCP/IP-based printing service that uses the LPD protocol |
| Telephony | M | Provides Telephony API (TAPI) support for programs that control telephony devices and IP-based voice connections on the local computer and, through the LAN, on servers that are also running the service |
| Telnet | M | Allows a remote user to log on to the system and run console programs using the command line |
| Terminal Services | D | Provides a multisession environment that allows client devices to access a virtual Windows 2000 Professional desktop session and windows-based programs running on the server |
| Trivial FTP Daemon | M | Implements the Trivial FTP Internet standard, which does not require a username or password; part of the Remote Installation Services |
| Uninterruptible Power Supply | M | Manages an uninterruptible power supply (UPC) connected to the computer |
| Utility Manager | M | Starts and configures accessibility tools from one window |
| Windows Installer | M | Installs, repairs, and removes software according to instructions contained in *.msi* files |
| Windows Internet Name Service (WINS) | A | Provides a NetBIOS name service for TCP/IP clients that have to register and resolve NETBIOS-type names |
| Windows Management Instrumentation | A | Provides system-management information |
| Windows Management Instrumentation Driver Extensions | M | Provides system-management information to and from drivers |
| Windows Media Monitor Service | A | Provides services to monitor client and server connections to the Windows Media services |
| Windows Media Program Service | A | Used to group Windows Media streams into a sequential program for the Windows Media Station Service |
| Windows Media Station Service | A | Provides multicasting and distribution services for streamlining Windows Media content |
| Windows Media Unicast Service | A | Provides Windows Media streaming content on-demand to networked clients |
| Windows Time | A | Sets the computer clock |
| Workstation | A | Provides network connections and communications |
| World Wide Web Publishing Service | A | Provides web connectivity and administration through the Internet Information Services snap-in |

### Service Dependencies

When Windows 2000 Server boots, its services are started in a specific order based on the dependencies between them. A dependency is a relationship in which one service cannot function without the other service running. For example, the Print Spooler service depends upon the Remote Procedure Call (RPC) service already running, while other services such as the Fax Service and Print Service for Macintosh themselves depend upon Print Spooler to function.

### Service Settings

There are several settings that can be configured for Windows 2000 services. These settings are assigned default values by the operating system when they are installed, but you can also modify them if you desire. These settings are configured using Services in Administrative Tools and include the following:

*Status*

The status of a service can be started, stopped, or paused. Pausing a service typically keeps existing client connections to the service open while preventing new client connections from forming, but with some services it may have a different effect.

*Startup type*

Services can be configured to start in three ways:

*Automatic*

The service starts running automatically when the system is booted. Most services have this setting, but services may fail to start should the associated files somehow become corrupted or if other services on which they depend fail to start properly. Use Services in Administrative tools to view whether a service that has been configured for automatic startup has in fact started up and is running properly.

*Manual*

The service must be manually started by the user or by a dependent service that requires it. (A service that is listed as manual startup, but which is running, was started automatically by another service that required it.)

*Disabled*

The service does not start upon boot and cannot be started by a user or dependent service.

*Log On As*

Services require a security context to run in and must therefore be assigned an account for authentication and access purposes. By default, most services run within the context of a built-in account called the Local System account, which grants the services all the rights and privileges to run as part of the operating system.

*Recovery*

If a service fails (terminates unexpectedly or fails to start when configured for automatic startup), you can configure several levels of recovery actions that are taken. These actions include taking no action, attempting to restart the service, running a designated file, and rebooting the computer. By default, no recovery actions are specified.

### Notes

- For information on how to configure, install, pause, resume, start, and stop services, see *service* in Chapter 4.

- Services are typically disabled for security reasons to prevent unauthorized users or services from starting them.

- Services can be enabled or disabled for each hardware profile on the machine. See *hardware profile* in this chapter for more information.

- Some services have additional settings that can be configured. For example, the SNMP Service has settings for Agent, Traps, and Security, which you can configure from the property sheet of the service.

### See Also

*hardware profile(3)*, *service(4)*, *Services(5)*

---

## shared folder

A folder whose contents are made available for network users.

### Description

To make the contents of a folder on the local machine accessible to users on other machines on the network, you must share it. A machine whose dedicated purpose is to host shared folders is usually called a file server, but any Windows 2000 server or workstation can have shared folders created on it. In Windows Explorer and My Computer, shared-folder icons appear as folder icons with a hand holding them.

Just sharing a folder isn't enough, however; you also need to assign suitable permissions to the folder to control who has access to it and what level of access they have. For folders on FAT or FAT32 volumes, you can use shared-folder permissions to do this, but shared-folder permissions have certain limitations:

- They can only be applied to the folder and its contents as a whole and cannot be applied to individual files within the folder.

- They are not very granular and offer only a limited degree of control over access by users to the folder.

A better way of securing shared folders is to locate them on NTFS volumes. This is because NTFS permissions are more granular than shared-folder permissions. NTFS permissions can also be assigned to individual files within a folder, giving administrators a much greater degree of access control. For more information about both NTFS permissions and shared-folder permissions, see *permissions* in this chapter.

#### Planning Shared Folders

When planning which folders to share, here are some tips to follow:

- Use share names that are intuitive to the users who will be accessing them. Examples are *Pub* for public folder, *Apps* for applications folder, *Home* for home folder, and so on. Be aware that certain share names could cause difficulties for client computers running specific Microsoft Windows operating systems that try to access them (see Table 3-38).

---

- Try to group folders according to security needs and then share their parent folder, instead of sharing each folder individually. For example, if you have three applications stored in the folders *App1, App2,* and *App3,* place each of these folders into a parent folder called *Apps* and then share the parent folder. The fewer shared folders there are, the easier it will be for users to locate them on the network, and the less browse-list traffic they will generate.

*Table 3-38: Shared Names Acceptable to Windows Operating Systems*

| Operating System | Maximum Share Name Length |
|---|---|
| Windows 2000 | 80 characters |
| Windows NT 3.51 and 4.0 | 80 characters |
| Windows 98 | 12 characters |
| Windows 95 | 12 characters |
| Windows for Workgroups 3.11 | 8.3 characters |
| Windows 3.1 | 8.3 characters |
| MS-DOS | 8.3 characters |

### Connecting to Shared Folders

Once a folder has been shared on a file server, there are several ways in which users can connect to it from their client computers:

- By browsing My Network Places on Windows 2000 Professional clients (or Network Neighborhood on Windows NT 4.0 Workstation, Windows 98, or Windows 95 clients). This is probably the simplest way of finding a shared folder and connecting to it.

- By using Windows Explorer on Windows 2000 Professional, Windows 98, or Windows 95 clients (or Windows NT Explorer on Windows NT 4.0 Workstation). This is really the same method as the first item earlier, but using the hierarchical two-pane window interface of Windows Explorer instead of the one-pane window of My Network Places.

- By clicking Start, selecting Run, and then typing the UNC pathname to the shared folder. You can do this on Windows 2000 Professional, Windows NT 4.0 Workstation, Windows 98, or Windows 95 clients. Note that if you type \\*server_name*\*share_name*, you can open a window displaying the contents of the specific share, while if you only type \\*server_name*, a window will open displaying all shares on the specified server.

- By mapping a drive letter to the shared folder on any version of Microsoft Windows from WFW 3.11 onwards. This method can be used when you need to access a shared folder from an application that does not support UNC pathnames, when you need to back up the contents of shared folders over the network, or if you simply need a convenient way of accessing a particular share that you use often. To map a drive, right-click on My Network Places, and select Map Network Drive to start the Map Network Drive Wizard.

Concepts 8

### Notes

- In order to share a folder, you must be a member of at least one of the following built-in groups to gain the necessary rights:

  — Administrators

  — Server Operators

  — Power Users

  The Server Operators group is only available on domain controllers, while the Power Users group is only present on member servers and Windows 2000 Professional client computers. The Administrators group is present on all Windows 2000 computers.

  In addition, if the folder you want to share is on an NTFS volume, you must have a minimum NTFS permission of Read for the folder in order to share it.

- If you copy a shared folder, the copy is not shared. However, the original shared folder remains shared.

- If you move a shared folder, the moved folder is not shared.

- Folders can be shared multiple times, each time with a different share name and different shared-folder permissions.

- To temporarily prevent all users from accessing a shared folder, stop sharing it. This will immediately disconnect any users who had connected to the folder to access its contents.

- You can change the share name of a shared folder without stopping sharing it first. If you change the actual name of the folder itself, however, it will no longer be shared.

- Windows 2000 Server automatically shares certain system folders for administrative purposes. See *administrative share* in this chapter for more information.

- You can also share printers over the network. See *printer* in this chapter for more information.

- Shared folders and shared printers are often simply called "shares" in Microsoft parlance.

- When you are mapping a network drive, you can connect as a different user if desired. For example, if you are an administrator working at an ordinary user's desktop machine and you need to access the contents of a share whose permissions are restricted to Administrators, you can connect to the share using your administrator credentials and the Map Network Drive Wizard.

- Shared folders can be published in Active Directory so that users can locate and connect to them more easily. See *shared folder* in Chapter 4 for the procedure.

### See Also

*administrative share(3), net share(7), net view(7), permissions(3), printer(3), shared folder(4), Shared Folders(5)*

## simple volume

A volume created from contiguous free disk space that resides on a single disk drive.

### See Also

*disks(3)*

## site

A group of well-connected computers.

### Description

While a domain is a logical grouping of computers connected for administrative purposes, a site is a physical grouping of computers that are well connected to each other from the point of view of network bandwidth. Specifically, a site must consist of computers that:

- Run the TCP/IP protocol and are located on one or more subnets (TCP/IP is necessary to operation of Active Directory)
- Are joined by a high-speed network connection (typically, a LAN connection of 10 Mbps or greater with a high available bandwidth, but in some cases slower dedicated WAN connections)

Sites are created within Active Directory to mirror the physical layout of a large network. Sites consist of one or more subnets and should mirror the physical connectivity of your network. Computers joined by LAN connections typically form a site, while slower WAN connections form the boundaries between different sites. You thus might have a Vancouver site, a Seattle site, and so on within your enterprise.

 Sites and domains do not need to correspond in a one-to-one fashion. For example, one domain may contain several sites, or one site may contain several domains.

#### Site Terminology

There are several terms that need to be understood when working with sites in Windows 2000:

*Site link*
> A connection between two sites. A site link is defined by four components:
>
> *Cost*
>> This is a number used to determine which site link will be preferred for replication when two sites are connected by multiple site links. The higher the cost number assigned to a site link, the lower the priority of the link as far as replication is concerned. A cost of 1 represents the highest priority for replication.

### Member sites

This specifies the names of the sites that are connected together by the site link. Most site links join two sites only, but it is possible to create backbone site links that link more than two sites together.

### Schedule

This specifies the times when replication will occur between the sites. You might typically use 15 minutes over fast WAN links and longer time intervals over slower links.

### Transport

This the method used for intersite replication and can be either:

#### RPCs over IP

Use this transport when your WAN links are dedicated (always on). RCPs are only supported by dedicated network links. Typically, this means using a leased line, such as a T1 line, for your WAN connection.

#### SMTP over IP

Use this transport for asynchronous WAN connections such as dial-up ISDN links. SMTP is Simple Mail Transport Protocol, the mail protocol used on the Internet, and allows replication updates to be stored and forwarded as email messages.

### Site link bridge

A connection between two or more sites using multiple site links. Each site link in a site-link bridge must have a site in common with another site link in the bridge. This enables the bridge to calculate the cost value between sites in different links of the bridge.

---

 You should not need to use site-link bridges in fully routed IP inter-networks, as site links are transitive. As a result, all site links belong by default to a default site-link bridge, and this is sufficient. You can disable the transitive nature of site links if you are using IP as your transport, and this will require that site-link bridges be created, but this is a lot of extra work and usually offers little gain in performance.

---

### Subnet

A collection of IP hosts with a common subnet mask and network ID. Each site can consist of one or more subnets on your network.

### Bridgehead server

A single domain controller used in each site for replication with other sites. You can let Windows 2000 automatically select and configure a bridgehead server, or you can manually define one for each site transport. Once you decide to manually specify a bridgehead server, however, the Knowledge Consistency Checker (KCC) no longer selects another bridgehead server if the designated one becomes unavailable.

## Using Sites

There are a number of ways in which creating sites can help optimize the performance of your Windows 2000 network.

### Logon Traffic

When a user attempts to log on to the network, the user's client computer contacts a domain controller to accomplish this. By default, Windows 2000 Professional client computers try to find a domain controller in their own site to authenticate the user. In this way valuable WAN-link bandwidth is conserved by not attempting to authenticate the user by remote domain controllers in other sites.

You may also want to have one global catalog server in each site to facilitate logons in a multidomain forest. This may not be practical, though, since increasing the number of global catalog servers can significantly increase network traffic due to the partial replication of Active Directory, which occurs when global catalog servers are maintained. For small single-domain sites, the best solution may be to place one domain controller there and configure it to host the global catalog as well. See *global catalog* in this chapter for more information.

### Replication Traffic

Sites can be used to schedule Active Directory replication traffic so that it occurs during off-peak hours. This gives administrators more control over replication traffic on their network. The reason is due to how the replication process works within a site (intrasite) and between sites (intersite):

#### Intrasite replication

Replication has low latency within a site, with the result that all domain controllers within a site almost always tend to be fully synchronized. If you make an update to Active Directory on one domain controller, this update is replicated to other domain controllers in the site five minutes after the update was made. The way it works is that the domain controller on which the update was made notifies its replication partners, which then pull the updates from it. The topology of intrasite replication between domain controllers in a site is configured automatically by the KCC, and it does not need any further manual configuration by administrators. (The KCC is usually smart enough to establish the optimal replication topology within a site.)

#### Intersite replication

Replication between sites can be scheduled to utilize slow intersite WAN links during off-peak hours. In addition, replication information is compressed by about a factor of 10 to make more efficient use of these slow links. Intersite replication does not use notifications the way intrasite replication does. Intersite replication is enabled by creating site links between different sites.

Compression is only used for intersite replication traffic when the information to be updated exceeds 50 KB.

### Distributed File System (Dfs)

If you have implemented Dfs on your network and have replicas of a shared folder located in different sites, users will be automatically directed to the replica in their own site first if one exists, again conserving valuable WAN link bandwidth between sites. See *Dfs* in this chapter for more information.

### Site-Enabled Applications

Finally, newer Active Directory–aware applications, such as Microsoft Exchange 2000 Server, can take advantage of sites to optimize messaging and replication traffic. More of these applications will become available as time goes by.

## Planning Sites

Implementing sites on your network requires planning. The following are some of the issues you need to consider when planning sites:

*Default-First-Site*
> When you install your first Windows 2000 domain controller, creating a forest root domain in a new forest, a default site is also created called the Default-First-Site. You can rename this site to something more descriptive before you start creating new sites.

*Site boundaries*
> Start by identifying the slow WAN links between different physical locations of your network, and use this information to create your sites.

*Subnets*
> Each site must consist of one or more IP subnets. Look for subnets that are joined by high-speed LAN or WAN connections in your enterprise, and use this information to create subnet objects in Active Directory Sites and Services, associating them with your site objects.

*Site links*
> Sites must be connected to each other by site links in order for replication to occur between each other. Select the appropriate transport, specify the cost, and schedule replication for your site links as desired.

*Domain controllers*
> Domain controllers should be placed where client computers can easily access them over high-bandwidth connections. Usually, the best solution is to place at least one domain controller in a site for each domain that is part of the site. The exception is when your site is a small branch office with only a few computers, in which case using the slow WAN link for logons would be acceptable.

*Notes*

- Do not create additional sites unless you need them, since it may result in inefficient use of network bandwidth or poor performance of domain controller logon and replication functions.

- Every site must have at least one site link for each site it is connected to, otherwise domain controllers in the site will never replicate with those in the other connected sites.

- If you schedule your site links to replicate only once a day (say at 3 a.m.), then replication latency may be unacceptably high in environments where frequent changes are made to user and group settings. Using a more aggressive schedule (once an hour) is recommended in most cases.

- If you have both a high-speed backbone link, such as a T3 link, and a slow redundant backup link, such as a 56-Kbps link, between two sites, you might configure a cost value of 1 for the backbone link and 100 for the redundant link. That way, the redundant link will never be used unless the high-speed backbone link is down.

- Multihomed computers can only belong to a single site.

- When SMTP is used as the transport for site links, the replication schedule is ignored.

- SMTP used as a replication transport consumes about twice the network bandwidth as RPCs over IP because updates need to be packaged in SMTP messages.

- SMTP can be used to replicate schema, configuration, and global catalog information between sites, but it cannot be used to replicate between domain controllers belonging to the same domain. If you use SMTP as your transport, then your sites should be separate domains.

*See Also*

*Active Directory(3), Active Directory Sites and Services(5), Dfs(3), domain(3,4), global catalog(3), site(4)*

---

## spanned volume

A volume that spans more than one disk drive and that is filled up sequentially disk-by-disk. Spanned volumes correspond to volume sets in Windows NT.

*See Also*

*disks(3)*

---

## standalone server

A Windows 2000 Server computer that is configured as part of a workgroup instead of a domain.

*See Also*

*workgroup(3)*

## standby

A power-management mode in which both the display and hard drive are powered down to save power.

*See Also*

*standby(4)*

## striped volume

A volume that spans more than one disk drive and is filled up in an interleaved fashion. Striped volumes correspond to stripe sets in Windows NT.

*See Also*

*disks(3)*

## system partition/volume

The partition or volume on which the hardware-specific Windows 2000 boot files, such as *Ntldr* and *Ntdetect.com*, are located.

*See Also*

*disks(3)*

## TCP/IP

The most widely implemented network protocol in use today.

*Description*

TCP/IP is a protocol that was originally implemented on Unix platforms but has now become the default network protocol on Microsoft Windows, Novell NetWare, and Apple Macintosh computing platforms. TCP/IP is routable and can be used for both local-area networks (LANs) and wide-area networks (WANs). You should use TCP/IP if:

- Your network is heterogeneous in character, consisting of different computing platforms and operating systems that all need to work together.

- You need connectivity with the Internet or want to deploy Internet technologies within a corporate intranet environment.

- You want to make use of the Active Directory component of Windows 2000 Server. (Active Directory requires TCP/IP.)

A full treatment of TCP/IP is beyond the scope of this book. What follows here is a brief summary of its important features. For more information see the books *TCP/IP Network Administration* by Craig Hunt and *Windows NT TCP/IP Network Administration* by Craig Hunt and Robert Bruce Thompson, both published by O'Reilly & Associates.

Windows 2000 includes a number of enhancements to TCP/IP that improve performance and manageability over earlier versions of Microsoft Windows. The main enhancements are:

- Support for APIPA, which allows client computers to be assigned IP addresses automatically without the need of a DHCP server. See "Automatic Private IP Addressing (APIPA)" in this article for more information.

- Support for dynamic recalculation of TCP window size and the ability to use large TCP windows to improve performance when large amounts of data are transmitted during a session. See Request For Comment (RFC) 1323 at *http://www.ietf.org/rfc/* for more information.

- Support for selective TCP acknowledgements to reduce the time retransmitting lost packets. See RFC 2018 for more information.

- Support for the TCP Round Trip Time Measurement option of RFC 1323 to improve performance over slow WAN links.

- Support for caching of resolved DNS name queries on client resolvers.

- Support for ICMP Router Discovery for discovering router interfaces that are not assigned manually or through DHCP. This feature is enabled using the Routing and Remote Access console, and a description of the feature can be found in RFC 1256.

- The ability to disable NetBIOS over TCP/IP (NetBT) for specific network connections. This feature improves performance when DNS is the only name-resolution method in use on the network. This is really an all-or-nothing decision, as a Windows 2000 computer with NetBT disabled can use Client for Microsoft Networks to connect to other Windows 2000 computers running File and Print Sharing for Microsoft Networks only if those computers also have NetBT disabled. Disabling NetBT means the computer can no longer use NetBIOS name-resolution methods such as WINS servers or *lmhosts* files. In most cases you will not use this feature as most networks will consist of a mix of Windows 2000 and legacy Windows clients and servers. For information on how to disable NetBT, see *WINS* in Chapter 4.

## IP Addressing

Each *host* (computer, network printer, router interface, and so on) on a TCP/IP network is generally characterized by three pieces of information:

### IP address

A logical 32-bit address that uniquely identifies the host on the network. IP addresses are expressed in dotted decimal form and consist of four octets separated by decimals with each octet ranging from decimal 0 through 255 (with some restrictions). An example of an IP address might be 172.16.11.245.

### Subnet mask

A 32-bit number that divides the IP address into two parts, a *network ID*, which uniquely identifies the network that the host resides on, and a *host ID*, which uniquely identifies the host on that particular network. For example, the subnet mask 255.255.0.0, when applied to the IP address 172.16.11.245, indicates that the network ID of the host is 172.16 while the host ID of the host is 11.245.

### Default gateway

A 32-bit address that identifies the default router interface to send packets that are directed to another network (or more accurately, that are directed to a different *subnet* on a TCP/IP *internetwork*) if no other route is specified. The default gateway is optional and is only necessary on networks consisting of more than one subnet or when packets are being sent between different networks.

### Managing TCP/IP

One aspect of managing TCP/IP is managing IP addresses on your network. Windows 2000 Server lets you assign IP addresses and other TCP/IP settings in three different ways:

### Manually by using static IP addresses

This method is suitable only for small deployments of fewer than a hundred machines or so. TCP/IP settings must be configured at the local console of each machine, so this method is unsuitable if the hosts are geographically separated. Since errors in assigning IP addresses can cause general problems with network communications, this method can be a lot of work to troubleshoot.

### Automatically by using DHCP

This is the default method for assigning TCP/IP settings on Windows 2000 machines. It makes use of one or more Dynamic Host Configuration Protocol (DHCP) servers, which maintain pools of available IP addresses, which lease these addresses to client computers that request them. DHCP should always be used on medium- to large-scale networks that run TCP/IP. DHCP can also be used by legacy Microsoft Windows platforms for configuring TCP/IP on machines. This includes Windows NT, Windows 95/98, and Windows for Workgroups 3.11.

### Automatic Private IP Addressing (APIPA)

If your Windows 2000 Server machine is configured to obtain an IP address by DHCP but no DHCP server is available on the network, the machine opts for assigning itself an address using Automatic Private IP Addressing. This method is an alternative to using DHCP on small- to medium-scale networks that use Windows 2000 and run DHCP. APIPA can only be used on Windows 2000 machines it is not supported by legacy versions of Microsoft Windows. For more information see "Automatic Private IP Addressing (APIPA)" in this article.

For more information on configuring TCP/IP settings, see *TCP/IP* in Chapter 4.

### Troubleshooting TCP/IP

Windows 2000 includes a comprehensive set of command-line utilities for testing and troubleshooting TCP/IP configurations and networks, including `arp`, `hostname`, `ipconfig`, `nbtstat`, `netstat`, `pathping`, `ping`, `route`, and `tracert`. For more information on any of these utilities, see their associated articles in Chapter 7.

*Automatic Private IP Addressing (APIPA)*

APIPA is an extension of DHCP implemented in Windows 2000 (and Windows 98) that allows computers to self-configure their IP address and subnet mask without the need of a DHCP server. The way it works is that a computer uses APIPA to randomly select a unique IP address from a block of IP addresses reserved by Microsoft for this purpose. This reserved IP block covers the address range 169.254.0.1 through 169.254.255.254, and together with the subnet mask 255.255.0.0 provides enough addresses for 64,024 hosts running on a single subnet. In real life, however, APIPA is intended for use on home or small business networks containing at most a few dozen machines, because:

- Only the IP address and subnet mask can be assigned using APIPA, and not default gateways or other TCP/IP settings that can be provided by DHCP servers and that are needed by TCP/IP networks connected to other networks or to the Internet.

- Only a single subnet can be created using APIPA, which is not of much use in an enterprise-level network.

To configure a computer to use APIPA, simply configure it to obtain an IP address automatically (see *TCP/IP* in Chapter 4 for the procedure). Then when the machine restarts, it first tries to contact a DHCP server, and if this fails, APIPA then kicks in and the machine selects an IP address for itself of the form 169.254.x.y. It then tests the uniqueness of the address on the network by broadcasting a DHCP-type message to the rest of the machines on the network to find out if any other machine is using this address. If there is no negative response, it assigns the address to itself along with the subnet mask 255.255.0.0. If, however, another computer claims to already be using the address, APIPA generates another address at random until a usable one is found. Then should a DHCP server later be installed on the network, computers that used APIPA to select an address will soon detect the DHCP server and request a new IP address and other TCP/IP settings from the server.

APIPA can cause problems on large networks, however. For example, if a DHCP server went down and client computers couldn't renew their leases, they would start using APIPA to assign themselves addresses. This would result in communications on the network breaking down because the machines that acquired new addresses using APIPA would be on a different subnet from those still holding their leased DHCP addresses. The solution is to disable APIPA entirely, but, unfortunately, the only way to do this is to use the registry. You disable APIPA on a specific network adapter by creating a new key called IPAutoconfigurationEnabled of type REG_DWORD within the subkey:

```
HKEY_LOCAL_MACHINE\
  SYSTEM\
    CurrentControlSet\
     Services\
       Tcpip\
         Parameters\
           Interfaces\
             GUID_of_network_adapter\
```

and assigning this new key the value 0. Change the value to 1 to re-enable APIPA on the adapter. On a multihomed machine with multiple network adapters, you can disable APIPA on all adapters by placing the IPAutoconfigurationEnabled key within the subkey:

```
HKEY_LOCAL_MACHINE\
  SYSTEM\
   CurrentControlSet\
    Services\
     Tcpip\
      Parameters\
```

If there are network connections that are not being used on servers (most importantly, domain controllers), they should either be disabled or have APIPA disabled. Otherwise, clients may get incorrect IP addresses when querying DNS.

### Notes

- Windows 2000 Server installs TCP/IP by default as its default network protocol.

- You should generally assign IP addresses manually to servers on your network, and let DHCP assign addresses automatically to client computers.

- Windows 98 also supports APIPA.

- If your network will be connected to the Internet, the best IP addressing scheme to follow is to assign addresses from the private IP address blocks reserved by the Internet Assigned Numbers Authority (IANA) and connect your network to the Internet using a firewall or proxy server that uses Net-Work Address Translation (NAT). The private IP addresses reserved by IANA are shown in Table 3-39 below. You can use these addresses as long as you are *not* directly connected to the Internet.

*Table 3-39: IP Address Blocks Reserved for Private Networks*

| Network ID | Subnet Mask | Range of Addresses |
|---|---|---|
| 10.0.0.0 | 255.0.0.0 | 10.0.0.1 to 10.255.255.254 |
| 172.16.0.0 | 255.240.0.0 | 172.16.0.1 to 172.31.255.254 |
| 192.168.0.0 | 255.255.0.0 | 192.168.0.1 to 192.168.255.254 |

### See Also

*DHCP(3,4), DNS(3,4), network protocol(3,4), TCP/IP(4), WINS(3,4)*

---

# Terminal Services

Lets users access the Windows 2000 desktop and run Windows applications on remote computers.

### Description

Terminal Services is an optional component of Windows 2000 Server that lets remote computers or devices run sessions that give users access to a Windows 2000 desktop even though Windows 2000 is not installed on the computers.

---

Despite the fact that the remote computers may have different hardware and operating systems installed on them, they all display the same standard Windows 2000 desktop generated by the terminal server. A single terminal server can serve multiple remote computers and allow them to access Windows-based applications running on the server.

The advantages of using Terminal Services include the following:

- Windows 2000 can be run on computers whose hardware configuration is insufficient to run Windows 2000 locally. This allows business to get more mileage out of old computers and to avoid or delay the costly upgrade cycle. The client needs only enough processing power to connect to the server and display the Windows 2000 desktop.

- Instead of using legacy hardware, companies can opt to purchase newer thin clients that have modern hardware but only enough processing power to function as Terminal Services Clients.

- Windows-based applications can be accessed similarly by users on older computers whose hardware and software would not support local installation of these applications.

- Installation, upgrading, configuration, and maintenance of Windows-based applications is simplified because these actions only need to be performed on the terminal server, not on the individual client computers.

- Administrators can perform remote administration from Terminal Services Clients, enabling them to perform actions that otherwise could only be performed locally at the servers, such as installing software.

- Security is enhanced by the fact that applications and data need not reside on the client. Communications between the terminal server and clients can be encrypted as well for increased security. Furthermore, administrators can shadow client sessions from a second client session, allowing them to fully monitor the actions of logged-on users.

- Support is enhanced by the fact that administrators can assume remote control of client sessions and input their own keyboard and mouse actions to demonstrate procedures to users or troubleshoot problems remotely.

For procedures on installing and using Terminal Services, see *Terminal Services* in Chapter 4.

### How Terminal Services Works

Terminal Services consists of three components, which work together:

*Terminal server*
This is a Windows 2000 Server computer with Terminal Services installed and configured on it. The terminal server receives keyboard and mouse input from the clients, processes them, and returns data that remotely displays the Windows 2000 desktop on the client.

*Terminal Services Client*
> A terminal session on the client opens a window on the local desktop of the client and displays the Windows 2000 desktop remotely generated by the terminal server.

*Remote Desktop Protocol (RDP)*
> This is an application-layer TCP/IP protocol based on the T.120 standard from the ITU. RDP is responsible for displaying GUI elements on the client to create the remote Windows 2000 desktop.

## Implementing Terminal Services

The following are some of the considerations for implementing Terminal Services on your network.

### Client Requirements

Terminal Services Client software is provided in two versions:

- 32-bit client for Windows 2000, Windows NT, Windows 98, and Windows 95
- 16-bit client for Windows for Workgroups

Table 3-40 shows the memory requirements for different Windows operating systems to run as Terminal Services Clients. The minimum video-system requirement is VGA.

*Table 3-40: Memory Requirements for Terminal Services Clients*

| OS Version | Memory |
|---|---|
| Windows 2000 | 32 MB |
| Windows NT 4.0 | 16 MB |
| Windows 98 | 16 MB |
| Windows 95 | 16 MB |
| Windows 3.11 | 16 MB |

Other Terminal Services Clients are also available:

- Windows Terminal thin-client devices have an embedded Terminal Services Client.
- Windows CE handheld PCs may have an embedded client also.
- Citrix MetaFrame (*http://www.citrix.com*) includes clients for non-Windows computers.

### Server Requirements

A Windows 2000 Server formatted with NTFS is required. The server requires a minimum of 4 MB (recommended 8 MB) of additional RAM for each client it will support. Microsoft recommends running Terminal Services on a member server, not a domain controller. (This is not for security reasons but because the member server can dedicate its resources to supporting only Terminal Services Clients.) Fast SCSI hard drives and a high-performance network adapter are also recommended.

### Application Requirements

Terminal Services supports most Windows-based applications with little or no additional configuration. These applications preferably should be 32-bit ones, as running 16-bit applications can reduce the efficiency of a terminal server considerably. Running MS-DOS applications on a terminal server provides poor performance and is not recommended.

### Licensing Requirements

If you are going to deploy Terminal Services on your network, you need the following to be legal:

*Windows 2000 Server license*
This was included with your purchased Windows 2000 Server product. Choose per-seat licensing mode to run your server as a terminal server.

*Windows 2000 Server Client Access License (CAL)*
Each computer or device that will connect to your terminal server requires a CAL in order to legally access operating-system services such as File and Print Services on the server. CALs must be purchased separately for each client computer regardless of what operating system it is running.

*Windows 2000 Terminal Services Client Access License*
Each computer or device that will connect to your terminal server requires a Terminal Services CAL. If your clients are Windows 2000 Professional, one Terminal Services CAL was included with your purchased product, which you can use for remote administration. Terminal Services CALs must be purchased separately for each client computer regardless of what operating system it is running.

For more information and to make sure you are legal in your deployment, see Microsoft's web site, *http://www.microsoft.com/licensing/*.

### Notes

- Terminal Services can only be used with TCP/IP as the network protocol.
- Older single-user applications will not run on terminal servers.

### See Also

*Terminal Services(4)*

---

## tree

A hierarchical structure of domains.

### Description

A tree consists of a root (top-level parent) domain and one or more child domains connected together in a hierarchical structure using two-way transitive trusts. When you install the first Windows 2000 domain controller in your enterprise, you automatically create:

- The root domain of your initial tree
- The forest root domain of your initial forest

When you create additional Windows 2000 domains, you can choose whether to:

- Add the new domain to an existing tree by making the new domain a child of your root domain.

- Make the new domain the root domain of a new tree within the forest.

A tree can consist of a single domain (its root domain), or it can consist of any number of domains arranged in hierarchical fashion to any degree. The domain above a given domain in the tree is its parent domain, while a domain below a given domain is its child domain. Any child domain can become the parent of a new child domain. The point, though, is that all domains in a tree share the same root, and each child has exactly one parent above it. For more information on domains, see *domain* in this chapter.

### Namespace

The key thing about domains in a tree is that they form a contiguous namespace in Active Directory. Since DNS is the name-locator system used by Active Directory, the DNS namespace of a tree is also contiguous. For example, if the root domain of a tree is *mtit.com*, then *vancouver.mtit.com* and *seattle.mtit.com* would be two examples of child domains of *mtit.com*, while *support.vancouver.mtit.com* and *sales.vancouver.mtit.com* would be two more child domains whose parent domain is *vancouver.mtit.com*.

---

 Child domains receive their names from their parent domains in a tree, so it is important to choose the name of the root domain of a tree carefully as all other domains in the tree will contain this root DNS name. See "Root Domain" in the article *domain* in this chapter for more information.

---

### Using Trees

You might want to create a multiple-domain tree for your enterprise if one or more of the following conditions apply:

- You company is large enough to consider using the complexity of a multi-domain implementation of Windows 2000 Active Directory. There is no hard and fast rule here for how big a company should be though; this is based essentially on your available IT resources and expertise, as well as on the other factors described later.

- Your company requires that IT administration be decentralized across multiple locations or divisions. Multiple domains are appropriate here because domains represent strong security boundaries for administration of users, groups, computers, and other resources. Domain Admins in one domain cannot administer resources in other domains unless they are explicitly given permission to do so.

- Your company requires distinct Group Policy security settings (such as password and account lockout settings) for different locations or divisions. This might even be for legal reasons—for example, if some of your subsidiaries are in foreign countries with different legal security requirements.

- Your WAN links are slow, and you want to keep replication traffic between different locations to a minimum and to control it more tightly. You could make each location both a separate domain in the tree and a separate site. This is because the only Active Directory information replicated between domains in a tree are the schema, the configuration information, and the global catalog. If you use a single domain with multiple sites instead, the site links between the sites require enough bandwidth to support the greater traffic that occurs during intradomain replication of Active Directory.

---

Because domains in a tree are linked together by transitive trusts, a user in one domain of a tree can access resources in any other domain in the tree, provided he has suitable permissions for accessing the resources.

---

### One Domain or Many?

One of the fundamental questions the enterprise architect needs to ask is whether to create one domain for the entire enterprise or many domains (either as one tree or many):

- If you use only one domain, you can still create structure within that domain by creating a hierarchy of OUs. Administrators can then apply different Group Policies to different OUs within the domain and delegate authority over different OUs to different trusted users.

- On the other hand, creating multiple domains automatically creates structure for applying Group Policies and also creates security boundaries for administration of Users, Groups, Computers, and other objects. Furthermore, using multiple domains partitions or segments the directory into smaller units since domains only store information about their own objects in Active Directory. There is also greater flexibility and control gained by applying Group Policy to domains instead of OUs, and authority over domains can be delegated to trusted users.

For more information on these various planning issues and to help you decide which is the best model for you, see the articles *Active Directory, domain, forest, OU,* and *tree* in this chapter.

### Using an Empty Root Domain

An option to consider for a company that requires decentralized administration of IT functions across multiple locations or divisions is to make use of a tree that has an empty root domain. For example, if MTIT Enterprises has the DNS domain name *mtit.com* and consists of two relatively independent offices in Vancouver and Seattle, you could implement a Windows 2000 tree for the company as follows:

- Create the root Windows 2000 domain *mtit.com* in one of the two locations. Add a few high-level administrator accounts to the Enterprise Admins group in this root domain. Do not create any OUs or any other Active Directory objects such as users, groups, computers, or printers in this domain. In other words, this root domain is empty except for a few enterprise-level administrator accounts.

- Create the domains *vancouver.mtit.com* and *seattle.mtit.com* as child domains of the root domain *mtit.com*. Let the members of the Domain Admins group in each of these two child domains create the users, groups, computers, printers, OUs, and other directory objects for their own domain.

---

 For extra security, you could require that Enterprise Admins use a smart card or some other hard-authentication method to log on to the network in order to further secure these powerful accounts.

---

### Notes

- When designing an Active Directory structure and a DNS namespace for your enterprise, start by seeing if a tree consisting of a single domain will suffice, since this is the simplest solution to implement. The advantages of a single-domain implementation include:

  — Easier user and group administration, since you don't need to create as many security groups

  — Greater security, since you will have fewer members in your Domain Admins group

  — Easier delegation of authority, since you have more control over delegating authority to OUs than to domains

- Instead of creating a domain tree with multiple domains, see if a single domain with a tree of OUs within it will suffice for your company. See *OU* in this chapter for more information.

- Note that whether Active Directory contains a tree of one domain or a tree of many domains, the number of objects that the directory can hold is still the same.

- All domains in a tree share common Active Directory schema and configuration information and a common global catalog.

### See Also

*Active Directory(3), domain(3,4), forest(3,4), OU(3,4), tree(3), trust(3,4)*

---

# *trust*

A secure communications channel between domains, which permits pass-through authentication between the domains so that a user in one domain can be authenticated by a domain controller in another domain.

## *Description*

Trusts (also called trust relationships) provide a mechanism for users in one domain to access resources in different domains. Windows 2000 supports several kinds of trusts described later in this article.

### *Transitive Trust*

Also called two-way transitive trusts, these are trusts established when new child domains are added to an existing tree or when a new root domain is added to an existing forest to form a new tree. These actions can be taken when you use the Active Directory Installation Wizard to promote a standalone Windows 2000 server to the role of domain controller to create a new domain rather than join an existing domain.

Transitive trusts are created and managed automatically between all domains in a forest and require no maintenance or configuration. Transitive trusts allow users to be authenticated by domain controllers in any domain in the forest. Transitive trusts operate using the Kerberos v5 authentication protocol (see the sidebar "Kerberos Authentication Within a Forest" in the article *forest* in this chapter for more information).

### *Shortcut Trust*

Although all domains in a Windows 2000 forest implicitly trust each other through the two-way transitive trusts that exist between adjacent domains in a domain tree and between the roots of each tree in the forest, you can also explicitly create two-way transitive trusts between two domains that are not adjacent to one another in the tree or between any two domains in different trees. These explicit two-way transitive trusts are called shortcut trusts, and they can be created to shorten the trust path between two domains in a forest when the users in one or both of these domains frequently need to access the resources in the other domain. By creating a shortcut trust between two domains in a forest, the Kerberos authentication process by which users are granted access to resources in different domains is considerably shortened in terms of the number of steps involved, reducing authentication traffic and speeding up the interdomain authentication process for users.

For information on Kerberos authentication, see the sidebar "Kerberos Authentication Within a Forest" in the article *forest* in this chapter. For information on how to create shortcut trusts between domains, see *trust* in Chapter 4.

### External Trust

An external trust explicitly created using the Active Directory Domains and Trusts console, which is part of the Administrative Tools program group on domain controllers. There are two different kinds of external trusts you can create in Windows 2000:

*One-way external trust*
> This type of trust is nontransitive and is similar to a Windows NT trust relationship. In a one-way trust, the trusting domain trusts the trusted domain. User accounts in the trusted domain are able to access resources in the trusting domain, provided they have suitable permissions given to them. You can explicitly establish a one-way external trust between a Windows 2000 domain and a Windows NT domain in either direction.

*Two-way external trust*
> This type of trust is also nontransitive and generally consists of two, explicitly created, one-way trusts in opposite directions between a Windows 2000 and a Windows NT domain.

### Notes

- Upgrading an existing Windows NT 4.0 network to Windows 2000 preserves all existing trusts; that is, one-way trusts remain one-way in nature.

- If you install a new Windows 2000 domain and you want its users in your existing Windows NT network to be a able to access resources in the new domain (and vice versa), you must create explicit trusts between the Windows NT and Windows 2000 domains using Active Directory Domains and Trusts.

### See Also

*Active Directory Domains and Trusts(5), domain(3,4), forest(3), tree(3), trust(4)*

---

## universal group

Type of group used to grant permissions for users to access resources in any domain.

### See Also

*group(3)*

---

## upgrade

Upgrading Windows NT systems and domains to Windows 2000.

### Description

This section focuses primarily on specific issues regarding upgrading Windows NT member servers, standalone servers, and domain controllers to Windows 2000 Server. For information about performing new installations of Windows 2000 Server, and for pre- and post-installation issues that also apply to upgrading, see *install* earlier in this chapter.

### Upgrading Versus Installing

*Installing* means putting Windows 2000 Server on a newly formatted partition (or putting it on a partition having another operating system to create a multiboot machine). *Upgrading* means replacing an earlier operating system (or earlier version of Windows 2000 Server) with Windows 2000 Server. Installing means that you have to specify all of the user- and computer-specific settings for your machine, either by answering prompts during Setup or by using answer files to perform automated installations. Upgrading means that the existing user- and computer-specific settings from the previous operating system are carried over as much as possible to Windows 2000 Server. Upgrading also means that your existing applications do not need to be reinstalled and reconfigured, provided of course that these applications are fully compatible with Windows 2000 Server.

You can upgrade the following operating systems to Windows 2000 Server:

- Windows NT 3.51 Server (provided Citrix software is not installed)

- Windows NT 4.0 Server

- Windows NT 4.0 Server, Terminal Server Edition

Note that Windows NT 4.0 Server, Enterprise Edition, can only be upgraded to Windows 2000 Advanced Server, not Windows 2000 Server.

You can also upgrade earlier versions of Windows 2000 Server to the final product. However, not all Beta or Release Candidate (RC) versions of Windows 2000 Server can be upgraded directly to the final product in one step:

- For member servers or standalone servers, you cannot upgrade Beta x to RCx. You can first upgrade Beta 3 to RC2 and then upgrade RC2 to the final version.

- For domain controllers you can upgrade RC2 or RC3 directly to the final version. RC1 must first be upgraded to RC2, while Beta 3 must be upgraded to RC1 then RC2 then to the final version.

For more information on upgrading Beta or Release Candidate versions of Windows 2000 Server to the final product, see the file *Read1st.txt* located in the root directory of the Windows 2000 Server CD.

### Which Servers to Upgrade First

When upgrading a Windows NT Server–based network to Windows 2000 Server, you have a choice of which servers to upgrade first:

*Upgrade member servers first*
    This approach provides your network with many of the advantages of Windows 2000 Server, including new management tools, group policies, support for USB and Plug and Play hardware, updated version of NTFS with support for encryption and disk quotas, new services, better printing support,

and so on. Without Active Directory, however, you must maintain your old Windows NT Server domains until you upgrade your domain controllers. Nevertheless, you may want to choose this method since it gives you many of the advantages of Windows 2000 Server while allowing you to buy time for learning the complexity of Active Directory.

*Upgrade domain controllers first*

This approach immediately provides you with all of the Windows 2000 Server features described earlier, plus the power and scalability of having Active Directory on your network. The downside is that you really have to know how Active Directory works before you start implementing it, since you don't want to create a directory structure only to have to tear it down and rebuild it later.

The key thing, of course, with upgrading your servers is to *always make a full backup of your system before you upgrade!* For a description of the procedures involved in upgrading domain controllers, see *upgrade* in Chapter 4.

**Preupgrading Issues**

See "Preinstallation Issues" in the article *install* earlier in this chapter.

**See Also**

*domain controller(3), install(3,4), member server(3), standalone server(3), upgrade(4)*

---

# user account

Credentials enabling a user to log on and access resources on a computer or domain.

**Description**

There are two kinds of user accounts in Windows 2000–based networks:

*Local user account*

Enables a user to log on to a member server or client computer to access resources on that machine

*Domain user account*

Enables a user to log on to a domain to access resources in the domain

Administrators can create, modify, rename, delete, and copy both kinds of user accounts. In addition, a series of built-in user accounts are created when Windows 2000 Server is installed on a computer or when Active Directory is installed on a Windows 2000 Server machine. These built-in accounts can be renamed but not deleted.

**See Also**

*domain user account(3), local user account(3), built-in user account(3), group(3)*

# user profile

A collection of files that stores the desktop configuration and personal settings of a user.

## Description

User profiles ensure that users have consistent desktop and application settings each time they log on to their machine. User profiles can also be stored on the network to enable users to access their desktop and personal settings from any machine on the network and can be configured to either allow or prevent users from modifying their settings.

A user profile stores information about a user's:

- Desktop settings, such as wallpaper, screen resolution, desktop icons, Start menu items, files stored in My Documents folder, and so on

- Network connections, such as mapped drives and network shortcuts to shared folders and printers located on network servers

### Types of User Profiles

There are three types of user profiles: local, roaming, and mandatory. These three types allow administrators a variety of ways of controlling users' desktop environments.

#### Local User Profile

These are user profiles stored the local machine. A local user profile (or local profile) for a user is created the first time a user logs on locally to a machine. These local profiles are stored by default in the folder *C:\Documents and Settings* in subfolders each named after the username of a user who has logged on locally to the machine at least once. For example, the local profile for Administrator will be located in the folder *C:\Documents and Settings\Administrator* and consists of a series of subfolders and files within this *\Administrator* folder.

When a user makes changes to her desktop (e.g., changes the wallpaper) and then logs off, the local profile is updated to reflect any changes made by the user during the session. When the user next logs on, the settings will reflect these changes made during the previous session.

If multiple users share use of the same machine, each user will have his own, separate, local profile stored in the folder *C:Documents and Settings\<user_name>*. Each user's settings will be preserved regardless of what the other users do while they are logged on to the machine.

#### Roaming User Profile

By storing users' profiles on a network file server and configuring users' accounts with information about where their profiles can be found, you give users the ability to roam around the network, log on to any client machine, and retrieve their own, personal, desktop settings for use on that machine. This is known as roaming user profiles (or roaming profiles) and is useful when users need to perform their work at multiple client computers.

When a user logs on to a machine using the roaming profile and makes changes to the desktop environment, these changes are saved when the user logs off. If the user then logs on to a different machine, the changes made on the first machine are reflected on the second. In other words, users can make changes to their roaming profiles, unless mandatory user profiles are implemented, as described next.

Roaming profiles are typically used in situations where users share their computers. For example, if you have 15 sales personnel sharing 5 computers (since most of the time they should be out drumming up contracts anyway), then you could implement roaming profiles for these users so that they can use whichever of the 5 computers are currently free. Another example would be if you had 10 trainers who need to access their email during coffee break. You could give them 2 computers to share and assign them roaming profiles (the cost-effective solution) or give them each a laptop (my own preference, but no one ever listens to me).

### Mandatory User Profile

A mandatory user profile (or mandatory profile) is a form of roaming user profile where the user cannot make changes to the profile. The user can, however, make changes to the desktop environment while logged on. But when they log off, the mandatory profile is not updated to reflect these changes. Mandatory user profiles are also sometimes referred to as mandatory roaming profiles and roaming mandatory profiles!

You might typically use mandatory profiles for naive users to prevent them from making changes to their desktop. Users sometimes like to install shareware and other software they have downloaded off the Internet, and sometimes such software can cause problems that necessitate costly intervention from technical support staff. Mandatory profiles prevent such changes to users' desktops and thus reduce the costs of supporting these users.

Another use for mandatory profiles might be to create a customized user profile that you assign to several users who need to perform the same type of tasks on their computers. You can create a default user profile that reflects the kind of desktop environment most conducive to their productivity, make this profile mandatory, and then assign it to each user.

### How User Profiles Work

When a user logs on to a Windows 2000 client computer for the first time, the following procedure occurs:

1. Windows 2000 checks if a roaming profile has been specified for the user by the administrator. If so, it downloads this roaming profile from the appropriate network file server and applies it to the user's desktop environment. When the user logs off, the roaming profile is updated on the file server to reflect any changes the user has made during the session.

2. If not, Windows 2000 checks if there is a network-default user profile. A *default user profile* is a kind of template from which all other user profiles are created. It is called the network-default user profile if it has the name Default User and is stored in the NETLOGON administrative share on all domain controllers.

If such a default profile exists on the domain controller that the client computer contacts, Windows 2000 downloads this profile and applies it to the user's desktop environment. When the user logs off, a local profile is created on the client computer for the user. The next time the user logs on, the local profile is used instead of the network-default profile.

3. If not, Windows 2000 loads the default, local user profile and applies it to the user's desktop environment. When the user logs off, a local profile is created on the client computer for the user. The next time the user logs on, the local profile is used instead of the local default profile.

### Notes

- Configuring a network-default user profile can simplify administration of Windows 2000 client machines. You can create a default user profile reflecting the kind of desktop environment you want all your ordinary users to have and store this on your domain controllers. Then when your users log on to their client computers for the first time, the default user profile will be used as a template for creating their own local profiles.

- While local profiles enable multiple users to share a single machine and maintain their own, separate, desktop environment, things can easily go wrong. For example, if one user logs on and deletes the executable for an application, other users will still have access to the shortcut for that application from their Start menu, but they obviously won't be able to run a program that is no longer there!

- Even if your ordinary users do not require the ability to roam, you may want to give your administrators this capability so they can perform administrative tasks from any machine in the network. On the other hand, in high security environments you may want to restrict administrative logon to a few selected machines.

- You do not need to make copies of mandatory profiles—multiple users can be assigned the same profile. If you do assign a single roaming profile to multiple users, make sure you configure the profile as mandatory. Otherwise, one user will change the wallpaper, and another user will complain about it!

### See Also

*domain user account(3)*

---

## Users

Built-in group for granting users the rights and permissions needed by ordinary network users.

### See Also

*built-in group(3)*

## *volume*

A hard disk subsystem that is configured to use dynamic storage consists of one of more volumes.

### See Also

*disks(3)*

## *WINS*

Stands for Windows Internet Name Service and is used to support NetBIOS name resolution for downlevel Windows clients.

### Description

In a mixed-mode network where you still have some Windows NT servers or workstations, you may need to implement WINS on one or more Windows 2000 servers in your network. WINS enables downlevel (pre–Windows 2000) Windows computers to resolve NetBIOS names into IP addresses without the need of using broadcasts.

 Some legacy/downlevel applications may rely on NETBIOS and would still require WINS even if legacy or downlevel systems no longer exist on the network.

For information on how to configure WINS servers, see *WINS* in Chapter 4.

### *How WINS Works*

WINS centralizes the registration of computer and domain NetBIOS names into a central WINS database on one or more WINS servers on your network. When NetBIOS computers start up, they register their name and IP address with the WINS servers. NetBIOS clients can then contact the WINS servers to resolve the registered computer's NetBIOS name into its IP address to establish network communications with it.

### *WINS Requirements*

To implement WINS on your network, you need to meet the following requirements:

#### *WINS server requirements*

A Windows 2000 Server computer with a static IP address and with the Windows Internet Name Service installed. A single WINS server can support up to about 5,000 WINS clients. Networks that require WINS should have at least two WINS servers for fault tolerance in case one becomes unavailable. WINS database replication can be configured to allow WINS servers to share a common WINS database.

*WINS client requirements*

All Microsoft Windows versions can function as WINS clients. The client must be configured with the IP address of at least one WINS server on the network.

### Other WINS Terminology

*Static mapping*

A NetBIOS name–to–IP address mapping that is manually created in the WINS database of a WINS server. Static mappings can be configured for servers that do not support WINS to allow WINS clients to resolve their names and access them.

*WINS proxy*

A proxy that listens to broadcasts from non-WINS clients, forwards them to a WINS server for name resolution, then broadcasts the result to the clients.

*Pull partner*

A WINS server that is configured to request WINS database updates from its replication partner at specific intervals. Pull partners are often configured over slow WAN links.

*Push partner*

A WINS server that is configured to notify its replication partners when it has accumulated the threshold number of WINS database updates it wants to pass on to its partners. Push partners are generally configured when fast LAN links connect WINS servers.

*Push/pull partner*

A WINS server that is configured as both a push and pull partner.

### See Also

*WINS(4)*

---

# workgroup

A collection of Windows 2000 computers where each computer manages its own security and where Active Directory is not implemented.

### See Also

*domain(3)*

# CHAPTER 4

# *Tasks*

This chapter covers the basic tasks and procedures relating to Windows 2000 Server and its administration. When looking up a particular administrative task to perform in this chapter, you can use the cross-references at the end of each article to find background information on related topics in this and other chapters in Part II, *Alphabetical Reference*.

Tasks are listed here alphabetically according to "topic." This means that to find information on how to share a printer, you would first look up the topic *printer* in this chapter. Within the topic *printer* you will then find a list of procedures that can be performed on printers, and these procedures are themselves listed in alphabetical order within the topic. For example, for the topic *printer* the procedures (tasks) you can follow are outlined as follows:

> Add a Printer
>> Installing a Printer for a Local Print Device
>> Installing a Printer for a Network-Interface Print Device
>> Making a Connection to a Print
> Configure Clients for Printing to a Printer
> Configure Permissions for a Printer
> Configure Properties of a Printer
>> General
>> Sharing
>> Ports
>> Advanced
>> Security
>> Device Settings
> Find a Printer
> Manage a Printer Using a Web Browser
> Pause a Printer
> Redirect a Printer
> Share a Printer
> Use a Printer Offline

Note that some procedures have subprocedures outlined under them. In this case, the subprocedure "Sharing" under the procedure "Configure Properties of a Printer" is a cross-reference to the procedure "Share a Printer" later in the topic. (Main procedures are identified using headers separate from secondary procedures for easier lookup.)

Procedures are shown as a series of steps separated by arrows ( → ) in what I call "gestalt menus." Steps are usually described concisely and are understood best when sitting at a Windows 2000 machine to follow along. For example, the procedure for sharing a printer is described as:

> Start → Settings → Printers → right-click on printer → Sharing → Shared As →
> <share_name>

which when working through it at the computer is obviously understood to mean:

> Click the Start button, choose Settings, then Printers, which opens the Printers window. Right-click on the printer you want to share in the window and select Sharing from the shortcut menu that appears. This opens the property sheet for the printer, with the focus on the Sharing tab of this property sheet. Select the Shared As option and type in the share name, that is, the name under which you want the printer to be shared on the network. Click OK when you are done, and close the Printers window.

Notice from the previous procedure that certain obvious steps are usually omitted, particularly steps like clicking OK to close a dialog box or clicking Finish to end a wizard. There are a few times, however, when these steps are outlined specifically if they seem confusing because of the number of dialog boxes currently open.) Since most Windows 2000 administrative tasks involve using the *Microsoft Management Console* (MMC), familiarity with this tool is important; see the beginning of Chapter 5, *Consoles*, for a quick introduction to the MMC and how to use it effectively. Note that selecting a node in the MMC console tree and clicking the Action button on the toolbar displays a drop-down Action menu that is identical to the shortcut menu that appears when you right-click on the node instead. In other words, the steps for creating a new domain-user account using the Active Directory Users and Computer console can be described as either:

- Select the OU that will contain the account → Action → New → User

- Right-click the OU that will contain the account → New → User

Both of these conventions are used indiscriminately in the chapter, depending on how the fancy took me. Remember also that the Action and shortcut menus are context sensitive, so if the option you need doesn't appear in them, you probably have the wrong item selected in the console. For example, when working with domain-user account in the Active Directory Users and Computers console:

- To create a new user, select an *organizational unit* (OU) to create it in. This will cause the New option to appear on the Action and shortcut menus.

- To delete an existing user, select the *user account* you want to delete. In this case there is no New option on the Action or shortcut menus.

Finally, at various places within a topic and also at the end of the topic, cross-references are used liberally to guide the reader to relevant articles elsewhere in this chapter and in other chapters. The form of these cross-references is to use parentheses to indicate the destination chapter: for example, *printer(3)* refers to the article entitled *printer* in Chapter 3, *Concepts*.

# Alphabetical List of Tasks

## Active Directory

Back up Active Directory, create objects in Active Directory, move an object to a different container within Active Directory, publish a shared folder, shared printer, or application in Active Directory, and restore Active Directory.

### Procedures

This article contains procedures for several tasks involving Active Directory, which do not fit easily elsewhere in this chapter. For more information about creating, configuring, and managing different Active Directory objects and other entities, see the following articles elsewhere in this chapter:

> *computer*
> *domain*
> *domain controller*
> *group*
> *OU*
> *site*
> *trust*

### Back Up Active Directory

See *Backup* in Chapter 6, *Utilities*, for information about this procedure.

### Create Objects Within Active Directory

> Open the Active Directory Users and Computers console → right-click a domain, container, or OU → New → select type of object to create

For more information on creating different objects, see *computer, group*, and *printer* elsewhere in this chapter.

### Move an Object to a Different Container Within Active Directory

> Open the Active Directory Users and Computers console → right-click a User, Group, Computer, Printer, or other object → Move

You can create OUs and move objects to these OUs to facilitate delegation and application of Group Policy. See *delegation* and *Group Policy Objects (GPOs)* in this chapter for more information.

### Publish a Resource in Active Directory

Publishing a resource means creating an object in Active Directory to represent the resource. This helps users locate the resource on the network in order to access it. Most resources, such as users, groups, computers, and printers, are published automatically in Active Directory. Two exceptions to this are shared folders on network file servers and shared printers that are managed by print servers not running Windows 2000 as their operating system.

#### Publish a Shared Folder

> Open the Active Directory Users and Computers console → right-click on the OU where you want to publish the shared folder → New → Shared Folder → specify a friendly name for the resource → specify the UNC path to the shared folder → OK

After publishing the folder, you can open its property sheet and add a description and a list of keywords to help users find the folder when they need it.

#### Publish a Shared Printer (Non-Windows 2000)

> Open the Active Directory Users and Computers console → right-click on the OU where you want to publish the printer → New → Printer → specify the UNC path to the printer → OK

Once users find this printer in Active Directory, they can connect to it or manage its properties depending on their permissions.

#### Publish an Application

If you are deploying software on client computers using Windows Installer technologies (see *Group Policy* in Chapter 3), then Windows Installer packages are published automatically in Active Directory when you add a new package to the Software installation container in a Group Policy Object (GPO). Some packages, however—particularly those you create using ZAP files (see *Windows Installer* in this chapter)—must be published manually in Active Directory, as follows:

> Open the Active Directory Users and Computers console → right-click on the OU to which the GPO for deploying the application is linked → Properties → Group Policy → select the GPO → Edit → {User | Computer} Configuration → Software Settings → Software installation → New → Package → Files of type → ZAP Downlevel application packages → specify UNC path to .*zap* file → Open → select .*zap* file → Open → OK

Publishing the application results in its appearance in Add/Remove Programs in the Control Panel for users or computers in the OU where the GPO is configured to deploy the application.

### Restore Active Directory

In the event of the Active Directory database becoming corrupted or destroyed due to system failure or some other reason, you can use Windows Backup to restore Active Directory.

You can only restore Active Directory if you have backed up the system-state data on your domain controller within the last 60 days. You should definitely backup your system-state data more frequently than this, and you should have more than one domain controller per domain for fault tolerance!

The procedure is as follows:

1. Reboot the domain controller, and press F8 to display the advanced startup options.

2. Start your system in Directory Services Restore Mode, which starts Windows 2000 but not the Active Directory service.

3. Log on using the local Administrator account for the system (the account you use when running the Recovery Console on a domain controller).

4. Run Windows Backup in restore mode to restore the system-state data from your backup set.

5. Reboot the domain controller into normal mode. Various consistency checks and reindexing of the directory database will occur at this point. Once this is completed, your domain controller is working again.

### Notes

- Only publish resources that change relatively infrequently to prevent unnecessary replication traffic from consuming valuable network bandwidth (especially over slow WAN links).

- If you move a published resource to a different server on the network, update the information about the resource in Active Directory to reflect this. In this way users can still connect to the resource without needing to know its new location. This is really the main benefit of publishing resources in Active Directory: it frees users from the need to memorize which server the resource is located on in the network.

### See Also

*Active Directory(3)*, *Backup(6)*, *computer(4)*, *delegation(4)*, *domain(4)*, *domain controller(4)*, *group(4)*, *Group Policy(3)*, *Group Policy Objects (GPOs)(4)*, *OU(4)*, *printer(4)*, *site(4)*, *trust(4)*, *Windows Installer(4)*

## auditing

Configure an audit policy, enable auditing of Active Directory, filesystem, and printer objects, and view audit events in the security log.

### Procedures

For a general discussion of auditing, see *auditing* in Chapter 3.

### Configure an Audit Policy

Audit policies can be configured:

- For individual computers in a workgroup by using Security Settings → Local Policies → Audit Policy in the Local Security Policy console.

- For individual computers in a domain by using the Local Computer Policy Computer Configuration → Windows settings → Local Policies → Audit Policy in a Group Policy console.

- For multiple computers on a network by creating a Group Policy Object and assigning it to a site, domain, or OU.

Once you have selected the Audit Policy container in the appropriate console, open each audit policy in the Details Pane by double-clicking on it, and enable it for success and/or failure auditing as desired.

See *Group Policy Objects (GPOs)* and *Local Security Policy* in this chapter for more information.

---

Here are a few tips on creating an audit policy:

— Don't audit everything: that's being paranoid and will create huge overhead on your system (your security log will be full in no time). Instead, be selective in what you audit, focusing on auditing failures for security tracking and on successes for resource access.

— Don't configure auditing on every computer in your network. Each computer has its own specific roles, resources, and vulnerabilities. You don't want to spend all your nights and weekends reviewing security logs!

— If you're going to audit successes for tracking resource usage, you probably want to archive your logs regularly. This will save you disk space.

— Auditing is of no use if you don't regularly check your security logs for problems. Schedule a time when you can do this.

---

### Enable Auditing of Active Directory Objects

As an example, to audit access to the Users container in the *mtit.com* domain:

Open the Active Directory Users and Computers console → View → toggle Advanced Features on → right-click on Users container → Properties → Security → Advanced → Auditing → Add → select user or group to audit → OK → select types of events to audit → OK

By default, on domain controllers the Everyone group is audited for the root domain and all objects beneath it in Active Directory. But auditing is not turned on in the audit policy portion of the local-policies section of the Domain Security Policy and Domain Controller Security Policy. Do not turn on auditing of Active Directory object access unless absolutely necessary, as it may result in a considerable performance hit on your domain controller.

### Enable Auditing of Filesystem Objects

You can only audit attempts by users to access these objects if they reside on an NTFS partition or volume. As an example, if you wanted to audit access to the file *C:\hello.txt*, you first need to configure your audit policy to turn on success and/or failure auditing of object access (see "Configure an Audit Policy" earlier in this article). Then use Windows Explorer or My Computer to enable auditing of the file as follows:

> Windows Explorer → right-click on *C:\hello.txt* → Properties → Security → Advanced → Auditing → Add → select user or group to audit → OK → specify types of filesystem events to audit regarding *hello.txt* → OK

Configuring auditing on many individual files is a lot of work. It's almost always better to configure auditing on folders instead, for then you can specify that the audit settings be applied to:

- This folder only
- This folder, subfolders, and files
- This folder and subfolders
- This folder and files
- Subfolders and files only
- Subfolders only
- Files only

The default choice is to pass audit settings on down the entire subtree of files and subfolders beneath the folder you are configuring, which is the typical choice.

### Enable Auditing of Printers

> Start → Settings → Printers → right-click on a printer → Properties → Security ▸ Advanced → Auditing → Add → select a user or group to audit → OK → specify types of printer events to audit → OK

Printer access can be audited for documents only, for the printer only, or for both.

### View Audit Events in the Security Log

You use Event Viewer to view the Security log and the audit events recorded in it. See *Event Viewer* in Chapter 5 for more information.

### Notes

- You must be a member of the Administrators group to configure an audit policy.

- Domain-level audit policies override locally configured ones.

- Audit access by the Everyone group if you are concerned about unauthorized users attempting to access file and print resources or Active Directory objects.

- Before configuring an audit policy, check the settings for the Security log in Event Viewer, and check the available space on your disk to make sure that old log events will not be overwritten unexpectedly.

### See Also

*auditing(3), event logs(3,4), Event Viewer(5), Group Policy(3,4), Local Security Policy(3,4)*

## backup and restore

Perform a backup or restore, and rebuild a server.

### Procedures

Windows 2000 Backup and Recovery Tools (also called Windows Backup) is opened by:

Start → Programs → Accessories → Backup

Windows Backup is assumed to be open for the following procedures. Backup and recovery can be performed and configured either using a wizard or the Explorer-like interface. (The following procedures use the wizards on the General tab.)

### Perform a Backup

The key steps in this wizard are:

*What to back up*
System-state data includes the registry and other critical files, including Active Directory, on domain controllers. See the sidebar "System-State Data" in the article *disaster recovery* in Chapter 3 for more information.

*Where to store the backup*
You can only select Tape Drive when a tape drive is actually attached. If you have a tape drive attached, enter the tape name in the second box.

Select File if you want to back up to a hard disk, removable disk, or network share. In this case you specify the absolute or UNC path to the backup file (.*bkf* file) you want to create.

*Advanced (optional)*
Click Finish instead to select the default settings here (shown in parentheses). Click Advanced to choose the backup method (normal), whether to verify data (no), use hardware compression (varies with device), append or replace the backup to the media (append), restrict access to the backup set to the owner and Administrator (recommended when backing up Active Directory,

but only available when you replace, not append), specify a backup label (date and time) and media label (date and time), and perform the backup now or schedule it for later (now). If you schedule a backup job, it appears on the Scheduled Job tab of Windows Backup.

### Perform a Restore

The key steps in this wizard are:

#### What to restore

Select and expand the media type (File or Tape), select and expand the media set (backup set), then select the data you want to restore.

#### Advanced (optional)

Click Finish instead to immediately restore the selected data to its original location without overwriting any existing files. Click Advanced to choose whether to restore to original location, an alternate location, or a single folder (this collapses the tree of folders and files into a single flat-folder structure), and choose the conditions for overwriting existing files during restore.

### Rebuild a Server

If using the ERD fails to repair a Windows 2000 server, you need to rebuild it. Rebuilding a server requires:

- A recent complete backup
- The Windows 2000 Server CD
- Documentation of your server and networking configuration

Use the following steps to rebuild a server:

1. Recreate the partitions on the hard drive.

2. Install Windows 2000 Server as a standalone server (member of a workgroup). Use the Setup defaults, as restoring the system-state data will restore the server's proper name, domain, and so on.

3. Restore the system-state data from the backup set.

4. Restore any remaining data for the server. This last step may require additional configuration if you have other applications installed on the server. See the documentation for those applications on how to restore them from a backup set.

### Notes

- You must be a member of the Administrators, Backup Operators, or Server Operators group to perform a backup (local or network) of computers in a domain.

- Before performing a backup, send a notification to users to close their files as Windows Backup does not back up files that applications have locked open. To send a message open the Computer Management console, connect to the server(s) being backed up, and:

> Right-click on Computer Management node → All Tasks → Send Console Message

- If you are backing up to a tape drive as your backup media, the tape drive must be attached to the computer on which you are running Windows Backup.

### See Also

*disaster recovery(3)*

---

# bindings

Enable and disable bindings, and rearrange the binding order.

### Procedures

To modify bindings, you use the Network and Dial-up Connections window as follows:

> Start → Settings → Control Panel → Network and Dial-up Connections → Advanced → Advanced Settings → Adapters and Bindings

Select the network connection whose bindings you want to configure, and then perform one of the following tasks:

*Enable or disable a binding*
  Select or deselect the checkbox for that binding.

*Rearrange the binding order*
  Select a binding and use the up or down arrows to change the binding order. The binding at the top of the list is the first one used.

### Notes

- You must be a member of the Administrators group to modify bindings.

- You can use the Provider Order tab to rearrange the order in which network and print providers attempt connections on the network. You should use this in conjunction with the Adapters and Bindings tab. For example, if you have both TCP/IP and NWLink installed as network protocols and both File and Printer Sharing for Microsoft Networks and Gateway (and Client) Services for NetWare installed on your network, but on an attached network segment you have mostly Microsoft clients running TCP/IP, then:

  — Select Adapters and Bindings, and move TCP/IP to the top of the list for File and Printer Sharing for Microsoft Networks.

  — Select Provider Order, and move Microsoft Windows Network to the top of the list of network providers.

### See Also

*bindings(3), Network and Dial-up Connections(6), network protocol(3,4)*

## computer

Configure and create computer accounts, and join a computer to a domain or workgroup.

### Procedures

Computer accounts are managed with Active Directory Users and Computers, while computers can be configured to join a workgroup or domain using Computer Management or System in the Control Panel.

#### Configure a Computer Account

> Open the Active Directory Users and Computers console → right-click on a computer account → Properties

This lets you change the group membership, location, and other properties of the account. There is typically not much you need to configure here, if anything, for computer accounts.

#### Create a Computer Account

When you join a computer to a domain, you are prompted to provide credentials for creating a computer account for the computer. The new account is represented by a Computer object that is located by default within the default Computers container within the domain container in Active Directory. You can create computer accounts directly using Active Directory Users and Computers, however:

> Open the Active Directory Users and Computers console → right-click on an OU → New → Computer → specify name of computer → OK

Once a computer account has been created (either manually or when the computer joined the domain), you can configure it (see "Configure a Computer Account" earlier in this article).

Computer accounts can be used together with Group Policy to manage policy settings on computers. You cannot link a Group Policy Object (GPO) to the default Computers container for a domain in Active Directory, so you may want to move your computer accounts (right-click on a computer → Move) to different OUs and link GPOs to those OUs to manage computer configuration settings. You can also add computer accounts to different groups and then filter Group Policy settings for accounts in those groups. See *Group Policy Objects (GPOs)* in this chapter for more information on procedures for configuring Group Policy.

*Join a Computer to a Domain or Workgroup*

Typically, you will join a machine to a domain when you run Setup to install Windows 2000 on the machine. However, if you have already installed Windows 2000 on a standalone computer or as part of a workgroup, you can join your machine to an existing domain. There are several ways to proceed:

- Start → Programs → Administrative Tools → Computer Management → right-click on Computer Management node

- Start → Settings → Control Panel → Administrative Tools → Computer Management → right-click on Computer Management node

- Start → Settings → Control Panel → System

- Right-click on My Computer → Properties

Whichever method you choose, continue as follows:

Network Identification → Properties → Member of → {Domain | Workgroup} → specify name of domain or workgroup → OK → specify administrator's username and password (for domain only)

---

Windows 2000 Professional includes a Network Identification Wizard for leading you through the steps of adding your computer to a domain or workgroup. Click the Network ID button on the Network Identification tab to run the wizard.

---

When a machine has been added to a domain, you have a choice in the Log On To Windows dialog box of logging onto either:

- The local computer using a local user account

- The domain using a domain user account

- Other trusted domains in the forest

---

You must log on to the domain using a domain user account in order to access domain resources. If you log on using a local user account, you may not be able to access the network resources you need.

---

*Notes*

- You must be a member of Domain Admins to create a computer account in a domain. In addition, this task can be delegated to non–Domain Admins.

- Other actions you can perform on computer accounts using Active Directory Users and Computers include the following:

  — Right-click on a computer → Disable. This breaks the computer's connection with the domain and prevents it from authenticating to the domain until you Enable it. Disabling a computer account does not remove it from Active Directory (use → Delete to do that).

— Right-click on a computer → Manage. This opens up Computer Management and connects to the selected computer to manage its resources.

— Right-click on a computer → Reset Account. If you reset a computer account, you must first remove the computer from the domain if you want it to rejoin the domain again.

• When specifying the name of the domain you want to join, you can specify either the full DNS name of the domain (e.g., *mtit.com*) or the downlevel (pre–Windows 2000) name of the domain (e.g., *HEADOFFICE*).

— To find the full DNS name (e.g., *mtit.com*) for a domain, use Control Panel → System → Network Identification on a domain controller that belongs to the domain.

— To find the downlevel name (e.g., *HEADOFFICE*) for a domain, select the domain node (e.g., *mtit.com*) in the console tree of Active Directory Users and Computers and go Action → Properties → General.

• Joining a domain creates a computer account for the machine in Active Directory. This account can be displayed in the Computers OU of the Active Directory Users and Computers console. Removing a computer from a domain (by making it join a workgroup instead) only disables its corresponding computer account in Active Directory (instead of deleting it). You still need to delete the computer account using Active Directory Users and Computers. See *computer name* in this chapter for more information.

• To join a domain, you must use credentials for a user account belonging to the Domain Admins group for the domain. The computer will reboot to complete the process of joining a domain.

### See Also

*computer name(4), domain(3,4), Group Policy Objects (GPOs)(4)*

---

## computer name

Display and modify the name of a Windows 2000 computer.

### Procedures

Open the System utility in the Control Panel, and then proceed as follows:

*Display computer name*
See the Network Identification tab. Click Properties → More to see the NetBIOS name.

*Modify computer name*
Network Identification → Properties → <computer_name> → enter your Administrator credentials

### Notes

- When you change the computer name, you will need to reboot the computer for the change to take effect.

- When you change the computer name, the NetBIOS name also changes. For example, if *ms1.mtit.com* is changed to *ps3.mtit.com*, the NetBIOS name is changed from *MS1* to *PS3*.

- You cannot change the computer name on a domain controller.

### See Also

*computer name(3), net name(7), System(6)*

---

## default user profile

Create and deploy a default user profile for new users.

### Procedures

Administrators can create a default user profile, which will be applied to each new user account when the user logs on to the domain for the first time. This allows administrators to provide users with a standardized desktop environment the first time they log on.

#### Create and Deploy a Default User Profile

1. Log on to a Windows 2000 Professional client computer as an ordinary user (e.g., Bob).

2. Configure the client computer to reflect the desktop environment you wish all your users to have.

3. Log off the client computer to create a local user profile *C:\Documents and Settings\Bob.*

4. Log on as Administrator and copy Bob's local profile to the NETLOGON share on a domain controller.

5. Rename the profile on the domain controller to Default User.

6. Copy the Default User profile to the NETLOGON share on all domain controllers in your domain.

Now when a new user first logs on to the domain, the default profile will be downloaded from the domain controller and copied to the *C:\Documents and Settings\<user_name>* folder on the client computer, where *<user_name>* is the name of the user's account. Subsequent logons by the user will load the local user profile stored in this folder.

### Notes

- The ordinary user account (Bob in the previous example) you log on with to create a default profile should be a dummy account used only for this purpose, and not an account used by an actual user.

- If the profile is named anything other than Default User, it will not be downloaded from the domain controller when the user first logs on.

---

- If the default user profile is downloaded to a client computer and the user makes changes to her desktop environment, the default profile is not modified when the user logs off; only the local user profile is modified.

  If the user then logs on to another client computer, however, she will download the default profile instead of her own customized profile. If users need to roam between machines and maintain their own customized profile, implement roaming user profiles instead.

### See Also

*user profile(3)*

---

## delegation

Delegate administration over a domain, OU, or Site object to users or groups, and modify Active Directory permissions assigned through the Delegation of Control Wizard.

### Procedures

The task of delegating authority over a domain or OU uses the Active Directory Users and Computers console, while delegating authority over a site uses the Active Directory Sites and Services console. In either case you may first need to connect to the domain or forest in order to administer it.

#### Delegate Authority over a Domain

Active Directory Users and Computers → right-click on domain → Delegate Control → Next → Add → select users or groups → OK → Next

At this point in the Delegation of Control Wizard, select the tasks you want to delegate to your designated users or groups. For example, you can delegate authority to:

- Join a computer to the domain
- Manage Group Policy links

Clicking Next then Finish ends the wizard.

Alternatively, you can select "Create a custom task to delegate," which allows you to delegate control of the domain and all the objects it contains to your designated users or groups, or you can delegate control of specific types of objects within the folder to these users or groups. For example, you could delegate control of all Computer objects within the domain to a specific group. Depending on which type of object you select, you can specify different Active Directory permissions to be delegated over that object to your users or groups. The range and complexity of permissions you can assign users and groups over specific Active Directory objects is quite staggering! The most common choice here is simply to grant specified users or groups Full Control permission over the types of objects you specify. For example, you could grant Full Control permission to all Computer objects in your domain to a CompAdmins global group you create. Members of this group can fully administer computers in the domain but cannot administer users, groups, printers, or other kinds of objects.

---

### Delegate Authority over an OU

This is similar to the previous task, except that:

- You select an OU instead of a domain in the console tree of Active Directory Users and Computers.

- The list of tasks available for delegation is more extensive than when delegating authority over a domain. Specifically, you can delegate the ability to:
  — Create, delete, and manage user accounts
  — Reset passwords on user accounts
  — Read all user information
  — Create, delete, and manage groups
  — Modify the membership of a group
  — Manage Group Policy links

### Delegate Authority over a Site Object

By Site object, I mean one of the following types of objects in the console tree of Active Directory Sites and Services:

- The Sites container
- A particular site (including the Default-First-Site-Name object)
- A Servers folder beneath a particular site object
- The Inter-Site Transports container
- The Subnets container

Let's look at delegating control over a particular site object:

> Active Directory Sites and Services → right-click on site → Delegate Control → Next → Add → specify users or groups → OK → Next

At this point you can either:

- Delegate the task Manage Group Policy links
- Create a custom task to delegate

If you select the latter, you then specify the types of objects you want to delegate control over and the level of permissions that will be assigned in Active Directory to your specified users and groups. See "Delegate Authority over a Domain" in this article for more information.

### Modify Delegated Permissions

You can modify (or remove) Active Directory permissions that have been assigned to users and groups using the Delegation of Control Wizard, but to do so requires making the advanced portions of Active Directory visible if you are dealing with domains or OUs:

> Active Directory Users and Groups → View → toggle Advanced Features on → right-click on domain or OU → Properties → Security → select user or group → modify or remove permissions as desired

### Notes

- It is generally best to delegate authority to groups instead of individuals as this simplifies administration when your company grows or reorganizes.

- You cannot delegate control over the Builtin folder.

- The Delegation of Control Wizard is only useful for allowing permissions over Active Directory objects, not for denying them. To deny permissions you need to use the procedure outlined in "Modify Delegated Permissions" earlier in this article.

- If you want to remove permissions assigned through using the Delegation of Control Wizard, you need to use the method outlined in "Modify Delegated Permissions" earlier in this article.

- If you are delegating control to Site objects other than a particular site container, there are no prespecified tasks you can delegate. You must specify the types of objects and levels of permissions to delegate.

### See Also

*Active Directory(3), delegation(3), domain(3,4), OU(3,4)*

---

## Dfs

Add a Dfs link, root, root replica, or shared folder, delete a Dfs root, modify Dfs client cache time, monitor the status of Dfs shared folders, set a Dfs replication policy, or take a replica offline.

### Procedures

The following procedures assume that you already have the Dfs console open (see *Distributed File System* in Chapter 5 for more information on the Dfs console). In most cases each procedure covers two cases:

*Standalone Dfs*
> This is implemented on a standalone Windows 2000 server that does not belong to a domain (it belongs to a workgroup instead).

*Domain-based Dfs*
> This is implemented on a Windows 2000 member server (not a domain controller) that belongs to a domain.

#### Add a Dfs Link to a Dfs Root

Standalone or domain-based Dfs:

> Right-click on Dfs root → New Dfs link → specify name for link → specify shared folder (on local or remote machine) to which link points → specify Dfs client cache time → OK

Once you have created a Dfs link, you can add additional Dfs shared folders to it (see "Add a Dfs Shared Folder" later in this article).

### *Add a Dfs Root*

Standalone Dfs:

> Action → New Dfs root → Next → Create a standalone Dfs root → Next → Next → {create a new share | specify an existing share} to which the Dfs root will point → Next → Finish

This creates a standalone Dfs root on the local server. The name of the Dfs root is the same as the name of the local shared folder to which it points. Unfortunately, if you elect to create a new share, you must type the absolute path on the local drive system to the folder you want to share (you cannot browse).

Domain-based Dfs:

> Action → new Dfs root → Next → Create a domain Dfs root → select local or trusted domain → click Browse to select a member server or domain controller within the domain Next → {create a new share | specify an existing share} to which the Dfs root will point → Next → specify name of Dfs root → Finish

You can create domain-based Dfs roots from either the local or a remote server.

---

If you try to create a Dfs root on a member server and the wizard fails with a message indicating that it cannot find the specified domain, or if the wizard gives an RPC error when you try to Browse to select a remote server on which to create your root, you may not have your member server's TCP/IP settings configured with a pre-ferred DNS server. As a result, the server will not have registered itself with the DNS server running on the domain controller using Dynamic DNS. Specify a preferred DNS server and reboot the member server to register it with DDNS.

You must reboot your server after you add a new Dfs root in order to enable your new Dfs root.

---

### *Add a Dfs Root Replica*

This option is not available for standalone Dfs. For domain-based Dfs:

> Right-click on Dfs root → New Root Replica → specify FQDN of host server (or browse Active Directory) → Next → {create a new share | specify an existing share} to which the Dfs root will point → Next → Finish

The entire Dfs root you select is now fault tolerant—if a Dfs client tries to connect to the root and the original host server is unavailable, Dfs will transparently redirect the client to the new host server where the root replica resides. Once you have created a root replica, you should configure a replication policy (see "Set a Dfs Replication Policy" later in this article).

### Add a Dfs Shared Folder

Standalone Dfs:

> Right-click a Dfs link → New Replica → specify shared folder (on local or remote machine) to which link points → OK

A Dfs link that points to multiple shared folders is said to contain a replica set.

Domain-based Dfs are the same as earlier, except that you can specify the replication policy as either Manual or Automatic. If you select Manual, then you can configure a replication policy later if you decide to do so. If you select Automatic, then the Replication Policy box opens immediately. To configure replication, see "Set a Dfs Replication Policy" later in this article.

### Delete a Dfs Root

> Right-click on Dfs root → Delete Dfs Root

This does two things:

- Removes the Dfs root node from the Dfs console
- Removes the actual Dfs root definition from the host server (destroys its associated Dfs tree)

If you just want to remove the Dfs root node from the console window—for example, to connect to a different root to manage it (although you can connect to multiple roots with the Dfs console)—do the following:

> Right-click on Dfs root → Remove Display of Dfs Root

The root will no longer be displayed in the Dfs console, but its associated Dfs tree still exists, Dfs is still enabled, and Dfs clients can still connect to the tree.

### Modify Dfs Client Cache Time

> Right-click on Dfs root or link → Properties → modify cache time

---

 By default, Dfs client cache time is set to 1,800 seconds or 30 minutes for Dfs links and to 300 seconds or 5 minutes for a Dfs root. You might want to increase these times if clients need frequent access to shared folders and if you don't create or delete shared folders often on your file servers (or change your Dfs tree frequently). This will lessen the network traffic associated with Dfs overhead.

---

### Monitor the Status of Dfs Folders

> Right-click on Dfs root or link → Check Status

A red circle with an "X" indicates that the link is unavailable. If a link points to multiple replicas, it is still available as long as at least one of its replicas is available.

Unfortunately, you must use Check Status to check each Dfs link (and the Dfs root) separately! This is a rather tedious exercise if you have an extensive Dfs tree.

### Set a Dfs Replication Policy

Once you have added a root replica to an existing domain-based Dfs root (or a second Dfs shared folder to an existing Dfs link), you can configure a replication policy:

> Right-click on Dfs root → Replication Policy

This opens the Replication Policy box (which has nothing to do with Group Policies). Specify one replica as the master by selecting it and clicking Set Master, then select the other replicas and Enable (or Disable) them for replication as desired. When data in one of the replicas changes, the appropriate files are replicated between them automatically.

### Take a Replica Offline

> Select Dfs link → right-click on replica in Details Pane → Take Replica Offline/Online

Note that this does not disconnect Dfs clients that are already connected to the replica; it just prevents new connections (soft disconnect, not hard).

### Notes

- You can create Dfs roots on both FAT and NTFS partitions, but NTFS is recommended because of its additional security and because it supports automatic replication of Dfs roots and shared folders (FAT supports only manual replication).

- Save the Dfs console configuration once you have your Dfs tree set up, and use the Dfs console to monitor the tree to ensure that Dfs shared folders are available. If a Dfs folder's status is unavailable, check to make sure the file server is running and connected to the network, that it hasn't been renamed, and that the shared folder that Dfs points to is still shared.

- Dfs shared folders don't need to be on Windows 2000 Server computers; they can be on downlevel servers (Windows NT) or even client computers (Windows 95 or 98). However, to get the full advantages of Dfs replication, use Windows 2000 Server computers only.

- You cannot replicate between Dfs shared folders on a single machine; the shared folders must be located on different machines.

- The property sheet for a domain-based Dfs root has an additional Security tab, which can be used to configure NTFS permissions on the root.

- Don't forget to reboot your server after creating a new Dfs root on it, in order for it to take effect!

### See Also

*Dfs(3), Distributed File System(5), shared folder(3,4)*

Tasks D

# DHCP

Add a DHCP server, activate a scope, authorize a DHCP server, create a reservation, create and modify a scope (ordinary, multicast, and superscope), display DHCP statistics, display active leases, install the DHCP Server service, pause or stop a DHCP server, reconcile a scope, and specify scope options, user classes, and vendor classes.

## Procedures

You perform most DHCP procedures using the DHCP console, which is accessed using:

> Start → Programs → Administrative Tools → DHCP

The following procedures assume that the DHCP console is already open. For more information on DHCP concepts and terminology, see *DHCP* in Chapter 3.

---

 You can also manage many aspects of DHCP servers from the command line using the netsh (Netshell) command. See *netsh* in Chapter 7, *Commands*, for more information.

---

### Add a DHCP Server

> Right-click on root (DHCP) node in console tree → Add Server → Browse → select computer → OK

This adds a DHCP server to the DHCP console so you can manage it. You can delete a server from the console by selecting Delete from the shortcut menu.

### Activate (or Deactivate) a Scope

> Right-click on Scope node → {Activate | Deactivate}

Only an activated scope responds to DHCP lease and renewal requests from client computers. Activation allows you to selectively control which scopes are available on a DHCP server.

It is recommended that you do not deactivate a scope unless you intend to retire and delete it from the server. This is because a DHCP server whose scope is deactivated will send out DHCPNAK packets to clients who attempt to contact it, which commences a recall of DHCP addresses in the subnet. A better way of pausing a scope (rendering it temporarily unresponsive) is to temporarily increase the exclusions on the scope to exclude all addresses in the scope.

### Authorize (or Unauthorize) a DHCP Server

To authorize or unauthorize a particular DHCP server:

> Right-click on DHCP server node → {Authorize | Unauthorize}

After a minute or two, press F5 to refresh and see if authorization was successful. The DHCP console doesn't refresh itself very well, and you need to select a particular DHCP server in the console tree before pressing F5 or selecting Action → Refresh.

To authorize one or more DHCP servers or display their authorization status:

Right-click root (DHCP) node → Manage authorized servers → Authorize → specify IP address of DHCP server → OK

Note that you must be a member of the Enterprise Admins group to authorize a DHCP server. Unauthorizing a DHCP server causes it to ignore all lease and renewal requests from DHCP clients until it is reauthorized.

 If you install the DHCP Server service on a domain controller, it should authorize itself automatically. If this does not occur, then authorize it manually.

You can also use Active Directory Sites and Services to delegate the ability to authorize DHCP servers to users who are not Enterprise Admins. To do this, open Active Directory Sites and Services and select:

View → Show Services Node → select Services node → right-click on NetServices node → Delegate Control → Next → Add → select users or groups → Add → OK → Next → select This folder → Next → select Full Control → Next → Finish

### Create a Reservation

Right-click on Reservations node → New Reservation

Enter the name and MAC address of the client computer for which you want to reserve an IP address.

 You can determine a computer's MAC address by going to the computer and running the `ipconfig /all` command from the command line. Windows 2000 Help says you can also determine it by opening the property sheet of a LAN connection in Network and Dial-up Connections, but this doesn't work.

### Create and Modify a Scope

A DHCP server must be authorized (see "Authorize (or Unauthorize) a DHCP Server" earlier in this article) before you can create a scope. After creating a scope, you must activate the scope (see "Activate (or Deactivate) a Scope" earlier in this article) so clients can lease addresses from the server.

### Create and Modify an Ordinary Scope

Right-click on DHCP server node → New Scope

This starts the New Scope Wizard, which prompts you for:

- A name and description for the scope.

- The first and last IP address of the range of IP addresses belonging to the scope.

- The subnet mask for the scope. (You can either enter it manually or select the number of bits used in the host ID—a nice touch for those of us who have forgotten the rules for subnetting!)

- Individual or blocks of IP addresses that should be excluded from the scope. (Enter only the start address if you want to exclude a single address.)

- The duration of the lease.

- DHCP scope options such as default gateway address, DNS domain name, addresses of DNS servers, and addresses of WINS servers on your network.

---

 At the end of the wizard you are prompted to activate your scope. I suggest you decline this so you can double-check your scope configuration carefully in the DHCP console before you activate it and have clients start to lease addresses.

---

To modify a scope once it has been created:

Right-click on Scope node → Properties → General

You can increase the range of IP addresses in a scope, but you cannot decrease it. To exclude additional IP addresses from an existing scope:

Right-click on Address Pool node → New Exclusion Range → specify start and end IP addresses (or only start address to exclude a single address)

Note that you cannot exclude addresses that are actively leased to clients. To remove an existing exclusion:

Select Address Pool → right-click on exclusion in Details Pane → Delete

To reconfigure scope options, see "Specify Scope Options" later in this article.

---

 If you want to change the IP address range of the scope to a different subnet, you must first remove all exclusions and options that conflict with the new subnet. Otherwise, you will receive the error message, "The specified range either overlaps an existing range or is not valid." An easier solution is usually to delete the scope entirely and create a new one. Be aware that you will have to release and renew IP addresses from your DHCP clients afterwards. The essential thing with DHCP is therefore that you plan it carefully before implementing it on your network.

---

### Create a Multicast Scope

> Right-click on DHCP server node → New Multicast Scope

This starts the New Multicast Scope Wizard, which prompts you for:

- A name and description for the scope.

- The start and end IP address of a range of class D (multicast) IP addresses. This range must be within 224.0.0.0 and 239.255.255.255.

- The number of hops that the multicast packets can traverse through routers on the internetwork.

- Exclusions to the specified range of IP addresses.

- Lease duration.

To modify a multicast scope once it has been created:

> Right-click on Multicast Scope node → Properties

On the Lifetime tab you can specify a specific date when the scope expires or allow it to exist indefinitely. Note that this is not the same as lease duration, which is specified on the General tab.

### Create a Superscope

> Right-click on DHCP server node → New Superscope

This starts the New Superscope Wizard, which prompts you for:

- A name for the superscope

- Which scopes you want to include in your superscope

You can now use the new Superscope node for your DHCP server in the console tree to display statistics for the superscope or activate/deactivate all scopes within the superscope. However, if you want to make further modifications to the scopes, you have to use their individual nodes, which are now beneath the Superscope node.

### Display Active Leases

> Select Address Leases node → read Details Pane

You can then right-click on an active lease in the Details Pane and delete it if you like. However, the client may request the address again, so you will also need to release the address to the client using `ipconfig /release`.

### Display DHCP Statistics

> Right-click on DHCP server node → Display Statistics

This window is manually refreshed by default. To cause it to refresh automatically, do the following:

> Right-click on DHCP server node → Properties → General → Automatically update statistics → specify time interval

If you create a scope and later want to delete it (to create a new one), first deactivate the scope and leave it in that condition until half the configured lease time elapses. Otherwise, you will have to manually release and renew IP addresses on each client using `ipconfig` once your new scope is created.

### Install the DHCP Server Service

Start → Settings → Control Panel → Add/Remove Programs → Add/Remove Windows Components → select Networking Services → Details → select the Dynamic Host Configuration protocol (DHCP) checkbox → OK

 If you want to uninstall the DHCP Server service, be sure to stop it first (see the next section "Pause or Stop a DHCP Server") to ensure that it uninstalls properly.

### Pause or Stop a DHCP Server

Right-click on DHCP server node → All Tasks → {Pause | Stop | Restart}

Restarting a DHCP server stops and then starts the DHCP Server service on the server in one step. A paused server can be resumed, and a stopped one started.

You can also perform these actions from the command line (see the following commands in Chapter 7):

- `net start dhcpserver`
- `net stop dhcpserver`
- `net pause dhcpserver`
- `net continue dhcpserver`

### Reconcile a Scope

Right-click on Scope node → Reconcile → Verify

Lets you fix any inconsistency in the DHCP database by comparing it with information stored in the registry. If everything is fine, you are prompted to click OK. If there are inconsistencies, the inconsistent addresses are displayed; select them and click Reconcile.

If the DHCP server database *dhcp.mdb* grows beyond 30 MB, you can manually compact it offline using the *Jetpack.exe* utility. At the command prompt, enter the following:

```
cd %SystemRoot%\system32\dhcp
net stop dhcpserver
jetpack dhcp.mdb tmp.mdb
net start dhcpserver
```

Note that this procedure may not be as necessary in Windows 2000 Server as it was in Windows NT Server since the Windows 2000 DHCP Server service performs periodic automatic online compaction of the DHCP database. Nevertheless, Microsoft recommends offline compaction of the DHCP server database once a month if your server manages 1,000 or more clients.

### Specify Scope Options

You can configure scope options at four levels:

*Server level*
Right-click on Server Options node → Configure Options → General → select option → enter required data

*Scope level*
Right-click on Scope Options node → Configure Options → General → select option → enter required data

*Class level*
Right-click on {Server | Scope} Options node → Configure Options → Advanced → select {User | Vendor} class → select option → enter required data

*Reserved client level*
Select Reservations node → right-click on reservation → Configure Options → General → select option → enter required data

The usual options to configure in Microsoft networks are 003, 006, 015, and, if you are using WINS, 044 and 046 as well. Each option requires you to specify information related to that option, as summarized in Table 4-1. For options involving IP addresses, you can optionally enter the name of the computer and click Resolve to determine its IP address. If you configure 044, then 046 must be configured as well. For 046 the typical choice is 0x8 if a WINS server is present on the network.

*Table 4-1: DHCP Scope Options and the Information You Need to Specify*

| Option | Information |
|---|---|
| 003 Router | IP addresses of default gateways |
| 006 DNS Servers | IP addresses of DNS servers |
| 015 DNS Domain Name | DNS name of local domain (e.g., *mtit.com*) |
| 044 WINS/NBNS Servers | IP addresses of WINS servers |
| 046 WINS/NBT Node Type | 0x1 = B-node (broadcast) |
| | 0x2 = P-node (peer) |
| | 0x4 = M-node (mixed) |
| | 0x8 = H-node (hybrid) |

### Specify User-Defined Classes

These are used to identify a DHCP client according to its type, such as mobile computer or dial-up connection. You might use this feature to specify DHCP options for all laptop computers on your network:

Right-click on DHCP server node → Define User Classes → Add → specify a display name and a binary or hexadecimal (ASCII) identifier for the class → OK

The binary or ASCII string set here must match the DHCP class ID string set on the DHCP client computers that are members of the user-defined class. Only Windows 2000 client computers can have a DHCP class ID string set on them, and this is done using the `ipconfig /setclassid` command (see *ipconfig* in Chapter 7).

After specifying the user-defined class, you can then configure user-defined scope options as follows:

> Right-click on Scope Options node → Configure Options → Advanced → specify User Class you created → General → specify options

### Specify Vendor-Defined Classes

These are used to identify a DHCP client according to its vendor, such as Compaq or Dell. You might use this feature to specify DHCP options for all Compaq computers on your network:

> Right-click on DHCP server node → Define Vendor Classes → Add → specify a display name and a binary or hexadecimal (ASCII) identifier for the class → OK

The binary or ASCII string set here must match the DHCP class ID string set on the DHCP client computers that are members of the vendor-defined class. Only Windows 2000 client computers can have a DHCP class ID string set on them, and this is done using the `ipconfig /setclassid` command (see *ipconfig* in Chapter 7).

After specifying the vendor-defined class, you can then configure user-defined scope options as follows:

> Right-click on Scope Options node → Configure Options → Advanced → specify Vendor Class you created → General → specify options

### Notes

- Exclude the IP addresses of computers like servers that have static IP addresses.

- If the configuration of your network rarely changes, you can increase the duration of DHCP leases or make it unlimited. If you frequently move computers around or have a lot of mobile computers, you can reduce the lease duration.

- Similarly, if you have a lot of extra, unassigned IP addresses, you can increase the duration of DHCP leases or make it unlimited. If you have barely enough addresses, reduce the lease duration.

- Deleting a superscope does not delete the child scopes within it.

- The DHCP Server service automatically creates audit logs called *DhcpSrvLog. xxx*, where the extension depends on the day of the week. This log can be used to troubleshoot problems with the DHCP Server service. The location of the log is specified using:

  > Right-click on DHCP server node → Properties → Advanced

You can disable the log by:

> Right-click on DHCP server node → Properties → General → deselect "Enable DHCP audit logging"

- You can modify the bindings (the network connections on which the DHCP server is operating) by:

> Right-click on DHCP server node → Properties → Advanced → Bindings

Note that WAN connections do not show up in this box.

- The DHCP Users group provides Read-only access to the DHCP console. They cannot modify the DHCP server settings. To give a user the ability to modify DHCP server settings, add the user to the DHCP Administrators group.

- If your DHCP server stops unexpectedly, check the System log in Event Viewer. If this doesn't help, check the DHCP Server Audit log.

### See Also

*DHCP(3,5), DHCP relay agent(3,4), DNS(3,4), ipconfig(7), netsh(7), TCP/IP(3,4)*

---

## DHCP and DNS

A new and useful feature of DHCP on Windows 2000 Server is how a DHCP server can update its DHCP client information on DNS servers that support Dynamic DNS (see *DNS* in Chapter 3). For this feature to work, your DHCP and DNS servers must both be running Windows 2000 Server. You must also configure your DNS server to support dynamic updates (see *DNS* in this chapter).

A properly configured DHCP server can update the following records on a DNS server for each DHCP client:

- A (Address) record, which specifies the hostname to IP address mapping.
- PTR (Pointer) record, which specifies a reverse DNS mapping.

You enable your DHCP server to automatically update DHCP client information on DNS servers by opening the DHCP console and:

> Right-click on server node → Properties → DNS → "Automatically update DHCP client information in DNS"

By default, Windows 2000 Professional clients, after they contact the DHCP server and lease an address, will themselves contact the DNS server directly to update their A records (the DHCP server will update the client's PTR record). Legacy Windows clients cannot do this, but you can configure the DHCP server to do this in their place by:

> Right-click on server node → Properties → DNS → "Enable updates for clients that do not support dynamic update"

---

## DHCP relay agent

Configure a DHCP relay agent, and enable or disable it on a router interface.

### Procedures

The procedures here apply when configuring a Windows 2000 Server computer to operate as a DHCP relay agent (not third-party routers). You must have Routing and Remote Access enabled on your computer to configure it as a DHCP relay agent (see *Routing and Remote Access* in Chapter 5). The following procedures assume that the Routing and Remote Access console is already open.

#### Configure a DHCP Relay Agent

Select server node → IP Routing node → right-click on DHCP Relay Agent → Properties → General → specify IP address of DHCP server

If you have several DHCP servers on the network, you should specify which one(s) can service DHCP clients on the subnet on which your relay agent resides.

#### Enable or Disable a DHCP Relay Agent on a Router Interface

Select server node → IP Routing node → right-click on DHCP Relay Agent → Properties → New Interface → General → select Relay DHCP Packets

You enable the relay agent on each network connection or interface on which you want it to operate.

### Notes

- To view DHCP relay-agent statistics, select the DHCP Relay Agent node in the console tree and read the Details Pane.

- When you enable a DHCP agent (see "Enable or Disable a DHCP Relay Agent on a Router Interface" earlier in this article), you can also specify a wait interval for the agent. This is the time in seconds the agent will wait between receiving a DHCP client-broadcast request and forwarding it to a DHCP server. This is a useful feature, for it allows you to provide backup for a local DHCP server. If the client broadcasts a DHCP message and the local DHCP server doesn't respond in the time specified, the message will be forwarded by the agent to a DHCP server on a remote subnet. In this way, if the local DHCP server goes down, DHCP can still operate on the subnet.

- If your Windows 2000 Server computer is multihomed and acting as an IP router, make sure you add the network interfaces, which connect to the network segments you want to enable the DHCP relay agent on, to the relay agent.

### See Also

*DHCP(3,4), DHCP relay agent(3), Routing and Remote Access(5)*

# *dial-up connection*

Configure a dial-up connection, configure advanced connection settings, connect to a private network or the Internet using a dial-up connection, create a dial-up connection to a private network or to the Internet, disconnect a connection, monitor the status of a dial-up connection, or share a connection.

## *Procedures*

For information on general terminology related to connections, see *connection* in Chapter 3. Described in this section are tasks relating to the following kinds of *outbound* connections:

- Dial-up connections to private networks
- Dial-up connections to the Internet

For tasks relating to *inbound* connections, see the following articles in this chapter:

*incoming connection*
　　Describes how to configure incoming connections on a standalone Windows 2000 server that is part of a workgroup

*remote-access server*
　　Describes how to configure incoming connections on a Windows 2000 domain controller or member server that is part of a domain

The tasks listed here (unless otherwise specified) assume that you have already opened the Network and Dial-up Connections window by:

　　Start → Settings → Network and Dial-up Connections

## *Configure a Dial-up Connection*

When you use the Network Connection Wizard to create a new outbound dial-up connection, you specify only minimal configuration information for the connection. Typically, you need to further configure the connection so that you can successfully and efficiently connect to the remote-access server at the remote private network or the modem bank at the ISP you are dialing. To configure a dial-up connection on a client machine:

　　Right-click on connection → Properties

The configuration options are the same whether you are configuring a dial-up connection to a private network or to the Internet. Following are some highlights of some of the more important settings on the five tabs of this property sheet.

### *General*

Click the Alternates button if you want to assign multiple phone numbers to a connection. You can then have the connection try each number in order until it succeeds in establishing a connection. You can also configure it so that successful numbers are moved to the top of the list for future connection attempts.

*Tasks*
*D*

Select the Show icon that's in the taskbar when connected. This will place a connection icon in the system tray, which will blink when data is being transferred. You can double-click on this icon to display the status of the connection and right-click on it to disable (terminate) the connection.

If you have more than one modem installed, you have additional options on this tab that let you:

- Specify which modem or modems will be used for this connection.

- Specify the order in which they are used to establish a connection. (If the first modem fails, then the next one in the list will be used.)

- Specify whether they will all call the same numbers.

### Options

This is where you specify redial attempts and whether the connection should automatically terminate after being idle for a period of time. You can also specify that the connection will automatically redial if it is dropped—this is useful for file transfers using FTP since Windows 2000 can resume a file transfer without needing to start all over from the beginning.

If you have more than one modem installed and you have enabled at least two of them for this connection on the General tab, you have the additional option of Multiple Devices on the Options tab. This new option can be specified as either:

*Dial all devices (the default selection)*
　　Use this to configure a PPP Multilink dial-up connection. (The remote-access server you are dialing must support PPP Multilink also.)

*Dial only the first available device*
　　Use this if you want to use multiple modems to provide fault tolerance for your connection.

*Dial devices only as needed*
　　Use this to configure a BAP connection for dynamic multilinking. (The remote-access server you are dialing must support BAP as well.) After you make this selection, click Configure to specify the conditions under which lines are added or dropped to your connection.

---

Multilink dial-up connections usually don't work if callback is configured on the remote-access server. This is because only one callback number can be stored on the server to call the client back, with the result that only the first line in a multilink connection is used. The exception is 2B+D ISDN connections in which both ISDN B channels can have the same number for callback.

---

### Security

Typical security gives you a series of preconfigured settings for authentication protocols and data-encryption schemes. In any case the remote-access client and server will negotiate the highest degree of security for authentication and data integrity that they are both configured to support. The three settings here are (in order of increasing security):

*Allow unsecured password (the default setting)*
    Allows any authentication protocol including PAP but does not encrypt data

*Require secured password*
    Does not allow PAP but can encrypt data

*Use smart card*
    Allows only smart-card authentication and can encrypt data

If you want more granular control over which authentication protocols and data-encryption schemes the dial-up client will support, select Advanced → Settings.

For more information on these different schemes and protocols, see *remote access* in Chapter 3.

---

 Since the default setting allows unsecured passwords to be transmitted over the connection, you may want to change this to provide greater security, especially when connecting to the Internet.

---

### Networking

You can specify that the remote-access server you are dialing into is either PPP or SLIP (it's almost always PPP nowadays). If PPP, then click Settings to configure advanced PPP features, such as software compression, if supported by the server you are calling. (All of these features are enabled by default, and it's best to leave them so.)

Usually a dial-up connection to the Internet will dynamically obtain a client IP address using DHCP, and this is what is configured by default for Internet Protocol (TCP/IP) properties. If you need to specify a static IP address for the client, you can do so here. Table 4-2 shows which commonly installed network components are enabled for dial-up connections to private networks and the Internet.

*Table 4-2: Network Components Enabled for Outbound Dial-up Connections*

| Component | Dial-up Connection to . . . | |
| --- | --- | --- |
| | *Private Network* | *Internet* |
| Internet Protocol (TCP/IP) | ✓ | ✓ |
| Client for Microsoft Networks | ✓ | No |
| File and Print Sharing for Microsoft Networks | No | No |

### Sharing

You can enable Internet Connection Sharing (ICS) here, which lets your computer act as a gateway to the Internet so that other computers on your network can access the remote private network or the Internet through your connection. You can also specify that the connection on your computer be dialed automatically when another computer on your network tries to access the remote network or Internet.

Once you enable this feature, you need to click Settings and specify the TCP and UDP ports on the client and server that are needed to run any network applications you want other computers to access through the connection. You should also specify ports for any Internet services that other computers need to access through the connection. Finally, you will need to configure other computers on your LAN to connect to the Internet through a LAN connection using the Internet Connection Wizard in the Accessories program group.

 Internet Connection Sharing (ICS) is a great feature for Small Office/ Home Office (SOHO) businesses, but in the enterprise it can cause problems. This is because when you enable this feature, Windows 2000 automatically reconfigures the TCP/IP settings on the computer to use Automatic Private IP Addressing (APIPA) to assign IP addresses based on a specially reserved network ID. As a result, you should not enable ICS on enterprise networks that use DNS or DHCP or that have static IP addresses assigned to machines, or subnet communications problems will result. If you want to use ICS for your SOHO, first configure Windows 2000 computers on your LAN to obtain an IP address automatically using APIPA and then install and configure ICS. See *TCP/IP* in Chapter 3 for more information on APIPA.

### Configure Advanced Connection Settings

I always found configuring Dial-up Networking in earlier versions of Microsoft Windows somewhat confusing, as various parts of the configuration must be done using different tools and different parts of the GUI. Unfortunately, Windows 2000 has not removed all of this confusion. Just when you've gone through all five tabs of the property sheet for your dial-up connection and think that the job of configuring the connection is finished, there are always the Advanced settings to consider.

These Advanced settings are configured using the Advanced menu option of the Network and Dial-up Connections window, a place that's easy to overlook. (Menu options casually appear and disappear in Windows 2000 depending on installed components, configured settings, or perhaps sometimes at the whim of the operating system.) The ones that are significant in the context of outbound dial-up connections are as follows.

### Operator-Assisted Dialing

This lets you toggle this feature on or off. If enabled, you double-click on a dial-up connection, pick up the telephone, and manually dial the number or ask the operator to do it. Once the number has been dialed, click Dial, wait for the modem to take control of the line (the modem has gone silent at this point), and hang up.

### Dial-up Preferences

This lets you configure autodial and callback, specifically:

*Autodial*

This lets you enable autodial, a feature that maps network addresses (IP addresses or DNS names) to connection destinations so that when destinations are referenced, the connection is automatically dialed. For example, if you click on a URL in a Word document, you will be prompted to choose a connection to access the destination. If you select your dial-up Internet connection in response to the prompt, Windows 2000 internally maps this connection to the URL so that the next time you click on the URL, the mapped connection will automatically be dialed. All this happens only if autodial is enabled, of course. (It is enabled but always prompts you first.)

*Callback*

This feature allows your dial-up client to request that the remote-access server call it back after the client attempts to initiate a connection. This is typically implemented for either of two reasons:

— So that phone line charges can be billed to the server instead of the client

— For extra security so that the server can confirm the location from where the client is calling

Callback can be enabled on the client, but it must also be required by the server in order for it to be used. The default setting causes a dialog box to be displayed on the client during the initial connection attempt, requesting that the user specify the phone number that the server should use to call the client back. Alternatively, you can require that the server always call the client back at a specified number to confirm the identity of the client by its location.

 The callback settings configured on the remote-access server override any callback settings you configure for the outbound dial-up connection on your client computer. The server can require callback, deny callback, or allow the client to set the callback procedure.

Tasks
D

### Advanced Settings

The relevant setting here is whether your local-area connection or your remote-access connection has priority as far as DNS and other network services are concerned. You can also try modifying the bindings and provider order to get better connection performance when you are running multiple LAN protocols and network clients or services.

### Connect to a Private Network or the Internet Using a Dial-up Connection

Either:

> Double-click on connection → Dial
> Right-click on connection → Connect → Dial

The only difference between initiating a dial-up connection to a private network and initiating one to the Internet is that you have the option with the former of specifying a different phone number to dial from a drop-down list and of specifying a different location from which you are dialing (although with an Internet connection you can also modify these settings in a more tedious way by Properties → General). Why Microsoft decided on this difference, I don't know. Also, the option of selecting a location will only be available for a dial-up connection to a private network if Use Dialing Rules is selected on the General tab of the connection's property sheet.

---

 The administrator on the remote network must first grant dial-in permission to the user before the user will be able to connect to the remote-access server using a dial-up connection. See *remote-access server* and *incoming connection* in this chapter for information on how to do this.

---

### Create a Dial-up Connection to a Private Network

Prior to making a new outbound dial-up connection, make sure you have your modem or ISDN adapter installed and functioning. Double-click the Make New Connection icon to start the Network Connection Wizard. Then select "Dial-up to private network," and specify:

- The phone number of the remote-access server you are connecting to (if you need to specify an area code, select "Use dialing rules").

- Whether the connection will be for your use only or for any user who can log on to your computer. If you select For All Users, then you have the option of sharing the connection to enable other computers on your local-area network to use your computer as a gateway to the remote network.

- A new name is suggested for the connection. A default name is suggested, but you should change this to help you remember what the connection does.

When you finish making your new connection, the Connect <connection_name> box opens, prompting you to dial the connection. You should specify the username and password that your connection will use in being authenticated by the remote network, and you can further configure your connection by clicking Properties.

## Create a Dial-up Connection to the Internet

Make sure you have your modem or ISDN adapter installed and configured before creating your new connection. Also check with your ISP that you have the information you need to configure your connection, such as:

- The IP address of the DNS server at the ISP

- The IP address or FQDN of the SMTP and POP3 servers at the ISP (if you will be using email)

- Whether you need a specific IP address or one is assigned automatically to your connection using DHCP

- Whether IP header compression should be enabled for PPP

- Any other configuration information you may require

To create a dial-up connection to the Internet, do the following:

Make New Connection → Next → Dial-up to the Internet → Next

This opens the Welcome to the Internet Connection Wizard, which leads you through the process of creating and configuring your connection. (Afterwards, you may need to further configure your connection manually.) The initial screen of this wizard offers three options, which determine the steps the wizard takes:

*I want to sign up for a new Internet account*
Use this option only if you don't already have an account with an ISP. If you select this option, the wizard will attempt to use your modem to dial the Microsoft Internet Referral Service to obtain a list of ISPs in your area. It will then guide you through the process of registering with an ISP to obtain a new account.

---

 I tried the Referral Service, but it responded with "Sorry, there are currently no Internet service providers available in your area through the Microsoft Internet Referral Service which support this feature. Click Next to manually restore your Internet settings." I always thought Winnipeg was a backwater—and now I know for sure!

---

*I want to transfer my existing Internet account to this computer*
This option also dials the Referral Service to help you obtain information about transferring your account to this computer.

*I want to set up my Internet connection manually, or I want to connect through a LAN*
To set up your Internet connection manually, you typically need the phone number for your ISP and the username and password for your Internet account obtained from your ISP. You can also optionally set up your email account by specifying your email address and the DNS names of your ISP's mail servers.

*Tasks*
*D*

If your network is connected to the Internet using a dedicated high-speed WAN link like a T1 line, specify that you want to connect through a local-area network (LAN). Windows 2000 will attempt to discover if there is a proxy server installed on the network and configure itself (you can also manually specify proxy settings if the server is not detected). Note that this procedure does not result in a new connection icon being created in the Network and Dial-up Connections window. Once you finish the wizard, Internet Explorer will automatically open and try to connect to MSN on the Internet. If you decide later that you want to use a dial-up Internet connection instead for accessing the Internet, open Internet Explorer and select:

Tools → Internet Options → Connection → deselect "Never dial a connection"

You can also start the Internet Connection Wizard by:

Start → Programs → Accessories → Communications → Internet Connection Wizard

### Disconnect a Connection

Either:

Double-click on connection → Disconnect
Right-click on connection icon in system tray (if enabled) → Disconnect

### Monitor the Status of a Dial-up Connection

Either:

Double-click on connection
Right-click on connection → Status
Double-click on connection icon in system tray (if enabled)

The General tab shows bytes sent and received since the connection was initiated and other network traffic information. The Details tab shows useful information about the type of server, IP address of server and client, type of authentication protocol used, and so on.

You can learn a lot about the capabilities of the access server your ISP is using from this tab. Try changing the settings on the Security tab of your connection's property sheet and then connecting and examining what is displayed on the Details tab of the status box. For example, I discovered this way that my ISP only supports PAP, which transmits passwords in clear text over the connection.

Another connection-monitoring alternative is to select View → Details in the Network and Dial-up Connections window. This lets you monitor the general status of all connections on your machine.

### Sharing a Connection

Right-click on connection → Properties → Sharing → Enable

For more information see "Sharing" under "Configure a Dial-up Connection" earlier in this article.

## Notes

- If you have multiple private networks or ISPs you need to connect to using a dial-up connection, you can make copies of an existing dial-up connection and rename and modify each copy as desired. Just right-click on the connection, and select Create Copy. You can copy dial-up, direct, and VPN connections.

- Specifying a high value for "Idle time before hanging up" for a dial-up connection does not guarantee that the connection won't be terminated earlier by the remote-access server, which typically has its own disconnect timer configured on it.

- Connections can be automated to run from batch files or scripts using the `rasdial` command (see Chapter 7).

- You must be a member of the Administrators group to create a connection.

## See Also

*connection(3), direct computer connection(4), incoming connection(4), local-area connection(4), Network and Dial-up Connections(6), remote access(3), remote-access server(4), Routing and Remote Access(5), TCP/IP(3), VPN connection(4)*

---

# direct computer connection

Configure, connect using, create, and monitor a direct computer connection between two computers.

## Procedures

The tasks listed here (unless otherwise specified) assume that you have already opened the Network and Dial-up Connections window by:

Start → Settings → Network and Dial-up Connections

In some cases the steps depend on whether your computer is a standalone server (belonging to a workgroup) or a domain controller or member server (belonging to a domain).

### Configure a Direct Computer Connection

There are two possibilities, the standalone server and the domain server.

#### Standalone Server

Right-click on connection → Properties

The tabs available here depend on whether you have created a Host or Guest connection. Some of the more important settings on these tabs are as follows:

#### General (Host)

By default, this connection is enabled to listen on all WAN or direct connection devices, so you probably need to disable it on some of them for the sake of security.

Make the connection icon visible on the taskbar as it simplifies the process of monitoring and terminating the connection.

*General (Guest)*

Here you can only specify one device that the connection will use.

*Users (Host)*

By default, devices such as handheld PCs that are directly connected to the computer using a cable or IR port can bypass authentication to simplify and speed up the connection process. Of course, this means that you should probably physically secure your computer so that strangers do not take advantage of this feature.

 If you enable data encryption on the Users tab of a Host connection's property sheet, you must also enable it on the Security tab of the Guest connection's sheet for it to work. I don't recommend using this feature since there is not much need to encrypt data travelling along a parallel cable between two computers—unless it's a very long cable!

*Options (Guest)*

Configure your redial and connection-prompting settings here.

*Security (Guest)*

See *dial-up connection* in this chapter for more information about configuring authentication protocols and encryption schemes.

*Networking (Host and Guest)*

Leave both Client for Microsoft Networks and File and Print Sharing for Microsoft Networks enabled for the connection to work properly.

*Sharing (Guest)*

Be aware that using connection sharing may screw up your TCP/IP settings (see *dial-up connection* in this chapter).

**Domain Controller or Member Server**

Configuring a direct computer connection of Guest type on a domain controller or member server follows the same steps as for doing this on a standalone server belonging to a workgroup (see the previous section).

A direct computer connection of Host type on a member server or domain controller is actually a type of inbound connection and is configured using the Routing and Remote Access console. For information on configuring inbound connections on these types of computers, see *remote-access server* in this chapter.

## Connect Using a Direct Computer Connection

Make sure the null-modem cable is attached (or that a clear line of sight exists between IR ports on the two computers). Then go to the Guest computer and either:

Double-click on connection → Connect
Right-click on connection → Connect → Connect

### Create a Direct Computer Connection

When you create a direct computer connection, you need to decide which of two roles you will assume:

*Host*

> The computer that listens for and responds to direct computer-connection attempts from Guests. A direct computer connection of Host type is a form of inbound connection.

*Guest*

> The computer that attempts to initiate a direct computer connection with a Host. A direct computer connection of Guest type is a form of outbound connection.

Once you create the connection, you may need to further configure it (see "Configure a Direct Computer Connection" earlier in this article).

---

 To enable an ordinary user to use a COM port on his computer for a direct computer connection, you must first log on as Administrator and configure a COM port to use an RS-232C null-modem cable. Do this as follows:

> Control Panel → Phone and Modem Options → Modems → Add → "Don't detect my modem" → Next → "Communications cable between two computers" → Next → select Port → Next → Finish

---

#### Standalone Server

> Double-click on Make New Connection → Next → "Connect directly to another computer" → Next → specify whether your computer is Host or Guest → select port → Next → specify who can use this connection → Next → specify a descriptive name for the connection → Finish

When you create a Host connection on a standalone server, you can specify any or all local user accounts for those who can use the connection. If you create a Guest connection, you must choose between allowing all users to use it or only yourself.

#### Domain Controller or Member Server

Creating a direct computer connection of Guest type on a domain controller or member server follows the same steps as for doing so on a standalone server belonging to a workgroup (see earlier in this article).

If you try to create a direct computer connection of Host type on a member server or domain controller, you are actually trying to create an inbound connection and the New Connection Wizard prompts you to switch to the Routing and Remote Access console to complete the process. For the steps involved in creating inbound connections on these types of computers, see *remote-access server* in this chapter.

### Monitor a Direct Computer Connection

Either:

> Double-click on connection
> Right-click on connection → Status
> Double-click on connection icon in system tray (if enabled)

### Notes

- Direct computer connections can work with RS-232C null-modem cables, DirectParallel ECP cables, modems, ISDN adapters, infrared ports, and similar devices.

- DirectParallel connections only work on standalone Windows 2000 servers and Windows 2000 Professional machines.

- A direct computer connection configured as a Host type is actually a form of inbound connection and is configured as such. For more information see *incoming connection* in this chapter.

- You must be a member of the Administrators group to create a connection.

### See Also

*connection(3), dial-up connection(4), incoming connection(4), local-area connection(4), Network and Dial-up Connections(6), remote access(3), remote-access server(4), Routing and Remote Access(5), VPN connection(4)*

---

# disk quota

Enable, enforce limits for, monitor quota entries, override, remotely manage, and set limits or warning levels for disk quotas.

### Procedures

Disk quotas need to be enabled before quota limits and warnings can be set. To enable and set disk quotas, you access the property sheet of an NTFS partition, volume, or logical drive. The property sheet can be accessed using:

- My Computer

- Windows Explorer

- Disk Management in the Computer Management console

The following procedures assume you have opened the property sheet for a disk using any of these methods.

Note that the Quota tab on the property sheet for a disk is confusing at first and not very well designed. This would have been a good place for one of Microsoft's famous "wizards" to be included.

### Enable Disk Quotas

Disk Properties → Quota → Enable quota management

---

 The traffic light on the Quota tab of a disk's property sheet indicates the status of disk quotas as follows:

*Green light*
Disk quotas are enabled.

*Red light*
Disk quotas are not enabled.

*Yellow light*
Disk quotas are enabled, but Windows 2000 is currently busy rebuilding the quota information.

---

### Enforcing Quota Limits

Disk Properties → Quota → "Deny disk space to users exceeding quota limit"

### Log Disk Quota Events

Disk Properties → Quota → "Log event when a user exceeds their quota (or warning) limit"

You can log quota-warning events, quota limit–exceeded events, or both. These events are logged to the System log and can be viewed using the Event Viewer console. See *Event Viewer* in Chapter 5 for more information.

### Monitor Quota Entries

To view how much of their allotted space users have filled on a disk on which quotas have been enabled, select:

Disk Properties → Quota → Quota Entries

Unfortunately, the information in this Quota Entries window is displayed as a flat-file database. So to keep things simple, you should probably not mix users from different OUs or domains when having them store work on a specific partition, volume, or logical drive. If you must mix users from different OUs or domains, select View → Containing Folder to more easily distinguish users from different domains and OUs.

Note that quota entries are visible only for users who have stored files on the volume on which disk quotas have been enabled. You can also use the Quota Entries box to set quotas for specific users who have not yet stored any files on the volume. Just select Quota → New Quota Entry to do this. You might do this if you know in advance that a few selected users may require different quota limits from the rest.

The first time the Quota Entries window is opened for a volume, the computer must contact a domain controller to resolve user SID numbers (which are used by NTFS to record volume usage) to user logon names. This may take a few seconds if there are a large number of users using the volume. Once the SIDs have been resolved to logon names, this information is stored locally on the quota-enabled volume. If new users have been created and the list of users displayed from this information stored locally in the Quota Entries window gets out of date, press F5 to refresh the user information from the nearest domain controller.

### Override Quota Limit

Once a global quota limit has been established for all users, it may be overridden with specific quota limits for individual users. For example, if a user is given work on a special project and needs greater than normal disk space, you can temporarily increase the quota specifically for that user by:

> Disk Properties → Quota → Quota Entries → double-click on user → modify quota warning and limit

### Remotely Manage Disk Quotas

You might expect that you could use Disk Management to configure disk quotas on remote computers, but this is not so. Instead you have to use the following indirect procedure, which makes use of the fact that the root of a partition or volume is shared in Windows 2000 as a hidden share that can only be accessed by administrators. Let's say you want to enable disk quotas on the NTFS volume *D:* drive on a remote Windows 2000 member server called *MS2*. Do the following from your local Windows 2000 computer while logged on as a domain administrator:

> Right-click on My Computer → Map Network Drive → select drive letter (e.g., *E:*) → specify UNC path (e.g., \\*MS2*\*D$*) → Finish

This opens a My Computer window showing the contents of *E:* drive. Click the Up One Level button on the toolbar and then:

> Right-click on *D$ on 'Ms2' (D:)* icon → Properties → Quota

You must be a member of the Administrators group on the remote computer to modify disk quotas remotely.

### Set Quota Limit

> Disk Properties → Quota → "Limit disk space to"

This sets a "soft limit" on the amount of disk space that can be used. The limit set here applies to all users individually. In order to make this a "hard limit," see "Enforcing Quota Limits" earlier in this article.

### Set Quota Warning

> Disk Properties → Quota → "Set warning level to"

You might typically set the quota-warning level to about 50% or 75% of the quota-limit value.

### Notes

- To view and modify disk quotas, you need to be a member of the Administrators group.

- Neither the Administrator account nor any member of the Administrators group is limited by any disk-quota settings.

- If a user tries to write to disk when her disk space has been exceeded, the error message "insufficient disk space" will appear.

- Note that if both "Enable quota management" and "Do not limit disk usage" are selected, quotas will not be tracked. This is an example of the confusing layout of the Quota property sheet.

- The quota limit is displayed for users as the capacity of the drive on which quotas have been configured. For example, if a quota limit of 25 MB is set on *G:* drive, any user who selects *G:* drive in Windows Explorer or My Computer will read that *G:* has a capacity of only 25 MB, regardless of the size of the physical disk on which *G:* exists.

- Note that enabling and setting quota limits on a disk for all users does not actually divide the disk up into segments of fixed size for each user. In the previous note, for example, user one and user two would both read the capacity of *G:* drive as 25 MB. If user one placed a 5-MB file named *stuff.dat* into the root of *G:* drive, the drive would show 5 MB of used space and 20 MB of free space. If user one then logged off and user two logged on, user two would also see the *stuff.dat* file in the root of *G:* drive, but this drive would display 0 bytes of used space and 25 MB of free space.

  The point is, it's not enough to set quotas to manage disk space for users. You also have to create home folders where they should store their work and set appropriate permissions on these folders.

- If a user finds he is reaching his limit and decides to delete files on the quota-enabled disk, he may discover after deleting that he still has the same space usage on the disk. This is because when a user deletes a file for the first time on a volume or partition, by default Windows 2000 creates a new Recycle Bin on the drive and simply moves the deleted files to the Recycle Bin, resulting in no net gain in free space. You can prevent this from occurring by configuring the Recycle Bin properties to restrict which drives can have a Recycle Bin on them.

- Disk quotas can only be assigned to users, not groups.

- Compressed files are tallied in their uncompressed state as far as disk quotas are considered.

- You can sort the users in the Quota Entries window by using View → Arrange Items and then specifying the sort field. A good choice would be to sort by status to see quickly which users have exceeded their quotas, which are in a warning state, and which are still within limits. A quicker alternative is to click on the column title for the field you want to sort by.

- You cannot use Shift-click or Ctrl-click to select multiple users in the Quota Entries window to modify their quota settings simultaneously. However, you can use Edit → Select All to change all settings simultaneously. This is an unfortunate oversight in Microsoft's implementation of this tool. You can also select multiple, contiguous users by using the mouse and dragging, provided you position the mouse pointer just inside the left-hand edge of the window. For a workaround to performing noncontiguous selects, see the next bullet.

- If you have a large number of users in the Quota Entries window, you can use Edit → Find to locate a specific user's quota entry by entering her logon name instead of scrolling down through the flat-file database displayed. If you have users from multiple domains using the volume, search for a user by entering either of these forms into the text box:

  — <domain_name>\<user_name>

  — <user_name>@<domain_name>

  You can also reuse the Find box to select multiple users and then modify their quota limits simultaneously in one operation.

- You can copy quota entries from one quota-enabled volume to another in one of two ways:

  — Use Quota → Export on the initial volume's Quota Entries window to save the settings to a file, then use Quota → Import on the destination volume's window to import the saved settings.

  — Simply drag selected quota entries from one Quota Entries window to the other.

- You can generate a report of disk-quota usage by opening the Quota Entries window for a volume, choosing Edit → Select All, and dragging the highlighted entries into the window of a program such as Microsoft Excel or even Microsoft Word.

### See Also

*disk quota(3), disks(3,4), Event Viewer(5)*

---

## disks

Add a disk, assign a drive letter or path, connect to disks remotely, create a logical drive or partition or volume, delete a partition or volume, extend a volume, format a disk, maintain disks, reactivate a disk, recover a failed or mirrored or RAID-5 volume, repair a partition or volume, rescan disks, restore disk configuration, revert a disk, update disk information, upgrade a disk, view status of a disk, and view status of a partition or volume.

### Procedures

Disk storage is managed in Windows 2000 Server with a snap-in called Disk Management. This snap-in is included as part of the Computer Management console or can be used to create a custom console. The procedures that follow assume that you have already opened Disk Management by either method.

---

Use Volume List view or Graphical view when you want to select a volume or partition (drive). Use Disk List view or Graphical view if you want to select a physical disk instead. See *Disk Management* in Chapter 5 for more information.

For most administrative tasks involving disks, you should be logged on as an Administrator in order to have sufficient rights.

### Add a Disk

The procedure for adding new disks to a system depends on whether the system supports hot swapping or not:

*Hot swapping supported*
>   Install the new disks, then open Disk Management, and select Action → Rescan Disks. If the change is not detected by Disk Management, reboot the system.

*Hot swapping not supported*
>   Install the new disks, and reboot the system.

To remove disks from a system, follow the same procedures as adding a disk listed earlier.

---

 If the status of a new disk appears as Foreign, you will need to import the disk. Foreign disks are disks that were previously used in other Windows 2000 Server systems and may contain partitions or volumes with data on them. Right-click on the disk whose status is Foreign, select Import Foreign Disk, and follow the wizard. After this is complete, select Action → Rescan Disks, and you should be able to access the existing volumes on the new disk. If you want to add disks containing a RAID-5 volume or mirrored volume, you must add all the disks in the complete volume or you will be unable to access any of the data stored on the disks.

---

### Assign a Drive Letter

As in previous versions of Microsoft Windows, you can identify partitions, logical drives, volumes, and CD-ROM drives on your system by assigning them a drive letter from *C* through *Z*. For example, to assign a drive letter do the following:

>   Right-click on the partition, drive, or volume → Change Drive Letter and Path → Add → assign a drive letter

See the next section in this article for a different method of identifying partitions, drives, and volumes in Windows 2000.

### Assign a Drive Path

You can mount a partition, logical drive, volume, or CD-ROM drive to an empty folder on an NTFS volume. This is also called assigning a drive path to the partition or volume. For example, to assign a drive path do the following:

>   Right-click the partition, drive, or volume → Change Drive Letter and Path → Add → "Mount in this NTFS folder"

*Tasks D*

You can either browse to an existing empty folder or create a new one on the fly. Be careful not to use an empty folder that you want to use for other purposes!

## Connect to Disks Remotely

How you manage disks on a remote computer depends on whether you are using Computer Management or using a custom console with the Disk Management snap-in installed. Using Computer Management means that you can manage all aspects of the remote computer, not just its disk subsystem. Using a custom Disk Management console means that you can manage the disks of several computers (local and remote) simultaneously. Connect using Computer Management or Disk Management as follows:

*Computer Management*

Right-click on Computer Management (local) node → "Connect to another computer" → Look in Entire Directory or a domain → select remote computer → OK

*Disk Management*

Console → Add/Remove snap-in → Add → Disk Management → Add → Another computer → Browse → Look in Entire directory or a domain → select remote computer → OK → Finish → Close → OK

You can only use Disk Management to administer disks on a remote computer that is in the same domain as the local computer or in a trusted domain. Furthermore, you must be a member of the Administrators or Server Operators group on the remote computer. (If you are in the same domain, this is not a problem.)

You are limited in which administrative tasks you can perform on remote disks using Disk Management. For example, you can remotely create and format a partition or volume, extend a volume, change a drive letter assignment, or upgrade a disk from basic to dynamic storage, but you cannot remotely defragment a disk, check it for errors, or access the various tabs on its property sheet. These limitations somewhat reduce the usefulness of using Disk Management as far as remote administration is concerned.

However, there is an indirect way of accessing the property sheet of a disk on a remote Windows 2000 computer, provided you are logged on as an Administrator. Here's what you have to do:

- Map a network drive to the disk (volume, partition, or logical drive) on the remote computer. You can do this using My Computer or Windows Explorer. Specify the UNC path to the remote drive, taking note that in Windows 2000, partitions and volumes are automatically shared using a hidden share name and with permissions for Administrator access only. For example, when mapping a drive to *F:* drive on remote computer *MS1*, your UNC path would be *\\MS1\F$*.

- Open My Computer or Windows Explorer, right-click on the network drive you created, and select properties. The property sheet displayed allows you to change the NTFS permissions on the root of the remote drive and to set disk quotas on the remote drive. Unfortunately, other tasks, such as running Disk Cleanup or Disk Defragmenter cannot be done this way, nor can you reshare the remote disk with a new share name.

Why Microsoft decided you had to take this workaround method to manage disks on remote computers instead of building this functionality into Disk Management escapes me!

### Create a Logical Drive

> Right-click on an extended partition → Create Logical Drive

This starts the Create Partition Wizard. The only option available is creating a new logical drive and then specifying its size, drive letter, and filesystem.

### Create a Partition

> Right-click on unallocated space on a basic disk → Create Partition

This launches the Create Partition Wizard, which lets you create either primary or extended partitions, assign it a drive letter, format the partition, and so on.

---

 When extended partitions are created, they are colored bright green (which, according to the legend, indicates free space). If you look closely, you will also see a dark green outline around the bright green area, indicating that the space is located in an extended partition. It is easy to miss this dark green outline and get confused!

---

### Create a Volume

> Right-click on unallocated space on a dynamic disk → Create Volume

This launches the Create Volume Wizard, which lets you create simple, spanned, striped, mirrored, and RAID-5 volumes. Simple volumes can be formatted using FAT, FAT32, or NTFS, but other types of volumes require NTFS. The steps are different depending on which type of volume you choose to create:

*Simple volume*
> The steps are similar to creating a partition (see "Create a Partition" earlier in this article), except that volumes can be either assigned a drive letter or mounted at an empty folder that supports drive paths.

*Spanned volume*
> To create a spanned volume, you extend a simple volume with unallocated space from another disk. If you extend it with space from the same disk, it will still be a simple volume.

*Mirrored volume*
> You can use the wizard to create a mirrored volume from scratch by selecting unallocated space from two different disks. You can also mirror an existing volume by right-clicking on the volume and selecting Add Mirror.

**Tasks D**

*Striped volume*

Select between 2 and 32 different disks having sufficient unallocated space. The maximum size of the striped volume you create is determined by the disk having the smallest amount of unallocated space. (Striped volumes use equal amounts of unallocated space from each disk.)

*RAID-5 volume*

This is the same as striped volume, except that at least three disks must be used to create a RAID-5 volume.

### Delete a Partition or Volume

Right-click on partition or volume → Delete

Note that you cannot delete:

* The system partition (where hardware-specific boot files such as *Ntldr* and *Ntdetect* are found)

* The boot partition (where the \ *Winnt* folder resides, which contains the Windows 2000 Server, operating-system files and support files)

* Any volume with an active paging file

To delete an extended partition, you must first delete any logical drives in the partition. Deleting a partition or volume is a permanent action and cannot be undone!

### Extend a Volume

Right-click on a simple volume → Extend Volume

This launches the Extend Volume Wizard, which lets you add unallocated space to an existing volume to make it bigger. If you extend a simple volume using contiguous or noncontiguous unallocated space on the same disk, it is still a simple volume, only larger. If you extend it using space on another disk, it becomes a spanned volume.

Note that you cannot extend a FAT or FAT32 volume, only NTFS. Furthermore, you cannot extend the System or Boot volume or any volume that was formerly a partition before you upgraded your disks from basic to dynamic storage. You can only extend simple volumes that you have created from unallocated space on dynamic disks using the Create Volume Wizard.

---

Problems can occur when you use Disk Management to change the configuration of a disk, so always do a full backup of your system before making changes to the disk configuration! For example, if you create and extend a simple volume, delete the volume, and then create a new simple volume in the same space on the disk, you won't be able to change the volume name, which possibly indicates that some corruption has occurred in the disk configuration database. This is another clear indication that Microsoft rushed Windows 2000 Server out the door without sufficient quality assurance.

---

### Format a Partition or Volume

To format a partition or volume, you can do any the following:

- Disk Management → right-click on partition or volume → Format
- My Computer → right-click on partition or volume → Format
- Windows Explorer → right-click on partition or volume → Format

The only advantage of using Disk Management is that it provides more options for choosing the allocation unit size, although this is generally best left at Default.

For more information on formatting, see *NTFS permissions* in this chapter.

### Maintaining Disks

Windows 2000 Server includes a number of utilities for maintaining volumes and partitions.

#### Disk Cleanup

Right-click on volume/partition → Properties → General → Disk Cleanup

Lets you free up space by deleting downloaded program files such as ActiveX controls and Java applets, temporary Internet files (cached web pages), other temporary (*.tmp* or *.temp*) files, or old indexing catalogs, by emptying the Recycle Bin or by compressing files older than a specified age. You can also uninstall unnecessary Windows components or applications.

#### Error Checking

Right-click on volume/partition → Properties → Tools → Disk Cleanup

This lets you run the Check Disk utility to check the selected volume or partition for corruption and attempt repair. This is the Windows 2000 equivalent of the ScanDisk tool in earlier versions of Windows.

---

 Don't start Check Disk unless you really want to—there's no way of canceling the operation once it has begun! Checking a disk can take a long time, especially if the option "Scan for and attempt recovery of bad sectors" is chosen, which is the equivalent of the Thorough test in the earlier ScanDisk utility.

---

#### Backup

Right-click on volume/partition → Properties → Tools → Backup Now

This opens the Windows 2000 Backup and Recovery Tools dialog box, which lets you schedule and run backup-and-restore jobs for selected files, folders, and drives. See *backup and restore* in this chapter for more information.

#### Defragmentation

Right-click on volume/partition → Properties → Tools → Defragment Now

This lets you run the Disk Defragmenter, a utility developed by Executive Software. Disk Defragmenter is also a snap-in for the Microsoft Management Console and is part of the Computer Management console. For more information see *Disk Defragmenter* in Chapter 5.

 Actually, when Defragment Now is selected in my gold version of Windows 2000 (build 2195), an error appears saying that you cannot run more than one instance of Disk Defragmenter. This seems to be because I have Computer Management open to access the Disk Management snap-in. If I create a custom console with only Disk Management and then click Disk Defragmenter, it works. This is a bug that will hopefully be corrected in a service pack.

### Reactivate a Disk

Should the status of a dynamic disk become Missing or Offline, first check to make sure the disk is attached properly and has power, and then:

Right-click on the disk or volume → Reactivate Disk or Volume

The disk status should return to Online. Table 4-3 shows the different possible disk-status indicators, their meanings, and what steps to take in each case.

*Table 4-3: Disk Status Indicators*

| Status | Description |
|---|---|
| Online | Disk OK. |
| Online (Errors)[a] | I/O errors found on the disk. Try reactivating the disk in case the problem is transient; otherwise, remove the disk and replace it. |
| Offline | Disk is disconnected, powered down, or corrupted. Check controller and power cables, and then try reactivating the disk. If this fails, remove the disk and replace it. |
| Foreign[a] | Disk has been moved to this system from another computer running Windows 2000. Import the foreign disk to make use of it. |
| Unreadable | Disk has I/O errors, hardware failure, or corrupted configuration database. Try rescanning disk or rebooting the system; otherwise, remove the disk and replace it. |
| Unrecognized | Unknown disk type, such as from a Unix system or with an OEM signature. Replace the disk. |
| No Media | No compact disc in CD-ROM drive, or no media in removable drive. |

[a] Dynamic volumes only.

### Recover a Failed Mirrored Volume

You can identify a failed mirrored volume in Disk Management as follows:

• The volume will be marked as Failed Redundancy.

• The disk that failed will be marked either Missing, Offline, or Online (Errors).

If the status of the failed disk is Online (Errors), then:

> Right-click on disk marked Online (Errors) → Reactivate Disk

If all goes well, the mirrored volume will regenerate and the disk status should read Healthy.

If the status of the failed disk is Missing or Offline, first make sure the disk is attached properly and has power, and then perform the steps listed earlier. If a disk will not reactivate (will not return to Healthy status), replace the failed disk. Then break the old mirror by:

> Right-click on the mirrored volume on the failed disk → Remove Mirror

Then create a new mirror by:

> Right-click on the good half of the broken mirror → Add Mirror

### Recover a Failed RAID-5 Volume

You can identify a failed RAID-5 volume in Disk Management as follows:

- The volume will be marked as Failed Redundancy.
- The disk that failed will be marked either Missing, Offline, or Online (Errors).

If the status of the failed disk is Online (Errors), then:

> Right-click on the disk marked Online (Errors) → Reactivate Disk

If all goes well, the RAID-5 volume will regenerate and the disk status should read Healthy. If the status of the failed disk is Missing or Offline, first make sure the disk is attached properly and has power, and then perform the steps listed earlier.

If a disk will not reactivate (will not return to Healthy status), replace the failed disk and then:

> Right-click on the RAID-5 volume on the failed disk → Repair Volume → select the disk that will replace the failed one

This will automatically regenerate the RAID-5 volume.

### Repair a Partition or Volume

Should the status of a partition or volume become Failed, first check to make sure the physical disk on which the partition or volume resides is attached properly and has power. If the underlying disk has status Missing or Offline, see "Reactivate a Disk" earlier in this article for what to do. This should return the disk status to Online and the failed volume should return to Healthy. If the volume still indicates Failed, try:

> Right-click on the failed volume → Reactive Volume

Note that you can only repair a failed volume if it is on a dynamic disk, not a basic disk.

Table 4-4 shows the different possible partition/volume status indicators, their meanings, and what steps to take in each case.

*Table 4-4: Partition- and Volume-Status Indicators*

| Status | Description |
| --- | --- |
| Healthy | Volume OK. |
| Healthy (At Risk)[a] | Displayed by all volumes on a disk where I/O errors have been detected anywhere on the disk. Reactivate the disk. |
| Initializing[a] | Normal at system startup. |
| Resynching | A mirrored volume is resynching its mirrors. Do not make any configuration changes while this is happening. |
| Regenerating | A RAID-5 volume is being regenerated. Do not make any configuration changes while this is happening. |
| Failed Redundancy | A disk has failed in a mirrored or RAID-5 volume. See "Recover a Failed Mirrored Volume" and "Recover a Failed RAID-5 Volume" earlier in this article. |
| Failed Redundancy (At Risk)[a] | A disk has failed in a mirrored or RAID-5 volume and I/O errors have also been detected. Reactivate the failed disk and proceed as listed earlier. |
| Failed | A disk has failed or become corrupted. Check the disk cables, then reactivate the disk if necessary. If it still doesn't display Healthy status, try reactivating the volume. |

[a] Dynamic volumes only.

### Rescan Disks

Action → Rescan Disks

Updates the hardware information on all hard drives and updates information about removable media, CD-ROM drives, volumes, partitions, filesystems, and drive letters. If you make configuration changes to your disks and this information does not show up properly in Disk Management, use Rescan Disks to rebuild the disk-configuration database on each disk. You should *always* perform this action after adding disks to or removing disks from your system. Rescanning disks can take a few minutes, so be patient.

### Restore Disk Configuration

Use this procedure if you are installing Windows 2000 Server on a machine already running Windows NT 4.0 Server. If you want to be able to use existing Windows NT mirror sets, volume sets, stripe sets, or stripe sets with parity on the machine:

1. First use the Windows NT administrative tool, Disk Administrator, to save the disk-configuration information for the system to a floppy disk.

2. Now install Windows 2000 on the system.

3. Finally, open Disk Management, select Action → Restore Basic Disk Configuration, insert the floppy, and follow the instructions.

Disk Management should now be able to access the existing Windows NT fault-tolerant volumes on the system.

### Revert a Disk

To change a dynamic disk back to a basic disk, you must first delete all volumes on the disk, and then:

Right-click on a dynamic disk → Revert to Basic Disk

---

If your dynamic disk contains the System or Boot partition, you will have to reinstall Windows 2000 Server after the reversion process is complete.

### Update Disk Information

After you have made changes to drive letters or filesystems, or created or deleted partitions or volumes, you should do the following:

> Action → Refresh

If you only have one hard drive on your system, however, this step doesn't seem to be necessary.

### Upgrade a Disk

Upgrading a disk converts it from basic to dynamic storage. You need to perform this if you want to make use of Windows 2000 fault-tolerant disk technologies such as mirrored volumes and RAID-5 volumes, or if you want to extend a volume, create a spanned volume, or create a striped volume. First close any programs running or files open on the disk you want to upgrade, and then:

> Right click on a disk → Upgrade to Dynamic Disk → select which basic disk(s) to upgrade → accept all prompts

Note that you must have at least 1 MB of unallocated space on the disk in order for conversion to be successful. This space is used to store the database that contains the configuration information of all physical disks in the system.

Table 4-5 shows how partitions, logical drives in extended partitions, mirror sets, volume sets, stripe sets, and stripe sets with parity are upgraded when you convert your disk subsystem from basic to dynamic storage.

To change a dynamic disk back to a basic disk, see "Revert a Disk" earlier in this article.

*Table 4-5: What Happens When Basic Storage Is Converted to Dynamic*

| Basic Storage Type Becomes . . . | This Dynamic Storage Type |
|---|---|
| Primary partition | Simple volume |
| Extended partition with logical drives and free space | Simple volumes (from logical drives) and unallocated space (from free space) |
| Mirror set | Mirrored volume |
| Volume set | Spanned volume |
| Stripe set | Striped volume |
| Stripe set with parity | RAID-5 volume |
| Unallocated space | Unallocated space |

**Tasks D**

Don't convert a disk from basic to dynamic storage if your system dual-boots with previous versions of Microsoft Windows and if you still want to be able to do so!

Also, if you are upgrading the System or Boot partitions, wait for drive activity to cease before logging on and accepting prompts after the system reboots, or errors can occur. Two reboots are required to upgrade the System or Boot partitions.

### View Disk Status

Make sure you use either Disk List view or Graphical view in the steps that follow; if you use Volume List view, you will end up with partition or volume properties, not disk properties:

> Right-click on a disk → Properties

The Disk Properties box that opens displays useful information about the current configuration and status of the disk. Some of the less-evident properties are:

*Disk*
> Is the logical number of the disk, starting with 0

*Type*
> Can be basic, dynamic, or removable storage

*Status*
> Can be online, offline, foreign, or unknown

*Device type*
> Can be IDE, EIDE, or SCSI

### View Status of Partition or Volume

Make sure you use Volume List view or Graphical view in the steps that follow; if you use Disk List view, you will end up with disk properties, not volume/partition properties:

> Right-click on a volume or partition → Properties

The Local Disk Properties box that opens displays useful information about the current configuration and status of the volume or partition selected. The following summarize the more interesting information on the various tabs of this sheet.

### General

You can enable compression for an entire NTFS drive or just for the files in the root directory. For more information about compression, see *files and folders* in Chapter 3. Indexing the drive speeds up searching for files and folders. For more information see *Indexing Service* in Chapter 5. For information on Disk Cleanup, see "Maintaining Disks" earlier in this article.

### Tools

These disk maintenance tools are described in "Maintaining Disks" earlier in this article.

### Hardware

This tab is the same no matter which partition or volume you select. It displays a summary of disk-storage configuration information for all disk drives attached to your system, whether they are hard disks, floppy drives, CD-ROM or DVD-ROM drives, or removable storage. By selecting one of the displayed disk drives and clicking Properties, you can get information about the status of the disk, enable write-caching for hard disks, update the driver for the disk controller, disable drives in the present hardware configuration, and so on.

 Write-caching is a technique that improves a disk's write performance by batching write operations and executing them when sufficient operations have accumulated or when the system is idle. Write-caching also increases the chance of data corruption, however, for if a system fails before a cached write operation was executed, data is lost. Write-caching is disabled by default on all hard drives.

### Sharing

This lets you share the volume or partition and configure shared-folder permissions on it. See *shared folder* in Chapter 3 for more information.

### Security

This lets you set NTFS permissions on the root of the drive. See *permissions* in Chapter 3 for more information.

### Quota

This lets you set disk quotas to limit how much disk space users can access. This is covered separately in the article *disk quota* in Chapter 3.

### Web Sharing

This lets you create a virtual directory in a selected web site managed by Internet Information Services (IIS) and associate this virtual directory with the root of the drive.

 If you try to open the property sheet for a partition or volume that has not yet been formatted, the hourglass appears for quite a while and then disappears with no property sheet appearing.

Likewise, Disk Management may take a long time to start when you have partitions or volumes that are not formatted.

## Notes

- You can also access volume/partition properties for each volume or partition on a disk from the Disk Properties box.

- You can also view some volume/partition status information in the columns of the Volume List view in Disk Management. Unfortunately, you cannot customize which columns are displayed here.

- The conversion of a disk from basic to dynamic storage should take place with no loss of data on the disk, but to be safe, you should always back up a basic disk before converting it to dynamic.

- You can even convert the System and Boot partitions from basic storage to dynamic, the only difference here being that a reboot is required to complete the process. Most disk-management operations in Windows 2000 can be performed without restarting the system—a big improvement over Windows NT.

- You can't extend the System or Boot volume, so make sure you give these volumes enough space when you install Windows 2000 Server on a machine.

- When extending a volume, Windows 2000 Server will use the smallest area of contiguous unallocated space it can find on the drive.

- A simple volume that has been extended with unallocated free space on the same disk will be displayed in graphical view as two or more regions having the same volume name and drive letter assignment.

- You can assign drive letter *B* to a partition, volume, or logical drive if you only have one floppy drive (*A:* drive) in your system. This gives you a total of 25 drive letters to work with (*B, C–Z*).

- Another quirk of Disk Management is that when you assign drive paths instead of drive letters to a partition or volume, the drive path is not displayed beside the partition or volume name in the main window the way drive letters are. To see your drive path assignments, you have to perform the additional step of selecting View → All Drive Paths from the Disk Management menu.

- To edit a drive path, you must first remove the path and then assign a new drive path to the partition or volume.

- Still another quirk of Disk Management concerns using it to share partitions and volumes over the network. Specifically:

  — If you have assigned a drive letter to a partition or volume, you can share it over the network by opening its property sheet directly:

    Right-click on the partition or volume in Disk Management → Properties → Sharing

  — If you assign a drive path to a partition or volume (i.e., if you mount it to an empty folder on an NTFS volume), then its property sheet when accessed from Disk Management is lacking the Sharing tab. This means you have to share it using some other tool like Windows Explorer!

- If you are using a removable storage device, you should assign this device a drive letter that is beyond those used by permanent partitions, volumes, and drives on your system.

- If you add or rearrange storage devices on your system, Windows 2000 Server maintains the existing drive letters and drive paths unchanged so applications won't fail. If you are going to remove a drive letter or drive path, you are warned that the action may cause applications associated with the letter or path to fail.

- Partitions, volumes, and logical drives can be assigned multiple drive paths, but only one drive letter.

- A quick format can only be performed on a partition or volume that was previously formatted.

- Basic storage is suitable in most cases except when you want to create fault-tolerant disks, in which case you must use dynamic storage.

- You should generally format all partitions and volumes using NTFS. The only time you might want to use FAT or FAT32 is when you want to dual-boot between Windows 2000 Server and another operating system such as Windows 98—something that in real life you are unlikely to want to do.

- When you add a new disk to a computer, the disk is automatically configured as a basic disk. If you are using dynamic storage with your other disks, convert the new disk to dynamic after it has been recognized by the system.

- Changing drive letters incautiously can drastically affect whether MS-DOS or legacy Microsoft Windows applications will be able to continue running on the system.

- Drive letters cannot be changed for the System or Boot partitions.

- Drive letter assignments in Windows 2000 are static: existing drive letter assignments are not changed when you install new disks or create new partitions or volumes.

- Resynchronization is the process whereby a stale copy of a mirrored volume is brought up-to-date. Stale mirrors typically occur when one disk in a mirrored volume is temporarily disconnected or down. Mirrored volumes on dynamic disks are resynchronized automatically. If you have an older mirror set on your system (by virtue of installing Windows 2000 Server on an existing Windows NT Server system), right-click on the volume and select Resynchronize Mirror to manually force resynchronization.

- Breaking a mirror separates it into two simple volumes that are no longer fault tolerant. Removing a mirror turns one half of a mirrored volume into unallocated space and the other half into a simple volume.

- Mounting a drive to an empty folder on a local NTFS volume lets you do some fancy things. For example:

  — Create a *C:\temp* folder for temporary program files and mount this to a simple volume on another physical disk. Extend the volume when it runs low on space.

  — Create a *C:\Users* folder for user data, and mount it to a volume on a different disk. Configure disk quotas for the mounted drive without the need to configure them on *C:* drive.

- You cannot upgrade basic disks to dynamic when the sector size exceeds 512 bytes.

- You cannot format a partition or volume that does not have either a drive letter or a mount point assigned to it.

- When you create a new partition or volume, Windows 2000 Server automatically shares it for administrative purposes. The share name is the drive letter with a dollar sign after it (e.g., *G$*), which makes it a hidden share that cannot be seen in My Network Places. The permissions for this share cannot be viewed or modified. You should not remove this hidden administrative share from the partition or volume or Disk Management may be unable to manage it remotely.

- Disk Management lets you do some disk-administration tasks simultaneously. For example, you can format one volume while simultaneously extending another. This is probably not a good idea to do on disks in a production environment. Be sure to back up your disks first before you try pressing Disk Management to the max!

### See Also

*backup and restore(4), Disk Defragmenter(5), disk quota(3,4), Disk Management(5), disks(3), files and folders(3,4), Indexing Service(5), NTFS permissions(4), permissions(3), shared folder(3)*

---

## DNS

Administer a DNS server, configure DNS clients, flush the resolver cache, install and configure the DNS Server service, and view the resolver cache.

### Procedures

This section deals only with some general tasks relating to DNS. Other procedures can be found in the following two articles in this chapter:

*DNS server*
> General tasks associated with DNS servers, such as creating zones, configuring scavenging, clearing the cache, and so on

*zone*
> Specific tasks such as creating and modifying resource records, configuring zone transfers, and so on

### Administer a DNS Server

Start → Programs → Administrative Tools → DNS

This opens the DNS console, which is the primary tool for administering DNS servers. See *DNS server* and *zone* in this chapter for more information about using this tool, and see *DNS* in Chapter 5 for additional general information about using this console.

---

An alternative method of performing DNS administration in Windows 2000 is to use the command-line tool *Dnscmd.exe*, which can be used to perform most of the tasks that can be done using the DNS console. *Dnscmd.exe* has the additional advantage that it can be used in scripts to perform automated administration of DNS servers, but its command-line syntax must be mastered in order to do this.

### Configure DNS Clients

The procedure you will use to configure client computers to contact DNS servers for name resolution depends on:

- The type of operating system on the client
- Whether DHCP or static IP addressing is used

The actual steps will vary depending on which version of Microsoft Windows your clients are running, but the general steps in configuring the client are as follows.

#### For Clients with Static IP Addresses

Configure the following information on the client computer:

- Specify the DNS hostname for the client computer.
- Specify the IP address of the primary (and possibly a secondary) DNS server.
- Specify a list of DNS suffixes that should be appended to unqualified DNS names to try to resolve them (optional).
- Enable the client to register its IP address with the DNS server using DNS dynamic updates (Windows 2000 clients only).

On Windows 2000 Professional clients, the first step is done during Setup, and the last three steps are done afterward on the DNS tab of the Advanced TCP/IP property sheet. Dynamic updates are configured by default on Windows 2000 computers.

On Windows 2000 Professional clients, you can specify a primary DNS suffix by:

> Right-click on My Computer → Properties → Network Identification → Properties → More → enter Primary DNS suffix for this computer

This suffix is appended to the computer name to produce the FQDN of the machine. When a Windows 2000 Professional client computer is part of a Windows 2000 domain, the primary DNS suffix is automatically set to the DNS name of the domain it belongs to. For example, if the FQDN of a client computer is *bob.mtit.com*, then the hostname is *bob* and the primary DNS suffix is *mtit.com*.

The primary DNS suffix of a client is used both for name registration (with the DNS server running Dynamic DNS) and name resolution (it is appended to the name of the remote computer that the client is trying to connect to). For example, if you type ping mary on the client computer at the command line, Windows 2000 attaches the primary DNS suffix if configured (or the DNS suffixes specified on the DNS tab of the Advanced TCP/IP property sheet) to the hostname *mary* and issues the ping.

### For Clients with IP Addresses Dynamically Assigned Using DHCP

Configure the following information on the client computer:

- Specify the DNS hostname for the client computer.

- Enable the client to register its IP address with the DNS server using DNS dynamic updates (Windows 2000 clients only).

Configure the following information on the DHCP server (see *DHCP* in this chapter for more information):

- Specify the IP addresses of primary and alternate DNS servers using DHCP option 6.

- Specify a list of DNS suffixes that should be appended to unqualified DNS names to try to resolve them (optional). Unfortunately, only one such suffix can be assigned using DHCP option 15; others have to be manually assigned at the client.

If no additional DNS suffixes are supplied on the DNS tab of the Advanced TCP/IP property sheet in Windows 2000, the primary DNS suffix is appended to the host-name to form the computer's fully qualified domain name (FQDN). To view or modify the primary DNS suffix, do the following:

Right-click on My Computer → Network Identification → Properties → More → View or Modify Primary DNS suffix of this computer → reboot

The primary DNS suffix can also be modified using Group Policy (see *Group Policy Objects (GPOs)* in this chapter).

You can speed up name queries to frequently accessed hosts by preloading the client resolver cache. On Windows 2000 clients, for example, open the *Hosts* file located in *%SystemRoot%\System32\drivers\etc* and add hostname-to-IP address mappings using the format outlined in the file. When the client tries to resolve a name, it tries its local resolver cache first; if this fails, then it contacts a name server. You can verify that these entries have been preloaded into the client cache by using the `ipconfig /displaydns` command from a command prompt on the client. The downside of this procedure is that name-resolution data on your clients could become stale if you make changes to your server infrastructure often.

### Flush the Resolver Cache

On a DNS client you can flush the contents of the resolver cache (the cached responses from a name query the client issued) by typing `ipconfig /flushdns` from the command line. You can do this if its contents become stale (for example, after you modify existing records on DNS servers).

---

 Remember that a DNS server also has a DNS client (resolver) running on it.

---

## Install the DNS Server Service

There are two ways to make your Windows 2000 server a DNS server: manually and using a wizard.

### Manual Installation and Configuration of DNS Server Service

To manually install the DNS Server service on a Windows 2000 standalone or member server, do the following:

1. Open the Internet Protocol (TCP/IP) Properties box by:

   Right-click on My Network Places → Properties → right-click on Local-Area Connection → Properties → select Internet Protocol (TCP/IP) → Properties

2. Assign the server a static IP address.

3. Specify the server's own IP address as its Preferred DNS server.

4. Install the DNS Server service by:

   Start → Settings → Control Panel → Add/Remove Programs → Add/Remove Windows Components → select Networking Services → Details → select Domain Name System (DNS)

5. Follow the prompts.

Once the DNS Server service is installed on your server, you have to configure it. This includes a variety of tasks, such as:

- Creating forward and reverse-lookup zones

- Adding host and PTR records to your zones

- Configuring zone transfers between DNS servers

For more information on these tasks, see *DNS server* and *zone* in this chapter. However, the initial configuration of your DNS server can be accomplished using the Configure DNS Server Wizard:

   Start → Programs → Administrative Tools → DNS → right-click on your DNS server in the console tree → Configure the server

This starts the Configure DNS Server Wizard and guides you through the process of creating a forward-lookup zone and other DNS server settings. If Active Directory is already on the network, you can optionally integrate your new zone with Active Directory by changing its zone type to Active Directory integrated (see *zone* in this chapter).

---

 The Configure DNS Server Wizard does not create a reverse-lookup zone, so you will need to do this manually afterwards.

---

*Wizard-Based Installation and Configuration of DNS Server Service*

An alternative to manual installation and configuration of DNS servers is to automatically install the DNS Server service when you run the Active Directory Installation Wizard to promote a member server to the role of domain controller. The domain controller also becomes a DNS server for the network.

The procedure is simplest when you make the first domain controller of your root domain your first DNS server as well:

1. Log on to your first Windows 2000 Server as Administrator.

2. Right-click on My Network Places → Properties → right-click on Local-Area Connection → Properties → select Internet Protocol (TCP/IP) → Properties → specify the IP address of the server itself as its Preferred DNS Server

3. Start → Run → dcpromo → OK

4. Follow the prompts.

When the process is finished, you have a DNS server that has a forward-lookup zone created on it and is configured for dynamic updates by Windows 2000 Professional clients.

---

 You may want to manually create and configure a reverse-lookup zone and PTR records within this zone (unless a different DNS server controls the reverse-lookup zone for your server) since the Active Directory Installation Wizard does not create this type of zone. You don't need reverse-lookup zones and PTR records for Active Directory to work, however, but should only create them if clients will need to resolve IP addresses into FQDNs (for example, for certain kinds of security authentication or for troubleshooting purposes).

---

*View the Resolver Cache*

To see what information is stored in the resolver cache on a DNS client, type ipconfig /displaydns from the command line. This displays both:

• Information received from name servers in response to recently issued name queries by the client

• Preloaded hostname-to-IP address mappings from the client's local *Hosts* file

The entries in the cache age and expire when the TTL associated with their record on the name server expire (entries in *Hosts* do not expire).

*Notes*

• You can start, stop, pause and resume the DNS Server service by:

— Start → Programs → Administrative Tools → DNS → right-click DNS server → All Tasks → {Start | Stop | Pause | Resume | Restart}

— net stop dns, net start dns, net pause dns, or net continue dns.

- You can stop or start the DNS Client service on a Windows 2000 computer by net stop "dns client" or net start "dns client". Stopping the DNS client also flushes the resolver cache.

### See Also

*DHCP(4), DNS(3,5), DNS server(4), Group Policy Objects (GPOs)(4), zone(4)*

## DNS server

Clear the server cache, configure a caching-only name server, configure a forwarder, configure scavenging, monitor a DNS server, specify boot method, and update server datafiles.

### Procedures

Administration of DNS servers is performed primarily from the DNS console (see *DNS* in Chapter 5 for general information about this tool). This section covers general tasks associated with DNS servers. For tasks relating to zones and zone files, see *zone* in this chapter. For other general tasks relating to setting up DNS on your network, see *DNS* in this chapter.

The procedures assume that you have opened the DNS console by selecting:

Start → Programs → Administrative Tools → DNS

### Clear the DNS Server Cache

Right-click on DNS server → Clear cache

This removes all resolved names from the server cache. The server cache contains information received from other name servers in response to recursive queries it has issued.

You might clear the server cache after you manually modify existing resource records within a zone (for example, if servers had their IP addresses changed). This will ensure that DNS clients querying the server will have names resolved from zone data and not from a stale server cache.

---

The server cache on a DNS server and the resolver cache on a DNS client are two different things, although both are present on a DNS server (since every DNS server must also be a DNS client).

---

### Configure a Caching-Only Name Server

Simply install the DNS Server service on a Windows 2000 server, and don't configure any forward or reverse-lookup zones on it.

### Configure a Forwarder

To configure a DNS server to forward received name queries to a different DNS server (called a forwarder):

Right-click on DNS server → Properties → Forwarders → select Enable Forwarders → specify IP addresses of forwarders

---

If you specify more than one forwarder, they are tried in order until one is contacted within the specified forward time-out period.

When a DNS server configured to use a forwarder receives a name query from a client, it simply forwards the query to the forwarder to handle. If the forwarder can't resolve the name, it returns a failure message to the original DNS server. The original DNS server can then either:

- Simply pass the failure message on to the client that issued the query

- Attempt to resolve the query itself from its own zone information

To choose the first option, on the Forwarders tab of the DNS server's property sheet, select the checkbox "Do not use recursion." This will make your DNS server simply forward all queries to the forwarder to handle.

### Configure Scavenging

Right-click on DNS server → Set Aging/Scavenging for all zones → select "Scavenge stale resource records"

Scavenging removes stale resource records from the DNS database. This is important mainly if you are using dynamic updates to maintain your DNS database. For example, if a DNS client configured to use dynamic updates shuts down improperly (for example, by turning the power off or removing the cable from its network card), then the DNS server is not aware that the client is gone and still resolves names directed towards the client. (If the client shuts down smoothly, its resource record is deleted from the DNS database when dynamic updates are used.)

You can manually initiate scavenging by:

Right-click on DNS server → "Scavenge stale resource records"

---

Be careful with enabling scavenging. If it is not configured properly, you may end up deleting resource records that should have been retained. Scavenging can be enabled on a per-server, per-zone, or per-record basis. See the *Windows 2000 Server Resource Kit* for more information on configuring DNS scavenging.

---

### Monitor a DNS Server

Windows 2000 DNS servers can perform self-monitoring actions on a scheduled basis to ensure they are functioning properly. To configure monitoring:

Right-click on DNS server → Properties → Monitoring → select type of test → specify test interval

A simple query means the DNS server must return a response without querying any other name servers. Selecting recursive query means that your DNS server can recursively query other name servers if necessary, which is a more complex test to perform and interpret.

You can also click Test Now to perform a test manually. Test results are PASS or FAIL.

### Specify Boot Method

Right-click on DNS server → Properties → Advanced → "Load zone data on startup" → select from where

The possibilities are:

*From registry*
The default on Windows 2000 member servers running the DNS Server service and not containing Active Directory integrated zones.

*From file*
The option to store your DNS server–configuration information in a boot file, an ASCII text file that uses BIND 4 format. You don't need this file for DNS on Windows 2000, but if you are importing your DNS information from an existing BIND 4.x.x name server, you can port the boot file from the BIND server to the Windows 2000 DNS server and then specify the setting described above.

*From Active Directory and registry*
The default on Windows 2000 domain controllers running the DNS Server service.

### Update Server Datafiles

At predefined update intervals, DNS servers automatically write changes in standard primary zones to their associate zone files on the server's disk. This information is also written to disk when a DNS server is shut down. To immediately write changes in standard primary zones to their associated zone files on the server's disk:

Right-click DNS server → Update Server Data Files

 When you make a change to an Active Directory integrated zone, the information is written immediately to Active Directory—the Update Server Data Files option has no effect for these zones.

### Notes

* Always have at least two DNS servers hosting each zone to provide fault tolerance for name resolution.

* To troubleshoot DNS server problems, you can use:

  — nslookup, which can be used to issue DNS queries and examine zone files on local and remote servers.

  — ipconfig, which can be used to view and flush the resolver cache and force dynamic updates by Windows 2000 clients.

— Event Viewer, which manages the DNS server log.

— The optional DNS log *%SystemRoot%\System32\Dns\Dns.log*, which keeps track of DNS server activity. This log is enabled and configured by:

> Start → Programs → Administrative Tools → DNS → right-click on DNS server → Properties → Logging → select logging options

You view the *Dns.log* in WordPad (it is in RTF format), not Notepad.

— The DNS console to monitor the DNS server by:

> Start → Programs → Administrative Tools → DNS → right-click on DNS server → Properties → Monitoring → select a test

- Here is a basic troubleshooting procedure for checking a DNS server if problems occur (stop at the step where the problem is resolved):

— Check Event Viewer first.

— Go to the client and try pinging the DNS server to test for basic network connectivity.

— At the client, open a command prompt and type `nslookup 172.0.0.1`. If you get the name of the client in response to this, your server is OK. If it gives "Server failure" as a response, the server may simply be too busy (or the reverse-lookup zone in which the client's PTR record exists may be paused—check the General tab of the property sheet for this zone on the server).

— If the response is "Request to server timed out" or "No response from server," then go to the server, open a command prompt, and type `net start dns`. If DNS is already started, then check the Interfaces tab on the property sheet of the server to make sure that the server is listening on the interface to which the client's subnet is connected.

- If a client queries a DNS server and receives incorrect information (wrong IP address for the queried FQDN), then you can troubleshoot the problem like this:

— Go to the client, and flush the resolver cache by typing `ipconfig /flushdns` at a command prompt.

— Type `nslookup IP_address_to_resolve IP_address_of_server`. If you get a correct response, the problem was a stale cache entry. If not, the zone information on your authoritative name servers is in error. If you were querying the primary name server (or if your DNS is integrated with Active Directory), check the resource records for your host and whether dynamic update is configured properly on the client. If you were querying a secondary name server, check if zone transfers are configured properly as well.

### See Also

*DNS(3,4,5), zone(4)*

# domain

Add a new UPN suffix for a domain, change the domain mode, create a new domain, and manage a domain.

## Procedures

These procedures assume that you already have the Active Directory Domains and Trusts console opened. For related procedures see *domain controller* and *trust* in this chapter, and *forest* and *tree* in Chapter 3.

### Add a New UPN Suffix for a Domain

Right-click on Active Directory Domains and Trusts (root node in console) → Properties → specify an alternative UPN suffix for the domain → Add

### Change the Domain Mode

You can change a mixed-mode domain to native mode, but not vice versa (unless you completely reinstall Windows 2000 on all your domain controllers). To change a domain from mixed mode to native mode, do the following:

Right-click on a domain → Properties → General → Change Mode

### Create a New Domain

See *domain controller* in this chapter.

### Manage a Domain

Right-click on a domain → Manage

This opens the Active Directory Users and Computers console with the focus in the console tree on the selected domain. You can use this console to manage users, groups, computers, and printers in the domain. For more information see *Active Directory Users and Computers* in Chapter 5.

## Notes

- For information on how to delegate authority for a domain, see *delegation* in this chapter. For information on creating a Group Policy for a domain, see *Group Policy Objects (GPOs)* in this chapter.

- Additional tabs are available on the property sheet for a domain when View → Advanced Features is selected.

- You can change a domain from mixed mode to native mode but not the reverse, so make sure you do not perform this action until your Windows NT domain computers have been completely upgraded to Windows 2000.

## See Also

*Active Directory Domains and Trusts(5)*, *Active Directory Users and Computers(5)*, *delegation(4)*, *domain(3)*, *domain controller(3,4)*, *forest(3)*, *Group Policy Objects (GPOs)(4)*, *tree(3)*, *trust(3,4)*

## domain controller

Change properties of, change role of, force replication of Active Directory on, manage, and promote or demote a domain controller.

### Procedures

The first step in each of these procedures identifies the console being used from Administrative tools (for the Active Directory Schema console see *schema* in this chapter). For related procedures see *domain* and *trust* in this chapter, and *forest* and *tree* in Chapter 3.

#### Change Properties of a Domain Controller

> Active Directory Users and Computers → Select domain → select OU → right-click on a domain controller → Properties

The important settings here are:

*General*
> The setting "Trust computer for delegation" should be selected, otherwise the Message Queuing Service cannot run on the machine.

*Location*
> Specifying a location will help users find the computer in Active Directory.

#### Change Role of a Domain Controller

See *domain controller* in Chapter 3 for a discussion of the five different operations-master roles that a Windows 2000 domain controller can assume.

To determine whether your domain controller is running in one of the following roles:

*Infrastructure master, PDC emulator, or relative ID master roles*
> Active Directory Users and Computers → right-click on Active Directory Users and Computers → Operations Master
>
> If an Infrastructure, PDC, or RID tab is visible, your domain controller is running in that role.

*Domain naming master role*
> Active Directory Domains and Trusts → right click on Active Directory Domains and Trusts → Operations Master

*Schema master role*
> Active Directory Schema → right-click on Active Directory Schema → Operations Master

To transfer a specific role to a different domain controller, open the appropriate console as shown earlier and:

> Right-click on the console root node → Connect to Domain → specify domain → OK → right-click on the console root node again → "Operations master" → select appropriate tab → Change

For transferring the schema master role, however, you instead do the following:

> Right-click on the console root node → Change Domain Controller → specify name → right-click on the console root node again → Operations Master → Change

### Force Replication of Active Directory on a Domain Controller

See "Force Replication over a Connection" in the article *site* in this chapter.

### Manage a Domain Controller

> Active Directory Users and Computers → Select domain → select OU → right-click on a domain controller → Manage

This opens the Computer Management console with the console connected to the domain controller. You can use this to manage services, disks, and other aspects of the domain controller. See *Computer Management* in Chapter 5 for more information.

### Promote or Demote a Domain Controller

Note that a DNS server must be available on the network in order to promote a standalone or member server to the role of domain controller. Promoting and demoting computers to the role of domain controller has certain drastic effects:

- If you promote a standalone server, any local user accounts on the machine will be lost. If you demote a domain controller, any domain user accounts in Active Directory will be lost if this is the last domain controller in the domain.

- Any cryptographic keys stored on the computer will be lost after promotion or demotion and should be exported if necessary.

- Any EFS-encrypted files will be inaccessible after promotion or demotion and should therefore be unencrypted before the action is taken.

To promote a standalone or member server to the role of domain controller, use the Active Directory Installation Wizard. There a number of paths you can take through the wizard depending on whether you are:

- Creating an additional domain controller for an existing domain

- Creating a new child domain within an existing tree in the forest

- Creating a new tree in the forest by creating a new root domain

- Creating a new forest by creating a new forest root

The steps later in this article outline the procedure for creating a new child domain (other procedures are similar):

> Start → Run → dcpromo → OK → Next → select "Domain controller for a new domain" → Next → "Create a new child domain in an existing tree" → Next → specify Enterprise Admin credentials and DNS name of forest root domain → Next → specify parent domain → specify name for child domain → Next (several times) select Permissions option → Next → specify password for Directory Services Restore Mode → Next → Next → reboot

When you create a new child domain, it may take a few minutes after the wizard has finished and the computer has rebooted before the transitive trust relationship between the parent and child domains has been fully established. (The key with Active Directory reconfiguration problems is often simply *wait a few minutes and try again.*) You may be able to log on to the new domain immediately using an account in the parent domain, but other interdomain operations may not function yet. See *trust* in this chapter to see how to verify a trust.

Specifying permissions compatible only with Windows 2000 servers will prevent user accounts logged on with Anonymous access from having the ability to view group memberships, something which Windows NT 4.0 allowed and which SQL Server requires. If you do select this option and an application on your promoted server fails to work properly, try adding the Everyone special identity to the Compatible Access security group and rebooting.

To demote a domain controller, use the same Active Directory Installation Wizard. Note that:

- If there are still other domain controllers in the domain, the domain controller you are demoting becomes a member server in the domain.

- If you are demoting the last domain controller in the domain, the domain controller becomes a standalone server.

You cannot remove the last domain controller from a domain if your domain is a parent for other domains (that is, if there are child domains beneath your domain in the local domain tree):

> Start → Run → **dcpromo** → OK → specify whether the server is the last domain controller in the domain → Next → specify an Enterprise Admins account for the forest → Next → specify a password for a new local Administrator account → Next → reboot

---

 If DNS records in the root domain were not updated correctly when your server was promoted to the role of domain controller (or if appropriate DNS records were not manually created for the new domain when Dynamic DNS is not enabled in your enterprise), then your attempt to demote the last domain controller in a child domain may fail. If this happens, try logging on to your domain controller using the local computer name instead of the domain name (select the computer name from the Log On To text box in the Log On To Windows dialog box) and running the wizard again.

---

### Notes

- Do not demote a domain controller if it is the only global catalog server in a domain, otherwise users may be unable to log on to the network. If this is the last domain controller in your domain, however, this is not an issue.

- If a domain controller you want to demote owns one or more of the operations-master roles, then transfer these roles to other domain controllers in the domain before demoting it. If this is the last domain controller in your domain, however, this is not an issue.

---

- Demoting the last domain controller in the root domain of a tree removes the tree from the forest. All other domain controllers in the tree must be demoted first, however.

- Demoting the last domain controller in the forest root domain of a forest removes the forest. All other domain controllers in the forest must be demoted first, however.

- For information on how to delegate authority for a domain, see *delegation* in this chapter. For information on creating a Group Policy for a domain, see *Group Policy Objects (GPOs)* in this chapter.

- Additional tabs are available on the property sheet for a domain controller when View → Advanced Features is selected.

- If an operations master becomes permanently unavailable (such as from a fatal crash) before you can transfer its role to a different domain controller, you can seize the role and apply it to an existing domain controller.

- You cannot demote a domain controller if Certificate Services is running on it; you have to remove this service first.

- When you use dcpromo, there must be a DNS server available on the network. If you are creating a new forest root domain and you have no DNS server, you are prompted to have the wizard automatically install and configure your computer as a DNS server, which is a good idea.

- Domain controller objects are located by default in the Domain Controllers OU within a domain, and they can be managed, moved to different OUs, and configured using Active Directory Users and Computers.

- The Active Directory Installation Wizard may fail if:

  — Your DNS server is not installed and functioning correctly.

  — The server you are running the wizard on does not have the IP address of the DNS server configured in its TCP/IP properties.

  — The clock on the server you are promoting is not synchronized with the clocks on other Windows 2000 domain controllers in your domain.

### See Also

*Active Directory Domains and Trusts(5)*, *Computer Management(5)*, *delegation(4)*, *domain(3,4)*, *domain controller(3)*, *forest(3)*, *Group Policy Objects (GPOs)(4)*, *schema(4)*, *tree(3)*, *trust(3,4)*

**Tasks
D**

## domain user account

Add members to a group, copy, create, delete, disable, find, modify properties of, move, open home page, rename, send mail, or unlock user accounts.

### Procedures

Domain user accounts are administered using the *Active Directory Users and Computers* console (see Chapter 5). After opening this console, expand the console tree and select the organizational unit (OU) in which the account is located or where it is to be created. Then proceed with the steps described in the following sections.

By default, built-in user accounts such as Administrator and Guest are located in the Users OU. When you create new domain user accounts, you can either locate them in the Users OU or create your own new OUs to contain these accounts. For example, you could:

- Create a single, new OU called Domain Users and locate all domain user accounts within this OU. This is the simplest solution and is preferred unless there is a compelling reason to locate user accounts in more than one OU.

- Create different OUs for domain users residing in different subsidiaries, in different geographical locations, or in different functional departments such as marketing, sales, support, and so on.

One good reason for creating your own OUs—even within a single-domain environment—is because you cannot link a Group Policy Object (GPO) to the default Builtin, Computers, or Users containers (since these are not OUs but special containers in Active Directory). For more information see *Group Policy* in Chapter 3.

### Add Members to a Group

This option is obscurely worded and means simply "add the selected account(s) to a group you specify":

Right-click on account(s) → "Add members to a group" → select group

Multiple accounts can be selected by the usual methods (e.g., Shift-click or Ctrl-click).

### Copy a User Account

Right-click on account → Copy

Similar to adding a user account as shown earlier, except that when you copy an account, the new account has many of the same properties as the original one. Properties that are copied for the new account include the account restrictions, account expiration date, user profile, home folder, logon script, group membership, RAS, and Terminal Services settings of the original account.

---

It is useful when creating a large number of accounts to create a series of account templates for the different categories of users in your enterprise. Then copy each template as needed to create accounts for your users, entering in only the personal information needed for each user. Make sure you disable account templates, as they should not be used for logging on to the network.

---

### Create a User Account

Right-click on OU → New → User

Then specify first and/or last name (at least one of these is required) and the user logon name. The full name and downlevel (pre–Windows 2000) logon name are then generated automatically from this information, but you can also define them

---

differently if desired. The wizard's second screen asks you to specify a password and account restrictions (see "Modify Properties of a User Account" later in this article for more information about account restrictions).

 You can also create multiple user accounts by importing a specially formatted *.csv* file using the bulk-import utility *csvde.exe* (see *csvde* in Chapter 7).

The first screen of the wizard can be confusing, so let's look in more detail at two pieces of information you specify there:

*User logon name*
This is the name that the user will use to log on to the network, which might be something like *marys* or *msmith* for user Mary Smith. User logon names must always be unique within the domain. What's confusing is that there is an unlabeled list box to the right of the text box for user logon name. This list box displays the name of the currently selected domain, but this domain name begins with an @ sign. The idea implied here is that the user logon name consists of two parts, an alias such as *marys* and a domain such as *@mtit.com*.

To create the account in a different domain, use the drop-down arrow in the list box. Note that you must be a member of the Administrator or Account Operators group in a domain to be able to create accounts in the domain.

*User logon name (pre–Windows 2000)*
This is the logon name that the same user will use when logging on to client computers running Windows NT Workstation, Windows 98, or earlier versions of Microsoft Windows. Once again, the confusion is that there are two text boxes for this logon name: the first one is already populated with the older NetBIOS name of the domain followed by a backslash, and the second one is populated with the user logon name or alias you typed in the previous step. For example, if *HEADQUARTERS* is the NetBIOS domain name associated with the domain *mtit.com*, then Mary Smith's downlevel logon name would be *HEADQUARTERS\marys*.

A user's downlevel logon name must also be unique within the domain. The NetBIOS domain name is determined when Active Directory is installed using the Active Directory Installation Wizard. This NetBIOS domain name can be found later using Active Directory Users and Computers by right-clicking on the domain node → Properties → General.

Full names must be unique within the OU in which the account resides. For example, there can be an account named Mary Smith in both the Accounting and Sales OUs within the *mtit.com* domain, provided that these accounts have different user logon names. You could do this by assigning Mary Smith in Accounting the logon name *marys@mtit.com* and Mary Smith in Sales the logon name *marys2@mtit.com*.

Tasks D

Accounts in different domains within a domain tree can also have identical full names. For example, there can be an account named Mary Smith in both the *mtit.com* and *ny.mtit.com* domains, where *mtit.com* is the parent domain and *ny.mtit.com* is the child domain. In this case the logon name for Mary Smith in *mtit.com* would be *marys@mtit.com*, while that for Mary Smith in *ny.mtit.com* would be *marys@ny.mtit.com*, ensuring their uniqueness.

### Delete a User Account

> Right-click on account → Delete

Deleting an account is an unrecoverable action. It's usually better to disable an account instead. For example, if Bob leaves the company and Susan will be coming to replace him, disable Bob's account when he leaves, rename it Susan, and enable it when Susan arrives to take Bob's place. This way Susan will have access to all the network resources that Bob had access to.

---

 The problem with deleting rather than disabling accounts is that when you delete an account, its security identifier (SID) becomes unusable. (The SID is the internal way by which Windows 2000 identifies the account.) Thus, if you delete the account *bobsmith* and then create a new account called *bobsmith*, the new account has a different SID from the old one and hence does not automatically inherit all the settings and access privileges that the old one had.

---

### Disable a User Account

> Right-click on account → Disable Account

When an account is disabled, it still exists but the user cannot log on using the account. Disabled accounts show up in Active Directory Users and Computers with a red X icon on them. To enable an account that has been disabled, select the account and then Action → Enable Account.

### Find a User Account

If you have a large number of user accounts, you can use the Find function of Active Directory Users and Groups to find the account you want to work with. You can find accounts in a particular domain or OU by:

> Right-click on domain or OU → Find

You can also change the focus of the Find Users, Contacts, and Groups box to search the entire directory. See *find* later in this chapter for more information.

### Modify Properties of a User Account

> Select account → Action → Properties

This opens the <user_name> property sheet, which lets you to modify the properties of the account. This sheet has a number of tabs, which function as follows.

---

### General, Address, Telephones, and Organization

These tabs let you specify personal information about the user. You should take time to populate these fields as you will then be able to search for users in Active Directory using search criteria such as name, address, organization, email, and so on. See *find* and *search* later in this chapter.

### Account

These settings are a superset of the account settings you specified when you created the account (see "Create a User Account" earlier in this article). Of interest on this tab are:

*Logon Hours*
> Lets you specify when users can log on to the domain. This can help prevent accounts from being misused during off-hours. If users are logged on and their hours expire, they cannot form new connections to shared resources in the domain, but they are not bumped off resources they are already connected to.

*Log On To*
> Lets you specify the NetBIOS names of client computers in the domain with which the user is permitted to log on to the domain. This can help prevent users from trying to access information stored on computers that belong to other users. By default, users can log on to the domain using any client computer in the domain.

---

 Despite what Microsoft says, it looks as if NetBIOS has not been entirely eliminated from Windows 2000: you must have NetBIOS over TCP/IP enabled on your network if you plan to use the Log On To restriction to control which client computers users can use to log on to the domain. This is needed so that Windows 2000 can determine from which computer the user is attempting to log on. Another annoyance is that in the Logon Workstations box, you cannot browse a list of client computers on the network; you have to know the computer's name in advance and type it in.

---

*Account Options*
> These are more commonly known as account restrictions. Note that selecting some options prevents others from being selected. The more commonly enabled options include:

*User must change password at next logon*
> This is a good choice in low- to medium-security environments because it forces users to take responsibility for managing their passwords and removes this burden from the administrator. In high-security environments, complex passwords may be created and assigned to users by the administrator.

Tasks
D

*User cannot change password*

Again, this is generally used in high-security environments, or at the other end of the scale, it can be used to prevent careless users from denying themselves access.

*Password never expires*

Note that an expired password and an expired account are two different things.

*Account is disabled*

See "Disable a User Account" earlier in this article.

*Account Expires*

By default, new accounts never expire.

---

 By configuring the security policy for the domain, you can change the default account options and expiration settings for new users you create. See *security policy* in this chapter for more information.

---

### User Profile

Lets you specify the network location of the user profile, the user's home folder, and a logon script that runs when the user logs on. See *home folder* and *logon script* in this chapter for more information.

---

 A better way of configuring logon scripts for users is to use Group Policy, which allows administrators to centrally manage startup, shutdown, logon, and logoff scripts for all users and computers in a domain. See *Group Policy* in Chapter 3 for more information.

---

### Remote Control

Lets you enable administrators to remotely observe and control a Terminal Services session being run by the user. See *Terminal Services* later in this chapter for more information.

### Terminal Services Profile

Lets you specify the network location of the user profile and user's home folder when Terminal Services is being used. See *Terminal Services* later in this chapter for more information.

### Member Of

Displays the groups to which the user belongs and lets you modify which groups the user belongs to. These groups can be either groups in the local domain or universal groups. See *group* in Chapter 3 for more information on the different kinds of groups in Windows 2000.

Leave the Primary Group as Domain Users unless you have Macintosh or POSIX clients and there is a reason you need to specify a different group.

---

### Dial-in

Lets you control whether and how the user can remotely connect via a dial-up connection to a remote-access server. For more information see *remote-access server* later in this chapter.

### Environment

Lets you specify the startup environment for a user who logs on using Terminal Services. See *Terminal Services* later in this chapter for more information.

### Sessions

Lets you configure time-out and reconnection settings for users who log on using Terminal Services. See *Terminal Services* later in this chapter for more information.

## Move a User Account

Right-click on account → Move → specify destination OU

## Open Home Page of a User Account

Right-click on account → "Open home page"

This opens up Internet Explorer as your default web client, unless you have other software installed such as Netscape Communicator. Make sure you have run the Internet Connection Wizard before using this feature, or you will be prompted to do so the first time you try to open a user's home page. If a home page is not specified on the General tab of the account's property sheet, you will get an error when you try to use this feature.

## Rename a User Account

Right-click on account → Rename → <new_user_account_name> → press Enter key → specify new first name, last name, display name, user logon name, and pre–Windows 2000 user logon name

Renaming an account allows you to transfer all the rights, permissions, and group memberships of an account to another user. You may want to do this when an employee is leaving the company and will be replaced by someone new who will take over her job. Simply rename the account with the new employee's username, then change the personal information on the account's property sheet to that of the new employee.

## Reset Password of a User Account

Right-click on account → Reset password → <new_password>

If a user forgets his password or it expires before he can change it, he will be unable to log on to the network with his user account. You will need to reset his password. See *password* in this chapter for more information.

 Checking "Force user to change password at next logon" does not get replicated immediately like the password. Therefore, it is best to reset the password and check this setting on a domain controller in the site where the user is located.

### Send Email to a User Account

Right-click on account → Send email

This opens up Outlook Express as your default mail client, unless you have other software installed such as Office 2000. Make sure you configure your mail client before using this feature, or you will be prompted to do so the first time you try to send mail to a user. If an email address is not specified on the General tab of the account's property sheet, you will get an error when you try to use this feature.

### Unlock a User Account

Right-click on account → Properties → Account → clear "Account Locked Out"

A user account is locked out when the user has violated the security policy for the domain. For example, if a user exceeds the number of failed logon attempts permitted by a policy, the user will receive an error message when she attempts to log on, informing her that her account has been locked out and must be unlocked by an administrator.

---

## *Naming Conventions*

Before you start creating user accounts for your enterprise, it is important to establish guidelines for naming conventions. These guidelines are needed to ensure that:

- Account names are simple and easy to remember for users
- Users with identical names will have unique accounts

Here are some considerations and recommendations for establishing naming conventions:

- User logon names can be up to 20 characters long and can include any characters except the following:
   `"/\[]:;|=,+#?<>`
- User logon names can have spaces in them, but this is generally not a good practice, since it may lead to unusable email addresses. For example, Bob Smart of the *mtit.com* domain could have the user logon name *bob smart@mtit.com*, but this would be unusable as an SMTP email address. Since email addresses are a separate attribute of a user's account, you could assign *bobsmart@mtit.com* as Bob Smart's email address, but this could confuse good old Bob ("Why do I use *bob smart* to logon to my machine but *bobsmart* in my email address?).
- Common naming conventions include: first name plus last initial, first initial plus last name, full name with spaces, full name without spaces, initials underscore department/OU, "T-" prefix for temporary employees, and so on. Use your imagination, but think of the users who will be using your accounts.

---

### Notes

- If you have to create a lot of user accounts, try selecting the desired OU and then use the keyboard shortcut Shift-F10 → N → U to open the New Object–User dialog box.

- If you select multiple user accounts in an OU, you can simultaneously perform any of the following tasks on them:

  Add members to a group
  Delete account
  Disable account
  Enable account
  Move account
  Open home page
  Send email

- When you create a new domain user account, it is automatically added to the Domain Users built-in global group, regardless of whether the new user account is created in the default Users organizational unit or in some other OU you created.

- As a security precaution, you should disable a user account when the user is going to be absent for an extended period—for example, on vacation. This is especially important for users who have some level of administrative access to network resources.

- Active Directory Users and Computers cannot be used to move user accounts between domains. Use the tool *MoveTree* instead, which can be found in the \\*Support*\\*Tools* directory on the Windows 2000 Server compact disc.

- You can rename the built-in Administrator account for additional security.

- If you are an administrator, create a second account for yourself and make it a member of the Domain Users group only. Use this second account for all nonadministrative work you do on the network, such as writing reports and checking your email. Use your administrator account only when its privileges are needed for some task.

- Make sure accounts for temporary employees have an expiration date.

### See Also

*Active Directory Users and Computers(5), csvde(7), domain user account(3), find(4), group(3), Group Policy(3), home folder(4), local user account(3,4), logon script(4), net accounts(7), net user(7), password(3,4), remote-access server(4), search(4), security policy(4), Terminal Services(4)*

---

# Emergency Repair Disk (ERD)

Create an Emergency Repair Disk, and repair a system using the ERD.

### Procedures

Use this procedure when your system fails to boot successfully to the point where you can log on. The ERD can only be used to repair system files, the partition

---

boot sector, and the startup environment for multiboot systems. To repair the registry, use the Recovery Console instead (see *Recovery Console* in this chapter).

### Create an ERD

Start → Programs → Accessories → Backup → General → Emergency Repair Disk → select "Also back up the registry" → insert a blank, formatted floppy → OK

### Repair a System Using the ERD

1. Boot the system using the four Windows 2000 boot floppies.

2. Select the Repair or Recover option.

3. Select the Emergency Repair Process.

4. Select the Fast Repair option, which attempts an automatic repair, or select Manual to manually specify which aspect of the system you want to attempt to repair.

5. Insert the ERD when requested and the Windows 2000 CD if system files need to be restored. (The CD may not be required if the *%SystemRoot%\ Repair* directory was successfully updated when the ERD was created.)

If the repair is successful, the system will restart and you will be able to log on. If not, you may need to rebuild your server (see *backup and restore* in this chapter).

### Notes

If you don't have the four boot floppies, you can create new ones by inserting the Windows 2000 CD and:

Start → Run → *<CD_drive>\Bootdisk\Makebt32.exe* → OK

### See Also

*backup and restore(4), disaster recovery(3), Recovery Console(4)*

---

# environment variable

Add, delete, and set environment variables.

### Procedures

Environment variables are created, deleted, and configured using the System utility in the Control Panel (see *System* in Chapter 6 for more information). You can also right-click on the root node of the Computer Management console to display or modify the environment variables for the computer to which the console is currently connected.

### Add or Delete an Environment Variable

Start → Settings → Control Panel → System → Advanced → Environment Variables → {New | Delete}

### Set an Environment Variable

To set (modify the value of) an environment variable from the GUI, you can use System in the Control Panel:

> System → Advanced → Environment Variables → select a variable → Edit → specify value

You can also rename variables this way, but you should exercise caution as renaming system variables could cause boot failures.

To set a variable from the command line, use the **set** command (see Chapter 7).

### Notes

- Only a member of the Administrators group can add, delete, or set the value of a system environment variable.

- Changes made by the currently logged-on user only affect the user environment variables for that user.

- You may have to reboot your system or close and reopen your application for the new value of an environment variable to take effect.

- Use the **setlocal** and **endlocal** commands to set environment variables that are local to a particular batch file.

### See Also

*environment variable(3), logon script(3), System(6)*

---

# event logs

Archive an event log, configure an event log, and monitor events using Event Viewer.

### Procedures

The following procedures assume that you either have the Event Viewer console open and are connected to the computer you want to manage and monitor event logs on, or have the Computer Management console open (which contains the Event Viewer snap-in as part of its set of system tools).

### Archive an Event Log

> Right-click on an event log → Save Log File as → specify filename and file type

See *event logs* in Chapter 3 for information about different file types for archiving event logs. Once a log has been archived, you can view it again by:

> Right-click on Event Viewer node → open Log File → select an archived log file → specify the type of log → specify a display name if desired → Open

### Configure an Event Log

To configure the size and retention settings of an event log, do the following:

> Right-click on an event log → Properties

---

The maximum log size can range between 64 KB and 4 GB (512 KB is the default). Monitor your logs and if they grow too quickly, increase the maximum log size so events don't get lost.

You can configure retention settings in one of three modes:

*Overwrite events as needed*

This is the default setting and means that circular logging is configured. Once the log becomes full, old events are deleted to make room for new ones. This setting can result in loss of important information and should be changed as soon as your server becomes operational on the network.

*Overwrite events older than seven days*

This is another form of circular logging. You can select this option if you know that your maximum log size is large enough to prevent your log from getting full, and if you regularly archive your log at the end of each logging interval and then clear the log to free up space for the next interval.

*Do not overwrite events*

Use this setting if you have adequate disk space for the event log, and when security and system functionality is a priority for your enterprise and you need to keep a long-life paper trail. You must monitor and archive the log periodically and manually clear the events before the log becomes full. Otherwise, if the log becomes full, Windows 2000 stops writing new events to the log.

---

 If you have configured auditing on your system and security is a concern, you can configure your system to shut down when the Security log becomes full. Set the retention setting on the log to "Do not overwrite events," then use *regedt32.exe* to create or assign the value of 1 to the REG_DWORD key called CrashOnAuditFail in:

HKLM\SYSTEM\CurrentControlSet\Control\Lsa

and reboot your machine (use caution editing the registry!) If the Security log fills up, the system will display a message saying "Audit failed" and will stop responding. To recover from this, reboot and log on as Administrator, open Event Viewer, archive the Security log if desired, and then clear it.

If you want your system to still be configured to stop when the log becomes full again, you need to recreate the above registry key at this point.

---

### Monitoring Events

Select an event log in the console tree to display a list of events in the Details Pane. Recent events are listed at the top by default, but you can sort by type, date, and other attributes by clicking on the heading of each column in the Details

Pane. Sorting by type lets you check for critical (error) events quickly; sorting by source helps you troubleshoot problems associated with specific services or devices; sorting by event ID helps you isolate specific conditions and system activities that cause problems. These methods help you quickly determine the frequency and severity of a problem. Note the event ID if you need to contact a Microsoft support technician:

Right-click on an event log → Properties → Filter

This is a powerful feature that lets you filter out unwanted events so you can focus on the problem at hand. The filter is automatically removed when you connect to a different computer.

Double-click on a particular event in the Details Pane to display more information about the event. Use the up or down buttons to scroll through events, and the other funny button to copy the details of the event to the clipboard so you can paste it into a document or email message.

### Notes

- If you right-click on an event log → Clear All Events, you can wipe out all the events in the log. The exception is the Security log: if you clear the events in this log, a single new event is generated in the log recording who cleared the Security log. You can't cover your tracks that easily!

- If you suspect your problem is hardware related, filter your System log to show only those events generated by that component.

### See Also

*auditing(3,4), event logs(3), Event Viewer(5)*

---

# files and folders

Compress, copy or move, customize a folder, encrypt, explore, modify attributes, modify a file association, open, search, secure, send to somewhere, share, and view properties of a file or folder.

### Procedures

Most operations on files and folders can be performed regardless of the underlying disk filesystem. For example, if you right-click on a folder, the same shortcut menu is displayed regardless of whether the underlying partition or volume is formatted using FAT, FAT32, or NTFS. Additional tasks can be performed on files and folders located on NTFS volumes, as indicated later in this article.

### Compress a File or Folder

Right-click on file or folder → Properties → General → Advanced → Compress contents → accept prompts

If you compress a folder, you will be prompted to choose between the following:

*Apply changes to this folder only*
> Compresses the folder but (contrary to what you might expect) does not compress any of the files in the folder. However, if you copy existing uncompressed files or save new files to this folder, they will be automatically compressed.

*Apply changes to this folder, subfolders, and files*
> Compresses the folder, all files within the folder, all subfolders within the folder, and all files within these subfolders. Use this option if you want to compress existing files within a folder.

To display compressed files and folders using an alternate color, open My Computer or Windows Explorer and select:

> Tools → Folder Options → View → "Display compressed files and folders with alternate color"

To compress an entire drive, select the drive in My Computer, Windows Explorer, or Disk Management and:

> Right-click on drive → Properties → General → "Compress drive"

### Copy or Move a File or Folder

Copying or moving files within or between NTFS volumes can affect their NTFS permissions, compression state, or encryption state. The rules are as follows.

#### Rule 1: NTFS Permissions

A file or folder *inherits* the NTFS permissions of its destination folder when it is:

- Copied from one location to another within an NTFS volume
- Copied from one NTFS volume to another
- Moved from one NTFS volume to another

A file or folder *retains* its NTFS permissions when it is moved from one location to another within an NTFS volume.

Finally, if you *save* a new file in a folder, the file inherits the NTFS permissions assigned to the folder.

#### Rule 2: Compression State

The rules are similar to those for NTFS: a file or folder *inherits* the compression state of its destination folder when it is:

- Copied from one location to another within an NTFS volume
- Copied from one NTFS volume to another
- Moved from one NTFS volume to another

A file or folder *retains* its compression state when it is moved from one location to another within an NTFS volume.

Finally, if you *save* a new file in a compressed folder, the file is saved in a compressed state.

### Rule 3: Encryption State

The rules are different from compression or NTFS permissions described earlier:

- An unencrypted file or folder moved or copied to an encrypted folder *becomes* encrypted, whether the destination folder is on the same NTFS volume or not.

- An encrypted file or folder moved or copied to an unencrypted folder *remains* encrypted, whether the destination folder is on the same NTFS volume or not.

Finally, if you *save* a new file in an encrypted folder, the file is saved as encrypted.

 If you copy or move encrypted files and folders to a remote computer, your encryption certificate and private key must be available on the remote computer or you will not be able to decrypt them from the remote computer. To avoid this complicated process, decrypt files and folders prior to copying them over the network. Otherwise, you will have to export your certificate and key from the local computer as a *.pfx* file to a floppy disk and then import it into your personal store on the remote computer.

The exception to this situation is if you have a roaming user profile configured on the network. In this case your encryption certificate and private key are stored on the file server where your profile is stored, and they are available from any machine you log on to.

### Rule 4: Copy/Move to Non-NTFS Volume

A file or folder loses its NTFS permissions, becomes uncompressed, and is decrypted when it is copied or moved to a FAT or FAT32 volume or a floppy drive.

### Rule 5: Other Attributes

Other file and folder attributes, such as Read-only, Hidden, and so on, are not affected in this way but are always retained whenever files are copied or moved.

## Customize a Folder

Open the folder using My Computer or Windows Explorer and:

Right-click on a blank spot in the window → Customize This Folder

This starts the Customize This Folder Wizard (see *My Computer* in Chapter 6 for more information).

## Encrypt a File or Folder

Right-click on file or folder → Properties → General → Advanced → Encrypt contents → accept prompts

---

### *EFS Recovery*

The default recovery policy, which is automatically created when the Administrator account first logs on to the computer (local user account) or domain (domain user account), establishes the Administrator account as a recovery agent for EFS on the computer or domain. This allows the Administrator to decrypt files that users have encrypted using EFS, which may be required if the user is sick or travelling, has lost his EFS key by having his system partition blow up, or quits and leaves your company suddenly.

In a domain environment the Administrator can log on to the user's computer, open the property sheet for the encrypted file or folder in Windows Explorer or My Computer, click the Advanced button on the General tab, and simply clear the Encrypt checkbox's contents to secure data.

If the computer is a standalone machine, the Administrator can use the Backup utility to make a backup of the encrypted files, restore the backup to the Administrator's computer where the EFS Recovery certificate is available, and proceed as stated earlier.

For more information on recovery policies and recovery agents, see *EFS* in Chapter 3.

---

If you encrypt a file, you will be prompted to choose between the following:

*Encrypt the file and the parent folder*
> This is the recommended choice, since files that are copied to or saved in encrypted folders are automatically encrypted.

*Encrypt the file only*
> By selecting "Always encrypt only the file," you can make this the default choice.

If you encrypt a folder you will be prompted to choose between the following:

*Apply changes to this folder only*
> Encrypts the folder but (contrary to what you might expect) does not encrypt any of the files in the folder. However, if you copy existing files or save new files to this folder, they will be automatically encrypted.

*Apply changes to this folder, subfolders, and files*
> Encrypts the folder, all files within the folder, all subfolders within the folder, and all files within these subfolders. Use this option if you want to encrypt existing files within a folder.

### Explore a Folder

Open Windows Explorer with the focus on the selected folder by:

> Right-click on selected folder → Explore

See *Windows Explorer* in Chapter 6 for more information.

---

## Remote Encryption

By default, you can modify most attributes of files and folders remotely, but you are not allowed to encrypt files and folders on remote computers. If you could, users storing files in a public or work folder might cause problems for one another, for when one user encrypts a file, others cannot decrypt and read it. Nevertheless, there may be situations when you want to enable files stored on remote computers to be encrypted from another location. To enable this feature, open the Active Directory Users and Computers console and do the following:

> Right-click on remote file server → Properties → "Trust computer for Delegation"

Enabling this setting allows services on the local system to issue requests to services running on the remote system by impersonating the remote system. Since this is an inherently insecure thing to do (it could make your network more susceptible to attack through Trojan Horse programs), you should enable this setting with care and only on a selected number of file servers. Once the setting is enabled, users who have files stored on the remote computer can encrypt and decrypt them by accessing their property sheet through a mapped network drive, Windows Explorer, or My Network Places.

Remember also that you cannot encrypt files on a remote computer unless you are their owner (or Administrator).

### Modify Attributes of a File or Folder

> Right-click on file or folder → Properties → General

On NTFS volumes, additional attributes are accessed using the Advanced button. You can modify attributes of files and folders on remote computers as follows:

- If the remote file or folder is in a shared folder, open Windows Explorer or My Network Places to find the share, and open the property sheet for the file or folder.

- If the remote file or folder is not in a shared folder, first map a network drive to the hidden share name for the root of the remote drive on which the file or folder resides. Then when the window for the mapped drive opens, open the property sheet for the file or folder.

This works with every attribute except encryption. See the sidebar entitled "Remote Encryption" for information on how to remotely encrypt files or folders.

### Modify a File Association

Each file in Windows 2000 is associated with a default program that is used to open it. Double-clicking on the file opens the file using this program. To change the program that is invoked when you open the file:

> Right-click on file → Properties → General → Change → select program

For more about file associations, see *My Computer* in Chapter 6.

Changing the file association for a file changes the association for all files of the same type! For example, if you select a text file *Test.txt* and change its associated program from Notepad to Paint, all files ending with *.txt* will now invoke Microsoft Paint when you try to open them!

### Open a File or Folder

To open a file using its default program (see "Modify a File Association" earlier in this article) or open a folder and display its contents, either double-click on it or:

Right-click on file or folder → Open

If you want to open a file using a different program (for example, if you wanted to open an *.html* file using Notepad), use Open With instead.

### Search a Folder for a File

Right-click on folder → Search

This opens the Search Assistant with the selected folder specified in the Look In box. See *search* later in this chapter for more information on how to use the Search Assistant.

### Secure a File or Folder

You can secure a file or folder using NTFS permissions (on NTFS volumes only, of course) by:

Right-click on file or folder → Properties → Security

See *permissions* in Chapter 3 for more information.

### Send a File or Folder to Somewhere

Right-click on file or folder → Send To → select destination

By default, there are four choices you can Send To:

*3 1/2-inch Floppy*
Copies the selected file or folder to a floppy disk.

*Desktop*
Creates a shortcut to the selected file or folder and places this shortcut on the Desktop so you can access the file or folder more easily.

*Mail Recipient*
Attaches the selected file or folder to a new email message in Microsoft Outlook Express and prompts you for the recipient. You should configure your Internet email settings using the Internet Connection Wizard before using this.

*My Documents*
Copies (does not move) the selected file or folder to the My Documents folder for the logged-on user.

Additional Send To options are created when other Windows 2000–compliant software is installed.

You can create a custom Send To option by editing your user profile (unless it is mandatory). To do this, first open My Computer and go to:

> Tools → Folder Options → View → "Show hidden files and folders"

Then browse your profile to locate the Send To folder. For example, if you are logged on as Administrator, open the folder:

> *C:\Documents and Settings\Administrator\SendTo*

Then right-click and create a new shortcut to the program or location you want to send files or folders to. For example:

— To Send To → Notepad, create a shortcut to *C:\Winnt\ notepad.exe.*

— To Send To → Pub on *Server12*, create a shortcut to \\*Server12\ pub.*

### Share a File or Folder

See *shared folder* later in this chapter for more information.

### View Properties of a File or Folder

> Right-click on a file or folder → Properties

See *files and folders* in Chapter 3 for where you can find additional information on these property sheet tabs.

### Notes

- Compressed files cannot be encrypted, and encrypted files cannot be compressed.

- System files cannot be encrypted unless the System attribute is removed. Encrypting system files is not recommended as it could cause the operating system to become unbootable.

- By selecting multiple files or folders in My Computer or Windows Explorer, you can perform many of the previously mentioned tasks simultaneously on the selected files or folders.

- When multiple files are selected and their collective properties viewed, a checked attribute checkbox with a gray interior indicates that some of the selected files have the attribute set and others have it cleared.

- If the Hidden attribute for a file has a checked attribute checkbox with a gray interior, it means the file has both its Hidden and System attributes set. To clear the System attribute for a file, you must use the `attrib` command (see Chapter 7). Do not do this carelessly, as operating-system files should normally remain marked as Hidden, System, and Read-only to protect them from accidental corruption or deletion!

- If you set the Hidden attribute for a file on the desktop and My Computer is configured to hide hidden files from view, the file will remain visible but ghosted until you log off and then log on again, at which time it will be hidden from view.

- If a compressed file is copied to a FAT or FAT32 permission, it will be uncompressed.

- If you rename an encrypted file, it remains encrypted.

### See Also

*attrib(7),  attribute(3),  compression(3),  EFS(3),  files  and  folders(3),  My Computer(6),  offline  files(3,4),  permissions(3),  search(4),  shared  folder(3,4), Windows Explorer(6)*

---

# find

Find users, contacts, groups, computers, printers, shared folders, or organizational units in Active Directory, or perform a custom search of Active Directory.

### Procedures

This procedure illustrates how an administrator can search Active Directory for a specific object or attribute (ordinary users search Active Directory differently by using Start → Search instead):

1. Open the Active Directory Users and Computers console, and select a domain or organizational unit (OU) from which to begin your search. If you select Entire Directory, then the entire global catalog is searched using your query.

2. Use Action → Find to open the Find Users, Contacts, and Groups dialog box.

3. Specify what type of objects to find:

   > Users, Contacts, and Groups
   > Computers
   > Printers
   > Shared Folders
   > Organizational Units
   > Custom search

4. Broaden the starting point for your search by selecting:

   > Entire directory
   > Local domain or any parent domain in the domain tree
   > The OU selected above

5. Formulate a search query using any or all of the available tabs:

   — The first tab allows you to formulate simple queries using basic attributes for the type of object specified, such as a user's name, the role of a computer, the location of a printer, and so on.

   — The Features tab (printers only) provides additional search attributes.

— The Advanced tab lets you search using pattern-matching on any combination of attributes for the selected type of directory object. Specify a field (attribute) to search on, a condition, and a value to search for. Conditions include:

> Starts with
> Ends with
> Is (exactly)
> Is not
> Present
> Not present

Once you have formulated your advanced query, click Add to add it to the list. Queries are processed in the order listed.

6. Select Find Now to begin the search.

7. Once the query results are generated, an administrator can right-click on an object in the search results box and perform various administrative actions on the object (the actions available depend on the type of object).

### Example

To find all user accounts in the Sales OU whose last names start with the letter "S," select the Sales OU in Active Directory Users and Groups, then select:

> Action → Find → Advanced → Field → User → Last Name → enter S in Value field → Add → Find Now

### Notes

• You can also search Active Directory for users, printers, and other objects by using the Search Assistant, which is opened from the Start menu by Start → Search → choose type of search. See *search* in this chapter for more information.

• You can sort your search results by clicking on the heading of any column. Select View → Choose Columns to display more columns in Details view.

• You can apply a filter to your search results by selecting View → Filter. For more on filters, see *Active Directory Users and Computers* in Chapter 5.

• Once you've found the specified objects (users, groups, printers, and so on), you can perform various actions on them by selecting them and either right-clicking or using the File menu. For example, you can rename, delete, add to a group, disable, reset the password, move to a different OU, send email to, open the web page of, or modify the properties of user accounts selected in your search results list box. You can perform most actions on multiple accounts at once.

• You can find *all* printers on the network (for example) by specifying that the entire directory be searched and then clicking Find Now without specifying any name or other attribute of a printer.

### See Also

*Active Directory Users and Computers(5), search(4)*

# folder redirection

Configure redirected folders, redirect all users' folders to the same share, redirect each user's folders to a different share, and redirect folders based on group membership.

## Procedures

Folder redirection is implemented by Group Policy, so it is assumed for these procedures that you already have a Group Policy Object (GPO) opened in a console for editing (see "Open a GPO" in the article *Group Policy Objects (GPOs)* later in this chapter).

### Configure Redirected Folders

Before you can configure the settings on a redirected folder, you need to redirect it. See the following procedures for how to do this. To configure a redirected folder:

> User Configuration → Windows Settings → Folder Redirection → right-click on a folder to redirect → Properties → Settings

If you want each user to have exclusive rights to his redirected folder, select Grant the user exclusive rights. If multiple users will be sharing the same redirected folder, clear this setting.

If you later unlink the GPO containing the folder-redirection policies from the OU where the users reside in Active Directory, you can specify whether to leave folders in their present (redirected) location or restore them to the local user profile for each user.

### Redirect All Users' Folders to the Same Share

> User Configuration → Windows Settings → Folder Redirection → right-click on a folder to redirect → Properties → Target → Setting → Basic → \\<server>\<share> → OK

For example, you could redirect the Start menu folder to \\<server>\<share> for all users and set the NTFS permission to Read for the Users group on the <share> folder. In this way all your users will have a common, standard Start menu that they can use but not modify.

### Redirect Each User's Folders to a Different Share

> User Configuration → Windows Settings → Folder Redirection → right-click a folder to redirect → Properties → Target → Setting → Basic → \\<server>\<share>\%<username>% → OK

Using the %<username>% replaceable variable in this case causes a separate subfolder named %<username>% to be created for each user within <share>.

### Redirect Folders Based on Group Membership

> User Configuration → Windows Settings → Folder Redirection → right-click on a folder to redirect → Properties → Target → Setting → Advanced → Add → Security Group Membership → Browse → select a group → OK → Target Folder Location → \\<server>\<share>\<folder> → OK

### Notes

The option "Move the contents of Application Data to the new location" should be left selected on the Settings tab, otherwise redirection will not occur!

### See Also

*folder redirection(3), Group Policy(3,4)*

---

## global catalog

Add an attribute to the global catalog, and create or move the global catalog to a different domain controller.

### Procedures

#### Add an Attribute to the Global Catalog

This procedure is useful to speed up search queries across domains for an attribute that is not included by default in the global catalog. For example, you might want to add the Phone Number attribute for User objects to the global catalog so users can search for other users' phone numbers easily in a multi-domain forest:

> Active Directory Schema → expand Attributes container → right-click on attribute → Properties → select "Replicate this attribute to the Global Catalog"

See *schema* in this chapter for more information on using the Active Directory Schema snap-in.

#### Create or Move a Global Catalog

To create a global catalog on the destination domain controller:

> Active Directory Sites and Services → expand destination Site container → expand destination Servers container → right-click on destination domain controller → Properties → General → select Global Catalog

To remove the global catalog from the original domain controller:

> Active Directory Sites and Services → expand original Site container → expand destination Servers container → right-click on original domain controller → Properties → General → deselect Global Catalog

### Notes

- Adding a new attribute to the global catalog results in a full synchronization of all Active Directory information for all domains in the forest, which can create a lot of network traffic, so schedule this operation during off hours.

- Don't create additional global catalog servers on a single domain unless you have multiple sites connected by slow WAN links. You should generally have one global catalog server per site if WAN connections between sites are slow. This is because clients need to be able to access the global catalog in order to log on to the network.

- The global catalog is created by default on the first domain controller in the forest root domain.

### See Also

*Active Directory(3), domain controller(3,4), global catalog(3)*

---

## group

Add members to, create, delete, find, modify properties, move, rename, or send mail to a group.

### Procedures

Domain local groups, global groups, and universal groups are administered using the *Active Directory Users and Computers* console (see Chapter 5). After opening this console, expand the console tree and select the organization unit (OU) in which the group is located or where it is to be created. Then proceed with the steps described in the following sections.

By default, two different types of built-in groups are created when Windows 2000 Server is installed, and these two types of groups are stored in two locations in Active Directory:

- Built-in domain local groups such as Administrators, Backup Operators, and Users are located in the Builtin OU.

- Built-in global groups such as Domain Admins, Domain Guests, and Domain Users are located in the Users OU.

When you create new groups, you can create them in the Users OU or create your own new OUs to contain these accounts. For example, you could:

- Create a single, new OU called Groups and locate all new groups you create within this OU. This is the simplest solution and is preferred unless there is a compelling reason to locate groups in more than one OU.

- Create one new OU for new domain local groups you create, another for new global groups you create, and one more for new universal groups you create.

For more information see *OU* in this chapter and in Chapter 3.

### Add Members to a Group

> Right-click on group → Properties → Members → Add → select domain → select members → Add

When adding members, you can select multiple user accounts by the usual methods (e.g., Shift-click or Ctrl-click). For another way to add members to a group, see "Add Members to a Group" in the article *domain user account* earlier in this chapter.

### Create a Group

> Right-click on OU → New → Group → <group_name> → specify type and scope

---

If you have to create a lot of groups, select the desired OU, and then use the keyboard shortcut Shift-F10 → N → G to open the New Object–Group dialog box.

Group names must be unique within the domain in which the group resides. By default, when you specify the group name, this also becomes the pre–Windows 2000 or downlevel group name as well, though these can be different if you desire. Downlevel group names are used in a mixed-mode environment to provide compatibility with Windows NT and earlier computers.

To create groups in a given domain, you must be a member of either the Administrators or the Account Operators built-in groups for that domain. When creating a group, any of the two group types may be combined with any of the three group scopes to give a total of six possible kinds of groups you can create. Note, however, that you cannot create universal groups if your domain is in mixed mode (see *mixed mode* in Chapter 3).

### Delete a Group

> Right-click on group → Delete

Deleting a group does not delete the members of the group.

---

Be careful before deleting a group from your enterprise. If you already have various permissions assigned to a group and you delete the group, you cannot regain those permissions by simply creating another group with the same name as the old group. This is because groups are internally represented within Active Directory by unique security identifiers (SIDs) assigned when the groups are created. When you create a new group with the same name as the deleted group, the new group will have a different SID, and the new group's permissions will need to be assigned again from scratch.

---

### Find a Group

If you have a large number of groups, you can use the Find function of Active Directory Users and Groups to find the group you want to work with. You can find groups in a particular domain or OU by:

> Right-click on domain or OU → Find

You can also change the focus of the Find Users, Contacts, and Groups box to search the entire directory. See *find* earlier in this chapter for more information.

To find all the groups of which a particular user is a member, do the following:

> Right-click on user account → Properties → Member Of

### Modify Properties of a Group

> Right-click on group → Properties

This opens the <group_name> property sheet, which lets you modify various properties of the group.

### General

Lets you change the type and scope of the group. You can always change the type of a group from security to distribution and vice versa, but there are restrictions on what scope conversions you can perform (see Table 4-6).

*Table 4-6: Allowed Conversions Between Group Scopes*

| | Can Be Converted to . . . | | |
|---|---|---|---|
| *Scope of group* | *Domain Local* | *Global* | *Universal* |
| Domain local | N/A | | ✓ |
| Global | | N/A | ✓ |
| Universal | ✓ | ✓ | N/A |

### Members

Lists the user accounts that belong to the group and lets you add new members or remove existing ones.

### Members Of

Lists other groups of which this group itself is a member. This can be:

- Domain local groups and universal groups from the local domain

- Universal groups from other domains in the current domain tree or forest

### Managed By

Lets you specify the user account or contact who is responsible for managing the selected group. If you select an existing user account or contact, the personal information for that user is automatically imported into the fields on this sheet.

## Move a Group

Right-click on group → Move → select destination OU

## Rename a Group

Right-click on group → Rename → <new_group_name>

## Send Mail to a Group

Right-click on group → Send mail

This opens up Outlook Express as your default mail client, unless you have other software installed, such as Office 2000. Make sure you configure your mail client before using this feature, or you will be prompted to do so the first time you try to send mail to a group.

### Notes

- Add users only to those groups that give the users just enough rights and permissions to access the resources they need on the network.

- Use built-in groups wherever possible to simplify the task of granting users rights and permissions to use network resources.

## *power scheme*

Create or modify a power scheme.

### *Procedures*

Use Power Options in the Control Panel to create or modify power schemes on the local machine.

#### *Create a New Power Scheme*

Start → Settings → Control Panel → Power Options → Power Schemes → select an existing scheme → configure {monitor | disk | standby} settings → Save As → give the scheme a new name

#### *Modify a Power Scheme*

Start → Settings → Control Panel → Power Options → Power Schemes → select a scheme → configure {monitor | disk | standby} settings

### *Notes*

You cannot use Computer Management or any other console to create or configure power schemes on a *remote* computer.

### *See Also*

*hibernation(3,4), Power Options(6), power scheme(3), standby(3,4)*

---

## *printer*

Add, configure clients for, configure permissions for, configure properties of, find, manage using a web browser, pause, redirect, share, and use a printer offline.

### *Procedures*

Managing printers is much the same as it was in Windows NT, with a few additions and enhancements. Printers can be administered three ways:

- Using the Printers folder, which can be accessed on the local machine by Start → Settings → Printers. New printers can be created in this folder using Add Printer, while existing ones can be administered by right-clicking on the printer icon. If you are not physically located at the print server, don't despair: as long as you are logged on with Administrator credentials (or as a user with Manage Printers permission for the printers on your network), you can manage shared printers on remote print servers located anywhere on your Windows 2000 network. First find the printer using any of the methods outlined in "Find a Printer" later in this article, and then right-click on its icon to select a task or open its property sheet.

- Using a web browser running on any computer. The functionality is more limited than using the Printers folder and uses a web-based interface instead of dialog boxes.

- Using the command line (very limited administrative capability this way).

While administering printers using the Printers folder is the faster and most familiar method, administration using a web browser has some advantages:

- Printers can be managed from any computer on the network regardless of what operating system it is running, as long as it is running a web browser.

- The web pages displayed can be printed out to generate reports that display the status of print devices managed by a given print server or display the contents of a printer queue.

- The web interface can be customized by creating additional HTML pages to display information such as a floor plan indicating where print devices and print servers are located.

But the disadvantages are:

- Only a few printer settings are displayed, and none of them can be modified. This will probably be corrected later in a service pack.

- Like most web interfaces, more mouse work is generally required to accomplish a task than by using the standard Windows dialog boxes and shortcut menus.

Web-based administration of printers is described later in this article in the section "Manage a Printer Using a Web Browser."

To install and configure a printer, you need to be a member of the Administrators group. To administer a printer, you need to have either Manage Printers or Manage Documents permission for that printer, depending on what kind of administration you want to perform. See *printer permissions* in Chapter 3 for more information.

You can also control printer administration through the use of group policies. These policies can be used to do the following:

- Modify the default behavior of the Add Printer Wizard.

- Prevent new printers from being published by default in Active Directory.

- Disable web-based management of printers and Internet printing.

For more information, see *Group Policy* in Chapters 3 and 4. If you can't perform some administrative task involving printers, there may be a Group Policy defined preventing you from doing so.

### Add a Printer

Start → Settings → Printers → Add Printer

This opens the Add Printer Wizard, which can be used to either:

- Install printer software directly on a print server. Microsoft calls this "installing a printer."

- Install printer software on a client computer. Microsoft calls this "making a printer connection."

In addition, when installing a printer on a print server, you can choose which of the following to install:

- A local print device, which is directly attached to the server using a serial, parallel, or USB cable.

- A network-interface print device, which is directly connected to a TCP/IP network using a network card installed in the printer.

---

## Windows Printing Terminology

Windows printing terminology can be confusing. A local print device is a print device that is connected directly to a print server, usually by a parallel cable. A *local printer*, however, is a software interface that is installed on a print server and can manage either a local or network-interface print device.

In the same vein, a network print device is a print device that is connected directly to the network. A *network printer*, however, is a software interface that is installed on a client computer to enable it to send print jobs to the print server.

In other words, you need to create two printers to be able to print over the network:

1. First create a local printer on the print server to manage the print device (which may be either the local or network-interface type). Make sure the local printer is shared so it can be seen by client machines on the network.
2. Now create a network printer on each client computer to which the user actually prints from the running application. The process of creating a network printer on the client makes a *connection* between the printer installed on the client computer and the printer installed on the print server.

When you add a printer and share it over a Windows 2000 domain-based network, the information about the printer is automatically published in Active Directory. Make sure you take the time to enter information into the Location and Comments fields when you run the Add Printer Wizard, since this information is also published in Active Directory and can be utilized when searching for specific printers on the network.

---

### Installing a Printer for a Local Print Device

Make sure the print device is attached to the print server and is turned on in case it is Plug and Play. Start the Add Printer Wizard, select Local printer, then follow the steps that involve selecting a port to which the print device is attached (usually LPT1), selecting the manufacturer and model, specifying the name of the printer, and so on. Make sure you share the printer if you plan to allow client machines to connect to it and print from over the network.

### Installing a Printer for a Network-Interface Print Device

Make sure the print device is connected to the network and is turned on. Start the Add Printer Wizard on the print server, and select Local printer (clear the Plug and Play checkbox). On the Select the Printer Port page of the wizard, select:

"Create a new port" → Standard TCP/IP Port → Next

This opens another wizard called Add Standard TCP/IP Printer Port. Specify the IP address of the print device (a port name is generated automatically from this information) and the type of network card the print device uses (try Generic if you're not sure). Clicking Finish closes this wizard and returns to the previous one, which you must then complete as in the previous section.

### Making a Connection to a Print Server

There are lots of ways you can connect a client computer to a shared printer that is managed by a remote print server (i.e., create a network printer on a client computer that lets users submit jobs to the print server). Once you have connected to the printer, you can print to it as if it was physically connected to your client computer. Once your Windows 2000 Professional client computer connects to the remote print server, it automatically downloads the necessary printer driver files to create the connection.

To connect to a remote printer, do any of the following on the client computer:

*   Start → Settings → Printers → Add Printer → Next → Network printer

    Then specify the remote printer you want to connect to by either locating it in Active Directory, browsing for it on the network, typing its name, or specifying its URL.

*   Start → Search → For Printers → enter search criteria → Find Now → select desired printer → right-click → Connect

*   Open the Active Directory Users and Computers console and:

    Select Domain → Action → Find → Find Printers → enter search criteria → Find Now → select desired printer → right-click → Connect

*   Find the remote printer in My Network Places, right-click on it, and select Connect from the shortcut menu.

*   Find the remote printer in My Network Places, and drag its icon into the Printers window.

*   Start → Run → *http://<print_server_name>/printers/* → OK → click on Printer link → Connect

    or:

    Start → Run → *http://<print_server_name>/printers/<printer_share_name>/printer/* → Connect

Either way, <print_server_name> can be the full DNS name of the remote print server, allowing you to connect to printers over the Internet, provided you have appropriate permissions on that printer. Of course, the remote Windows 2000 print server must be running Internet Information Services (IIS), which is installed by default.

- Open Internet Explorer, and use either of the URLs listed in the previous bullet. You must be running Internet Explorer 4.0 or higher to connect to a printer (this is not an issue with Windows 2000 Professional clients). You can also add the printer to your list of favorites for easy access to the print queue.

USB, IEEE 1394, and IR print devices are automatically detected by Windows 2000 when you connect them to the appropriate port on the computer. The Found New Hardware Wizard is then invoked to walk you through the process. You only need to use Add Printer in the Printers folder when your print device is not detected by the operating system. Ports for these devices are not listed on the Ports tab unless the device is already installed.

Parallel-port print devices are not automatically detected when you attach them to an LPT port on a Windows 2000 computer. However, when you run the Add Printer Wizard, make sure that "Automatically detect my printer" is selected, which should successfully detect and help install most modern, bidirectional, parallel-port print devices.

### Configure Clients for Printing to a Printer

The configuration needed on client computers depends on the operating system installed on them:

*Windows 2000/98/95 clients*
No client configuration is necessary. The first time the client computer makes a connection to the shared printer, it automatically downloads the appropriate printer driver (provided you have made this driver available on the print server).

*Windows NT/3.x and MS-DOS clients*
You need first to manually install the printer driver on the client computer.

*Macintosh clients*
Services for Macintosh must be installed and configured.

*Unix clients*
TCP/IP Printing (LPD) must be installed and configured.

*NetWare clients*
File and Print Services for NetWare must be installed and configured. (This must be obtained separately.)

### Configure Permissions for a Printer

Start → Settings → Printers → right-click on printer → Properties → Security

Then specify printer permissions for a user or group by:

Add → select domain → select user or group → Add → OK → allow or deny permissions

*Tasks*
*P*

Not all combinations of permissions are permitted. For example, if you allow Manage Printers, then Print is also allowed. Similarly, you cannot simultaneously allow and deny Print permission for the same user or group.

For more granular control of printer permissions, click Advanced. See *printer permissions* in Chapter 3 for more information about advanced printer permissions. The Advanced button can also be used to take ownership of a printer and to set up auditing of the printer. See *ownership* and *auditing* in this chapter for more information.

### Configure Properties of a Printer

> Start → Settings → Printers → right-click on printer → Properties

This opens the printer's property sheet to allow you to configure various printer settings. The most popular settings administrators generally configure are:

- Setting priorities between printers for different groups of users
- Creating a printer pool to handle increased load
- Sharing an additional printer to handle increased load

Let's look at some highlights from the various tabs. Note that some printers may have additional device-specific tabs. For example, a color printer will have an additional tab called Color Management. Other tabs may be supplied by the vendor's printer driver.

#### General

Assigning a location to a printer helps you find it in Active Directory.

Printing preferences set here on print servers will be default settings for all users. Users can override these settings by opening their own Printers folders, right-clicking on a printer icon, and selecting Printing Preferences.

#### Sharing

See "Share a Printer" later in this article.

#### Ports

This lets you specify and configure the port to which the print device is attached. To redirect a printer to a different port or device, see "Redirect a Printer" later in this article. To add a TCP/IP port for a network interface print device, see "Add a Printer" earlier in this article.

*Printer pooling* lets you connect one logical printer to multiple, physical print devices. Jobs that are sent to the printer are then distributed between the different print devices according to availability. This might be an option if your users make heavy demands on an existing printer and are frequently standing in line to pick up jobs. To make use of printer pooling, you must ensure that all printers in the pool use the same printer driver. (The best is to use identical print devices, but similar devices that use the same driver are acceptable.) To enable printer pooling, check the "Enable printer pooling" checkbox, and select the ports to which the print devices are attached.

### Advanced

If several printers send jobs to the same print device (see *printer* in Chapter 3), you can control what happens by specifying the printer priority and available print times for each printer. Priorities range from 1 (lowest) to 99 (highest), and jobs from printers with higher priority are printed first. To assign different printer priorities to two different groups of users, you must create a printer for each group, assign a priority to each printer, set permissions so each group can only use one of the printers, and then instruct each group concerning which printer to use.

Spooling documents returns control to the application sooner than printing directly to the printer, but you must ensure you have adequate disk space for the spooling process. Mismatched documents occur, for example, when a letter-size document is being printed to a device whose only tray contains legal-size paper. Keeping printed documents causes them to remain in the queue so they can be resubmitted, but this can use up disk space quickly (if you have this feature enabled, disabling it will purge the print queue). Enabling the advanced printing feature is recommended unless printing problems occur relating to page order, pages per sheet, or other advanced features.

Clicking the New Driver button starts the Add New Printer Driver Wizard, which lets you install new or updated printer drivers for your print device. Note that this is not the same as the Additional Drivers button on the Sharing tab, which lets you install drivers for clients running other versions of Windows. You can also update printer drivers over the Internet by using Windows Update (Start → Windows Update). Whatever way you do it, you need to be a member of the Administrators group to update a driver.

A *separator page* is a file that contains printer commands and is used to switch between different printing modes—for example, from PostScript to PCL—and to separate print jobs with a printed page identifying the document being printed. Table 4-12 lists the different types of separator pagefiles available. Note that some printers can automatically detect which language a print job uses and switch mode accordingly.

*Table 4-12: Separator Pagefiles*

| File | Function |
|------|----------|
| *Pcl.sep* | Switch an HP print device to PCL mode. A page is printed before each document. |
| *Pscript.sep* | Switch an HP print device to PostScript mode. A page is *not* printed before each document. |
| *Sysprint.sep* | Used with PostScript print devices to print a page before each document. |
| *Sysprtj.sep* | Same as *Sysprint.sep*, but uses Japanese characters. |

In order to use the Printing Defaults button to set default choices for page orientation, default printer tray, number of copies, and other settings, you must have Manage Printers permission. However, users who have Print permission can override these default settings and configure their own personal printing settings by:

Start → Settings → Printers → right-click on printer → Printing Preferences

### Security

See "Configure Permissions for a Printer" earlier in this article.

### Device Settings

A form is a paper size such as letter, legal, A4, envelope#10, and so on. If your printer has multiple trays, you can assign a form to a particular tray or let Windows 2000 automatically detect the paper tray for each form.

### Find a Printer

To administer a printer, you first need to find it. Information about shared printers is stored in Active Directory and can be found using either of the following procedures:

* Open the Active Directory Users and Computers console, select the entire directory or the domain in which the printer is located (if known), and then:

    Action → Find → Find Printers → specify search criteria → Find Now

* If you leave the search criteria blank and click Find Now, all printers in the selected domain or container will be displayed.

    Start → Search → For Printers

See also *find* and *search* in this chapter.

---

 You can also find a printer simply by browsing My Network Places until you locate the remote print server managing the desired printer. Once you have found the appropriate server, double-click on its icon to see the shared printers on the server. Don't stop here, however, as opening the property sheet for one of these shared printer icons gives only minimal information. Instead, you need to double-click on the Printers folder that is displayed for the remote print server you are viewing, and then right-click on a printer icon to administer it or open its property sheet.

Once you've found the Printers folder on a remote print server in My Network Places, simply drag this folder into your own local Printers folder to provide a quick way of finding and administering remote printers on your network.

---

### Manage a Printer Using a Web Browser

The Default Web Site of Internet Information Services 5.0, which is installed by default on Windows 2000 Server, has a virtual directory called Printers, which contains an Active Server Pages (ASP) application that enables administrators to remotely manage printers using a web browser. This ASP application is located in the \\*Winnt\\web\\printers* folder.

To display the status, location, model, and current number of jobs queued for all printers managed by a given print server, use Internet Explorer or some other browser to open the following URL: *http://<print_server_name>/printers/*.

---

Here *print_server_name* can be the computer name, IP address, or fully qualified DNS name of the print server, e.g.:

*http://dc1/printers/*
*http://dc1.mtit.com/printers/*
*http://172.16.11.140*

To manage a specific printer on the print server, you can either:

- Follow the previous step, and then click on the hyperlinked name of the printer you want to manage.

- Open the URL *http://<print_server_name>/<printer_share_name>/*.

- Select Start → Settings → Printers → select printer → Get More Info

Either method opens a page that allows you to view and manage the print queue, view basic printer properties, pause or resume the printer or specific documents, and so on. By printing out the page displayed, you can produce:

- A printer status report for all printers managed by a print server

- Configuration settings for a given printer

- The status of documents in a given print queue

### Pause a Printer

Start → Settings → Printers → right-click on printer → Pause Printing

Pause a printer if there is a problem with the device, such as a paper jam. Pausing a printer does not delete jobs pending in the queue. To resume or restart printing after you have fixed the problem, repeat the steps listed earlier.

Taking a printer offline also pauses printing. See "Use a Printer Offline" later in this article.

### Redirect a Printer

If a print device fails, you can redirect the pending jobs to a different print device as long as the new printer uses the same printer driver as the current one. You can even redirect jobs to a print device managed by a different print server than the one you normally use. To do this, open the property sheet for the printer and:

Ports tab → Add Port → Local Port → New Port → specify \\<*print_server_ name*>\<*print_share_name*> → OK

If the new print device is managed by the same print server as the current one, redirecting jobs is easier: just change the port select to the port used by the new printer.

### Share a Printer

Windows 2000 Server shares printers by default when you create them (Windows 2000 Professional does not), but if you decided not to share the printer when you created it, you can share it later by:

Start → Settings → Printers → right-click on printer → Sharing → Shared As → <*share_name*>

If your shared printer will be used not just by Windows 2000 Professional client machines, but also by client machines running legacy versions of Microsoft Windows (Windows NT 3.1/3.51/4.0 or Windows 95/98), you will need to install additional drivers for these legacy operating systems on your shared printer. To do this, use the Additional Drivers button on the Sharing tab. The Windows 2000 Server compact disc includes printer drivers for Windows 2000, Windows NT 4.0, Windows 98, and Windows 95.

Select the "List in the Directory" checkbox if you want to publish the printer in Active Directory (which is what you probably want to do). This makes it easier for users to find specific printers on the network. You cannot publish a printer unless it has been shared first.

If you are running a mixed-mode network with some computers running legacy versions of Microsoft Windows, you can publish information about non–Windows 2000 shared printers in Active Directory so that Windows 2000 clients can search for them. To do this, open the Active Directory Users and Computers console, select the organizational unit (OU) or other container in which you want to publish the printer, and proceed as follows:

> Action → New → Printer → enter UNC path to printer → OK

There is also a sample script \ *Winnt\System32\pubprn.vbs*, which shows how to use the Windows Scripting Host to publish non–Windows 2000 printers from the command line.

You can also stop sharing a printer. Be sure to notify users, however, so that their jobs will not be lost.

How printer drivers are updated on the client depends on the particular Windows client operating system being used:

- Every time a Windows 2000 Professional or Windows NT 4.0 Workstation client connects to the Windows 2000 print server to print a document, it checks to make sure that it has the latest version of the driver. If the server has a newer driver, the client automatically downloads and installs it.

- Windows NT 3.51 Workstation clients only check for new drivers on the server when the local Spooler service on the client is restarted (typically when the machine is rebooted).

- Windows 95 and Windows 98 clients cannot automatically download new drivers from the server; you must install these drivers manually on the clients.

### Use a Printer Offline

> Start → Settings → Printers → right-click on printer → Use Printer Offline

This is similar to pausing a printer except that jobs pending remain in the print queue even if you shut down and restart the print server.

### Notes

- When viewing a print queue using a web browser, the page is automatically refreshed when jobs enter or leave the queue.

- If a printer is added and then deleted from a print server, the printer driver is not deleted from the hard disk. If you then reinstall the printer, you have the option of either keeping the existing driver or replacing it with a new one. This can be useful for troubleshooting problems associated with printer drivers.

- When adding a printer, keep the printer name short (no more than 31 characters) to ensure legacy applications will be able to print to it.

- If you cannot find a printer using the Find Printers box, you may have deselected the "List in the Directory" checkbox on the Sharing tab of the printer's property sheet.

- If you need to clear all documents from a print queue, do this:

  Start → Settings → Printers → select printer → right-click → Cancel All Documents

  This is useful if unprintable documents become stuck in the queue.

- Many of the options available when you right-click on a printer icon in the Printers folder are also available from:

  — The File menu of the Printers window when the desired printer is selected in that window

  — The Printer menu of the print-queue window for the selected printer

- You cannot redirect selected jobs to a different print device; you can only redirect all jobs.

- When enabling printer pooling for print devices having different speeds, add the port for the fastest print device first, since this will be the default device to which jobs are sent when all devices in the pool are idle.

- If you configure a printer's port as File, jobs will be printed to a file on the client machine, and users will be prompted for a filename.

- If you do use printer pooling, make sure the pooled devices are physically near each other, not on different floors—unless you want to give your users lots of exercise climbing stairs!

- Using separator pages can be a good idea if you have multiple users printing to the same print device. These pages help users identify their jobs and can ease the crowd around the device.

- Selecting View → Details in the Printers window allows you to quickly see the status of all printers managed by the print server.

- To pause or resume a printer, take a printer offline, share a printer and perform many other common administrative tasks involving printers, you need Manage Printers permission (see *printer permissions* in Chapter 3).

- The standard port monitor, which connects a Windows 2000 printer to a TCP/IP network-interface print device, is a big improvement over the old LPRMON print monitor of Windows NT. LPRMON must still be used, however, for printing to print devices connected to Unix print servers.

- The Performance console (which replaces the Windows NT tool called System Monitor) includes a Print Queue object, which can be used for remote monitoring of print queues, giving administrators useful statistics about job errors, cumulative pages printed, and so on.

- If printing fails because a job becomes stuck in the print spooler, you can try stopping and restarting the print spooler. If printing still fails, stop the spooler again and manually delete the print job from the spooler folder, then restart the spooler. To stop or restart the spooler you can:

  — Open the Computer Management console and select:

      Services and Information → Services → Print Spooler → Action → Start or Stop

  — Open a command prompt and type net stop spooler or net start spooler.

  Stopping the print spooler may stop other services such as the Fax Service, which will need to be restarted afterwards.

- The document currently being printed cannot be redirected.

- When accessing a printer using a web browser to print over the Internet, Windows 2000 first tries to connect to the remote printer using RPCs (in case it is on the local LAN or intranet). If this fails, it uses the Internet Printing Protocol (IPP), which is encapsulated by HTTP. Either way, the end result is transparent to the user printing the document.

### See Also

*auditing(4), find(4), Group Policy(3), Group Policy Objects (GPOs)(4), net print(7), ownership(4), printer(3), printer permissions(3), print queue(4), print server(4), search(4)*

---

## printer permissions

Assign and modify standard and special permissions on a printer.

### Procedures

Printer permissions are a means for controlling the level of access to shared printers on a Windows 2000 network. Printers must be shared on the network for printer permissions to be assigned to them.

To assign printer permissions, you must first be able to access the icon of the shared printer. You can do this using Windows Explorer, My Network Places, or from the Search Results of the Search Assistant accessed through Start → Search → For Printers. The following procedures assume you have already located the icon for the printer that you have shared and whose permissions you want to assign or modify.

### Assign Standard Printer Permissions

> Right-click on shared printer → Properties → Security → Add → select domain → select user or group → Add → OK → allow or deny printer permissions → Apply or OK

Unless you allow or deny different permissions, when you assign printer permissions to a user or group, the default permission assigned is Allow Print.

You can select more than one user or group at a time in the "Select Users, Computers, or Groups" dialog box.

When you try to allow or deny different combinations of printer permissions, you will discover that not all combinations are allowed. For example, if you try to allow Manage Printers, the Print checkbox under "Allow" also automatically becomes checked. Table 4-13 shows the permissible combinations of printer permissions that can be assigned using the Security tab. This table works only if you are allowing permissions; if you both allow and deny permissions, other combinations are possible.

*Table 4-13: Allowable Combinations of Printer Permissions*

| Selecting . . . | Automatically Selects . . . | | |
|---|---|---|---|
| | Print | Manage Printers | Manage Documents |
| Print | ✓ | | |
| Manage Printers | ✓ | ✓ | |
| Manage Documents | | | ✓ |

### Assign Special Print Permissions

> Right-click on shared printer → Properties → Security → Advanced → Add → select domain → select user or group → OK → allow or deny special permissions

Like assigning standard print permissions, assigning a special printer permission by selecting one checkbox may cause others to magically become selected or deselected as well (i.e., not all combinations of special print permissions are possible). Furthermore, you cannot allow and deny a permission at the same time.

You also have the option of applying your special permissions to either:

> This printer and documents (the default)
> This printer only
> Documents only

### Modify Standard Printer Permissions

> Right-click on shared printer → Properties → Security → select name → allow or deny printer permissions

For more information see "Assign Standard Printer Permissions" earlier in this article.

Tasks
P

#### Modify Special Printer Permissions

>Right-click on shared printer → Properties → security → Advanced → select name → View/Edit

For more information see "Assign Special Print Permissions" earlier in this article.

#### Notes

- Inheritance is not an issue with printer permissions.

- Don't assign special permissions unless absolutely necessary. Keep permissions simple to ease troubleshooting when things go wrong.

- There is no print security for Macintosh clients on your network—if they can send a job to a printer on your network, it will print.

#### See Also

*offline files(4)), ownership(4), permissions(3), printer(3,4), shared-folder permissions(4)*

---

## print queue

Manage jobs in the print queue.

#### Procedures

To open a print queue for a given printer, do the following:

>Start → Settings → Printers → double-click on the printer icon

Once the print queue window is open, you can manage documents pending for that printer.

#### Manage Print Jobs

Select a document in the queue, and then use the Documents menu to pause, resume, cancel, or restart a job. You might typically pause a document if there is a problem printing it (e.g., margins too small), while you pause the printer itself if a problem such as a paper jam occurs. Resuming a paused document starts printing it from where it left off, while restarting a paused document prints the entire document again from the beginning.

You can also drag jobs to change their print order, depending on your permissions and whose jobs are in the queue.

Documents → Properties lets you specify a print priority and printing schedule for the selected job. This overrides the settings on the Advanced tab of the printer's property sheet, which specifies the default priority and schedule for all jobs printed using that printer. You can also specify a logon name to indicate which user is to be notified when the job is done (the logon name of the user who submitted the job is entered by default). Make sure as well that notifications are enabled on the print server (see *print server* in this chapter).

### Notes

- The Printer menu is similar to what you get when you right-click on the printer icon within the Printers folder.

- You can also right-click on a printer icon within the Printers folder if you want to pause or resume a printer instead of just a particular document, or if you want to cancel all documents pending for a printer.

- If you cancel all documents for a printer, the job currently printing will finish.

- If you are an ordinary user, you will only be able to manage your own jobs within the print queue, not those of other users.

- You need at least the Manage Documents printer permission if you want to configure priority, schedule, and notifications for all documents sent to the printer.

- Double-clicking on a job in the queue also opens the properties for that document.

### See Also

*net print(7), print server(4), printer(3,4), printer permissions(3)*

---

## print server

Configure print-server settings.

### Procedures

You can display and configure various settings that are common to all print devices managed by the print server.

### Configure Print Server

Start → Settings → Printers → File → Server Properties

This opens the Printer Server Properties box. Here are some highlights of the various tabs.

### Forms

In addition to displaying available forms for the device, you can create new ones by specifying the paper size. Be sure to save your form definition if you want to use it again.

### Ports

Similar to the Ports tab on the property sheet for a printer, but this only lets you create and configure ports, not assign them to a specific printer. The information shown in the three columns of the list box here are:

*Port*
   The name of the available port

*Description*
   The port monitor associated with the port

*Printer*
   The printers that use the port

The types of ports you can add are as follows:

*Local port*
> Typically, used to add a new local port when you want to redirect the jobs pending in the printer's queue to another print device. See *printer* earlier in this chapter for more information on redirecting a printer. For the various types of local ports you can create, see the note at the end of this section.

*Standard TCP/IP port*
> Used for network-interface print devices that have their own built-in Ethernet card.

*LPR port*
> Used for printers managed by Unix print servers. You must first install Print Services for Unix first on the Windows 2000 computer before you can create an LPR port, and you must know the full DNS name or IP address of the network-interface print device or the Unix server running LPD to which it is connected. See the sidebar "Print Services for Unix" for more information on Print Services for Unix.

*Hewlett-Packard network port*
> Used for older HP network-interface print devices with JetDirect cards that use DLC instead of TCP/IP. You must install the DLC protocol on the Windows 2000 computer before you can create a Hewlett-Packard network port.

*AppleTalk printing device port*
> Used for printing from Macintosh clients. You must install AppleTalk protocol on the Windows 2000 computer before you can create an AppleTalk printing device port.

You can also add new ports when running the Add Printer Wizard (see *printer* earlier in this chapter).

---

There are three kinds of local ports you can create on a Windows 2000 print server:

— A filename (e.g., *C:\<path>\<filename>*). Any job sent to this port is written to the specified file, overwriting previous ones (this is essentially printing to a file).

— A shared printer (e.g., *\\<print_server>\<printer>*). Any job sent to this port is handled by the remote printer specified (this is essentially redirecting a printer).

— NUL. This sends jobs to never-never land. It's used mainly for testing purposes.

Parallel and serial ports are also local ports, but Windows 2000 generally detects this hardware automatically.

---

## Print Services for Unix

This Windows 2000 component provides line printer remote (LPR) and line printer daemon (LPD) services to allow cross-platform printing between Unix and Windows 2000. LPR is the client-side Unix printing utility that enables a user to send a job to a Unix print server running LPD. In Windows 2000, the two new services provided by Print Services for Unix are:

- LPRMON, which enables Windows 2000 print servers to send print jobs to Unix print servers running LPD. In other words, LPRMON enables Windows clients to print to Unix printers via the Windows 2000 print server running LPRMON.

- LPDSVC, which emulates LPD on Windows 2000 print servers. In other words, LPDSVC enables Unix clients to send print jobs to the Windows 2000 print server running LPDSVC.

Note that once you have installed these services, you must change the startup configuration of LPDSVC from Manual to Automatic. Use Services in the Computer Management console to do this.

Note also that not all Unix systems use the same LPR specification, so establishing printing interoperability between Windows 2000 and Unix platforms can sometimes be problematic.

### Drivers

This lists the various printer drivers installed on the server. If a printer driver should somehow become corrupt, you can Update (reinstall) it here by clicking Add to start the Add New Printer Driver Wizard (see *printer* earlier in this chapter). You can also use this wizard to add (install) drivers for legacy Windows clients such as Windows NT, 98, or 95.

Select an installed driver and click Properties to list the various files that make up the printer driver and see where they are stored on the server.

You can also install printer drivers from the Sharing tab of each printer's property sheet. The main advantage of doing it here on the Drivers tab of Server Properties is that if your print server is used to manage multiple print devices of the same type, you can update drivers for these in one step.

### Advanced

This lets you specify the location where jobs will be spooled. This is useful if your current drive is filling up and you want to move the spool folder to a different drive. Make sure you stop the spooler service prior to moving the spool folder, and restart the spooler service or reboot the server afterwards. Use the Services node in Computer Management to stop and start the spooler service.

Don't locate the spool folder on the *%SystemRoot%* volume, that is, the volume where the \ *Winnt* folder is located (typically *C:* drive). If users print lots of long jobs, it could fill up all available space on the drive and cause the system to hang.

By default, spooler events are logged to the System log in event Viewer. You may want to turn off information events to reduce the amount of noise in the log. If you make changes to these settings, you must stop and restart the spooler service.

You can specify that notifications be sent when printing jobs are finished. These notifications can be sent to either the users or the computers submitting the jobs. If notifications are sent to computers and the user who submitted the job has logged off their client machine, the next user who logs on to the machine will receive the notification. So you should generally specify that users be notified instead of computers if roaming user profiles are configured on the network. Again, be sure to stop and restart the spooler service after changing this setting.

### Notes

- If the spooler folder is located on an NTFS volume, make sure Change permission is assigned to the Users group. Otherwise, they won't be able to print.

- To delete a form you created, you must first deselect Create a New Form.

### See Also

*printer(3,4)*

## Recovery Console

Install the Recovery Console, run the Recovery Console from the Windows 2000 CD, use the Recovery Console to repair a system.

### Procedures

The normal procedure is to install the Recovery Console on a computer before you need it. In an emergency, though, you can run the console from the Windows 2000 CD (see later in this article).

#### Install the Recovery Console

1. Insert the Windows 2000 CD.

2. Open a command prompt, and change the current directory to *<CD_drive>*\ *I386*.

3. Type winnt32 /cmdcons.

The Recovery Console is installed on the system partition in \ *Cmdcons*.

### Run the Recovery Console from the Windows 2000 CD

If you installed the Recovery Console on a computer but the partition on which it is installed becomes corrupt, you can run the console directly from the Windows 2000 CD. To do this:

1. Boot the system using the four Windows 2000 boot floppies.

2. Select the Repair or Recover option.

3. Select the Recovery Console.

4. Insert the Windows 2000 CD.

### Use the Recovery Console to Repair a System

To repair a system with the Recovery Console, perform the following steps:

1. Restart the system and when the boot-loader menu appears, select Microsoft Windows 2000 Recovery Console.

2. Enter the number of the Windows 2000 installation you want to use (use 1 unless you have a multiboot system).

3. Enter the password for the local Administrator account on the computer.

4. Type `help` to see a list of the commands supported by the Recovery Console.

5. Type `command` /? to show the syntax for a specific command.

6. To quit the Recovery Console and reboot, type `exit`.

See *disaster recovery* in Chapter 3 for a list of commands you can use at the Recovery Console.

### See Also

*disaster recovery(3)*

---

# recovery options

Specify what will happen if the operating system halts unexpectedly.

### Procedures

When the operating system halts unexpectedly, a blue screen called a stop screen is typically displayed. The information on this screen can be used by qualified Microsoft support technicians to determine the cause of the failure. Recovery options let you specify what actions will occur when a fatal system error occurs:

Start → Settings → Control Panel → System → Advanced → Startup and Recovery

You can then specify:

- Whether an event will be written to the system log when the error occurs. This error can then be displayed after rebooting by using the Event Viewer console (this is assuming that you are able to reboot the system).

- Whether an alert message will be sent to administrators when the error occurs.

- Whether the contents of system memory will be dumped to a log file when the error occurs. By default, this log file is *C:\Winnt\memory.dmp*. A complete memory dump requires enough free disk space to contain all of physical memory (RAM) plus an additional 1MB. To reduce the size of the dump log, you can select Write kernel information only. Microsoft support technicians can then analyze your dump log to help determine the cause of the crash.

- Whether to reboot automatically after the other recovery actions are performed.

The first two options on the previous list only work if part of the pagefile is located on the boot partition and this portion is equal to at least the amount of physical memory (RAM) plus 1 MB.

Be careful in selecting the "Automatically reboot" option. If the stop error should occur during rebooting—for example, due to the failure of a hardware device that is critical for the boot process—the computer may enter a cycle of endless reboots.

### Notes

- You must be a member of the Administrators group to configure recovery options on your computer.

- You can configure recovery options on remote computers by:

  Start → Programs → Administrative Tools → Computer Management → right-click on root node in console tree → "Connect to another computer" → select computer → OK → right-click on root node again → Properties → Advanced → Startup and Recovery

- The Windows 2000 Server Help file lists other recovery options that have been withdrawn from the final release of the product.

### See Also

*Computer Management(5), System(6)*

## remote-access server

Add a remote-access server, configure a remote-access server (various subtasks), create a remote-access policy, enable the Routing and Remote Access Service, grant remote-access permission to a user, manage a connected remote-access client, manage a downlevel Windows NT 4.0 RAS server, monitor a remote-access server, monitor connected remote-access clients, and start, stop, pause, resume, or restart a remote-access server.

### Procedures

The Routing and Remote Access console is used to configure inbound connections on a Windows 2000 domain controller or member server belonging to a domain. To configure inbound connections on a standalone server, use Network and Dial-up Connections (see *incoming connection* in this chapter for more information).

To configure outbound connections on any Windows 2000 computer, use Network and Dial-up Connections (see *dial-up connection, direct computer connection,* and *VPN connection* in this chapter for more information).

Unless otherwise specified, the tasks in this section assume that you have already opened the Routing and Remote Access console by:

Start → Programs → Administrative Tools → Routing and Remote Access

### Add a Remote-Access Server

Right-click on Server Status → Add Server → specify computer

Note that this simply adds an existing remote-access server to the Routing and Remote Access Server console so that you can administer the server; it does not cause the specified computer to assume the role of a remote-access server. To make a Windows 2000 server into a remote-access server, see "Enable Routing and Remote Access Service" later in this article.

### Configure a Remote-Access Server

Rather than going through all the settings on the various property sheets of objects in the Routing and Remote Access console, this section covers some of the most common or important settings on a task-by-task basis, listed in alphabetical order.

#### Configure a Remote-Access Server as a Network Gateway

Remote-access servers can either grant remote clients access to resources:

- On the remote-access server alone

- On any server in the local network

In the second case, the remote-access server functions as a network gateway, allowing remote clients to access other servers on the LAN through the remote-access server. To enable your server as a network gateway for an IP-based remote-access server:

Right-click on server → IP → Enable IP routing → Allow IP-based remote access and demand-dial connections

#### Configure Security on a Remote-Access Server

Right-click on server → Properties → Security

There are a variety of ways you can configure security on a remote-access server. For example, your authentication provider, which determines how remote-access clients are authenticated by your server, can be either:

*Windows Authentication*
Authentication is performed by either Active Directory or a Windows NT 4.0 PDC, depending on whether you are running your network in native or mixed mode.

*RADIUS*
Authentication is performed by a RADIUS server if one exists on the network. You can configure a Windows 2000 server as a RADIUS server by installing the optional Internet Authentication Service (IAS) component of Windows 2000 Server.

Similarly, your accounting provider (which keeps track of remote-access sessions and connection attempts) can be either of the same two choices as listed earlier.

Once you select your authentication and accounting providers, you can also configure which authentication protocols will be supported by your remote-access server. To do this:

> Right-click on server → Properties → Security → Authentication Methods

By default, for added security only MS-CHAP (Versions 1 and 2) are enabled on a Windows 2000 remote-access server. If your clients can only use weaker authentication protocols, you must enable them here. For more information on the various authentication protocols and what they do, see *remote access* in Chapter 3.

### Configure a Static IP-Address Pool for Remote-Access Clients

> Right-click on server → IP → Static address pool → Add → specify Start and End IP addresses

You should select addresses whose range forms a standard subnet since there is no option here for specifying the subnet mask. If you specify addresses in a subnet different from the address of the LAN adapter of the server, you must add static routes to the server's routing table to enable the server to forward packets between the LAN and WAN connections (or you could enable an IP routing protocol on the server instead).

---

 If you are using IPX or AppleTalk instead of IP, the IP tab of the server's property sheet will be replaced with an IPX or AppleTalk tab instead.

---

### Enable a Remote-Access Server

> Right-click on server → General → Remote access server

Selecting this option enables your server to accept connections from both dial-up and VPN clients.

---

 The Router option is used to configure your server as a router instead of a remote-access server. (It is possible for one server to assume both roles). LAN routing requires two or more network adapters be installed in the machine (multihomed computer), while demand-dial routing can route between LAN and WAN connections. To run your server in the role of a remote-access server, you do not need to select the Router option.

---

### Configure Logging Options for a Remote-Access Server

To configure which remote-access events will be logged in the System log:

> Right-click on server → Properties → Event Logging → specify logging level

---

To configure settings for the IAS log file:

> Expand server node → select Remote Access Logging → right-click on Local File → Properties → specify log file settings

### Enable Multilink on a Remote-Access Server

> Right-click on server → PPP → Multilink connections

If you are going to use Multilink (PPPMP or BAP), you also need to specify the phone numbers for your device:

> Expand server container → right-click on Ports → Properties → select device → Configure → Phone number for this device

### Enable Remote Access for a Specific Device

> Expand server container → right-click on Ports → Properties → select device → Configure → Remote-access connections (inbound only)

The difference between a device and a port is as follows:

*Device*
> Hardware (modem, modem bank, null-modem cable, and so on) or software (WAN Miniport), which can be used to create a physical or logical point-to-point connection between two computers. A WAN Miniport is a software driver that acts as a kind of virtual modem bank for VPN connections. Windows 2000 includes two types of WAN Miniport drivers, PPTP and L2PT.

*Port*
> A logical communications channel that supports a single point-to-point connection between two computers. A port can be considered a subdivision of a multiport device.

Windows 2000 Server automatically creates ten WAN Miniport virtual ports when you enable Routing and Remote Access Service on the server. These virtual ports are used for accepting incoming connections from VPN clients; five are of PPTP type, while the rest are L2TP. You can increase the number of virtual ports up to 1,000 to support more simultaneous connections from VPN clients by:

> Expand server container → right-click on Ports → Properties → select WAN Miniport (<type>) → Configure → specify Maximum ports → reboot

When a remote VPN client connects to your remote-access server to establish a VPN connection with the server, it uses the highest-numbered virtual port available. The client first tries to connect to an L2TP port (which requires the client have a digital certificate installed that the server can recognize) and, if this fails, it uses PPTP instead.

### Create a Remote-Access Policy

The following procedures assume that you have a remote-access server running on a Windows 2000 domain controller or member server that is part of a domain, and that the Windows 2000 domain is running in native mode. For more information on remote-access policies, see *remote access* in Chapter 3.

First delete the existing, Default, remote-access policy by:

Expand server container → Remote Access Policies → right-click on "Allow access if dial-in permission is enabled" → Delete

At this point no user accounts can connect to your remote-access server unless remote-access permission is explicitly allowed on the Dial-in tab of the user account's property sheet in Active Directory Users and Computers. (To have remote access controlled by policies, leave the user account Dial-in settings set to "Control access through Remote Access Policy.")

Now create a new remote-access policy by:

Right-click on Remote Access Policies container → New Remote Access Policy → specify a descriptive name for the policy → Next → add conditions to the policy

Some of the more common conditions you might specify in a remote-access policy include:

*Calling Station ID*
Specifies the remote client's phone number for callback-verification purposes

*Day and Time Restrictions*
Indicates which days of the week and times of the day the policy will be applied

*Windows-Groups*
Specifies which Windows 2000 domain-based (global or universal) groups the user must belong to in order for the policy to be applied

After specifying conditions (you must specify at least one condition—if in doubt which, then specify Day and Time Restrictions) continue to create the new policy by:

Next → {Grant | Allow} remote-access permission

If your policy is designed to grant users remote-access permission, select Grant. Remember, you can create multiple remote-access policies with some granting permission and others denying it. Policies are evaluated one at a time in the order in which they are listed until a policy is found that matches (does not conflict with) the user account and client connection settings:

Next → Edit Profile → specify profile settings

Specifying profile settings is optional. Some of the more important settings on the six tabs here include the following:

*Dial-in Constraints*
You can restrict the duration of user sessions if you have limited dial-in ports on your remote-access server. It's also good to configure the connection to disconnect automatically if it is idle for more than about five minutes.

*IP*
You should generally leave the IP Address Assignment Policy set to "Server settings define policy." Configuring packet filters is an extra layer of complexity that should be done carefully; otherwise, connections may be accepted, but users will not be able to access the resources they need on the remote corporate network.

*Multilink*

Multilink settings can be left at "Default to server settings." If you are short of modems, you can disable Multilink using this profile setting.

*Authentication*

Try to specify only the most secure authentication protocols that your remote clients can negotiate. Only select Unauthenticated Access for direct computer connections using null-modem cables.

*Encryption*

The encryption schemes you select here can be negotiated by the server with the client. If your clients are Windows 2000 computers and use VPN connections, then deselect No Encryption and Basic Encryption, leaving only Advanced selected. This will enable MPPE 56 to be used for data encryption.

*Advanced*

These settings are typically used when RADIUS is implemented on your network and should not be modified for basic remote access.

Click Finish to create your new remote-access policy. To further edit the policy, double-click on it. If you have multiple policies created, right-click on them and select Move Up or Move Down to change the order in which they are matched.

### Enable Routing and Remote Access Service

You must first enable the Routing and Remote Access Service on a domain controller or member server before it can accept incoming connections from clients. Enabling this server also preconfigures the server to support one of five different remote-access server roles. To enable the service:

Right-click on server → Configure and Enable Routing and Remote Access → Next

At this point in the Routing and Remote Access Server Setup Wizard prompts you to select a role for the remote-access server. The five different remote-access roles are discussed later in this article, but further configuration of the server is explained in this article for only one of them, the "Manually configured server" role. If you can understand the configuration options for this role, you can easily configure the other roles as well.

 If you later decide to change the role of your remote-access server, you can remove the existing configuration and then run the Routing and Remote Access Server Setup Wizard again. To remove the existing configuration of a remote-access server:

Right-click on server → Disable Routing and Remote Access

Alternatively, you can reconfigure the settings on your server to assume a new role if you have a deep enough understanding of these settings. It's generally easier to rerun the wizard, however.

### Internet-Connection Server

Selecting this option and clicking Next lets you choose between:

#### Set up Internet Connection Sharing (ICS)

Choosing this option results in a message informing you that if you want to enable ICS, you should do the following to an existing dial-up, VPN, or incoming connection in the Network and Dial-up Connections window:

> Right-click on connection → Properties → Sharing → Enable

Since you cannot create an incoming connection on a domain controller or member server using the Network Connection Wizard, however, do not use this option.

#### Set up a router with the Network Address Translation (NAT) routing protocol

Choosing this option lets you configure your server to perform Network Address Translation (NAT). This enables your server to provide secure Internet access for computers on different network connections, including your local-area connection. Note that this option is designed only for Small Office/Home Office (SOHO) use as it requires computers on your LAN to obtain their IP addresses using Automatic Private IP Addressing (APIPA) instead of DHCP or static addressing (see *TCP/IP* in Chapter 3 for information on APIPA). Selecting this option does the following:

— Configures your server's network adapter with the IP address 192.168.0.1 and subnet mask 255.255.255.0 with no default gateway.

— Enables routing on your dial-up port so that computers on your LAN can connect to the Internet through your server. If your Internet connection is not a dedicated connection, such as a leased line, the wizard enables dial-on-demand for the outbound connection on the server.

— Adds the NAT routing protocol and binds both the LAN and Internet interfaces on the server to the NAT protocol.

In addition to configuring the Internet-connection server, you also need to configure other computers on your LAN to:

— Use APIPA to obtain their IP address and subnet mask.

— Use the address of the network adapter on your Internet-connection server as their default gateway and DNS server address.

### Remote-Access Server

This lets you configure your server to function as a basic remote-access server that can accept incoming connections from dial-up clients using a modem or ISDN adapter. The Routing and Remote Access Server Setup Wizard guides you through the following steps in configuring a basic remote-access server:

• Add additional LAN protocols to the ones currently installed if remote-access clients need them.

• Specify how IP addresses will be assigned to clients, either using a DHCP server or a range of addresses you specify here. If you choose DHCP server, you first need to ensure that your DHCP server is configured properly and working.

- Configure your server to use an existing RADIUS server (if one is already set up). To configure a Windows 2000 server as a RADIUS server, use the optional Internet Authentication Service (IAS) component.

Once these basic settings are configured, the Routing and Remote Access Service starts on your server. At this point you probably need to further configure your remote-access server and configure a remote-access policy—these steps are discussed elsewhere in this article.

### Virtual Private Network (VPN) Server

This lets you configure your server to accept incoming VPN connections from remote computers over the Internet. The basic steps here are the same as for "Remote-Access Server" earlier in this article, but the resulting configuration is enabled to accept incoming VPN connections instead of ordinary incoming dial-up connections by using the WAN Miniports (virtual ports) created by default on the server.

### Network Router

This lets your network communicate with other networks through this server. In other words, you are configuring your server to act as a router. After running the wizard, you need to ensure that your network adapters have suitable IP-address settings, and you may also need to set up routing protocols on them (if you want to implement this feature in your network).

### Manually Configured Server

This starts the Routing and Remote Access Server service on the server with default settings. No further information is required from the administrator while running the wizard, other than the fact that once the service is installed, you are prompted to start it. You can then manually configure settings on the server to configure it for any of the basic roles described earlier or for a custom role you design.

---

 Selecting the "Manually configured server" option in the wizard is a bit misleading. What it really means is that no configuration at all is performed by the wizard on your server other than installing the Routing and Remote Access Service. Once this is done, it is now up to you to "manually configure your server" so that it can perform the routing or remote-access functions you want it to perform. It is easier to select one of the other four options to perform the initial basic configuration of your server for the specific role you want it to perform.

---

### Grant Remote-Access Permission to a User

Start → Programs → Administrative Tools → Active Directory Users and Computers → expand domain → Users → right-click on a domain user account → Properties → Dial-in → Allow access

You can also set the callback option for the user here.

*Tasks*
*R*

You can only choose to control access through a remote-access policy if you have all domain controllers running Windows 2000; that is, if you are running in native mode. The same is true for assigning a static IP address to a remote-access client.

If your network is running in mixed mode (combination of Windows NT and Windows 2000 domain controllers), you can use User Manager for Domains, the Windows NT user administration tool, to grant users remote-access permission and set their callback option.

### Manage a Connected Remote-Access Client

Expand server node → select Remote Access Clients → right-click on a user

You have two options:

- Select Disconnect to immediately disconnect the remote VPN client. No warning message appears on the client's machine.

- Select Send Message to send a brief message to the client—for example, to warn the client that you are about to disconnect it. A dialog box will pop up on the client to display this message. You can also select Send To All to send a message to all connected clients—for example, when you are going to take the VPN server offline for maintenance.

### Manage a Downlevel Windows NT 4.0 RAS Server

Start → Run → `rasadmin` → OK

This opens the Windows NT 4.0 Server administrative tool called Remote Access Admin, which is included in Windows 2000 Server in order to manage downlevel RAS servers. For more information on using this tool, see Eric Pearce's *Windows NT in a Nutshell* from O'Reilly.

### Monitor a Remote-Access Server

Select the Server Status node in the console tree to view the state of each server and the number of ports in use in the contents pane. Make sure Details view is selected from the menu.

### Monitor Connected Remote-Access Clients

If you select the Remote Access Clients container for your server in the console tree, the Details Pane displays the names of connected clients in the form *<domain>\<username>*, the time since the user connected, and the number of ports in use by the user (which is one unless it is a multilink connection). Note that the information in the Details Pane does not refresh automatically by default, so you should do the following:

Right-click on root node in console tree → toggle Auto Refresh on → right-click again on root node → Refresh Rate → specify refresh interval in seconds

You can display further information about a connected client by:

Right-click on user → Status

This displays the username connected, bytes in and out and other network-traffic information, and the IP address given to the client. (If you have created a static IP pool on the server, then IP addresses are assigned to clients in round-robin order starting with the lowest available address, and a client which disconnects and then reconnects is assigned the next higher address above its previously assigned one).

---

 You can also select the Ports container for your server in the console tree and then right-click on an Active port to view the status of the connection or disconnect the port.

---

### Start, Stop, Pause, Resume, or Restart a Remote-Access Server

Right-click on server → All Tasks → {Start | Stop | Pause | Resume | Restart}

Restart first stops and then restarts the server immediately.

### Notes

- Clients that can connect to Windows 2000 remote-access servers include Windows 2000, Windows NT, Windows 95/98, Windows for Workgroups, MS-DOS, and Apple Macintosh.

- Standalone Windows 2000 remote-access servers (see *incoming connection* in this chapter) support the following dial-up user configuration options:

  — Allow/deny remote access to clients or control access through a remote-access policy.

  — Verify caller ID

  — Configure callback options

  — Assign a static IP address to the client

  — Apply static routes

  If you upgrade your server to a domain controller using the Active Directory Installation Wizard, it is installed in mixed mode by default and its remote-access server configuration is maintained. However, since mixed mode is designed to support both Windows NT and Windows 2000 domain controllers, only a subset of the above dial-in user configuration options are available (in order to be compatible with Windows NT RAS servers), namely:

  — Allow/deny remote access to clients

  — Configure callback options

  If you then change your remote-access server (which is also a domain controller) from mixed mode to native mode, all of the previous dial-in user configuration options are available again.

- If dial-in or VPN clients can't connect to your remote-access server, there are a number of things you can check:

  — Check the modem, modem bank, or other hardware at both the client and the server.

  — Make sure the Routing and Remote Access Service is started on the server by:

    Routing and Remote Access console → select Server Status → check server in Details Pane

    To start a stopped server:

    Routing and Remote Access console → select Server Status → right-click on server in Details Pane → All Tasks → Start

  — Make sure the remote-access server is enabled for remote access by:

    Routing and Remote Access console → right-click on server → Properties → General → "Enable this computer as a remote-access server"

  — Make sure your dial-in or VPN (PPTP/L2TP) ports are enabled for inbound connections by:

    Routing and Remote Access console → expand server container → right-click on Ports → select device → Configure → select "Remote access connections"

    If all your remote-access ports are active, you can add additional ports (easy for VPN ports).

  — Make sure you have allowed remote access for the client's user account and that if there is a remote-access policy configured, that the policy does not deny the user access.

  — Make sure your client supports the correct network protocol, that you have assigned the client addresses from a correct pool, that you have allowed sufficiently lax authentication and encryption methods on the server, that a connection can be successfully negotiated with the client, that the client is using appropriate credentials, that the client supports the correct tunneling protocol for VPN connections, that the phone number on the client is configured correctly for a dial-up connection, and so on. There are lots of things that can go wrong with remote access!

### See Also

connection(3), dial-up connection(4), direct computer connection(4), incoming connection(4), local-area connection(4), Network and Dial-up Connections(6), remote access(3), Routing and Remote Access(5), TCP/IP(3), VPN connection(4)

## rights

Assign or withhold a system right to a user or group.

### Procedures

Assigning rights to users and groups is more complex in Windows 2000 than in the earlier Windows NT operating system because of Group Policy. System rights are configured using the following node in the Group Policy console tree:

Policy root node → Computer Configuration → Windows Settings → Local Policies → User Rights Assignment

Here the policy root node could be:

- The Local Computer Policy
- The Default Domain Policy
- Any custom GPO created for a site, domain, or OU

You can configure user rights settings at any of these policy levels, but the effect will depend upon the result of combining together the Local Security Policy settings and those of the various Group Policies that are applied to the computer. Specifically:

- To assign rights to users or groups on a standalone Windows 2000 Server computer or a Windows 2000 Professional client computer that is part of a workgroup, you configure the User Rights Assignment settings of the Local Security Policy on the computer.

- To assign rights to users or groups on a domain controller, member server, or client computer belonging to a domain, you can assign rights both at the Local Security Policy level and at the level of any Group Policy Objects configured for the site, domain, OU. The effective rights assigned to a user or group are determined by the following order in which policy settings are applied in a domain:

  1. Local Security Policy
  2. Group Policy for sites
  3. Group Policy for domains
  4. Group Policy for OUs

Each succeeding level may override policies set at the previous levels. In particular, the Default Domain Policy overrides the Local Security Policy where their settings conflict, so assigning rights using Local Security Policy may not guarantee that those rights will be available. As a result, in a domain-based environment the usual way to assign or withhold system rights is to do so using Group Policy (using the Default Domain Policy or custom GPOs configured on OUs).

To view the currently effective system rights assignments on a computer, do the following:

Open the Local Security Policy console → expand Local Policies → select User Rights Assignment → view effective setting in Details Pane

You can also double-click on a policy setting to see in detail what rights are locally assigned to users and groups and what the effective policy settings are for those users and groups.

See *Group Policy Objects (GPOs)* and *Local Security Policy* in this chapter for more information on how these features work.

### See Also

*Group Policy(3,4), Local Security Policy(3,4), rights(3)*

# roaming user profile

Create, customize, and share a roaming user profile.

## Procedures

To enable users to roam between client computers and still have their personal desktop and network settings, user profiles must be stored in a shared folder on a centrally available server. This share:

- Can be located on any domain controller or member server in the domain (but is usually located on a member server)
- Can have any share name (but is usually given the name Profiles)
- Should be shared with Full Control permission assigned to the Authenticated Users group (instead of to the Everyone group)

### Create a Roaming Profile

This procedure outlines how to change a user's local profile into a roaming one:

1. Open the Active Directory Users and Computers console, and expand the console tree to select the organizational unit (OU) where the user's account resides (by default, this is the Users OU).
2. Select account → Action → Properties → Profile tab.
3. Enter the following as the Profile Path setting:

    \\server_name\shared_folder_name\user_name

   where:

   — *server_name* is the name of the server where the share for storing roaming profiles is located.

   — *shared_folder_name* is the name of the share where the roaming profiles will be stored (typically called Profiles).

   — *user_name* is the user's logon name.

When the user next logs on, his local user profile will be copied from the *C:\Documents and Settings\<user_name>* folder on the client computer to the shared folder on the server. The user will then be able to roam.

Note that in step 3, you can use the replaceable variable %username% instead of manually specifying *user_name* (the user's logon name). Windows 2000 will then automatically replace %username% with the logon name of the user whose roaming profile is being configured. For example, to create a roaming profile for user MaryS (Mary Smith) to be stored in the Profiles folder on member server MS1, enter the UNC path \\ms1\profiles\%username% into the Profile Path box.

When MaryS next logs on to her client computer, the roaming profile folder \\*ms1\ profiles\marys* will be created on the server.

### Customize a Roaming Profile

Instead of making a user's own local profile her roaming one, administrators can first create a customized roaming profile and then assign it the user, thus delivering a preconfigured desktop environment for the user wherever she logs on to the network.

Accomplishing this is a complicated process involving a number of steps. To make it easier to understand, let's say we want to create a customized roaming profile for user MaryS (Mary Smith) and store this profile in the Profiles folder on member server MS1. To do this, first create a customized profile template on a client computer as follows:

1. Log on to a Windows 2000 client computer using a dummy user account (you may need to create this account first). The dummy account should be used for creating profile templates only and should not be assigned to any users on your network. I'll use Dummy as the logon name of my dummy account. Logging on as Dummy will create the local profile folder *C:\Documents and Settings\Dummy* on the client machine.

2. While logged on as Dummy, configure the client computer to reflect the desktop environment you wish your roaming user (Mary) to have.

3. Log off the client computer to update your local profile with the changes you have made. Your local profile is now the desired template profile you wished to create for Mary.

Now you will copy the template profile to the server and specify who can use it. Log on to the client computer as Administrator and proceed as follows:

4. Control Panel → System → User Profiles → select template profile → Copy To

5. In the Copy To dialog box, enter the full UNC path to the new profile folder where the roaming profile will be stored on the server (this folder doesn't exist yet). In my example, I want to assign the roaming profile to Mary. In the "Copy profile to" text box enter the following (don't click OK yet):

    \\server_name\shared_folder_name\user_name

   or in the example:

    \\ms1\profiles\marys

6. Now specify the user who is permitted to use the roaming profile. What this does is assign appropriate NTFS permissions to the new profile folder and its contents. Do this as follows:

    Change → select user account (i.e., marys) → OK

7. Finally, use Active Directory Users and Computers to specify the path where the user's roaming profile is located. For the user Mary, this means:

    Select account → Action → Properties → Profile tab → enter \\ms1\ profiles\marys in the Profile path text box → OK

When the user (Mary) next logs on, her roaming profile will be downloaded to her client computer, overwriting any local profile for her on the machine.

### Share a Roaming Profile

You can also assign a single roaming profile to several users. You might do this for a group of users belonging to the same department and having similar job functions, such as for all the accountants in the Finance department. Proceed as follows:

1. First create a global group. Then make the users (those who will be assigned the same roaming profile) members of this group. As an example, let's call this group Accountants.

2. Now proceed as in steps 1 through 7 of "Customize a Roaming Profile" earlier in this section, with the following changes:

   — In step 5, give the new roaming profile a name that describes its use for the users in the group. For example, you could make the profile name the same as the group name (in the example, it would be \\ms1\ profiles\accountants).

   — In step 6, select the group (Accountants) using the Change button. This will permit each member of the group to use the roaming profile.

   — Complete step 7 for each user account that is a member of the group (it would have been nice if there was a faster way of doing this than one at a time).

### Notes

- Only members of the Administrators group can manage user profiles.

- The Profiles folder should be created and shared before you create any roaming user profiles.

- Locate your Profiles share on a member server instead of a domain controller to improve performance. This is because user profiles can be quite large, thus slowing the network while they are being copied to the client computer during logon or back to the server during logoff. In particular, the contents of a user's My Documents folder are part of his user profile, and any documents that have been changed during the user's session are copied to the server when the user logs off. Locating the Profiles share on a member server thus helps to speed the logon process and reduce the load on domain controllers.

- If a user cannot log on or receives an error message when logging on, the user's roaming profile may be corrupted. Delete both the user's roaming profile (on the server where it is stored) and the user's local profile (on the user's client machine); when the user next logs on, a new local profile will be created for the user from the default profile, and when she logs off, this local profile will be copied to the server and become her roaming profile.

- If you are going to share roaming profiles among multiple users, you probably want to make them mandatory. This is because any changes made to the desktop environment by one of the users will be reflected in the desktops of all users sharing the same profile.

- Unfortunately, you cannot assign a roaming profile to all members of a group by simply assigning it to the group; you must instead assign it to each user within the group individually.

### See Also

*local user profile(4), mandatory user profile(4), user profile(3)*

---

## schema

Add a new attribute to an existing class, or create a new attribute or class in the schema.

### Procedures

Before you can use the Active Directory Schema snap-in, you must register it by:

   Start → Run → `regsvr32 schmmgmt.dll` → OK → OK

Next you need to create a custom administrative console by adding the Active Directory Schema snap-in to a blank MMC console (see the beginning of Chapter 5 for information on how to create and save a custom console). Call this new console Active Directory Schema for easy reference.

As an extra precaution, before you can use this console to modify the schema, you must also create a value for a registry key on the domain controller on which you will be running the console (this should be the schema operations master in the domain). You can do this by:

   Active Directory Schema → right-click on Active Directory Schema → Operations Master → select "The Schema may be modified on this Domain Controller."

Note that this dialog box displays which domain controller in your domain is your schema master. Alternatively, you can open *regedt32* and navigate to the registry key:

   HKEY_LOCAL_MACHINE
     \SYSTEM
       \CurrentControlSet
         \Services
           \NTDS
             \Parameters

Create a new value called Schema Update Allowed of type REG_DWORD, and set its value to 1.

---

 Do not modify the schema unless you really have to and unless you really know what you're doing! Careless changes can wreak havoc with Active Directory.

---

### Add an Attribute to a Class

Active Directory Schema → expand Active Directory Schema → right-click on a class → Properties → Attributes → Add

### Create a New Attribute

Active Directory Schema → expand Active Directory Schema → right-click on Attributes → Create Attribute → Continue

The information you specify in the Create New Attribute box depends on the type of attribute you want to create. As an example, let's say you want to create a new attribute called FavoriteSong to document users' favorite songs in Active Directory. You could enter the following information:

*Common name*
FavoriteSong

*LDAP display*
FavoriteSong

*Unique X500 object ID*
1.2.840.156244.1 (assuming you have registered 1.2.840.156244 with the ISO)

*Syntax*
Case insensitive string

*Minimum*
0

*Maximum*
100

Click OK to create the attribute.

### Create a New Class

Active Directory Schema → expand Active Directory Schema → right-click on Classes → Create Class → Continue → specify identification, inheritance, and type → Next → specify mandatory and optional attributes → Finish

### Notes

- You must be a member of the Schema Admins group to modify the schema. The Administrator account is a member of this group by default.

- You can deactivate a class or attribute you created by double-clicking on it and selecting Deactivate.

- You cannot deactivate the default schema classes and attributes created when Active Directory is installed.

### See Also

*Active Directory(3), schema(3)*

## search

Search for files or folders, computers, printers, people, or Internet content using the Search Assistant.

### Procedures

There are four ways to open the Search Assistant from the Start menu:

> Files or Folders
> Printers
> People
> On the Internet

The first choice (Files or Folders) is the most general, however, since it lets you access the other three choices as well.

#### Search for Files or Folders

> Start → Search → For Files or Folders → select type of search

This opens the main Search Assistant window, which can be used for finding not just files and folders but also computers, printers, people, or even web content on the Internet. Search Assistant uses the Active Desktop or web-type interface of My Computer on Windows 2000, but it is inconsistent since for some functions it opens a separate dialog box instead.

You select the type of search to perform by using the links found at the bottom of the left window pane. This is somewhat inconvenient as you have to scroll down to access these links unless your monitor is set to 1024×768 pixel resolution or higher. Here are some additional details for each type of search you can perform:

#### Files or Folders

> This is the default choice. Lets you search for files or folders located on local hard drives, mapped network drives, or shared folders on the network. You can use various search criteria to narrow your search, including filename, date the file was created or modified, file type (extension), and file size in KB. You can search for files that contain a specific text string, and toggle advanced search features such as preserving case (default is off) or whether to search subfolders (default is on). The wildcards * and ? are supported for all text fields.

> Once you find a file or folder, you can open it using its associated application (or run it if it is an executable) and otherwise manipulate it by right-clicking and using the context menu.

#### Computers

> Lets you search for computers by name within Active Directory. You can also enter the first portion of a computer name and use the * and ? wildcards.

> Once you find a computer, you can open a window displaying shared folders and printers on the computer, open the parent folder containing the computer, or display its properties using the context menu.

*For Printers*

Opens a separate dialog box called Find Printers that can be used to search for network printers in Active Directory. You can search for printers anywhere in the directory or by domain, and you can search by printer name, location, model, or for printers with specific features such as double-sided printing or collation.

Once you find a printer, you can connect to it, display its properties, or open its print queue by right-clicking and using the context menu.

*For People*

Opens a separate dialog box called Find People that can be used to search for people (that is, user accounts and groups) either in Active Directory, in the local machine's address book, or on the Internet by using online directory services such as Bigfoot, WhoWhere, Yahoo!, and so on. You can search for people by name, email address, and several other common criteria.

Once you find someone, you can access a subset of the properties of his account, send him email, telephone him, open his home page, or add him to the address book. Some of these actions are not possible unless certain settings are configured, however. For example, you can't send someone email unless his account has an email address configured.

*On the Internet*

Lets you search for web content on the Internet using Internet Explorer. Specify a search category, enter your query, and click Search.

**Search on the Internet**

Start → Search → On the Internet

See "On the Internet" in the previous variable list.

**Search for Printers**

Start → Search → For Printers

See "For Printers" in the previous variable list.

**Search for People**

Start → Search → For People

See "For People" in the previous variable list.

**Notes**

- You can also open the Search Assistant by:
  - Right-click on My Computer → Search
  - Right-click on My Network Places → Search for Computers
  - Click the Search button on the toolbar in Windows Explorer or Internet Explorer
- Administrators can also use the Find function in the Active Directory Users and Computers console to find users, groups, computers, printers, shared folders, and other information published in Active Directory. See *find* in this chapter for more information.

- You can also select File → Save Search to save your search results. This is available only for searches for Files or Folders and Printers.

- Enabling the Indexing service will speed up the file-searching capabilities of Search Assistant.

- There are several other ways in Windows 2000 of getting to Search Assistant:

  My Computer → Search button
  My Network Places → Search button
  Windows Explorer → Search button

- For People does not distinguish between user accounts and groups in its search results.

- The address book can be opened either by Start → Accessories → Address Book or by Start → Run → *wab.exe*. The address book is used primarily on Windows 2000 Professional client machines to store contact information for applications such as Microsoft Outlook Express and Microsoft NetMeeting.

### See Also

*find(4)*

---

## security policy

Configure a security policy, and create or import a security template.

### Procedures

See *security policy* in Chapter 3 for information on different types of security policies.

#### Configure a Security Policy

You can edit the security settings in the Default Domain Policy on a domain controller for your domain by:

  Start → Administrative Tools → Domain Security Policy → modify settings as desired

The preferred method, however, is to create custom Group Policy Objects (GPOs) linked to the domain and selected OUs using Active Directory Users and Computers. You then configure the security settings in each GPO as desired (see *Group Policy* in Chapter 3 for a description of these different settings) by opening the GPO (see *Group Policy Objects (GPOs)* in this chapter for how) and:

  Computer Configuration → Windows Settings → Security Settings → modify settings as desired

---

 Account Policies security settings only have an effect when they are configured in a GPO linked to a domain, not an OU.

---

### Create a Security Template

To speed the process of configuring security settings, you can create a template containing predefined security settings. Windows 2000 includes a number of default templates that are described in *Local Security Policy* in Chapter 3, but you can also create your own security templates using the Security Templates snap-in. Add this snap-in to a new or existing MMC console and do the following:

Right-click the template search path node → New Template → specify a name and description → OK → select and expand the new template in the console tree → double-click on a policy → define this policy setting in the template → specify parameters → repeat for as many policies as need to be configured

Once you create a new security template, you can import it into a GPO to apply it to computers in a domain or OU (see the next section) or use it to analyze security on a local computer (see *Local Security Policy* in this chapter).

### Import a Security Template

You can import either one of the default security templates included in Windows 2000 or a custom template you have created (see "Create a Security Template" earlier in this article). To do this, open the desired GPO and:

Computer Configuration → Windows Settings → right-click on Security Settings → Import Policy → select *.inf* file for template → Open

### See Also

*Group Policy(3,4,5), Local Security Policy(3,4), security policy(3)*

---

## service

Configure, install, pause, resume, restart, and stop services.

### Procedures

The main tool for administering services on the local computer is the Services console in the Administrative Tools program group. A more powerful tool that can administer services on both local and remote machines, including downlevel Windows NT servers, is the Computer Management console, also in Administrative Tools. We focus here on using the Services console because the steps are similar but fewer. If you use Computer Management, you must first connect to the computer whose services you want to manage (see *Computer Management* in Chapter 5). You can also start, stop, pause, resume, and configure services from the command line using net commands.

### Configure a Service

Start → Programs → Administrative Tools → Services → right-click on a service → Properties

By selecting different tabs, you can configure different settings for the selected service:

*General*

Lets you configure the startup type for the service, change the status of the service, and view the path to the executable for the service

*Log On*

Lets you configure the security context (account) in which the service will run and the hardware profiles in which the service is enabled

*Recovery*

Lets you configure recovery actions to take place when the service fails

*Dependencies*

Lets you view the dependencies between the selected service and other services on the machine

For more information about these different service settings, see *service* in Chapter 3. You can also use the net config command from the command line to configure two important services: the Server service and the Workstation service. See *net config* in Chapter 7 for more information.

### Install a Service

Several dozen services are installed by default during a typical installation of Windows 2000 Server. You can install additional services in several ways:

- Start → Settings → Control Panel → Add/Remove Programs → Add/Remove Windows Components

  This lets you install or remove optional components of Windows 2000 Server. Many of these components are associated with specific services.

- Start → Settings → Network and Dial-up Connections → right-click on Local-Area Connection → Properties → Install → Service → Add → select service

  This lets you install various optional networking services such as file and print sharing services.

- By installing other Microsoft BackOffice applications such as Microsoft Exchange Server or by installing many third-party products for Windows 2000 Server.

### Pause a Service

Start → Programs → Administrative Tools → Services → right-click on a service → Pause

You can only pause a service that is running.

### Resuming a Service

Start → Programs → Administrative Tools → Services → right-click on a service → Resume

You can only resume a service that has been paused.

### Restart a Service

Start → Programs → Administrative Tools → Services → right-click on a service → Restart

You can only restart a service that has been stopped.

### Stop a Service

Start → Programs → Administrative Tools → Services → right-click on a service → Stop

You can stop a service that is either paused or running.

### Notes

- You must be logged on as a member of the Administrators group to configure service settings.

- Some services cannot be paused or stopped, such as the Plug and Play service.

- Some services can be stopped but not paused, such as the DNS Client service.

- To quickly stop and restart a running service, do the following:

    Right-click on running service → Restart

- If you pause a service upon which other services depend, the dependent services are not paused but may not function as expected.

- If you stop a service that has dependent services, these dependent services will also be stopped. You will then have to restart all of the stopped services independently since, unfortunately, you cannot select multiple services in Services and restart them.

- The Server service, which is fundamental to file sharing functionality, has some special behaviors to note:

    — If you pause the service, users will be unable to form new connections with the server. The exception is that members of the Administrators and Server Operators group will still be able to form new connections with the server.

    — If you stop the Server service on a remote computer, you will no longer be able to administer it remotely using Computer Management. You will have to go to the console of the remote computer and restart the service locally.

- Some services have more than four tabs on their property sheet. An example is the SNMP Service, which has three additional tabs.

- The only services you can configure from the command line are the Server and Workstation services.

- If you modify services and the computer fails to boot properly upon restarting, try booting to safe mode.

- When configuring reboot as a recovery action, you can create a custom message sent to remote users warning them of the impending reboot and can also specify the time interval before it takes place. For example, you might want to warn connected users before stopping the Server service since this will terminate their connections, causing them to lose unsaved work.

- The Services and Applications container in Computer Management not only contains the Services node but also other nodes enabling more detailed configuration of services such as DHCP, DNS, Indexing, IIS, Message Queuing, Telephony, WINS, and WMI Control.

### See Also

*Computer Management(5), net config(7), net config server(7), net config worksta-tion(7), net continue(7), net pause(7), net start(7), net stop(7), service(3), Services(5)*

## shared folder

Create or modify a shared folder, publish a shared folder in Active Directory.

### Procedures

To create a shared folder, you first create the folder and then share it. Afterwards, you can modify the shared folder by changing the permissions assigned to it, or changing the name under which it is shared, change the caching setting for offline use, share the folder under additional names, or stop sharing it.

You can create and manage shared folders in two different ways in Windows 2000:

- By accessing folder properties from the desktop or using Windows Explorer. This method is analogous to how one worked with shared folders in Windows NT 4.0.

- By using the new Computer Management console. This method is analogous to using the Windows NT administrative tool, Server Manager, but is easier and more powerful.

The advantages of using the new method (Computer Management) are:

- You can connect to remote machines and share folders without having to know the absolute path to the folder on the machine's drive.

- You can view hidden and administrative shares that are not visible in My Computer, My Network Places, or Windows Explorer.

- You are presented with a uniform view of all shares on a machine in a single window.

- You can view session information, open files for users connected to shared folders, send messages to those users, and disconnect all or selected sessions and open files.

- You can create custom consoles using the Shared Folders snap-in to allow users to manage shared folders on a specific machine.

Note that you must be a member of either the Administrators, Server Operators, or Power Users group to be able to create or modify shared folders. For further background information on planning and implementing shared folders on your network, see *shared folder* and *permissions* in Chapter 3.

### Create or Modify a Shared Folder (Old Method)

Select the folder using one of the following methods:

- My Computer
- Windows Explorer

Now create a new shared folder:

Right-click on folder → Properties → Sharing → Share this folder

Then specify the following:

*Share name (required)*
This is the name by which the shared folder will be visible on the network, and it need not be the same as the folder's name itself. The maximum length for a share name is 80 characters.

*Comment*
See "Notes" later in this article.

*User limit*
The number of concurrent client connections possible to the shared folder depends on the number of client access licenses (CALs) you have purchased.

*Permissions*
The default permission assigned to a newly created shared folder is Full Control for Everyone. If you add an ordinary user to the access list for a shared folder, the default permission assigned to the user is Read. See *permissions* in Chapter 3 for information on shared-folder permissions.

*Caching*
See *offline files* in Chapters 3 and 4.

*New Share*
You can share the folder under additional share names. For example, *C:\Public* could be shared first using the default share name Public and then shared a second time using the share name *Pub*. Note that this option is only available once you have shared the folder for the first time. Each time you share a folder, you can assign different permissions and connection limits to the new share.

To modify an existing shared folder:

Right-click on folder → Properties → Sharing

Then make changes to the folder's permissions, change the share name, change the caching settings for offline access, reshare the folder under additional names, or stop sharing the folder as desired.

### Create or Modify a Shared Folder (New Method)

To create a new shared folder on the *local* machine using the Computer Management console, open this console from the Start menu and then select:

Computer Management → System Tools → Shared Folders → Shares → Action → New File Share

To create a new shared folder on a *remote* machine using Computer Management, open this console from the Start menu and then select:

> Computer Management → Action → "Connect to another computer" → select computer → System Tools → Shared Folders → Shares → Action → New File Share

Either way, the Create Shared Folder Wizard opens to walk you through the process of creating a new shared folder. Typically, you will select the folder you want to share, specify a share name (usually the same as the folder name), and accept the remaining defaults in the wizard.

To modify a shared folder using Computer Management, proceed as earlier except:

> . . . → Shares → select shared folder → Action → Properties

Alternatively, instead of using Computer Management to manage shared folders, you could open a new MMC console, add the Shared Folders snap-in, save your console in Administrative Tools, and then use this console to create and manage shared folders on a specific machine. See *Shared Folders* in Chapter 5 for more information.

### Publish a Shared Folder in Active Directory

Publishing shared folders in Active Directory makes it easier for users to locate shared resources on the network. You should share the folder first before you publish it. To publish a shared folder in Active Directory, open the Active Directory Users and Computers console and:

> Right-click on a domain → New → Shared Folder → specify name → specify UNC path to shared folder

You can also publish shared folders to an OU within a domain instead of to the domain itself. For example, you could create an OU called Shares to contain all published shared folders in a domain.

### Notes

- Keep the share name the same as the folder name to simplify administration of shared folders.

- If you add a dollar sign ($) as a suffix to the share name for a shared folder, it becomes a hidden folder that doesn't appear in My Network Places or Windows Explorer. A client can still access the folder, though, if they know the exact share name—so this method should not be used for securing a shared folder. Use permissions instead to control access to the folder.

- To make things easier for users when there are a large number of shared folders on the network, specify a Comment for each shared folder that describes what the folder is used for or what it contains. These comments are visible to users in My Network Places and Windows Explorer.

- Shared folders on Windows 2000 Professional client computers support a maximum of 10 concurrent connections when Maximum Allowed is specified for User Limit.

- A good suggestion is to create all shared folders on NTFS volumes. Then leave the shared-folder permissions at their default setting (Full Control for Everyone), and manage folder access using the more granular NTFS permissions. For more information on shared-folder and NTFS permissions and how they combine, see *permissions* in Chapter 3.

- There is little reason to create multiple shares for a single folder using New Share. Keep things simple when you are creating and managing shared folders.

- If you have shared a folder more than once, an additional option called Remove a Share appears on the Sharing tab of the folder's property sheet.

- Do not stop sharing a folder while users are connected to it, or they may lose their data. Instead, first send a console message to all users connected to the share, indicating that they should save their work. Do this by opening the Computer Management console and selecting:

  System Tools → Shared Folders → Action → Send Console Message

- If you modify the permissions on a shared folder to grant users or groups access to the folder, but users complain that they still do not have the access you promised them, tell them to either:

  — Log off and then log on again (simplest).

  — Close all network connections from the client to the server where the share resides (for example, by disconnecting network drives to that machine), and then make new connections to the server.

  Other things you can check if this doesn't work include:

  — Check their network connection.

  — Check which groups the user belongs to and what level of access these groups have to the resource.

  — If the resource is located on an NTFS volume, make sure the user has NTFS permissions explicitly assigned to his user account or to a group to which he belongs.

### See Also

*offline files(3,4), permissions(3), shared folder(3), shared-folder permissions(4), Shared Folders(5)*

---

## shared-folder permissions

Assign and modify permissions on a shared folder.

### Procedures

Shared-folder permissions are an alternate means for controlling the level of access to file resources on Windows 2000–based file servers. As discussed in *permissions* in Chapter 3, the primary means for controlling the level of access to file resources on an NTFS volume is to assign them suitable NTFS permissions. When the folder is shared over the network, the shared-folder permissions can be left at their default setting of Full Control for Everyone or can be customized as desired, with the result that the NTFS and shared-folder permissions are combined.

To assign shared-folder permissions, you must first be able to access the icon of the shared folder. You can do this using Windows Explorer, My Network Places, or from the Search Results of the Search Assistant accessed through Start → Search → For Files or Folders. The following procedures assume you have already located the icon for the folder that you have shared and whose permissions you want to assign or modify.

### Assign Shared-Folder Permissions

Right-click on shared folder → Sharing → Permissions → Add → select domain → select user or group → Add → OK → allow or deny shared-folder permissions → Apply or OK

Unless you allow or deny different permissions, when you assign shared-folder permissions to a user or group, the default permission that is assigned is Allow Read.

You can select more than one user or group at a time in the "Select Users, Computers, or Groups" dialog box.

When you try to allow or deny different combinations of shared-folder permissions, you will discover that not all combinations are allowed. For example, if you try to allow Full Control, then all three checkboxes under Allow automatically become checked. Table 4-14 shows the permissible combinations of shared-folder permissions that can be assigned using the Sharing tab. This table works only if you are allowing permissions; if you both allow and deny permissions, other combinations are possible.

*Table 4-14: Allowable Combinations of Shared-Folder Permissions*

| Selecting . . . | Full Control | Change | Read |
|---|---|---|---|
| | *Automatically Selects . . .* | | |
| Full Control | ✓ | ✓ | ✓ |
| Change | | ✓ | |
| Read | | | ✓ |

### Modify Shared-Folder Permissions

Right-click on shared folder → Sharing → Permissions → select name → allow or deny shared-folder permissions

For more information see "Assign Shared-Folder Permissions" earlier in this article.

### Notes

- To assign shared-folder permissions, the folder must of course be shared.

- Unlike NTFS and print permissions, there are no advanced (special) shared-folder permissions you can configure.

- To learn more about how to create and manage shared folders on the network, see *shared folder* in Chapters 3 and 4.

- If you do modify the default shared-folder permissions, make sure you understand how NTFS and shared-folder permissions combine. See *permissions* in Chapter 3 for more information.

### See Also

*net share(7), offline files(4), ownership(4), permissions(3), printer permissions(4), shared folder(3,4), Shared Folders(5)*

---

## shutdown

Gracefully shut down the operating system so the machine can be turned off for maintenance, repair, or some other purpose.

### Procedures

Ctrl-Alt-Del → Shutdown

### Notes

- Use this method to shut down a machine prior to powering it off, since it causes open files to be closed and saves operating-system configuration information. Do not shut down a machine simply by powering it off since this could cause loss of data.

- By default, you must log on to a Windows 2000 Server machine before you can shut it down.

### See Also

*logon(3), log on(4)*

---

## site

Check the replication topology, configure a site, site link, or subnet, create an Active Directory connection, site, site link, or subnet, designate a preferred bridgehead server, move a server to a different site, and rename the Default-First-Site.

### Procedures

Sites, site links, and subnets are created and modified using the Active Directory Sites and Services console, which the following procedures assume to be opened. Make sure you are logged on as a member of the Enterprise Admins group.

#### Check the Replication Topology

The following procedure can be used to check the existing replication topology to determine whether it is optimal. The process checks whether domain controllers are available in each site and whether new ones have been added to sites, and then uses site link cost values to recalculate an optimal topology for intersite replication. If new Active Directory connections are required, these will be automatically created by the process:

---

Expand the Sites container → expand a site → expand the Servers container → expand a server → right-click on NTDS Settings → All Tasks → Check Replication Topology

### Configure a Site

Expand the Sites container → right-click on a site → Properties

The main thing to configure here is Location, which makes it easier to find sites in Active Directory when there are many of them. You can also apply Group Policy to the site (see *Group Policy Objects (GPOs)* in this chapter).

### Configure a Site Link

Expand the Inter-Site Transports container → select transport (IP or SMTP) → right-click on a site link → Properties

The key settings here are on the General tab:

*Cost*

Choose a lower cost value for a WAN connection with higher bandwidth and reliability to give preference to that connection when there are multiple links between sites. Dial-up connections such as ISDN should have a relatively high cost value for similar reasons. The lower-valued cost will always be used unless it is unavailable.

*Replication interval*

The minimum replication interval is 15 minutes, and the maximum is 10,080 minutes (1 week). A typical choice is every few hours or so. Click the Change Schedule button to specify times and days of the week when the link will be unavailable for replication if needed.

### Configure a Subnet

Expand the Subnets container → right-click on a subnet → Properties

The main thing you can configure here is Site on the Subnet tab. This lets you associate the selected subnet with a different site if desired.

### Create an Active Directory Connection

To manually create a connection between a domain controller in one site and one in a different site, you can do the following:

Expand the Sites container → expand a site → expand the Servers container → expand a server → right-click on NTDS Settings → New Active Directory Connection → select target domain controller

---

 Manually creating Active Directory connections is not usually necessary, as Active Directory creates these connections automatically between domain controllers in different sites. It is generally better to check the replication topology instead, using the procedure described earlier, which creates additional Active Directory connections if they are needed to optimize intersite replication.

---

### Create a New Site

Right-click on Sites container → New Site → specify a name for the site → select a site link to associate with this site → OK

Once you create a new site, you should add subnets for it to the Subnet container (see "Create a New Subnet" later in this article). You should then typically promote a member server in the site to the role of domain controller to facilitate user logons and specify the licensing computer for the site to ensure you're legal.

---

You can delete any site you create, but you cannot delete the Default-First-Site: you can only rename it to something else. Note that you can, however, delete the DEFAULTSITELINK that was created for the Default-First-Site.

---

### Create a New Site Link

Right-click on Inter-Site Transports container → right-click on a transport (IP or SMTP) → New Site Link → specify a name → add sites to the site link → OK

Once you create a new site link, you should configure its settings (see "Configure a Site Link" earlier in this article.)

### Create a New Subnet

Right-click on Subnets → New Subnet → specify network ID and subnet mask → select a site to associate with this subnet → OK

When you specify the network ID and subnet mask, it is automatically displayed in the form *w.x.y.z/n*, where *w.x.y.z* is the network ID and n is the number of ones in the binary form of the subnet mask.

### Designate a Preferred Bridgehead Server

Bridgehead servers are domain controllers used for replication with other sites:

Expand the Sites container → expand a site → select Servers container → right-click on a server → Properties → select transport → Add

### Force Replication over a Connection

Use this procedure to force a domain controller in one site to replicate with one in a different site. The first domain controller is the one selected in the Servers container of the first site, while the second domain controller is the one specified on the Active Directory Connection tab of the property sheet for the selected connection:

Expand the Sites container → expand a site (the first site) → expand the Servers container → expand a server (the first domain controller) → select NTDS Settings → right-click on a connection → Replicate Now

To view the second site and second domain controller:

... → select NTDS Settings → Properties → Active Directory connection → read Site and Server information

### Move a Server to a Different Site

Expand the Sites container → expand a site → select Servers container → right-click on a server → Move → select target site → OK

This procedure is typically used to move a domain controller from one site to another to optimize replication and logon traffic for the target site.

### Rename the Default-First-Site

Expand Sites container → right-click on Default-First-Site → Rename → specify a friendly name for the site

## Notes

- To delegate control of sites:

    Right-click on a site → Delegate Control

    See *delegation* in this chapter for more information.

- A site link must contain at least two sites.

- Replication schedules for site links are ignored when the transport is SMTP over IP, so don't configure a schedule in this case unless a scheduled dial-up WAN connection is used.

- If you have two or more site links configured as a site-link bridge, the cost of the bridge is calculated as the sum of the costs of the links within the bridge.

- You can delegate authority over sites, subnets, and Inter-Site Transports (see *delegation* in this chapter). You can apply Group Policy to sites as well (see *Group Policy Objects (GPOs)* in this chapter).

- Manually created Active Directory connections will not be affected when Check Replication Topology is used to optimize intersite.

- You cannot use SMTP as an intersite transport unless you have installed a certificate authority (CA) in your enterprise and installed certificates on your domain controllers. This is necessary to ensure the authenticity of SMTP replication messages as they may be sent over the unsecure Internet.

## See Also

*Active Directory(3)*, *Active Directory Sites and Services(5)*, *delegation(4)*, *Group Policy Objects (GPOs)(4)*, *site(3)*

---

# standby

Configure automatic standby settings or manually enter standby mode.

## Procedures

Use Power Options in the Control Panel to configure the actions or conditions that lead to your computer being placed in standby mode.

---

### Configure Automatic Standby

Start → Settings → Control Panel → Power Options → Power Schemes → select your default scheme → configure interval of inactivity that triggers standby mode

### Manually Enter Standby

Start → Shutdown → Standby

You can also configure your system so that pressing the power button causes it to enter standby mode instead of powering off completely:

Start → Settings → Control Panel → Power Options → Advanced → select Standby in the "When I press the power button on my computer" list box

### Notes

- Make sure that you save all your work before you enter (or allow your machine to enter) standby mode, since any data stored only in physical memory (RAM) will be lost when standby occurs.

- You can password protect your computer during standby by:

    Power Options → Advanced → "Prompt for password when computer goes off standby"

    Note that the same password is used for both standby and hibernation modes.

- Press the power button to leave standby mode.

- Standby mode consumes minimal power for the processor and system board, as opposed to powering off which causes your system to consume no power at all. The advantage is that the system can return from standby mode more quickly than rebooting from a powered-off condition.

- Servers should not generally be allowed to enter standby mode since they are often in demand 24 hours a day.

### See Also

*hibernation(3,4), Power Options(6), power scheme(3,4), standby(3)*

---

## startup options

Specify whether and how long the boot menu is displayed during startup.

### Procedures

The boot menu is the menu showing available operating systems and is displayed during startup. The boot menu is constructed from the entries in a Hidden, Read-only, System text file called *boot.ini*, which resides in the root directory of the boot partition. Although you can edit this file by hand, it is not recommended as a corrupted *boot.ini* file may prevent your system from booting:

Start → Settings → Control Panel → System → Advanced → Startup and Recovery

---

You can then specify:

- Which operating system the computer will automatically boot if you do not respond to the boot menu

- Whether the boot menu is displayed or not and how long it is displayed before the default choice is automatically made

### Notes

- You must be a member of the Administrators group to configure startup options on your computer.

- You can configure startup options on remote computers by:

  Start → Programs → Administrative Tools → Computer Management → right-click on root node in console tree → "Connect to another computer" → select computer → OK → right-click on root node again → Properties → Advanced → Startup and Recovery

- If there is only one operating system installed on the computer, the boot menu is not displayed during startup.

- Setting the time of the "Display list of operating systems" to zero seconds causes the boot menu to be bypassed and the default operating system to be loaded automatically.

### See Also

*Computer Management(5), recovery options(4), System(6)*

---

# TCP/IP

Configuring the TCP/IP network protocol.

### Procedures

For information on how to install TCP/IP and other networking protocols, see *network protocol* earlier in this chapter. For a general overview of TCP/IP concepts and functionality, see *TCP/IP* in Chapter 3.

### Configuring TCP/IP

First you need to access the Internet Protocol (TCP/IP) property sheet for your computer:

- If you are configuring TCP/IP for a local-area connection, then do the following:

  Start → Settings → Network and Dial-up Connections → select a local-area connection → Properties → select Internet Protocol (TCP/IP) → Properties

- If you are configuring TCP/IP for a dial-up or VPN connection, then do the following:

  Start → Settings → Network and Dial-up Connections → select a dial-up or VPN connection → Properties → Networking → select Internet Protocol (TCP/IP) → Properties

Now use the Internet Protocol (TCP/IP) property sheet to make various changes to your TCP/IP configuration, as described later in this article.

### Additional Default Gateways

To assign additional default gateways to a network connection, use Advanced → IP Settings → Default gateways → Add.

### Additional IP Addresses and Subnet Masks

To assign additional IP addresses and subnet masks to a network connection, use Advanced → IP Settings → IP addresses → Add. You can assign as many IP addresses as you like to the connection. A typical use of this feature is creating multiple virtual servers for hosting different web sites on a single Windows 2000 Server running Internet Information Services (IIS).

### Assign a Metric

The metric for the network connection is the cost in hops of using this connection to route packets. The metric you specify here is entered into the routing table for the network interface (see *route* in Chapter 7 for more information about routing tables). The default value is 1, and this should usually not be changed unless you want to shape the flow of traffic over your internetwork, and then only if you are dealing with a multihomed Windows 2000 Server operating in the role of a router.

### Configuration Method

To manually assign an IP address, subnet mask, and default gateway, choose "Use the following IP address." To use DHCP or APIPA for obtaining TCP/IP settings, select "Obtain an IP address automatically" (see the section "Automatic Private IP Addressing (APIPA)" in the article *TCP/IP* in Chapter 3 for more information on APIPA, and see *DHCP* in this chapter for information on Dynamic Host Configuration Protocol).

### DNS Client Configuration

You can either manually specify the IP address of a preferred and alternate DNS server, or if you are using DHCP, you can select "Obtain the DNS server address automatically." You can also add IP addresses for additional DNS servers, modify the order in which these servers are queried by resolvers, and perform other DNS client configuration actions by Advanced → DNS (see *DNS* in Chapters 3 and 4 for more information on configuring Domain Name System clients).

### Optional TCP/IP Configuration

You can perform advanced configuration such as enabling IP security (IPsec) or TCP/IP filtering using Advanced → Options. IPsec is discussed elsewhere while TCP/IP filtering is discussed in the sidebar "TCP/IP Filtering."

### WINS Client Configuration

You can manually specify the IP addresses of WINS servers on your network, or you can use DHCP to assign these addresses. You can also manually enable or disable NetBIOS over TCP/IP (NetBT), obtain NetBT settings from a DHCP server, and enable or disable NetBIOS name resolution using *lmhosts* files using Advanced → WINS (see *WINS* in Chapters 3 and 4 for more information on configuring Windows Internet Name Service clients).

## TCP/IP Filtering

To protect your computer or simply to manage the bandwidth utilized by incoming network traffic, you can control which types of incoming TCP/IP traffic are accepted by your computer. TCP/IP filtering works with broadcast, multicast, and directed packets. Note that on a multihomed machine (multiple network adapters), filter settings apply globally to all adapters. This feature was previously called TCP/IP Security in Windows NT 4.0. To configure TCP/IP filtering, just open the Internet Protocol (TCP/IP) property sheet and select:

> Advanced → Options → TCP/IP filtering → Properties → Enable TCP/IP Filtering (all adapters) → Permit Only → specify {TCP ports | UPD ports | IP protocols}

Note that you can also filter traffic using the Routing and Remote Access Service or by installing a firewall or proxy server application on your machine.

Be careful when configuring TCP/IP filtering that you don't block traffic that is essential to your network's operation! For example, blocking UDP ports 67 and 68 would cause problems with DHCP.

### Notes

- Any TCP/IP settings you configure manually on a computer will override similar settings obtained from a DHCP server.

- A good practice on multihomed machines is to configure only a default gateway on the first adapter. If both adapters have gateways configured, the second gateway is only used if the first one is unavailable.

- Configure multiple default gateways for a single adapter if your network topology is complex enough to allow alternate routes between subnets. This way if a router fails, communications can still be maintained.

- If your computer is configured to obtain an IP address automatically from a DHCP server but the server does not provide your computer with a default gateway, you either need to reconfigure the DHCP server to provide a default gateway or manually configure a TCP/IP address and subnet mask on the client in order to assign it a default gateway.

- To test your TCP/IP configuration, use the command-line utilities `ping` and `ipconfig` (see Chapter 7).

- Use the `pathping` or `tracert` command-line utilities to test the configuration and operation of routers on a TCP/IP internetwork (see Chapter 7).

- Use the `netstat` command-line utility to view the current TCP/IP protocol, routing, and connection statistics (see Chapter 7).

### See Also

*arp(7), DHCP(3,4), DNS(3,4), hostname(7), ipconfig(7), nbtstat(7), netstat(7), network protocol(3,4), nslookup(7), pathping(7), ping(7), route(7), TCP/IP(3), tracert(7), WINS(3,4)*

## *Terminal Services*

Configure Terminal Services, create client installation disks, establish a terminal session, install Terminal Services, install Terminal Services Client, manage and monitor terminal sessions, and terminate a terminal session.

### *Procedures*

Installing Terminal Services on a Windows 2000 server adds four new consoles to the Administrative Tools program group:

* Terminal Services Manager
* Terminal Services Configuration
* Terminal Services Licensing
* Terminal Services Client Creator

The following procedures start with one of these consoles unless otherwise specified.

### *Configure Terminal Services*

There are two nodes in the console tree of the Terminal Services Configuration console, as follows.

#### *Connections*

This lets you configure global settings for client connections to the terminal server. Double-click on a connection node to open its property sheet, then configure settings as desired. Of special importance here are:

*General*
Specify the level of encryption to be used to protect data from the client to the server. Using High requires the 128-bit encryption add-on to Windows 2000.

*Logon Settings*
Specify a user that can automatically log on using this connection.

*Sessions*
Configure timeout values for both active and idle sessions, and either disconnect the client or terminate the session when the limit is reached.

*Environment*
Configure wallpaper and a startup program for the client.

*Remote Control*
Enable and configure remote-control settings for the client. Typically, you should specify that a user's permission is required before assuming remote control of a session (this should be company policy).

*Client Settings*
Specify various printer, COM port, and clipboard mappings for the client.

*Network Adapter*
> Specify the maximum number of terminal sessions allowed. Consider your server's resources when configuring this setting.

*Permissions*
> Leave as Full Control if you want to disconnect, remotely control, and perform other actions on user sessions.

### Server Settings

This contains settings that let you configure different aspects of the terminal server, specifically:

*Terminal server mode*
> Specify either remote administration or application server mode. To change modes, use Add/Remove Programs in the Control Panel to uninstall and then reinstall Terminal Services, selecting the new mode during reinstallation.

*Delete temporary folders on exit*
> Leave the default setting at Yes for best performance.

*Use temporary folders per session*
> Leave the default setting at Yes for best performance.

*Internet Connector licensing*
> Enable this feature to allow up to 200 concurrent users to connect anonymously to a terminal server over the Internet. These users must not be employees of your business. This feature is only available when running in application server mode.

*Active Desktop*
> Disable this feature if you need to conserve resources on your terminal server.

*Permissions Compatibility*
> Configure permissions for Windows 2000 or legacy clients.

### Create Client Installation Disks

> Terminal Services Client Creator → select 16- or 32-bit client → insert floppies

You need 4 floppies for 16-bit clients, and 2 for 32-bit ones. Do not write-protect the floppies afterward, or you will not be able to install Terminal Services Client using them.

### Establish a Terminal Session

To connect to a terminal server, you start the Terminal Services Client on the computer. The method for doing this depends on the version of Windows on the computer (use Start → Programs → Terminal Services client → Terminal Services Client on 32-bit Windows, for example). In the Terminal Services Client box that appears, specify:

*Server*
> Enter either the name or IP address of a terminal server on the network.

*Screen area*
> The screen resolution you choose for the Terminal Services Client is not dependent on the screen resolution of the terminal server itself.

*Available servers*
> You can also select a terminal server from the list of available servers displayed here.

*Enable data compression*
> Use this if you are connecting over a slow network connection such as a modem.

*Cache bitmaps to disk*
> Selecting this option caches desktop GUI elements to the local cache on the client and improves performance.

Click Connect to establish a connection. A new window will open on the client computer displaying the Windows 2000 desktop, and a Log On to Windows dialog box will appear requesting credentials to access the terminal server. Enter your domain credentials here.

---

 You can open multiple terminal sessions on a single client computer. Each session can use the same domain credentials or different ones.

---

### Install Terminal Services

Terminal Services can be installed during Setup or afterward using Add/Remove Programs in the Control Panel (the latter method is described here):

> Control Panel → Add/Remove Programs → Add/Remove Windows Components → select Terminal Services and Terminal Services Licensing → Next

At this point you must choose the mode in which you wish to run your terminal server:

*Remote administration mode*
> This mode is used for remotely administering the server using terminal Services. If you use Windows 2000 Professional clients, you need no further licensing (see "Licensing Requirements" in the article *Terminal Services* in Chapter 3).

*Application server mode*
> This mode is used when you want clients to be able to run Windows-based applications on the terminal server. If you select this mode, you must set up your Terminal Services Licensing server and purchase necessary licenses within 90 days. If you select this mode, you are next required to specify whether permissions should be configured to support only Windows 2000 applications or also legacy Windows-based applications. Afterwards, you are warned about any currently installed applications which may not function properly once Terminal Services is installed and which may need to be reinstalled if Terminal Services is removed from the server.

Next you are required to specify the location where the Terminal Services licensing database will be located for your domain/workgroup or for the entire enterprise. At this point, files are copied from the Windows 2000 CD and the installation is completed.

The results of installing Terminal Services on a server include the following new consoles in the Administrative Tools program group:

*Terminal Services Manager*
    Manage and monitor processes and sessions on the terminal server

*Terminal Services Configuration*
    Manage server settings and protocol configuration settings on the terminal server

*Terminal Services Licensing*
    Manage Terminal Services CALs for the domain or enterprise

*Terminal Services Client Creator*
    Create sets of floppy disks for installing Terminal Services Client software on client computers

Once you install Terminal Services, you need to configure it (see "Configure Terminal Services" earlier in this article).

### Install Terminal Services Client

You first need to create installation disks (see "Create Client Installation Disks" earlier in this article). Make sure the client is connected to the network. Insert the first installation disk and select:

    Start → Run → `A:\setup.exe` → OK

Enter your name and organization, accept the licensing agreement, accept the default location, and choose whether the client will be used by all users on this computer or only the current user. Installation then completes by copying files.

---

You can also share the directory *%SystemRoot%\System32\Clients\ Tsclient* on the terminal server to allow users to access *Setup.exe* in the appropriate subfolder and install Terminal Services over the network instead of using floppies.

To install Terminal Services Client on the terminal server itself, use Windows Explorer or My Computer to find and double-click on the file *%SystemRoot%\System32\Clients\Tsclient\Win32\Setup.exe.*

---

### Manage and Monitor Terminal Sessions

Open the Terminal Services Manager on the terminal server (or preferably, establish a terminal session with the server and run the console within this session). Terminal Services Manager should display the active terminal servers in your enterprise (if not, you can right-click on All Listed servers → Find Servers in All Domains).

Select a terminal server in the console tree to display the active users, sessions, and processes in the Details Pane. The session labeled as Console is the user logged on locally to the Terminal server (if any). Terminal sessions are labeled as RDP-Tcp#n, where n is the number of the session since startup. The session labeled as RDP-Tcp is the listening state, which allows the server to respond to new connection attempts by clients. Right-click on a user or session in the Details Pane and variously:

- Connect to a new session (you are disconnected from your previous one).

- Disconnect from a session (you need Full Control permission to disconnect another user's session). This leaves the session running on the server, and the user can reconnect to it if she desires.

- Send a pop-up message to the connected user.

- Assume remote control of a user's session (you need Full Control permission to disconnect another user's session). The remote user will typically be prompted whether he wants to allow you to assume control of the session. By default, you terminate a remote-control session using the hot key Ctrl plus an asterisk (*) on the numeric key pad of your keyboard.

- Reset a session (delete it from the server, disconnecting the user). Don't do this carelessly or users can lose their work.

- Display the status of a session in bytes and frames sent and received, % errors, and so on.

- Log a user off from a session (this terminates the session on the server as well).

You can also right-click on a process and terminate it for any user or session.

Expand a terminal server container in the console tree, and select a session beneath it to display the processes running in that session and various session information, including the username, client computer name and IP address, client color depth and screen resolution used, level of encryption, and other information.

### Terminating a Terminal Session

There are two different ways you can end a terminal session:

*Disconnect from the session*
In the terminal session window, do the following:

> Start → Shut Down → Disconnect → OK

This leaves the session running on the server, and the user can reconnect to the session later if desired. This feature is useful if the user needs to start a time-consuming process on the server, such as running a complex query against a large database, and then disconnect to free up system resources.

*Log off from the session*
In the terminal session window, do the following:

> Start → Shut Down → Log off → OK

This is the preferred method for ending a terminal session as it stops the session on both the server and the client. Stopping the session on the server frees up resources for other sessions. Make sure you save your work before doing this.

## Notes

- The remote-control feature of Terminal Services can only be configured using Terminal Services Manager when Terminal Services Manager itself is run within a terminal session.

- Closing the terminal session window by clicking the close gadget in the top left corner of the window disconnects the session but leaves it running on the server.

- Resetting the RDP-Tcp listening session terminates all sessions on the server.

- To log on to a terminal server, users must be enabled to do so (they are by default). To enable or disable a user for running terminal sessions, open the Active Directory Users and Computers console, open the property sheet for the user, select the Terminal Services Profile tab, and select or clear the checkbox "Allow logon to terminal server."

### See Also

*Terminal Services(3)*

# trust

Create an external trust, create a shortcut trust, or verify a trust.

### Procedures

Trusts are managed using the Active Directory Domains and Trusts console, and the following procedures assume that you have this console open.

### Create an External Trust

External trusts are one-way trusts in which a trusting domain trusts a trusted domain. You might typically create external trusts between:

- A Windows 2000 domain and a legacy Windows NT domain

- Two Windows 2000 domains in different forests

Before you create a one-way trust, you need to decide which domain is the trusting domain and which the trusted one. The trusting domain typically contains the shared resources that need to be accessed, while the trusted one contains the user accounts who need to access these resources. Creating a one-way trust involves two steps—one of which is performed on a domain controller in the domain that will be the trusting one, and the other on a domain controller in the domain that will be the trusted one (the order doesn't matter).

For example, let's say you want to establish a one-way trust from the root domain of forest A (the trusting domain) and the root domain of forest B (the trusted domain). The steps involved are as follows:

- In the domain that will be the trusted one (root domain in forest B):

  Right-click on a domain → Properties → Trusts → click bottom Add button → specify DNS name of domain that will be the trusting one (root domain of forest A) → specify a password → OK

- In the domain that will be the trusting one (root domain in forest A):

   Right-click on a domain → Properties → Trusts → click top Add button → specify DNS name of domain that will be the trusted one (root domain of forest B) → specify same password as earlier → OK

---

 Note that explicitly creating an external trust between the root domains of two forests allows authentication only between these two domains, not between other domains in the two forests. In other words, external trusts are not transitive.

---

In order to establish a trust with another domain, the domain controller must be able to resolve the DNS name of the other domain. If it can verify the DNS name of the domain, it then offers to try to verify that the trust has been established. To do this, you are required to enter administrator credentials in the remote domain.

### Create a Shortcut Trust

To create a shortcut trust between two domains in a Windows 2000 forest, follow the same procedure as in "Create an External Trust" earlier in this article.

### Verify a Trust

   Right-click on a domain → Properties → Trusts → select a trusted or trusting domain → Edit → Verify

If the trust is working, a dialog box will confirm this. If the trust has failed, a series of dialog boxes will lead you through the process of re-establishing the trust relationship between the domains. You can verify both implicit (transitive) and explicit (external or shortcut) trusts this way.

### Notes

- You can revoke an external trust between two domains by:

   Right-click on the trusted or trusting domain → Properties → Trusts → select trusted or trusting domain → Remove

- An external trust displays as External in the Relationship column of the Trusts tab.

- You create a two-way external trust by creating two one-way trusts, one in each direction.

- You cannot revoke transitive trusts, as these are created and maintained automatically.

### See Also

*Active Directory Domains and Trusts(5), domain(3,4), domain controller(3,4), trust(3)*

# upgrade

Upgrading Windows NT domains, domain controllers, member servers, and stand-alone servers to Windows 2000 Server.

## Procedures

The actual upgrade procedures are almost identical to the procedures for installing fresh versions of Windows 2000 Server as described in *install* earlier in this chapter. Only additional issues are covered here.

### Upgrading a Windows NT Domain

Upgrading a domain means upgrading all the domain controllers in the domain. The important issues are:

- Make sure your servers meet all the hardware requirements for upgrading to Windows 2000 Server. See *install* earlier in this chapter for more information.

- Make sure you have your Windows 2000 domain structure planned out ahead of time. This includes determining the number of domains, domain trees, and forests you want to have in your new network. See *domain*, *tree*, and *forest* in Chapter 3 for more information.

- Do the upgrade at night or on the weekend when user activity is low or zero.

- Ensure that your domain controllers have fully replicated with each other prior to upgrading them.

- Be sure to back up your domain controllers prior to upgrading them.

- Disconnect one backup domain controller (BDC) from your network prior to upgrading the domain. This way you have a way of ensuring users can still log on should the upgrade of the domain fail or become problematic. If things really go wrong, you can then promote this BDC to the role of PDC and then recreate additional BDCs.

- You must upgrade the primary domain controller (PDC) first for each domain. See "Upgrading a Domain Controller" later in this article for more information on the procedure involved. After the upgrade is complete, test your new Windows 2000 domain controller thoroughly before upgrading anything else on your network.

- Once your PDC (or PDCs) are upgraded, you can then upgrade your BDCs. Windows 2000 member servers and Windows 2000 Professional desktop machines can be upgraded either before or after domain controllers.

If you have a Windows NT member server configured as a remote-access server (RAS) on your network, make sure you upgrade it *before* your last BDC is upgraded. This is because RAS servers depend on domain controllers for authenticating users. An alternative is to weaken Active Directory permissions on your Windows 2000 domain controllers so that Windows NT RAS servers are able to use them for authenticating users.

### Before Upgrading Any Windows NT Server

Some general steps you should consider before upgrading any Windows NT domain controller, member server, or standalone server to Windows 2000 Server include:

- Read the *Readme.doc* file in the root directory of the Windows 2000 Server compact disc to make sure your installed applications will work properly after your operating system has been upgraded from Windows NT 4.0 Server to Windows 2000 Server. This may make or break whether you go ahead and upgrade your server or not.

- Perform a full backup of your server.

- If you have a mirror set, break the mirror prior to upgrading, then re-create the mirror set after the upgrade is complete.

- If any partitions have been compressed using a third-party compression utility, make sure you uncompress them first.

- If you are using a UPS, disconnect it.

- Disable any virus-protection software.

### Upgrading a Domain Controller

The Setup procedure is almost the same as for performing a fresh installation of Windows 2000 Server as described in *install* earlier in this chapter. There are only a few important points:

- The Setup Wizard prompts you for whether you want to create:

  — A new domain or a child domain of an existing domain. Choose New Domain for your first PDC since a PDC actually *defines* a domain. For the other PDCs, the choice you make depends upon the domain model you want to create.

  — A new forest or a domain tree within an existing forest. Choose New Forest for your first PDC. For the other PDCs, the choice you make depends upon the domain model you want to create.

- Setup prompts you for where you want to locate your Sysvol directory and your Active Directory data and log file (must be an NTFS partition). Make sure you choose a partition with enough free space—when the SAM database on a Windows NT domain controller is upgraded to Active Directory, it may occupy as much as ten times the disk space as the original SAM database.

- For backward-compatibility reasons, upgraded domain controllers are in mixed mode by default. This means that:

  — Windows 2000 member servers and Windows 2000 Professional desktop machines see the upgraded domain controller as a Windows 2000 domain controller.

  — Windows NT servers and workstations see it as a Windows NT primary domain controller (PDC).

*Upgrading a Member Server*

There are no special issues involved here. See *install* earlier in this chapter for the general procedure.

*Upgrading a Standalone Server*

There are no special issues involved here. See *install* earlier in this chapter for the general procedure.

## Notes

- When upgrading your first BDC, you must make sure your upgraded PDC is working and available on the network. And when you upgrade your other BDCs, you must ensure that at least one upgraded domain controller is available on the network. This is because when a BDC is upgraded, it must copy the Active Directory data from an existing Windows 2000 domain controller.

- Once you have upgraded all of your Windows NT domains and domain controllers to Windows 2000, you can switch your domain controllers from mixed mode to native mode. Note that this step is irreversible. See *mixed mode* in Chapter 3 for more information.

## See Also

*domain(3,4)*, *forest(3)*, *mixed mode(3)*, *install(3,4)*, *tree(3)*, *upgrade(3)*

---

# VPN connection

Configure a VPN connection, configure advanced connection settings, connect using a VPN connection, create a new VPN connection, and monitor the status of a VPN connection.

## Procedures

For information on general terminology related to remote-access connections, see *remote access* in Chapter 3. Described in this section are tasks relating to creating and configuring *outbound* VPN connections on Windows 2000 computers.

For tasks relating to *inbound* connections, see the following articles in this chapter:

*incoming connection*
> Describes how to configure incoming connections on a standalone Windows 2000 server that is part of a workgroup

*remote-access server*
> Describes how to configure incoming connections on a Windows 2000 domain controller or member server that is part of a domain

The tasks listed here (unless otherwise specified) assume that you have already opened the Network and Dial-up Connections window by:

> Start → Settings → Network and Dial-up Connections

## Configure a VPN Connection

When you use the Network Connection Wizard to create a new outbound VPN connection, you specify only minimal configuration information for the connection. Typically, you need to further configure the connection so that you can successfully and efficiently connect to the VPN remote-access server on the remote private network. To configure a VPN connection on a client machine:

Right-click on connection → Properties

Following are some highlights of some of the more important settings on the five tabs of this property sheet:

### General

The VPN remote-access server (the server on the remote private network that accepts inbound VPN connections) must be identified using either its IP address or fully qualified domain name (FQDN).

If your client computer is connected to the Internet through a LAN connection using a dedicated or leased line, you can deselect "Dial another connection first."

---

 In order to establish a VPN connection with the remote private network, you first need to establish a connection with the Internet. Unfortunately, you can specify only one dial-up connection for your VPN connection to use. It would have been nice if you could create and assign multiple dial-up connections to the VPN connection so that if the first one failed to connect to the Internet, the next one would be tried, and so on.

---

Select the Show icon in the taskbar when connected. This will place a connection icon in the system tray, which will blink when data is being transferred. You can double-click on this icon to display the status of the connection and right-click on it to disable (terminate) the connection.

### Options

This is where you specify redial attempts and whether the connection should automatically terminate itself after being idle for a period of time. You can also specify that the connection will automatically redial if it is dropped—this is useful for file transfers using FTP since Windows 2000 can resume a file transfer without needing to start all over from the beginning.

### Security

Typical security gives you a series of preconfigured settings for authentication protocols and data-encryption schemes. In any case, the remote-access client and server will negotiate the highest degree of security for authentication and data integrity that they are configured to support. The default setting here is to require a secured password (any authentication method may be used except PAP) and to

---

require data encryption (necessary because data is being transmitted over an insecure link, namely the Internet). If you want more granular control over which authentication protocols and data-encryption schemes the dial-up client will support, select Advanced → Settings. For more information on these different schemes and protocols, see *remote access* in Chapter 3.

If you want to try to be authenticated by the VPN server on the remote private network using your currently logged-on user credentials, select "Automatically use my Windows logon name and password."

### Networking

By default, the setting "Type of VPN server I am calling" is configured as Automatic. This means that Windows 2000 will determine whether the remote VPN server uses PPTP or L2TP as its tunneling protocol (L2TP is tried first as it is more secure, but it requires that your client computer be configured with a digital certificate acceptable to the remote server).

By default, all your currently installed networking components are enabled for your VPN connection since these types of connections provide a very secure method for connecting to a remote private network. Once you are connected, it is as if you are directly connected using a secure, dedicated LAN connection and can both access shared resources on the private network and share your own resources for others to access.

### Sharing

You can enable Internet Connection Sharing (ICS) here, which lets your computer act as a gateway so that other computers on your local network can access the remote private network or the Internet through your connection. You can also specify that the connection on your computer be dialed automatically when another computer on your network tries to access the remote network or Internet. See *dial-up connection* in this chapter for more details.

### Configure Advanced Connection Settings

See "Configure Advanced Connection Settings" in *dial-up connection* in this chapter.

### Connect Using a VPN Connection

Either:

> Double-click on connection → Dial
> Right-click on connection → Connect → Dial

---

 The administrator on the remote network must first grant dial-in permission to the user before the user will be able to connect to the remote-access server using a VPN connection. See *remote-access server* and *incoming connection* in this chapter for information on how to do this.

---

## Create a New VPN Connection

Make sure you have a dial-up Internet connection configured on your client computer (or dedicated Internet connection configured on your local-area network) and that the VPN remote-access server on the remote private network is installed and configured before you create and test an outbound VPN connection on your client computer.

Double-click the Make New Connection icon to start the Network Connection Wizard. Then select "Connect to a private network through the Internet," and specify:

- Whether to automatically dial the initial connection to the Internet when you try to connect to your remote private network using your VPN connection. You can specify which of several dial-up connections to use if you have more than one configured on your client computer.

- The IP address or FQDN of the VPN remote-access server you want to connect to on the remote private network.

- Whether the connection will be available for everyone who uses the client computer or only for yourself. If you select For All Users, then you have the option of sharing the connection so that other client computers on your local-area network can use your VPN connection to connect to the remote private network through your machine.

- A friendly name for your connection to help you remember what remote private network it is used to connect to.

When you finish making your new VPN connection, you are prompted to use your dial-up connection to connect to the Internet. Once you are connected to the Internet, you are then prompted to connect to the VPN remote-access server on the remote private network using your new VPN connection (you need to specify the username and password for your VPN connection). If the Internet connection can be established but the VPN connection fails, the Internet connection is also terminated.

## Monitor the Status of a VPN Connection

Either:

Double-click on connection
Right-click on connection → Status
Double-click on connection icon in system tray (if enabled)

The General tab shows bytes sent and received since the connection was initiated, as well as other network traffic information. The Details tab shows useful information about the type of server, IP address of server and client, type of authentication protocol used, and so on. For example, for a VPN connection between a Windows 2000 Professional client machine and a Windows 2000 remote-access server, typical information displayed on the Details tab might be as follows:

Server type: PPP
Transports: TCP/IP
Authentication: MS CHAP V2
Encryption: MPPE 56
Compression: MPPC
PPP multilink framing: On
Server IP address: 172.16.11.128
Client IP address: 172.16.11.130

Another connection-monitoring alternative is to select View → Details in the Network and Dial-up Connections window. This lets you monitor the general status of all connections on your machine.

### Notes

- Windows 2000, Windows NT 4.0, Windows 98, and Windows 95 client computers can establish VPN connections with a Windows 2000 remote-access server, but note that:

  — All of these clients have built-in support for PPTP except Windows 95, which requires the installation of the optional Windows Dial-Up Network 1.3 Performance & Security Upgrade component.

  — Only Windows 2000 clients support L2TP.

  — Windows NT 3.5x does not support VPN connectivity.

- You can also create a VPN connection across a LAN between a VPN client and remote-access server (instead of over a dial-up WAN link). Just configure the client and server to use their LAN connection as their Internet connection using the Internet Connection Wizard in the Communications subgroup of the Accessories program group.

### See Also

*connection(3), dial-up connection(4), direct computer connection(4), incoming connection(4), local-area connection(4), Network and Dial-up Connections(6), remote access(3), remote-access server(4), Routing and Remote Access(5)*

---

## web site

Configure a web site, create a virtual directory, and create a web site.

### Procedures

These procedures use the Internet Information Services console, which is opened by:

Start → Programs → Administrative Tools → Internet Services Manager

### Configure a Web Site

Expand a server node in the console tree → right-click on a web site → Properties

This opens the property sheet for the site and contains a wealth of configuration options. Some of the more important ones include:

*Web Site*

Displays the web site identification information (IP address, port number, and host header name), which you can modify. You can also limit the number of concurrent HTTP connections to your server, enable IIS logging on any directories so configured, and specify the logging format.

*Operators*

Lists users who have limited rights for administering aspects of a web site (for example, they can configure a new default home page, but they cannot create a new web site).

*Performance*

Lets you tune how your web site responds to clients and specify the maximum amount of bandwidth your site can use (useful on servers hosting multiple sites).

*Home Directory*

Displays and lets you modify the location of the home directory for the site. You can also reconfigure IIS permissions, enable logging on the home directory (must first be globally enabled on the Web Site tab), enable automatic indexing of the site using the Windows 2000 Indexing service, enable directory browsing (lets clients list the contents of the directory when the home page is missing), and configure various advanced settings related to Active Server Pages (ASP) applications (beyond the scope of this book).

*Documents*

Lets you specify the filename for the default home page (more than one can be specified). If no home page is present and directory browsing is disabled on the Home Directory tab, the server returns an error to the browser attempting to access the site.

*Directory Security*

Lets you specify the authentication methods allowed for the site (Anonymous, Basic, Digest, or Windows Integrated), allow or deny access to the site by clients on the basis of IP address or domain name, and enable/configure SSL for encrypted HTTP sessions (requires Certificate Services to be configured in your enterprise).

*Server Extensions*

Allows you to configure your IIS server to support content creation and management by clients running Microsoft FrontPage.

For a more detailed discussion of configuring web sites on IIS, see my book *Administering IIS5* (McGraw-Hill).

### Create a Virtual Directory

Expand a server node in the console tree → right-click on a web site → New → Virtual directory → Next → enter an alias → Next → specify path to mapped directory → Next → specify IIS permissions for virtual directory → Next → Finish

The path you specify can be local (absolute path) or remote (UNC path to shared folder on network). The alias for the virtual directory is used in the URL to direct the HTTP client (web browser) to the content in the mapped directory. See *Internet Information Services (IIS)* in Chapter 3 for more information.

Once you have created a virtual directory, you can configure various aspects of it by:

> Expand a web site node → right-click on virtual directory → Properties

The range of settings is a subset of those explained in "Configure a Web Site" earlier in this article.

You can also create virtual directories quickly using *web sharing*. This is a feature built in to Windows Explorer and My Computer. To create a virtual directory using web sharing, do the following:

> Open Windows Explorer or My Computer → right-click on the folder you want to associate with your new virtual directory → Properties → Web Sharing → select the web site in which the virtual directory will reside → "Share this folder" → specify an alias for the virtual directory → specify IIS permissions for the directory → OK

Close and reopen Internet Services Manager to see the new virtual directory in the console tree (refreshing the view may not work).

The main limitation is that web sharing can only be used to create local virtual directories on the IIS server.

### Create a Web Site

First connect to a remote IIS server if you are not creating the web site on the local one. To do this:

> Right-click on Internet Information Services node → Connect → specify name or IP address of server

To create a new web site on the connected server:

> Right-click on server node → New → web site → Next → enter a description → Next

The key screen here is called IP Address and Port Settings. Each web site on an IIS server must be uniquely identified by the following parameters (any two web sites must differ by at least one of these parameters):

*IP address*
> Specify the IP address for which the server will respond with the web site to an HTTP request from the client. You can bind multiple IP addresses to your network adapter and give each web site on the server a unique address. This is typically used when the server is running at an ISP and must host multiple web sites, each of which has a registered DNS domain name.

*Tasks V*

If you leave the IP address set at All Unassigned, your web site becomes the new default web site. That is, when an HTTP client (web browser) tries to access the server using an IP address that is bound to the network adapter but not used for an existing web site, the server responds to the client by returning the default web site's home page.

*Port*

Leave the port set at 80 to allow HTTP clients to transparently access the web site on the server. Changing the port to a different value (use a value above 1023 so you don't conflict with established well-known port-number assignments) means that the client must know the port-number of the site in order to access it. (The client must specify the port number in the URL by appending it after the domain name using a colon prefix, e.g., *http://www.mtit.com:6523.*) You can change the port number to hide a site from all but those who know the port number for the site.

*Host header name*

When servers have a limited pool of IP addresses to work with but need to host many web sites, different sites can have the same IP address and port number but different host header names. A host header name is essentially the full DNS name for the site (the DNS name must be registered with ICANN and configured on your DNS server).

After specifying the identification information, do the following:

Next → specify path to home directory → select or deselect "Allow anonymous access" → Next → specify IIS permissions for web site

IIS permissions are different from NTFS ones and are combined to determine whether access will be granted to content or not. After specifying permissions, click Next to end the wizard and create the new web site. After creating a site, you may need to further configure it (see "Configure a Web Site" earlier in this article).

*See Also*

*Internet Information Services (IIS)(3)*

## Windows Installer

Add a new package for deployment, add software modifications to a package, change the deployment method for a package, configure default deployment settings for all packages, configure deployment settings for a package, create and assign software categories, modify file-extension priorities, redeploy software, remove deployed software, and upgrade deployed software using Windows Installer technologies.

## Procedures

For an overview of how software can be automatically deployed on client computers using Windows Installer technologies, see the section "Software Installation" in the article *Group Policy* in Chapter 3.

Prior to configuring your method of software deployment, you need to perform the following preparatory steps:

*Create or obtain a Windows Installer package*
> A Windows Installer package (an *.msi* file) must first be created or obtained for the application you want to remotely deploy on your client computers. You may obtain a package from Microsoft or a third-party vendor, or you may create your own package using a third-party packaging tool.

*Create a software distribution point*
> Share a folder on a file server on your network, and assign users Read and Execute permissions on the contents of the share. Then create a subfolder that has the same name as the application you want to deploy, and store the *.msi* package file and any other files required for the application in the subfolder.

*Create or edit a GPO*
> If you want to deploy software for all User or Computer objects within a container (a site, domain, or OU), you need either to create a new Group Policy Object (GPO) and link it to the container or to edit an existing GPO that is linked to the container. See *Group Policy Objects (GPOs)* in this chapter for general information about creating and linking GPOs.

The remaining procedures assume that you have already opened the GPO for editing (see "Open a GPO" in the article *Group Policy Objects (GPOs)* in this chapter) unless otherwise specified.

 If you need to deploy an application that does not come from the vendor with a Windows Installer package file (*.msi* file), you can obtain a third-party packaging tool such as WinINSTALL to create your own packages. WinINSTALL is available from OnDemand Software, Inc. at *http://www.ondemand.com*. WinINSTALL is also included in Microsoft Systems Management Server. WinINSTALL LE is included on the Windows 2000 Server CD for this purpose.

### Add a New Package for Deployment

> Select {Computer | User} Configuration → Software Settings → right-click on Software installation → New → Package → select package → Open

At this point you have three options to select from:

*Assigned*
> This causes the application to be automatically deployed the next time the user logs on (if User Configuration was chosen) or the client computer boots up (if Computer Configuration was chosen). You can further configure the package for deployment by right-clicking the package in the Details Pane to open its property sheet.

*Published*
> This causes the application to appear as available for installation in Add/Remove Programs in the Control Panel, as well as automatically installed if the user double-clicks on a file whose file association matches the application. You can further configure the package for deployment by right-clicking the package in the Details Pane to open its property sheet.

*Advanced published or assigned*
> This simply opens the property sheet for the new package and lets you configure the deployment method (assigned or published) and other options.

After you add a new package, you can further configure the deployment method, add software modifications, or create software categories. See the relevant headings in this article for more.

### Add Software Modifications to a Package

You can only add and remove software modifications when you are preparing to deploy the package. You cannot add software modifications to the application once it has been installed on the client machines. Transform files (*.mst* files) are typically supplied by the vendor that created the package:

> Select {Computer | User} Configuration → Software Settings → Software installation → right-click a package → Properties → Modifications → Add → select an *.mst* file → Open → OK

If you have multiple software modifications added, they are applied in the order listed here.

### Change the Deployment Method for a Package

> Select {Computer | User} Configuration → Software Settings → Software installation → right-click a package → select a new deployment method

If your package is assigned, you can change it to published. If published, you can either:

- Leave it as published, but enable or disable automatic installation by users double-clicking on the appropriate file association for the application.

- Change it to assigned.

### Configure Default Deployment Settings for All Packages

> Select {Computer | User} Configuration → Software Settings → right-click Software installation → Properties

The key options to configure on these tabs are:

*General*
> You can change the location where your packages are assumed to be stored. The default location is on domain controllers in the relevant GPT within the Sysvol share:

> > *Sysvol\\<domain>\Policies\<GPT_GUID>\Machine\Scripts\Startup*

You can configure deployment options so that new packages are automatically published or assigned by default, so that a dialog box prompts whether you want to assign or publish the packages, or so that the property sheet for the package lets you configure its deployment options in detail.

The Basic installation, user-interface option enables automatic installation using the default, Windows Installer, package settings. Maximum allows users to manually specify the installation options instead. Most *.msi* packages support both of these options.

If you want the application to be automatically uninstalled when the GPO containing the software-installation policy no longer applies to the users and computers for which it was configured (either by unlinking the GPO from the OU or by moving users and computers to a different OU), then select "Uninstall the applications" when they fall out of the scope of management.

*File extensions*
See "Modify File-Extension Priorities" later in this article.

*Categories*
See "Create and Assign Software Categories" later in this article.

### Configure Deployment Settings for a Package

Select {Computer | User} Configuration → Software Settings → Software installation → right-click a package → Properties

The key options here on the Deployment tab are:

- Deployment Type lets you change how your software will be deployed (either Assigned or Published). If you choose Published, then you can enable or disable either or both of the two installation methods used for installing published software (by document activation or by using Add/Remove Programs).

- You can choose to have the application automatically installed when the GPO used to deploy software is unlinked from the OU or when the User or Computer objects are moved to a different OU where the GPO does not apply.

- Select the Basic installation, user-interface option for automatic installation using the default, Windows Installer, package settings. If you want to allow users to specify installation options instead, select Maximum. Most *.msi* packages support both these options.

- If your deployment is replacing a version previously installed manually (not using Group Policy) on client computers, click Advanced and select "Remove previous installs of this product."

### Create and Assign Software Categories

To create a new category for software you are publishing:

Select {Computer | User} Configuration → Software Settings → right-click on Software installation → Properties → Categories → Add → enter a category name → OK

---

## *Deploying ZAP Files*

If a vendor doesn't supply a Windows Installer package (*.msi* file) for their application and you don't have a third-party utility such as WinINSTALL for creating packages, you can create a Zero Administration for Windows (ZAP) file to deploy your application. A ZAP file is a text file with a *.zap* extension, which contains instructions that can be used to deploy software using the Software Installation and Maintenance feature of Windows 2000. ZAP files have certain limitations, however:

- They can be used only to publish software, not assign it.

- Setup usually requires user interaction on the client computers when the software is being installed.

- If a deployed application becomes corrupt, it will be reinstalled instead of repaired.

- Users must be granted necessary permissions on client computers to perform the installation.

A typical ZAP file could be created using Notepad and might look like this:

```
[Application]
FriendlyName = Word 97
SetupCommand = setup.exe /unattend

[Ext]
DOC=
```

The location of the *SetupCommand* file is relative to the location of the ZAP file itself, so it is simplest to place them in the same folder on the network-distribution point. Specifying *DOC=* as a file extension causes Setup to be run automatically when a *.doc* file is double-clicked (document activation).

---

Once the category is created, you can assign it to a package:

> Select {Computer | User} Configuration → Software Settings → Software installation → right-click on a package → Properties → Categories → select a category → Select

### *Modify File-Extension Priorities*

If you are deploying two different versions of an application that create files with the same file extension, you can specify which extension's priority will be used to deploy published software using document activation (i.e., double-clicking on a document). To do this:

> Select {Computer | User} Configuration → Software Settings → right-click on Software installation → Properties → File extensions → use Up or Down buttons

---

The application at the top of the list will be the one installed. This affects all users or computers that have the currently selected GPO applied to them.

### Redeploy Software

Use this procedure to apply a fix (service pack or patch) to a deployed application. This only works if the fix comes as a Windows Installer package file (an *.msi* file). First place the fix in the appropriate location (where the original package file was placed). Then, to apply the fix, open the GPO that was used to deploy the application and:

> Select {Computer | User} Configuration → Software Settings → Software installation → right-click on a package → All Tasks → Redeploy application → Yes

### Remove Deployed Software

> Select {Computer | User} Configuration → Software Settings → Software installation → right-click on a package → All Tasks → Remove

You can either choose to have the application removed immediately (i.e., when users' client computers next reboot or users next log on), or you can leave existing deployments as they are and prevent any new deployments from occurring. Either action removes the policy for the package from the Software-installation container in the GPO, but does not delete the package itself from its distribution point. If you choose to leave existing deployments intact, users may be able to delete them manually using Add/Remove Programs in the Control Panel, depending on Group Policy settings for their domain or OU.

### Upgrade Deployed Software

To deploy a newer version of software you have already deployed using Group Policy, add a new package for the upgraded version of the software (see "Add a New Package for Deployment" earlier in this article). Then do the following:

> Select {Computer | User} Configuration → Software Settings → Software installation → right-click on the new package → Properties → Upgrades → Add → Browse → select package for previous version → OK → specify whether to uninstall previous application first or perform the upgrade over it → OK

The previous version may have been selected automatically with the right uninstallation/upgrade option. At this point, if you select the option "Required upgrade for existing packages," then a mandatory upgrade will be performed, replacing the previous version with the new version when the client computers boot up next or the user logs on next. If you deselect this option, the upgrade will be optional and users can choose whether to continue working with the previous version or upgrade to the new version.

Note that upgrading a deployed application to a new version is different from applying a service pack or a fix to the application. To apply a service pack or fix to a deployed application, see "Redeploy Software" earlier in this article.

### Notes

- You can use the Distributed File System (Dfs) to create a single, fault-tolerant share point for all your software-deployment activities in the enterprise. See *Dfs* in this chapter for more information.

- When you create your distribution point, use a hidden shared folder (append a dollar sign "$" to the share name) to prevent your users from browsing the folder's contents.

### See Also

*Dfs(4)*, *Group Policy(3,4)*

---

## WINS

Configure WINS clients, configure a WINS proxy, configure WINS replication, create a static mapping, and install WINS.

### Procedures

The following procedures use the WINS console in Administrative tools (available when WINS is installed) unless otherwise specified.

#### Configure WINS Clients

You can configure WINS clients either manually or automatically using DHCP. For Windows 2000 clients, do the following:

*Manual*

Start → Settings → Network and Dial-up Connections → right-click on Local-Area Connection → Properties → Internet Protocol (TCP/IP) → Properties → Advanced → WINS → select Enable NetBIOS over TCP/IP → Add → specify IP address of primary WINS server → Add → OK

Specify a secondary WINS server if there is one.

*Automatic*

Configure DHCP scope options 044 and 046 on the DHCP server (see *DHCP* in this chapter).

#### Configure a WINS Proxy

To configure a Windows 2000 server to act as a WINS proxy, use *regedt32.exe* to change EnableProxy from 0 to 1 in the following registry key:

HKLM\System\CurrentControlSet\Services\NetBT\Parameters

You should have no more than two WINS proxies per subnet. Make sure you also configure the WINS proxy computer as a WINS client.

#### Configure WINS Replication

Select a WINS server → right-click on Replication Partners → New → Replication Partner → specify the IP address of the replication partner → OK

You can specify whether your replication partner is a push, pull, or push/pull partner using the Advanced tab on the property sheet for the replication partner.

### Create a Static Mapping

Select a WINS server → right-click on Active Registrations → New → Static Mapping → specify computer name and IP address of non-WINS client → OK

If you make an error entering a static mapping, delete it and recreate it.

### Install WINS

First configure TCP/IP so that the WINS server is a WINS client for itself (that way the server will register itself in its WINS database). To do this, select:

Start → Settings → Network and Dial-up Connections → right-click on Local-Area Connection → Properties → Internet Protocol (TCP/IP) → Properties → Advanced → WINS → select Enable NetBIOS over TCP/IP → Add → specify IP address of server → Add → OK

Now install WINS as follows:

Control Panel → Add/Remove Programs → Add/Remove Windows Components → Networking Services → Details → Windows Internet Name Service (WINS) → OK

### Notes

- If you manually configure the addresses of WINS servers for a Windows 2000 WINS client, the settings take precedence over settings obtained using DHCP.

- You can specify up to 12 WINS servers when configuring a Windows 2000 computer as a WINS client. The first two are the primary and secondary WINS servers, and the rest are backup WINS servers.

### See Also

*DHCP(4)*, *WINS(3)*

---

## zone

Add a resource record to a zone, configure zone transfer, convert a zone, create a new zone, create a subdomain, display type of zone, enable dynamic updates, force a zone transfer, and modify a resource record.

### Procedures

Administration of DNS zones is performed primarily from the DNS console (see *DNS* in Chapter 5 for general information about this tool). This section covers specific tasks associated with zones and zone files. For general tasks relating to DNS servers, see *DNS server* in this chapter. For other general tasks relating to setting up DNS on your network, see *DNS* in this chapter.

The procedures assume that you have opened the DNS console by:

Start → Programs → Administrative Tools → DNS

### Add a Resource Record to a Zone

You can manually create resource records in a zone as follows:

Right-click on a zone → <specify>

where <specify> can be the following:

*New Host*
Creates an A record for a host. (This option is only available for forward-lookup zones.) You can optionally create an associated PTR record simultaneously.

*New Pointer*
Creates a PTR record for a host. (This option is only available for reverse-lookup zones.)

*New Alias*
Creates a CNAME record to map an alias to a host.

*New Mail Exchanger*
Creates an MX record for an SMTP mail forwarding host.

*Other New Records*
Lets you create any type of resource record (use this mainly to create NS records).

---

If you are using Dynamic DNS to create and maintain your DNS database with dynamic updates from clients or DHCP servers, you may not need to create any resource records manually—other than for those hosts that do not support DDNS. This certainly makes DNS administration a snap, but it works primarily in an all–Windows 2000 network. See the sidebar "Windows 2000 Clients and Dynamic Updates" in this article.

---

### Configure Zone Transfer

Right-click on a zone → Properties → Zone Transfers

Lets you enable/disable zone transfers, restrict which secondary name servers can perform zone transfers with the primary name server, and specify whether the primary servers should automatically notify specified secondary servers when zone information has been updated on the primary. The default is to allow zone transfers with any secondary servers and to notify all secondary servers listed on the Name Servers tab. (The Name Servers tab lists all those name servers, both primary and secondary, that are authoritative for the zone.)

In addition, you can further configure zone transfer by:

Right-click on a primary zone → Properties → Start of Authority (SOA)

The important settings here are:

*Refresh interval*

This specifies how often a secondary name server will contact its master name server for zone updates, which by default is every 15 minutes.

*Retry interval*

This specifies how long a secondary server will wait before attempting to contact a master name server after a failed attempt at contacting it, which by default is every 10 minutes.

*Expire interval*

This specifies how long the secondary server will retry before it stops responding to client requests for name resolution as the second server's DNS information is probably out-of-date. The default is one day.

*Minimum TTL*

This specifies the amount of time for which the DNS server will cache information it receives from other name servers in response to a recursive query it issues. Making the TTL smaller makes the DNS database information more consistent across the various DNS servers for the zone, but it also increases DNS network traffic and the load on the DNS servers. Windows 2000 DNS servers can also cache negative responses to name-query requests.

---

On stable networks whose configuration does not frequently change, you can try increasing the zone-transfer settings to reduce zone-transfer traffic. If name resolution starts to become erratic on the network, lower the settings again.

---

### Convert a Zone

You can convert a zone from one type to another:

Right-click on a zone → Properties → General → Change → select a zone type

You can convert a primary zone to an Active Directory integrated zone, but only if the DNS server is also a domain controller.

---

If you convert a primary zone to a secondary, you must specify the IP address for the master zone.

---

### Create a New Zone

Right-click on a DNS server node → New zone

This starts the New Zone Wizard. The path through the wizard depends on where the zone information will be stored. There are three types of zones you can create:

*Active Directory integrated zone*

To create a forward-lookup zone, specify the name of the zone (e.g., *mtit.com*) and click Finish. Nothing more is required.

If you create a reverse-lookup zone, the easiest thing to do is to specify the network-ID portion of the IP-address group for the zone, as this automatically creates the name for the zone in the standard *in-addr.arpa* format. For example, if you specify *172.16.13* as the network ID, the zone is automatically named *13.16.172.in-addr.arpa*.

---

 You can create Active Directory integrated zones only on DNS servers that are domain controllers, not on DNS servers that are member servers or standalone servers.

---

What happens if you delete a zone? If you try to delete an Active Directory zone you get a prompt asking if you also want to delete the zone from Active Directory as well (which will remove it from all DNS servers running as domain controllers). If you elect not to delete it from Active Directory, then the zone information is removed only from the server's registry but still remains in Active Directory. If the Advanced tab of the DNS server's property sheet has "Load data on startup" set to From Active Directory and Registry, then after the next refresh interval the zone information will be restored from Active Directory and the zone will be recreated on the server.

*Standard primary zone*

To create a forward-lookup zone, you can either have the wizard create a new zone file (for example, the zone file for the zone *mtit.com* would be *mtit.com.dns*) or specify an existing file as your zone file. (This file must be located in *%SystemRoot%\System32\Dns* and must be a properly formatted text file.)

To create a reverse-lookup zone, specify the network ID for the zone as earlier for Active Directory integrated zones. The zone file is automatically named after the reverse-lookup zone; for example, a zone of *13.16.172.in-addr.arpa* would have a zone file *13.16.172.in-addr.arpa.dns*.

*Standard secondary zone*

Creating a standard secondary zone is similar to creating a standard primary zone except that you need to specify the IP address of the DNS server from which the secondary zone will copy its zone information (in other words, the master name server for the secondary). There can be more than one master listed for each secondary, and they will be tried in order until one is contacted. If the secondary zone cannot contact a master name server, it is marked in the DNS console with a red circle and a white "X" to indicate that the zone transfer has failed.

When you create a new zone, Windows 2000 automatically populates the zone file with an SOA record (to define the zone) and an NS record for the DNS server itself.

If you create an Active Directory integrated zone on one domain controller and then create the same zone on a different domain controller before the first one has replicated, the zone on the first domain controller will be deleted and any changes you made to the version of the zone will be lost. The rule is, don't create the same zone on more than one domain controller; create it on one domain controller, and let the zone information replicate to other domain controllers.

### Create a Subdomain

Right-click on a zone → New Domain → specify name of subdomain

For example, if your existing zone is authoritative in the *mtit.com* domain, you could create a subdomain called *sales* within the same zone. You only need to specify the name *sales* for the new subdomain, not the full name *sales.mtit.com*. Creating subdomains is a way of adding structure to the DNS namespace of your company.

### Display Type of Zone

Right-click on a zone → Properties → General → Type

Alternatively, you can select either the Forward Lookup Zones or Reverse Lookup Zones node in the console tree and read the type of zone in the contents pane when the view is Details.

### Enable Dynamic Updates

To allow a zone to be automatically updated by dynamic updates:

Right-click on a zone → Properties → General → Allow dynamic updates → {No | Yes | Only secure updates}

The option for secure updates is available only for Active Directory integrated zones and only allows updates to be received from clients that have been authorized in Active Directory. This protects zone information from being altered by unauthorized users.

### Force a Zone Transfer

To force a secondary name server to update its secondary zone from its master name server:

Right-click on a secondary zone → Transfer from master

To force a master name server to notify its secondary name servers that they should contact it to initiate a zone transfer:

Right-click on a zone → Properties → Start of Authority (SOA) → Increment

## Windows 2000 Clients and Dynamic Updates

Windows 2000 clients are configured by default to attempt to register their names and IP addresses in Active Directory using dynamic updates. This can be toggled on or off by:

> Right-click on My Network Places → Properties → right-click on Local-Area Connection → Properties → select Internet Protocol (TCP/IP) → Properties → Advanced → DNS → select/deselect "Register this connection's addresses in DNS"

By default, Windows 2000 clients can send dynamic updates for:

- DHCP-configured adapters
- Statically configured adapters
- Remote-access adapters (substitute the suitable connection for the Local-Area Connection in the previous procedure)

Windows 2000 clients dynamically register their A resource records with the DNS server every 24 hours or when:

- A DHCP lease is renewed or a new lease is obtained
- The TCP/IP configuration on the client changes
- An IP address is added or removed for a static adapter
- A Plug and Play event occurs

You can force a client to reregister its A record with DNS servers by typing `ipconfig /registerdns` at the command line on the client. With Windows NT clients that use DHCP to perform dynamic updates, use `ipconfig / release` and `ipconfig /renew` instead.

If a DHCP lease expires, the client also de-registers its A record with DNS servers.

With dynamic updates, the whole process of administering DNS in an organization becomes much simpler. Windows 2000 also supports Secure Dynamic Updates using the GSS Algorithm. By default, if a Windows 2000 client attempts a dynamic update and fails (for example, because the zone on the DNS server has been configured to accept only secure dynamic updates), the client then tries to negotiate a secure dynamic update instead. However, you can edit a registry entry on the client to ensure that it always attempts a secure dynamic update instead. Simply add the UpdateSecurityLevel entry to the following registry key:

> HKLM\CurrentControlSet\Services\Tcpip\Parameters

and set the value of the entry to 256 to ensure that only secure dynamic updates are attempted.

The DNS clients must also be configured, however, to send dynamic updates to the DNS server for Dynamic DNS to work. See *DNS* and *DHCP* in this chapter for more information.

This increments the version number of the zone on the master name server, indicating to secondary servers that the zone has been updated and that they should initiate a zone transfer with the primary.

To force a zone transfer when you are using Active Directory integrated zones, you must force Active Directory multimaster replication to occur. You can do so by opening Active Directory Sites and Services from Administrative Tools and expanding the following nodes in the console tree:

> Root node → Sites → select a site → Servers → select your domain controller (DNS server) → NDTS settings

Right-click on the object in the Details Pane that represents the link to the domain controller with which you want to immediately replicate, and select Replicate Now.

### Modify a Resource Record

> Select zone → double-click on a resource record in the Details Pane

### Notes

- You can create multiple zones, both forward and reverse lookup, on a single DNS server.

- If the person responsible for administering a DNS zone should change, make sure you modify the SOA record for the zone to update the email address of the zone administrator. The DNS Server service sends email to this address automatically when query errors and other conditions arise. Note that the email address substitutes the usual @ symbol with a period (.); for example, specify *info.mtit.com* instead of *info@mtit.com*.

### See Also

*DHCP(4), DNS(3,4,5), DNS server(4)*

# CHAPTER 5

# *Consoles*

This chapter begins with a tutorial on the Microsoft Management Console (MMC). You will learn how to create new administrative tools or consoles by adding or removing snap-ins and how to work effectively with consoles. Although you can perform most Windows 2000 Server administrative tasks without ever creating and configuring your own custom MMC console, it's a good idea to learn these skills as custom consoles can simplify administration when you have many servers or when administration is distributed between different members of a team.

After this comes the main part of this chapter, an alphabetical reference guide to the standard Windows 2000 Server administrative tools and the various snap-ins that can be installed in the MMC to create custom consoles. These consoles and snap-ins are cross-referenced to Chapter 3, *Concepts*, for background information on the concepts involved, to Chapter 4, *Tasks*, for descriptions of how to perform specific administrative tasks using them, and to other chapters in Part II, *Alphabetical Reference*, of this book as applicable.

## *The Microsoft Management Console*

Windows 2000 Server administration is based largely upon a software framework called the Microsoft Management Console (MMC). The MMC is an application that in itself has no administrative functionality, but in which other software components called *snap-ins* can be installed and utilized. These snap-ins each provide basic administrative functionality for some component or aspect of Windows 2000 Server. When one or more snap-ins are installed in the MMC, the result is called a *console*.

### *Administrative Tools*

Windows 2000 Server includes a number of preconfigured consoles and utilities called *administrative tools*. These tools can be launched by shortcuts found in the Administrative Tools program group or in Administrative Tools in the Control Panel. Table 5-1 shows the default set of administrative tools installed during Typical Setup on a Windows 2000 Server computer configured in the role of a member server.

While most administrative tools in Windows 2000 Server are implemented as MMC consoles, a few of the administrative tools listed in Tables 5-1 through 5-3 are implemented differently: as wizards, dialog boxes, Windows applications, or command-line utilities. The two terms *administrative tool* and *console* are thus not exactly synonymous, even though in common usage they are often treated as such. See Table 5-4 for a list of these nonconsole administrative tools.

*Table 5-1: Default Set of Administrative Tools on a Windows 2000 Member Server*

| Administrative Tool | Function |
| --- | --- |
| Component Services | Manage COM components and COM+ applications |
| Computer Management | Manage disks, shares, services, and other resources on local and remote computers |
| Configure Your Server | Add and configure components and services to customize the role of your server |
| Data Sources | Configure connectivity with data providers |
| Distributed File System | Manage files distributed across multiple servers as if they reside in one location on the network |
| Event Viewer | Monitor events in various logs |
| Internet Services Manager | Manage the WWW, FTP, SMTP, and NNTP services |
| Licensing | Manage licensing for your enterprise |
| Local Security Policy | Manage security settings for the local computer using Group Policies |
| Performance | Collect and display performance information |
| Routing and Remote Access | Manage dial-up and virtual private network (VPN) remote-access services |
| Server Extensions Administrator | Manage FrontPage server extensions for creating web content with Microsoft FrontPage |
| Services | Manage Windows 2000 services |
| Telnet Server Administrator | Manage the Telnet Server service |

When a Windows 2000 member server is promoted to the role of domain controller, several new administrative tools are installed on the computer. These are listed in Table 5-2 and are used to manage Active Directory, the Domain Name System (DNS), and security settings for the domain and the domain controller.

*Table 5-2: Additional Administrative Tools on Domain Controller*

| Administrative Tool | Function |
| --- | --- |
| Active Directory Domains and Trusts | Manage domains and trusts |
| Active Directory Sites and Services | Manage replication of Active Directory |
| Active Directory Users and Computers | Manage users, groups, and computers |
| DNS | Manage DNS for the network |

*Consoles*

*Table 5-2: Additional Administrative Tools on Domain Controller (continued)*

| Administrative Tool | Function |
|---|---|
| Domain Controller Security Policy | Manage security settings for the domain controller using Group Policies via a shortcut to a Group Policy Object (GPO) |
| Domain Security Policy | Manage security settings for the domain using group policies via shortcut to a GPO |

Windows 2000 Server includes a number of optional components, which are not installed by default. These optional components can be installed afterwards as desired by using:

Start → Settings → Control Panel → Add/Remove Programs → Add/Remove Windows Components

Examples of some of these optional components include:

- Certificate Services
- Additional Internet Services such as FTP and NNTP
- Management and Monitoring tools such as Network Monitor, SNMP, and Connection Manager
- Message Queuing Services
- Additional Networking Services such as DHCP and WINS
- Other Network File and Print Services such as File and Print Services for Macintosh and Print Services for Unix
- Remote Installation Services
- Terminal Services and Terminal Services Licensing
- Windows Media Services
- Remote Storage

Installing some of these optional components with Add/Remove Windows Components causes additional administrative tools to be installed (see Table 5-3); installing other optional components does not install any additional administrative tools since these components are automatically configured.

*Table 5-3: Additional Administrative Tools Installed*

| Administrative Tool | Function |
|---|---|
| Certification Authority | Manages PKI digital certificates |
| Connection Manager Administration Kit | Manages Connection Manager Service Profiles |
| DHCP | Manages IP addresses using Dynamic Host Configuration Protocol (DHCP) |
| Internet Authentication Service | Manages authentication, authorization, and accounting for dial-up and VPN users using RADIUS |
| Network Monitor | Captures and analyzes frames on the network |
| QoS Admission Control | Manages end-to-end bandwidth for network traffic |

*Table 5-3: Additional Administrative Tools Installed (continued)*

| Administrative Tool | Function |
|---|---|
| Remote Storage | Automatically archives infrequently used files to a tape library |
| Terminal Services Client Creator | Creates sets of floppy disks for installing Terminal Services Client software on client computers |
| Terminal Services Configuration | Manages server settings and protocol configuration settings on the terminal server |
| Terminal Services Licensing | Manages Terminal Services CALs for the domain or enterprise |
| Terminal Services Manager | Manages and monitors processes and sessions on the terminal server |
| Windows Media | Manages computers running Windows Media Services |
| Windows Media Performance | Monitors the performance of Windows Media Services |
| WINS | Manages NetBIOS–to–IP address mappings using the Windows Internet Name Service (WINS) |

As mentioned previously, a few administrative tools are *not* implemented as MMC consoles. These tools are summarized in Table 5-4.

*Table 5-4: Administrative Tools Not Implemented as MMC Consoles*

| Tool | How It's Implemented |
|---|---|
| Configure Your Server | Wizard |
| Connection Manager Administration Kit | Wizard |
| Data Sources (ODBC) | Windows dialog box |
| Licensing | Windows application |
| Network Monitor | Windows application |
| Terminal Services Client Creator | Windows dialog box |
| Telnet Server Administration | Command-line utility |
| Windows Media Administrator | Web application |

You can install a full set of administrative tools on any Windows 2000 Professional or Server computer directly from the Windows 2000 Server compact disc. This makes it possible for administrators to manage all aspects of a Windows 2000 network from a single workstation.

To install the administrative tools locally, just do the following:

- Insert the Windows 2000 Server CD-ROM.

- Start → Run → *CD_drive*\I386\Adminpak.msi → OK.

- Follow the prompts in the wizard.

- Note that Service Pack 1 for Windows 2000 includes an updated set of the Administrator Tools. These tools are not updated when installing the Service Pack. Therefore, you should always install this newer set of tools.

*Consoles*

## The Console Window

Let's look at one particular administrative tool as an example of a preconfigured MMC console. The tool we will look at is Computer Management, which is used to manage a variety of resources on both local and remote computers. You can launch the Computer Management console in several ways:

- Start → Programs → Administrative Tools → Computer Management

- Start → Settings → Control Panel → Administrative Tools → Computer Management

- By using My Computer or Windows Explorer to browse the *%SystemRoot%\ system32* folder and double-clicking on the file *compmgmt.msc*

- From the command line by typing:

      %SystemRoot%\system32\compmgmt.msc

- By opening a new (blank) MMC console (or opening an existing console in author mode) and adding the Computer Management snap-in to create a custom MMC console

The last three of these methods will be considered later on, but for now let's consider the Computer Management console I have opened (see Figure 5-1).

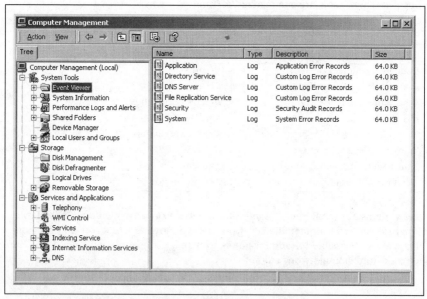

*Figure 5-1: The Computer Management console*

Computer Management is a typical example of an administrative tool that is implemented as an MMC console. It consists of a single window with two panes:

*Left pane*
   Displays a tree-like structure of different nodes called the console tree. The root node identifies the snap-in involved (Computer Management) and also displays which computer is currently being managed (local computer).

Beneath the root node are three containers (System Tools, Storage, and Services and Applications) whose only purpose is to group together the nodes under them according to function or usage—these nodes themselves being either leaf nodes (nodes that cannot contain other nodes) or further containers.

*Right pane*

Also called the Details Pane, what is displayed in this pane depends entirely on which node is selected in the left pane of the console tree. In Figure 5-1 we have selected Event Viewer under System Tools in the left pane, and the right pane displays a simple list showing the various logs that are managed by this tool. But the Details Pane can also contain much more complex elements including multiple subpanes, graphic elements, web pages, and more, depending on the node selected in the console tree.

Besides the other usual Windows gadgets (title bar, control gadget, sizing gadgets, status bar), there is also a toolbar displayed in the console window. This toolbar is context sensitive, meaning that it changes depending on which node you select in the console tree or which object you select in the Details Pane. The toolbar typically includes several drop-down menus such as Action and View, usually providing the same set of options you obtain in the shortcut menu when you right-click on a node in the console tree or an object in the Details Pane.

The real power of the MMC, however, resides in the capability of creating your own custom MMC consoles. Custom consoles can contain any snap-ins you wish and can be arranged into a console tree in any fashion you desire. Some of the reasons you might want to create custom consoles include:

- Creating a console that can be used to manage the resources on more than one computer at a time (the preconfigured administrative tool called Computer Management can only connect to one computer at a time)

- Creating a console that can be used to manage a limited subset of resources on a computer and then assigning this console to a junior-level administrator

- Creating a console with multiple windows arranged just the way you like it

- Creating a console with shortcuts to frequently used nodes and objects to facilitate easy administration of those nodes and objects

Let's walk through the process of creating a custom console that can be used to manage resources simultaneously on two computers running Windows 2000 Server.

## Creating and Saving a Console

Log on as an Administrator, and open a blank MMC console using one of the following methods:

- Start → Run → mmc → OK

- Use My Computer or Windows Explorer to browse the *%SystemRoot%\system32* folder and double-click on the file *mmc.exe*

- Type mmc at the command line

Figure 5-2 shows a blank MMC console in which no snap-ins have been installed yet.

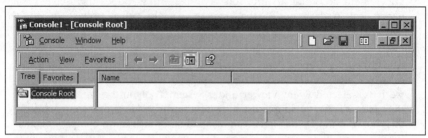

*Figure 5-2: Blank MMC console*

Now let's add some snap-ins for managing the local computer and two remote computers running Windows 2000 Server. To add a Computer Management snap-in for managing the local computer, do the following:

Console → Add/Remove Snap-in → Add

This opens the Add/Remove Standalone Snap-in dialog box, which lists the various standalone snap-ins available for installing on the system (see the sidebar "Windows 2000 Professional" for information on the two types of snap-ins). You can add as many of these snap-ins to a console as you like, and you can add multiple instances of any snap-in to manage different computers or simply to give different views of the same snap-in. Table 5-5 lists the snap-ins included with Windows 2000 Server. (Terminal Services snap-ins are only available when Terminal Services and Terminal Services Licensing are installed, and additional snap-ins are provided by third-party vendors for Windows 2000 applications they produce.) If the table entry under Required Component is "None," the snap-in is present when a Typical Setup of Windows 2000 Server has been performed; otherwise, the associated required component must be installed before the snap-in becomes available in the Add/Remove Standalone Snap-in box.

---

Many of the administrative tools listed in Tables 5-1 through 5-3 are named identically to the snap-in that they contain. For example, the Computer Management console in the Administrative Tools program group contains the Computer Management snap-in. To confuse things, however, a few administrative tools are named differently from their associated snap-ins. For example, the Internet Services Manager console in Administrative Tools contains the Internet Information Services snap-in. Finally, some administrative tools contain more than one snap-in. For example, the Performance console in Administrative Tools contains both the Performance Logs and Alerts snap-in and the ActiveX control called System Monitor.

---

## *Windows 2000 Professional*

The administrative tools for Windows 2000 Professional are hidden away in the Control Panel, presumably to make users less likely to use them and cause problems for tech support to solve. By default, the following tools are available in the Administrative Tools utility in the Control Panel:

- Component Services
- Computer Management
- Data Sources (ODBC)
- Event Viewer
- Local Security Policy
- Performance
- Services
- Telnet Server Administrator

If you open a new MMC console you can add the following limited set of snap-ins to create your own custom tools:

- ActiveX Control
- Certificates
- Component Services
- Computer Management
- Device Manager
- Disk Defragmenter
- Disk Management
- Event Viewer
- Fax Service Management
- Folder
- Group Policy
- Indexing Service
- IP Security Policy Management
- Link to Web Address
- Local Users and Groups
- Performance Logs and Alerts
- Removable Storage Management
- Security Configuration and Analysis
- Security Templates
- Services
- Shard Folders
- System Information
- WMI Control

You can of course also install the Windows 2000 Server Administration Tools on a Windows 2000 Professional computer using the Windows 2000 Server compact disc (see the note earlier in this section).

*Consoles*

*Table 5-5: Snap-ins Included with Windows 2000 Server*

| Snap-in | Required Component |
| --- | --- |
| Active Directory Domains and Trusts | None |
| Active Directory Sites and Services | None |
| Active Directory Users and Computers | None |
| ActiveX Control | None |
| Certificates | None |
| Certification Authority | Certificate Services |
| Component Services | None |
| Computer Management | None |
| Device Manager | None |
| DHCP | Dynamic Host Configuration Protocol (DHCP) |
| Disk Defragmenter | None |
| Disk Management | None |
| Distributed File System | None |
| DNS | Domain Name System (DNS) |
| Event Viewer | None |
| Fax Service Management | None |
| Folder | None |
| FrontPage Server Extensions | None |
| Group Policy | None |
| Indexing Service | None |
| Internet Authentication Service (IAS) | None |
| Internet Information Services | None |
| IP Security Policy Management | None |
| Link to Web Address | None |
| Local Users and Groups | None |
| Performance Logs and Alerts | None |
| QoS Admission Control | None |
| Remote Storage | Remote Storage |
| Removable Storage Management | None |
| Routing and Remote Access | None |
| Security Configuration and Analysis | None |
| Security Templates | None |
| Services | None |
| Shared Folders | None |
| System Information | None |
| Telephony | None |
| Terminal Services Client Creator | Terminal Services |
| Terminal Services Configuration | Terminal Services |
| Terminal Services Licensing | Terminal Services Licensing |
| Terminal Services Manager | Terminal Services |
| WINS | Windows Internet Name Service (WINS) |
| WMI Control | None |

In the Add/Remove Standalone Snap-in dialog box, select the Computer Management snap-in and click Add. This opens a dialog box prompting you to specify the computer that the snap-in will manage (see Figure 5-3). If you select "Another computer," you have to browse Active Directory to locate the remote computer you want to manage. If the snap-in cannot connect to this remote computer (for example, if the remote computer is down), then you will not be able to complete the installation of the snap-in into the console.

You can also use this dialog box to toggle whether you can specify the computer you want to manage when you open the console from the command line. This is discussed later on in this chapter in the section "Running consoles from the command line."

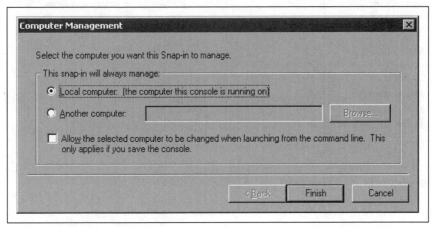

*Figure 5-3: Specifying which computer will be managed by the selected snap-in*

Note that the dialog box in Figure 5-3 does not appear for every snap-in you try to install. For example, some snap-ins can only manage services on the local computer and not on remote ones, while other snap-ins can only manage services on domain controllers. Furthermore, for some snap-ins the dialog box includes different options than the ones displayed in Figure 5-3. For example, when you install the Shared Folders snap-in, you can choose to display all three subnodes (Shares, Sessions, and Open Files) or just one of them. Or when you install the Certificates snap-in, you must specify whether the snap-in will be used to manage certificates for your user account, the service account, or the computer account. Table 5-6 summarizes the various options offered when installing a new snap-in into a console. When no options are indicated, the snap-in either can only manage the local computer or, by default, it manages the function for all computers in the enterprise.

*Consoles*

*Table 5-6: Options When Installing a New Snap-in into a Console*

| Snap-in | Manage Local or Remote Computer | Select Computer from Command Line | Other Options |
|---|---|---|---|
| Active Directory Domains and Trusts | | | |
| Active Directory Sites and Services | | | |
| Active Directory Users and Computers | | | |
| ActiveX Control | | | Starts the Insert ActiveX Control Wizard |
| Certificates | | | Specify whether to manage the user, service, or computer account |
| Component Services | | | |
| Computer Management | ✓ | ✓ | |
| Device Manager | ✓ | | |
| Disk Defragmenter | | | |
| Disk Management | ✓ | | |
| Distributed File System | | | |
| DNS | | | |
| Event Viewer | ✓ | ✓ | |
| Fax Service Management | ✓ | | |
| Folder | | | |
| FrontPage Server Extensions | | | |
| Group Policy | ✓ | ✓ | |
| Indexing Service | ✓ | | |
| Internet Authentication Service | ✓ | | |
| Internet Information Services | | | |
| IP Security Policy Management | ✓ | | Can manage domain policy for current or different domain |
| Link to Web Address | | | Specify URL |
| Local Users and Groups | ✓ | ✓ | |
| Performance Logs and Alerts | | | |
| QoS Admission Control | | | |
| Removable Storage Management | ✓ | ✓ | |

*Table 5-6: Options When Installing a New Snap-in into a Console (continued)*

| Snap-in | Manage Local or Remote Computer | Select Computer from Command Line | Other Options |
|---|:---:|:---:|---|
| Routing and Remote Access | | | |
| Security Configuration and Analysis | | | |
| Security Templates | | | |
| Services | ✓ | ✓ | |
| Shared Folders | ✓ | ✓ | Can also display one or all subnodes |
| System Information | ✓ | | |
| Telephony | | | |
| WMI Control | ✓ | | Can specify credentials when managing remote computers |

In the example, you want to install two instances of the Computer Management snap-in into our console: one to manage the local computer and the other to manage a remote computer. After selecting "Local computer," accept the remaining prompts (Finish → Close → OK) to install the snap-in for managing the local computer. Then to add a snap-in for managing the remote computer, simply repeat the previous steps, except that instead of selecting "Local computer," select "Another computer" and browse Active Directory to locate the remote computer you want to manage.

You now have your finished console, but before you do any work with it, you should save it, so perform the following steps:

Console → Save → **Manage Two Computers** → Save

This saves the console as a *.msc* file, which stands for Management Saved Console (also known as a Microsoft Common Console Document). By default, this file is saved in the personal Administrative Tools program group of the local user profile for the currently logged-on user. If you are logged on as Administrator, then by default the saved file will be located in the folder:

\*Documents and Settings\Administrator\Start Menu\Programs\*
*Administrative Tools*

Figure 5-4 shows your custom console. If you close this console, you should now be able to reopen it by selecting:

Start → Programs → Administrative Tools → Manage Two Computers

The administrative tools created when Windows 2000 Server is installed (or when optional components are added later) are located in the folder \*Documents and Settings\All Users\Start Menu\Programs\Administrative Tools*. Administrative Tools in the Control Panel is a shortcut to this folder, which explains why when you create your own custom console, it is not found in Administrative Tools in the Control Panel.

*Consoles*

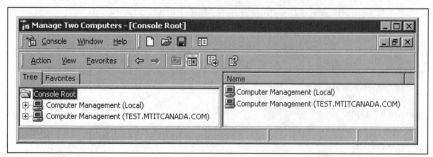

*Figure 5-4: Custom console with local and remote Computer Management nodes*

## Standalone Versus Extension Snap-ins

There are actually two types of snap-ins for the MMC:

*Standalone snap-ins*

Also simply referred to as snap-ins, these are basic, administrative software components that can be added to the console tree of a new or existing console window. You add a standalone snap-in to a console by selecting:

Console → Add/Remove Snap-in → Add → select standalone snap-in → Add

*Extension snap-ins*

Also simply called extensions, these cannot be added by themselves to the console tree, but instead must be added together with a suitable standalone snap-in. Extensions provide additional administrative functionality for some of the objects controlled by the standalone snap-in with which they are associated. You add or remove an extension snap-in by selecting:

Console → Add/Remove Snap-in → Extensions → select a snap-in from "Snap-ins that can be extended"

To add all extensions for the selected snap-in, select the "Add all extensions" checkbox (this is checked by default). To add only the extensions you want for the selected snap-in, first deselect the "Add all extensions" checkbox for that snap-in. Then deselect any extensions you don't want for that snap-in, leaving the remaining ones selected.

Note that some standalone snap-ins share the same extensions, and you can enable an extension for one snap-in while disabling it for different snap-ins in the same console. However, if you have multiple instances of the same standalone snap-in in a console, disabling an extension for one instance disables it for all instances of the same snap-in.

Microsoft documentation says that if a "snap-in becomes damaged, try adding another instance of the same snap-in to the console, configuring it as needed, and then remove the first instance of the snap-in." Why a snap-in should become *damaged* is not clear, but this is probably useful advice to remember with a new product like Windows 2000.

Although normally you can only add snap-ins for components that are already installed on your computer, you can also add snap-ins that are published in Active Directory. These are identified in the Add/Remove Standalone Snap-ins dialog box by having the description "Not Installed" in the Vendor column. When you add these snap-ins, the Windows Installer Wizard may appear, prompting you to add the appropriate Windows component to your system. This applies to both stand-alone and extension snap-ins.

## Customizing a Console

Now that a console for managing the local and a remote computer has been created, let's see what can be done to customize this console. Customizing a console is the process of personalizing and configuring it to make using it quick and simple.

### Using the View menu

You can use the View menu to:

- Change the default view of how objects in the Details Pane are displayed. You probably want to use View → Detail so that any columns of status information present in the console are displayed.

- Hide or remove various elements of the MMC window using View → Customize. For example, with some administrative tools, such as the Services console, there is only one node in the console tree, so hiding the console tree might be a good idea.

One of the customization options under View → Customize is to remove the View menu itself! If you later decide that you want to bring it back, use Customize View under the System menu. (The System menu is accessed using the gadget at the top left-hand corner of a window.)

If you have selected Detail view, you can rearrange columns by dragging and you can sort rows by clicking on column headers in the Details Pane (this doesn't work for all snap-ins).

Some snap-ins also provide a Filter item on the View menu, which can be used to filter what is displayed in the Details Pane.

### Customizing the console tree

A Folder is a standalone snap-in that simply provides a container for other snap-ins; it does not have any inherent administrative functionality. You can add folders to the console tree to group together snap-ins according to computer, site, network, domain, department, and so on.

For example, if we plan on adding more Computer Management snap-ins for managing additional remote computers, we might add a Folder snap-in for grouping together the remote computers we are managing, and rename this Folder snap-in "Remote Computers," (see Figure 5-5). Continuing our previous example, do the following:

> Console → Add/Remove Snap-in → Add → Folder → Add → Close → OK → right-click on New Folder → Rename → Remote Computers

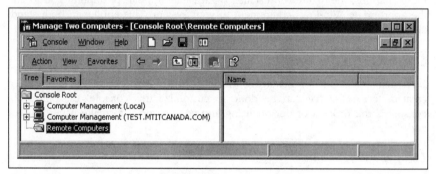

*Figure 5-5: Custom console with new folder added but snap-ins in wrong position*

The problem is that we how have the situation shown in Figure 5-5, where our new container is in the same level of the console tree as our two Computer Management snap-ins. We need to move the snap-in for the remote computer into the Remote Computers folder. Unfortunately, Microsoft made this process more complicated than it need be. In fact, there is no way of moving snap-ins around the console tree once they have been added to the tree! Our only recourse is to remove the existing snap-in for the remote computer and add it again, this time making sure that we add it to the Remote Computers folder instead of to Console Root:

> Console → Add/Remove Snap-in → select Computer Management (<remote_computer_name>) → Remove → select Remote Computers folder from "Snap-ins added to" list box → Add → select Computer Management → Add → Another computer → Browse → select remote computer → OK → Finish → Close → OK

This now gives us what we want (see Figure 5-6) and tells us the clear moral of the story regarding customizing the console tree: plan what you want to do before you start! You can obviously continue this process to build incredibly complex consoles (if you have nothing better to do).

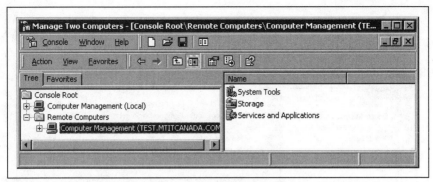

*Figure 5-6: Custom console with new folder and snap-ins in correct position*

### Adding favorites

A quick way of switching to specific places on a complex console tree is to add favorites to your console. Once you have selected the particular node in the console tree you want to bookmark, use Favorites → Add to Favorites from the toolbar to create a favorite to that node. (Unfortunately, favorites only map to nodes in the console tree, not to specific objects in the Details Pane for that node). You can even group favorites in different folders if you have a lot of them. Once you have created your favorites, you can access them in two different ways:

*Using favorites on the toolbar*
> This method expands the console tree until the bookmarked node is selected, displaying its associated objects in the Details Pane.

*Using the Favorites tab in the left-hand pane*
> Selecting this tab hides the console tree entirely and displays the list of favorites as hyperlinks. Clicking on a link will display the associated objects for that favorite in the Details Pane.

### Creating new child windows

You can create new child windows within the MMC main window and root these windows at any node within the console tree. For example, to create a new child window whose root node is System Tools under Computer Management (Local), do this:

> Right-click on System Tools under Computer Management (Local) → New Window from Here

You can tile or cascade multiple child windows. More importantly, you can use this procedure to create custom consoles for junior administrators by closing the original child window, thus restricting their access to peripheral portions of the console tree. In the previous example, closing the original child Window leaves a console whose root node is System Tools for the local computer (see Figure 5-7).

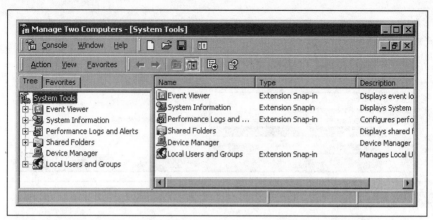

*Figure 5-7: Custom console rooted at System Tools for the local computer*

### Adding taskpad views and tasks

The real customization power of the MMC is found in taskpad views. A *taskpad view* is a page in the Details Pane of a console to which you can add shortcuts to performing specific *tasks*, such as running wizards, opening property sheets, selecting menus, opening web pages, and running command-line utilities and scripts. Taskpad views can make life easier for junior administrators by providing a single location from which various administrative tasks can be performed. Taskpad views can also make complex administration tasks easier by providing a single location from which the property sheets and menus from many different snap-ins can be accessed.

Let's walk through the process by creating a taskpad view. You first need to decide which node in the console tree your taskpad view will be attached to, and you should think about the various tasks you want to incorporate into that view. Then right-click on the selected node to start the New Taskpad View Wizard, which leads you through the following steps:

*Taskpad Display*
Select how the taskpad view will be displayed, including how (or whether) the objects in the Details Pane will be displayed, and whether normal or pop-up text is used to caption shortcuts.

*Taskpad Target*
Select whether the taskpad view will apply only to the current node in the console tree, or to all nodes of the same type as the selected one, and specify whether the taskpad view will become the default display in the Details Pane for all nodes of the selected type.

*Name and Description*
Specify a name for the taskpad view and a brief description.

Once the New Taskpad View Wizard is finished, you can then run the New Task Wizard and add tasks to your taskpad. (The New Task Wizard starts automatically when the New Taskpad View Wizard ends.) Let's walk through the process of adding new tasks to the taskpad view using the New Task Wizard:

---

*Command type*
Specify the kind of task you want to perform, which includes:

*Menu command*
Run a command from a menu. Specify any menu command available for any node in the console tree or from objects in the list in the Details Pane.

*Shell command*
Run a script, start a program, or open a web page. Specify the path and file for the command or script you want to run, a list of parameters, the directory to start in, and the type of window the command or script will run in. You can select any program files to run here (*.exe*, *.com*, *.bat*, *.cmd*, *.pif*) or specify a URL.

*Navigation*
Select a view to display from your list of favorites. This also causes the selected node to receive the focus in the left pane of the console.

*Name and Description/Task icon*
Once you have specified the details of the task, identify the shortcut that launches the task by assigning it a name, a short description, and an icon. You can the launch the task by clicking its shortcut in the taskpad view.

Once you have created your taskpad view, you can modify it by selecting Action → Edit Taskpad View. This allows you to change the display options of the taskpad view, launch the New Task Wizard to create new tasks, or modify, remove, and rearrange existing tasks in the taskpad view. You can also delete your taskpad view to return to the normal Details Pane view. Figure 5-8 shows some of the power of using taskpad views.

*Figure 5-8: Taskpad view for Event Viewer on the local computer*

You can switch between a taskpad view and the normal Details Pane by using the tabs at the bottom of the right pane—they are easy to miss. You can also create as many taskpad views as you like for a given node in the console tree and use these tabs to switch easily between them. However, keep the name of a taskpad view short so that the space used by these tabs will be minimized; if these tabs go to the edge of the console window, there is no gadget for scrolling them.

### Setting console options

Once you have created and customized a console, you should specify a console name, associated icon, and the mode in which the console will be opened. These options are specified using Console → Options, and the most important of these is specifying the console mode, of which there are four possibilities:

*Author mode*
Users have full rights to customize the console as they desire, including adding or removing snap-ins, creating new child windows, creating taskpad views, and accessing all portions of the console tree. Author mode is typically used only for creating and customizing new consoles. Once they are configured appropriately, they should be assigned one of the user modes to prevent them from being modified by users. Consoles opened in author mode have a second menu bar with the options Console, Window, and Help—consoles opened in user mode do not have this menu.

*User mode—full access*
Users have full access to the console tree but cannot add or remove snap-ins or change console properties.

*User mode—limited access, multiple window*
Users have access only to the visible portion of the console tree. Users can open new windows but cannot close existing ones. Users cannot add or remove snap-ins or change console properties.

*User mode—limited access, single window*
Users have access only to the visible portion of the console tree. Users cannot open new windows or close existing ones. Users cannot add or remove snap-ins or change console properties.

In addition, when any of the user modes is selected, you can also toggle whether users can customize the console view or use context menus (right-click) in task-pads in the console.

If a console has been set to one of the user modes, it will have no Console menu when it is opened the next time. If you later want to make changes to your console, you need to open it in author mode. Since there is no Console menu, you cannot do this using Console → Options; you need another way of opening the console in author mode. You have several choices:

- If the console is an existing administrative tool:

  Right-click on Start button → Open All Users → Programs → Administrative Tools → right-click on selected shortcut → Author

- If the console is a custom console saved in the user's profile:

  Right-click on Start button → Open → Programs → Administrative Tools → right-click on selected shortcut → Author

- You can also perform the above steps on the actual *.msc* file for the console if you can find it in My Computer or Windows Explorer. Table 5-7 lists the various preconfigured *.msc* files (administrative tools) for Windows 2000 Server and where they are located.

- You can also open any console in author mode from the command line by using the /a switch:

  ```
  mmc path\console_name.msc /a
  ```

---

If you are logged in as an ordinary user and need to perform some quick administrative task using a console, you can run the console using your Administrator credentials as follows:

— Right-click on console shortcut → Run as → specify credentials

— Use the runas command from the command line (see Chapter 7, *Commands*)

---

*Table 5-7: Windows 2000 Server .msc Files and Locations*

| File | Administrative Tool | Location |
| --- | --- | --- |
| *acssnap.msc* | QoS Admission Control | *\system32* |
| *certmgr.msc* | Certificates | *\system32* |
| *certsrv.msc* | Certification Authority | *\system32* |
| *ciadv.msc* | Indexing Service[a] | *\system32* |
| *comexp.msc* | Component Services | *\system32\Com* |
| *compmgmt.msc* | Computer Management | *\system32* |
| *dcpol.msc* | Domain Controller Security Policy | *\system32* |
| *devmgmt.msc* | Device Manager[a] | *\system32* |
| *dfrg.msc* | Disk Defragmenter[a] | *\system32* |
| *dfsgui.msc* | Distributed File System | *\system32* |
| *dhcpmgmt.msc* | DHCP | *\system32* |
| *diskmgmt.msc* | Disk Management[a] | *\system32* |
| *dnsmgmt.msc* | DNS | *\system32* |
| *domain.msc* | Active Directory Domains and Trusts | *\system32* |

*Table 5-7: Windows 2000 Server .msc Files and Locations (continued)*

| File | Administrative Tool | Location |
|------|---------------------|----------|
| dompol.msc | Domain Security Policy | \system32 |
| dsa.msc | Active Directory Users and Computers | \system32 |
| dssite.msc | Active Directory Sites and Services | \system32 |
| eventvwr.msc | Event Viewer[a] | \system32 |
| faxserv.msc | Fax Service Management | \system32 |
| fpmmc.msc | FrontPage Server Extensions | \Program Files\Microsoft Shared\ Web Server extensions\40\bin |
| fsmgmt.msc | Shared Folders[a] | \system32 |
| gpedit.msc | Group Policy | \system32 |
| ias.msc | Internet Authentication Service | \system32 |
| iis.msc | Internet Information Services | \system32\inetsrv |
| lusrmgr.msc | Local Users and Groups | \system32 |
| msinfo32.msc | System Information[a] | \Documents and Settings\ Administrator\Start Menu\ Programs\Administrative Tools |
| ntmsmgr.msc | Removable Storage | \system32 |
| ntmsoprq.msc | Removable Storage Operator Requests | \system32 |
| perfmon.msc | Performance | \system32 |
| rrasmgmt.msc | Routing and Remote Access | \system32 |
| rsadmin.msc | Remote Storage | \system32 |
| secpol.msc | Local Security Settings | \system32 |
| services.msc | Services[a] | \system32 |
| tapimgmt.msc | Telephony | \system32 |
| tscc.msc | Terminal Services Configuration | \system32 |
| winsmgmt.msc | WINS | \system32 |
| wmimgmt.msc | Windows Management Infrastructure (WMI) | \system32 |
| wmtperf.msc | Windows Media Performance | \system32\Windows Media\ Server |

[a] Normally part of Computer Management.

### Saving consoles

If a console is in author mode, you are prompted to save any changes you have made when you try to close it. If it is in one of the three user modes, whether the changes you have made are saved or not depends on the setting:

> Console → Options → "Do not save changes to this console" checkbox

If the checkbox is checked, changes made by users will not be saved when they close the console. Remember, this setting can only be configured when the console is in author mode!

### Distributing consoles

You can distribute custom consoles that you've created to other administrators by:

- Saving or copying them to a network share with appropriate permissions set to preclude access by anyone except administrators. You may also want to publish the location of the *.msc* file in Active Directory so they can search for it using the Search Assistant.

- Right-clicking on the *.msc* file in My Computer or Windows Explorer and using the Send To option to email the file to other administrators or to copy it to a floppy disk to hand around.

- Any other creative way you can think of.

---

 You can also run the MMC on computers running Windows NT, Windows 98, and Windows 95, provided they are part of a Windows 2000 domain.

---

### Running consoles from the command line

You can run a console from the command line as long as you know the directory where the *.msc* file is stored (see Table 5-7 earlier in this chapter). To run a console, open a command prompt and type either:

```
mmc path\console_file.msc
```

or:

```
path\console_file.msc
```

unless you are in the current directory where the *.msc* file is stored, in which case you can type either:

```
mmc console_file.msc
```

or just:

```
console_file.msc
```

Note that the *.msc* extension must be specified in order to open the console.

There are some optional switches you can append to the above commands:

/a   Opens a saved console in author mode so you can modify the console.

/computer=computer_name
    Opens the console and connects to the specified computer. This switch is supported by Computer Management (*compmgmt.msc*) and related consoles.

/server=domain_controller_name
    Opens the console and connects to the specified domain controller. This switch is supported by Active Directory Users and Computers (*dsa.msc*).

`/domain=domain_name`

Opens the console and connects to a domain controller in the specified domain. This switch is supported by Active Directory Users and Computers (*dsa.msc*).

---

### *Group Policies and Consoles*

You can restrict what users are able to do when creating and configuring custom MMC consoles by using Group Policies. Using Group Policies allows you to:

- Restrict which snap-ins may be installed in a custom console

- Restrict which users and groups are allowed to open consoles in author mode

To configure these restrictions, first open the appropriate Group Policy Object (GPO). For example, to set restrictions on MMC use for the local computer, do the following:

Start → Run → mmc → OK → Console → Add/Remove Snap-in → Add → Group Policy → Add → Local Computer → Finish → Close → OK

This opens the appropriate GPO. Now browse the console tree as follows, starting from the root node:

Local Computer Policy → User Configuration → Administrative Templates → Microsoft Management Console

Double-click on a restriction in the Details Pane, and configure it as desired.

On the other hand, if you want to use Group Policies to restrict MMC usage for the entire domain, it might be easier to proceed as follows:

Start → Programs → Administrative Tools → Active Directory Users and Computers → right-click on domain node → Properties → Group Policy → select Default Domain Policy → Edit

This opens the appropriate Default Domain Policy object. As earlier, browse the console tree starting from the root node:

Default Domain Policy → User Configuration → Administrative Templates → Microsoft Management Console

For more information see *Group Policy* in Chapters 3 and 4.

---

## MMC Keyboard Accelerators

Finally, for the mouse-weary, there is an extensive set of keyboard shortcuts you can use to work with the main window, console tree, and active child window in the console. These are summarized in Tables 5-8 to 5-10.

*Table 5-8: Keyboard Accelerators for Navigating the Console Window*

| Accelerator | Function |
| --- | --- |
| Tab or F6 | Moves forward between panes in the active console window |
| Shift-Tab or Shift-F6 | Moves backward between panes in the active console window |
| Ctrl-Tab or Ctrl-F6 | Moves forward between console windows |
| Ctrl-Shift-Tab or Ctrl-Shift-F6 | Moves backward between console windows |
| Plus Sign (+) on the numeric keypad | Expands the selected item |
| Minus Sign (-) on the numeric keypad | Collapses the selected item |
| Asterisk (*) on the numeric keypad | Expands the whole console tree below the root item in the active console window |
| Up Arrow | Moves the selection up one item in a pane |
| Down Arrow | Moves the selection down one item in a pane |
| Page Up | Moves the selection to the top item visible in a pane |
| Page Down | Moves the selection to the bottom item visible in a pane |
| Home | Moves the selection to the first item in a pane |
| End | Moves the selection to the last item in a pane |
| Right Arrow | Expands the selected item |
| Left Arrow | Collapses the selected item |
| Alt–Right Arrow | Moves the selection to the next item (same as the Forward arrow on the toolbar) |
| Alt–Left Arrow | Moves the selection to the previous item (same as the Back arrow on the toolbar) |

*Table 5-9: Keyboard Accelerators for Accessing Menu Commands That Act on the Main Console Window*

| Accelerator | Function |
| --- | --- |
| Ctrl-O | Opens a saved console |
| Ctrl-N | Opens a new (blank) console and closes the existing one |
| Ctrl-S | Saves the open console |
| Ctrl-M | Adds or removes a console item |
| Ctrl-W | Opens a new window |
| F5 | Refreshes all console windows |
| Alt-Spacebar | Displays the MMC window menu |
| Alt-F4 | Closes the active console window |

*Table 5-10: Keyboard Accelerators for Accessing Menu Commands That Act on the Active Console Window Pane*

| Accelerator | Function |
| --- | --- |
| Ctrl-P | Prints the current page or active window pane |
| Alt–Minus Sign | Displays the window menu for the active console window |
| Shift-F10 | Displays the Action (shortcut) menu for the selected item |
| Alt-A | Displays the Action (shortcut) menu for the active console window |

*Consoles*

*Table 5-10: Keyboard Accelerators for Accessing Menu Commands That Act on the Active Console Window Pane (continued)*

| Accelerator | Function |
|---|---|
| Alt-V | Displays the View menu for the active console window |
| Alt-F | Displays the Favorites menu for the active console window |
| F1 | Opens the Help topic (if any) for the selected item |
| F5 | Refreshes the content of all console windows |
| Ctrl-F10 | Maximizes the active console window |
| Ctrl-F5 | Restores the active console window |
| Alt-Enter | Displays the Properties dialog box (if any) for the selected item |
| F2 | Renames the selected item |
| Ctrl-F4 | Closes the active console window (if there is only one console window, this closes the console) |

# Alphabetical List of Consoles

Because a default set of administrative tools is installed when you install Windows 2000, I decided to cover two types of items in this alphabetical reference section:

*Snap-ins*

Snap-ins are identified in this reference section by the single puzzle piece icon ( ![puzzle] ). By adding a snap-in to a new (blank) console, you can give the console the desired administrative functionality. For example, by adding the Disk Management snap-in to a new console, you can create a console that can be used exclusively to administer disks. Similarly, by adding a snap-in to an existing console, you can add the additional administrative functionality of that snap-in to the console. The snap-ins listed here are common for Windows 2000 administration. Some of these are only available when certain optional components of Windows 2000 Server are installed, and these are appropriately identified when this is the case.

The snap-ins covered here are the ones used for day-to-day administration of Windows 2000–based networks. Each article describes, where possible, the basic purpose and functionality of the snap-in, general configuration options, and a typical console tree for a console with the snap-in installed in it, and cross references to concepts in Chapter 3 and tasks in Chapter 4 that involve the snap-in.

*Administrative tools*

Administrative tools are identified in this alphabetical reference by the hammer icon ( ![hammer] ). Windows 2000 Server has a preconfigured set of consoles and utilities to enable you to perform common administrative tasks. These tools can be accessed from the Start menu using Start → Programs → Administrative Tools. Note that while most of these administrative tools are implemented as MMC consoles, a few of them are not implemented this way. These are only mentioned here and then cross-referenced to further information found in Chapter 6, *Utilities*.

Here are some additional notes concerning symbols used in this chapter:

- A particular entry in this chapter may have both symbols, since it may be both a snap-in ( ![snap-in icon] ) and a preconfigured administrative tool ( ![tool icon] ). An example of this is Event Viewer.

- Some administrative tools and snap-ins are installed by default only on domain controllers, and these tools are further identified by the globe icon ( ![globe icon] ).

- A few extensions to snap-ins are separately covered in this section, and these are identified by the two connected puzzle pieces icon ( ![puzzle icon] ).

---

# Active Directory Domains and Trusts

Administers various aspects of domains and trusts.

## Description

Active Directory Domains and Trusts is used for managing external trusts between domains (including trusts with Windows NT domains), changing the mode of a domain from mixed to native, and specifying alternative UPN suffixes for domains. These are important issues, but you won't use this tool very often in your day-to-day administration of Windows 2000.

Active Directory Domains and Trusts performs similar functions to those provided by the Windows NT administrative tool called User Manager for Domains (but of course, it also supports additional functions that are new to Windows 2000).

### Using Active Directory Domains and Trusts

You can access Active Directory Domains and Trusts by either:

- Start → Programs → Administrative Tools → Active Directory Domains and Trusts

- Installing the Active Directory Domains and Trusts snap-in into a new or existing console.

The console tree for this tool displays the various domains and trees in the forest. A typical console tree looks like this:

Active Directory Domains and Trusts
    Forest root domain (root domain of first tree)
        Child domain
        Child domain . . .
    Root domain of next tree . . .

Child domains can be nested to any level in the tree—not just level two as displayed earlier. The console tree here shows the hierarchy of domains and trees in the forest for your enterprise. See *Active Directory, domain, domain controller, forest, tree,* and *trust* in Chapter 3 for more information on these concepts.

### Action Menu

Select the Active Directory Domains and Trusts node to connect to a particular domain controller, thus retrieving the information needed to display the hierarchy of domains and trees in the forest. Typically, using any domain controller in the local domain is fine, but you can browse a domain for a list of available domain controllers and specify the one to which you wish to connect. You can also display the current domain-naming operations master and change this role to a different domain controller in the domain—for example, if the present domain-naming operations master is going to be taken down for maintenance. See *domain controller* in Chapter 3 for an explanation of single-master operations roles.

Select any domain in the console tree to change the mode of the domain from mixed to native or manage external trusts between the domain and some other domain.

Right-click on any domain, and select Manage to open an Active Directory Users and Computers console with the focus on the domain you selected. See *domain* and *trust* in Chapter 4 for information on specific procedures relating to these issues.

### View Menu

There are just the standard options here, namely selecting which columns to display in the Details Pane, specifying the icon size and display method, and customizing the appearance of the MMC console window.

### See Also

*Active Directory(3,4), domain(3,4), domain controller(3,4), forest(3), mixed mode(3), native mode(3), tree(3), trust(3,4)*

---

## Active Directory Sites and Services

Manages directory replication between different sites.

### Description

Active Directory Sites and Services is used for creating sites and subnets that mirror the physical and geographical topology of your network. You can then configure how and when Active Directory replication occurs between different sites to optimize bandwidth usage over slow WAN links between sites. If your implementation of Windows 2000 is at one physical location only, then you may not use this tool at all. If you have multiple branch offices or subsidiaries at different locations, however, expect to use this tool, especially during the implementation stage when you are tuning network traffic over slow WAN links.

There is no comparable Windows NT tool to Active Directory Sites and Services. Windows NT administrators manage directory replication between remote domain controllers by configuring various registry settings instead.

### Using Active Directory Sites and Services

You can access Active Directory Domains and Trusts by either:

* Start → Programs → Administrative Tools → Active Directory Sites and Services

* Installing the Active Directory Sites and Services snap-in into a new or existing console

The console tree for this tool displays the sites in your enterprise and the links between them. A typical console tree looks like this:

```
Active Directory Sites and Services
    Inter-Site Transports
        IP
            Site link
            Site link . . .
        SMTP
            Site link
            Site link . . .
    Site
        Servers
            Server
                NTDS Settings
                    Active Directory connection
                    Active Directory connection . . .
            Server . . .
    Site . . .
    Subnets
        Subnet
        Subnet . . .
```

The three first-level containers here are:

*Inter-Site Transports*

This contains the various site links between your different sites, grouped together depending on whether they use RPCs or SMTP messages to replicate directory information between sites.

*Sites*

These are one or more containers for the various sites in your enterprise. The Default-First-Site is created by default when you install your first domain controller in your forest root domain. Other sites are created using this tool to reflect the different physical or geographical locations of portions of your Windows 2000 network. Each site can contain one or more server objects, which are typically domain controllers. Each site also contains NTDS Site Settings for scheduling directory replication. Each server object contains an NTDS Settings object that represents the directory (*Ntds.dit* file). This file is located on an NTFS partition on the domain controllers and contains the Active Directory connections for the domain controller.

*Subnets*

This contains the various subnets in your network, each of which is associated with one of your sites.

See *site* in Chapter 3 for more information about sites, subnets, and directory replication.

The objects in the Server container for a site can also be member servers and not just domain controllers. This allows you to delegate authority over all servers (both domain controllers and member servers) in a given site.

### Action Menu

Under the Action menu, you can select the following:

*Active Directory Sites and Services node*
Select this to administer a target forest or to connect to a particular domain controller in the forest, thus retrieving the information needed to display the hierarchy of sites and subnets in the enterprise.

*Sites, Inter-Site Transports, or Subnets container*
Select this in order to delegate authority to administer these portions of Active Directory to trusted users in your enterprise. You can also delegate individual sites or just the Servers container within a site. See *delegation* in Chapters 3 and 4 for more information on the subject of delegation.

*A site*
Select this to link a Group Policy Object (GPO) to that site. See *Group Policy* in Chapters 3 and 4 for more information.

*A particular server within the Servers container in a site*
Select this if you want to move the server to a different site.

*A particular Active Directory connection in the NTDS Settings container of any
domain controller*
Select this to manually force directory replication to occur with that domain controller.

For information on various tasks involving this tool, see *domain controller* and *site* in Chapter 4.

### View Menu

In addition to the standard options of selecting the icon size, display method, and which columns to display in the Details Pane, as well as customizing the appearance of the MMC console window, there are also:

*Filter Options*
Filter different kinds of objects, which is useful in a complex enterprise involving many sites

*Show Services node*
Display an additional hidden portion of Active Directory (the Services container); there is nothing here relating to day-to-day administration

### See Also

*Active Directory(3,4), delegation(3,4), domain controller(3,4), Group Policy(3,4), site(3,4)*

# Active Directory Users and Computers

Manages and publishes information in Active Directory.

## Description

Active Directory Users and Computers is one of the Windows 2000 tools you will use frequently as an administrator. Use this tool to:

- Create and manage objects representing users, groups, computers, and printers on your network.

- Publish information about shared folders and downlevel Windows NT printers in Active Directory.

- Create hierarchies of organizational units (OUs) to facilitate delegation and the implementation of Group Policy in your enterprise.

- Manage certain aspects of domain controllers, including some single-master operation roles.

- Link GPOs to domains and OUs.

- Delegate authority over OUs to trusted users in your enterprise.

### Using Active Directory Users and Computers

You can access Active Directory Users and Computers by either:

- Start → Programs → Administrative Tools → Active Directory Users and Computers

- Start → Programs → Administrative Tools → Active Directory Domains and Trusts → right-click on a domain → Manage

- Installing the Active Directory Users and Computers snap-in into a new or existing console

The console tree for this tool displays the hierarchy of OUs and other containers that make up the structure of your selected domain. A typical console tree looks like this:

        Active Directory Domains and Trusts
            OU
                OU
                OU . . .
            OU . . .
            Builtin
            Computers
            Domain Controllers
            Foreign Security Principals
            Users
            OU . . .

A *security principal* is an object in Active Directory that is automatically assigned a security identifier (SID) and is associated with an actual user or computer on the network. Security principles can be granted access rights to network resources and can be authenticated by domain controllers. You can create security principals (User and Computer objects) using Active Directory Users and Computers. See *computer* and *domain user account* in Chapter 4 for information.

A *foreign security principal* is an object representing a user or computer from trusted domains outside the local forest. Foreign security principals are stored in the Foreign Security Principals container (they are not visible unless Advanced Features is toggled on using the View menu). Active Directory creates these foreign security principals automatically, and you should not modify the properties of these objects.

---

OUs can be nested to any level in the hierarchy, not just level two as displayed earlier. OUs are not present unless they are explicitly created; the remaining five containers are defaults created when Active Directory is installed. You can move objects between containers to organize them better for purposes of delegation and Group Policy application. For more information see *Active Directory, domain, tree, forest,* and *OU* in Chapter 3. For additional hidden containers, see "View Menu" later in this article.

### Action Menu

Under the Action menu you can select the following:

*Active Directory Users and Computers node*
Select this to connect to a domain, domain controller, or a specific operations master in the domain to administer it. Selecting a domain allows you to manage and publish resources (users, groups, computers, and so on) in the domain.

*A domain*
Select this to delegate authority for the domain to trusted users and to apply Group Policy to the domain. Right-click on a domain and select Find to locate published information in the domain (see *find* in Chapter 4).

*An OU*
Select this to delegate authority for the OU to trusted users and to apply Group Policy to the OU. Right-click on an OU and select Find to locate published information in the OU. See *delegation* and *Group Policy* in Chapter 3 for more information.

*A User, Computer, Group, or other object*
Select one of these to administer. The actions you can perform depend on the type of object. For example, right-clicking on a Computer object and selecting Manage will open a Computer Management console with the selected computer having the focus.

For information on specific tasks you can perform on these different objects, see *built-in group* and *built-in user account* in Chapter 3, and *computer, domain, domain controller, domain user account,* and *group* in Chapter 4.

### View Menu

In addition to the standard options, there are also:

*Users, Groups, and Computers as containers*
This allows User, Group, and Computer objects to be displayed in the console tree as containers. You might think that selecting a Group object in the console tree would display the group's members in the Details Pane, but unfortunately this is not so, so the feature has little usefulness.

*Advanced Features*
This toggles on or off the following hidden containers in Active Directory:

— LostAndFound

— System

The System container has subcontainers representing various networking services you have installed, such as Dfs, DNS, RAS, and so on. You should not modify any objects in these containers unless you are instructed to do so by qualified technicians.

Advanced Features also displays two hidden tabs for objects in Active Directory:

*Object tab*
This displays the path to the object in Active Directory.

*Security tab*
This lets you set permissions on an object in Active Directory to control who can display it using Search and who can manage or modify it.

*Filter Options*
This lets you set up a filter to display one or more types of published objects. If your directory contains numerous objects, this may be more helpful than Find (discussed earlier).

### See Also

*Active Directory(3,4), built-in group(3), built-in user account(3), computer(4), delegation(3,4), domain(3,4), domain controller(3,4), domain user account(3,4), find(4), forest(3), group(3,4), Group Policy(3,4), OU(3)*

---

## Computer Management

Manages resources on local or remote computers.

### Description

Computer Management is the default tool for managing numerous aspects of local and remote Windows 2000 servers. Using Computer Management, you can perform common administrative tasks such as:

**Consoles C**

- Displaying device configuration information
- Installing and upgrading device drivers
- Starting and stopping services
- Creating and managing network shares
- Disconnecting users from network shares
- Managing disks and volumes
- Monitoring event logs
- Monitoring system performance counters
- Managing networking services

For administrators familiar with Windows NT 4.0 Server, the Computer Management console performs functions similar to those provided by numerous NT administrative tools, such as Disk Administrator, Event Viewer, Performance Monitor, Server Manager, and Windows NT Diagnostics. In addition, if optional networking services such as the DHCP or DNS Server services are installed, Computer Manager takes the place of the NT tools DHCP Manager and DNC Manager.

In short, Computer Manager can be used to administer most aspects of Windows 2000 computers, with the notable exceptions of anything to do with Active Directory and Group Policy.

### Using Computer Management

You can access Computer Management in numerous ways:

- Start → Programs → Administrative Tools → Computer Management
- Start → Programs → Administrative Tools → Active Directory Users and Computers → right-click on a computer → Manage
- Right-click on My Computer → Manage
- Installing the Computer Management snap-in into a new or existing console

The console tree for this tool displays a node for each snap-in integrated into Computer Management. A typical console tree looks like this:

```
Computer Management
    System Tools
        Event Viewer
        System Information
        Performance Logs and Alerts
        Shared Folders
        Device Manager
        Local Users and Groups
    Storage
        Disk Management
        Disk Defragmenter
        Logical Drives
        Removable Storage
    Services and Applications
```

Telephony
WMI Control
Services
Indexing Service
Internet Information Services
Message Queuing
[additional services]

Here [additional services] represents other optional networking components, which may be installed on the computer, and includes DHCP, DNS, Fax Service, RAS Server, Services for Macintosh, WINS, and so on.

Unlike other snap-ins for the MMC, Computer Management actually consists of a broad selection of standalone and extension snap-ins integrated into a single, hierarchical console tree. These snap-ins are grouped together under three first-level containers in the console tree:

*System Tools*
Contains tools for managing users and groups, shared folders, performance and event logs, and devices

*Storage*
Contains tools for managing all storage devices

*Services and Applications*
Contains tools for managing various services

For more information about the various snap-ins integrated into Computer Management, see the articles on those snap-ins in this chapter. For example, to find information on the Disk Management node in the Storage container in Computer Management, see *Device Manager* in this chapter.

**Action Menu**

Select the root node in the console tree to connect to a remote computer you want to manage (Computer Management connects to the local computer by default). You can also send a console message to the user on the remote computer.

---

 Right-clicking on the Computer Management root node and selecting Properties opens the System utility from the Control Panel (see *System* in Chapter 6), but only displays three of the five tabs for that utility. What's nice about this is that you can display and modify this information even on remote computers, which the System utility in the Control Panel cannot do.

---

For information on what you can do with any of the nodes in the System Tools, Storage, and Services and Applications containers, see the article for the associated snap-in in this chapter.

### View Menu

In addition to the standard options of selecting the icon size, display method, and which columns to display in the Details Pane, as well as customizing the appearance of the MMC console window, there are also various other options that appear only when you select a particular node in the console tree (for more on these options, see the articles in this chapter on the various snap-ins that are integrated into Computer Management).

### Notes

- You must be a member of the Administrators group for the computer you want to manage if you want to use Computer Management to modify the administrative properties of a system.

- If the root node of the Computer Management console tree is labeled "Computer Management (Local)," then you are managing the local computer. Otherwise, the root node identifies the remote computer using either its NetBIOS name (if DNS is not configured on the network) or its fully qualified domain name (if DNS is configured).

### See Also

*Device Manager(5), Disk Defragmenter(5), Disk Management(5), Event Viewer(5), Indexing Service(5), Internet Information Services(5), Local Users and Groups(5), Logical Drives(5), Performance Logs and Alerts(5), Services(5), Shared Folders(5), System(6), System Information(5)*

---

## Configure Your Server

Configures a role for your server.

### Description

This administrative tool is not implemented as a snap-in or console but instead as a rather wimpy wizard that tries to do everything. The wizard is run the first time you log on as Administrator after installing or upgrading your computer to Windows 2000 Server. The wizard provides the following options:

*Home*
Connects you to Microsoft's web site where you can read a zillion white papers on Windows 2000.

*Register*
Registers your copy of Windows 2000 Server.

*Active Directory*
Installs Active Directory on your server (starts the Active Directory Installation Wizard) or manages Active Directory if it is already installed. (Clicking the Manage link simply opens the Active Directory Users and Computers console.)

*File Server*
Runs a wizard to share a folder or opens Computer Management to do it manually.

---

*Print Server*
> Adds a printer by running the Add Printer Wizard or manages existing printers in the Printers folder.

*Web Server*
> Installs IIS and creates virtual directories or installs Windows Media Services.

*Networking*
> Opens the Network and Dial-up Connections folder or installs DHCP, DNS, Remote Access, or Routing.

*Application Server*
> Installs and configures Component Services or Terminal Services.

*Advanced*
> Installs Message Queuing, the Windows 2000 Support Tools, and so on.

### Notes

The Windows 2000 Support tools are a subset of the tools and utilities included in the *Windows 2000 Server Resource Kit.*

## Data Sources (ODBC)

Configures data sources for ODBC database connectivity.

### Description

In Windows NT this tool was called ODBC and was found in the Control Panel. In Windows 2000 it has been updated a bit and moved to the Administrative Tools program group. The tool is implemented as a dialog box, not a console, and its actual title is ODBC Data Source Administrator.

The main function of this tool is to add, configure, and remove data sources by associating an ODBC driver with a data-source name or DSN. Applications on the computer can then use the data source to interact with a database on the local computer or on a remote computer on the network.

The dialog box has seven tabs:

*User DSN*
> Can be used by the current user only and is local to the computer. (Local data sources are stored in the \*Program Files\Common Files\ODBC\Data Sources* folder.) To create a user DSN, click Add to specify an ODBC driver for the database. Then specify a name for the DSN, the location of the database file you want to access, and various configuration options that vary depending on the type of database you are accessing.

*System DSN*
> Can be used by any logged-on user or by any service running on the computer and is local to the computer. You add a system DSN the same way you add a user DSN.

*File DSN*

Can be used by any logged-on user and need not be local to the computer. (In other words, these data sources can also be stored on a shared folder on a remote computer on the network.) You add a file DSN the same way you add a user DSN.

*Drivers*

Displays the ODBC drivers you have installed on your computer.

*Tracing*

Creates a log of ODBC driver calls for debugging data-source problems.

*Connection Pooling*

Enables pooling of ODBC connections for selected drivers (double-click on a driver to enable this) and configures connection-pooling timeouts. Connection pooling allows idle connections to be reused without re-establishing a new connection and can significantly improve database-access performance, for example with Active Server Pages (ASP) applications running on Internet Information Services (IIS).

*About*

Displays version information about ODBC core files.

## Device Manager

Displays and manages hardware on local and remote computers.

### Description

Device Manager makes it easy to manage hardware devices by providing a simple GUI interface for performing actions such as:

- Enabling, disabling, and uninstalling devices

- Installing updated drivers for devices

- Diagnosing IRQ conflicts and other resource conflicts

- Manually reconfiguring IRQ and other resource settings to resolve conflicts

- Generating a printed report of your computer's hardware-configuration settings to aid in future troubleshooting efforts

The Windows 2000 Device Manager console has no counterpart in Windows NT since that platform was not Plug and Play. It does have a counterpart with a tab in the System utility on Windows 95 and Windows 98, however.

With the Plug and Play functionality of Windows 2000, you should need to use Device Manager only rarely since Windows 2000 should automatically prompt you when new hardware is added and should resolve most resource conflicts itself. However, you may find yourself using Device Manager when:

- You obtain updated device drivers from the manufacturers and want to install them on your system.

- Your system contains legacy devices that cannot have their resource settings properly assigned by the Windows 2000 Plug and Play enumerator.

### Using Device Manager

You can access Device Manager in several ways:

- Start → Programs → Administrative Tools → Computer Management → System Tools → Device Manager

- Start → Settings → Control Panel → System → Hardware → Device Manager

- Right-click on My Computer → Properties → Hardware → Device Manager

- Right-click on My Computer → Manage → System Tools → Disk Management

- Installing the Device Manager snap-in into a new or existing console

Using Computer Management or a custom console with the Device Manager snap-in installed, you can connect to either a local or remote computer. If you connect to a remote computer, however, you can display the hardware settings but cannot modify them (only devices on the local computer can be managed using Device Manager). The other methods for opening Device Manager only allow you to display and manage devices on the local computer, not on remote ones.

The console tree for this tool only displays the root Device Manager node. The actual hierarchy of device types and devices is displayed in the Details Pane, which is kind of odd, as it would have made more sense to display the device types in the left-hand pane instead. A typical Details Pane looks like this:

```
Root node (computer name)
    Computer
    Disk Drives
    Display Adapters
    DVD/CD-ROM drives
    Floppy disk controllers
    Floppy disk drives
    IDE ATA/ATAPI controllers
    Keyboards
    Mice and other pointing devices
    Modems
    Monitors
    Network adapters
    Ports (COM & LPT)
    Sound, video, and game controllers
    System devices
    Universal Serial Bus controllers
```

Each device-type node contains nodes for each instance of that device type installed. Note that there are alternate ways of displaying device information using this tool (see "View Menu" later in this article). If a certain type of device is not installed on the computer, the container for that device type is not displayed.

For general information see *hardware* in Chapter 3.

### Action Menu

With any node selected, you can choose "Scan for hardware changes." (Doing this for a particular device-type node does not scan just for changes for that type of device, but for all device types.) This forces Windows 2000 to scan your system for new hardware that was not properly detected when you installed the hardware, or to scan your system when you have manually changed hardware settings on a device and want these changes recognized by the operating system. Normally when you reboot, this hardware scan is performed automatically, but if you have installed hardware that does not require a reboot and the system did not detect it, forcing a scan could cause it to be detected properly. If hardware is detected, the Found New Hardware Wizard appears, leading you through a series of prompts. If this wizard does not appear, you can force its appearance using Control Panel → Add/Remove Hardware.

For information on how to enable, disable, install, uninstall, scan, update drivers for, and modify resource settings for devices, see *hardware* in Chapter 4.

You should exercise caution using Device Manager: by making improper changes to your hardware-resource settings, you can easily render your system inoperable. Make sure you have an understanding of computer-hardware configurations before attempting to manually change these settings.

### View Menu

In addition to being able to customize the MMC appearance, you can use the View menu to change the way in which devices are displayed in Device Manager. There are four different views possible:

*Devices by type*
> Groups devices by type. For example, all network adapters are grouped together under the Network Adapters node.

*Devices by connection*
> Groups devices by connection. For example, all devices connected to the PCI bus are grouped together under the PCI Bus node.

*Resources by type*
> Groups devices by type of resource used: IRQ, I/O, DMA, or memory.

*Resources by connection*
> Same as previous view except that a secondary grouping is included according to system board or PCI bus connection.

There are also the following additional options:

*Show Hidden Devices*
> Toggles the display of non–Plug and Play devices as well as devices that have been removed from the system but whose drivers have not been uninstalled.

*Print*
> Prints a report of your hardware devices and the resources they use. You have several different print options for different kinds of reports.

### Notes

- Device Manager is integrated into the System Tools section of the Computer Management console for easy access.

- When you first have your computer up and running, use Device Manager to print a complete report of the hardware configuration, and file this report somewhere safe. It may be useful later on should hardware problems occur. Make sure you update this report whenever you install new hardware or reconfigure existing hardware.

- If you are using a custom Device Manager console, use View → Customize → deselect Console Tree (or just click the Show/Hide button on the toolbar) to hide the console tree. This makes the left pane disappear—it only displays the root node anyway, and there is nothing you can do with that node.

- Make changes to hardware-resource settings sparingly—when you manually change a device setting, this change becomes fixed and leaves Windows 2000 less flexibility when assigning remaining resources to Plug and Play devices.

### See Also

*Add/Remove Hardware(6), Computer Management(5), hardware(3,4), System(6)*

---

## Disk Defragmenter

Defragments hard disks on the local computer to improve performance.

### Description

Fragmentation is generally less of an issue with NTFS volumes than with FAT or FAT32 volumes, since NTFS usually needs fewer disk accesses than FAT to locate all the fragments of a file. However, a significant performance improvement in disk access can be achieved by regularly defragmenting all volumes and partitions, including NTFS volumes and partitions, on a Windows 2000 computer. Disk Defragmenter achieves this performance gain by:

- Consolidating fragments of files and folders by moving them to one location so that each file and folder occupies a contiguous segment of space on the volume. Disk Defragmenter consolidates all fragments of each file into a single contiguous block of space, but different files may occupy different blocks of contiguous space after defragmentation. In other words, Disk Defragmenter does not cause all files on the volume to be grouped into a single contiguous region of space on the disk.

- Consolidating free space to make it less likely that new files will become fragmented. Disk Defragmenter typically does not attempt to completely consolidate all free space on the volume, however, since this generally provides little improvement in performance.

For administrators familiar with Windows NT 4.0 Server, there was no tool for defragmenting disks. On the Tools tab of a volume's property sheet (accessed through My Computer or Windows NT Explorer), there was in fact a ghosted-out button labeled Defragment Now, which required third-party disk-defragmenter software to be installed in order to work.

### Using Disk Defragmenter

You can access Disk Defragmenter several ways:

- Start → Programs → Administrative Tools → Computer Management → Storage → Disk Defragmenter

- Start → Programs → Accessories → System Tools → Disk Defragmenter

- My Computer or Windows Explorer → right-click on local disk → Properties → Tools → Defragment Now

- Right-click on My Computer → Manage → System Tools → Disk Defragmenter

- Installing the Disk Defragmenter snap-in into a new or existing console

The console tree has only the root node Disk Defragmenter. The right-hand pane displays in the top pane the volumes you can defragment, and in the bottom, the status of defragmentation. You can run Disk Defragmenter in two modes:

*Analysis*

Determines the amount of file fragmentation present and indicates whether defragmenting the disk is worthwhile. After analyzing a volume, the Analysis Display graphic box displays the volume's the initial state of fragmentation using the color-coded legend at the bottom of the screen.

*Defragmentation*

Defragments the disk and displays the progress in the Defragmentation Display graphic box.

### Action Menu

This allows you to analyze or defragment the selected volume, partition, or logical drive. You can pause or stop the analysis or defragmentation process at any time. Both the analysis and defragmentation processes produce reports you can view, save, and print. Note that only the report gives an accurate view of the defragmentation state of the volume; the graphical displays are only approximate since they cannot resolve individual clusters into colored regions due to screen-resolution limits.

 Although it is possible to use your computer while a disk is being defragmented, this is generally not a good idea as the system will be slow to respond due to the overhead of the defragmentation process. Making changes to files during defragmentation can also considerably lengthen the defragmentation process. Instead, pause or stop defragmentation, perform the work you have to do, and then restart defragmentation.

### View Menu

Just the usual MMC customization options here.

### Notes

- Disk Defragmenter is integrated into the System Tools section of the Computer Management console for easy access.

- You must be a member of the Administrators group to use Disk Defragmenter.

- System files cannot be defragmented using Disk Defragmenter. This includes the Master File Table (MFT), located at the beginning of each NTFS volume, and the paging file. Any other open files on the system will also not be defragmented, so it is a good idea to close all running applications and open files prior to starting defragmentation.

- Use Disk Defragmenter during times of light or no usage—for example, late at night.

- You can safely defragment the system and boot volumes, but do so when activity is light.

- The key figure in an analysis or defragmentation report is the Average Fragments Per File, which should be as close to 1 as possible. A value of 1.25, for example, would indicate 25% defragmentation on the volume.

- Always analyze a volume before defragmenting it—analyzing takes much less time and can determine whether defragmentation will really be useful or not.

- Volumes to which frequent file changes are written should be defragmented more frequently. An example would be the volume on a member server where users' home folders are stored.

- Defragmenting disks once a month is usually sufficient for most purposes. Unfortunately, you cannot use Scheduled Tasks to schedule defragmentation of disks, nor can you run more than one instance of Disk Defragmenter at a time on a computer, nor can you use Disk Defragmenter to defragment disks on remote computers. For a more powerful version of Disk Defragmenter, contact Executive Software (*sales@executive.com*), the makers of the Disk Defragmenter snap-in.

### See Also

*Computer Management(5), disks(3,4)*

---

## Disk Management

Manages disks on local and remote computers.

### Description

Disk Management can be used for managing both local and remote disk subsystems. You can use it to perform such administrative tasks as:

- Adding or removing disks

- Creating and managing partitions and volumes, including fault-tolerant volumes

- Performing disk-maintenance tasks such as defragmenting, backing up, and checking a disk for errors

- Configuring disk quotas and permissions and sharing disks for use over the network

For administrators familiar with Windows NT 4.0 Server, Disk Management performs similar functions to those provided by the NT administrative tool called Disk Administrator.

### Using Disk Management

You can access Disk Management either by:

- Start → Programs → Administrative Tools → Computer Management → Storage → Disk Management

- Right-click on My Computer → Manage → System Tools → Disk Management

- Installing the Disk Management snap-in into a new or existing console

The console tree for this tool only displays the root Disk Manager node. By default, the top section of the Details Pane displays a list of partitions and volumes on the system, while the bottom section displays a graphical representation of the partitions or volumes on each installed hard disk (see "View Menu" later in this article on how to change these views).

For general information see *disks* and *disk quota* in Chapter 3.

### Action Menu

Under the Action menu you can select the following:

*Console tree root node*
    Select this to rescan all disks or restore a previous disk configuration.

*Installed hard disk*
    Select this to display its status and vendor information, create partitions or volumes, change the storage mode from basic to dynamic, import a disk drive from a different machine, and so on.

*Partition or volume*
    Select this to format it, change its drive letter, extend it, add a mirror, or open its property sheet to configure disk quotas, NTFS permissions, share the volume, and so on.

For information on how to perform hard-disk administrative tasks, see *disks* and *disk quota* in Chapter 4.

### View Menu

In addition to the usual MMC customization options, you have the following:

*Top and Bottom*
    Display any two of the following three status-and-configuration views in the Details Pane:

*Disk List*
        Provides information about the physical disks (hard drives, CD-ROM drives, and so on) in your system

*Volume List*
> Provides information about the partitions, volumes, and logical drives on your hard disks

*Graphical View*
> Shows information about the partitions, volumes, and logical drives on your disks using color-coded regions

Bottom also lets you hide the bottom pane entirely. (This is useful if you have a lot of disks or volumes on your system.)

*Settings*
> Changes the color coding and horizontal scaling of the regions in Graphical view.

*All Drive Paths*
> Displays any drive paths on a disk system that is configured for dynamic storage. A drive path is created when you mount a volume to an empty folder on an NTFS volume (see *disks* in Chapter 3 for more information).

## Notes

Device Manager is integrated into the System Tools section of the Computer Management console for easy access.

## See Also

*Computer Management(5), disks(3,4), disk quota(3,4)*

---

## Distributed File System

Creates and administers a Dfs tree.

## Description

Distributed File System integrates shared folders on local and remote servers into a single, consolidated hierarchy called a Dfs tree. This benefits both administrators, who can centrally manage shared folders across an enterprise, and users, who can find and access shared folders more easily.

Windows NT 4.0 administrators will recall that limited Dfs functionality was supplied by Service Pack 3 for Windows NT 4.0 Server.

### Using Distributed File System

You can access Distributed File System by:

- Start → Programs → Administrative Tools → Distributed File System

- Installing the Distributed File System snap-in into a new or existing console

The console tree for this tool displays the various Dfs links in the Dfs tree. A typical console tree looks like this:

    Distributed File System
        Dfs root
            Dfs link
            Dfs link . . .

---

Select a Dfs link to display its associated replicas (network shared folders) in the Details Pane. Additional Dfs roots can be configured, but only one per Windows 2000 server. For background information on Dfs, see *Dfs* in Chapter 3.

### Action Menu

Under the Action menu you can select the following:

*Distributed File System node*
Select this to add a new Dfs root, or select an existing one in your enterprise.

*Dfs root node*
Select this to create an new Dfs link, add a replica to the root, check the status of the root, and configure its security settings.

*Dfs link*
Select this to add a new replica to the link, check the status of the link, and configure its security settings. With a link selected, you can take each of its replicas offline and check their status.

See *Dfs* in Chapter 4 for information on specific procedures relating to implementing and configuring Dfs.

### View Menu

Just the standard options here, namely selecting the icon size, display method, and which columns to display in the Details Pane, as well as customizing the appearance of the MMC console window.

### Notes

Dfs on Windows 2000 only allows Dfs-link hierarchies one level deep within a Dfs root (i.e., midlevel junctions are not allowed). If you want to create a Dfs tree more than one level deep, there is a workaround: link an existing Dfs link to a Dfs root on a different server. (This is called an inter-Dfs link, in which the target of a Dfs link is the shared folder of a new Dfs root.) You can chain together Dfs roots this way (Dfs root–Dfs link–Dfs root–Dfs link– . . . ) to create hierarchies as deep as you like. This is only a workaround, however.

### See Also

*Dfs(3,4)*

---

# DNS

Configures and administers a local or remote DNS server.

### Description

DNS is used for administering all aspects of Windows 2000 DNS servers. Since DNS is fundamental to the operation of Active Directory, expect to use this tool from time to time to configure DNS (unless all your computers are Windows 2000 Server and Professional, which can use Dynamic DNS to automatically create their own resource records on Windows 2000 DNS servers) and troubleshoot any DNS problems that may arise.

---

DNS performs similar functions to those provided by the Windows NT administrative tool called DNS Manager, but includes support for Dynamic DNS and other aspects of DNS not supported by Windows NT.

### Using DNS

You can access DNS by either:

- Start → Programs → Administrative Tools → DNS

- Start → Programs → Administrative Tools → Computer Management → Services and Applications → DNS

- Installing the DNS snap-in into a new or existing console

The console tree for this tool displays the connected DNS server and the zones configured on it. A typical console tree looks like this:

```
DNS
    DNS server name
        Forward Lookup Zones
            Root zone
            Zone
            Zone . . .
        Reverse Lookup Zones
            Zone
            Zone . . .
```

The root zone is identified by a dot (.) while the other zones represent your Windows 2000 domains (which are named as DNS domains). Reverse-lookup zones are optional. For more information on how DNS works, see *DNS* in Chapter 3.

### Action Menu

Under the Action menu you can select the following:

*DNS node*
> Select this to connect to a different DNS server.

*Server node*
> Select this to create a new zone, stop and start the DNS Server service, clear the DNS server cache, and configure various aspects of the DNS server.

*Forward or Reverse Lookup Zone containers*
> Select these to create a new zone in either of them.

*A zone*
> Select this to add new resource records to the zone, allow updates using Dynamic DNS, configure zone-transfer settings, and configure other aspects of the zone. Select a resource record within a zone to display its properties, or view these properties in the Details Pane when a zone is selected.

See *DNS*, *DNS server*, and *zone* in Chapter 4 for information on specific procedures relating to administering DNS.

### View Menu

In addition to the usual options of selecting the icon size, display method, and which columns to display in the Details Pane, as well as customizing the appearance of the MMC console window, you also have:

*Filter*

Lets you filter information displayed by name or portion of a name, which is especially useful to manage zones that have large numbers of resource records.

*Advanced*

Displays a hidden container showing the cached-name lookups stored in the DNS server cache. Right-click on this folder to clear the cache.

Additionally, when the server node is selected, a Messages option appears in the View menu. This is supposed to toggle on viewing current messages in the results pane, but I haven't seen it work yet.

### Notes

Device Manager is integrated into the System Tools section of the Computer Management console for easy access.

### See Also

*Computer Management(5), DNS(3,4), DNS server(4), zone(4)*

---

## Domain Controller Security Policy

A Group Policy Object (GPO) used for configuring domain-controller security settings.

### Description

The Domain Controller Security Policy shortcut in Administrative Tools opens the Default Domain Controller Security GPO for the domain in an MMC console window with the Group Policy snap-in installed. The entire GPO is not displayed, however. Only the policy subtree Computer Configuration → Windows Settings → Security Settings is displayed and available, allowing a quick way of configuring security settings for domain controllers in your domain using Group Policy.

See *Group Policy* in Chapter 3 for an explanation of GPOs and also *Group Policy Objects (GPOs)* in Chapter 4 for information on specific procedures relating to administering GPOs.

### Notes

Modifying the Domain Controller Security Policy does not change the default security templates or any custom templates you have created.

### See Also

*Domain Security Policy(5), Group Policy(3,4), Local Security Policy(3,4,5)*

## Domain Security Policy

A Group Policy Object (GPO) used for configuring domain security settings.

### Description

The Domain Security Policy shortcut in Administrative Tools opens the Default Domain Security GPO for the domain in an MMC console window with the Group Policy snap-in installed. The entire GPO is not displayed, however. Only the policy subtree Computer Configuration → Windows Settings → Security Settings is displayed and available, allowing a quick way of configuring security settings for domains using Group Policy.

See *Group Policy* in Chapter 3 for an explanation of GPOs and also *Group Policy Objects (GPOs)* in Chapter 4 for information on specific procedures relating to administering GPOs.

### Notes

Modifying the Domain Security Policy does not change the default security templates or any custom templates you have created.

### See Also

*Domain Security Policy(5), Group Policy(3,4), Local Security Policy(3,4,5)*

## Event Viewer

Monitors event logs on local and remote computers.

### Description

Event Viewer shows events recorded in the Application, Security, and System logs. These logs provide administrators with crucial information concerning component failures, invalid logon attempts, application errors, and other problems that may occur.

For administrators familiar with Windows NT 4.0 Server, Event Viewer performs similar functions to those provided by the NT administrative tool of the same name.

#### Using Event Viewer

You can access Event Viewer by:

- Start → Programs → Administrative Tools → Event Viewer
- Start → Programs → Administrative Tools → Computer Management → System Tools → Event Viewer
- Installing the Event Viewer snap-in into a new or existing console

The console tree for this tool typically looks like this:

Event Viewer
    Application Log
    Security Log
    System Log
    Directory Service
    DNS Server
    File Replication Service

The first three logs are present on all Windows 2000 computers. As for the remaining three:

- Directory Service is only on domain controllers (see *domain controller* in Chapter 3).

- DNS Server is only on servers that have the DNS Server service installed (see *DNS* in Chapter 3).

- File Replication Service is only on servers that have Dfs configured (see *Dfs* in Chapter 3).

For more information see *event logs* in Chapter 3.

**Action Menu**

Under the Action menu, you can select the following:

*Root node*
    Select this to connect to a remote computer whose event logs you want to monitor or to open an archived event log file.

*Particular log*
    Select this to display its logged events in the Details Pane. Double-click on an event to display additional information concerning the event.

For information on how to perform administrative tasks with event logs, see *event logs* in Chapter 4.

**View Menu**

In addition to the standard options of selecting which columns to display in the Details Pane and customizing the appearance of the MMC console window, there are also the following options (which only appear when an event log is selected):

*All Records*
    Displays all events recorded in the log (i.e., turns off any filter you created).

*Filter*
    Lets you create a filter to display only certain kinds of events. This is a very useful feature as event logs tend to grow unmanageably large otherwise.

*Newest First or Oldest First*
    Changes the order of the events (easier, though, is to just click the Date column header in the Details Pane).

*Find*
    Lets you search a log for a particular type of event. This is a powerful adjunct feature to Filter, and it's particularly useful if you are searching for all instances of a particular event in order to gauge its frequency (which may be a measure of its seriousness).

### Notes

Event Viewer is integrated into the System Tools section of the Computer Management console for easy access.

### See Also

*auditing(3,4)*, *Computer Management(5)*, *Dfs(3)*, *DNS(3)*, *domain controller(3)*, *event logs(3,4)*

---

# Group Policy

Opens a Group Policy Object (GPO) for editing.

### Description

Group Policy is used to configure existing GPOs. You cannot use it to create a new GPO—to do this use either:

*Active Directory Users and Computers*
Creates GPOs linked to domains and OUs

*Active Directory Sites and Services*
Creates GPOs linked to sites

There is no equivalent Windows NT 4.0 administrative tool since that platform did not support Group Policy. (Windows NT has a feature called System Policy, which was used for modifying registry settings on computers in the domain, but this reflects only a small part of what Group Policy in Windows 2000 is all about.)

#### Using Group Policy

The usual way of opening a GPO is through either Active Directory Users and Computers or Active Directory Sites and Services. For example, to open a GPO linked to a domain, do the following:

> Start → Programs → Administrative Tools → Active Directory Users and Computers → right-click on a domain → Properties → Group Policy → select a GPO → Edit

This opens a new console with the Group Policy snap-in installed and the focus on the GPO you selected. You cannot change the focus of this console to a different GPO.

However, you can create a custom MMC console and install the Group Policy snap-in into it. When you install the snap-in, you must also specify which GPO the console will manage. For example, to open a GPO for a domain:

> Start → Run → mmc → OK → Console → Add/Remove Snap-in → Add → Group Policy → Add → Browse → Look in → select domain → select GPO → OK → Finish → Close → OK

The advantage of this method is that if you save the console, you can then open the GPO directly from the Administrative Tools program group.

*Consoles*
*G*

Before you click Finish, you can select the option "Allow the focus of the Group Policy Snap-in to be changed when launching from the command line. This only applies if you save the console."

The console tree for a GPO typically looks like this:

GPO name
    Computer Configuration
        Software Settings
        Windows Settings
        Administrative Templates
    Computer Configuration
        Software Settings
        Windows Settings
        Administrative Templates

There are many levels of nodes here. For an explanation of the different categories of GPO settings, see *Group Policy* in Chapter 3.

### Action Menu

Select the root node (GPO name) to display the sites, domains, or OUs to which the GPO is linked, to disable the Computer or User Configuration portions of the GPO if they are not needed (speeds up processing), or to restrict access to the GPO using NTFS permissions.

The first- and second-level containers have no properties to configure, but deeper into a GPO you will find the GPO settings that can be configured by accessing their property sheets. For more information on configuring GPO settings, see *Group Policy Objects (GPOs)* in Chapter 4.

### View Menu

In addition to the standard options of selecting the icon size, display method, which columns to display in the Details Pane, as well as customizing the appearance of the MMC console window, if you select the root node (GPO name), then you can select DC Options in order to specify which domain controller will be selected when Group Policy is selecting a domain controller. It's strange that this option is in the View menu instead of the Action menu. The three options available are:

- Use the one with the Operations Master token for the PDC emulator
- Use the one used by the Active Directory snap-ins
- Use any available domain controller

The first option is enabled by default, as GPOs are created and edited by default on the domain controller running the PDC emulator role. Leave this setting alone for safety's sake. This is because if one administrator opens a particular GPO on this domain controller, it is locked so that no other administrator can simultaneously modify the same GPO. The only reason you might select one of the other options is if your domain spans several sites with slow WAN links between them, in which case you'll get a better response by selecting a more available domain controller. Care must be taken in this case that no other administrator in the domain can edit the same GPO at the same time on a different domain controller, or data corruption might result.

You can also use Group Policy itself to enforce which domain controllers can be used for creating GPOs. The policy setting is:

User Configuration\
 Administrative Templates\
  System\
   Group Policy\
    Group Policy domain controller selection

### See Also

*Domain Controller Security Policy(5)*, *Domain Security Policy(5)*, *Group Policy(3,4)*, *Local Security Policy(5)*

## Indexing Service

Indexes documents and document properties on your disks.

### Description

The Indexing Service runs in the background and extracts index information from documents stored on your hard drives. This information is used to create catalogs that can be used to search all documents on your drives for:

- Key words or phrases

- Document properties such as author name or file size

The types of documents that can be automatically indexed include documents created in Microsoft Office 95 or later, text files, web pages, and any other document type for which a filter has been obtained and installed. Filters are software components that allow the Indexing Service to extract index information from specific types of documents. Third-party vendors of document-creation software often provide filters for their document types.

---

The Windows NT 4.0 Option Pack includes an Index Server component that is similar to the one included here. When Windows 2000 is installed, the Indexing Service is not started. Do not start the Indexing Service unless you have sufficient hardware resources to support it, specifically:

— Enough free disk space to contain the catalogs. This is about 15% of the space used by documents stored on NTFS partitions or 30% on FAT partitions.

— Enough RAM—the more the better.

---

The Indexing Service is configured to operate automatically in the background once it is started, with no additional manual configuration required. There are configuration options that advanced administrators can use for certain purposes, however. For a fuller treatment of how the Indexing Service works and what you can do with it, see my book *Administering IIS5* (McGraw-Hill).

### Using Indexing Service

Access the Indexing Service by either:

* Start → Programs → Administrative Tools → Computer Management → Services and Applications → Indexing Service
* Installing the Indexing Service snap-in into a new or existing console

The console tree for this tool typically looks like this:

Indexing Service
    System
    Web
    Catalog
    Catalog . . .

The two default catalogs are:

*System*
    Used to catalog system-volume information on the computer, specifically the contents of the \\*Documents and Settings* folder and the entire *C:* drive

*Web*
    Used to catalog the \\*Inetpub* folder and related folders for Internet Information Services (IIS)

For information on how to create and configure new catalogs, see my book *Administering IIS5* (McGraw-Hill).

The Startup setting for the Indexing Service is set to Manual. To start the Indexing Service on a machine, select:

Start → Programs → Administrative Tools → Computer Management → Services and Applications → right-click Indexing Service → Start → Yes

Once the Indexing Service is started, it will automatically catalog documents on your machine during idle periods. You can watch the progress of indexing in the Details Pane (scroll to see the last column, called Status). The initial indexing process may take hours; when new documents are saved or existing ones modified, catalogs are updated more quickly.

After the catalogs are fully updated, search for text within files on your hard drive by using:

Start → Search → Containing Text → specify keywords → Search Now

This will be significantly faster than before. You can also query a catalog directly by using:

Start → Programs → Administrative Tools → Computer Management → Services and Applications → Indexing Service → select a catalog → double-click on Query a Catalog in the Details Pane

## Notes

- The Indexing Service is integrated into the Services and Applications section of the Computer Management console.

- You must be a member of the Administrators group to manage the Indexing Service.

- The Indexing Service respects NTFS security: users will only see those documents in a query result for which they have at least Read permission.

- Don't run antivirus or backup software in the background when the Indexing Service is running, as these programs lock files and will cause the Indexing Service to time out when trying to access these files.

## See Also

*Computer Management(5), search(4)*

---

# Internet Information Services

Manages HTTP, FTP, and other Internet protocols on local or remote computers.

## Description

Internet Information Services (IIS) is mainly used to create and configure a Windows 2000 Server computer in the role of a web server for either public use on the Internet or private use on a corporate intranet.

The related Windows NT 4.0 Server administrative tool was called Internet Services Manager. An updated version of IIS, which was managed using Version 1.0 of the MMC, was included in the Windows NT 4.0 Option Pack.

### Using Internet Information Services

You can access IIS by:

- Start → Programs → Administrative Tools → Internet Services Manager

- Start → Programs → Administrative Tools → Computer Management → Services and Applications → Internet Information Services

- Installing the Internet Information Services snap-in into a new or existing console

A typical console tree looks like this:

    Internet Information Services
        Server name
            Default Web Site
            Administration Web Site
            Web Site
            Web Site . . .

Other nodes such as Default SMTP Virtual Server or Default NNTP Virtual Server may be present if these components are installed. For general information on IIS, see *Internet Information Services (IIS)* in Chapter 3. For information on how to create and configure a web site or virtual directory, see *web site* in Chapter 4. And for detailed information see my book *Administering IIS5* (McGraw-Hill).

### Notes

IIS is integrated into the Services and Applications section of the Computer Management console.

### See Also

*Computer Management(5), Internet Information Services (IIS)(3), web site(4)*

---

## Licensing

Manages licenses for your Windows 2000–based enterprise.

### Description

In Windows NT this administrative tool was called License Manager. In Windows 2000 it is similarly implemented as a dialog box instead of an MMC console.

The Windows 2000 tool is very similar to the old one, and it is used for centrally administering licenses for the operating system, clients, and other applications on Windows 2000 or Windows NT computers in your enterprise. You can use it to view licensing information using the four tabs:

*Purchase History*
    Display when and how many licenses you purchased at different times.

*Products View*
    Display how many licenses you have for each type of product.

*Clients (Per Seat)*
    View user licensing information or revoke a user's license. (Revoking a license returns it to the pool of available Per Seat licenses for the product.)

*Server Browser*
    Select a domain or computer to administer its licenses. For example, you can add or remove licenses from the server or change the licensing mode for the server from Per Server to Per Seat (a permanent change).

In any of these views, you can use the menu to add newly purchased CALs to the licensing database.

### See Also

*Licensing(6)*

---

## Local Security Policy

A Group Policy Object (GPO) used for configuring local security settings.

### Description

The Local Security Policy shortcut in Administrative Tools opens the security settings for the local computer in an MMC console window with the Group Policy snap-in installed. See *Local Security Policy* in Chapter 3 for background information and *Local Security Policy* in Chapter 4 for information on specific tasks.

---

## Notes

- A computer's Local Security Policy settings are stored in:

  *%SystemRoot%\System32\grouppolicy*

- Computers can have only one Local Security Policy object.

## See Also

*Group Policy(3,4), Local Security Policy(3,4)*

---

## Local Users and Groups

Creates and manages local users and local groups on a Windows 2000 member server or a Windows 2000 Professional workstation.

### Description

Local users are user accounts that exist in the security database of the local computer; similarly, local groups are groups that exist only on the local computer. On Windows 2000 Server computers configured as member servers, you can use local users and groups to grant permissions and rights on the computer, but their usefulness is limited to workgroup settings. When in a domain environment, use domain user accounts, global groups, and domain local groups instead, which you can create and manage using the *Active Directory Users and Computers* console discussed earlier in this chapter. For more information see *local user account* and *local group* in Chapter 3.

For administrators familiar with Windows NT 4.0 Server, the Local Users and Groups snap-in performs functions similar to those provided by the NT administrative tool called User Manager.

#### Using Local Users and Groups

You can access Local Users and Groups by either:

- Start → Programs → Administrative Tools → Computer Management → System Tools → Local Users and Groups

- Installing the Local Users and Groups snap-in into a new or existing console

The console tree looks like this:

Local Users and Groups
    Users
    Groups

The two subnodes are as follows:

*Users*
    Contains built-in local user accounts, plus additional local user accounts that you create. The built-in local user accounts typically include Administrator, Guest (disabled), and other accounts such as the built-in account for anonymous access to Internet Information Services and the user account for Terminal Services (depending on which Windows 2000 services are installed on the computer).

*Consoles*
*L*

---

*Groups*

Contains built-in local groups, plus additional local groups that you create. The built-in local groups typically include Administrators, Backup Operators, Guests, Power Users, Replicator, and Users.

For background information see *local user account* and *local group* in Chapter 3.

**Action Menu**

Select either the Users or Groups container to create a new local user account or new local group. For more information on creating and configuring these items, see *local user account* and *local group* in Chapter 4.

**View Menu**

Just the standard options here, namely selecting the icon size, display method, and which columns to display in the Details Pane, as well as customizing the appearance of the MMC console window.

**Notes**

- You must be a member of the local Administrators group to use this console.

- Local Users and Groups is also used to manage local users and groups on Windows 2000 Professional computers that are used as standalone (non-networked) computers.

- You cannot use Local Users and Groups on a domain controller—the snap-in is displayed under Computer Management as disabled in this case.

**See Also**

*local group(3,4), local user account(3,4)*

## Logical Drives

Manages both local and mapped drives on local and remote computers.

**Description**

Logical Drives is an extension to the Computer Management snap-in that lets you manage partitions, volumes, logical drives, and mapped network drives on either local or remote computers. Logical Drives connects through Windows Management Instrumentation (WMI) to obtain the required information to display.

 There are two different meanings to the phrase "logical drive" in the previous paragraph. A logical drive can refer to either:

— A volume created within an extended partition on a basic disk

— A primary partition, volume within an extended partition, dynamic volume, or mapped network drive on a computer

### Using Logical Drives

You can access Logical Drives by either:

- Start → Programs → Administrative Tools → Computer Management → Storage → Logical Drives

- Installing the Computer Management snap-in into a new or existing console (do not disable the Logical Drives extension)

When Logical Drives is selected in the console tree, the right-hand pane displays attached floppies, CD-ROMs, and all partitions and volumes on attached hard disks as local mappings, while mapped network drives are displayed with their associated share names and remote computer names (for example, *PUB* on *MS1*).

### Action Menu

Select a logical drive to display the property sheet of the drive. With FAT/FAT32 drives you can only modify the volume label, while with NTFS drives you can also modify the NTFS permissions on the root of the drive. (Any permissions set on the root of an NTFS partition or volume are inherited by all future files and folders you create on that volume.) You cannot modify any of the properties of mapped network drives.

### Notes

- To use Logical Drives to modify drive properties, you must be a member of the Administrators group.

- If you create new volumes or new mapped drives while running Computer Management, you will not be able to see these under Logical Drives unless you shut down and restart the Computer Management console—in other words, there is no way of refreshing the view in Logical Drives.

- To manage logical drives on a remote computer, right-click the root node of Computer Management and select "Connect to another computer."

### See Also

*Computer Management(5), disks(3,4)*

---

## Performance

Logs performance data and displays it.

### Description

Performance lets you collect system performance data into logs and then view and analyze these logs to determine system bottlenecks, establish trends in resource usage, and forecast needed hardware upgrades.

For administrators familiar with Windows NT 4.0 Server, the Performance console performs functions similar to those provided by the NT administrative tool called Performance Monitor.

### Using Performance

You can access Performance by:

- Start → Programs → Administrative Tools → Performance
- Install the Performance Logs and Alerts snap-in and the System Monitor ActiveX control into a new or existing console.

The console tree typically looks like this:

Console Root
    System Monitor
    Performance Logs and Alerts
        Counter Logs
        Trace Logs
        Alerts

Console Root is simply a folder that contains two snap-ins:

### Performance Logs and Alerts

This lets you collect and log data for monitoring the performance of processor, memory, disk, network, and other subsystems of your computer. For more information see *Performance Logs and Alerts* in this chapter.

### System Monitor

An ActiveX control that lets you display performance logs using the chart, histogram, and report views familiar to administrators who have used the Windows NT administration tool, Performance Monitor. You can display these logs either while they are being created (real-time mode) or by opening previously saved performance logs and selecting the performance objects and counters you want to view.

### Notes

- Unfortunately, the Performance console does not include the facility for connecting to remote computers to manage performance logs on those computers. Instead, the Performance console can only manage performance logs on the local computer. However, by using the Computer Management console, which includes Performance Logs and Alerts under System Tools, you can connect to a remote computer and manage performance logs on that computer. You cannot, however, view them using Computer Management unless you also install the ActiveX control called System Monitor into the console. See *Performance Logs and Alerts* in this chapter for more information.

- You can use Performance to view performance logs created on a remote computer by logging on as an Administrator and opening the log file on the remote computer. Performance logs are stored by default in *C:\PerfLogs*, a directory that is created the first time you run Performance Logs and Alerts. To open a log on a remote computer, type \\<*remote_computer_name*>\C$\ *PerfLogs* in the File Name box, and then select the log you want to display.

### See Also

*Computer Management(5)*, *Performance Logs and Alerts(5)*

# Performance Logs and Alerts

Creates and manages performance logs and alerts.

## Description

Performance Logs and Alerts enables administrators to collect and log data for monitoring the performance of processor, memory, disk, network, and other subsystems of their computers. This information can then be used to analyze and optimize the performance of network servers.

For administrators familiar with Windows NT 4.0 Server, the Performance Logs and Alerts snap-in performs functions similar to those provided by the NT administrative tool, Performance Monitor. However, Performance Logs and Alerts can only be used to collect performance data and not to view it. To view and analyze performance data, use the administrative tool called Performance, which includes the ActiveX control called System Monitor. For more information see *Performance* in this chapter.

### Using Performance Logs and Alerts

You can access Performance Logs and Alerts by:

- Start → Programs → Administrative Tools → Computer Management → System Tools → Performance Logs and Alerts

- Start → Programs → Administrative Tools → Performance → Performance Logs and Alerts

- Installing the Performance Logs and Alerts snap-in into a new or existing console

The console tree typically looks like this:

```
Performance Logs and Alerts
    Counter Logs
        Log
        Log . . .
    Trace Logs
        Log
        Log . . .
    Alerts
        Alert
        Alert . . .
```

The three first-level containers are:

*Counter Logs*
> Creates and configures counter logs, which collect performance data at specific time intervals using various counters you specify

*Trace Logs*
> Creates and configures trace logs, which record data only when certain system events occur, such as a page fault or a disk I/O operation

*Alerts*
> Creates and configures alerts, which trigger upon actions like starting a log or sending a message when a performance counter goes outside a range specified

### Action Menu

Under the Action menu you can select the following:

*Counter Logs*

> Select this to create a new counter log by giving it a name, adding counters for different performance objects, and specifying a sampling interval, log-file format, and schedule for collecting performance data. The default is to start logging immediately when you select the log in the Details Pane. (Log icons in the Details Pane are green when collecting data and red when stopped.) Select the log to stop logging or reconfigure the settings for the log.

*Trace Logs*

> Select this to create a new trace log by giving it a name, enabling the system provider or one or more nonsystem providers, and specifying a log file format, schedule for collecting performance data, and buffer settings. The default is to start logging immediately when you select the log in the Details Pane. Select the log to stop logging or reconfigure the settings for the log.

*Alerts*

> Select this to create a new alert by giving it a name, adding counters for different performance objects, specifying an alert threshold value for each counter, specifying an action to occur when an alert is generated, and specifying a schedule for the alert. The default is to run an alert immediately when you select the alert in the Details Pane. Select the alert to stop it or reconfigure its settings.

Counter and trace logs are stored in the *C:\Perflogs* folder by default. Use the System Monitor control in the Performance console in Administrative Tools to open a log and display it for analysis.

### View Menu

Just the standard options here, namely selecting the icon size, display method, and which columns to display in the Details Pane, as well as customizing the appearance of the MMC console window.

### Notes

- Performance Logs and Alerts is integrated into the System Tools section of the Computer Management console for easy access.

- When you create a new console using the Performance Logs and Alerts snap-in, you are not given the option of specifying which computer you will manage. By default, a new Performance Logs and Alerts console can only create and configure performance logs on the local computer. However, by using the Computer Management console, which includes Performance Logs and Alerts under System Tools, you can connect to a remote computer and collect performance logs on that computer.

### See Also

*Computer Management(5), Performance(5)*

## Server Analysis and Optimization

The process of analyzing and optimizing the performance of servers may seem like an art, but to a certain extent it can also be approached systematically like a science. The basic process involves six different stages of work:

1. The first step is to *create a baseline* by logging performance data to determine what the behavior of the system is like in the normal working environment. The baseline should always include information concerning the four major resource groups of every server: processor, memory, disk, and network subsystems.

2. Once a baseline has been established, *systematically collect performance data* over a period of time to establish trends in resource usage that might indicate future problems. The data stored in performance logs can be viewed using the Performance console or can be exported to other applications such as Microsoft Excel for further analysis.

3. The next step involves *characterizing the system workload*. This may involve determining how many users the server is able to support, what the response time is for different requests, and so on. What usually happens at this stage is that a bottleneck is identified. A *bottleneck* is the system resource that is limiting overall system performance. What's mysterious about this stage is that the bottleneck might not be what it at first seems to be. For example, if the disk subsystem is too active during heavy workload, it may be a problem with the disks or their drivers, but more likely the cause is insufficient memory, which results in excessive paging to disk. Thus, sustained high disk activity may indicate that memory is a bottleneck for the system. By examining several different performance counters, the experienced system administrator can determine what the true underlying cause of the bottleneck is. Once a bottleneck has been identified and resolved (for example, by adding more RAM), a new baseline should be re-established, and additional data should be collected over time to determine if there is a second bottleneck hiding underneath the first.

4. The fourth step is to *define expectations of system responsiveness*. This means predicting how the system will behave under different levels of load and what the peak sustained capabilities of the system can be.

5. When these defined expectations are compared with both existing trends in system usage and your company's business plan, you can then *forecast your future resource needs*. Will you need to upgrade your server or add an additional server within the next six months? At this point you should be able to make predictions concerning questions like this.

6. Finally, you should ensure that you have a *long-term monitoring plan* in place. Performance data should be regularly logged and analyzed, predictions for resource usage should be tested, and records should be kept for both technical and business purposes.

*Consoles*
*P*

## Routing and Remote Access

Configures and manages a remote-access server or router.

### Description

Routing and Remote Access can be used to configure a Windows 2000 server for the role of:

- A dial-up networking server (remote-access server)
- A virtual private networking server (VPN server)

In addition, it can be used for:

- Configuring a direct cable connection between two computers for the purposes of file transfer between them
- Configuring a multihomed machine to function as a router using RIP or OSPF as a routing protocol

Routing and Remote Access performs remote-access server functions similar to the Windows NT administrative tool, Remote Access Admin, and more specifically to the Routing and RAS Admin tool installed with the optional Routing and Remote Access Service (RRAS) component for Windows NT 4.0 Server.

### Using Routing and Remote Access

You can access Routing and Remote Access by:

- Start → Programs → Administrative Tools → Routing and Remote Access
- Installing the Routing and Remote Access snap-in into a new or existing console

By default, Routing and Remote Access Service is configured for manual startup on a Windows 2000 server, so the console tree initially looks like this:

```
Routing and Remote Access
    Server Status
    Server Name
```

where Server Name is the local computer. To start the Routing and Remote Access Service on the local computer, right-click on Server Name and select Configure and Enable Routing and Remote Access. This starts a wizard that leads you through the process of configuring the computer as a remote-access server or router.

Once the server has been configured, the console tree typically looks like this:

```
Routing and Remote Access
    Server Status
    Server Name
        Routing Interfaces
        Ports
        Remote Access Clients
        IP Routing
        Remote Access Policies
        Remote Access Logging
    Server Name . . .
```

Depending on the role in which the server is configured (remote-access server, VPN server, router, or manually configured server), some of the six nodes under Server Name may not be present. For more information on remote-access features and capabilities in Windows 2000, see *remote access* in Chapter 3.

### Action Menu

Under the Action menu you can select the following:

*Routing and Remote Access*
> Select this to add additional remote-access servers to the console tree and to configure the interval at which the console refreshes when Auto Refresh is enabled.

*Server Status*
> Select this to see the status of your remote-access servers in the Details Pane.

*Server Name node*
> Select this to pause, start, and restart the Routing and Remote Access Service on the server or disable the service (remove the remote-access server configuration from the server). You can also change the role of the server, specify providers for authentication and accounting, and manage IP routing and PPP settings on the server.

*Routing Interfaces*
> Select this to display the physical or logical interfaces over which packets are forwarded. These can be LAN, demand-dial, or IP-tunnel interfaces. (You can create new demand-dial or IP-tunnel interfaces, but LAN interfaces are created automatically when network adapters are installed.) Depending on the type of interface, you may be able to connect or disconnect it, enable or disable it, configure dial-out credentials and hours, change the device associated with the interface, configure which networking services function over the interface, and configure other properties of the interface.

*Ports*
> Select this to display and configure the devices (modems, modem banks, logical WAN Miniports, and so on) supported by RRAS on the server. The Details Pane displays the point-to-point connections that are configured and their statuses. (If you have a single-port device such as a modem, the port and the device are indistinguishable.) Double-click on a port to display more details of its status.

*Remote Access Clients*
> Select this to view the connected dial-up or VPN clients in the Details Pane and disconnect them or view their status.

*IP Routing*
> Select this to configure a multihomed server as a router.

*Remote Access Policies*
> Select this to create a new Remote Access Policy for controlling remote access for users. The Details Pane displays the Remote Access Policy created when the Routing and Remote Access Service is enabled on the server.

*Consoles*
*8*

*Remote Access Logging*
> Select this to view the remote-access log file, and double-click on the file to configure its logging settings.

See *remote-access server* in Chapter 4 for information on specific procedures relating to configuring remote-access servers.

### View Menu

Just the standard options here, namely selecting the icon size, display method, and which columns to display in the Details Pane, as well as customizing the appearance of the MMC console window.

### See Also

*remote access(3), remote-access server(4)*

---

## Security Configuration and Analysis

Analyzes and configures security on the local computer.

### Description

Using this tool to analyze and configure security settings on the local computer, you can:

- Import security templates created using the Security Templates snap-in into a computer-specific data store (database), merging or overwriting successive templates to create a composite template that you can save or export.

- Compare the current (effective) security settings on the local computer with settings stored in the database, displaying the differences for easy recognition. (A green check mark next to a setting means the current setting and the template setting agree; a red X means there is a difference; no mark means both the current setting and template setting are Not Defined.)

- Apply a security template to the Local Security Policy on the computer so that it takes effect immediately. If after performing analysis you choose to accept the current settings, the corresponding value in the database is modified to match.

There is no Windows NT 4.0 administrative tool corresponding to Security Configuration and Analysis.

### Using Security Configuration and Analysis

You access Security Configuration and Analysis by installing the snap-in in a new or existing MMC console. The first time you use this tool, the console tree has only the Security Configuration and Analysis root node. When you select this node, instructions for using the tool are displayed in the Details Pane.

### Action Menu

Select Security Configuration and Analysis to create a new database or open an existing one. To create a new database, you must first import a security template. You can then import additional templates into the database, either merging them with previously imported template settings or overwriting the existing settings.

You can also directly modify security settings in the database once you have completed the analysis procedure described next.

Next, you analyze your computer to compare the settings in the database with the system's current local security settings. After analysis the console tree typically looks like this:

> Security Configuration and Analysis
> > Account Policies
> > Local Policies
> > Event Log
> > Restricted Groups
> > System Services
> > Registry
> > File System

After analysis, select Security Configuration and Analysis again to display a logged description of the results of the analysis. Then, if desired, expand the different containers to display the differences between the database settings and the system's current security settings (differences marked with red X as explained earlier). For more information on these different security settings, see *Group Policy* and *Local Security Policy* in Chapter 3.

Finally, you can either:

- Immediately apply the security-template settings you imported into the database to the computer's Local Security Policy by right-clicking on Security Configuration and Analysis and selecting Configure Computer Now. Choose this approach if you only have a few computers to configure. Changes will be applied when you reboot your computer. If your computers are part of a domain in which Group Policy is configured, however, be aware that the security settings you configure locally on your computers may be overwritten when Group Policy is applied. For more information see *Local Security Policy* in Chapter 4.

- Export your database settings to a security template, which you can then import into a Group Policy Object (GPO). Choose this approach if you have a domain configuration with multiple computers to configure. For more information see *Group Policy Objects (GPOs)* in Chapter 4.

### View Menu

Just the standard options here, namely selecting the icon size, display method, which columns to display in the Details Pane, as well as customizing the appearance of the MMC console window.

### Notes

- To create and modify security templates, see *Security Templates* in this chapter.
- The *Secedit.exe* command-line utility can be used to perform batch analysis on multiple computers in a domain, but you must view the results of the analysis using Security Configuration and Analysis.

### See Also

*Group Policy(3,4,5)*, *Local Security Policy(3,4,5)*, *Security Templates(5)*

## Security Templates

Defines security templates that can be applied to a Group Policy Object (GPO) to define its security settings.

### Description

A security template is an *.inf* file containing different security settings for a GPO. Windows 2000 includes a number of default security templates, which can be viewed using this tool. These default templates represent typical security settings for different levels of security (low, medium, or high) on different roles of computers (domain controllers, member servers, or workstations). The default templates can also be used as a basis for creating custom templates, which can then be imported into a GPO.

Security Templates has some similarity to the Windows NT 4.0 Server administrative tool, System Policy Editor, but goes well beyond it.

#### Using Security Templates

You access Security Templates by installing the snap-in in a new or existing MMC console. A typical console tree looks like this:

```
Security Templates
    Template Search Path
        Template
        Template . . .
```

The list of templates includes the default templates plus any additional ones you define. For information on the default security templates, see *Local Security Policy* in Chapter 3.

#### Action Menu

Under the Action menu you can select the following:

*Security Templates*
> Select this to define a new template search path.

*Template Search Path (C:\WINNT\Security\Templates by default)*
> Select this to create a new template or delete an existing one. You can use Save As to save a copy of an existing template under a different name and then modify it. (This can save time over defining a new template from scratch.) If you do create a new template, be sure to save it.

*Template*
> Select a template to display and modify the template's security settings using the Details Pane.

A security template can be applied to a local computer to modify its Local Security Policy settings by using a console with the Security Configuration and Analysis snap-in installed in it. See *Security Configuration and Analysis* in this chapter for more information, as well as *Local Security Policy* in Chapter 4.

A security template can also be imported into a GPO using the Group Policy console. This can simplify the administration of Group Policy on the network. See *Group Policy Objects (GPOs)* in Chapter 4 for procedures.

### View Menu

Just the standard options here, namely selecting the icon size, display method, and which columns to display in the Details Pane, as well as customizing the appearance of the MMC console window.

### See Also

*Group Policy(3,4,5), Local Security Policy(3,4,5), Security Configuration and Analysis(5)*

---

## Services

Manages services on local and remote computers.

### Description

Services starts, stops, pauses, resumes, and configures startup and recovery settings for services on both local and remote computers, including computers running Windows NT 4.0 Server. You can also view the various dependencies between services so you can see the effect of stopping or pausing services.

The corresponding Windows NT 4.0 tool is Services in the Control Panel.

### Using Services

You can access Services by:

- Start → Programs → Administrative Tools → Computer Management → Services and Applications → Services

- Installing the Services snap-in into a new or existing console

The console tree displays only the Services root node, while the various Windows 2000 services and their statuses are displayed in the Details Pane. For background information see *service* in Chapter 3.

### Action menu

Under the Action menu you can select the following:

*Services*
Select this to send a console message to all users currently connected to the connected server. You might do this, for example, if you were going to pause or stop the Server service, telling users to close their files in order to avoid losing work.

*A service in the Details Pane*
Select this to start, stop, pause, resume, or restart the service. Double-click on a service to open its property sheet in order to configure the startup type, account context, and recovery settings for the service. For more information on procedures see *service* in Chapter 4.

### View Menu

Just the standard options here, namely selecting the icon size, display method, and which columns to display in the Details Pane, as well as customizing the appearance of the MMC console window.

### Notes

- Services is also found in the Services and Applications section of the Computer Management console.

- If you are using a custom Services console, you can hide the console tree using View → Customize → deselect Console Tree (or use the Show/Hide button on the toolbar). This gives you a better view of the settings of the various services.

- Services does not refresh automatically—use Action → Refresh to display the current state of all services on your system.

### See Also

*Computer Management(5), service(3,4)*

---

## Shared Folders

Creates and manages shared folders on local and remote computers.

### Description

Shared Folders makes it easy to create and manage shares on local and remote computers, as well as to stop and reconfigure shares, terminate user sessions, and close files.

For administrators familiar with Windows NT 4.0 Server, the Shared Folders snap-in performs functions similar to those provided by the NT administrative tool called Server Manager.

### Using Shared Folders

You can access Shared Folders by either:

- Start → Programs → Administrative Tools → Computer Management → System Tools → Shared Folders

- Installing the Shared Folders snap-in into a new or existing console

The console tree looks like this:

    Shared Folders
        Shares
        Sessions
        Open Files

Shares displays information about shared resources (folders, volumes, printers, directories, or named pipes) on the computer, including the share name, the path to the shared resource, the type of network connection (Windows, Macintosh, or NetWare), and the current number of connected users.

Sessions displays information about network users currently connected to shared resources on the computer, including the username and computer name of each connected user, the type of network connection, the number of files the user has open on the computer, how much time has elapsed since the user first connected to the computer, and the amount of time since his last activity on the computer.

Open Files displays information about files currently open on the computer by users connecting over the network, including the name of the file (or print job or named pipe), who has opened it, the type of network connection, the number of locks on the resource (if any), and the permission granted to the user for the resource.

For general information on shared folders, see *shared folder* in Chapter 3.

### Action Menu

Under the Action menu you can select the following:

*Shared Folders*
> Select this to send a console message to users who have active sessions with that server.

*Shares*
> Select this to create a new file share on the server using the Create Shared Folder Wizard. You can also send a console message to all users who have active sessions with that server. Selecting an existing share in the Details Pane allows you to stop sharing the share and to access the properties of the share for modifying shared-folder permissions, NTFS permissions, maximum number of sessions, and file-caching settings.

*Sessions*
> Select this to disconnect all sessions from the server. Selecting a particular session in the Details Pane lets you close that session alone.

*Open Files*
> Select this to disconnect all open files from the server. Selecting a particular open file in the Details Pane lets you close that file alone.

For more on creating and configuring shared folders, see *shared folder* in Chapter 4.

The capability to send a console message is actually implemented by means of a snap-in extension to Shared Folders called Send Console Message. If for some reason you wish to do so, you can create a custom Shared Folders console that does not have the capability to send a console message by:

> Start → Run → mmc → OK → Console → Add/Remove Snap-in → Add → Shared Folders → Add → Finish → Close → Extensions → deselect "Add all extensions" → deselect Send Console Message → OK

You would think that if you wanted to modify the permissions on a share, you would proceed somewhat like this:

1. Send a console message to inform connected users to close files and disconnect from the share.

2. Stop sharing the share by right-clicking on share → Stop Sharing.

3. Modify the permissions on the share by right-clicking on share → Properties

4. Restart sharing the share again by right-clicking on share → Restart Sharing

Unfortunately, there is no Restart Sharing option on the Action or shortcut menu. When you stop sharing a share, it disappears from the list of shares under the Shares node, which means you need to recreate the share and all its permissions and settings again.

### View Menu

Just the standard options here, namely selecting the icon size, display method, and which columns to display in the Details Pane, as well as customizing the appearance of the MMC console window.

### Notes

- Shared Folders is also found in the System Tools section of the Computer Management console.

- To use Shared Folders to manage Windows 2000 Server computers, you need to be a member of either the Administrators or Server Operators group.

- Note that the information displayed in Shared Folders is not updated automatically. To update the display, use Action → Refresh.

- You should always send a console message to users before disconnecting them so they have time to close files and save their work. This applies whether you want to terminate sessions, close files, or stop sharing a shared folder.

- If you stop sharing an administrative share, it may disrupt network communications with the server and remote management of the server. If you do stop an administrative share, you should reboot the server to restore the appropriate permissions on the share.

- When you create a custom Shared Folders console, you specify in advance which computer this console will manage. You cannot switch the focus to a different computer once the console has been created, though you have the option to do this if you launch the console from the command line. If you are using Shared Folders as part of Computer Management, however, you can switch the focus to a different computer using the Action menu.

- When you create a custom Shared Folders console, you also have the option of displaying all three subnodes or any single subnode you specify. In this way, for example, you can create a Shared Folders console that displays only the open sessions on the server.

- Open Files displays files opened by other users on the network but not files opened by yourself.

- A named pipe is a mechanism by which local or remote processes can exchange information. Sessions display administrative connections to remote computers as named pipes, and these sessions cannot be closed using Shared Folders (since to do so would interfere with the operation of the Shared Folders console itself).

### See Also

*Computer Management(5), shared folder(3,4)*

# System Information

Views system-configuration information for local or remote computers.

## Description

System Information provides comprehensive information for troubleshooting problems with hardware, drivers, and other software components on the connected computer. This information is either queried in real time or accessed from the registry, depending on the type of information needed. System Information displays hardware- and software-configuration information for a computer but cannot be used to make changes to this information. Use Device Manager to change hardware settings for a computer (see *Device Manager* in this chapter).

For administrators familiar with Windows NT 4.0 Server, the System Information snap-in performs functions similar to those provided by the NT administrative tool called Windows NT Diagnostics.

### Using System Information

You can access System Information by:

- Start → Programs → Administrative Tools → Computer Management → System Tools → System Information
- Start → Programs → Accessories → System Tools → System Information
- Installing the System Information snap-in into a new or existing console

The console tree typically looks like this:

```
System Information
    System Summary
    Hardware Resources
    Components
    Software Environment
    Internet Explorer 5
```

System Summary contains general information such as operating-system version, computer name, processor type, BIOS version, and memory.

Hardware Resources contains hardware information such as IRQ settings, I/O ports, DMA, and mapped memory. The Conflicts/Sharing node is useful for identifying possible device conflicts.

Components contains information about device drivers for keyboard, mouse, video, storage, network, modem, and multimedia. The Problem Devices node is useful for identifying devices with driver problems.

Software Environment contains detailed information about the software currently running on the computer, including device drivers, environment variables, print jobs pending, current network connections, tasks running (in more detail than that shown by Taskbar), and the status of installed services. It also displays the installed program groups and their shortcuts, programs in the Startup group, and OLE registration information.

Internet Explorer 5 contains information about the version, proxy configuration, cache settings, digital certificates, and security-zone settings for Internet Explorer.

### Action Menu

Select any folder in the console tree to save the information in the folder to a text file. You can then print this information as a report for documentation purposes. You should do this every time you update hardware or software on a server. You can also save system information in a proprietary format as a System Information file, which you can later open and display in the System Information console, which is considerably more readable than a text file.

 When you save system information in a text file, only the information for the selected node and its subnodes in the console tree is saved. However, when you save the information in a System Information file, it saves all of the system information regardless of which node you have selected.

Use Action → Find to search System Information for a specific keyword. You can restrict the search to the subtree under the selected node, and you can also restrict the search to categories (names of nodes).

If you are using a custom System Information console instead of Computer Management, then it is not immediately obvious how to connect to a different computer to view its system-configuration information (there is no "Connect to another computer" option under the Action menu). To accomplish this, however, simply use Action → Properties → Another computer → <computer_name>. Note that it doesn't matter which node is selected when you choose Properties.

### View Menu

Basic gives you a default set of system information for the computer.

Advanced gives you additional information, particularly about device drivers, services, and the working sets of running processes. This might be of use when troubleshooting device or application problems.

### Tools Menu

A handy feature of System Information is that you can directly run various Windows tools using the Tools menu. (These tools are scattered throughout the Control Panel, the System program group under Accessories, and various other hidden places, so it is nice to be able to access them all from one location here.) These Windows tools include:

*Disk Cleanup*
    Deletes unnecessary files from disks

*Dr. Watson*
    Configures the program error debugger, Dr. Watson

*DirectX Diagnostic Tool*
  Displays and modifies the DirectX settings for your computer

*Hardware Wizard*
  Runs the Add/Remove Hardware Wizard

*Network Connections*
  Opens the Network and Dial-up Connections window

*Backup*
  Opens the Windows 2000 Backup and Recovery Tools dialog box

*File Signature Verification Utility*
  Checks for system files that have not been properly signed

*Update Wizard Uninstall*
  Removes packages previously installed using Windows Update

*Windows Report Tool*
  Collects information about your system and creates a report that can be used by Microsoft support specialists to troubleshoot problems associated with your computer

 If you select the System Information node under System Tools in Computer Management, the View and Tools menus will magically appear. This context-sensitive appearance and disappearance of whole menus in the Microsoft Management Console can be disturbing at first, and it occurs regardless of whether you have enabled or disabled Personalized Menus using the Taskbar properties.

### Notes

- System Information is also found in the System Tools section of the Computer Management console.

- New hardware or software installed on your system may add new nodes to System Information.

### See Also

*Computer Management(5), Device Manager(5)*

## Telnet Server Administration

Configures the Windows 2000 Telnet Server service.

### Description

The Telnet service enables a Windows 2000 server to function as a Telnet server so that remote Telnet clients can run character-mode applications on the server. The Telnet service supports only two concurrent Telnet client sessions (Services for Unix supports up to 63 concurrent sessions).

*Consoles*
*T*

Telnet Server Administration is not implemented as an MMC console but as a command-line application. When you start this tool, you are prompted to select an option from the following list:

*0*  Quits the Telnet Server Administration application and closes the command-prompt window.

*1*  Lists the current users who have connected to the server using Telnet client software, giving their name, domain, computer, session ID, and log time.

*2*  Terminates the session of a user you select.

*3*  Lists registry settings you can display or modify to configure the operation of the Telnet service. These options include:

   *0*  Exit this menu and return to the main menu

   *1*  Specify 1 to allow users from trusted domains to access the server or 0 to allow only local users

   *2*  Specify 1 for Ctrl-A to represent Alt or 0 for Ctrl-A to represent Ctrl-A (VT100 emulation mode only)

   *3*  Specify a period ( . ) to configure the local domain to be the default domain (provided option 1 is set to 1), or otherwise specify the name of the default domain (must be a trusted domain)

   *4*  Specify the path and current options of the shell, which by default is:

   > *%SystemRoot%\System32\Cmd.exe /q /k*

   *5*  Specify the path of the Telnet Server Logon Script, which by default is:

   > *%SystemRoot%\System32\login.cmd*

   *6*  Specify the maximum number of failed logon attempts allowed before a connection is terminated

   *7*  Specify 0 for clear-text authentication (Telnet client user enters *username* and *password*); 1 to try NTLM authentication (Telnet client user is logged on transparently to the Telnet service using her current credentials), but if this fails use clear-text authentication; 2 to allow only NTLM authentication (restart the service for this to take effect)

   *8*  Specify the Telnet listening port (TCP port 23 by default)

*4*  Starts the Telnet service. (Startup for this service is set to Manual by default.)

*5*  Stops the Telnet service.

### Notes

- You must be logged on as a member of the Administrators group to use this tool.

- The Windows 2000 Telnet service is limited to two inbound connections.

- Modify the *%SystemRoot%\System32\Login.cmd* file using a text editor to change the banner that displays when a Telnet client connects to the Telnet server or to run specific programs when users log on to the Telnet server.

- You can also run this tool from the command line by typing `tlntadmn`.

### See Also

*telnet(7)*

## Terminal Services Client Creator

Creates a set of floppy disks to install Terminal Services Client software on a computer.

### Description

This tool is only available when Terminal Services and Terminal Services Licensing components are installed on a Windows 2000 server. The tool is implemented not as an MMC console but as a Windows dialog box that lets you create installation disks for either:

- 16-bit Terminal Services Client software (4 floppies)
- 32-bit Terminal Services Client software (2 floppies)

Terminal Services Client Creator corresponds to the administrative tool of the same name on the Windows NT Server 4.0, Terminal Server Edition platform.

For more information see *Terminal Services* in Chapter 4.

### See Also

*Terminal Services(3,4)*

---

## Terminal Services Configuration

Manages server settings and protocol-configuration settings on the terminal server.

### Description

This tool is only available when Terminal Services and Terminal Services Licensing components are installed on a Windows 2000 server. It is used to configure server and connection settings for Terminal Services.

Terminal Services Configuration corresponds to the administrative tool, Terminal Server Client Connection Configuration, on the Windows NT Server 4.0, Terminal Server Edition platform.

#### Using Terminal Services Configuration

You can access Terminal Services Configuration by:

- Start → Programs → Administrative Tools → Terminal Services Configuration
- Installing the Terminal Services Configuration snap-in into a new or existing console

The console tree typically looks like this:

```
Terminal Services Configuration
    Connections
    Server Settings
```

For background information see *Terminal Services* in Chapter 3.

*Consoles*
*T*

### Action Menu

Under the Action menu you can select the following:

*Connections*

> Select this to create a new Terminal Services connection, specifying the connection type, encryption level, authentication method, whether to enable remote control, a name for the connection, transport type, and network adapter to use. (Each connection must have either a unique connection type, transport type, or network adapter.) Connections are displayed in the Details Pane and can be renamed, disabled, or reconfigured as desired.

*Server Settings*

> Select this to display or modify server-configuration settings, including the terminal server mode, permissions compatibility, behavior of temporary folders, and other settings. Double-click on a setting in the Details Pane to modify it.

For more information on procedures, see *Terminal Services* in Chapter 4.

### View Menu

Just the standard options here, namely selecting the icon size, display method, and which columns to display in the Details Pane, as well as customizing the appearance of the MMC console window.

### See Also

*Terminal Services(3,4)*

---

## Terminal Services Licensing

Manages Terminal Services CALs for the domain or enterprise.

### Description

This tool is only available when Terminal Services and Terminal Services Licensing components are installed on a Windows 2000 server. It is used to activate a Terminal Services Licensing server and configure licensing information.

Terminal Services Licensing corresponds to the administrative tool called Terminal Server License Manager on the Windows NT Server 4.0, Terminal Server Edition platform.

### Using Terminal Services Licensing

You can access Terminal Services Licensing by:

> Start → Programs → Administrative Tools → Terminal Services Licensing

The console tree typically looks like this:

> All Servers
> > Server Name
> > > Existing Windows 2000 License
> > > Existing Windows 2000 License . . .
> > Server Name . . .

For background information see *Terminal Services* in Chapter 3.

---

### Action Menu

Under the Action menu you can select the following:

*All Servers*
    Select this to connect to a different licensing server in your enterprise.

*Server Name*
    Select this to activate a licensing server, install licenses, or open a property sheet to specify your licensing program and company information.

For more information on administering Terminal Services, see *Terminal Services* in Chapter 4.

### View Menu

Essentially just the standard options here, namely selecting the icon size, display method, and which columns to display in the Details Pane, as well as customizing the appearance of the MMC console window. You can also use this menu to refresh console information.

### See Also

*Terminal Services(3,4)*

---

## Terminal Services Manager

Manages and monitors processes and sessions on the terminal server.

### Description

This tool is only available when Terminal Services and Terminal Services Licensing components are installed on a Windows 2000 server. It is used to display information about current Terminal Services sessions and processes running on a terminal server.

Terminal Services Manager corresponds to the administrative tool called Terminal Server Administration on the Windows NT Server 4.0, Terminal Server Edition platform.

#### Using Terminal Services Manager

You can access Terminal Services Manager by:

    Start → Programs → Administrative Tools → Terminal Services Manager

The console tree typically looks like this:

```
All Listed Servers
    Domain
        Terminal Server
            RDP-Tcp (listener)
            Console
            RDP-Tcp#1
            RDP-Tcp#2 . . .
        Terminal Server . . .
    Domain . . .
```

The domains are listed in a flat order regardless of their hierarchy in the forest. For background information see *Terminal Services* in Chapter 3.

 You should run Terminal Services Manager in a Terminal Services Client session window if you want to take advantage of advanced features such as remote control.

### Action Menu

Under the Action menu you can select the following:

*All Listed Servers*
Select this to find and connect to all terminal servers in all domains.

*A domain*
Select this to find and connect to all terminal servers in the domain.

*A Terminal Server*
Select this to connect to or disconnect from and to display in the Details Pane the currently connected users, current sessions, and processes running on the server. For each user, session, or process you can variously disconnect, send a message, display the status, log off, reset, enable remote control, or terminate it (depending on the context).

For more information on procedures see *Terminal Services* in Chapter 4.

### View Menu

In addition to the standard options of selecting the icon size, display method, and which columns to display in the Details Pane, as well as customizing the appearance of the MMC console window, you can also expand or collapse the console tree in various ways and toggle on or off the display of system processes. (Toggle this off to help you determine which applications a Terminal Services Client is using.)

### Tools Menu

Selecting Options lets you configure the refresh interval for the console and for dialog boxes and several other options.

### See Also

*Terminal Services(3,4)*

---

# WINS

Manages the Windows Internet Name Service (WINS).

### Description

WINS is a service that maps NetBIOS names to IP addresses for computers on a network. It is is included with Windows 2000 Server for interoperability with legacy Windows NT 4.0 networks. WINS corresponds to the administrative tool called WINS Manager on Windows NT Server 4.0.

---

### Using WINS

You can access WINS by:

- Start → Programs → Administrative Tools → WINS

- Installing the WINS snap-in into a new or existing console

The console tree typically looks like this:

```
WINS
     Server Status
     WINS Server
          Active Registrations
          Replication Partners
```

For background information see *WINS* in Chapter 3.

### Action Menu

Under the Action menu you can select the following:

*WINS*
> Select this to add a new WINS server to the console, toggle the display of servers by name or IP address, show the DNS names of WINS servers, or validate the WINS cache on startup.

*Server Status*
> Select this to display the status of connected WINS servers in the Details Pane and to configure the refresh interval for this display.

*A WINS server*
> Select this to display server statistics, scavenge the WINS database for expired records, initiate WINS replication with another WINS server, back up the WINS database, and configure various WINS server settings.

*Active Registrations*
> Select this to display WINS database records by name or by owner, create a static mapping for non-WINS clients, import an *LMHOSTS* file, and perform other actions. Double-click on an active registration (WINS database record) in the Details Pane to display more information about it.

*Replication Partners*
> Select this to add a new WINS replication partner, configure replication settings, and force replication to occur.

For more information on administering WINS servers, see *WINS* in Chapter 4.

### View Menu

Just the standard options here, namely selecting the icon size, display method, and which columns to display in the Details Pane, as well as customizing the appearance of the MMC console window. The exception is when you select Active Registrations, as you can flip between Find By Name Results and Find By Owner Results using the View menu.

### See Also

*WINS(3,4)*

## CHAPTER 6

# *Utilities*

This chapter covers miscellaneous utilities and GUI elements of Windows 2000. In particular, the following items are covered in this chapter:

- All the Control Panel utilities, although some of them are covered only briefly since they are only of peripheral interest to administrators.
- Some of the Start menu shortcuts, particularly from the Accessories program group and its various subgroups. User-oriented utilities such as Paint and games such as Solitaire are omitted.
- All of the standard desktop elements, including the taskbar and icons such as My Computer and My Network Places.

In general, new or useful features of these items are emphasized, while familiar or tangential features are overlooked. Items are cross-referenced where appropriate to other chapters in Part II, *Alphabetical Reference*.

 Many of the utilities listed in this chapter can also be run from the command line or Run box. For example, Accessibility Options can be run by:

— Command interpreter → `control access.cpl`

— Start → Run → `control access.cpl`

## *Alphabetical Reference of Utilities*

### *Accessibility Options*

Configures the accessibility features of Windows 2000.

#### *To Launch*

- Start → Settings → Control Panel → Accessibility Options
- Command interpreter → `control access.cpl`

## Description

Accessibility Options opens a property sheet with five tabs to configure Windows 2000 for easier use by individuals with various types of physical impairments. The key features on these tabs are as follows:

*Keyboard*
> Enables StickyKeys, FilterKeys, and ToggleKeys:
>
> *StickyKeys*
>> Executes simultaneous keystrokes such as Ctrl-Alt-Del by pressing one key at a time. Once enabled, this feature is turned on or off by pressing the Shift key five times in succession.
>
> *FilterKeys*
>> Configures Windows to ignore brief or repeated keystrokes. Once enabled, this feature is turned on or off by depressing the Right Shift key for eight seconds.
>
> *ToggleKeys*
>> Causes Windows 2000 to emit a sound when the Caps Lock, Num Lock, or Scroll Lock keys are depressed. Once enabled, this feature is turned on or off by depressing the Num Lock key for five seconds.

*Sound*
> Enables SoundSentry and ShowSounds. These features are:
>
> *SoundSentry*
>> Causes Windows 2000 to flash the desktop, active window, or active caption bar when a system sound is generated—for example, to indicate an operating-system warning.
>
> *ShowSounds*
>> Causes applications designed for Windows 2000 to display captions for sounds they generate.

*Display*
> Enables High Contrast, which switches the color scheme to white on black or some other high-contrast color scheme. Once enabled, this feature is turned on or off by pressing Left Alt–Left Shift–Print Screen.

*Mouse*
> Enables MouseKeys, which uses the keyboard to perform mouse functions. Once enabled, this feature is turned off or on by pressing Left Alt–Left Shift–Num Lock or by pressing only Num Lock.

*General*
> Configures accessibility options to turn off automatically after not being used for a certain number of minutes, to indicate by a sound or warning message when an accessibility feature is turned on or off, to apply the configured settings for the logged-on user only or for all new users who log on, and to configure SerialKey settings for an alternative input device to be used instead of the keyboard and mouse.

*Utilities*
*A*

### Notes

- This Control Panel utility is not present unless the Accessibility Wizard component of Windows 2000 has been installed.

- An alternate way of configuring accessibility options is by using the Accessibility Wizard:

  Start → Programs → Accessories → Accessibility → Accessibility Wizard

- There are additional accessibility features that are not enabled or configured using Accessibility Options in the Control Panel. These include:

  Magnifier
  Narrator
  On-Screen Keyboard
  Utility Manager

For more information see the article on each utility in this chapter.

### See Also

*Magnifier(6), Narrator(6), On-Screen Keyboard(6), Utility Manager(6)*

---

## Accessibility Wizard

Walks you through the process of configuring accessibility options on your computer.

### To Launch

- Start → Programs → Accessories → Accessibility → Accessibility Wizard
- Command interpreter → `accwiz.exe`

### See Also

*Accessibility Options(6)*

---

## Add/Remove Hardware

Adds or removes hardware devices.

### To Launch

- Start → Settings → Control Panel → Add/Remove Hardware
- Command interpreter → `control hdwwiz.cpl`
- Right-click on My Computer → Properties → Hardware → Hardware Wizard

### Description

Add/Remove Hardware opens a wizard that walks you through the process of installing new hardware devices or removing existing ones. Most of the time, this is not necessary with Windows 2000 as Plug and Play devices are usually detected and installed automatically without the need to reboot the system. Should the system require a reboot, Found New Hardware starts and completes the installation.

Add/Remove Hardware is typically used for installing legacy (non–Plug and Play) devices, in which case you skip the Plug and Play option and manually specify the type and model of the device from a list displayed by the wizard.

You can also run Add/Remove Hardware to unplug or eject a device such as a removable drive. If you need to do this frequently with a device, there is an option in the wizard to place an icon in the system tray, which can be used for this purpose.

### Notes

- You may need to be logged on as an Administrator to install a Plug and Play device if user interaction is required during the installation process. You must be logged on as an Administrator to use Add/Remove Hardware to install a legacy (non–Plug and Play) device.

- You may be asked to supply the disk or CD-ROM containing the device drivers for the device if Windows 2000 does not have them.

- To update a device driver for a device, use Device Manager, which is in the System Tools folder in Computer Management. See *Device Manager* in Chapter 5, *Consoles*, for more information.

- Group Policy can prevent the running of this wizard on a computer belonging to a domain.

- If you encounter errors when installing a Plug and Play device, check Event Viewer for more information on Plug and Play events.

- Plug and Play devices can also be detected and installed by using Action → Scan for Hardware Changes in Device Manager.

- Plug and Play devices are typically uninstalled automatically when you disconnect them from the computer.

- Legacy (non–Plug and Play) devices can by uninstalled using Device Manager. This does not delete the drivers for the device from the hard disk.

- Make sure your hardware is on the Hardware Compatibility List (HCL) before attempting to install it. See *Hcl.txt* in the Support folder on your Windows 2000 CD.

- If you install a legacy device, you also manually specify the resource settings (IRQ, I/O, and so on) for the device. This means that if a resource conflict arises afterwards that involves the device, Windows 2000 will not be able to reconfigure the settings that you configured manually. This is a good reason for only using Plug and Play hardware with Windows 2000.

### See Also

*Device Manager(5)*, *hardware(3,4)*

# Add/Remove Programs

Installs or uninstalls applications.

## To Launch

- Start → Settings → Control Panel → Add/Remove Programs
- Command interpreter → `control appwiz.cpl`

## Description

Add/Remove Programs opens a dialog box with the following options:

### Change or Remove Programs

Displays the currently installed programs and lets you update or uninstall them. You can sort this list of installed programs by name, size, frequency of use, or date last used.

### Add New Programs

Installs a new program from a floppy or CD, or using the Windows Update web site, which is a part of Microsoft's web site that contains new Windows features, system updates, and device drivers. If you have published software to Active Directory using Group Policy, these applications will appear here as programs you can install over the network. See *Group Policy* in Chapter 3, *Concepts*, and *Active Directory* in Chapter 4, *Tasks*, for more information.

### Add/Remove Windows Components

Installs optional components of Windows 2000, such as the Indexing Service.

## Notes

- Many programs have their own installation utility—if so, use this utility instead of Add/Remove Programs to install, uninstall, or add/remove components of the program.

- Programs published using Group Policy may be grouped into different categories. You may need to browse these categories in order to select the right one.

- You must be logged on as an Administrator to install or remove optional Windows components.

- When you run Add/Remove Programs within a Terminal Services session as Administrator, it installs programs files into the *%SystemRoot%* path instead of the *%homepath%* path for the logged-on user. This is done so that any user who logs on may use the installed program.

## See Also

*Active Directory(4)*, *Group Policy(3)*, *Windows Installer(4)*

# Administrative Tools

Launches different Windows 2000 administrative tools.

## To Launch

Start → Settings → Control Panel → Administrative Tools

### Description

The shortcuts in this folder are essentially the same as those available through Start → Programs → Administrative Tools. The only difference is that any custom tools you create (by adding snap-ins to an MMC console) are displayed through the Start menu but not in the Control Panel folder.

If you hate the Start menu, open Administrative Tools in the Control Panel, select List view from the toolbar, and size and relocate the window so that the tools are easily available from the desktop.

### Notes

- On Windows 2000 Professional computers this folder contains only the following limited set of preconfigured MMC consoles:

  Component Services
  Computer Management
  Data Sources (ODBC)
  Event Viewer
  Local Security Policy
  Performance
  Services
  Telnet Server Administrator

  By default, these tools are not displayed from the Start menu, but this can be changed by using the Advanced settings of the Taskbar Properties (see *Taskbar* in this chapter).

- You can install a full set of tools for administering Windows 2000 Server computers on a Windows 2000 Professional workstation. To do this, insert the Windows 2000 Server CD, open the *I386* folder, double-click on *Adminpak.msi*, and follow the prompts. This automatically adds the Administrative Tools program group to Programs in the Start menu, and it also adds the new tools to the Administrative Tools folder in the Control Panel. You can remove the tools you added using Add/Remove Programs in the Control Panel.

### See Also

The various administrative tools are covered individually in Chapter 5.

---

## Backup

Backs up and restores system files and datafiles.

### To Launch

- Start → Programs → Accessories → System → Backup
- Windows Explorer or My Computer → right-click on a drive → Properties → Tools → Backup
- Computer Management → Storage → Disk Management → right-click on a drive → Properties → Tools → Backup
- Command interpreter → `ntbackup.exe`

---

### Description

Backup opens a property sheet with four tabs. The key settings here are:

*Welcome*

> Performs or schedules a backup or restore using step-by-step wizards and creates a new Emergency Repair Disk (ERD). Up-to-date backups and ERDs are an essential part of a good disaster-recovery plan (see *disaster recovery* in Chapter 3).

*Backup*

> Manually configures a backup job by selecting volumes, folders, or files to back up, a backup destination, and a backup medium. When you select Start Backup, you are given the option of scheduling the job instead of performing it immediately and configuring other job settings. See *backup and restore* in Chapter 4 for more information on performing backups.

*Restore*

> Restores a backup job to its original location or an alternate location. See *backup and restore* in Chapter 4 for more information on performing restores.

*Schedule Jobs*

> Displays scheduled backup jobs and creates a new job by running the Backup Wizard discussed earlier. Click on a job icon (not just on the data square where the icon resides but on the icon itself) to display or modify the schedule details for the job or delete the job entirely.

There are also some menu options that are important to be aware of:

*Job*

> Creates a new job, starts a job, and saves or loads selection scripts. A selection script is a description of which volumes, folders, and files should be backed up.

*Tools*

> In addition to running the Backup and Restore Wizards and creating an ERD, lets you catalog a backup job medium (creates an on-disk catalog), delete a catalog (use if you have a damaged or lost tape and you want to delete it from the on-disk catalog), view or print a backup job report, and configure a number of options for how the tool operates. These options include the following:
>
> — The default backup type (normal, incremental, and so on)
>
> — The verbosity of the backup log (detailed, summary, or none)
>
> — When and whether to overwrite existing files during a restore
>
> — Which special files should always be excluded from backup jobs
>
> — Whether to verify backups, use media catalogs, backup mounted drives, and show alerts under various conditions

## Notes

Scheduled backup jobs also appear in the Scheduled Tasks folder in the Control Panel and can be reconfigured there.

### See Also

*backup and restore(4), disaster recovery(3), Emergency Repair Disk (ERD)(4), Scheduled Tasks(6)*

---

# Command Interpreter

Performs text-based command-line functions.

### To Launch

- Start → Programs → Accessories → Command Prompt
- Command interpreter → cmd
- Command interpreter → start cmd (opens a new window)

### Description

The Windows 2000 command-line interpreter, *cmd.exe*, is similar to that of Windows NT but has been enhanced with additional features. Windows 2000 also enhances the usefulness of the interpreter with new services and command-line utilities. For example:

- Windows 2000 includes all the commands available in Windows NT, plus some important new ones:

  — The powerful netsh (Netshell) command that can be used for administering networking components on local or remote computers from the command line. This is accomplished through the use of Helper DLLs, which extend the functionality of netsh for specific networking services such as DHCP, WINS, and Routing and Remote Access.

  — Sets of commands for administering Certificate Services, Cluster Service, Removable Storage, Site Server ILS Service, and Terminal Services from the command line.

- Both Windows 2000 Server and Professional include a Telnet Server service, which is a real boon to remote administration. Using the telnet command on one computer, you can log on to a remote computer and remotely execute any text-based command in the Windows 2000 repertoire.

- The Windows 2000 command line includes an enhanced autocompletion feature that is turned on by typing cmd /f:on at a command prompt. Instead of typing the complete names of files and folders in commands, you can just enter the first letter or two of the file or folder name and press Ctrl-D to complete the name.

- The secondary logon feature (runas command) lets you run commands from a command-interpreter window using one set of credentials while logged on to the computer using a different set of credentials. For example, you can use runas to run commands as an Administrator while logged on to the computer as an ordinary user.

*Utilities
C*

The rest of this article deals with configuring the command-interpreter window once it is open. See *cmd* in Chapter 7, *Commands*, for options to open a new instance of the command prompt.

### Configuring the Command Interpreter

To configure the properties of a command-interpreter window, right-click on the title bar of the command-interpreter window, and select Properties. This opens a property sheet with four tabs. The key settings here are:

*Options*
Switches the command interpreter between full screen and a window (you can switch between them using Alt-Enter), enables QuickEdit (which lets you cut and paste using a mouse instead of the tedious Edit menu), enables Insert mode (which lets you insert text at the present cursor position instead of overwriting previous text there), and configures the number of commands that can be remembered in the command-history buffer (you access previously typed commands by using the Up and Down Arrow keys).

*Font*
Specifies a font size and name for use in the command-interpreter window.

*Layout*
Lets you specify the window and buffer size. Window size refers to the width in characters and height in lines of the command-interpreter window. Buffer size refers to the virtual size of the window when you use the horizontal and vertical scroll bars. It's a nice touch that the default buffer size is now 300 lines instead of the 25 lines it was in Windows NT.

*Colors*
Lets you specify colors for the screen text and background and for popup text and background.

### Notes

- When you change the properties of a command-interpreter window and click OK, a dialog box appears asking you whether you want to apply the properties to the current command-interpreter window only (in which case the settings vanish when you close this window) or to future windows of the same title or started from the same shortcut (in which case the changes you made are persistent). If you want your settings to be persistent, you can avoid this annoyance by selecting Defaults instead of Properties when you right-click on the title bar of the command-interpreter window.

- You can cause the command-history buffer to discard duplicates, but I find this tends to get in the way of my thinking. (I like to remember the way things happened and expect history not to be rewritten.)

### See Also

*cmd(7)*, *netsh(7)*, *runas(7)*

# Control Panel

Configures and customizes various aspects of the operating system and your computer's hardware.

## To Launch

- Start → Settings → Control Panel
- Command interpreter → `control`

## Description

The Windows 2000 Control Panel is similar to that of earlier versions of Windows with a few tools renamed or modified. Table 6-1 shows the various Control Panel utilities on Windows 2000 Professional and Server platforms, with a note for those that are only present when optional components or services are installed. For more information on any Control Panel utility, see its corresponding article in this chapter.

*Table 6-1: Control Panel Utilities on Windows 2000 Server/Professional*

| Utility | Server? | Professional? | Note |
|---|:---:|:---:|---|
| Accessibility Options | ✓ | ✓ | Accessibility Wizard must be installed |
| Add/Remove Hardware | ✓ | ✓ | |
| Add/Remove Programs | ✓ | ✓ | |
| Administrative Tools | ✓ | ✓ | |
| CSNW | | ✓ | Client Services for NetWare must be installed |
| Date/Time | ✓ | ✓ | |
| Display | ✓ | ✓ | |
| Fax | ✓ | | Fax Service must be enabled |
| Folder Options | ✓ | ✓ | |
| Fonts | ✓ | ✓ | |
| Game Controllers | ✓ | ✓ | |
| GSNW | ✓ | | Gateway (and Client) Services for NetWare must be installed |
| Internet Options | ✓ | ✓ | |
| Keyboard | ✓ | ✓ | |
| Licensing | ✓ | ✓ | |
| Mouse | ✓ | ✓ | |
| Network and Dial-up Connections | ✓ | ✓ | |
| Phone and Modem Options | | ✓ | |
| Power Options | ✓ | ✓ | |
| Printers | ✓ | ✓ | |
| Regional Options | ✓ | ✓ | |
| Scanners and Cameras | ✓ | ✓ | |
| Scheduled Tasks | ✓ | ✓ | |

*Utilities*
*C*

*Table 6-1: Control Panel Utilities on Windows 2000 Server/Professional (continued)*

| Utility | Server? | Professional? | Note |
|---|---|---|---|
| Sounds and Multimedia | ✓ | ✓ | |
| System | ✓ | ✓ | |
| Users and Groups | | ✓ | |
| Wireless Link | ✓ | ✓ | An Infrared Data Association (IrDA) device must be installed |

### Notes

Installing some third-party programs may add additional vendor-specific utilities to the Control Panel.

### See Also

See the article for each Control Panel utility in this chapter.

## CSNW

Configures Client Service for NetWare.

### To Launch

- Start → Settings → Control Panel → CSNW
- Command interpreter → `control nwc.cpl`

### Description

CSNW is present only on Windows 2000 Professional computers on which the additional networking component, Client Service for NetWare, has been installed (see *Network and Dial-up Connections* in this chapter). CSNW allows Windows computers to directly access file and print resources on a Novell NetWare 2.x, 3.x, or 4.x server.

CSNW opens as a dialog box that allows you to configure a preferred NetWare server (if the NetWare server is using bindery security), the default tree and context for the connection (if the NetWare server is running NDS), and various logon script and print options.

### See Also

*GSNW(6), Network and Dial-up Connections(6), NWLink(3)*

## Date/Time

Configures the internal clock on the local machine.

### To Launch

- Start → Settings → Control Panel → Date/Time
- Right-click on taskbar → Adjust Date/Time
- Command interpreter → `control timedate.cpl`

## Description

There are two tabs on this property sheet:

*Date&Time*
> Specifies the current date and time for the internal system clock on the local machine

*Time Zone*
> Chooses a time zone for the machine and specifies whether to adjust the clock for daylight-savings time when appropriate

Date/Time is really only necessary in a workgroup scenario (see "Notes" later in this article).

## Notes

- There are several ways to solve the problem of time synchronization for computers in a domain:

  — Windows 2000 member servers and client computers automatically synchronize themselves with Windows 2000 domain controllers, which automatically synchronize themselves with the PDC emulator, which is typically the first domain controller installed in the forest root domain. This PDC emulator should itself be synchronized to an external time server (such as a Windows 2000 member server or clocking device) using the net time command. Otherwise, the System log will show repeated W32Time error events telling you to do so.

  — If you also have downlevel (Windows NT) computers, use the net time command in a logon script on your domain controllers to synchronize these downlevel computers with your Windows 2000 domain controllers.

- Since Windows 2000 domain controllers use sequence numbers in order to identify directory-replication messages instead of time stamps, having the clocks of your domain controllers accurately synchronized is not critical. The exception is if changes were made to an object's attributes on two domain controllers simultaneously, which does not normally occur unless administrators specifically connect to domain controllers other than the default to make these changes. In this case the timestamp becomes the deciding factor in resolving conflicts. On the other hand, in a multidomain scenario where Kerberos authentication is used to provide access to resources across domain boundaries, Kerberos tickets are time stamped, which means that clock synchronization is important.

## See Also

*net time(7)*

## Disk Cleanup

Deletes unnecessary files from your disks.

### To Launch

- Start → Programs → Accessories → System → Disk Cleanup
- Windows Explorer or My Computer → right-click on a drive → Properties → General → Disk Cleanup
- Computer Management → Storage → Disk Management → right-click on a drive → Properties → General → Disk Cleanup
- Command interpreter → `cleanmgr.exe`

### Description

If you run Disk Cleanup using the first method listed earlier, you must first specify the drive (partition, volume, or logical drive) you want to clean up. Disk Cleanup will then calculate how much free space can be recovered from the drive (if the drive is large and has many files, this could take a few minutes).

At this point Disk Cleanup opens as a property sheet with two tabs. The key settings here are:

*Disk Cleanup*
> Specifies one or more cleanup operations to perform on your disk. These operations include deleting downloaded program files such as Java applets and ActiveX controls, deleting temporary Internet files (cached web pages and images), deleting other temporary files such as *\*.tmp* files or files stored in a *\temp* folder, emptying the Recycle Bin, and compressing old files that you have not accessed for some specified time interval (the default is 50 days). For each operation, the space you can gain by running Disk Cleanup is displayed. You can also view the names of files before you delete them.

*More Options*
> Removes any optional Windows components or installed programs that you deem unnecessary. This essentially opens Add/Remove Programs and lets you decide what you want to remove.

### See Also

*Add/Remove Programs(6), disks(3)*

## Disk Defragmenter

Defragments drives on your computer.

### To Launch

- Start → Programs → Accessories → System → Disk Defragmenter
- Windows Explorer or My Computer → right-click on a drive → Properties → Tools → Defragment Now

- Computer Management → Storage → Disk Management → right-click on a drive → Properties → Tools → Defragment Now
- Command interpreter → dfrg.msc

### See Also

*Disk Defragmenter(5)*

---

## Display

Configures the video display.

### To Launch

- Start → Settings → Control Panel → Display
- Right-click on desktop → Properties
- Command interpreter → control desk.cpl

### Description

Display opens a property sheet that typically has six tabs, unless the driver for your video card has added additional tabs or removed/renamed existing ones. The key features on the standard tabs are:

*Background*
Selects a bitmap or other image file as your screen background. If you have Active Desktop enabled, you can also choose an HTML file or define a pattern.

*Screen Saver*
Enables a screensaver and configures power settings (see *Power Options* in this chapter).

*Appearance*
Chooses a scheme for displaying colors and fonts on your desktop. You can also create your own custom schemes.

*Web*
Enables Active Desktop so you can display web content directly on the desktop. Once enabled, you can add or remove web content from your Active Desktop, make the content available when your Internet connection is offline, download fresh content on a scheduled basis or when you choose Synchronize from the Tools menu of My Computer, specify the number of links deep the content should be downloaded, set a limit to how much disk space will be used for the content, specify which kinds of web content to download, and configure an email address to notify when content changes.

---

 Active Desktop is a powerful feature but is rarely enabled in an enterprise environment. It also seems to be waning in popularity, as evidenced by the paucity of sample items to download in Microsoft's Active Desktop Gallery site.

---

*Effects*

Enables various desktop visual effects. Many of these effects are annoying and waste processor power. You can also change icons for standard items on your desktop.

*Settings*

Changes the screen resolution and color depth on the fly, usually without rebooting. There are additional settings here if you have multiple monitors configured (see the sidebar "Multiple-Monitor Support" in this article). Select Advanced to open a second property sheet with the following tabs:

*General*

Selects the font size for your display and specifies whether Windows 2000 should be restarted after changes are made to the display settings (some older video cards may require this).

*Adapter*

Displays the drivers and resources for your video adapter (same effect as using Device Manager in Computer Management) and displays all the video scan modes supported by the adapter.

*Monitor*

Displays the drivers and resources for your monitor (same effect as using Device Manager in Computer Management) and displays all the refresh frequencies supported by the monitor.

*Troubleshooting*

Manages the hardware acceleration feature of your video adapter. Use Full unless you are experiencing graphics problems with certain applications.

*Color Management*

Configures the default color profile for your monitor. Click Add for a list of color profiles you can choose from.

### Notes

- You can also enable Active Desktop by using the General tab of Folder Options. See *Folder Options* in this chapter for more information.

- Be careful not to select a video refresh frequency/screen resolution combination that your monitor cannot support, as you may damage your monitor if you do so. When in doubt, select a lower refresh setting.

### See Also

*Folder Options(6), Power Options(6)*

---

## Fax

Configures fax settings for the Fax Service.

### To Launch

- Start → Settings → Control Panel → Fax
- Command interpreter → `control fax.cpl`

---

## *Multiple-Monitor Support*

By installing additional video adapters, you can connect up to 10 monitors to a single Windows 2000 computer, each displaying a different portion of a larger virtual desktop. How you do this may depend on the types of display adapters you are using (PCI and AGP cards are supported) and the BIOS. One adapter is chosen as the primary display, and it cannot be disabled (which explains why multiple-monitor support may not function on laptops in which the docking station contains its own display adapter that disables the laptop's display when it is docked).

Usually the displays are ordered by PCI slot. You simply turn off your computer, install another PCI or AGP video card, and turn on the computer. Windows 2000 detects the new card and installs drivers for it. At this point, you use the Settings tab in the Control Panel's Display utility to extend the Windows desktop onto your new monitor, using the icon on this tab for the new monitor. Then select Identify on this tab to show the identification number for each monitor icon displayed there. You can drag the monitor icons to arrange them as desired. You will then be able to drag GUI objects from one monitor to another effortlessly.

A few more notes about multiple-monitor support:

- The logon box is always displayed on the primary monitor.

- When you open an application, it displays first in the primary monitor.

- Each monitor's display options can be configured separately with regard to color depth and screen resolution.

### Description

The Windows 2000 Fax Service can send and receive faxes using a fax modem. When you install a fax modem, Windows 2000 detects the modem's capabilities, installs the Fax Service, and creates a Fax printer in the Printers folder. Simply print to this printer from an application such as Word to send a fax, or use the Fax utility in the Accessories program group.

You use this Control Panel utility to:

- Specify user information for faxes you send

- Create and manage your personal cover pages

- Configure notifications for sent or received faxes

- Enable manual answer for single-line service

Use the Advanced Options tab to add a new Fax printer or to open Fax Service Management, an MMC console that can be used to:

- Enable a computer to receive a fax (by default, when the Fax Service is enabled, your machine is configured to send a fax but not to receive a fax)

- Configure permissions for using a fax device

- Configure number of rings for receiving and number of retries for sending
- Specify storage locations for sent and received faxes

**Notes**

Fax is available on Windows 2000 Server computers only, not Windows 2000 Professional.

---

## Folder Options

Lets you configure how folders are displayed, including the desktop.

### To Launch

- Start → Settings → Control Panel → Folder Options
- Any open folder on the desktop → Tools → Folder Options

### Description

Folder Options opens a property sheet with four tabs that let you configure different aspects of how folders behave when you browse through them on the desktop. The folders that can be affected by this control include:

Windows Explorer
My Computer
My Network Places
My Documents
Control Panel

Folder Options can also be used to enable or disable Active Desktop, a feature of Windows 2000 that lets you place web content directly on the desktop. The key features on these tabs are as follows:

*General*

Includes four important settings on this tab:

*Active Desktop*

Enables or disables Active Desktop on your computer. Activating it requires additional processor power and essentially makes your desktop a web page to which other web content can be added. The default is to use the classic desktop.

*Web View*

Specifies whether your folders will be displayed as web pages. The default is to enable web content in folders. You may want to disable Web View to optimize use of your desktop real estate.

*Browse Folders*

Specifies whether a new window will be opened when you try to open a folder icon by double-clicking on it. The default is to open new folders in the existing window where the folder icon is displayed.

*Click items as follows*

Specifies whether you must single- or double-click on icons to open them. The default is double-click, but if we all switched to single-click, the incidence of carpal tunnel syndrome might drop precipitously.

---

*View*

Configures various options for how files and folders are displayed, such as whether to display hidden folders, file extensions, and so on.

*File Types*

Displays file extensions for registered file types. When programs are installed, new file associations may be created and registered automatically, and they will be displayed here.

*Offline Files*

Enables offline files on your computer. See *offline files* in Chapter 3 for more information.

## Notes

- Settings configured here affect all desktop folders.

- You can also enable Active Desktop by:

    Right-click on desktop → Active Desktop → Show Web Content

- Adding web content to Active Desktop is easy:

    Right-click on desktop → Active Desktop → New Desktop Item

    This opens a dialog box that lets you enter the URL or browse for an HTML document or picture to display on your desktop. Visit Gallery takes you to Microsoft's web site where you can download additional content for your desktop.

- To change which web content items are displayed on your Active Desktop, do the following:

    Right-click on desktop → Active Desktop → Customize My Desktop

    This opens the Display utility from Control Panel with focus on the web tab of this utility (see *Display* in this chapter).

## See Also

*Display(6), offline files(3), Windows Explorer(6)*

---

# Fonts

Displays and manages the fonts on your computer.

## To Launch

Start → Settings → Control Panel → Fonts

## Description

Fonts opens a folder containing the installed fonts on your system. Use the File menu to install new fonts, double-click on a font to see what it looks like or print out a sample, and use the View menu to group fonts according to similarity.

### Notes

- When you are installing fonts from a mapped network drive, if you deselect the option "Copy fonts to Fonts folder," then you can add fonts to your system without having them occupy disk space on your local drive.

- You can also drag a font into the Fonts window to install it.

## Game Controllers

Adds and manages joysticks and game pads.

### To Launch

- Start → Settings → Control Panel → Game Controllers
- Command interpreter → `control joy.cpl`

### Description

Since this book is on Windows 2000 administration and since most companies frown on employees playing games, I'll skip this one!

## GSNW

Configures Gateway (and Client) Services for NetWare.

### To Launch

- Start → Settings → Control Panel → GSNW
- Command interpreter → `control nwc.cpl`

### Description

GSWN is present only on Windows 2000 Server computers on which the additional networking component, Gateway (and Client) Services for NetWare, has been installed (see *Network and Dial-up Connections* in this chapter). GSNW allows Windows 2000 computers to access file and print resources on a Novell NetWare 2.x, 3.x, or 4.x server by using the GSNW server as a gateway. In this way, the Windows computers do not need NetWare client software to be installed on them. GSNW should be viewed as a temporary solution for occasional access to NetWare resources, however.

GSNW opens as a dialog box that allows you to configure a preferred NetWare server (if the NetWare server is using bindery security), the default tree and context for the connection (if the NetWare server is running NDS), and various logon scripts and print options. Select Gateway to open a second dialog box to enable the gateway, to specify a gateway account that has suitable access rights on the NetWare server, and also to create shares for selected NetWare volumes.

### See Also

*CSNW(6), Network and Dial-up Connections(6), NWLink(3)*

## HyperTerminal

Provides terminal access to remote computers.

### To Launch

- Start → Programs → Accessories → Communications → HyperTerminal
- Command interpreter → `hypertrm.exe`

### Description

HyperTerminal uses a modem to connect to remote computers that support terminal access. Using terminal programs such as HyperTerminal used to be a popular way of transferring files until the Internet took over everything. Hyper-Terminal is still sometimes useful to administrators because it can be used for connecting to older routers to manage settings through a command-line interface. To use HyperTerminal this way, connect a straight-through serial cable from one of your computer's COM ports to a serial port on the router. Then create a new HyperTerminal connection for the COM port, and configure the port settings (usually 8N1).

 Telnet is an alternative to HyperTerminal for configuring routers, but only if the router has an IP address preconfigured at the factory. Most modern routers now support web-based administration, which is much easier to learn and use.

### See Also

*telnet(7)*

## Internet Connection Wizard

Helps you configure your Internet connection.

### To Launch

- Start → Programs → Accessories → Communications → Internet Connection Wizard
- Command interpreter → `icwconn1.exe`

### Description

The first time you start Internet Explorer or Outlook Express on your computer, the Internet Connection Wizard automatically runs. If you select any option other than "I want to set up my Internet connection manually," the wizard uses your modem to dial a number that connects you with a web site Microsoft has set up to help you find a provider in your area. (I tried this for my area and drew a blank, even through there are dozens of ISPs in my town.)

To configure a manual connection, the wizard helps you to either:

- Create a dial-up connection using a modem. You need to know your ISP's dial-in phone number and the username and password your provider has assigned you. You can optionally set up your email account as well if you know the IP addresses or DNS names of your provider's SMTP and POP/IMAP servers. Once you are finished, your new connection can be found in Network and Dial-up Connections if you need to reconfigure it.

- Connect through your LAN. Select this option if you are on a corporate network with a dedicated leased-line connection to your ISP, such as a T1 line. In this case you may have to configure proxy server settings if the wizard can't detect your proxy server (if your network has one).

### See Also

*Network and Dial-up Connections(6)*

---

## Internet Explorer

Browses any resource on the local computer, the network, or the Internet.

### To Launch

- Start → Programs → Internet Explorer
- Desktop → Internet Explorer
- Taskbar → Internet Explorer
- Start → Run → enter URL → OK
- My Computer → Address bar → enter URL
- My Network Places → Address bar → enter URL
- Windows Explorer → Address bar → enter URL
- Command interpreter → start iexplore
- Command interpreter → start *URL* (starts Internet Explorer and accesses the file specified by *URL*)

### Description

Microsoft is right when they claim that Internet Explorer (IE) is more than just a web browser: it really appears to function as an integrated part of the operating system. Not only can you use it to browse the Web by entering a URL into the File → Open box or Address bar, but you can also browse your local computer's filesystem by entering a local path (such as *C:\Winnt*) or connect to shared resources on the network by entering a UNC path (such as *\\giggles\stuff*). In fact, when you enter a local or UNC path, the menu options and toolbar buttons switch to those for My Computer or My Network Places. In fact, all four browsing tools (Internet Explorer, Windows Explorer, My Computer, and My Network Places) are really different appearances of the same program, and their general properties are covered in the article *Windows Explorer* in this chapter. This present article focuses on the differences between IE and the other personalities of this schizophrenic program.

### Menu Options

While the menu options for My Computer are context sensitive, those for IE are fixed, which perhaps indicates that IE is not as fully integrated into the operating system as Microsoft claims it to be. In fact, a simple experiment proves that this is so. With Internet Information Services installed, open the properties of the Default Web Site, and enable directory browsing on the Home Directory tab while disabling default documents on the Documents tab. Now use IE to open the URL *http://localhost*, and you will see a listing of the files contained in the *C:\Inetpub\ wwwroot* folder on your machine. What's significant is that this listing is quite different from what you would get if you typed *C:\Inetpub\wwwroot* into the Address bar of My Computer or Windows Explorer. This indicates the fundamental difference between IE and the other three tools, which is confirmed by the fact that if you type `start iexplore` at the command line, you open IE, while if you type `start explorer`, you open Windows Explorer. So they really are two different programs, but the amazing thing is that to the user, the transition between browsing resources on the local computer and on the Internet can seem absolutely seamless.

Since this book is not about IE, however, I won't delve any deeper into the various menu and toolbar options here.

### Notes

To open the Internet property sheet for configuring IE without opening IE itself:

- Right-click on IE icon on desktop → Properties
- Start → Run → `control inetcpl.cpl`

### See Also

*My Computer(6), My Network Places(6), Synchronize(6), Windows Explorer(6)*

---

## Keyboard

Customizes the behavior of your keyboard.

### To Launch

- Start → Settings → Control Panel → Keyboard
- Command interpreter → `control main.cpl keyboard`

### Description

Keyboard is a property sheet that has three tabs. The key settings are:

*Speed*
> Modifies the repeat rate and delays and the cursor blink rate.

*Input Locales*
> Adds new keyboard layouts for different languages. If you enable the keyboard-layout indicator in the system tray, you can easily switch between different layouts when you need to type in different languages. You can also specify a hot key to switch between locales or to a specific locale.

*Utilities
K–L*

*Hardware*
> Displays the drivers and resources for your keyboard (same effect as using Device Manager in Computer Management).

### Notes

If you right-click on the keyboard-layout indicator in the system tray and select Properties, the Regional Options utility from the Control Panel opens.

### See Also

*Device Manager(5)*

---

## Licensing

Manages licensing locally on a server.

### To Launch

- Start → Settings → Control Panel → Licensing
- Command interpreter → `control liccpa.cpl`

### Description

Licensing opens a dialog box to:

- Add or remove per-server client-access licenses (CALs) on the local server.
- Change the licensing mode from per server to per seat (a one-time, one-way operation).
- Configure the interval at which the local server replicates its licensing information to the site-license server.

### Notes

- If you plan to use Windows 2000 Server on a standalone non-networked computer, you can set the number of concurrent per-server licenses to zero.
- Once a server is changed to per-seat mode, you add CALs using the Licensing dialog box (see *Licensing* in Chapter 5).
- Licenses removed from a server can be allocated to a different server.

### See Also

*Licensing(5)*

---

## Magnifier

A cool tool for visually impaired individuals.

### To Launch

- Start → Programs → Accessories → Accessibility → Magnifier
- Command interpreter → `magnify.exe`

---

## Description

Magnifier displays a magnified version of a specified desktop region in a section at the top of the screen. You can drag the border of the magnified section so it covers up to half the screen, drag the section to the bottom or side of the screen, or have it float for different positioning.

When you start Magnifier, you are prompted to specify the following settings in a dialog box:

- The magnification level to use. (The default is 2X, and this is probably sufficient in most cases.)

- What portion of the desktop Magnifier should display. You can choose to track the mouse cursor, to track the keyboard focus (as in currently selected buttons and gadgets), or to follow text editing in an application such as WordPad. (By default, all three options are selected.)

- Whether the magnified section should use the default desktop colors or inverted colors (very cool). If you select High Contrast Mode, then the entire screen is placed in that mode, but you can also invert the colors so that the magnified section looks different from the rest of the desktop.

- The Start Minimized option. If you select Start Minimized, the Settings dialog box initially runs out of the way on the taskbar.

## Notes

Unfortunately, you cannot use nonintegral magnification factors such as 1.5X.

## See Also

*Accessibility Options(6), Narrator(6), On-Screen Keyboard(6), Utility Manager(6)*

---

# Message Queuing

Configures aspects of the Message Queuing service.

## To Launch

- Start → Settings → Control Panel → Message Queuing
- Command interpreter → `control msmq.cpl`

## Description

The Message Queuing service provides a communications infrastructure for asynchronous data transfer between applications. The tabs on this property sheet let you specify a storage location for Message Queuing files and logs and let you register digital certificates for the service in Active Directory. There is nothing of interest here unless you are a developer working with Message Queuing to build distributed applications.

## Notes

This Control Panel utility is not present unless the Message Queuing Service component of Windows 2000 has been installed.

## *Mouse*

Customizes the behavior of the mouse.

### *To Launch*

* Start → Settings → Control Panel → Mouse
* Command interpreter → `control main.cpl`

### *Description*

Mouse has four tabs on its property sheet. The key settings are:

*Buttons*
> Switches between right- and left-handed operation, specifies whether to use single- or double-click to open items (see *Folder Options* in this chapter for another way of configuring this), and configures the double-click speed.

*Pointers*
> Customizes your mouse pointer. Use a large pointer with a shadow to enhance visibility on laptops.

*Motion*
> Customizes the pointer speed and acceleration. You can also cause the mouse to snap to the default button in dialog boxes if desired.

*Hardware*
> Displays the drivers and resources for your mouse (same effect as using Device Manager in Computer Management). You can also configure mouse movement to bring the computer out of standby mode.

### *See Also*

*Folder Options(6)*

---

## *My Computer*

Browses any resource on the local computer, network, or Internet.

### *To Launch*

* Desktop → My Computer
* My Network Places → click the My Computer link (web content must first be enabled using Folder Options)
* Windows Explorer → select My Computer in left pane → click Folders button on toolbar
* Internet Explorer → type C: in Address bar → press Enter → click Up button on toolbar
* Command interpreter → `start c:` → press Enter → click Up button on toolbar
* Command interpreter → `explorer` → press Enter → click Up button on toolbar

### Description

My Computer is an all-in-one browsing tool that can be used to browse the file-system of the local computer, shared folders and printers on the network, objects in Active Directory, and web content on the Internet. Really, this tool is just another incarnation of Windows Explorer—as is My Network Places—so for further discussion of this tool, see *Windows Explorer* in this chapter.

### Notes

Right-clicking on My Computer on the desktop lets you do some useful things. Here are the options in the Context menu:

*Open*
> Opens a folder displaying the drives (floppy, hard, mapped, CD-ROM, and so on) on the local computer.

*Explore*
> Does the same as Open, except it displays the folder using the two-pane Windows Explorer view.

*Search*
> Opens the Search Assistant with the focus on searching for files and folders on the local computer (see *search* in Chapter 4).

*Manage*
> Opens Computer Management (see *Computer Management* in Chapter 5).

*Map Network Drive*
> Maps a drive letter to a shared folder on a local or remote computer.

*Disconnect Network Drive*
> Deletes a drive-letter mapping created earlier.

*Create a Shortcut*
> Creates a shortcut to My Computer and places it on the desktop.

*Rename*
> Renames My Computer. It's a really good idea to rename My Computer so it displays the actual name of your computer.

*Properties*
> Has the same result as selecting:
>> Start → Settings → Control Panel → System

### See Also

*Computer Management(5), Internet Explorer(6), My Network Places(6), search(4), Synchronize(6), System(6), Windows Explorer(6)*

---

# My Documents

A user-specific folder for storing personal files.

### To Launch

- Desktop → My Documents
- My Computer → click Up button on toolbar → My Documents

---

- Windows Explorer → My Documents → click Folders button on toolbar
- My Network Places → click Up button on toolbar → My Documents
- Internet Explorer → type C: in Address bar → press Enter → click Up button on toolbar → My Documents

To open your personal My Documents folder from the command line, first right-click on My Documents on your desktop, and select Properties. Right-click on the Target folder location, and select Copy. Then type cd at the command line, and paste the path to My Documents into the command.

### Description

My Documents is a desktop folder that is actually part of the currently logged-on user's profile. Since each user who logs on to a Windows 2000 computer has a local profile created for him in the Documents and Settings folder, each user has his own separate My Documents folder for storing his personal documents. My Documents is also the default location for opening and saving files in applications designed for Windows 2000.

The Target tab on the property sheet for My Documents displays the current location of My Documents for the logged-on user and lets you specify a different target location. This can either be a folder on the local computer or a shared folder on the network. Moving My Documents folders to a network share has two advantages:

- The central location allows users' work files to be backed up more easily.
- Users with roaming profiles can access their work files from any computer on the network.

The downside is that when a user logs on, the contents of My Documents are copied to the local computer, and when the user logs off, the contents are copied back again. A better solution is to use the folder-redirection feature of Group Policy (see *Group Policy* in Chapter 3).

### Notes

- Windows 2000 computers can use home folders instead of My Documents to store their work on a network file server (see *home folder* in Chapter 3). This is provided to maintain backward compatibility with Windows NT clients in a network that has not yet been fully migrated to Windows 2000.
- You can use Folder Options in the Control Panel to remove My Documents from the desktop (see *Folder Options* in this chapter).
- Consider encrypting My Documents with EFS to provide laptop users with greater security for their data.

### See Also

*Folder Options(6), Group Policy(3,4), home folder(3,4)*

# My Network Places

Browses for network resources.

## To Launch

- Desktop → My Network Places
- My Computer Places → click the My Network Places link (web content must first be enabled using Folder Options)
- Windows Explorer → select My Network Places in left pane → click Folders button on toolbar
- Internet Explorer → type C: in Address bar → press Enter → click Up button on toolbar twice → double-click on My Network Places
- Command interpreter → `start c:` → press Enter → click Up button on toolbar twice → double-click on My Network Places
- Command interpreter → `explorer` → press Enter → click Up button on toolbar twice → double-click on My Network Places

## Description

My Network Places is an all-in-one browsing tool that can be used to browse the filesystem of the local computer, shared folders and printers on the network, objects in Active Directory, and web content on the Internet. Really, this tool is just another incarnation of Windows Explorer—as is My Computer—so for a general discussion of this tool, see *Windows Explorer* in this chapter.

### Inside My Network Places

One thing to note, however, are the kinds of icons that are displayed when you open My Network Places by double-clicking on it:

*Add Network Place*
   This starts a wizard that can be used to create shortcuts to network resources such as shared folders (enter a UNC path) or web and FTP sites (enter a URL). Note that if you specify a URL, the wizard must be able to connect to the remote web or FTP site in order to create the shortcut.

   If you try to specify a resource by browsing for it instead of entering the path, you can also select the Printers or Scheduled Tasks folders on a local or remote computer. But when you try to complete the wizard, an error occurs telling you the network name cannot be found. This is a small bug in the wizard.

*Entire Network*
   This browses the domains, workgroups, computers, shared folders, and printers on your network. Double-clicking Entire Networks displays one or more of the following items, depending on the configuration of your network (if you have web content enabled in Folder Options under the Tools menu, you also have to click the "entire contents" link to display the following items):

   *Microsoft Windows Network*
      Displays the domains and workgroups in your network.

   *NetWare or Compatible Network*
      Displays the NetWare servers on your network.

*Directory*

Displays the publicly readable portions of Active Directory for the local forest. The folder initially shows only the root domains of each tree in the forest. Double-click on a root domain to display the OUs and default containers in that domain, along with any first-level child domains in that tree. Double-click on an OU to browse the objects within it, and double-click on an object to display its publicly readable properties. If you are logged on as an Administrator in the domain, you can modify the displayed properties for Active Directory objects. Double-clicking on a published shared folder opens the folder and displays its contents. Right-clicking on a computer object and selecting Manage opens Computer Management for the computer.

*Network Share*

This represents a shortcut to a shared folder, web, or FTP site you created using the Add Network Place Wizard described earlier. Note that Windows 2000 sometimes creates some network shares automatically—for example, the "SYSVOL on <server>" shortcut in My Network Places on domain controllers, where <server> is the first domain controller in the forest root domain.

*Computers Near Me*

This takes the place of Entire Network if your computer belongs to a work-group instead of a domain.

### Notes

Right-clicking on My Network Places on the desktop does some useful things. Here are the options in the Context menu:

*Open*

See "Inside My Network Places" earlier in this article.

*Explore*

Does the same as Open except it displays the folder using the two-pane Windows Explorer view.

*Search for Computers*

Opens the Search Assistant with the focus on searching for computers in the local forest (see *search* in Chapter 4).

*Who Am I*

Displays credentials of logged-on user (only present when NetWare connectivity is enabled using CSNW or GSNW).

*Map Network Drive*

Maps a drive-letter to a shared folder on a local or remote computer.

*Disconnect Network Drive*

Deletes a drive-letter mapping created earlier.

*Create a Shortcut*

Creates a shortcut to My Network Places and places it on the desktop.

*Rename*

> Renames My Network Places. It's a really good idea to rename My Network Places so it displays the DNS name of your domain.

*Properties*

> Has the same result as doing:

> Start → Settings → Control Panel → Network and Dial-up Connections

### See Also

*Internet Explorer(6), My Computer(6), Network and Dial-up Connections(6), search(4), Windows Explorer(6)*

---

## Narrator

A not-so-cool tool for visually impaired individuals.

### To Launch

- Start → Programs → Accessories → Accessibility → Narrator
- Command interpreter → `narrator.exe`

### Description

If you have speakers and a sound card installed on your computer, you can use Narrator to read aloud text you type, the contents of folders, menu items, dialog box buttons, and system events. This is a great idea in principle, but it's poorly implemented since the amount of information read aloud is often overwhelming.

When you start Narrator, the key options you can choose are:

*Announce events on screen*

> This is the option that generates way too much talk and should be disabled.

*Read typed characters*

> Not very useful because it doesn't read words—only letters you type.

*Voice*

> This customizes Narrator's voice. One thing you should do immediately is slow it down a bit, as the default setting reads too fast. Even slowed down, there are some words I just can't make out.

### Notes

Pressing Ctrl is supposed to shut this tool off, but sometimes Narrator responds by saying "Control! Control!" instead.

### See Also

*Accessibility Options(6), Magnifier(6), On-Screen Keyboard(6), Utility Manager(6)*

## Network and Dial-up Connections

Creates and manages LAN/WAN connections.

### To Launch

- Start → Settings → Control Panel → Network and Dial-up Connections
- Start → Programs → Accessories → Communications → Network and Dial-up Connections
- Command interpreter → `control ncpa.cpl`

### Description

Network and Dial-up Connections opens a folder that by default contains two icons:

*Make New Connection*

Starts the Network Connection Wizard, which walks you through the process of creating a private or public dial-up connection, VPN connection, direct computer (null-modem cable) connection, or incoming connection for remote access. For more information see *connection* in Chapter 3.

*Local-Area Connection*

Displays the status (speed, uptime, packets sent and received) and lets you configure which networking services are bound to your network adapter card (see *local-area connection* in Chapter 4).

Additional connection icons will be displayed if they have been created. You can also use the folder menu to perform certain operations regarding connections:

*File*

Enables or disables a connection, accesses the properties of a connection, or creates a new connection.

*Advanced*

Configures the following functions:

*Operator-Assisted Dialing*

When toggled on, lets you pick up the phone and either dial the connection manually or ask the operator to do so. When you are finished, click the Dial button to initiate the connection, and then hang up once the modem has control. This works with dial-up connections only.

*Dial-up Preferences*

Configures autodial and callback for a dial-up connection. Autodial attempts to re-establish a severed connection, while callback can be used to enhance security or reverse the charges to the remote-access server. Callback must also be enabled on the remote-access server for it to function on the client.

*Network Identification*

Opens the System utility in the Control Panel and displays the Network Identification tab (see *System* in this chapter).

*Advanced Settings*
> Enables or disables how services and protocols are bound to different connections and changes the order in which network providers service the connections. If you have multiple providers (such as file/print services for both Windows and NetWare), then changing the order may improve performance for clients connecting to these resources.

*Optional Networking Components*
> Adds or removes optional Windows 2000 networking components.

### Additional Networking Components

Not all aspects of Windows 2000 are readily visible at first. For example, selecting Add/Remove Windows Components in the Add/Remove Programs utility in the Control Panel and adding everything listed there won't result in certain networking clients, services, and protocols being installed on your computer. To install these additional networking components, do the following:

> Start → Settings → Control Panel → Network and Dial-up Connections → right-click on Local-Area Connection → Properties → Install

Then select the type of networking component you want to install, namely:

*Client*
> These components enable your computer to access resources on a network. The clients you can install include:

*Client for Microsoft Networks*
> This client lets your computer access resources on other computers running Microsoft Windows, such as on a Windows 2000 computer running File and Printer Sharing for Microsoft Networks (see later in this list). This component is installed by default during a typical Setup.

*Client Service for NetWare*
> Available on Windows 2000 Professional computers only, this client lets your computer access resources on Novell NetWare 2.x, 3.x, or 4.x servers that use either bindery or NDS security. See *CSNW* in this chapter for more information.

*Gateway (and Client) Services for NetWare*
> Available on Windows 2000 Server computers only, this client lets your computer function as a gateway to allow Windows workstations to access resources on NetWare servers without the need of installing NetWare client software on the workstations. See *CSNW* in this chapter for more information.

*Service*
> These components provide services to other computers on the network. The services you can install include:

*File and Printer Sharing for Microsoft Networks*
> Lets shared resources on your computer be accessed by other computers on the network that are running Client for Microsoft Networks (see earlier in this list). This component is installed by default during a typical Setup.

QoS Packet Scheduler
: Provides network traffic–control services for TCP/IP.

SAP Agent
: Advertises servers and addresses on an IPX network.

Protocols
: This enables communication over a network. The protocols you can install include:

TCP/IP
: The default protocol and the one used on the Internet. See *TCP/IP* in Chapter 3 for more information.

NWLink
: Microsoft's version of IPX/SPX for connectivity with NetWare servers. Installing either Client Service for NetWare or Gateway (and Client) Services for NetWare automatically installs NWLink NetBIOS and NWLink IPX/SPX/NetBIOS Compatible Transport Protocol. See *NWLink* in Chapter 3 for more information.

NetBEUI
: Microsoft's legacy protocol used for small workgroup LANs. See *NetBEUI* in Chapter 3 for more information.

AppleTalk
: Connection to Apple Macintosh computers.

DLC
: The primary connection to older network-interface print devices for network printing.

### Notes

The first time you try to create a new connection, Windows may prompt you to specify TAPI location information (country and area code) if you haven't already done so using Phone and Modem Options in the Control Panel.

### See Also

*connection(3), CSNW(6), direct computer connection(4), GSNW(6), local-area connection(4), NetBEUI(3), NWLink(3), remote access(3), remote-access server(4), System(6), TCP/IP(3), VPN connection(4)*

---

## On-Screen Keyboard

A neat utility for motor-impaired individuals or when your keyboard conks out.

### To Launch

* Start → Programs → Accessories → Accessibility → On-Screen Keyboard
* Command interpreter → `osk.exe`

## Description

On-Screen Keyboard displays a floating keyboard that can be used to enter text or respond to any dialog box or prompt. There are a number of customization options you can select from the menu:

*Keyboard*
> This switches between standard or enhanced keyboards and between regular or block layout.

*Settings*
> If you have a sound card and speakers, you can have Keyboard generate an audible click whenever you click on a key. You can also configure Keyboard to type when you hover over a key instead of clicking it, or even when you use a joystick. You can change the font used on Keyboard itself to make it more readable if you desire.

## See Also

*Accessibility Options(6), Magnifier(6), Narrator(6), Utility Manager(6)*

---

# Phone and Modem Options

Configures modem properties and dialing rules.

## To Launch

- Start → Settings → Control Panel → Phone and Modem Options
- Command interpreter → `control telephon.cpl`

## Description

Phone and Modem Options opens a property sheet with three tabs. The key settings are:

*Dialing Rules*
> Configures locations from which you may dial. The minimum information to specify when creating a new location is a location name, country, and area code. You can configure a location to use a calling card automatically if desired.

*Modems*
> Displays the installed modems, installs new modems or removes existing ones, and configures the properties of an installed modem. The properties for a modem vary and are usually configured automatically when the modem is installed. Some settings you might want to adjust are the speaker volume and the disconnect-if-idle timer. For standard (default) modem drivers these settings cannot be changed.

*Advanced*
> Displays the installed TAPI providers and lets you configure their settings when using advanced telephony applications.

---

## Power Options

Configures energy-saving features for your computer.

### To Launch

- Start → Settings → Control Panel → Power Options
- Command interpreter → `control powercfg.cpl`

### Description

Power Options opens a property sheet with four tabs. The key settings are:

*Power Schemes*

> Selects between the default power schemes shown in Table 6-2. To create a custom scheme, modify an existing scheme and save it under a different name. Note that only a subset of these options may be configurable if you have an older computer whose BIOS is not compliant with the Advanced Configuration and Power Interface (ACPI) standard.

*Advanced*

> Displays an icon in the system tray. This is handy and can be used to switch quickly between a power scheme or to open Power Options for further configuration.

> If your BIOS is ACPI-compliant, you can also configure your computer to prompt you for your password when it returns from standby or hibernation mode (see *hibernation* and *standby* in Chapter 3). Finally, you can configure the power button on your box to do any of the following: switch to standby mode, switch to hibernate mode, or power off the machine.

*Hibernate*

> Enables support for hibernation. This tab is only present on machines with an ACPI-compliant BIOS.

*UPS*

> Displays the status of and configures an uninterruptible power supply unit (if present).

*Table 6-2: Default Power Schemes*

| Scheme | Turn off Monitor | Turn off Hard Disks | System Standby | System Hibernates |
|---|---|---|---|---|
| Home/Office Desk | 20 min | Never | Never | Never |
| Portable/Laptop | 15 min | 30 min | 20 min | 1 hr |
| Presentation | Never | Never | Never | Never |
| Always On | 20 min | Never | Never | Never |
| Minimal Power Management | 15 min | Never | Never | Never |
| Max Battery | 15 min | Never | 20 min | 45 min |

### Notes

- Additional tabs may be displayed on certain machines. For example, laptop computers may show an Alarms tab that can be used to configure an alarm to warn you when your battery is about to run out.

- Make sure your hard drive or monitor supports automatic power down before using this feature.

### See Also

*hibernation(3), standby(3)*

---

## Printers

Adds, removes, and manages local and network printers.

### To Launch

- Start → Settings → Control Panel → Printers
- Start → Settings → Printers

### Description

Printers opens a folder that by default contains only one icon, Add Printer, which launches a wizard for adding a new local or network printer. If printers are already installed, icons representing them will be present in this folder as well. For more information on adding and managing printers, see the following articles:

- In Chapter 3, see *print device, print server, printer, printer driver,* and *printer permissions.*

- In Chapter 4, see *print queue, print server, printer,* and *printer permissions.*

### Notes

The options on the File menu vary depending on which icon (if any) is selected in this folder.

### See Also

*print device(3), printer(3,4), printer driver(3),  printer permissions(3,4), print queue(4), print server(3,4)*

---

## Recycle Bin

Temporary storage for deleted items.

### To Launch

Desktop → Recycle Bin

## Description

The Recycle Bin is a temporary storage location where deleted items are kept in case you want to undelete them. The property sheet for this object allows you to configure its size and behavior as follows:

*General*

> This tab lets you decide whether to configure separate Recycle Bin settings for each drive or whether to use one common setting for all local drives (the default). If you select the latter, you can specify the maximum size to which the Recycle Bin on each drive can grow (default is 10% of each drive). Otherwise, you can choose to delete files permanently instead of simply moving them to the Recycle Bin when you delete them using a file-management utility such as Windows Explorer or My Computer.

*Other tabs (one for each local drive)*

> If you specify on the General tab that you will "Configure drives independently," then you can specify the maximum Recycle Bin size for each drive on your system.

To empty the Recycle Bin, right-click and use the Context menu. This permanently deletes all items stored in it.

To view the files within Recycle Bin, double-click on it to open it as a folder on your desktop. You can then select files you want to restore and move them to their original location by selecting File → Restore.

## Notes

- Make the Recycle Bin big enough to meet your needs, since once it fills up, any further items moved to it will permanently delete earlier ones to make room.

- If you try to delete a file that is larger than the capacity of your Recycle Bin, it is permanently deleted instead.

- Files deleted from floppies and other removable media are not moved to the Recycle Bin but are permanently deleted instead. This is also true of files deleted from network shares.

- If you enable disk quotas on a disk, each user who deletes a file from the disk will have a separate Recycle Bin created for her on that disk. As a result, a deleted file still counts against her quota (unless she holds down the Shift key when deleting the file, which permanently deletes it instead of moving it to her Recycle Bin). If you later disable disk quotas on the drive, you may end up with multiple Recycle Bins on the drive.

---

# Regional Options

Customizes language, currency, and other settings for your locality.

## To Launch

- Start → Settings → Control Panel → Regional Options
- Command interpreter → `control intl.cpl`

---

## Description

Regional Options opens a property sheet with six tabs. The key settings are:

*General*
> Specifies your locale (combination of geographical location and language) and which language groups should be installed on your computer. Specify the locale before doing anything, as this automatically affects the settings available on the other tabs.

*Numbers, Currency, Time, and Date*
> Configures conventions for displaying numbers, currency, time, and date information.

*Input Locales*
> Displays the installed locales. If you have more than one locale installed, you can switch between them using an icon in the system tray (must be enabled) or a specified keystroke sequence. Note that this tab is also present in the Keyboard utility in the Control Panel (see *Keyboard* in this chapter).

## Notes

Settings configured here are used by other Windows programs such as Word.

## See Also

*Keyboard(6)*

---

# Scanners and Cameras

Installs and configures scanners and digital cameras.

## To Launch

- Start → Settings → Control Panel → Scanners and Cameras
- Command interpreter → `control sticpl.cpl`

## Description

Scanners and Cameras is a property sheet with only one tab, Devices, which can be used to install and configure a scanner or digital camera. The installation wizard automatically tries to detect the device using Plug and Play first. If this fails, you can select it from a list or supply a driver disk. Once the device is installed, you can open a property sheet to configure it (settings vary with device).

## Notes

You must be a member of the Administrators group to use this utility.

---

# Scheduled Tasks

Schedules tasks to run automatically.

## To Launch

- Start → Settings → Control Panel → Scheduled Tasks
- Start → Programs → Accessories → System → Scheduled Tasks

---

### Description

Scheduled Tasks opens a folder that by default contains only one icon, Add Scheduled Task, which starts a wizard to help you schedule a task. The wizard leads you through the following steps:

- Select a common task from the list, or browse to locate any executable.
- Give the task a descriptive name so you will remember what it does (important if you schedule a lot of tasks).
- Specify when the task should execute:
  — Daily at a specific time, weekdays only, or every $n$th day
  — Weekly on a specific day(s) at a specific time for $n$ weeks
  — Monthly on a specific month(s) at a specific day or date
  — Only once (specify date and time)
  — Whenever your computer restarts
  — Whenever you log on
- Enter your credentials to authorize the task to run.

You can further configure your task by selecting the "Open Advanced properties for this task when I click finish" checkbox. For example, you may need to specify certain command-line switches for your task to run properly; enter these in the Run text box on the Task tab of your task's property sheet. Enclose the executable and switches with double quotes if there are spaces in the path or command syntax.

---

 Task Scheduler is actually just a GUI for the old reliable at command. If you create a task using the at command, it appears in the Scheduled Tasks folder as ATxxxx, where xxxx is a numeric identifier. However, if you then modify the properties of this task in Scheduled Tasks, you will no longer be able to see it using the at command. Better therefore to stick to one method or the other, either the at command or Task Scheduler.

---

#### Managing Tasks

Some of the ways you can manage scheduled tasks are as follows:

- After you create a task, you can test it by:

    Right-click on the task → Run

- You can disable a task while leaving it scheduled by:

    Right-click on the task → Properties → clear the Enabled checkbox

- If you want to stop a task that is running, do this:

    Right-click on the task → End

For some reason programs started by Task Scheduler may take a minute or more to actually terminate when you end them this way.

---

The Advanced menu on the Scheduled Tasks folder has several useful options:

*Stop Using Task Scheduler*
> Stops Task Scheduler from running. The next time you start your computer, however, Task Scheduler will not automatically start again, and you will have to use Services in Computer Management to reconfigure its startup settings.

*Pause Task Scheduler*
> Pauses the service and prevents any tasks from running. To resume the service, select Continue Task Scheduler.

*Notify Me of Missed Tasks*
> Configures Task Scheduler to notify you by a pop-up message when a task cannot be run.

*AT Service Account*
> Specifies an account other than the System account as a security context within which scheduled tasks are run.

*View Log*
> Opens the Task Scheduler log in Notepad. This log includes information both on tasks and the state of the service itself. The most recent data is at the bottom of the file. Note that this file is described incorrectly as *SchedLog.txt* in Windows 2000 Help (it is actually *SchedLgU.txt* and is in *%SystemRoot%*). A quick way to check the status of a task is to make sure the Scheduled Tasks folder is set to Details view and scroll to the Status column.

---

You can add and configure tasks on remote computers by:

> My Network Places → Entire Network → Entire Contents → Microsoft Windows Network → domain → computer → Scheduled Tasks

This works on Windows 2000, Windows NT, and Windows 95/98 computers, except that on Windows 95/98 computers you need to enable remote administration for your account and share the drive where the Scheduled Tasks folder is located.

---

### Remote Tasks

To view scheduled tasks on a remote computer, expand My Network Places to find the icon for the remote computer, then expand the computer's icon to display its Scheduled Tasks folder. Select View → Details to see full information about the task. You must have suitable permissions on the remote computer in order to modify or delete a scheduled task.

To copy a scheduled task to a remote computer, just drag or copy it between your Scheduled Tasks folder and the remote one. You can also email a task (*.job* file) to a user and have him drag the task into his Scheduled Tasks folder.

### Notes

- The user who configures the task usually doesn't need to be logged on at the time the task runs unless user input is required when the task runs.

- If task A has started task B and you end task A, task B will still run.

- Removing a task does not remove the executable that the task runs.

- You can also create a task on your local computer and then use My Network Places to drag the task into the Scheduled Tasks folder of a remote computer.

- You can find out the command-line switches for many programs by typing *program_name* /? at the command prompt.

- Make sure your computer's internal clock is set to the correct date and time if you want your tasks to execute as expected. If a task executes at an unexpected time, check your computer's date and time settings.

- To schedule a task to run only after the computer has been idle for a period of time, use:

  > Right-click on the task → Properties → Settings → configure Idle Time settings

  Note that "idle time" does not refer here to low processor usage, but to keyboard/mouse inactivity.

- You can also schedule a task by dragging a program, batch file, or document into the Scheduled Tasks folder.

- Don't try to schedule the Backup system tool (see *Backup* in this chapter) using Scheduled Tasks, as Backup has its own scheduling feature. (Backup jobs that are scheduled using Backup are, however, displayed in the Scheduled Tasks folder.)

### See Also

*at(7), Backup(6)*

---

## Sounds and Multimedia

Configures multimedia devices and system sounds.

### To Launch

- Start → Settings → Control Panel → Sounds and Multimedia
- Command interpreter → control mmsys.cpl

### Description

Sounds and Multimedia opens a property sheet with three tabs. The key settings are:

*Sounds*

    Assigns or modifies a sound associated with a system event. You can also save your settings as a sound scheme for easy configuration.

---

*Audio*

Configures sound playback, sound recording, and MIDI settings, provided you have suitable devices installed.

*Hardware*

Displays the drivers and resources for your installed sound devices (same effect as using Device Manager in Computer Management).

---

## Synchronize

Ensures that you have the most current version of files when working offline.

### To Launch

- Start → Programs → Accessories → Synchronize
- Command interpreter → `mobsync.exe`

### Description

If you have configured your computer to use offline files (or if you are using Internet Explorer in Offline mode), you can use Synchronize to ensure that the same versions of your offline files (or offline web pages) can be found on both the local computer and the network (or the Internet).

Synchronize opens a dialog box listing the files and web pages you have marked for offline use. If you select an offline file and click Properties, the Offline Files folder opens up displaying the locally cached versions of the files and their synchronization status (see *offline files* in Chapter 3 for more information). Click Synchronize to manually synchronize the selected offline files, or click Setup to configure automatic synchronization of selected offline items:

- When you log off from or log on to your computer. Different actions can occur for each network connection in the Network and Dial-up Connections folder.

- When your computer is idle for a specified interval of time. (You can prevent synchronization from occurring on laptops running on batteries to conserve power.)

- On a scheduled basis that you specify.

If you select an offline web page in Synchronize and click Properties, a property sheet opens allowing you to reconfigure the offline settings for the page. To make a web page available for offline use, first open the page using Internet Explorer, then add it to your list of favorites, making sure you select the checkbox "Make available offline." Click the Customize button as you add the favorite to specify a link depth to download, whether you will synchronize content manually (using Tools → Synchronize in Internet Explorer or using Synchronize in the Accessories program group) or automatically (using a schedule you define). Once you finish adding the favorite, the web page will automatically be downloaded to the local cache. To view offline web pages with Internet Explorer, select File → Work Offline, and then select the page from your favorites list.

### See Also

*offline files(3, 4)*

# System

Manages various system settings on the computer.

## To Launch

- Start → Settings → Control Panel → System
- Right-click on My Computer → Properties
- Command interpreter → control sysdm.cpl

## Description

System is a catch-all for a variety of different system-related configuration tasks, including:

- Specifying your computer name and whether your computer belongs to a domain or a workgroup
- Creating and managing hardware profiles, and installing and managing hardware devices
- Configuring user profiles, performance options, environment variables, and startup and recovery options

System opens a property sheet that has five tabs. The key settings here are:

*General*
Displays important system and network information concerning the machine.

*Network Identification*
Displays and modifies the computer name, name of the domain or workgroup to which the computer belongs, primary DNS suffix, and pre–Windows 2000 NetBIOS computer name.

*Hardware*
Opens the Add/Remove Hardware Wizard (see *Add/Remove Hardware* in this chapter), Device Manager (see *Device Manager* in Chapter 5), and creates and manages hardware profiles on your computer (see *hardware profile* in Chapter 3). It also configures how Windows 2000 will react when you try to install new software that is not signed with a digital signature (install all files, warn about unsigned files, or block installation of unsigned files).

*User Profiles*
Displays the user profiles that are set up on your computer and lets you change them between local and roaming types, provided a roaming profile has already been configured for the user (see *user profile* in Chapter 3).

*Advanced*
This tab contains three additional items:

*Performance Options*
Gives priority to either foreground applications or background services. If this is a server, select Background services to optimize performance over the network.

You can also adjust virtual memory settings here by specifying the drive(s) the pagefile will be stored on, the initial and maximum size of the pagefile, and the maximum size of the registry. See *pagefile* in Chapter 3 for more information.

*Environment Variables*

Displays and configures user and system variables (see *environment variable* in Chapter 3).

*Startup and Recovery*

Configures which operating system is the default on a multiboot machine (or whether to automatically boot to the operating system or the Recovery Console on a machine that has the Recovery Console installed), how long the boot menu is displayed (there is no boot menu displayed if there is only a single operating system installed and no Recovery Console), what action to take when a system failure occurs, as well as what debugging information should be saved (debugging information can be used by Microsoft support specialists to determine the cause of a system failure, but this is a last course procedure).

### Notes

- You can also access system properties by:

  Start → Programs → Administrative Tools → Computer Management → right-click on Computer Management → Properties

  Note that this method only gives the General, Network Identification, and Advanced tabs, however.

- On Windows 2000 Professional machines, the Network Identification tab of System includes an option called Network ID, which launches the Network Identification Wizard. This wizard asks you questions about how your computer will be used and then joins a domain, creates a local user, or performs other suitable actions.

### See Also

*Add/Remove Hardware(6), Device Manager(5), domain(4), environment variable(3), hardware(3), hardware profile(3), pagefile(3), user profile(3)*

---

## System Information

Displays current system information.

### To Launch

- Start → Programs → Accessories → System → System Information
- Start → Programs → Administrative Tools → Computer Management → System Tools → System Information
- Command interpreter → `msinfo32.exe`

### See Also

*System Information(5)*

## Taskbar

Used for launching applications and managing the windows of running applications.

### Description

The taskbar contains the Start button for launching Windows 2000 tools and utilities using shortcuts. Open programs are displayed as blocks on the taskbar that can be used to minimize or restore each program's window. The taskbar can be widened or dragged to any side of the screen, but it cannot float.

Right-clicking on the taskbar reveals a Context menu with several useful options:

*Toolbars*

Hides or displays the following toolbars, which can be superimposed upon the taskbar, be dragged to a different side of the screen, or float on the desktop:

*Address*

Lets you enter a URL, UNC path, local path, or Windows command and open or run it. This is pretty cool, because you can type cmd to open a command-prompt window or My Documents to open the *My Documents* folder, and so on. You can even toggle the "Address" title off to save taskbar real estate.

*Links*

Displays your Internet Explorer links toolbar. You can drag shortcuts to any resource (local, network, or Internet) onto this toolbar.

*Desktop*

Displays a toolbar with shortcuts to desktop items.

*Quick Launch*

Displays buttons to launch Internet Explorer or Outlook Express, or minimize all open windows to display the desktop. These buttons are activated by a single click. You can add additional buttons by dragging icons onto the taskbar to create shortcuts.

*New Toolbar*

Selects a folder such as My Computer or My Network Places and creates a new toolbar containing the items in the selected folder (you can also do this by dragging My Computer or My Network Places onto the taskbar). You can even squish a web page flat into a new toolbar (why is the question!)

*Task Manager*

Displays information about running programs and processes (see *Task Manager* in this chapter).

*Properties*

Customizes the appearance of the taskbar. A new item here is Use Personalized Menus, which when enabled will hide items that you have not recently used in the Start menu. This annoying feature should be one of the first things you disable after you install Windows 2000 on your computer!

Selecting the Advanced tab displays or hides certain shortcuts from the Start menu, such as Administrative Tools, Favorites, and Logoff. You can also turn certain shortcuts into expanding menus, such as the Control Panel, My Documents, Network and Dial-up Connections, and Printers. This can be frustrating at first: if you configure Network and Dial-up Connections as an expanding Start menu item, you can access connections but not the parent folder itself. Since certain connection settings can only be configured using the Advanced menu on the Network and Dial-up Connections folder, this seems a disadvantage. There is a way around it, however: just click Start to open the Start menu, point to Settings, point to Network and Dial-up Connections, then right-click on Network and Dial-up Connections, and select Open from the Context menu to open the desired folder. One final setting on the Advanced tab is "Scroll the Programs menu," which is useful when you have a full set of Administrative Tools or a lot of custom consoles in your Administrative Tools program group.

### Notes

If you display a toolbar such as the Links bar and then drag it off the taskbar, you can display additional instances of this toolbar. This is probably a bug.

### See Also

*Task Manager(6)*

---

## Task Manager

Displays information about running programs and processes.

### To Launch

* Right-click on taskbar → Task Manager
* Ctrl-Alt-Del → Task Manager
* Command interpreter → `taskmgr.exe`

### Description

Task Manager opens a property sheet with three tabs:

*Applications*
Displays the foreground programs currently running on the computer and lets you switch to a program, end the program, or find the process associated with the program. You can also launch a new program if you know its associated executable file. You can use the View menu to change the speed at which the display here is updated.

*Processes*
Displays the processes currently running on the computer and lets you end a process, end the process tree of which this process is the root, or modify the priority of the process. Do not indiscriminately modify the priority of running processes or your system may stop responding. You can use the Options menu to hide or view 16-bit processes that are running, and the View menu to change the speed at which the display here is updated or to display additional columns of information about running processes.

*Performance*

Graphically displays CPU and virtual-memory usage and gives various real-time statistics about processes and memory. Double-click on a graph to expand it vertically. Use the View menu to change the update speed, display each CPU separately on multiprocessor machines, or display the activity of kernel processes.

## Users and Passwords

Creates and manages local users and passwords.

### To Launch

Start → Settings → Control Panel → Users and Passwords

### Description

On Windows 2000 Professional computers, Users and Passwords opens a property sheet with two tabs. The key settings here are:

*Users*

Adds a new local user account to your computer and specifies the local group to which the new user should belong. You can also change the group membership of existing accounts. If your computer belongs to a domain, you can grant a domain user account membership in one of your local groups to grant access privileges to the account for resources on your computer. Note that the list of user accounts displayed in the list box are the local user accounts on the computer, regardless of whether the computer belongs to a workgroup or a domain. You can change the password of any account you select in the list box.

Another setting you specify on this tab is whether you need a user account at all in order to use the computer. (Standalone, non-networked, Windows 2000 Professional computers have no need for a password if they are only being used by one individual and are physically secure.)

*Advanced*

Displays or adds digital certificates to the computer if a computer with Certificate Services is configured on your network. You can also open the Local Users and Groups snap-in to perform additional management of user and group accounts. See *Local Users and Groups* in Chapter 5.

You can also require that users press Ctrl-Alt-Del to log on, guarding against Trojan horse attacks that might masquerade this escape sequence. This setting should always be left enabled.

### Notes

This utility is not present on Windows 2000 Server computers belonging to a domain.

### See Also

*domain user account(3), local user account(3), Local Users and Groups(5)*

## Utility Manager

A utility for managing other accessibility tools.

### To Launch

- Start → Programs → Accessories → Accessibility → Utility Manager
- Command interpreter → `utilman /start`

### Description

Utility Manager configures which of the accessibility tools (Magnifier, Narrator, or On-Screen Keyboard) should start automatically when Windows starts (or when Utility Manager is opened). Narrator runs by default when Utility Manager is opened.

### Notes

- You must be an Administrator to configure these settings.

- You can also start Utility Manager by using the keyboard accelerator Windows Logo Key–U.

### See Also

*Accessibility Options(6), Magnifier(6), Narrator(6), On-Screen Keyboard(6)*

## Windows Explorer

Browses any resource on the local computer, the network, or the Internet.

### To Launch

- Start → Programs → Accessories → Windows Explorer
- Right-click on My Computer → Explore
- Right-click on My Network Places → Explore
- Internet Explorer → type `C:` in Address bar → press Enter → click Folders button on toolbar
- Command interpreter → `explorer`

### Description

Windows Explorer is an all-in-one browsing tool that can be used to browse the filesystem of the local computer, shared folders and printers on the network, objects in Active Directory, and web content on the Internet. Other similar tools (My Computer and My Network Places) are simply different views of Windows Explorer. While Internet Explorer is a different tool (see *Internet Explorer* in this chapter), it cooperates seamlessly with Windows Explorer to give a unified browsing experience from the local computer to the Internet.

Windows Explorer displays resources in a familiar two-pane view called Explorer view, with the left pane showing the hierarchy of resources being browsed and the right pane displaying the contents of the folder, volume, or other container object selected in the left pane.

*Utilities
W*

There are many useful and interesting menu options and toolbar buttons on this tool. It's virtually impossible to fully document everything, though, since the menus here are context sensitive and vary depending on the type of file selected. Some of the more useful features include the following:

*Search button (toolbar)*
> This changes the left pane to the Search Assistant and searches for files or folders on local or remote computers (see *search* in Chapter 4).

*History button (toolbar)*
> This changes the left pane to a History folder that lists files you have recently accessed.

*View → Thumbnails*
> This new view displays a thumbnail image of files and is particularly useful for identifying images and web pages in a folder.

*View → Customize This Folder*
> This starts a wizard to help you customize the folder by adding a background picture or folder comment, or basing it on an HTML template. For example, you could modify an HTML template to customize it with your company's logo.

*Favorites*
> This menu option is not just for web pages; it can also be used to provide fast access to local drives or folders and to shares on the network.

*Tools → Folder Options*
> See *Folder Options* in this chapter for information.

*Tools → Synchronize*
> See *Synchronize* in this chapter for information.

### See Also

*Folder Options(6), Internet Explorer(6), My Computer(6), My Network Places(6), search(4), Synchronize(6)*

---

# Windows Update

Updates your computer with new Windows system files and device drivers.

### To Launch

- Start → Windows Update
- Start → Settings → Add/Remove Programs → Add New Programs → Windows Update
- Internet Explorer → Address bar → *http://windowsupdate.microsoft.com*
- Command interpreter → `wupdmgr.exe`

### Description

Windows Update makes sure you always have the latest versions of Windows 2000 system files and device drivers. You must have an Internet connection in order to use it though, because Windows Update simply connects to the *http://windowsupdate.microsoft.com* web site and runs ActiveX controls for updating your system.

The first time you use this feature, go to the Product Updates page and select Yes when prompted to install the required ActiveX controls such as Microsoft Active Setup. Then follow the instructions posted on the site to update your system.

### Notes

The *http://windowsupdate.microsoft.com* site now has a Critical Update Notification control you can install on your computer. If you install this control, each time you connect to the Internet the control will check with *http://windowsupdate. microsoft.com* to see if any critical system-update files have been posted that you should install.

## Wireless Link

Configures an infrared, wireless, network connection.

### To Launch

* Start → Settings → Control Panel → Wireless Link
* Command interpreter → `control irprops.cpl`

### Description

Wireless Link configures wireless network communications using an infrared device supporting the Infrared Data Association (IrDA) protocols. IrDA devices are detected and installed automatically using Plug and Play when they are connected to a serial COM port on the computer (laptops may have built-in IrDA ports).

Wireless Link opens a property sheet with different tabs. The key settings here are:

*General*
Displays the properties of your IrDA device and indicates whether it is working properly.

*IrDA Settings*
Displays the status, usage, maximum connection speed, and other settings of your IrDA device. These settings generally do not need to be configured, although you can try lowering the maximum connection rate if you are experiencing communications problems with your link.

*File Transfer*
Sends files over an IrDA link and displays the Wireless Link icon in the system tray.

*Image Transfer*
Transfers image files from a digital camera to your computer.

*Utilities*
*W*

# CHAPTER 7

# *Commands*

Although the main way of administering Windows 2000 Server is through the GUI-based Microsoft Management Console, many administrative tasks can be performed using the command line instead. This chapter describes important commands and utilities that can be accessed from the Windows 2000 command prompt. These commands can be used interactively from the command line or can be scheduled for use in batch files to perform various administrative tasks.

A large number of these commands are the same as those in Windows NT, though sometimes new switches or options have been added to enhance their functionality. In addition, there are some commands and utilities in this chapter that are new to Windows 2000 and are indicated as such. However, this chapter is not intended as a tutorial in using the command line. The reader is assumed to be familiar with basic DOS commands, such as `dir` and `copy`, and with creating simple batch files.

The entries in this chapter are also cross-referenced to the other chapters in Part II, *Alphabetical Reference*, of this work. For example, if you look up the `net print` command in this chapter, you may find cross-references such as the following:

- To understand how printing works in Windows 2000, look up *printer* in Chapter 3, *Concepts*.

- For detailed instructions about adding and configuring printers, managing printers through a web browser, or any other administrative task involving printers, look up *printer* in Chapter 4, *Tasks*.

- To stop the print spooler because of a corrupt job in the queue, you can use Services in Computer Management, an MMC console described in the article *Services* in Chapter 5, *Consoles*.

- To learn how to configure printers using the Printers folder in the Control Panel, see *Printers* in Chapter 6, *Utilities*.

## *Alphabetical List of Commands*

The Windows 2000 commands listed in this chapter are grouped into the following five categories:

- General commands
- Net commands
- Netshell commands
- TCP/IP commands
- Miscellaneous commands

The Netshell (netsh) commands are a major addition to Windows 2000, which enable command-line administration of DHCP, DNS, Routing and Remote Access, and WINS services. Administrators upgrading from Windows NT may want to familiarize themselves with these carefully.

Commands are grouped according to category and are cross-referenced when necessary. Command-line switches and options are explained, and examples are given to help illustrate their use.

Many additional command-line utilities are available in the Windows 2000 Server Resource Kit from Microsoft Press. Despite the number of pages (almost 8,000) and weight (23 lbs!) of the resource kit, it is well worth buying because of the additional utilities included in it.

A whole different paradigm in programmatic administration of Windows 2000 is afforded by a tool called the Windows Scripting Host (WSH), which allows scripts to be executed from either the desktop or the command line. WSH can be used for either interactive or batch scripting of administrative tasks. The scripting engine supports VBScript and JScript and is extensible to support other scripting languages such as Perl and REXX. Since knowing a scripting language is a prerequisite of using WSH, this tool is not covered here and is better suited to a book of its own.

## *General Commands*

These commands are used to perform various administrative tasks. Many of these commands will be familiar to administrators who have worked with Windows NT. I've skipped many familiar commands such as dir and cd, as the reader is likely to be familiar with these. I've concentrated instead on commands of special interest to administrators, commands new to Windows 2000, and commands whose syntax has been updated in Windows 2000.

## *at*

Schedules jobs (commands or programs) to run on a computer at a specified time and date. It can also be used to display the currently scheduled jobs.

### *Syntax*

```
at [\\computername] [ [id] [/delete] | [/yes] ]
at [\\computername] time [/interactive] [/every:date[,...] |
next:date[,...] ] command
```

### *Options*

`none`

Displays scheduled jobs.

`\\computername`

Specifies the name of the remote computer on which the job is run. (If omitted, the job executes on the local computer.)

`id`

Is the identification number assigned to the scheduled job.

`/delete`

Removes a job from the list of scheduled jobs. (If `id` is omitted, all scheduled jobs on the specified computer are canceled.)

`/yes`

Executes the scheduled job without prompting for confirmation.

`time`

Specifies when the command is to run (syntax is `hours:minutes` in 24-hour notation).

`/interactive`

Lets the scheduled job interact with the desktop of the user logged on when the job runs.

`/every:date[,...]`

Runs the job on specified day(s) of the week or month. Use `M,T,W,Th,F,S,Su` for days or the numbers 1 through 31 for dates, and separate with commas. (If omitted, the current date is used.)

`/next:date[,...]`

Runs the job on the next occurrence of the specified day or date.

`command`

Is the command, program (*.exe* or *.com* file), or batch file (*.bat* or *.cmd* file) scheduled to run. Enclose the command in quotes if it includes spaces. If a path is required, use an absolute path for commands run on the local machine and a UNC path (\\*server*\*share*) for remote computers. (Don't use mapped drive letters since these may depend on the user who is logged on.)

### *Examples*

To display all scheduled jobs on server *BOB*:

```
at \\BOB
```

Typical output might be:

```
Status ID   Day           Time      Command Line
-----------------------------------------------------
         1   Each M W F   2:00AM    \\BOB /yes c15.bat
```

To display information about job 12 on *BOB*:

**at \\BOB 12**

To delete job 4 on the local server:

**at 4 /delete**

To execute a command that is not a simple executable, precede it with cmd /c since the at command does not automatically load the command interpreter (*cmd.exe*) prior to executing commands. For example, to synchronize the clock of the current server with *BOB* daily at 3 a.m.:

**at 03:00 /every:M,T,W,Th,F,S,Su "cmd net time \\BOB /set /yes"**

## Notes

- For a GUI command scheduler see *Scheduled Tasks* in Chapter 6. Note that jobs scheduled with at are displayed in the Scheduled Tasks folder, but if you then modify the parameters of the job using Scheduled Tasks, you can no longer access it from the command line using at.

- You need to be a member of the local Administrators group to use this command.

- The Task Scheduler service must be running to use this command. Use the Services console to start this service if necessary. (By default, this service is set to start automatically when the system is booted.)

- Scheduled jobs are stored in the registry and are not lost if you restart the Scheduled Tasks service.

- The current directory for executing a scheduled command is *%SystemRoot%*.

- Scheduled jobs run as background processes, and no output is displayed on the screen. You can redirect screen output to a file instead by using the redirection symbol (>).

- If you change the system time on a computer after scheduling a job to run on it, be sure to synchronize the command scheduler with the new time by typing at without options.

- If a scheduled job uses a mapped drive letter to connect to a network share, be sure to schedule a second job that disconnects the drive when you are finished using it; otherwise, the drive letter will not be available from the command prompt.

## See Also

*Scheduled Tasks(6)*

## *attrib*

Displays, modifies, or removes file attributes such as Read-only, Archive, System, and Hidden.

### Syntax

```
attrib [+r | -r] [+a | -a] [+s | -s] [+h | -h] [ [drive:] [path]
filename] [/s [/d] ]
```

### Options

*[drive:][path] filename*
Indicates location and name of the directory, file, or set of files whose attributes you want to set or clear. (The wildcards ? and * can also be used.)

+r  Sets Read-only attribute (useful for protecting users from themselves).

-r  Clears Read-only attribute.

+a  Sets Archive attribute (indicates files that have changed since the last backup was performed).

-a  Clears Archive attribute.

+s  Sets System attribute. (System files are generally protected operating-system files.)

-s  Clears System attribute.

+h  Sets Hidden attribute. (By default, hidden files are not displayed in Windows Explorer.)

-h  Clears hidden attribute.

/s  Sets or clears attributes recursively, starting from the current directory and extending to all subdirectories.

/d  Sets or clears attributes on directories only (new to Windows 2000).

### Examples

Display the attributes of all directories and files in the current directory:

**attrib**

List the attributes of *C:\boot.ini* (used to create the Boot Loader menu):

```
attrib C:\boot.ini
A  SH    C:\boot.ini
```

Note that the Archive (A), System (S), and Hidden (H) attributes are set on this file.

Remove the System and Hidden attributes of *boot.ini* so the file can be modified (leave the archive attribute unchanged):

```
attrib C:\boot.ini -s -h
```

View the attributes again:

```
attrib C:\boot.ini
A        C:\boot.ini
```

## Notes

- The file with the System or Hidden attribute set must have these attributes cleared before you can change any other attributes for that file.

- To display or view advanced attributes such as encryption and compression state, see *cipher* in this chapter.

## See Also

*attribute(3)*, *cipher(7)*

## *cacls*

Displays or modifies access control lists (ACLs) of files and directories on NTFS volumes.

### Syntax

```
cacls filename [/t] [/e] [/c] [/g username:perm] [/r username [...] ]
[/p username:perm [...] ] [/d username [...] ]
```

### Options

`filename [filename...]`
Displays ACLs of specified file(s)

`/t` Recursively applies changes to ACLs of specified files, starting from the current directory and extending to all subdirectories

`/e` Merges changes into an ACL instead of overwriting it

`/c` Ignores errors during the process of modifying an ACL

`/g username:perm`
Grants *username* one of the following permissions:

N   None (new to Windows 2000)

R   Read

C   Change (Write)

F   Full Control

`/r username`
Revokes all permissions for *username*

`/p username:perm`
Replaces one of the following permissions for *username*:

N   None

R   Read

C   Change (Write)

F   Full Control

`/d username`
Explicitly denies access to *username*

**Commands**

## Examples

Display the ACL for the directory *C:\ WINNT*:

```
cacls C:\winnt
C:\WINNT NT AUTHORITY\Authenticated Users:R
        NT AUTHORITY\Authenticated Users:
               (OI)(CI)(IO)(special access:)
                      GENERIC_READ
                      GENERIC_EXECUTE
        BUILTIN\Server Operators:C
        BUILTIN\Server Operators:(OI)(CI)(IO)C
        BUILTIN\Administrators:F
        BUILTIN\Administrators:(OI)(CI)(IO)F
        NT AUTHORITY\SYSTEM:F
        NT AUTHORITY\SYSTEM:(OI)(CI)(IO)F
        BUILTIN\Administrators:F
        CREATOR OWNER:(OI)(CI)(IO)F
        Everyone:R
```

Table 7-1 explains the various symbols used in the output of `cacls`.

*Table 7-1: Symbols Used in cacls Command*

| Symbol | Description |
|--------|-------------|
| C | Container (directory) |
| O | Object (file) |
| I | Inherit (taking on the permissions of the parent directory) |
| OI | Object Inherit (any files created in this directory will inherit this ACL) |
| CI | Container Inherit (any subdirectories created in this directory will inherit this ACL) |
| IO | Inherit Only (ACL does not apply to the directory, only to subdirectories) |

## Notes

- `cacls` cannot be used to create special permissions, only standard permissions. In this sense it is less granular than the GUI.

- You can specify more than one file or user in a command.

- `cacls` cannot be used to set permissions on the root of an NTFS volume that is mounted to a folder on a different NTFS volume.

- To use `cacls` in a batch file, you need to provide a way of automatically answering prompts it may generate. Since `calcs` doesn't have a /y switch to do this, use the Echo command to pipe "y" as input in response to an "Are You Sure?" message that `cacls` might generate. To do this, use:

  ```
  Echo y | cacls filename /g username:perm
  ```

- A practical use for `cacls` is to add the Administrators group automatically to the access control list (ACL) for users' home directories. See Knowledge Base article Q180464 on Microsoft TechNet for several scripts for doing this.

## See Also

*permissions(3), offline files(4), shared-folder permissions(4)*

# *chkdsk*

Verifies and fixes the integrity of a filesystem on a disk.

## *Syntax*

```
chkdsk [volume [ [[path] filename] ] ] [/f] [/v] [/r] [/x] [/i] [/c]
[/l[:size] ]
```

## *Options*

**none**

Displays status of current drive.

***volume***

Specifies drive to check. This can be a drive letter followed by a colon, a volume mount point, or a volume name.

***[path] filename***

Lists specific file(s) to check using **chkdsk** (wildcards are acceptable).

**/f**  Fixes any disk errors found.

**/v**  Verbose mode (displays the name of each file checked).

**/r**  Recovers readable information from bad sectors.

**/l[:*size*]**

Specifies log-file size (NTFS only). Current size is displayed if no size is specified.

**/x**  Forces volume to dismount first if necessary (NTFS only and new to Windows 2000) and fixes any disk errors found. Note that all open handles to the disk are then invalid. You cannot force-dismount the system volume.

**/i**  Performs a quick check of index entries only (NTFS only).

**/c**  Speeds check by ignoring cycles within folder structure (NTFS only).

The following options are new to Windows 2000 and are available only when running the Recovery Console (see *Recovery Console* in Chapter 4):

**/p**  Performs an exhaustive check on the drive regardless of whether **chkdsk** is marked to run (does not fix errors).

**/r**  Recovers readable information from bad sectors (implies /p).

## *Examples*

Check drive *C:*, but don't fix any errors found:

**chkdsk C:**

Typical output might be:

```
The type of the file system is NTFS.

WARNING!  F parameter not specified.
Running CHKDSK in read-only mode.
```

```
CHKDSK is verifying files (stage 1 of 3)...
File verification completed.
CHKDSK is verifying indexes (stage 2 of 3)...
Index verification completed.
CHKDSK is verifying security descriptors (stage 3 of 3)...
Security descriptor verification completed.
CHKDSK is verifying Usn Journal...
Usn Journal verification completed.
Windows found problems with the file system.
Run CHKDSK with the /F (fix) option to correct these.

  2096450 KB total disk space.
  1758220 KB in 23870 files.
     8056 KB in 1407 indexes.
        0 KB in bad sectors.
    72348 KB in use by the system.
    12544 KB occupied by the log file.
   257826 KB available on disk.

     2048 bytes in each allocation unit.
  1048225 total allocation units on disk.
   128913 allocation units available on disk.
```

Note that errors were found. To try to correct these, run:

**chkdsk C: /f**

The output is now:

```
The type of the file system is NTFS.
Cannot lock current drive.

Chkdsk cannot run because the volume is in use by another
process.  Would you like to schedule this volume to be
checked the next time the system restarts? (Y/N)
```

Press "Y" to schedule chkdsk to run at the next reboot. Note, however, that running chkdsk on the active partition may generate spurious errors. (On NTFS volumes chkdsk identifies unreferenced security descriptions as errors, whereas they simply take up space.)

### Notes

- You must be a member of the Administrators group to use chkdsk.

- chkdsk can take hours (or days) to run on very large volumes. To speed up chkdsk, use the /i and /c options, which omit certain checks on the volume.

- If you choose to fix errors using chkdsk /f, there is a possibility of data loss (especially on FAT partitions), so you are prompted to confirm whether chkdsk should make the necessary changes to the file-allocation table. Also, always make a full backup of volumes containing important data before running chkdsk /f on them.

- The file *%SystemRoot%\System32Autochk.exe* is required by chkdsk in order to run. Autochk writes a message to the application log for each drive checked.

- You can also check a disk for errors from the GUI using the Check Disk button on the Tools tab of a disk's property sheet (see *disks* in Chapter 4 for more information).

- chkdsk cannot repair corruption in the master file table (MFT) for an NTFS volume. If you have a file or directory that you cannot open, rename, copy, or delete from an NTFS volume, back up the volume to tape—excluding the problem file from the backup job—and then restore the volume.

- See the recover command in this chapter for information about recovering physically damaged files.

### See Also

*chkntfs(7), disks(3,4), recover(7), Recovery Console(4)*

---

## chkntfs

Displays or specifies whether to schedule automatic filesystem checking (using chkdsk) to be run at startup.

### Syntax

```
chkntfs volume [...]
chkntfs /d
chkntfs /t[:time]
chkntfs /x volume [...]
chkntfs /c volume [...]
```

### Options

*volume* [...]
    Displays the filesystem of the volume(s) and, if automatic file checking is scheduled, whether the volume has been corrupted. (If so, then run chkdsk /f.) The volume may be identified by a drive letter with colon, a volume mount point, or a volume name.

/d  Restores default behavior—except countdown time—for automatic file checking (use this switch alone). In other words, all drives will be checked at startup, and those found to be dirty will have chkdsk run against them.

/t[:*time*]
    Displays or specifies countdown time for automatic filesystem checking (new to Windows 2000).

/x  Excludes specified volume from being checked (even if volume is marked for running chkdsk). To exclude multiple volumes, list them in one command. (This option is not accumulative.)

/c  Checks the specified volume at startup. (This option is accumulative.)

### Examples

To display the filesystem on drive *C:* and its current state:

```
chkntfs c:
The type of the file system is NTFS.
C: is not dirty.
```

To show the countdown time for automatic filesystem checking:

```
chkntfs /t
```
The AUTOCHK initiation count down time is set to 10 seconds.

To change the countdown time to 60 seconds:

```
chkntfs /t:60
```

To specify that only *C:* will be checked at startup on a system that also has *D:* and *E:* as fixed drives:

```
chkntfs /d
chkntfs /x C: D: E:
chkntfs /c C:
```

The explanation for the previous example is as follows:

- The first command resets the default setting, which causes all volumes to be checked at startup.

- The second command excludes all volumes from being checked.

- The third command schedules *C:* alone for checking.

### Notes

- You must be a member of the local Administrators group to use the chkntfs command.

- The default behavior of chkntfs is to check all volumes at startup.

- Don't set the countdown time to zero, as checking the filesystem can be very time consuming and the user will then be unable to cancel this operation. (chkdsk cannot be stopped once it is running.)

### See Also

*chkdsk(7)*

---

## cipher

Displays or modifies the encryption state of files and directories on NTFS volumes. This command is new to Windows 2000.

### Syntax

```
cipher [/e | /d] [/s:directory] [/a] [/i] [/f] [/q] [/h] [/k]
[pathname [...] ]
```

### Options

none
: Lists encryption state of current directory and its files.

*pathname* [...]
: Specifies files or directories to be processed.

/e  Encrypts specified directories.

/d  Decrypts specified directories.

**/s:***directory*
    Recursively processes all subdirectories in specified directory (cannot be used more than once in a single command).

**/a**  Processes specified files. (If there is no matching file, the switch is ignored.)

**/i**  Ignores errors during processing.

**/f**  Forces encryption/decryption of specified files even if they have already been encrypted/decrypted.

**/q**  Switches to quick (nonverbose) output.

**/h**  Shows files with Hidden or System attributes. (These files are not encrypted or decrypted.)

**/k**  Creates a new EFS key for the current user (use this switch alone).

## Examples

To view the encryption state of files and directories in the root of *H:* drive:

```
cipher h:\*
Listing h:\
New files added to this directory will not be encrypted.

U doc1.txt
E doc2.txt
U pub
```

To encrypt the *pub* folder shown earlier:

```
cipher /e h:\pub
Encrypting directories in h:\

pub             [OK]

1 directorie(s) within 1 directorie(s) were encrypted.
```

New files added to *pub* now will be encrypted. To encrypt only the file *doc3.txt* in *pub*:

```
cipher /e /a h:\pub\doc3.txt
Encrypting files in h:\pub\

doc3.txt           [OK]

1 file(s) [or directorie(s)] within 1 directorie(s) were encrypted.
```

## Notes

• Wildcards work with files but not directories.

• You cannot encrypt system or compressed files.

## See Also

*EFS(3), files and folders(3,4)*

*Commands*

# *cmd*

Runs a new instance of the command-line shell.

## *Syntax*

    cmd [/a | /u] [/q] [/d] [/e:on | /e:off] [/f:on | /f:off] [/v:on |
    /v:off] [ [/s] [/c | /k] command]

## *Options*

> Opens a new command shell.

*command*

> Runs the specified command in the current command shell.

/c  Executes command and then exits the shell. (The remainder of the command following the /c switch is processed as a command line.)

/k  Executes command and continues running the shell. (The remainder of the command following the /k switch is processed as a command line.)

/s  If the first character after /c or /k is a quote and the /s switch is used, strips the leading and final closing quotes and retains any other quotes in the line as part of the command (new to Windows 2000).

/q  Disables Echo.

/d  Disables running AutoRun commands, which are stored in the registry and executed by default whenever cmd is run (new to Windows 2000). The registry locations are:

> HKLM\Software\Microsoft\Command Processor\AutoRun
> HKCU\Software\Microsoft\Command Processor\AutoRun

/a  Sets output to ANSI.

/u  Sets output to Unicode.

/t:*bf*

> Specifies background and foreground colors using hexadecimal numeric codes of the color command (type color /? for a list of codes).

/e:[on | off]

> Enables or disables command-shell extensions (enabled by default), which extend the functionality of the following commands: del (erase), color, cd (chdir), md (mdir), prompt, pushd, popd, set, setlocal, endlocal, if, for, call, shift, goto, start, assoc, and ftype.

/f:[on | off]

> Enables or disables filename and directory name completion characters (disabled by default), which use Ctrl-D and Ctrl-F for directory and filename completion, respectively (new to Windows 2000).

/v:[on | off]

> Disables delayed environment-variable expansion (disabled by default and new to Windows 2000). If enabled, you can use the exclamation character (!) to substitute the value of environment variables at runtime.

## Examples

To turn autocompletion on:

`cmd /f:on`

To change to the *C:\Program Files* directory using autocompletion:

`cd p`

Then press Ctrl-D several times until "Program Files" appears, and then press Enter.

## Notes

- To close a new command shell, type `exit`.
- Use double quotes to enclose commands that contain spaces.
- Use `&&` to separate multiple commands surrounded by quotes in a single command line.
- Note that `/x` is the same as `/e:on` and `/y` is the same as `/e:off` for backwards compatibility with the Windows NT command shell.

## See Also

*runas(7)*

---

## convert

Converts FAT and FAT32 volumes to NTFS.

## Syntax

`convert volume /fs:ntfs [/v] [/nametable:filename]`

## Options

`volume`

Specifies the volume to convert. A drive letter with colon, a volume mount point, or a volume name can identify this volume.

`/fs:ntfs`

Converts the volume to NTFS (required).

`/v` Verbose.

`/nametable:filename`

Creates a temporary table of the filenames that need to be changed when converting to NTFS. (Use this if you have strange filenames that prevent conversion from completing properly.)

## Examples

Convert *F:* drive from FAT32 to NTFS:

```
convert F: /fs:ntfs
The type of the file system is FAT32.
Enter current volume label for drive F: F32
Determining disk space required for file system conversion...
```

*Commands*

```
Total disk space:              614400 KB
Free space on volume:          613160 KB
Space required for conversion:   6083 KB
Converting file system
Conversion complete
```

Note that for safety purposes you have to enter the volume label of the volume you want to convert. If you typed the convert command and then opened Windows Explorer or My Computer to determine the necessary volume label, be sure to close that tool before entering the label or you might get this:

**convert f: /fs:ntfs**
```
The type of the file system is FAT32.
Enter current volume label for drive F: F32
Convert cannot gain exclusive access to the F: drive,
so it cannot convert it now.  Would you like to
schedule it to be converted the next time the
system restarts (Y/N)?
```

### Notes

- The current drive cannot be converted.

- If a drive is almost full, convert may not run successfully. Delete some files, and try again.

- Check for Winlogon events in the application log if automatic conversion fails at boot.

### See Also

*disks(3,4)*

---

## diskperf

Enables disk performance counters for the Performance console (see *Performance* in Chapter 5).

### Syntax

```
diskperf [-y[d|v] | -n[d|v] ] [\\computername]
```

### Options

**none**
Displays current status of disk performance counters on local machine.

*computername*
Specifies computer on which to view or set disk performance counters. (The default is local machine.)

-y  Enables disk performance counters for both physical and logical drives upon rebooting.

-yd
Enables disk performance counters for physical drives only upon rebooting (new to Windows 2000).

---

-yv

Enables disk performance counters for logical drives only upon rebooting (new to Windows 2000).

-n    Disables disk performance counters for both physical and logical drives upon rebooting.

-nd

Disables disk performance counters for physical drives only upon rebooting (new to Windows 2000).

-nv

Disables disk performance counters for logical drives only upon rebooting (new to Windows 2000).

### Examples

Enable both physical and logical disk performance counters on the local machine upon rebooting:

```
diskperf -y
Both Logical and Physical Disk Performance counters on this system are
now set to start at boot.
```

### Notes

By default, only physical disk performance counters are enabled; logical counters must be specifically enabled. If you change the default setting, you can later restore them with diskperf -yd.

### See Also

*Performance(5)*

---

## mountvol

Creates, deletes, or displays a volume mount point. Windows 2000 lets you mount an NTFS volume to an empty directory on another NTFS volume (see *disks* in Chapter 3). This command is new to Windows 2000.

### Syntax

```
mountvol [drive:]path volume_name
mountvol [drive:]path /d
mountvol [drive:]path /l
```

### Options

Displays existing mount points (if any) and volumes that can be targeted for new mount points

[*drive:*]*path*

Specifies a directory (must be empty and on an NTFS volume) where the mount point will reside

*Commands*

*volume_name*
>     Indicates the volume name targeted for the mount point (must be the GUID
>     of the volume)

/d   Deletes the mount point

/l   Lists the mounted volume name for the specified directory

## Examples

Display volumes on which empty directories can be targeted as mount points:

**mountvol**
```
Possible values for VolumeName along with current mount points are:

    \\?\Volume{efc6cef2-cd37-11d3-8139-806d6172696f}\
        C:\

    \\?\Volume{886dfe07-d034-11d3-8142-0000b4a04774}\
        E:\

    \\?\Volume{886dfe08-d034-11d3-8142-0000b4a04774}\
        F:\

    \\?\Volume{886dfe09-d034-11d3-8142-0000b4a04774}\
        G:\

    \\?\Volume{b5349550-d58e-11d3-8144-0000b4a04774}\
        H:\

    \\?\Volume{0b77be43-ccff-11d3-b77a-806d6172696f}\
        D:\

    \\?\Volume{0b77be42-ccff-11d3-b77a-806d6172696f}\
        A:\
```

Notice that the Help file for mountvol is also printed (here omitted). We'll now
create the empty directory *C:\accounting* and mount *H:* drive to this directory.
Working in the current directory, which is *C:*, we do the following:

**md accounting**
**mountvol accounting \\?\Volume{b5349550-d58e-11d3-8144-0000b4a04774}**

To see if it worked:

**dir accounting**
```
Volume in drive C has no label.
Volume Serial Number is D839-4CFA

 Directory of C:\accounting

06/22/2000   01:40p                    46 doc1.txt
06/22/2000   01:44p                    30 doc2.txt
06/22/2000   02:12p        DIR            pub
            2 File(s)            76 bytes
            1 Dir(s)     497,959,936 bytes free
```

What is displayed above is the contents of *H:* drive, which is mounted to the empty folder *C:\accounting.*

## Notes

- You can create mount points using Disk Management as well (see "Assign a Drive Path" in *disks* in Chapter 4).

- Mount points can be used if you are running out of drive letters for local volumes and to expand the space on a volume without reformatting it or replacing the hard drive (just add a mount path to another volume). You can also use one volume with several mount paths to enable access to all your local volumes using a single drive letter.

- Don't delete a mount point using Windows Explorer or del /s, as this will remove the target directory and all its subdirectories. Use mountvol /d to remove a mount point instead.

## See Also

*disks(3,4)*

---

# popd

Changes back to the directory stored by pushd (see *pushd* later in this chapter).

## Syntax

```
popd
```

## Options

None.

## Examples

Here's a simple example of how popd together with pushd can be used in a batch file to return to the directory in which the batch file was started:

```
@echo off
' Batch file to delete all .TXT files in a specified directory
pushd %1
del *.txt
popd
```

## Notes

The pushd/popd buffer is cleared after each time the command is used.

## See Also

*pushd(7)*

# pushd

Stores the name of the current directory and then changes to the specified directory (for use by the popd command earlier in this chapter).

## Syntax

    pushd [path | ..]

## Options

path
>    The directory to make the current directory

## Examples

To store the current directory (here *C:\\*) and change to *C:\pub*:

    **pushd C:\pub**
    C:\pub>

See popd earlier in this chapter to see what you can do with this.

## Notes

pushd supports relative paths and accepts either a network path or a local drive letter and path. If a network path is specified, a temporary drive letter is created, and pushd then switches the current drive and directory to the specified directory on the temporary drive. popd then deletes the temporary drive letter when it is used.

## See Also

*popd(7)*

---

# recover

Tries to recover a file from a defective disk.

## Syntax

    recover [drive:][path]filename

## Options

[*drive:*] [*path*] *filename*
>    The file you want to recover

## Examples

Recover the file *doc1.txt* in the root of *H:* drive:

    **recover H:\doc1.txt**
    The type of the file system is NTFS.
    Press ENTER to begin recovery of the file on drive H:

    459264 of 459264 bytes recovered.

### Notes

- **recover** reads the specified file sector by sector and recovers data on good sectors. (Data on bad sectors is lost.)
- You cannot use wildcards.

---

## *runas*

Runs a program using alternate credentials than those currently being used. This command is new to Windows 2000.

### Syntax

```
runas [/profile] [/env] [/netonly] /user:credentials program
```

### Options

`/user:credentials`

User credentials for running the program. (The syntax is *user@domain* or *domain\user* for domain accounts and *user@computer* or *computer\user* for local accounts.)

`program`

Program to be run.

`/profile`

User's profile (may need to be loaded for some programs).

`/env`

Current network environment instead of user's local environment.

`/netonly`

For remote access.

### Examples

To open a command shell using the default Administrator account for the domain while logged on as an ordinary domain user:

```
runas /user:administrator@mtitworld.com cmd
Enter password for administrator@mtitworld.com: ********
Attempting to start "cmd" as user
    "administrator@mtitworld.com"...
```

A second command shell now opens with the following in the title bar:

*cmd (running as administrator@mtitworld.com)*

To run Computer Management using the administrator account JaneD from the domain *mtitworld.com*:

```
runas /user:janed@mtitworld.com "mmc
    %windir%\system32\compmgmt.msc"
```

To open a command shell to administer a server in a different forest using credentials in that forest:

```
runas /netonly /user:credentials cmd
```

**runas** can also be invoked from the GUI. For example, to open the Display utility in the Control Panel using alternate credentials, select:

Start → Settings → Control Panel → hold down Shift → right-click Display → Run as . . . → enter credentials

This is easier than remembering how to do it from the command line:

```
runas /user:credentials "control
    %windir%\system32\desk.cpl"
```

## Notes

- It's a good idea for administrators to have two accounts: an ordinary user account for performing daily tasks, such as checking email or writing reports, and an administrator account for performing administrative tasks. The usefulness of **runas** is that administrators can perform tasks requiring Administrator credentials while logged on as an ordinary user, making it unnecessary to log off and then on again.

- Another name for using **runas** is using the "secondary logon."

- **runas** works with programs (*\*.exe*), saved MMC consoles (*\*.msc*), and Control Panel items.

- **runas** cannot be used to start items, such as Windows Explorer, the Printers folder, and desktop items. However, you can work around this by using the Processes tab of Task Manager to kill the current shell (*Explorer.exe*) and then the New Task button on the Applications tab to run the following command:

```
runas /user:domain\administrator explorer.exe
```

- You can create a shortcut to an item such as a saved MMC console and configure it to always run using a specific set of credentials.

- **runas** may not be able to run programs stored on a network share since the credentials used to start the program may be different from the credentials used to connect to the network share. This may make **runas** unable to gain access to the share.

- The Runas Service must be running in order to use the **runas** command.

- If you use **runas** at the command line without the `/profile` option, the default user profile is used instead of the profile of the user being impersonated. For example, if the command being invoked by **runas** saves a file in My Documents; it saves it in My Documents for the default user, not the user being impersonated by **runas**. If you use the **runas** option from the shortcut menu in Windows Explorer, the `/profile` option is specified by default.

## See Also

*cmd(7)*

## *start*

Runs a program or command.

### *Syntax*

```
start ["title"] [/d path] [/i] [/min] [/max] [/separate | shared]
[/low | /normal | /high | /realtime | /abovenormal | /belownormal]
[/wait] [/b] [program] [parameters]
```

### *Options*

none
> Opens a new command-shell window.

program [parameters]
> Specifies a program or command to run, with optional parameters.

"title"
> Is displayed in title bar.

/d path
> Indicates startup directory.

/i  Passes the startup environment for cmd to the new window.

/min
> Starts window minimized.

/max
> Starts window maximized.

/separate
> Indicates a 16-bit Windows program run in separate memory.

/shared
> Indicates a 16-bit Windows program run in shared memory.

/low
> Runs application using idle priority.

/normal
> Runs application using normal priority.

/high
> Runs application using high priority.

/realtime
> Runs application using real-time priority.

/abovenormal
> Runs application using above-normal priority class (between normal and high).

/belownormal
> Runs application using below-normal priority class (between normal and low).

*Commands*

/wait
    Starts application and waits for it to end.

/b  When executing a Windows command using `start`, prevents a new command-interpreter window from being opened to run the command. In this case use Ctrl-Break instead of Ctrl-C to interrupt the application.

### Examples

To start a new command-shell window with the title "Testing Connection" and continuously `ping` host 172.16.11.39 until Ctrl-C is pressed:

```
start "Testing Connection" ping -t 172.16.11.39
```

To start Computer Management from the command line:

```
start mmc %windir%\system32\compmgmt.msc
```

or simply:

```
mmc %windir%\system32\compmgmt.msc
```

### Notes

*   Using `start` to run a Windows command (such as `dir`, `chkdsk`, and so on) opens a new command-interpreter (`cmd`) window to execute the command. This window implicitly runs using the /k option, which means that the new window stays open after the command is run. See *cmd* in this chapter for more info.

*   When executing a 32-bit GUI application using `start`, control is returned to the command prompt immediately. When a Windows command or command script is run, however, the command or script must first terminate before control is returned to the command shell.

*   If command extensions are enabled (as they are by default), you can use `start` to open a document or file using its associated application. For example, to open *readme.doc* using Word, you can type:

```
start readme.doc
```

### See Also

*cmd(7)*

# Net Commands

This group of commands is used to manage Windows 2000 networking services, user and group accounts, file sharing, printing, and so on.

---

## net

Allows command-line administration of certain aspects of network connectivity and security.

### Syntax

```
net [option]
```

---

## Options

*Net.exe* must be used with one of the following options to give it a specific focus:

accounts
> Manages password and logon requirements for user accounts

computer
> Adds or removes computer accounts from the domain

config
> Displays whether Server and Workstation services are running and configures these services

continue
> Continues paused services

file
> Displays a list of shared files that are open and closes them

group
> Creates global groups or modifies their membership

help
> Provides quick help for a net command from the command line

helpmsg
> Provides information on net-command error messages

localgroup
> Creates local groups or modifies their membership

name
> Adds or removes an alias for the computer

pause
> Pauses a service

print
> Manages printer queues and print jobs

send
> Sends a message to users or computers on the network

session
> Manages sessions between a server and connected clients

share
> Manages shared folders

start
> Manages services

statistics
> Displays statistics for the Workstation or Server service

stop
> Stops a service

time
> Synchronizes the clock on the local machine with a time server

*Commands*

use
> Manages connections with shared resources

user
> Manages user accounts

view
> Lists domains, computers, and shared resources

Since these options are independent of each other and cannot be combined in a single command, you can think of them as a family of net commands instead of a single command with distinct options. In the rest of this section, the individual members of this family are considered in detail.

### Notes

- To see the syntax of a net command from the command line, type net help followed by the option that defines the command. For example, to see the syntax for net accounts, type net help accounts.

- All net commands also accept the following options:

  /y  Automatically answers yes to any prompt generated by the command (useful in batch files).

  /n  Automatically answers no to prompts.

### See Also

*net accounts(7), net computer(7), net config(7), net continue(7), net file(7), net group(7), net help(7), net helpmsg(7), net localgroup(7), net name(7), net pause(7), net print(7), net send(7), net session(7), net share(7), net start(7), net statistics(7), net stop(7), net time(7), net use(7), net user(7), net view(7)*

---

## net accounts

Manages password and logon requirements for user accounts.

### Syntax

```
net accounts [/forcelogoff:{minutes | no}] [/minpwlen:length]
[/maxpwage:{days | unlimited}] [/minpwage:days] [/uniquepw:number]
[/domain]
```

### Options

none
> Current password and logon settings.

/forcelogoff:[*minutes* | no]
> Time to wait before terminating a user session when account or password expires. (The default is no, which means user is not forced to log off.) A warning is sent to the user telling him to save his work.

/minpwlen:*length*
> Minimum number of characters required for password. (The default is 6, and the allowed range is 0–127.)

**/maxpwage:**[*days* | unlimited]

Maximum number of days passwords are valid before expiring. (The default is 90, and the allowed range is 1–49,710.) unlimited means passwords never expire. The value of **/maxpwage** must exceed **/minpwage**.

**/minpwage:***days*

Minimum number of days before a user is allowed to change her password. (The default is 0, and the allowed range is 0–49,710.) Choosing 0 means users can change their passwords anytime.

**/uniquepw:***number*

Specification of password history by requiring users to not repeat a password for *number* password changes. (The default is 5, and the allowed range is 0–24.)

**/lockoutthreshold:***number*

Maximum number of failed logon attempts before account is locked. (Allowed range is 1–999.)

**/lockoutduration:***minutes*

How long a locked account remains locked before being automatically unlocked. (Allowed range is 1–99,999.)

**/lockoutwindow:***minutes*

Maximum time between two consecutive failed logon attempts before the account is locked. (Allowed range is 1–99,999.)

**/domain**

On member servers and workstations, an indication that net accounts settings apply to domain accounts rather than local ones. (On Windows 2000 domain controllers, this is the default setting anyway and is not needed.)

**/sync**

A holdover from Windows NT that caused backup domain controllers to synchronize with the primary domain controller (where net accounts made its changes to the domain directory database). It is mentioned in Windows 2000, but doesn't work.

## Examples

Display the current password and logoff settings:

```
net accounts
Force user logoff how long after time expires?: Never
Minimum password age (days): 0
Maximum password age (days): 42
Minimum password length: 0
Length of password history maintained: 18
Lockout threshold: Never
Lockout duration (minutes): 30
Lockout observation window (minutes): 30
Computer role: PRIMARY
The command completed successfully.
```

*Commands*

### Notes

- The Netlogon Service must be running to use net accounts.

- To manage password and logon restrictions for a domain, see *Group Policy* in Chapter 3.

- If net accounts displays the computer role as PRIMARY, the computer is a domain controller; if SERVER, it is a standalone server.

### See Also

*domain user account(3,4), Group Policy(3,4), local user account(3,4), net group(7), net localgroup(7), net user(7)*

---

## net computer

Adds or removes computer accounts to or from the domain.

### Syntax

```
net computer \\computername {/add | /del}
```

### Options

\\computername

Indicates name of computer to add to or remove from the domain

/add

Adds a computer account

/del

Removes a computer account

### Examples

Add a computer account for the Windows 2000 server *GEORGE*:

```
net computer \\george /add
The command completed successfully.
```

If you now open the Active Directory Users and Computers console, you will find a new computer account for *GEORGE* in the Computers container for the current domain.

### Notes

- This command is not available on machines running Windows 2000 Professional.

- Using this command, you can create computer accounts for member servers and workstations, but not for domain controllers.

- Computer accounts are created on the PDC emulator.

### See Also

*Active Directory Users and Computers(5), computer(4), net(7)*

## net config

Displays whether Server and Workstation services are running.

### Syntax

```
net config {server | workstation}
```

### Options

none
> Verifies whether Server and Workstation services are running

### Notes

To configure the Server and Workstation services, see *net config server* and *net config workstation* later in this chapter.

### See Also

*net config server(7), net config workstation(7)*

---

## net config server

Control settings for the Server service.

### Syntax

```
net config server [/autodisconnect:minutes] [/srvcomment:"text"]
[/hidden:{yes | no}]
```

### Options

none
> Shows current settings.

/autodisconnect:*minutes*
> Sets the maximum idle time before disconnecting user sessions. (The default is 15, and the allowed range is 1–65535.) Specify -1 to never disconnect a user.

/srvcomment:"*text* "
> Displays the comment when the **net view** command is used. (Maximum length is 48 characters.) Be sure to use the quotes.

/hidden:[yes | no]
> Hides the server name from the **net view** command. (The default is no.)

### Examples

Display the configuration of the Server service on the local machine:

```
net config server
Server Name                   \\TEST
Server Comment                Hello
Software version              Windows 2000
Server is active on
   NetBT_Tcpip_{54414D01-02DA-4783-B931-C9AC7A70EDDD}
   (0000b4a04774)
```

```
NetBT_Tcpip_{54414D01-02DA-4783-B931-C9AC7A70EDDD}
  (0000b4a04774)
NetbiosSmb (000000000000)
NetbiosSmb (000000000000)
Nbf_{54414D01-02DA-4783-B931-C9AC7A70EDDD}
  (0000b4a04774)
Nbf_NdisWanNbfOut{0D374F9E-C395-4C81-BDFA-
  FC1503D82B34} (f46f20524153)
Nbf_NdisWanNbfIn{AEDAF533-9187-477C-BDF7-
  07B657D13D4F} (f25920524153)
NwlnkNb (0000b4a04774)
Nbf_NdisWanNbfOut{0EC56659-6FD4-4E8A-BF83-
  146D25681D8B} (f6f420524153)
Nbf_NdisWanNbfIn{160A090E-ACA6-4D63-95E3-
  6E111EB3A6D4} (f2e620524153)
Nbf_NdisWanNbfOut{033CCCCB-D120-4913-A25F-
  3DD13FE9E915} (f46f20524153)
NwlnkIpx (000000000001)
```

```
Server hidden                        No
Maximum Logged On Users              Unlimited
Maximum open files per session       16384
Idle session time (min)              15
The command completed successfully.
```

Table 7-2 shows the fields displayed.

*Table 7-2: Fields Displayed in net config server Command Output*

| Field | Description |
|---|---|
| Server name | UNC name of server |
| Server comment | "Text" value specified |
| Software version | Windows 2000 |
| Server is active on | Protocols bound to service |
| Server hidden | Yes or no |
| Maximum logged on users | Unlimited for Windows 2000 Server and 10 for Windows 2000 Professional |
| Maximum open files per session | 16,384 |
| Idle session time (minutes) | 15 minutes by default |

Disconnect user sessions after 5 minutes of inactivity:

**net config server /autodisconnect:5**
```
The command completed successfully.
```

## Notes

- Changes made using this command take effect immediately and are permanent.

- It is better to modify Server service parameters by editing the registry directly instead of using this command with any of its three switches. The reason is that using this command permanently saves the current settings of the Server service to the registry and disables autotuning of the Server service. Autotuning is a mechanism by which Windows 2000 tries to maintain optimum performance for the Server service. For example, if you add more memory to your server after running net config server /autodisconnect:5, the result is that Windows 2000 will be unable to automatically configure itself to make best use of the additional memory. Note, however, that using net config server without any additional parameters does not have this negative effect. To learn how to undo this problem, see Knowledge Base article Q128167 on Microsoft TechNet.

- To configure the Workstation service, use net config workstation.

### See Also

*net config(7), net config workstation(7)*

---

## net config workstation

Control settings for the Workstation service.

### Syntax

```
net config workstation [/charcount:bytes] [/chartime:msec]
[/charwait:sec]
```

### Options

none
  Shows current settings.

/charcount:*bytes*
  Number of bytes buffered before sending data to a COM device. (The default is 16, and the allowed range is 0–65,535.) If /chartime:msec is specified, then the first one satisfied is used.

/chartime:*msec*
  Time in milliseconds data is buffered before sending it to a COM device. (The default is 250, and the allowed range is 0–65,535,000.) If /charcount:bytes is specified, then the first one satisfied is used.

/charwait:*sec*
  The maximum time Windows 2000 waits for a COM device to become available when it has data to send. (The default is 3,600, and the allowed range is 0–65,535.)

### Examples

Display the configuration of the Server service on the local machine:

```
net config workstation
Computer name                 \\TEST
Full Computer name            test.mtit.com
User name                     Administrator

Workstation active on
    Nbf_{54414D01-02DA-4783-B931-C9AC7A70EDDD}
      (0000B4A04774)
    Nbf_NdisWanNbfIn{AEDAF533-9187-477C-BDF7-
      07B657D13D4F} (F25920524153)
```

```
Nbf_NdisWanNbfIn{160A090E-ACA6-4D63-95E3-
    6E111EB3A6D4} (F2E620524153)
Nbf_NdisWanNbfOut{0D374F9E-C395-4C81-BDFA-
    FC1503D82B34} (F46F20524153)
Nbf_NdisWanNbfOut{033CCCCB-D120-4913-A25F-
    3DD13FE9E915} (F46F20524153)
Nbf_NdisWanNbfOut{0EC56659-6FD4-4E8A-BF83-
    146D25681D8B} (F6F420524153)
NwlnkNb (0000B4A04774)
NetbiosSmb (000000000000)
NetBT_Tcpip_{54414D01-02DA-4783-B931-C9AC7A70EDDD}
    (0000B4A04774)
```

```
Software version                Windows 2000
Workstation domain              MTITCANADA
Workstation Domain DNS Name     mtitcanada.com
Logon domain                    MTITCANADA
COM Open Timeout (sec)          0
COM Send Count (byte)           16
COM Send Timeout (msec)         250
The command completed successfully.
```

Table 7-3 shows the fields displayed.

*Table 7-3: Fields Displayed in net config workstation Command Output*

| Field | Description |
|---|---|
| Computer name | UNC name of computer |
| User name | Currently logged-on user |
| Workstation active on | Lists protocols and interfaces bound to the service |
| Software version | Windows 2000 |
| Workstation domain | Domain workstation belongs to |
| Logon domain | Domain of currently logged-on user |
| COM Open Timeout (sec) | Value of `charwait` |
| COM Send Count (byte) | Value of `charcount` |
| COM Send Timeout (msec) | Value of `chartime` |

### Notes

- Changes made take effect immediately and are permanent.
- To configure the Server service, use net config server.

### See Also

*net(7), net config server(7)*

## net continue

Continues paused services.

### Syntax

```
net continue service
```

## Options

*service*
> The paused service to continue

## Examples

Continue the Server service:

**net continue server**
The Server service was continued successfully.

## Notes

- Service names with embedded spaces require double quotes around them.

- This command will only restart paused services, not stopped ones.

## See Also

*net pause(7), net start(7), net stop(7)*

---

# net file

Displays a list of shared files that are open and closes them.

## Syntax

    net file [id [/close] ]

## Options

none
> Lists the shared files on the server that are open

*id*
> Represents the identification number of the file

/close
> Closes the file

## Examples

To display a list of shared files open on the server:

```
net file
ID      Path                   User name          # Locks
--------------------------------------------------------
15      \PIPE\lsarpc           BACH$              0
2765    G:\pub\mydoc.txt       ADMINISTRATOR      0
The command completed successfully.
```

To close the open file:

```
net file 2765 /close
The command completed successfully.
```

### Notes

- `net file` should be typed on the console of the server where the shared file is located.

- `net files` has the same effect as `net file`.

- Closing a file removes any locks on the file.

- Use the Shared Folders node in Computer Management to manage shared files with the GUI (see *Shared Folders* in Chapter 5).

### See Also

*net session(7), net share(7), net use(7), net view(7), Shared Folders(5)*

---

## net group

Creates global groups or modifies their membership.

### Syntax

```
net group [groupname [/comment:"text"] ] [/domain]
net group groupname {/add [/comment:"text"] | /delete} [/domain]
net group groupname username [...] {/add | /delete} [/domain]
```

### Options

none
> Lists global groups on the server.

*groupname*
> Is the name of a group to create, delete, or modify the membership of.

/comment:"*text*"
> Describes a group (up to 48 characters).

/domain
> If omitted, performs the command on the local computer (which must be a domain controller). To manage groups from a workstation, use this switch.

*username*[...]
> Adds or removes user account(s) from the group (separate with spaces).

/add
> Creates a new group or adds existing users to an existing group.

/delete
> Deletes a group or removes users from a group.

### Examples

List all global groups in the domain:

```
net group
Group Accounts for \\TEST
-----------------------------------------------------

*Cert Publishers
*DnsUpdateProxy
```

```
*Domain Admins
*Domain Computers
*Domain Controllers
*Domain Guests
*Domain Users
*Group Policy Creator Owners
The command completed successfully.
```

Create a new global group called Support, and give it the description "Support staff":

**net group support /add /comment:"Support staff"**
```
The command completed successfully.
```

Add users sally and mktulloch to Support:

**net group support sally mktulloch /add**
```
The command completed successfully.
```

View the membership of Support:

**net group support**
```
Group name        support
Comment           Support staff
Members

-------------------------------------------------------
mktulloch               sally
The command completed successfully.
```

### Notes

- net group can also be typed net groups.

- Use double quotes around group names with embedded spaces, such as "domain users."

- When viewing the output of net group, an asterisk preceding a group name indicates that it includes both users and groups.

### See Also

*Active Directory Users and Computers(5)*, *group(3,4)*, *net accounts(7)*, *net local-group(7)*, *net user(7)*

---

## net help

Provides quick help for a net command from the command line.

### Syntax

```
net help command
net command /help
```

### Options

none
> Shows a list of net commands

command
> Represents the net command you need help with

---

## Examples

To get help information on the net computer command:

```
net help computer
The syntax of this command is:
NET COMPUTER \\computername {/ADD | /DEL}
NET COMPUTER adds or deletes computers from a domain database. This
command is available only on Windows NT Servers.
\\computername    Specifies the computer to add or delete from the domain.
/ADD              Adds the specified computer to the domain.
/DEL              Removes the specified computer from the domain.
```

The same result can be obtained by typing:

```
net computer /help
```

To get only the syntax of net computer:

```
net computer /?
The syntax of this command is:
NET COMPUTER \\computername {/ADD | /DEL}
```

## See Also

*net helpmsg(7)*

---

# net helpmsg

Provides information on net-command error messages.

## Syntax

```
net helpmsg message#
```

## Options

**message#**
> Four-digit error-message number from a net command.

## Examples

View a nonexistent share on the server (spelling mistake):

```
net share pubb
This shared resource does not exist.
More help is available by typing NET HELPMSG 2310.
```

Find out what error message 2310 means:

```
net helpmsg 2310
This shared resource does not exist.
EXPLANATION
The share name you specified does not exist.
ACTION
Check the spelling of the share name.
To display a list of resources shared on the server, type:
    NET SHARE
```

## See Also

*net help(7)*

---

# net localgroup

Creates local groups or modifies their membership.

### Syntax

```
net localgroup [groupname [/comment:"text"] ] [/domain]
net localgroup groupname {/add [/comment:"text"] | /delete} [/domain]
net localgroup groupname username [...] {/add | /delete} [/domain]
```

### Options

none
>    Lists local groups on the server.

groupname
>    Is the name of a group to create, delete, or modify the membership of.

/comment:"text"
>    Describes a group (up to 48 characters).

/domain
>    If omitted, performs the command on the local computer (which must be a domain controller). To manage groups from a workstation, use this switch.

username[...]
>    Adds or removes user account(s) from the group (separate with spaces).

/add
>    Creates a new group or adds existing users to an existing group.

/delete
>    Deletes a group or removes users from a group.

### Examples

List all local groups in the domain:

```
net localgroup
Aliases for \\TEST

-------------------------------------------------------
*Account Operators    *Administrators            *Backup Operators
*DHCP Administrators   *DHCP Users                *DnsAdmins
*Guests                *NetShow Administrators    *Pre-Windows 2000 Compatib
*Print Operators       *RAS and IAS Servers       *Replicator
*Server Operators      *Users                     *WINS Users
The command completed successfully.
```

Create a new local group called Color Printers:

```
net localgroup "Color Printers" /add
The command completed successfully.
```

Add the Domain Users global group to the Color Printers local group:

```
net localgroup "Color Printers" "domain users" /add
The command completed successfully.
```

Commands

List the members of Color Printers:

```
net localgroup "Color Printers"
Alias name       Color Printers
Comment
Members
----------------------------------------------------
Domain Users
The command completed successfully.
```

### Notes

- net localgroup can also be typed net localgroups.

- Use double quotes around group names with embedded spaces, such as "domain users."

- When viewing the output of the command, an asterisk preceding a group name indicates that it includes both users and groups.

### See Also

*Active Directory Users and Computers(5), group(3,4), net accounts(7), net group(7), net user(7)*

---

## net name

Adds or removes an alias for the computer.

### Syntax

```
net name [alias [/add | /delete] ]
```

### Options

none
> Displays a list of names for which the computer will accept messages.

alias
> Specifies an alias (up to 15 characters).

/add
> Adds an alias. (This switch is optional, as it is implied.)

/delete
> Removes an alias.

### Examples

Display the names that your computer responds to for messages sent over the network using the Messenger service:

```
net name
Name
-------------------------------------------------
TEST
NETSHOWSERVICES
The command completed successfully.
```

Add the alias `hellothere` for the computer:

**net name hellothere /add**
The message name HELLOTHERE was added successfully.

## Notes

- Aliases must be unique to the network and may not be the same as a computer name or username elsewhere on the network. If an alias duplicates an existing computer name and either machine is rebooted, the Messenger service will fail to start on the restarted machine.

- The Messenger service must be running.

## See Also

*computer name(3)*, *net send(7)*

---

## net pause

Pause a service.

### Syntax

    net pause *service*

### Options

*service*
> The service to pause

### Examples

Pause the Server service:

**net pause server**
The Server service was paused successfully.

Restart (continue) the paused Server service:

**net continue server**
The Server service was continued successfully.

### Notes

- Services whose names have embedded spaces must be enclosed in quotes:

      net pause "Net Logon"

- If a service is paused, users previously connected to resources managed by the service remain connected. The same is not true of stopping a service, which forcibly disconnects users from resources. However, not all services can be paused (for example, the Remote Procedure Call Service RPCSS), and the effect of pausing a service depends on the service involved. For example:

  *Server service*
  > Pausing this service prevents users from forming new connections to shared resources on the server (existing connections are unaffected). Administrators can still connect to the server even if the Server service is paused.

*Commands*

*Workstation service*

Pausing this service has no effect on the user's logon session and network connections. However, if the user tries to print to a network printer, the request will be redirected to a local printer.

*Netlogon service*

Pausing this service prevents the affected computer from processing logon requests.

• You should pause services on a server before stopping them. This will give the user time to save work and disconnect from resources. After pausing a service, send connected users a message indicating that you will soon be stopping it and that they should save their work (see *net send* in this chapter).

## See Also

*net continue(7), net send(7), net start(7), net stop(7)*

---

## net print

Manages printer queues and print jobs.

### Syntax

```
net print \\computername\sharename
net print [\\computername] job# [/hold | /release | /delete]
```

### Options

`computername`
Indicates the print server

`sharename`
Indicates share name of the printer

`job#`
Represents identification number of print job

`/hold`
Holds a print job waiting in a queue and lets other jobs bypass it (use with `job#`)

`/release`
Releases a job that is on hold

`/delete`
Deletes a job from the queue

### Examples

Display jobs in print queue of printer *HPLASERJ* on print server *TEST*:

```
net print \\test\hplaserj
Printers at \\test

Name              Job #   Size       Status
-----------------------------------------------------
hplaserj Queue     1 jobs             *Printer Active*
    administrator   3   17500         Printing
The command completed successfully.
```

Look at details of job 3 earlier:

**net print \\test 3**
Print job detail

```
Job #              3
Status             Printing
Size               17500
Remark             Untitled - Notepad
Submitting user    administrator
Notify             administrator
Job data type      NT EMF 1.
Job parameters
Additional info
The command completed successfully.
```

Delete job 3 from the queue:

**net print \\test 3 /delete**
The command completed successfully.

### Notes

- To find the share name of your shared printer, type **net share** at the command line.

- If a print server has multiple shared printers, each printer has its own print queue. However, jobs in different print queues on the same server cannot have the same job ID number.

### See Also

*net session(7), net share(7), net use(7), net view(7), printer(3,4), Printers(6), Services(5)*

---

## net send

Send a message to users or computers on the network.

### Syntax

```
net send {name | * | /domain[:name] | /users} message
```

### Options

*name*
Sends the message to a specific recipient, which can be:

— A logged-on user (user logon name)

— A computer name (NetBIOS name)

— A computer alias (see *net name* in this chapter)

\* Broadcasts the message to all registered NetBIOS names in the domain or workgroup

/domain[:*name*]
Broadcasts the message to all names in the local domain or a specified domain

/users
  Sends the message to all users connected to the server

*message*
  Is the actual message sent (no quotes required)

## Examples

Send the message "Save your work—rebooting in 5 minutes" to all users who have open sessions with the server:

```
net send /users Save your work--rebooting in 5 minutes
```

## Notes

- In order for a user to receive messages, the Messenger service must be running.

- Use quotation marks for computer names or usernames that have embedded spaces in them.

- Messages can be up to 128 characters in length.

- The message queue, which temporarily stores messages for the Messenger service, can store a maximum of only 6 messages; any further messages will be ignored if the previous ones are not acknowledged.

- net send * is the same as net send /domain.

- Broadcast messages (* and /domain options) are sent over all network protocols. For example, if you have both TCP/IP and NWLink installed, then messages will appear twice on receiving machines. Messages sent to specific recipients are received only once, however.

- Broadcast messages are received only on the local subnet unless routers are specifically configured to forward NetBIOS Name Query packets.

- Messages sent using the /user option are sent to each session established with the server. If a user has three sessions open with the server, the message will be received three times.

## See Also

*Computer Management(5), net name(7), Shared Folders(5)*

---

# net session

Manage sessions between a server and connected clients.

## Syntax

```
net session [\\computername] [/delete]
```

## Options

none
  Displays information about all sessions on the server.

\\computername
  Specifies the client whose sessions with the server you want to manage.

---

**/delete**

Terminates the session between the server and the specified client, or between the server and all clients if *computername* is unspecified. Files that were opened during the session are closed.

## Examples

View current sessions on the server:

```
net session
Computer     User name     Client Type    Opens Idle time
--------------------------------------------------------
\\172.16.11.100  BACH$    Windows 2000     1    07:04:11
\\172.16.11.104  TEST$    Windows 2000     0    00:00:00
\\BACH    ADMINISTRATOR   Windows 2000     1    07:02:32
\\TEST    ADMINISTRATOR   Windows 2000     0    05:01:42
\\TEST    ADMINISTRATOR   Windows 2000     0    07:16:08
The command completed successfully.
```

View details of the session between client *BACH* and server *TEST*:

```
net session \\bach
User name        ADMINISTRATOR
Computer         BACH
Guest logon      No
Client type      Windows 2000 2195
Sess time        07:04:06
Idle time        07:02:40


Share name      Type     # Opens
-----------------------------------------------
pub             Disk     1
The command completed successfully.
```

Terminate the session with *BACH*:

```
net session \\bach /delete
The session from BACH has open files.
Do you want to continue this operation? (Y/N) [N]: y
The command completed successfully.
```

## Notes

- **net sessions** is equivalent to **net session**.

- A session is initiated when a client machine successfully contacts a server—for example, to access a shared folder or printer.

- A client can only establish one session with a server but can have many connections to resources on the server.

- Use **net send** to warn clients to save their work before terminating their connections with the server.

## See Also

*net file(7), net share(7), net use(7), net view(7), Shared Folders(5)*

*Commands*

## net share

Manage shared resources.

### Syntax

```
net share sharename

net share sharename=drive:path [/users:number | /unlimited]
[/remark:"text"] [/cache:Manual | Automatic | No]

net share sharename [/users:number | /unlimited] [/remark:"text"]
[/cache:Manual | Automatic | No]

net share {sharename | devicename | drive:path} /delete
```

### Options

**none**

A list of information about all shares on the server

**sharename**

The name of the share (may differ from actual name of folder or printer shared)

**drive:path**

Absolute path of a folder to share or unshare

**/users:number**

Maximum number of users who can simultaneously connect to the share

**/unlimited**

No limit to number of users who can simultaneously connect to the share

**/remark:"text"**

Description of share

**/delete**

Used to unshare (stop sharing) the share

**/cache**

Undocumented option for configuring share caching for offline folders (new to Windows 2000—see "Notes" later in this article)

### Examples

List all shared resources on the local machine:

```
net share
Share name   Resource                      Remark
-----------------------------------------------------------
C$           C:\                           Default share
IPC$                                       Remote IPC
print$       C:\WINNT\System32\            Printer Drivers
             spool\drivers
H$           H:\                           Default share
ADMIN$       C:\WINNT                      Remote Admin
```

| | | | |
|---|---|---|---|
| G$ | G:\ | Default share | |
| F$ | F:\ | Default share | |
| E$ | E:\ | Default share | |
| CertConfig | C:\CAConfig | Certificate Services configuration | |
| CertEnroll | C:\WINNT\System32\ | Certificate Services share | |
| | CertSrv\CertEnroll | | |
| NETLOGON | C:\WINNT\SYSVOL\sysvol\ | Logon server share | |
| | mtitcanada.com\SCRIPTS | | |
| pub | G:\pub | | |
| SYSVOL | C:\WINNT\SYSVOL\sysvol | Logon server share | |
| Tool | E:\Tool | | |
| BROTHER | \\SELKIRK\BROTHER | Spooled | \\SELKIRK\BROTHER |
| HPLaserJ | LPT1: | Spooled HP | LaserJet 5L |

The command completed successfully.

View details of *PUB* share:

**net share pub**

| | |
|---|---|
| Share name | pub |
| Path | G:\pub |
| Remark | |
| Maximum users | No limit |
| Users | |

The command completed successfully.

Unshare the *PUB* share:

**net share pub /delete**
Users have open files on pub.  Continuing the
  operation will force the files closed.
Do you want to continue this operation? (Y/N) [N]: **y**
pub was deleted successfully.

Reshare *PUB*:

**net share pub=G:\pub**
The command completed successfully.

## Notes

- Enclose the absolute path in quotes if it contains embedded spaces.

- If you delete a shared folder using net share /delete, the share may still be visible in My Computer and Windows Explorer even if you reboot. The workaround is to press F5 to flush the cached information.

- The /cache option can be used to configure the share-caching mode to be used when offline folders are implemented (see *offline files* in Chapter 3). For a full description of this option, see Knowledge Base article Q214738 on Microsoft TechNet.

## See Also

*net file(7), net session(7), net use(7), net view(7), offline files(3), Shared Folders(5)*

**Commands**

## *net start*

Manages services.

### *Syntax*

    net start *service*

### *Options*

A list of services currently running on the machine.

*service*

The service you want to start. This can be: alerter, client service for netware, clipbook server, content index, computer browser, dhcp client, directory replicator, event log, ftp publishing service, hypermedia object manager, logical disk manager, lpdsvc, media services management, messenger, fax service, microsoft install server, net logon, network dde, network dde dsdm, nt lm security support provider, ole, plug and play, remote access connection manager, remote access isnsap service, remote access server, remote procedure call (rpc) locator, remote procedure call (rpc) service, schedule, server, simple tcp/ip services, site server ldap service, smartcard resource manager, snmp, spooler, task scheduler, tcp/ip netbios helper, telephony service, tracking service, tracking (server) service, ups, windows time service, and workstation.

### *Examples*

Display the services running on the local machine:

```
net start
These Windows 2000 services are started:
    Alerter
    Application Management
    Certificate Services
    COM+ Event System
    Computer Browser
    DHCP Client
    DHCP Server
    Distributed File System
    Distributed Link Tracking Client
    Distributed Link Tracking Server
    Distributed Transaction Coordinator
    DNS Client
    DNS Server
    Event Log
    File Replication Service
    File Server for Macintosh
    FTP Publishing Service
    IIS Admin Service
```

```
        Indexing Service
        Internet Authentication Service
        Intersite Messaging
        IPSEC Policy Agent
        Kerberos Key Distribution Center
        License Logging Service
        Logical Disk Manager
        Logical Disk Manager Administrative Service
        Message Queuing
        Messenger
        Microsoft Search
        Net Logon
        Network Connections
        Network News Transport Protocol (NNTP)
        NT LM Security Support Provider
        Plug and Play
        Print Server for Macintosh
        Print Spooler
        Protected Storage
        Remote Access Connection Manager
        Remote Procedure Call (RPC)
        Remote Procedure Call (RPC) Locator
        Remote Registry Service
        Remote Storage Engine
        Remote Storage File
        Remote Storage Media
        Removable Storage
        RunAs Service
        SAP Agent
        Security Accounts Manager
        Server
        Simple Mail Transport Protocol (SMTP)
        Simple TCP/IP Services
        Site Server ILS Service
        SNMP Service
        Still Image Service
        System Event Notification
        Task Scheduler
        TCP/IP NetBIOS Helper Service
        TCP/IP Print Server
        Telephony
        Windows Installer
        Windows Internet Name Service (WINS)
        Windows Management Instrumentation
        Windows Management Instrumentation Driver Extensions
        Windows Media Monitor Service
        Windows Media Program Service
        Windows Media Station Service
        Windows Media Unicast Service
        Windows Time
        Workstation
        World Wide Web Publishing Service
The command completed successfully.
```

*Commands*

Start the Fax Service:

**net start "Fax Service"**
The Fax Service service is starting.
The Fax Service service was started successfully.

## Notes

- Use quotation marks to enclose service names containing embedded spaces.

- Starting services can have unexpected effects due to service dependencies.

- Certain services are available only on Windows 2000 Server and not on Windows 2000 Professional, such as File Service for Macintosh, Gateway Service for Netware, Microsoft DHCP Service, Print Service for Macintosh, and Windows Internet Name Service.

- The GUI tool for managing services is the Services console (see *Services* in Chapter 5).

## See Also

*net continue(7), net pause(7), net stop(7), Services(5)*

---

## net statistics

Displays statistics for the Workstation or Server service.

### Syntax

    net statistics {workstation | server}

### Options

**none**
Lists services running for which statistics can be displayed

**workstation**
Displays statistics for Workstation service

**server**
Displays statistics for Server service

### Examples

Display statistics for Server service:

**net statistics server**
Server Statistics for \\TEST
Statistics since 6/14/2000 4:21 PM

    Sessions accepted            6
    Sessions timed-out           0
    Sessions errored-out         2
    Kilobytes sent               4056
    Kilobytes received           7421
    Mean response time (msec)    0
    System errors                0
    Permission violations        0
    Password violations          0

```
Files accessed                          3149
Communication devices accessed          0
Print jobs spooled                      0
Times buffers exhausted
  Big buffers                           0
  Request buffers                       0
The command completed successfully.
```

Display statistics for Workstation service:

**net statistics workstation**
```
Workstation Statistics for \\TEST
Statistics since 6/14/2000 4:21 PM

Bytes received                          7848390
Server Message Blocks (SMBs) received   80932
Bytes transmitted                       33602893
Server Message Blocks (SMBs) transmitted 80791
Read operations                         8338
Write operations                        70
Raw reads denied                        0
Raw writes denied                       0
Network errors                          0
Connections made                        3024
Reconnections made                      0
Server disconnects                      1
Sessions started                        214
Hung sessions                           1
Failed sessions                         0
Failed operations                       0
Use count                               1693
Failed use count                        3
The command completed successfully.
```

Use more to display Server service statistics one screen at a time:

```
net statistics server | more
```

### Notes

- net stats has the same result as net statistics.

- Use the net statistics command to display performance information for the specified service.

---

# net stop

Stops a service.

## Syntax

```
net stop service
```

## Options

**service**

The service you want to stop. See *net start* in this chapter for a list of services you can start and stop.

## Examples

To stop the Server service:

```
net stop server
These workstations have sessions on this server:
172.16.11.100        TEST                TEST
BACH                 BACH                172.16.11.104
Do you want to continue this operation? (Y/N) [Y]: y
These workstations have sessions with open files on this server:
172.16.11.100           172.16.11.104
Do you want to continue this operation? (Y/N) [N]: y
The following services are dependent on the Server service.
Stopping the Server service will also stop these services.
   Net Logon
   Message Queuing
   Distributed File System
   Computer Browser
Do you want to continue this operation? (Y/N) [N]: n
```

To stop the Net Logon service:

```
net stop "net logon"
The Net Logon service is stopping.
The Net Logon service was stopped successfully.
```

To restart Net Logon:

```
net start "net logon"
The Net Logon service is starting..........
The Net Logon service was started successfully.
```

## Notes

- Stopping a service removes its associated resources from memory.

- Where possible before stopping a service, pause the service first and then send a message to connected users that the service is about to be stopped. This gives users time to save their work and disconnect. See *net pause* and *net send* in this chapter.

- You cannot stop the Fax Service as this service functions on demand and stops automatically when there are no faxes to send or receive.

## See Also

*net continue(7)*, *net pause(7)*, *net send(7)*, *net start(7)*, *Services(5)*

---

## net time

Synchronizes the clock on the local machine with a time server.

### Syntax

```
net time [\\computername | /domain[:domainname] |
/rtsdomain[:domainname] ] [/set]
net time [\\computername] /querysntp
net time [\\computername] /setsntp[:ntp server list]
```

## Options

none
> A display of the current date and time on the time server

\\*computername*
> The time server for the domain (can be any Windows 2000 server)

/domain[:*domainname*]
> The domain where the time server resides

/rtsdomain[:*domainname*]
> The domain where a Reliable Time Server resides (see the upcoming sidebar "Synchronizing Windows 2000 Machines in a Windows NT 4.0 Domain")

/set
> An option forcing synchronization to occur

/querysntp
> The name of the Network Time Protocol (NTP) server for the domain (see the sidebar "Synchronizing Windows 2000 Machines in a Windows NT 4.0 Domain")

/setsntp[:*ntp server list*]
> A list of IP addresses or DNS names of NTP time servers for the domain (see the sidebar "Synchronizing Windows 2000 Machines in a Windows NT 4.0 Domain")

## Examples

Synchronize the clock on the local machine with time server *BACH*:

```
net time \\bach /set
Current time at \\bach is 6/26/2000 11:18 PM
The current local clock is 6/26/2000 11:16 PM
Do you want to set the local computer's time to match
  the time at \\bach? (Y/N) [Y]: y
The command completed successfully.
```

Verify that the previous command worked:

```
net time
Current time at \\TEST is 6/26/2000 11:18 PM
The command completed successfully.
```

## Notes

- Synchronization of clocks is important for activities such as directory replication to function properly. (Updates are time-stamped to resolve collisions.)

- Use net time \\*timeserver* /set /yes in a logon script to synchronize the clocks of all machines with *timeserver*, which should have a reliable clock itself.

- /s no longer works for /set as it did in Windows NT.

# Synchronizing Windows 2000 Machines in a Windows NT 4.0 Domain

If you have Windows 2000 computers belonging to a Windows NT 4.0 domain, you may find this event in the System event log:

```
"Source: W32Time
Type: Warning
Event ID: 64
```

Because of repeated network problems, the time service has not been able to find a domain controller to synchronize with for a long time. To reduce network traffic, the time service will wait 960 minutes before trying again. No synchronization will take place during this interval, even if network connectivity is restored. Accumulated time errors may cause certain network operations to fail. To tell the time service that network connectivity has been restored and that it should resynchronize, execute w32tm /s from the command line.

The reason for this error message is that Windows 2000 has a time synchronization service called W32Time that is used for synchronizing clocks of Windows 2000 computers. As a result, Windows 2000 clients and member servers always try to synchronize their clocks with a Windows 2000 domain controller. If they can't find such a domain controller (as in a Windows NT 4.0 domain), then the W32Time service cannot succeed.

The solution is to edit the *%SystemRoot%\W32time.ini* file on a Windows NT 4.0 domain controller so that LocalNTP=yes and then type the following commands on the domain controller:

```
net stop w32time
w32time -update
net start w32time
```

Then go to your Windows 2000 clients and member servers, and type the following command:

```
net time /setsntp:domaincontroller
```

where *domaincontroller* is the one previously configured.

If your Windows NT 4.0 domain controller is using Timeserv instead of W32Time, then just substitute this in the previous procedure.

Note, however, that running net time /setsntp:*domaincontroller* on a Windows 2000 computer alters the default registry settings for the W32Time service. So if you later plan to migrate your domain to Windows 2000, you need to restore the W32Time settings to their default values by editing the following registry key:

HKLM\SYSTEM\CurrentControlSet\Services\W32Time\Parameters

Just delete the value ntpserver and change the type value from ntp to nt5DS.

*—Continued—*

Configuring and synchronizing time on Windows 2000/NT networks is a complex topic. For more information see the following Knowledge Base articles on Microsoft TechNet: Q156460, Q174557, Q216734, Q223184, Q224799, Q232255, and Q258059.

## *net use*

Manages connections with shared resources.

### *Syntax*

```
net use [devicename | *] [\\computername\sharename[\volume]
[password | *] ] [credentials] [ [/delete] | [/persistent:{yes | no}] ]
```

where `credentials` represents one of:

```
[/user:[domainname\]username]
[/user:[dotted domain name\]username]
[/user:[username@dotted domain name]
net use {devicename | *} [password | *] /home
net use [/psersistent:{yes | no}]
```

### *Options*

`none`

> A list of current network connections.

`devicename`

> The resource to connect/disconnect. (Specify *D:* to *Z:* for drives and *LPT1:* to *LPT3:* for printers, or use an asterisk to assign the next available device name.)

`\\computername\sharename[\volume]`

> The shared resource to connect/disconnect. `volume` represents a NetWare volume to connect/disconnect (requires Client Service for NetWare or Gateway Service for NetWare).

`[password | *]`

> Password required for the resource. An asterisk causes a prompt for the password when the command is run.

`/user:[domainname\]username`

> Domain to connect from and username to use for establishing the connection (if required). If `domainname` is omitted, the current logon domain is used.

`/delete`

> Termination of the connection. (If an asterisk is used for the connection, then all network connections are disconnected.)

`/home[password | *]`

> Connection of a user to the home directory.

**/persistent:[yes | no]**

yes makes the connection being made and subsequent connections persistent (saves them and restores them at next logon). no makes the connection being made and subsequent connections nonpersistent, but existing persistent connections remain so (use /delete to remove persistent connections).

## Examples

Display a list of currently connected mapped network drives:

```
net use
New connections will be remembered.
Status  Local  Remote            Network
-------------------------------------------------
OK      I:     \\leonardo\swynk     Microsoft Windows Network
OK      J:     \\leonardo\transfer  Microsoft Windows Network
The command completed successfully.
```

Notice above that all connections are currently persistent.

View details of *I:* connection:

```
net use I:
Local name      I:
Remote name     \\leonardo\swynk
Resource type   Disk
Status          OK
# Opens         0
# Connections   1
The command completed successfully.
```

Display a list of connections on server *BACH*:

```
net view \\bach
Shared resources at \\bach
Share name    Type    Used as   Comment
-------------------------------------------------
NETLOGON      Disk              Logon server share
one           Disk
source        Disk
SYSVOL        Disk              Logon server share
test2         Disk
test3         Disk
y1            Disk
y2            Disk
y3            Disk
The command completed successfully.
```

Map the drive letter *P:* to the share TEST2 on *BACH*:

```
net use p: \\bach\test2
The command completed successfully.
```

Disconnect mapped drive *P:* previously connected:

```
net use p: /delete
p: was deleted successfully.
```

## Notes

- Use quotes to enclose *computername* if it contains embedded spaces.

- You cannot disconnect from a share if it is your current drive or if it is locked by an active process.

## See Also

*Computer Management(5), net file(7), net session(7), net share(7), net view(7), Shared Folders(5)*

---

# net user

Manages user accounts.

## Syntax

```
net user [username [password | *] [options] ] [/domain]
net user username {password | *} /add [options] [/domain]
net user username [/delete] [/domain]
```

## Options

Lists user accounts on computer or domain (see /domain later in this list).

username [password | *] [options]

Indicates user account (up to 20 characters long) and password (up to 127 characters long) to manage. An asterisk prompts for a password when the command is run. *options* specifies account options, which can include:

/active:[no | yes]

Enables or disables the account (enabled is default).

/comment:"text"

Indicates a descriptive comment up to 48 characters long.

/countrycode:nnn

Uses Country/Region codes to specify language file for user's Help and error messages (use 0 for default Country/Region code).

/expires:[date | never]

Represents the account expiration date (use mm/dd/yy, dd/mm/yy, or mmm,dd,yy format depending on the Country/Region code).

/fullname:"name"

Indicates the user's full name.

/homedir:path

Indicates path to user's home directory.

/passwordchg:[yes | no]

Specifies whether users can change their password (default is yes).

/passwordreq:[yes | no]

Specifies whether a password is required (default is yes).

*Commands*

`/profilepath:[path]`
> Indicates path to user's logon profile.

`/scriptpath:path`
> Indicates path to user's logon script, which must be relative to:
>
> *%Systemroot%\System32\Repl\Import\Scripts*

`/times:[times | all]`
> Represents logon hours allowed (use `day[-day][,day[-day]] ,time [-time][,time[-time]]`, in one-hour time increments with days spelled out or abbreviated as `M,T,W,Th,F,Sa,Su` and hours in 12- or 24-hour notation). Using a null (blank) value means the user can never log on.

`/usercomment:"text"`
> Specifies the "user comment" for the account.

`/workstations:{computername[,...] | *}`
> Specifies up to eight workstations from which the user can log on (separate using commas). An asterisk means the user can log on from any machine.

`/domain`
> Manages domain accounts instead of local accounts on Windows 2000 Professional machines. (On Windows 2000 Server machines domain accounts are managed by default.) Domain accounts are updated on the PDC emulator of the computer's primary domain.

`/add [options]`
> Adds the account (see earlier in this list for options).

`/delete`
> Removes the account.

### Examples

Display a list of user accounts on a domain controller *TEST*:

```
net user
User accounts for \\TEST
-------------------------------------------------------
Administrator        Guest            ILS_ANONYMOUS_USER
IUSR_MS3             IUSR_TEST        IWAM_MS3
IWAM_TEST            krbtgt           mktulloch
NetShowServices      sally            TsInternetUser
The command completed successfully.
```

If you executed the previous command on a Windows 2000 Professional workstation, you would need to add the `/domain` switch.

View details of user account Sally:

```
net user sally
User name                sally
Full Name                sally
Comment
User's comment
Country code             000 (System Default)
```

```
Account active              Yes
Account expires             Never
Password last set           6/23/2000 11:56 AM
Password expires            8/5/2000 10:44 AM
Password changeable         6/23/2000 11:56 AM
Password required           Yes
User may change password    Yes
Workstations allowed        All
Logon script
User profile
Home directory
Last logon                  Never
Logon hours allowed         All
Local Group Memberships
Global Group memberships    *support          *Domain Users
The command completed successfully.
```

Add user account FredP (for Fred Penner) with high-security password KDj59Pw8, allowing the user to log on between 8 a.m. and 5 p.m. from Monday to Friday, prohibiting the user from changing his password himself, and restricting the user to logging on from the workstation named *PRO115*:

```
net user fredp KDj59Pw8 /add /fullname:"Fred Penner"
    /times:M-F,8am-5pm /passwordchg:no
    /workstations:PRO115
The command completed successfully.
```

Since you made an error entering FredP's password, you need to change it:

```
net user fredp *
Type a password for the user:********
Retype the password to confirm:********
The command completed successfully.
```

Generate a report listing all users in the computer's primary domain:

```
net user  /domain > users.txt
```

### Notes

net users has the same effect as net user.

### See Also

*Active Directory Users and Computers(5)*, *domain user account(3,4)*, *local user account(3,4)*, *net accounts(7)*, *net group(7)*, *net localgroup(7)*

---

## net view

Lists domains, computers, and shared resources.

### Syntax

```
net view [\\computername [/cache] | /domain[:domainname] ]
net view /network:nw [\\computername]
```

## Options

Lists computers in current domain.

\\*computername*

Represents the computer whose shared resources you want to display.

/domain[:*domainname*]

Represents the domain whose available computers you want to display. (To display all domains on the network, just omit *domainname*.)

/network:*nw*

Shows available servers on a NetWare network, or if a computer name is specified, then the resources available on that computer.

## Examples

List all available computers in current domain:

```
net view
Server Name          Remark
---------------------------------------------
\\TEST               Hello
The command completed successfully.
```

List all available domains:

```
net view /domain
Domain
---------------------------------------------
MTIT
MTITCANADA
MTITCORP
MTITWORLD
The command completed successfully.
```

List available computers in *MTITWORLD* domain:

```
net view /domain:mtitworld
Server Name          Remark
---------------------------------------------
\\BACH
The command completed successfully.
```

List shared resources on *BACH* in *MTITWORLD* domain:

```
net view \\bach
Shared resources at \\bach
Share name   Type     Used as   Comment
---------------------------------------------
NETLOGON     Disk               Logon server share
one          Disk
source       Disk
SYSVOL       Disk               Logon server share
test2        Disk
test3        Disk
```

```
y1          Disk
y2          Disk
y3          Disk
The command completed successfully.
```

You can get the same result with:

**net view \\bach.mtitworld.com**

You can also use the computer's IP address.

### Notes

If you try to view the shared resources on a computer and get a System Error 51 or 53 message, File and Printer Sharing for Microsoft Networks is not enabled on the computer or its appropriate network interface.

### See Also

*net file(7), net session(7), net share(7), net use(7), Shared Folders(5)*

# Netshell Commands

This group of commands is a major addition to Windows 2000 and enables command-line administration of networking services such as DHCP, DNS, Routing and Remote Access, and WINS. Netshell (*netsh.exe*) is a command-line scripting tool that can administer these services on local or remote computers in both interactive and batch mode. It functions by providing a shell from which you can enter different contexts for administering each service. *Contexts* are provided by helper DLLs, which extend Netshell's functionality by providing service-specific command sets. Some contexts have subcontexts as well, which are described later in this section.

Netshell supports two kinds of commands:

*Global commands*
> These can be run within any context and provide general functionality to the shell.

*Context-specific commands*
> These are commands specific to a given context (see later in this section).

The various contexts and subcontexts that are currently supported by Netshell (more may be added later in the next version of Windows 2000) include the following:

*AAAA*
> Configures the AAAA component that is used by both Routing and Remote Access and Internet Authentication Service

*DHCP*
> Configures DHCP servers

> *Server*
>> Subcontext for configuring a specific DHCP server

*Interface*
> Configures demand-dial interfaces

> *IP*
>> Subcontext for configuring IP demand-dial interfaces

*RAS*
> Configures remote-access servers

> *IP, IPX, NETBEUI, Appletalk, AAAA*
>> Possible subcontexts for configuring RAS

*Routing*
> Configures IP and IPX routing

> *IP, IPX*
>> Possible subcontexts for configuring routing

*WINS*
> Configures WINS servers

---

 For some reason, there are a couple of Windows 2000 services that require different command-line tools for administering them and are not supported by Netshell. Specifically, DNS servers can be configured from the command line using dnscmd, and Dfs can be configured using dfscmd. These utilities are discussed later in this chapter. Surprisingly, there is no utility for command-line administration of web servers.

---

Netshell can be run in two command modes:

*Interactive (online) mode*
> Commands typed at the Netshell prompt (netsh>) are executed immediately.

*Batch (offline) mode*
> Commands typed at the Netshell prompt are collected and then run as a batch job using the commit command. Note that this is only for router-configuration commands in the routing context.

In addition, you can create a text file containing a script of Netshell commands and then run the script using the -f switch or exec command (see *Global Context* later in this chapter).

The remainder of this section covers:

- The syntax of netsh
- Command set for Netshell global context
- Command sets for each Netshell context

## netsh

Configures networking services from the command line.

### Syntax

```
netsh [-a Aliasfile] [-c Context] [-r RemoteComputer] [command |
-f Scriptfile]
```

### Options

**-r *RemoteComputer***

Specifies the remote computer on which Netshell commands are to be executed. The computer can be specified using its computer name (NetBIOS or DNS name) or IP address. If this option is omitted, the commands are executed on the local computer.

**-a *Aliasfile***

Specifies an alias file to use, which is a file containing a list of Netshell commands together with an alias to allow the commands to be used by just typing the alias name (useful for mapping commands on other platforms, such as Unix, to specific Netshell commands).

**-c *Context***

Opens the Netshell shell and switches immediately to the specified context.

***command***

Specifies any Netshell global command to be executed immediately (see "Examples" later in this article).

**-f *Scriptfile***

Runs the Netshell commands found in the file *Scriptfile* (include path).

### Examples

Open the Netshell shell:

```
C:\>netsh
netsh>
```

Open the Netshell shell in the DHCP context to configure DHCP interactively:

```
C:\>netsh -c dhcp
dhcp>
```

Open the Netshell shell, switch to the IP subcontext of the Interface context, obtain IP address information about the network interface, and return to the command shell:

```
C:\>netsh -r 172.16.11.104 -c interface ip show address
Configuration for interface "Local Area Connection"
    DHCP enabled:           No
    IP Address:             172.16.11.104
    SubnetMask:             255.255.255.0
    Default Gateway:        172.16.11.196
    GatewayMetric:          1
    InterfaceMetric:        1
C:\>
```

*Commands*

## Global Context

Commands available in every Netshell context.

### Subcontexts

AAAA
DHCP
Interface
RAS
Routing
WINS

### Commands

`..`    Returns to previous context.

`?`    Displays help for this context.

`aaaa`
Enters the AAAA context (see later in this section).

`abort`
Discards any changes made while in Offline mode.

`add helper DLLfilename`
Installs a new Helper DLL to extend the functionality of Netshell. The DLLs included with Windows 2000 Server are:

*Ipmontr.dll*
Routing DLL

*Ifmon.dll*
Interface DLL

*Rasmontr.dll*
Remote-access server DLL

*Dhcpmon.dll*
DHCP server DLL

*Winsmon.dll*
WINS server DLL

*Aaaamon.dll*
AAAA component DLL

`alias [aliasname [[string]...]]`
Displays all aliases or the specified alias, or assigns string values to the specified alias.

`bye`
Exits the shell (can also use `quit` or `exit`).

`commit`
Commits Netshell router commands collected in Offline mode and sends them to the router.

`delete helper DLLfilename`
Removes an installed Helper DLL.

dhcp
> Enters the DCHP context (see later in this section).

dump *filename*
> Dumps or appends the configuration to the specified text file.

exec *scriptfile*
> Executes a text file containing a series of Netshell commands.

help
> Same as ?.

interface
> Enters the Interface context (see later in this section).

offline
> Changes to offline mode. All router commands entered into the shell are collected and can later be sent to the router using the commit or online commands.

online
> Changes to online mode. All commands entered into the shell are executed immediately.

popd
> Pops a context from the stack.

pushd
> Pushes current context onto the stack.

ras
> Enters the RAS context (see *RAS Context* later in this section).

router
> Enters the Router context (see *router Context* later in this section).

set machine
> Sets the current machine on which to operate.

set mode [mode=[offline | online]]
> Changes the Netshell mode.

show [alias | helper | mode]
> Shows all defined aliases, installed Helper DLLs, or the current Netshell mode.

unalias *aliasname*
> Removes an alias.

wins
> Enters the WINS context (see *WINS Context* later in this section).

## Examples

First use Notepad to create a text file called *Script.txt*, containing the following Netshell commands, to display the authentication mode and types currently enabled on a Windows 2000 remote-access server:

```
ras
show authmode
show authtype
..
```

*Commands*

Now start the Netshell shell:

```
C:>netsh
```

Check that you are in Online mode:

```
netsh>show mode
online
```

Run the script:

```
netsh>exec C:\script.txt
authentication mode = standard
Enabled Authentication Types:
Code          Meaning
-------------------------------------------
MSCHAP        Microsoft Challenge-Handshake
   Authentication Protocol.
MSCHAPv2      Microsoft Challenge-Handshake
   Authentication Protocol version 2.
netsh>
```

If you are in the Windows 2000 command shell, you can run the script directly:

```
C:\>netsh -f Script.txt
```

### Notes

- There is supposed to be a flush command for removing commands collected in Offline mode, but this doesn't seem to work in the current release.

- The dump command outputs the current configuration of Netshell-configurable services on the machine as a series of Netshell commands. The dumped file can then be run on a different machine using the exec command to configure that machine identically to the first. The only problem is that a number of the configuration settings are not dumped properly! See Knowledge Base article Q254252 on Microsoft TechNet for how to edit the dump file manually to fix it.

---

## *aaaa Context*

Configures Internet Authentication Services (IAS), which is the Microsoft implementation of Remote Authentication Dial-In User Service (RADIUS) in Windows 2000. The "aaaa" stands here for "authentication, authorization, auditing, and accounting" (and has nothing to do with the AAAA record of DNS as defined in RFC 1886!)

### Subcontexts

None

### Commands

In addition to global-context commands, the following additional commands are available in this context:

**? or help**
> Lists these commands

**set config blob=*data***
> *data* sets the configuration of the aaaa engine and must be in Base64 format (as, for instance, that dumped by the show command)

**show [config | version]**
> Dumps the configuration of the aaaa engine in Base64 form or displays the version of the engine (currently Version 0)

## Examples

```
C:\>netsh
netsh>aaaa
aaaa>show config

# aaaa configuration script.
# Known Issues and limitations:
# Import/Export between different versions is not be supported.
# IAS.MDB Version = 0
pushd aaaa
set config blob=\
/bEAAAEAAFN0YW4AZGFyZCBKZXQIIERCAZAAtW4DAGJgCcJV6alnAHJAPwCcfp+QAP+FmjHF\
ebrtADC838ydY9nkAMOfRvuKvE7nAHTsNzzLnPqnANEo5nI5imA1ABt7NpT937EWAHsTQ64g\
...
...
A7ACI/wD\
\
*
popd
# End of aaaa show config
aaaa>
```

# dhcp Context

Configures DHCP servers.

## Subcontexts

> Server
> Scope
> Mscope

## Commands

**? or help**
> Displays these commands.

**list**
> Lists available DHCP commands (more verbose than help).

**dump**
> Dumps the configuration of the DHCP server as a series of Netshell commands.

add server [*servername* | *serveraddress*]
> Adds a DHCP server to the list of authorized DHCP servers stored in Active Directory. You can specify either the DNS name or IP address of the server.

delete server [*servername* | *serveraddress*]
> Removes a DHCP server from the list of authorized DHCP servers.

show server
> Lists all authorized DHCP servers in the current domain.

server [\\*servername* | *serveraddress*]
> Enters the subcontext for the specified DHCP server, which enables you to configure the DHCP server using the add, delete, initiate, scope, mscope, set, and show commands. These commands and their options are summarized in Table 7-4.

> Note that the scope and mscope commands enter new subcontexts. The Scope context is used for configuring a specific scope on the server, and Mscope is used for configuring multicast scopes. The commands available in these subcontexts are shown in Tables 7-5 and 7-6.

---

You can tell what context you are currently in by the command prompt during a Netshell session. For example:

```
C:\>netsh
netsh>dhcp
dhcp>server \\mydhcp
dhcp server>
```

In the previous example, you move from the Windows command shell to the Netshell global context (netsh>), then to the DHCP context (dhcp>), and finally to the DHCP server context (dhcp server>), which is a subcontext for a particular DHCP server. From here you could move deeper into the subcontext of a particular scope on the specified server, and so on.

---

*Table 7-4: Commands Available in DHCP Server Subcontext*

| Command | Option | Description |
|---------|--------|-------------|
| add | class | Adds a class to the server |
| | mscope | Adds a multicast scope to the server |
| | optiondef | Adds a new option to the server |
| | scope | Adds a scope to the server |
| delete | class | Deletes a specific class from the server |
| | mscope | Deletes a multicast scope from the server |
| | optiondef | Deletes an option from the server |
| | optionvalue | Deletes an option value from the server |
| | scope | Deletes a scope from the server |
| | superscope | Deletes a superscope from the server |
| initiate | auth | Initiates retry authorization with the server |
| | reconcile | Checks and reconciles the database for all scopes under the server |

*Table 7-4: Commands Available in DHCP Server Subcontext (continued)*

| Command | Option | Description |
|---------|--------|-------------|
| mscope | *mscope-name* | Switches to the mscope identified by the Mscope name |
| scope | *scope-ip-address* | Switches to the scope identified by the IP address |
| set | auditlog | Sets the audit log parameters for the server |
| | databasebackupinterval | Sets the database backup interval of the current server |
| | databasebackuppath | Sets the database backup path for the server |
| | databasecleanupinterval | Sets the database cleanup interval |
| | databaseloggingflag | Sets/resets the database logging flag |
| | databasename | Sets the name of the server database file |
| | databasepath | Sets the path of the server database file |
| | databaserestoreflag | Sets/resets the database restore flag |
| | detectconflictretry | Sets the number of conflict detection attempts by the DHCP server |
| | dnsconfig | Sets the Dynamic DNS configuration for the server |
| | optionvalue | Sets the global option value for the server |
| | server | Sets the current server in the server mode |
| | userclass | Sets the global user class name for subsequent operation |
| | vendorclass | Sets the global vendor class name for subsequent operation |
| show | all | Displays all information for the server |
| | auditlog | Displays the audit log settings for the server |
| | bindings | Displays binding information for the server |
| | class | Displays all available classes for the server |
| | detectconflictretry | Displays the detect-conflict-retry settings |
| | dnsconfig | Displays the Dynamic DNS configuration for the server |
| | mibinfo | Displays Management Information Base (MIB) information for the server |
| | mscope | Displays all multicast scopes for the server |
| | optiondef | Displays all options for the server |
| | optionvalue | Displays all option values that are set for the server |
| | scope | Displays all available scopes under the server |
| | server | Displays the current server |
| | dbproperties | Displays server database-configuration information |
| | serverstatus | Displays the current status for the server |
| | userclass | Displays the currently set, user class name |
| | vendorclass | Displays the currently set, vendor class name |
| | version | Displays the current version of the server |

*Commands*

Table 7-5: *Commands Available in DHCP Server Scope Subcontext*

| Command | Option | Description |
|---------|--------|-------------|
| add | excluderange | Adds a range of excluded addresses to the current scope |
| | iprange | Adds a range of IP addresses to the current scope |
| | reservedip | Reserves an IP address for use by a specified MAC address in the current scope |
| delete | excluderange | Deletes an exclusion range of previously excluded IP addresses in the current scope |
| | iprange | Deletes a range of IP addresses from the current scope |
| | optionvalue | Removes or clears an assigned scope option value from the current scope |
| | reservedip | Deletes a reservation for an IP address in the current scope |
| | reservedoptionvalue | Removes an option value assigned for a reserved client in the current scope |
| initiate | reconcile | Checks and reconciles the current scope |
| set | comment | Sets the comment for the current scope |
| | name | Sets the name of the current scope |
| | optionvalue | Sets an option value for the current scope |
| | reservedoptionvalue | Sets the comments for the current scope |
| | scope | Sets the scope to be used in subsequent operations |
| | state | Sets/resets the state of the current scope to either an active or inactive state |
| | superscope | Sets the superscope to be used in subsequent operations |
| show | clients | Displays all available Version 4 clients for the current scope |
| | clientsv5 | Displays all available Version 5 clients for the current scope |
| | excluderange | Displays all currently excluded ranges of IP addresses for the current scope |
| | iprange | Displays all available address ranges for the current scope |
| | optionvalue | Displays all option values that are set for the current scope |
| | reservedip | Displays all currently reserved IP addresses for the current scope |
| | reservedoptionvalue | Displays all currently set option values for a reserved client IP address in the current scope |
| | scope | Displays information for the current scope |
| | state | Displays the state of the current scope, indicating whether it is active or inactive |

*Table 7-6: Commands Available in DHCP Server Mscope Subcontext*

| Command | Option | Description |
|---------|--------|-------------|
| add | excluderange | Adds a range of excluded addresses to the current multicast scope |
| | iprange | Adds a range of IP addresses to the current multicast scope |
| delete | excluderange | Deletes an exclusion range of previously excluded IP addresses in the current multicast scope |
| | iprange | Deletes a range of IP addresses from the current multicast scope |
| initiate | reconcile | Checks and reconciles the current multicast scope |
| set | comment | Sets the comment for the current multicast scope |
| | lease | Sets the lease duration for multicast scope IP addresses |
| | mscope | Sets the multicast scope to be used in subsequent operations |
| | name | Sets the name of the current multicast scope |
| | state | Sets/resets the state of the current multicast scope to either an active or inactive state |
| | ttl | Sets the time-to-live (TTL) value for the current multicast scope |
| show | clients | Displays all available clients for the current multicast scope |
| | excluderange | Displays all currently excluded ranges of IP addresses for the current multicast scope |
| | iprange | Displays all available IP address ranges for the current multicast scope |
| | lease | Displays the current lease duration settings for the multicast scope |
| | mibinfo | Displays Management Information Base (MIB) information for the current multicast scope |
| | mscope | Displays information for the current multicast scope |
| | state | Displays the state of the current multicast scope, indicating whether it is active or inactive |
| | ttl | Displays the time-to-live (TTL) value for the current multicast scope |

*Commands*

### Examples

Configure the scope on the DHCP server with IP address 172.16.11.104:

```
C:\>netsh
netsh>dhcp
dhcp>server 172.16.11.104
dhcp server>show scope
```

```
=========================================================
Scope Address   - Subnet Mask    - State    - Scope Name
=========================================================
172.16.11.0    - 255.255.255.0  -Active   -Building 14
```

```
Total No. of Scopes = 1
Command completed successfully.
```

Switch to subcontext of the defined scope:

```
dhcp server>scope 172.16.11.0
Changed the current scope context to 172.16.11.0 scope.
```

Show the range of IP addresses in the current scope:

```
dhcp server scope>show iprange
=========================================================
Start Address   -    End Address    -    Address Type
=========================================================
172.16.11.220  -    172.16.11.240   -    DHCP ONLY
No. of IPRanges : 1 in the Scope : 172.16.11.0.
Command completed successfully.
```

Show addresses excluded from the scope:

```
dhcp server scope>show excluderange
======================================
   Start Address   -    End Address
======================================
   172.16.11.233   -   172.16.11.233
No. of ExcludeRanges : 1 in the Scope : 172.16.11.0.
Command completed successfully.
```

To exclude the addresses 172.16.11.236 through 172.16.11.238 from the scope, first check the syntax for adding an exclusion range:

```
dhcp server scope>add excluderange ?
To exclude a range of IP addresses from distribution by the scope.
Syntax:
  add excluderange StartIP EndIP
Parameters:
  StartIP        - The starting IP address of the
                   exclusion range.
  EndIP          - The ending IP address of the
                   exclusion range.
Example:        add excluderange 10.2.2.10 10.2.2.20
This command excludes IP addresses in the range 10.2.2.10 to 10.2.2.20
from distribution in the scope.
```

Exclude the addresses:

```
dhcp server scope>add excluderange 172.16.11.236  172.16.11.238
Command completed successfully.
```

Verify the results:

```
dhcp server scope>show excluderange
========================================
    Start Address    -    End Address
========================================
    172.16.11.233   -   172.16.11.233
    172.16.11.236   -   172.16.11.238
No. of ExcludeRanges : 2 in the Scope : 172.16.11.0.
Command completed successfully.
```

Quit the Netshell shell:

```
dhcp server scope>quit
C:\>
```

## Notes

- You must be a member of the Enterprise Admins group to configure DHCP servers.

- Netshell's DHCP context is particularly useful for managing remote DHCP servers over slow WAN links where using the remote-administration Terminal Server mode to run the GUI DHCP management tool would result in poor performance.

## See Also

*DHCP(3,4)*

---

## interface Context

Configures router interfaces for Routing and Remote Access Service.

### Subcontexts

IP

### Commands

? or help
> Displays these commands.

add interface name=*iname* type=[tunnel | full]
> Adds an interface to the router, specifying its name (*iname*) and type (tunnel for VPN interfaces and full for demand-dial interfaces). The name of the interface must be in quotes if it contains spaces.

delete interface name=*iname*
> Removes the specified interface.

dump
> Dumps the configuration of the interfaces for the Routing and Remote Access Service as a series of Netshell commands.

reset all
> Resets the router configuration by deleting all interfaces.

show interface [name=*iname*]
> Displays the name, type, and current state of each interface on the router. If no name is specified, all interfaces are displayed.

`show credentials name=`*iname*

Displays the credentials needed to connect to each interface.

`set interface name=`*iname* `admin=[enabled | disabled]`
`connect=[connected | disconnected] [newname=`*newiname*`]`

Sets the current state of the WAN interface called *iname* to either `enabled` or `disabled`. If `connected` is specified, the interface is automatically enabled. *Newiname* is used only for renaming the default LAN interface.

`set credentials name=`*iname* `user=`*username* `domain=`*domainname*
`password=`*password*

Specifies the credentials needed to connect to an interface.

`ip`

Switches to the IP subcontext to further configure IP interfaces on the router. The commands available in this subcontext are listed in Table 7-7.

*Table 7-7: Commands Available in Interface IP Subcontext*

| Command | Options | Description |
|---------|---------|-------------|
| add | address | Adds an IP address to the specified interface |
|  | dns | Adds a static DNS server address |
|  | wins | Adds a static WINS server address |
| delete | address | Deletes an IP address or default gateway from the specified interface |
|  | arpcache | Flushes the ARP cache for one or all interfaces |
|  | dns | Deletes the DNS server from the specified interface |
|  | wins | Deletes the WINS server from the specified interface |
| dump |  | Dumps a configuration script |
| set | address | Sets the IP address or default gateway to the specified interface |
|  | dns | Sets DNS server mode and addresses |
|  | wins | Sets WINS server mode and addresses |
| show | address | Displays IP addresses |
|  | config | Displays IP addresses and other information |
|  | dns | Displays the DNS server addresses |
|  | icmp | Displays ICMP statistics |
|  | interface | Displays IP-interface statistics |
|  | ipaddress | Displays IP addresses |
|  | ipnet | Displays IP net-to-media mappings |
|  | ipstats | Displays IP statistics |
|  | joins | Displays multicast groups joined |
|  | offload | Displays the offload information |
|  | tcpconn | Displays TCP connections |
|  | tcpstats | Displays TCP statistics |
|  | udpconn | Displays UDP connections |
|  | udpstats | Displays UDP statistics |
|  | wins | Displays the WINS server addresses |

## Examples

Display interfaces on router:

```
C:\>netsh
netsh>interface
interface>show interface
Admin State    State      Type         Interface Name
-------------------------------------------------------
Enabled       Connected   Loopback     Loopback
Enabled       Connected   Internal     Internal
Enabled       Connected   Dedicated    Local Area Connection
```

Switch to IP subcontext and view details of interfaces:

```
interface>ip
interface ip>show interface
MIB-II Interface Information
-------------------------------------------------------
Index:                              1
User-friendly Name:                 Loopback
GUID Name:                          Loopback
Type:                               Loopback
MTU:                                32768
Speed:                              10000000
Physical Address:
Admin Status:                       Up
Operational Status:                 Operational
Last Change:                        0
In Octets:                          0
In Unicast Packets:                 0
In Non-unicast Packets:             0
In Packets Discarded:               0
In Erroneous Packets:               0
In Unknown Protocol Packets:        0
Out Octets:                         0
Out Unicast Packets:                0
Out Non-unicast Packets:            0
Out Packets Discarded:              0
Out Erroneous Packets:              0
Output Queue Length:                0
Description:                        Internal loopback interface for
                                    127.0.0 network


Index:                              2
User-friendly Name:                 Local Area Connection
GUID Name:                          {54414D01-02DA-4783-B931-C9AC7A70EDDD}
Type:                               Ethernet
MTU:                                1500
Speed:                              10000000
Physical Address:                   00-00-B4-A0-47-74
Admin Status:                       Up
Operational Status:                 Operational
Last Change:                        0
In Octets:                          4722820
```

```
In Unicast Packets:                16263
In Non-unicast Packets:            6698
In Packets Discarded:              0
In Erroneous Packets:              0
In Unknown Protocol Packets:       8151
Out Octets:                        2970151
Out Unicast Packets:               21769
Out Non-unicast Packets:           3745
Out Packets Discarded:             0
Out Erroneous Packets:             0
Output Queue Length:               0
Description:                       Realtek RTL8029(AS) Ethernet Adapt
(Microsoft's Packet Scheduler)
```

Display IP address info for "Local Area Connection" interface:

```
interface ip>show address "Local Area Connection"
Configuration for interface "Local Area Connection"
    DHCP enabled:                  No
    IP Address:                    172.16.11.104
    SubnetMask:                    255.255.255.0
    Default Gateway:               172.16.11.196
    GatewayMetric:                 1
    InterfaceMetric:               1
```

Before adding a second IP address for this interface, first check the syntax for the add address command:

```
interface ip>add address ?
Usage: add address [name=]string [[addr=]IP address
  [mask=]IP subnet mask][[gateway=]IP address
  [gwmetric=]integer]
Parameters:
    name       - The name of the IP interface.
    addr       - The IP address to be added for
                 the interface.
    mask       - The IP subnet mask for the
                 specified IP address.
    gateway    - The default gateway for the
                 specified IP address.
    gwmetric   - The metric to the default
                 gateway.
Remarks: Adds IP addresses and default gateways to an interface
configured with static IP addresses.
Examples:
add address "Local Area Connection" 10.0.0.2 255.0.0.0
add address "Local Area Connection" gateway=10.0.0.3
  gwmetric=2
The first command adds a static IP address of 10.0.0.2 with a subnet mask
of 255.0.0.0 to the Local Area Connection interface. The second command
adds the IP address of 10.0.0.3 as a second default gateway for this
interface with a gateway metric of 2.
```

Add a second IP address 172.16.11.105 for this interface:

```
interface ip>add address "Local Area Connection"
                172.16.11.105 255.255.255.0
Ok.
```

Verify the result:

```
interface ip>show address "Local Area Connection"
Configuration for interface "Local Area Connection"
    DHCP enabled:              No
    IP Address:                172.16.11.104
    SubnetMask:                255.255.255.0
    IP Address:                172.16.11.105
    SubnetMask:                255.255.255.0
    Default Gateway:           172.16.11.196
    GatewayMetric:             1
    InterfaceMetric:           1
interface ip>
```

You can also verify that the address was successfully added by accessing the TCP/IP property sheet for this interface in the GUI:

Right-click on My Network Places → Properties → right-click on Local-Area Connection → Properties → select Internet Protocol (TCP/IP) → Properties → Advanced

### See Also

connection(3), dial-up connection(4), direct computer connection(4), incoming connection(4), local-area connection(4), Network and Dial-up Connections(6), RAS Context(7), remote access(3), remote-access server(4), router Context(7), Routing and Remote Access(5), VPN connection(4)

---

## RAS Context

Configures a remote-access server.

### Subcontexts

AAAA
Appletalk
IP
IPX
NETBEUI

Only commands for the IP subcontext are covered in this section. For a list of commands in a different subcontext, switch to that subcontext and type help.

### Commands

? or help
   Displays these commands.

aaaa
   Switches to AAAA subcontext.

`add authtype type=[PAP | SPAP | MD5CHAP | MSCHAP | MSCHAPv2 | EAP]`
Specifies additional types of authentication that the RAS server can negotiate.

`add link type=[SWC | LCP]`
Specifies additional link properties that can be used for PPP negotiation.

`add multilink type=[MULTI | BACP]`
Specifies additional multilink types that can be used for PPP negotiation.

`add registeredserver name=domainname server=RASservername`
Registers the RAS server in Active Directory.

`appletalk`
Switches to Appletalk subcontext.

`delete [authtype | link | multilink | registeredserver] [options]`
Removes a RAS authentication, PPP link, or PPP multilink type, or unregisters a RAS server in Active Directory (see the add commands earlier in this article for the syntax).

`dump`
Dumps the configuration of the remote-access server as a series of Netshell commands.

`ip`
Switches to IP subcontext. The commands available in this subcontext are listed in Table 7-8.

`ipx`
Switches to IPX subcontext.

`netbeui`
Switches to NETBEUI subcontext.

`set authmode mode=[STANDARD | NODCC | BYPASS]`
STANDARD means all clients must be authenitcated, NODCC bypasses authentication for direct cable connections, and BYPASS means authentication is not required for any type of device.

`set tracing component=componentname state=[ENABLED | DISABLED]`
Turns extended tracing on or off for the specified component (use an asterisk to represent all components).

`set user name=username dialin=[PERMIT | DENY | POLICY]`
`[cbpolicy=[NONE | CALLER | ADMIN] cbnumber=callbacknumber]`
Configures the RAS properties for the specified user, including whether the user is specifically allowed or denied the right to dial in, whether this is determined by the remote-access policy, and whether the user can use callback when dialing in.

`show activeservers`
Causes the server to listen for RAS server advertisements.

`show authmode`
Displays the current authentication mode of the RAS server.

show **authtype**
> Displays the authentication types currently enabled on the server.

show **client**
> Lists RAS clients currently connected to the server.

show **link**
> Displays the types of link properties that the server currently uses for PPP negotiation.

show **multilink**
> Displays the types of multilink types that the server currently uses for PPP negotiation.

show **registeredserver** domain=*domainname* server=*RASservername*
> Verifies whether the specified RAS server is registered in Active Directory for that domain.

show **tracing** component=*componentname*
> Displays whether extended tracing is enabled for the specified component. (If no component is specified, then the state of tracing is displayed for all components.)

show **user** name=*username* mode=[PERMIT | REPORT]
> Displays the RAS settings for the specified user—or for all users, if no user-name is specified. PERMIT displays only those users whose dial-in setting is currently set to PERMIT, while REPORT displays all users in the current domain.

*Table 7-8: Commands Available in RAS IP Subcontext*

| Command | Options | Description |
|---------|---------|-------------|
| add | Range | Adds a range of IP addresses to the static address pool for the server |
| delete | Pool | Deletes all ranges from the static IP-address pool |
| | Range | Deletes the specified range from the static IP-address pool |
| dump | | Dumps the IP-address configuration information of the RAS server as a series of Netshell commands |
| set | Access | Specifies whether RAS clients should be given access to the network beyond the RAS server |
| | Addrassign | Specifies the method used by the RAS server for assigning IP addresses to clients |
| | Addrreq | Specifies whether RAS clients are allowed to request their own IP addresses from the server |
| | Negotiation | Specifies whether IP is negotiated for client RAS connections |
| show | Config | Shows the current IP configuration of the RAS server |

## Examples

Enter RAS context of Netshell:

```
C:\>netsh
netsh>ras
ras>
```

*Commands*

Display the authentication mode and types currently configured on the server:

```
ras>show authmode
authentication mode = standard
ras>show authtype
Enabled Authentication Types:
Code           Meaning
-------------------------------------------
MSCHAP         Microsoft Challenge-Handshake
               Authentication Protocol.
MSCHAPv2       Microsoft Challenge-Handshake
               Authentication Protocol version 2.
```

Check whether the RAS server *test.mtitcanada.com* is registered in Active Directory:

```
ras>show registeredserver domain=mtitcanada.com
       server=test
The following RAS server is registered:
  RAS Server:  test
  Domain:      mtitcanada.com
```

Check if user Sally is currently allowed to dial in to the RAS server:

```
ras>show user name=sally
User name:          sally
Dialin:             policy
Callback policy:    none
Callback number:
```

The default remote-access policy denies all users RAS dial-in permission, so specifically assign Sally this permission and enable callback:

```
ras>set user name=sally dialin=permit cbpolicy=admin
       cbnumber=555-777-1212
User name:          sally
Dialin:             permit
Callback policy:    admin
Callback number:    555-777-1212
```

Switch to the IP subcontext:

```
ras>ip
ras ip>
```

Show the IP configuration of the RAS server (this is not the IP address of the server's interface, but rather how it provides clients with IP addresses when they connect):

```
ras ip>show config
RAS IP config
  Negotiation mode:       allow
  Access mode:            all
  Address request mode:   deny
  Assignment method:      auto
  Pool:
```

### Notes

Use the **set user** command in a batch file or script to automatically configure RAS dial-in settings for a collection of users.

### See Also

*connection(3), dial-up connection(4), direct computer connection(4), incoming connection(4), interface Context(7), local-area connection(4), Network and Dial-up Connections(6), remote access(3), remote-access server(4), router Context(7), Routing and Remote Access(5), VPN connection(4)*

---

## router Context

Configures a router (a multihomed Windows 2000 Server computer with the Routing and Remote Access Service installed and enabled).

### Subcontexts

IP
>    autodhcp
>    dnsproxy
>    IGMP
>    NAT
>    OSPF
>    Relay
>    RIP

IPX
>    NETBIOS
>    RIP
>    sap

Only commands for the IP subcontext are covered in this section. For a list of commands in the IPX subcontext, switch to that subcontext and type **help**.

### Commands

**? or help**
>    Displays these commands.

**dump**
>    Dumps the configuration of the router as a series of Netshell commands.

**ip**
>    Switches to IP subcontext. The commands available in this subcontext are listed in Table 7-9. Within the IP subcontext are the following deeper subcontexts: autodhcp, dnsproxy, IGMP, NAT, OSPF, Relay, and RIP. The commands for these subcontexts are listed in Tables 7-10 through 7-16.

**ipx**
>    Switches to IPX subcontext.

**reset**
>    Resets the IP-address configuration of the router to a clean state.

**show helper**
>    Details IP and IPX Helper DLLs for the routing context.

---

*Commands*

*Table 7-9: Commands Available in Routing IP Subcontext*

| Command | Options | Description |
|---|---|---|
| add/delete/<br>set/show | interface | Adds, deletes, configures, or displays general IP-routing settings on a specified interface |
| | filter | Adds, deletes, configures, or displays IP packet filters on a specified interface |
| | rtmroute | Adds, deletes, configures, or displays a nonpersistent Route Table Manager route |
| | persistentroute | Adds, deletes, configures, or displays persistent routes |
| | preference-<br>forprotocol | Adds, deletes, configures, or displays the preference level for a routing protocol |
| | scope | Adds, deletes, or displays a multicast scope |
| add/delete/<br>show | boundary | Adds, deletes, or displays multicast boundary settings on a specified interface |
| add/set | ipiptunnel | Adds or configures an IP-in-IP interface |
| autodhcp | | Switches to routing IP autodhcp subcontext (see Table 7-10) |
| dnsproxy | | Switches to routing IP dnsproxy subcontext (see Table 7-11) |
| igmp | | Switches to routing IP IGMP subcontext (see Table 7-12) |
| nat | | Switches to routing IP NAT subcontext (see Table 7-13) |
| ospf | | Switches to routing IP OSPF subcontext (see Table 7-14) |
| relay | | Switches to routing IP Relay subcontext (see Table 7-15) |
| rip | | Switches to routing IP RIP subcontext (see Table 7-16) |
| set/show | loglevel | Configures or displays the global IP-logging level |
| show | helper | Displays all Netsh utility subcontexts of IP |
| | protocol | Displays all running IP-routing protocols |
| | mfe | Displays multicast forwarding entries |
| | mfestats | Displays multicast forwarding entry statistics |
| | boundarystats | Displays IP multicast boundaries |
| | rtmdestinations | Displays destinations in the Route Table Manager routing table |
| | rtmroutes | Displays routes in the Route Table Manager routing table |

*Table 7-10: Commands Available in Routing IP autodhcp Subcontext*

| Command | Options | Description |
|---|---|---|
| set/show | global | Configures or displays global DHCP-allocator parameters |
| | interface | Configures or displays DHCP-allocator settings for a specified interface |
| | exclusion | Adds or deletes an exclusion from the DHCP-allocator range of addresses |

*Table 7-11: Commands Available in Routing IP dnsproxy Subcontext*

| Command | Options | Description |
|---------|---------|-------------|
| set/show | global | Configures or displays global DNS proxy parameters |
| | interface | Configures or displays DNS proxy parameters for a specified interface |

*Table 7-12: Commands Available in Routing IP IGMP Subcontext*

| Command | Options | Description |
|---------|---------|-------------|
| set/show | global | Configures or displays IGMP global settings |
| add/delete/ set/show | interface | Adds, deletes, configures, or displays IGMP on the specified interface |
| add/delete | staticgroup | Adds or deletes a static multicast group for the specified interface |
| show | grouptable | Displays the IGMP host-groups table |
| | ifstats | Displays the IGMP statistics for each interface |
| | iftable | Displays the IGMP host groups for each interface |
| | proxygrouptable | Displays the IGMP group table for the IGMP proxy interface |
| vshow | rasgrouptable | Displays the group table for the internal interface used by the remote-access server |

*Table 7-13: Commands Available in Routing IP NAT Subcontext*

| Command | Options | Description |
|---------|---------|-------------|
| set/show | global | Configures or displays global Network Address Translation (NAT) settings |
| add/delete/ set/show | interface | Adds, deletes, configures, or displays NAT settings for a specified interface |
| add/delete | addressrange | Adds or deletes an address range to the NAT-interface public-address pool |
| | addressmapping | Adds or deletes a NAT address mapping |
| | portmapping | Adds or deletes a NAT port mapping |

*Table 7-14: Commands Available in Routing IP OSPF Subcontext*

| Command | Options | Description |
|---------|---------|-------------|
| set/show | global | Configures or displays global OSPF settings |
| add/delete/ set/show | interface | Adds, removes, configures, or displays OSPF on a specified interface |
| | area | Adds, removes, configures, or displays an OSPF area |
| | virtif | Adds, removes, configures, or displays an OSPF virtual interface |
| add/delete/ show | range | Adds, removes, configures, or displays a range to a specified OSPF area |
| | neighbor | Adds, removes, configures, or displays an OSPF neighbor |
| | protofilter | Adds, removes, configures, or displays routing information sources for OSPF external routes |

*Commands*

*Table 7-14: Commands Available in Routing IP OSPF Subcontext (continued)*

| Command | Options | Description |
|---------|---------|-------------|
|         | routefilter | Adds, removes, configures, or displays route filtering for OSPF external routes |
| show    | areastats | Displays OSPF area statistics |
|         | lsdb | Displays the OSPF link-state database |
|         | virtifstats | Displays OSPF virtual-link statistics |

*Table 7-15: Commands Available in Routing IP Relay Subcontext*

| Command | Options | Description |
|---------|---------|-------------|
| set | global | Configures DHCP Relay Agent global settings |
| add/delete/ set | interface | Adds, removes, or configures DHCP Relay Agent settings on a specified interface |
| add/delete | dhcpserver | Adds or removes a DHCP-server IP address to or from the list of DHCP-server addresses |
| show | ifbinding | Displays IP-address bindings for interfaces |
|      | ifconfig | Displays DHCP Relay Agent configuration for each interface |
|      | ifstats | Displays DHCP statistics for each interface |

*Table 7-16: Commands Available in Routing IP RIP Subcontext*

| Command | Options | Description |
|---------|---------|-------------|
| set/show | flags | Configures advanced settings of RIP for IP on a specified interface |
|          | global | Configures global RIP-for-IP settings |
| add/delete/ set/show | interface | Adds or configures RIP-for-IP settings on a specified interface |
| add/delete | peerfilter | Adds or removes a RIP peer filter |
|            | acceptfilter | Adds or removes a RIP route filter to or from the list of routes being accepted |
|            | announcefilter | Adds or removes a RIP route filter to or from the list of routes being announced |
| add/delete/ show | neighbor | Adds or removes a RIP neighbor |
| show | globalstats | Displays global RIP parameters |
|      | ifbinding | Displays IP-address bindings for interfaces |
|      | ifstats | Displays RIP statistics for each interface |

## Examples

Reset routing tables in router to clean configuration:

```
C:\>netsh
netsh>routing
routing>reset
routing>
```

Switch to IP subcontext and display routing table:

```
routing>ip
routing ip>show rtmroutes

Prefix    Protocol  Prf  Met  Gateway  Vw  Interface
----------------------------------------------------
0.0.0.0/0        NetMgmt 10   1  172.16.11.196  UM
  Local Area Connection
127.0.0.0/8      Local  1    1  127.0.0.1      U
  Loopback
127.0.0.1/32     Local  1    1  127.0.0.1      U
  Loopback
172.16.11.0/24    Local  1   1  172.16.11.104  UM
  Local Area Connection
172.16.11.0/24    Local  1   1  172.16.11.105  UM
  Local Area Connection
172.16.11.104/32  Local  1   1  127.0.0.1      U
  Loopback
172.16.11.105/32  Local  1   1  127.0.0.1      U
  Loopback
172.16.255.255/32 Local  1   1  172.16.11.104  UM
  Local Area Connection
172.16.255.255/32 Local  1   1  172.16.11.105  UM
  Local Area Connection
224.0.0.0/4      Local  1    1  172.16.11.104  U
  Local Area Connection
224.0.0.0/4      Local  1    1  172.16.11.105  U
 Local Area Connection
255.255.255.255/32 Local 1   1  172.16.11.104  U
  Local Area Connection
255.255.255.255/32 Local 1   1  172.16.11.105  U
  Local Area Connection
```

Show IP protocols used:

```
routing ip>show protocol
Type        Vendor      Protocol
----------------------------------------------------
General     -           Protocol Priority
General     -           Multicast Boundaries
General     -           Global Info
Multicast   Microsoft   IGMP
Unicast     MS-0000     DHCP
```

Switch to Relay subcontext, and show DHCP Relay global settings:

```
routing ip>relay
routing ip relay>show global
DHCP Relay Global Configuration Information
----------------------------------------------------
Logging Level                    : Errors Only
Max Receive Queue Size           : 1048576
Server Count                     : 0
```

### See Also

*connection(3), dial-up connection(4), direct computer connection(4), incoming connection(4), interface Context(7), local-area connection(4), Network and Dial-up Connections(6), remote access(3), remote-access server(4), RAS Context(7), Routing and Remote Access(5), VPN connection(4)*

---

## WINS Context

Configures a WINS server.

### Subcontexts

Server

### Commands

? *or* help
> Displays these commands.

list
> Lists available WINS commands (more verbose than help).

dump
> Dumps the configuration of the WINS server as a series of Netshell commands.

server [\\*servername* | *serveraddress*]
> Enters the subcontext for the specified WINS server, which enables you to configure the WINS server using the add, check, delete, init, reset, set, and show commands. These commands and their options are summarized in Table 7-17.

*Table 7-17: Commands Available in WINS Server Subcontext*

| Command | Options | Description |
|---------|---------|-------------|
| add | name | Registers a name to the server |
| | partner | Adds a replication partner to the server |
| | pngserver | Adds a list of persona non grata servers for the current server |
| check | database | Checks the consistency of the database |
| | name | Checks a list of name records against a set of WINS servers |
| | version | Checks the consistency of the version number |
| delete | name | Deletes a registered name from the server database |
| | partner | Deletes a replication partner from the list of replication partners |
| | records | Deletes or tombstones all or a set of records from the server |
| | owners | Deletes a list of owners and their records |
| | pngserver | Deletes all or selected persona non grata servers from the list |
| init | backup | Initiates backup of the WINS database |

---

*Table 7-17: Commands Available in WINS Server Subcontext (continued)*

| Command | Options | Description |
|---------|---------|-------------|
| | import | Initiates import from an *lmhosts* file |
| | pull | Initiates and sends a pull trigger to another WINS server |
| | pullrange | Initiates and pulls a range of records from another WINS server |
| | push | Initiates and sends a push trigger to another WINS server |
| | replicate | Initiates replication of the database with replication partners |
| | restore | Initiates restoring of the database from a file |
| | scavenge | Initiates scavenging of the WINS database for the server |
| | search | Initiates search on the WINS database for the server |
| reset | statistics | Resets the server statistics |
| set | autopartnerconfig | Sets the automatic-replication partner-configuration information for the server |
| | backuppath | Sets the backup parameters for the server |
| | burstparam | Sets the burst-handling parameters for the server |
| | logparam | Sets the database and event-logging options |
| | migrateflag | Sets the migration flag for the server |
| | namerecord | Sets Interval and Timeout values for the server |
| | periodicdbchecking | Sets periodic database-checking parameters for the server |
| | pullpartnerconfig | Sets the configuration parameters for the specified pull partner |
| | pushpartnerconfig | Sets the configuration parameters for the specified push partner |
| | pullparam | Sets the default pull parameters for the server |
| | pushparam | Sets the default push parameters for the server |
| | replicateflag | Sets the replication flag for the server |
| | startversion | Sets the start version ID for the database |
| show | browser | Displays all active, domain master browser [1Bh] records |
| | database | Displays the database and records for the specified server |
| | info | Displays configuration information |
| | name | Displays detailed information for a particular record in the server |
| | partner | Displays pull or push (or both) partners for the server |
| | partnerproperties | Displays default partner configuration |
| | pullpartnerconfig | Displays configuration information for a pull partner |
| | pushpartnerconfig | Displays configuration information for a push partner |

**Commands**

*Table 7-17: Commands Available in WINS Server Subcontext (continued)*

| Command | Options | Description |
|---------|---------|-------------|
| | reccount | Displays number of records owned by a specific server |
| | recbyversion | Displays records owned by a specific server |
| | server | Displays the currently selected server |
| | statistics | Displays the statistics for the WINS server |
| | version | Displays the current version counter value for the WINS server |
| | versionmap | Displays the owner ID to Maximum Version Number mappings |

### Examples

Open a Netshell shell, and switch to the subcontext of a WINS server with IP address 172.16.11.104:

```
C:\>netsh
netsh>wins
wins>server \\172.16.11.104
***You have Read and Write access to the server 172.16.11.104***
```

Display configuration settings of WINS server:

```
wins server>show info

WINS Database backup parameter
~~~~~~~~~~~~~~~~~~~~~~~~~~~~~~~~~~~~~~~~~~~~~~~~~~~~~~~~~~~~~~
Backup Dir                       : Not Set
Backup on Shutdown               : Not Set

Name Record Settings(day:hour:minute)
~~~~~~~~~~~~~~~~~~~~~~~~~~~~~~~~~~~~~~~~~~~~~~~~~~~~~~~~~~~~~~
Refresh Interval                 : 006:00:00
Extinction(Tombstone) Interval   : 004:00:00
Extinction(Tombstone) TimeOut    : 006:00:00
Verification Interval            : 024:00:00

Database consistency checking parameters :
~~~~~~~~~~~~~~~~~~~~~~~~~~~~~~~~~~~~~~~~~~~~~~~~~~~~~~~~~~~~~~
Periodic Checking                : Disabled

WINS Logging Parameters:
~~~~~~~~~~~~~~~~~~~~~~~~~~~~~~~~~~~~~~~~~~~~~~~~~~~~~~~~~~~~~~
Log Database changes in Jet.Log  : Not Set
Log details events to event log  : Not Set

Burst Handling Parameters :
~~~~~~~~~~~~~~~~~~~~~~~~~~~~~~~~~~~~~~~~~~~~~~~~~~~~~~~~~~~~~~
Burst Handling State             : Not Set
```

Display records in WINS server's database:

```
wins server>show database {172.16.11.104}
Description of different fields in the Record Table
~~~~~~~~~~~~~~~~~~~~~~~~~~~~~~~~~~~~~~~~~~~~~~~~~~~~~~~~~
NAME               = Name of the Record. Up to 16
                     characters
T                  = Type of Record : D - Dynamic,
                     S - Static
S                  = State of the Record : A - Active,
                     R - Released, T - Tombstoned
VERSION            = LowPart ( in Hex)
G                  = Address Group : U - Unique,
                     N - Group, I - Internet,
                     M - Multihomed, D - Domain Name.
IPADDRESS          = List of IP Addresses associated
                     with the Name.
EXPIRATION DATE    = Expiration Time Stamp for the Name
                     Record.


~~~~~~~~~~~~~~~~~~~~~~~~~~~~~~~~~~~~~~~~~~~~~~~~~~~~~~~~~
NAME    -T-S- VERSION -G- IPADDRESS - EXPIRATION DATE
~~~~~~~~~~~~~~~~~~~~~~~~~~~~~~~~~~~~~~~~~~~~~~~~~~~~~~~~~
Retrieving database from the Wins server 172.16.11.104
??__MSBROWSE__?[01h]-D-A- 1      -N- 172.16.11.104  -
                                 7/8/2000 3:40:31 PM
MTITCANADA     [1Bh]-D-A- 1f8     -U- 172.16.11.104  -
                                 7/7/2000 8:57:56 AM
IS~TEST        [00h]-D-A- 2       -U- 172.16.11.104  -
                                 7/8/2000 6:24:33 PM
Total No. of records retrieved for server 172.16.11.104 : 3
Total No. of records displayed : 3
Command completed successfully.
```

Note that some WINS records may contain characters that cannot be displayed, which are represented in the example above by question marks.

### See Also

*WINS(3,4,5)*

# TCP/IP Commands

These commands are used for administering various aspects of TCP/IP and for interoperability with Unix machines in a heterogeneous networking environment. There have been relatively few changes to these commands from Windows NT to Windows 2000.

*Commands*

# arp

Resolves IP addresses into media access control (MAC) addresses and caches them for reuse.

## Syntax

```
arp -s IPaddress MACaddress [interfacenumber]
arp -d IPaddress [interfacenumber]
arp -a [IPaddress] [-N interfacenumber]
```

## Options

**-a** `[IPaddress]`

Resolves the specified IP address into its associated MAC address by querying the Address Resolution Protocol (ARP) cache on the local machine. (If no address is specified, then all cached IP-to-MAC address mappings are displayed.)

**-g** `[IPaddress]`

Same as **-a**.

**-N** `interfacenumber`

Specifies the network adapter whose ARP cache is to be queried. (Each network adapter has its own ARP cache on a multihomed machine.) Use **arp -a** to determine the number of each interface. If **arp** is used without **-N** on a multi-homed machine, the first interface found is used.

**-d** `IPaddress [interfacenumber]`

Removes the IP-to-MAC address mapping from the local ARP cache for the specified IP address and interface. If no *IPaddress* is specified, the top entry in the ARP cache is removed.

**-s** `IPaddress MACaddress [interfacenumber]`

Adds a static IP-to-MAC address mapping to the local ARP cache for the specified interface. The MAC address must be expressed in hexidecimal form as 12 characters, in groups of 2, separated by dashes. Static ARP mappings are persistent until the system reboots.

## Examples

View the ARP cache on the local machine:

```
arp -a
Interface: 172.16.11.104 on Interface 0x2
  Internet Address      Physical Address      Type
  172.16.11.100         00-40-95-d1-29-6c     dynamic
```

ping the host named *LEONARDO* to determine its IP address, and add a mapping for it to the local ARP cache:

```
ping -n 1 leonardo
Pinging leonardo [172.16.11.39] with 32 bytes of data:
Reply from 172.16.11.39: bytes=32 time<10ms TTL=32
Ping statistics for 172.16.11.39:
  Packets: Sent = 1, Received = 1, Lost = 0 (0% loss),
Approximate round trip times in milli-seconds:
  Minimum = 0ms, Maximum =  0ms, Average =  0ms
```

Verify that an IP-to-MAC address mapping for *LEONARDO* (172.16.11.39) has been added to the local ARP cache:

```
arp -a
Interface: 172.16.11.104 on Interface 0x2
  Internet Address      Physical Address       Type
  172.16.11.39          00-40-95-d1-32-90      dynamic
  172.16.11.100         00-40-95-d1-29-6c      dynamic
```

Add a static mapping for *LEONARDO* to the local ARP cache:

```
arp -s 172.16.11.39 00-40-95-d1-32-90
```

Verify the static mapping:

```
arp -a
Interface: 172.16.11.104 on Interface 0x2
  Internet Address      Physical Address       Type
  172.16.11.39          00-40-95-d1-32-90      static
  172.16.11.100         00-40-95-d1-29-6c      dynamic
```

### Notes

- For one host to communicate with another on a TCP/IP network, the first host uses **arp** to resolve the second host's IP address into its corresponding MAC address. This MAC address is then used to provide a destination address for Ethernet or token-ring frames sent from the first host to the second. **arp** caches these IP-to-MAC address mappings for a short time (from 2 to 10 minutes) to reduce the number of ARP broadcasts needed.

- **arp** is a useful tool for troubleshooting TCP/IP networks as it can be used to find the MAC address of any host on the local subnet, provided that the IP address for the host is known.

- **arp** can only be used to view the ARP cache on the local machine, not on remote ones.

- To reduce broadcast traffic and speed up TCP/IP communications, you can add static mappings to the ARP cache on client machines. This lets clients resolve IP addresses of commonly used servers on the network from the clients' local ARP caches instead of using ARP broadcasts.

- To make static ARP cache mappings persistent across reboots, add **arp** commands to a batch file and run the file at system startup.

### See Also

*ping(7)*

---

## finger

Provides information about a user on a remote system.

### Syntax

```
finger [-1] [username]@computername [...]
```

## Options

-l   Verbose output.

[*username*] @*computername*

The user you want to finger on the remote system—that is, the user about whom you want to obtain information. If *username* is omitted, then finger obtains information concerning all users on the remote system.

## Examples

In general, the output to the finger command will depend on the system being queried. For example, here are the instructions displayed when using finger on a hypothetical Unix host at university BlahBlah.edu and the results of fingering a user named mitch:

```
finger help@blahblah.edu
[blahblah.edu]
Welcome to the finger daemon at blahblah.edu! By default, the finger
command displays in multi-column format the following information about
each logged-in user:
   o   User Name
   o   Nickname, you can use this to send to
         nickname_lastname@blahblah.edu.
   o   The send_email_to field is the address to use
         to send this person email.
   o   Campus address
   o   Campus phone
   o   Project
We don't show login info, or idle time since these ids never actually
login, this is a client-server system.

Different types of queries:
    alias/netid lookup - finger jwh2@blahblah.edu
    name lookup - finger howell@blahblah.edu
                  finger jim@blahblah.edu
```

If you get a message that says "Too many returns for your query" then you will have to refine your query:

```
finger mitch@blahblah.edu
[blahblah.edu]
Information from BlahBlah's Network Identity Directory...
-------------------------------------------------------

Your query returned   2 matches:

Name:           Mitchell K Sillyness
Nickname: Mitch
Send Email To:  mks@graphics.blahblah.edu
Campus Phone:   607-555-1212
Campus Address: 580 Smith Hall
Local Phone:
Local Address:
Project:
```

```
Name:           Mitch H. McNobody
Nickname:
Send Email To:  mhm12@blahblah.edu
Campus Phone:
Campus Address:
Local Phone:
Local Address:
Project:

   . . .
```

### Notes

The remote machine must be running the finger daemon or service. If it isn't, you'll get "Connection refused" in response to using the `finger` command. Windows 2000 Server does not include a finger service, only a command-line finger client.

## *ftp*

Transfers files to or from a computer running the FTP Server service.

### Syntax

```
ftp [-v] [-n] [-i] [-d] [-g] [-s:filename] [-a] [-w:windowsize]
[hostname]
```

### Options

-a  Uses any local interface for the endpoint of the FTP data connection. (The FTP data connection is used for transferring files and is different from the FTP control connection, which is used for sending FTP commands between the client and server.)

-d  Enables debugging mode, which displays all FTP commands sent between the client and server.

-g  Disables globbing (filename expansion) so that wildcards can be used within local paths and filenames without being interpreted by the shell.

-i  Disables interactive prompting when multiple files are being transferred.

-n  Disables autologon to establish a control connection with the remote host, but nothing else.

-s:*filename*
    Executes a series of FTP commands stored in a text file as a batch job.

-w:*windowsize*
    Specifies the amount of data that can be transferred before requiring that the receiving end issue a configuration. The defaul, transfer buffer size is 4,096 bytes.

-v  Disables showing responses of remote FTP connections.

*hostname*
>    Identifies the computer name (DNS or NetBIOS name) or IP address of the remote computer you want to connect to using FTP (this must be the last parameter on the line).

### FTP Commands

There is a whole separate set of FTP-specific commands you can use when you run ftp in interactive mode. Here are some of the more commonly used ones:

!   Escapes from an interactive FTP session to the command shell *cmd.exe* in order to execute the command, then returns to the FTP session.

ascii
>    Sets file transfer type to ASCII for transferring text files. ASCII is the default type, the other being binary.

binary
>    Sets file transfer type to binary for transferring binary files such as image files and Word documents.

bye *or* close *or* quit
>    Terminates an FTP session with the remote server and exits the FTP shell.

cd *remotedirectory*
>    Changes to the specified directory on the remote server.

delete *remotefilename*
>    Deletes the file from the current directory on the remote server.

dir [*remotedirectory*] [*localfilename*]
>    Displays a directory listing of the specified remote directory (or the current remote directory if none is specified). If a filename is specified, the listing is saved with this name on the local machine instead of being displayed.

disconnect
>    Terminates an FTP session with the remote server, but stays within the FTP shell.

get *remotefilename* [*localfilename*]
>    Transfers the specified file from the remote server to the local machine, renaming it as well if *localfilename* is specified.

hash
>    Displays one hash character (#) each time 2,048 bytes are transferred (useful for displaying the progress when downloading large files).

help [*command*]
>    Lists the available FTP commands or displays a short description of the specified command.

lcd *localdirectory*
>    Changes to the specified directory on the local computer.

ls [*remotedirectory*] [*localfilename*]
>    Same as dir earlier in this list.

mget *remotefilenames*
>    Gets multiple files (see get earlier in this list).

mput *localfilenames*
>    Puts multiple files (see put later in this list).

open *hostname* [*port*]
>    Opens an FTP connection to the specified remote computer. *hostname* can be a computer name (DNS or NetBIOS name depending on the network) or IP address. *port* is only required if the remote server is listening on a different TCP port than the standard FTP one, which is port 21.

prompt
>    Toggles prompting for confirmation by user (default is on).

put *localfilename* [*remotefilename*]
>    Transfers the specified file from the local machine to the remote server, renaming it as well if *remotefilename* is specified.

pwd
>    Displays the name of the current directory on the remote server.

remotehelp [*command*]
>    Displays a list of FTP commands understood by the remote server or describes a particular command.

user *username*
>    Logs on to the remote server as *username* and then prompts you for a password.

### Examples

Run FTP in interactive mode:

```
C:\>ftp
ftp>
```

Open a session with an FTP server:

```
ftp> open 172.16.11.104
Connected to 172.16.11.104.
220 test Microsoft FTP Service (Version 5.0).
```

Log on to the server as "anonymous":

```
User (172.16.11.104:(none)): anonymous
331 Anonymous access allowed, send identity (e-mail name) as password.
Password: ********
230 Anonymous user logged in.
```

Display the current directory on the server:

```
ftp> pwd
257 "/" is current directory.
```

List the contents of the current directory on the server:

```
ftp> ls
200 PORT command successful.
150 Opening ASCII mode data connection for file list.
hello.txt
226 Transfer complete.
ftp: 11 bytes received in 0.04Seconds 0.28Kbytes/sec.
```

*Commands*

Download the file *hello.txt* from the server to the client:

```
ftp> get hello.txt
200 PORT command successful.
150 Opening ASCII mode data connection for hello.txt(12 bytes).
226 Transfer complete.
ftp: 12 bytes received in 0.00Seconds 12000.00Kbytes/sec.
```

Escape from the FTP shell momentarily and run the command type C:\hello.txt on the client, which should display the contents of the text file if it was successfully downloaded from the server:

```
ftp> !type C:\hello.txt
Hello there!ftp>
```

Note that the file contains the line of text "Hello there!"

Close the connection with the server and terminate the interactive FTP session:

```
ftp>quit
221
C:\>
```

## Notes

- The ftp command is a client, as opposed to an FTP service or daemon, which resides on the server.
- Windows 2000 Server includes an FTP Server service as part of its Internet Information Services (IIS). By default, the home or root directory of this service is mapped to the directory *C:\Inetpub\ftproot* on the server.
- FTP is inherently insecure as it transmits passwords in clear text.
- To use ftp in batch mode, do the following:
  - Go through an interactive FTP session, and copy it to a text editor such as Notepad.
  - Edit out the responses, leaving only the commands.
  - Use the -s switch to run the batch file with ftp.

## See Also

*Internet Information Services(5)*

---

# hostname

Displays the hostname of the local machine.

## Syntax

```
hostname
```

## Options

None

---

### Examples

Display the hostname of the computer whose full DNS name is *test.mtitcanada.com*:

```
hostname
test
```

### Notes

To display or modify the hostname using the GUI:

Right-click on My Computer → Properties → Network Identification

---

# ipconfig

Displays the current TCP/IP settings of the local machine.

### Syntax

```
ipconfig [/all | /release [adaptername] | [/renew [adaptername] |
flushdns | /registerdns | /showclassid adaptername | /setclassid
adaptername [newclassID] ]
```

### Options

Displays the IP address, subnet mask, and default gateway for each interface on the machine.

/all

Yields verbose output showing additional TCP/IP settings.

/release [*adaptername*]

Releases an IP address acquired using DHCP. On a multihomed machine, specify an adapter name using the name that appears for the adapter when you type ipconfig without parameters.

/renew [*adaptername*]

Requests a new IP address from a DHCP server (only available when the computer is configured as a DHCP client).

/displaydns

Displays the contents of the local DNS name cache on the client (new to Windows 2000). When DNS is used to resolve a DNS name into an IP address, the results are temporarily cached.

/flushdns

Flushes the list of locally cached DNS names on the client (new to Windows 2000). Flushing the cache removes these mappings and can be useful when troubleshooting DNS-related problems. Flushing the DNS cache on the client does not remove mappings that have been preloaded from the local *Hosts* file. (You must remove these mappings from the *Hosts* file to do this.)

/registerdns

Causes the client to re-register its hostname with DNS servers without restarting the client machine (new to Windows 2000). This may also be used in conjunction with Dynamic DNS.

---

**/showclassid** *adaptername*

Displays all the DHCP class IDs allowed for the adapter (new to Windows 2000). Windows 2000 DHCP clients support DHCP class options that can be viewed using this command and configured using `ipconfig /setclassid`.

**/setclassid** *adaptername* [*newclassID*]

Changes the DHCP class ID for the adapter (new to Windows 2000).

### Examples

Display summary of TCP/IP settings on local machine:

```
ipconfig
Windows 2000 IP Configuration
Ethernet adapter Local Area Connection:
   Connection-specific DNS Suffix  . :
   IP Address. . . . . . . . . . . : 172.16.11.105
   Subnet Mask . . . . . . . . . . : 255.255.255.0
   IP Address. . . . . . . . . . . : 172.16.11.104
   Subnet Mask . . . . . . . . . . : 255.255.255.0
   Default Gateway . . . . . . . . : 172.16.11.196
```

Display full details:

```
ipconfig /all
Windows 2000 IP Configuration
   Host Name . . . . . . . . . . . : test
   Primary DNS Suffix  . . . . . . : mtitcanada.com
   Node Type . . . . . . . . . . . : Hybrid
   IP Routing Enabled. . . . . . . : No
   WINS Proxy Enabled. . . . . . . : No
   DNS Suffix Search List. . . . . : mtitcanada.com
Ethernet adapter Local Area Connection:
   Connection-specific DNS Suffix  . :
   Description . . . . . . . . . . : Realtek
                 RTL8029(AS) PCI Ethernet Adapter
   Physical Address. . . . . . . . : 00-00-B4-A0-47-74
   DHCP Enabled. . . . . . . . . . : No
   IP Address. . . . . . . . . . . : 172.16.11.105
   Subnet Mask . . . . . . . . . . : 255.255.255.0
   IP Address. . . . . . . . . . . : 172.16.11.104
   Subnet Mask . . . . . . . . . . : 255.255.255.0
   Default Gateway . . . . . . . . : 172.16.11.196
   DNS Servers . . . . . . . . . . : 172.16.11.104
                                     172.16.11.100
```

Display contents of client DNS name cache:

```
ipconfig /displaydns
Windows 2000 IP Configuration
```

```
localhost.
-----------------------------------------------------
      Record Name . . . . . : localhost
      Record Type . . . . . : 1
      Time To Live  . . . . : 31338848
      Data Length . . . . . : 4
      Section . . . . . . . : Answer
      A (Host) Record . . . :
                          127.0.0.1

1.0.0.127.in-addr.arpa.
-----------------------------------------------------
      Record Name . . . . . : 1.0.0.127.in-addr.arpa
      Record Type . . . . . : 12
      Time To Live  . . . . : 31338847
      Data Length . . . . . : 4
      Section . . . . . . . : Answer
      PTR Record  . . . . . :
                          localhost

bach.mtitworld.com.
-----------------------------------------------------
      Record Name . . . . . : bach.mtitworld.com
      Record Type . . . . . : 1
      Time To Live  . . . . : 261
      Data Length . . . . . : 4
      Section . . . . . . . : Answer
      A (Host) Record . . . :
                          172.16.11.100

test.mtitcanada.com.
-----------------------------------------------------
      Record Name . . . . . : test.mtitcanada.com
      Record Type . . . . . : 1
      Time To Live  . . . . : 2665
      Data Length . . . . . : 4
      Section . . . . . . . : Answer
      A (Host) Record . . . :
                          172.16.11.104

      Record Name . . . . . : test.mtitcanada.com
      Record Type . . . . . : 1
      Time To Live  . . . . : 2665
      Data Length . . . . . : 4
      Section . . . . . . . : Answer
      A (Host) Record . . . :
                          172.16.11.105
```

Flush client DNS name cache:

**ipconfig /flushdns**
Windows 2000 IP Configuration
Successfully flushed the DNS Resolver Cache.

Verify that client DNS name cache has been flushed:

```
ipconfig /displaydns
Windows 2000 IP Configuration

    localhost.
    ------------------------------------------------------
        Record Name . . . . . : localhost
        Record Type . . . . . : 1
        Time To Live  . . . . : 31338835
        Data Length . . . . . : 4
        Section . . . . . . . : Answer
        A (Host) Record . . . :
                         127.0.0.1
```

Note the mapping that remains in the cache. This is preloaded from the *Hosts* file on the client.

Re-register client's DNS information with DNS server:

```
ipconfig /registerdns
Windows 2000 IP Configuration
Registration of the DNS resource records for all adapters of this
computer has been initiated. Any errors will be reported in the Event
Viewer in 15 minutes.
```

Display DHCP class IDs for the client on the "Local-Area Connection" adapter:

```
ipconfig showclassid "Local Area Connection"
Windows 2000 IP Configuration
DHCP Class ID for Adapter "Local Area Connection":
DHCP ClassID Name . . . . . . . . : Default BOOTP Class
DHCP ClassID Description  . . . . : User class for BOOTP Clients
```

## Notes

The Windows 2000 client, DNS name cache also supports negative caching of unresolved or invalid DNS names. However, these negative DNS responses are cached for only a short period of time.

## See Also

*DNS(3), ping(7)*

---

# lpq

Displays the status of a print queue on a TCP/IP print server running the LPD daemon.

## Syntax

```
lpq -S servername -P printername [-1]
```

## Options

**-S** *servername*
> The name or IP address of the LPD print server

**-P** *printername*
> The name of the print queue on the server

**-l** Verbose output

## Examples

Display status of print queue for the network printer *BROTHER* on *TEST*:

```
lpq -S 172.16.11.104 -P brother
    Windows 2000 LPD Server
    Printer \\172.16.11.104\brother

Owner Status Jobname Job-Id Size Pages Priority
-------------------------------------------------------
Administrator Printing Test Page 513 103793 0 0
```

## Notes

- `lpq` can query non-LPD print servers as well (for example, Microsoft Windows print servers). You cannot use `lpr` to send jobs to these print servers, however.
- You can query the TCP/IP print queue on the local machine by typing:

        lpq -S localhost -P printername

## See Also

*lpr(7)*

---

# lpr

Prints a file to a TCP/IP print server running the LPD daemon.

## Syntax

    lpr -S servername -P printername [-C classname] [-J jobname] [-o option]
    [-x] [-d] filename

## Options

**-S** *servername*
> Indicates the name or IP address of the LPD print server.

**-P** *printername*
> Indicates the name of the print queue on the server.

**-C** *classname*
> Specifies something to identify the output as your job (otherwise, the hostname of your computer will be used). This appears on the banner page (if enabled on the print server).

-J *jobname*
> Specifies the name of your job (otherwise, the filename of the file you are printing will be used). This appears on the banner page (if enabled on the print server).

-o *option*
> Specifies the type of file being printed (the default is ASCII text). For example, specify .PS as the option when printing PostScript files.

-x Provides backward compatibility for printing to LPD servers running older versions of SunOS.

-d Transfers the datafile before the control file, if needed by the LPD server.

*filename*
> Indicates the file you are printing.

### Examples

Send a job to queue *HPLASERJ* on LPD server 172.16.11.104:

```
lpr -S 172.16.11.104 -P hplaserj -C Mitchell -J
   Testing C:\hello.txt
```

Use lpq to check the queue to verify if the job is pending.

### See Also

*lpq(7)*

---

## nbtstat

Displays statistics and current connections for NetBT (NetBIOS over TCP/IP).

### Syntax

```
nbtstat [ [-a computername] [-A IPaddress] [-c] [-n] [-r] [-R] [-RR] [-s]
[-S] [interval] ]
```

### Options

-a *computername*
> Displays the NBT name table on the specified remote computer.

-A *IPaddress*
> Same as -a except that IP address of remote computer is used.

-c Displays contents of NetBIOS name cache on local machine. This shows the NetBIOS names on the network that have been successfully resolved into IP addresses.

-n Lists the NetBIOS names registered by the local machine. The "registered" field shows whether the name has been registered using broadcasts (B-node) or WINS servers (other node types).

-r Displays statistics for NetBIOS name resolution on the local machine.

-R  Purges all NetBIOS name–to–IP address mappings from the local NetBIOS name cache and then preloads mappings from the *lmhosts* file that have the #PRE specifier.

-RR
Releases and refreshes all NetBIOS names for the local machine (new to Windows 2000).

-s  Shows all current NetBIOS sessions, listing remote computers by NetBIOS names.

-S  Shows all current NetBIOS sessions, listing remote computers by IP addresses.

*interval*
Causes the output to be refreshed every *interval* seconds until Ctrl-C is pressed.

## Examples

Purge NetBIOS name–to–IP address mappings in the local NBT name cache:

```
nbtstat -R
Successful purge and preload of the NBT Remote Cache Name Table.
```

View the local NBT cache:

```
nbtstat -c
Local Area Connection:
Node IpAddress: [172.16.11.104] Scope Id: []
    No names in cache
```

Ping server *BACH* to resolve its NetBIOS name into its IP address:

```
ping bach
Pinging bach [172.16.11.100] with 32 bytes of data:

Reply from 172.16.11.100: bytes=32 time<10ms TTL=128
Reply from 172.16.11.100: bytes=32 time<10ms TTL=128
Reply from 172.16.11.100: bytes=32 time<10ms TTL=128
Reply from 172.16.11.100: bytes=32 time<10ms TTL=128

Ping statistics for 172.16.11.100:
Packets: Sent = 4, Received = 4, Lost = 0 (0% loss),
Approximate round trip times in milli-seconds:
Minimum = 0ms, Maximum =  0ms, Average =  0ms
```

Check if the resolved name (*BACH*) and its IP address mapping (172.16.11.100) have been cached on the local machine:

```
nbtstat -c
Local Area Connection:
Node IpAddress: [172.16.11.104] Scope Id: []

        NetBIOS Remote Cache Name Table

Name    Type          Host Address    Life [sec]
---------------------------------------------------
BACH    <00>  UNIQUE    172.16.11.100      597
```

Display a list of NetBIOS names registered for the local machine:

```
nbtstat -n
Local Area Connection:
Node IpAddress: [172.16.11.104] Scope Id: []


                NetBIOS Local Name Table

        Name                    Type        Status
        ---------------------------------------------
        TEST            <00>  UNIQUE      Registered
        MTITCANADA      <00>  GROUP       Registered
        MTITCANADA      <1C>  GROUP       Registered
        TEST            <20>  UNIQUE      Registered
        MTITCANADA      <1B>  UNIQUE      Registered
        TEST            <03>  UNIQUE      Registered
        NETSHOWSERVICES<03>  UNIQUE      Registered
        MTITCANADA      <1E>  GROUP       Registered
        MTITCANADA      <1D>  UNIQUE      Registered
        .._MSBROWSE__.<01>  GROUP       Registered
        INet~Services <1C>  GROUP       Registered
        IS~TEST........<00>  UNIQUE      Registered
```

The fact that one of the previous NetBIOS names has the <1C> suffix indicates that the local machine is a domain controller.

Display the list of NetBIOS names registered by the remote machine called *BACH* (this is also a handy way of obtaining the MAC address of *BACH*):

```
nbtstat -a bach
Local Area Connection:
Node IpAddress: [172.16.11.104] Scope Id: []


                NetBIOS Remote Machine Name Table

        Name                    Type        Status
        ---------------------------------------------
        BACH            <00>  UNIQUE      Registered
        BACH            <20>  UNIQUE      Registered
        MTITWORLD       <00>  GROUP       Registered
        MTITWORLD       <1C>  GROUP       Registered
        MTITWORLD       <1B>  UNIQUE      Registered
        BACH            <03>  UNIQUE      Registered
        MTITWORLD       <1E>  GROUP       Registered
        INet~Services <1C>  GROUP       Registered
        IS~BACH........<00>  UNIQUE      Registered
        MTITWORLD       <1D>  UNIQUE      Registered
        .._MSBROWSE__.<01>  GROUP       Registered
        ADMINISTRATOR <03>  UNIQUE      Registered


        MAC Address = 00-40-95-D1-29-6C
```

Display current NBT session statistics on the local machine:

```
nbtstat -S
Local Area Connection:
Node IpAddress: [172.16.11.104] Scope Id: []

                    NetBIOS Connection Table

LocalName   State      In/Out  RemoteHost    Input   Output
-------------------------------------------------------------
TEST   <00>Connected   Out     172.16.11.39   320KB   721KB
TEST   <00>Connected   Out     172.16.11.94   711KB   185KB
TEST   <00>Connected   Out     172.16.11.100    5KB     8KB
TEST   <03>Listening
```

## Notes

nbtstat is most useful when troubleshooting name-resolution problems in mixed Windows 2000/Windows NT networks where NetBIOS is still being used. (NetBIOS can be disabled in the TCP/IP properties of Windows 2000 machines and is not really needed in pure Windows 2000 networks.) The various fields of the output from nbtstat are:

Input
   Bytes received over the connection

Output
   Bytes sent over the connection

In/Out
   Whether the connection is inbound or outbound

Life
   How long the entry will remain in the name table cache before being purged

Local Name
   The local NetBIOS name associated with the connection

Remote Host
   The name or IP address of the remote computer

Type
   The type of the NetBIOS name, which can be either a unique name or a group name

State
   Current state of the connection (see Table 7-18)

*Table 7-18: Possible States of an NBT Connection*

| State | Description |
|---|---|
| Accepting | An inbound session is in the process of being accepted. |
| Associated | A connection endpoint has been created and associated with an IP address. |
| Connected | A session has been established. |
| Connecting | A session is in the connecting phase during which the name-to-IP address mapping of the destination is being resolved. |
| Disconnected | The local machine has issued a disconnect and is waiting for confirmation from the remote machine. |

*Table 7-18: Possible States of an NBT Connection (continued)*

| State | Description |
|-------|-------------|
| Disconnecting | A session is in the process of disconnecting. |
| Idle | An endpoint has been opened but cannot receive a connection. |
| Inbound | An inbound session is in the connecting phase. |
| Listening | An endpoint is available for an inbound connection. |
| Outbound | A session is in the connecting phase during which the TCP connection is being formed. |
| Reconnecting | A session is attempting to reconnect after failure to connect. |

### See Also

*WINS(3,4,5)*

---

## netstat

Displays statistics and current connections for TCP/IP.

### Syntax

```
netstat [-a] [-e] [-n] [-s] [-p protocol] [-r] [interval]
```

### Options

-a   Lists all TCP/IP connections and their current statuses.

-e   Displays frame statistics for network adapters (can be used with –s option).

-n   Lists addresses and port numbers as numbers instead of trying to resolve them using DNS. This is useful if DNS isn't working properly and you want to avoid long timeouts when using netstat.

-p *protocol*
  When used in conjunction with –s option, displays statistics for the specified protocol, which can be either TCP, UDP, ICMP, or IP.

-r   Displays the routing table.

-s   Displays statistics and connections for all TCP/IP protocols.

*interval*
  Causes the output to be refreshed every *interval* seconds until Ctrl-C is pressed.

### Examples

Show statistics for Ethernet frames:

```
netstat -e
Interface Statistics

                         Received              Sent
Bytes                    48446148          43795441
Unicast packets            195267            207067
Non-unicast packets         12311              6830
Discards                        0                 0
Errors                          0                 0
Unknown protocols           15400
```

Show statistics for TCP protocol and the current state of TCP connections:

```
netstat -s -p tcp
```

```
TCP Statistics
   Active Opens                      = 7631
   Passive Opens                     = 4689
   Failed Connection Attempts        = 269
   Reset Connections                 = 380
   Current Connections               = 23
   Segments Received                 = 160892
   Segments Sent                     = 173884
   Segments Retransmitted            = 680
```

```
Active Connections
 Proto  Local Address       Foreign Address                        State
 TCP    test:ldap           test.mtitcanada.com:4208               ESTABLISHED
 TCP    test:ldap           test.mtitcanada.com:4216               ESTABLISHED
 TCP    test:ldap           test.mtitcanada.com:4229               ESTABLISHED
 TCP    test:ldap           test.mtitcanada.com:4233               ESTABLISHED
 TCP    test:1110           test.mtitcanada.com:ldap               CLOSE_WAIT
 TCP    test:4208           test.mtitcanada.com:ldap               ESTABLISHED
 TCP    test:4216           test.mtitcanada.com:ldap               ESTABLISHED
 TCP    test:4229           test.mtitcanada.com:ldap               ESTABLISHED
 TCP    test:4233           test.mtitcanada.com:ldap               ESTABLISHED
 TCP    test:ldap           test.mtitcanada.com:3993               TIME_WAIT
 TCP    test:ldap           test.mtitcanada.com:3994               TIME_WAIT
 TCP    test:ldap           test.mtitcanada.com:4001               TIME_WAIT
 TCP    test:ldap           test.mtitcanada.com:4007               TIME_WAIT
 TCP    test:ldap           test.mtitcanada.com:4232               ESTABLISHED
 TCP    test:microsoft-ds   test.mtitcanada.com:4009               ESTABLISHED
 TCP    test:1026           test.mtitcanada.com:1233               ESTABLISHED
 TCP    test:1026           test.mtitcanada.com:1334               ESTABLISHED
 TCP    test:1224           test.mtitcanada.com:ldap               CLOSE_WAIT
 TCP    test:1227           test.mtitcanada.com:3268               CLOSE_WAIT
 TCP    test:1233           test.mtitcanada.com:1026               ESTABLISHED
 TCP    test:1298           LEONARDO:netbios-ssn                   ESTABLISHED
 TCP    test:1300           BACH:1026                              ESTABLISHED
 TCP    test:1334           test.mtitcanada.com:1026               ESTABLISHED
 TCP    test:3712           test.mtitcanada.com:ldap               CLOSE_WAIT
 TCP    test:3936           test.mtitcanada.com:ldap               CLOSE_WAIT
 TCP    test:3995           BACH:ldap                              TIME_WAIT
 TCP    test:3996           BACH:microsoft-ds                      TIME_WAIT
 TCP    test:3998           test.mtitcanada.com:microsoft-ds       TIME_WAIT
 TCP    test:4001           test.mtitcanada.com:ldap               TIME_WAIT
 TCP    test:4008           BACH:ldap                              TIME_WAIT
 TCP    test:4009           test.mtitcanada.com:microsoft-ds       ESTABLISHED
 TCP    test:4010           test.mtitcanada.com:epmap              TIME_WAIT
 TCP    test:4011           test.mtitcanada.com:1026               TIME_WAIT
 TCP    test:4012           test.mtitcanada.com:epmap              TIME_WAIT
 TCP    test:4013           test.mtitcanada.com:1026               TIME_WAIT
 TCP    test:4232           test.mtitcanada.com:ldap               ESTABLISHED
```

*Commands*

### Notes

The fields in the output of `netstat` are:

`Proto`
> The name of the protocol used for the connection.

`Local Address`
> The name (or IP address) and port number (or descriptor) for the connection on the local machine. An asterisk means that the port has not yet been established.

`Foreign Address`
> The name (or IP address) and port number (or descriptor) for the connection on the remote machine. An asterisk means that the port has not yet been established.

`State`
> The connection state (TCP only). This is typically either:

> `LISTEN`
>> TCP is waiting for a connection at this port.

> `ESTABLISHED`
>> An active TCP connection has been established at this port.

> If the state is any of the following, the TCP/IP connection is in the process of being established or torn down using a three-way TCP handshake:

>> CLOSED
>> CLOSE_WAIT
>> FIN_WAIT_1
>> FIN_WAIT_2
>> LAST_ACK
>> SYN_RECEIVED
>> SYN_SEND
>> TIME_WAIT

### See Also

*TCP/IP(3, 4)*

---

## nslookup

Diagnostic utility for displaying information stored in DNS servers.

### Modes

`nslookup` has two modes of operation:

*Interactive*
> In this mode, an `nslookup` shell is opened so that any sequence of `nslookup` commands can be run one at a time. Enter interactive mode by typing:

> `nslookup`

*Noninteractive*

In this mode, only a single nslookup command is run, after which you return to the command prompt. The syntax is:

    nslookup -command host DNSserver

*-command*

One of the nslookup commands listed later in this article. The hyphen is part of the syntax.

*host*

The IP address or hostname of the host whose DNS information you want to obtain from the DNS server. If you use a hyphen, the prompt changes to nslookup interactive mode.

*DNSserver*

The IP address or hostname of the DNS server you want to query. (If omitted, the default DNS server for the local machine is used.)

## Commands

? *or* help

Briefly describes these commands.

exit

Quits the interactive mode of nslookup.

finger [*username*]

Fingers the current computer for a list of currently logged-on users. If you specify *username*, then the information for that user is obtained.

ls [*option*] *dnsdomain* [[> | >>] *filename*]

Lists (or redirects to a file) different subsets of resource records for the specified DNS domain depending on the option selected, specifically:

*-t querytype*

Lists all records of the specified type (see Table 7-19)

-a  Lists aliases of hosts in the DNS domain (same result as using -t CNAME)

-d  Lists all records for the DNS domain (same result as using -t ANY)

-h  Lists operating-system information for the DNS domain (same result as using -t HINFO)

-s  Lists well-known services of host in the DNS domain (same result as using -t WKS)

lserver *dnsdomain*

Sets the default server to the specified DNS domain using the initial server.

root

Sets the default server to the DNS root server *ns.nic.ddn.mil* (same result as using lserver ns.nic.ddn.mil). Use set root to change the default root server.

server *dnsdomain*

Sets the default server to the specified DNS domain using the current default server.

`set all`

Displays the configuration of `nslookup` (how it performs lookups).

`set class=value`

Modifies the query class, which can be IN (Internet class), CHAOS (Chaos class), HESIOD (MIT Athena Hesiod class), or ANY (any class). The default is IN (the other classes are obsolete).

`set [no]debug`

Enables or disables debugging mode, which is very verbose (default is **no**).

`set [no]d2`

Enables or disables exhaustive debugging mode, which is incredibly verbose (default is **no**).

`set [no]defname`

Appends the default DNS domain name to each query (default is **yes**).

`set domain=dnsdomain`

Switches the default DNS domain to the one specified. This name will be appended to all `nslookup` queries if **defname** is specified.

`set [no]ignore`

Reports or ignores packet errors (default is **ignore**).

`set port=value`

Modifies the default TCP/UDP port for the DNS name server port. (This is port 53 by default.)

`set querytype=value`

Specifies the types of resource records to obtain from the DNS server (see Table 7-19). The default is Address (A) record.

`set [no]recurse`

Enables or disables recursion whether the DNS server should query other DNS servers if it cannot respond with the requested information. (Default is **yes**.)

`set retry=number`

Specifies the number of retries that can be performed by `nslookup` when querying a DNS server until it gives up (default is four times).

`set root=DNSserver`

Specifies the root server (affects the `root` command earlier in this article). The default is `ns.nic.ddn.mil`.

`set [no]search`

Toggles whether each DNS domain name in the search list should be appended to a request until a response is received (default is **yes**).

`set srchlist DNSdomain1[/DNSdomain2/...]`

Specifies the DNS domain-name search list (up to six DNS servers can be specified).

`set timeout=seconds`

Modifies the initial time in seconds that `nslookup` waits for a response to its first request (default is five seconds).

set type=*value*

Specifies the type of records to be requested from a DNS server (see Table 7-19).

set [no]vc

Specifies that a virtual circuit should be used when sending requests to a DNS server (default is no).

view *filename*

Displays the output of any previous commands that have been redirected to files.

*Table 7-19: Values for querytype Parameter for nslookup Commands*

| Value | Description |
|---|---|
| A | Computer's IP address |
| ANY | All types of data |
| CNAME | Canonical name for an alias |
| GID | Group identifier of a group name |
| HINFO | Computer's CPU and operating-system type |
| MB | Mailbox domain name |
| MG | Mail group member |
| MINFO | Mailbox or mail-list information |
| MR | Mail rename domain name |
| MX | Mail exchanger |
| NS | DNS name server for the named zone |
| PTR | Hostname (if the query is an IP address) or pointer to other info |
| SOA | DNS domain's start-of-authority record |
| TXT | Text information |
| UID | User identifier |
| UINFO | User information |
| WKS | Well-known service description |

## Examples

Start nslookup in interactive mode:

```
C:\>nslookup
Default Server:  izzy.mtitworld.com
Address:  172.16.11.99
>
```

Switch default DNS server to *BACH*:

```
> server bach.mtitworld.com
Default Server:  bach.mtitworld.com
Address:  172.16.11.100
```

Specify that only Address (A) records should be queried:

```
> set query=A
```

*Commands*

Resolve host *BEETHOVEN* in domain *mtitworld.com* into its IP address:

```
> beethoven.mtitworld.com
Server:   bach.mtitworld.com
Address:  172.16.11.100
Name:     beethoven.mtitworld.com
Address:  172.16.11.101
```

Query default DNS server for all A records in its database:

```
> ls mtitworld.com
[bach.mtitworld.com]
 mtitworld.com.                  A        172.16.11.100
 mtitworld.com.         NS       server=bach.mtitworld.com
 gc._msdcs                       A        172.16.11.105
 gc._msdcs                       A        172.16.11.103
 gc._msdcs                       A        172.16.11.104
 gc._msdcs                       A        172.16.11.100
 bach                            A        172.16.11.100
 beethoven                       A        172.16.11.101
 chopin                          A        172.16.11.102
 distrib                         A        172.16.11.103
 franck.distrib                  A        172.16.11.103
 handel                          A        172.16.11.70
 chopin.vancouver                A        172.16.11.102
```

### Notes

* nslookup commands must be 255 characters or less.

* To look up a computer not in the current DNS domain, append a period to the name. For example, type beethoven.otherdomain.com. at the interactive nslookup prompt.

* Use exit or Ctrl-C to escape from an nslookup session.

* An unrecognized command is interpreted as a hostname.

* For more information on using nslookup, see *DNS and BIND* by Paul Albitz and Cricket Liu and *DNS on Windows NT* by Paul Albitz, Matt Larson, and Cricket Liu, both published by O'Reilly & Associates.

### See Also

*DNS(3,4)*

---

## pathping

Combines the features of ping and tracert to trace packet loss due to routers over a routed path through an internetwork. pathping is new to Windows 2000 and gives additional information that neither of these commands provides.

### Syntax

```
pathping [-n] [-h maxhops] [-g hostlist] [-p msec] [-q queries] [-w msec]
[-t] [-R] [-r] target
```

## Options

**-g** *hostlist*
>  Permits consecutive hosts to be separated by intermediate gateways along *hostlist*

**-h** *maxhops*
>  Specifies maximum number of hops to traverse (the default is 30 hops)

**-n**  Does not resolve IP addresses to hostnames

**-p** *msec*
>  Specifies how many milliseconds to wait between consecutive pings (default is 250 msec, or 0.25 sec)

**-q** *queries*
>  Specifies number of queries issued to each host along the route (default is 100 queries)

**-R**  Checks which routers support Resource Reservation Setup Protocol (RSVP)

**-T**  Checks which routers do not have layer-2 priority configured

**-w** *msec*
>  Specifies how many milliseconds to wait for a reply (default is 3,000 msec or 3 seconds)

*target*
>  Identifies hostname or IP address of remote target host

## Examples

Use pathping to check for congestion along the route from *test.mtitcanada.com* to *www.gov.mb.ca*:

```
pathping -n www.gov.mb.ca
Tracing route to www.gov.mb.ca [198.163.12.46]
over a maximum of 30 hops:
  0   205.200.52.64
  1   205.200.52.1
  2   205.200.52.6
  3   205.200.28.66
  4   205.200.27.54
  5   192.35.252.242
  6   198.163.12.46


Computing statistics for 150 seconds...
                Source to Here    This Node/Link
  Hop  RTT      Lost/Sent = Pct   Lost/Sent = Pct   Address
  0                                                 205.200.52.64
                                   0/ 100 =  0%       |
  1    128ms    0/ 100 =  0%       0/ 100 =  0%     205.200.52.1
                                   0/ 100 =  0%       |
  2    122ms    0/ 100 =  0%       0/ 100 =  0%     205.200.52.6
                                   0/ 100 =  0%       |
  3    138ms    0/ 100 =  0%       0/ 100 =  0%     205.200.28.66
                                  15/ 100 = 15%       |
```

| 4 | 132ms | 5/ 100 = | 5% | 6/ 100 = | 6% | 205.200.27.54 |
|---|---|---|---|---|---|---|
|   |   |   |   | 0/ 100 = | 0% | \| |
| 5 | 124ms | 7/ 100 = | 7% | 0/ 100 = | 0% | 192.35.252.242 |
|   |   |   |   | 1/ 100 = | 1% | \| |
| 6 | 127ms | 6/ 100 = | 6% | 0/ 100 = | 0% | 198.163.12.46 |

Trace complete.

### Notes

pathping first displays the route taken to the remote target in the fashion of the tracert command. After an indicated period of time during which pathping collects necessary statistics, it displays the efficiency of the route by showing:

Hop
>    Local host zero. Each remote host along the route increments the hop count by one.

RTT
>    Round-trip time along the route.

Source to Here Lost/Sent = Pct
>    Cumulative packets lost by this point along the route, expressed as both a fraction and a percentage. pathping sends 100 ICMP packets to each host along the route, so the results are statistical (and therefore don't add up when comparing different hops).

This Node/Link Lost/Sent = Pct
>    Packets lost on this hop (between this host and the previous one), expressed as both a fraction and a percentage. There are actually two sets of results here:
>
>    — Loss rates for routers (indicated with the IP address in the Address column). When this is high, the router is congested.
>
>    — Loss rates for links (indicated with | in the Address column). When this is high, the link is congested.

Address
>    IP address of each host along the route.

### See Also

*ping(7)*, *tracert(7)*

---

## ping

Tests TCP/IP connectivity with a remote host.

### Syntax

ping [-t] [-a] [-n *number*] [-l *bytes*] [-f] [-i *TTL*] [-v *TOS*] [-r *number*] [-s *hops*] [ [-j *hostlist*] | [-k *hostlist*] ] [-w *msec*] *host* [...]

## Options

-a  Resolves IP addresses to hostnames.

-f  Sets the Do Not Fragment flag in the packets to prevent them from being fragmented by routers along the route.

-i *TTL*

Sets the time-to-live field in the packets.

-j *hostlist*

Routes packets using the specified list of remote hosts (up to 9). Consecutive hosts can be separated by intermediate gateways (loose source routing).

-k *hostlist*

Routes packets using the specified list of remote hosts (up to 9). Consecutive hosts cannot be separated by intermediate gateways (loose source routing).

-l *bytes*

Indicates number of bytes in each ECHO packet. (The default is 32 bytes, and the maximum is 65,527 bytes.)

-n *number*

Specifies the number of ICMP ECHO packets to send. (The default is 4 packets.)

-r *number*

Records the route of the outgoing packet and the returning packet in the Record Route field. (The minimum number of hosts you can specify is 1, and the maximum is 9.)

-s *hops*

Specifies the timestamp for the number of hops specified by *number*.

-t  Continues pinging the host until interrupted using Ctrl-C.

-v *TOS*

Sets the Type of Service field in the packets.

-w *msec*

Specifies time-out interval in milliseconds.

*host*

Indicates IP address or hostname of remote host(s) being pinged.

## Examples

ping a remote host:

**ping www.gov.mb.ca**
Pinging www.gov.mb.ca [198.163.12.46] with 32 bytes of data:

Reply from 198.163.12.46: bytes=32 time=140ms TTL=250
Reply from 198.163.12.46: bytes=32 time=130ms TTL=250
Reply from 198.163.12.46: bytes=32 time=120ms TTL=250
Reply from 198.163.12.46: bytes=32 time=110ms TTL=250

Ping statistics for 198.163.12.46:
Packets: Sent = 4, Received = 4, Lost = 0 (0% loss),
Approximate round trip times in milli-seconds:
Minimum = 110ms, Maximum =  140ms, Average =  125ms

### Notes

- By default, ping sequentially sends four 32-byte ICMP ECHO packets to the remote host and waits one second for a reply.

- If you can ping the remote host by IP address but not by hostname, there is probably a DNS problem.

### See Also

*pathping(7), tracert(7)*

---

# rcp

Stands for remote copy command, which copies files between the client and a host running the rshd daemon.

### Syntax

```
rcp [-a | -b] [-h] [-r] [hostname][.username:]source [hostname]
[.username:]destination
```

### Options

-a  Switches to ASCII mode (the default), which converts end-of-line control characters between MS-DOS and Unix format.

-b  Switches to binary mode (used to copy binary files such as images).

-h  Also copies hidden files.

-r  Recursively copies all subdirectories and their contents.

*hostname*[.*username*]

Specifies the destination host running the rshd daemon and the credentials used for accessing the server (only needs to be specified if different from those of logged-on user). If *hostname* is omitted, then the destination is the local machine. If *hostname* is specified as a full DNS name such as *george. mtit.com*, then the username must be specified; otherwise, the last part of the DNS name (here *.com*) will be interpreted as the username.

*source*

Indicates files or directories to be copied (include path if needed).

*destination*

Specifies target directory on rshd machine (path can be absolute or relative).

### Examples

Recursively copy the pub directory and its contents from the local machine to a remote Unix machine as user mitcht:

**rcp -r C:\pub bongo.mitcht:/tmp**

This will create the directory */tmp/pub* on *BONGO* and copy the contents of *C:\pub* to this directory.

## Notes

- Windows 2000 does not include a rshd deamon, so rcp is used mainly for copying files between Windows 2000 and Unix machines.

- rcp does not prompt for a password before copying. You get around this by using the *.rhosts* file in the user's home directory on the rshd server to specify which remote hostnames and usernames are allowed to use rcp to copy files to or from the rshd server.

---

## *rexec*

Stands for remote execute command, which runs commands on remote machines running the **rexec** service.

### Syntax

```
rexec remotehost [-l username] [-n] command
```

### Options

*remotehost*
  The remote machine running the **rexec** service.

*-l username*
  The credentials used to run the command on the remote host.

*-n*  Redirection of standard input of **rexec** to NULL. (Try using this for commands that run interactively.)

*command*
  The command to remotely execute (enclose in quotes if there are embedded spaces).

### Examples

Perform a directory listing on the Unix machine *BONGO* as user mitcht by remotely executing the ls command:

```
rexec bongo -l mitcht "ls ~"
Password (bongo:): ********
doc
fig
read.ps
```

Note that **rexec** prompts for a password before executing the command remotely.

### Notes

- **rexec** copies standard input to the remote command.

- The **rexec** terminates when the remote command has been executed.

- **rexec** cannot be used to run some common interactive Unix commands such as emacs (use telnet to do this instead).

### See Also

*rsh(7), telnet(7)*

# route

Displays and modifies the routing table on the local machine.

## Syntax

```
route [-f] [-p] [command [destination]] [MASK netmask] [gateway]
[METRIC metric] [IF interface]
```

## Options

-f  Flushes all routes (gateway entries) from the routing table. (If combined with other options, this causes the table to be flushed prior to executing the other options.)

-p  When used with the add command, causes the added route to be persistent across reboots; when used with the print command, only lists persistent routes.

## Commands

print
   Displays the contents of the routing table.

add *destination* MASK *netmask* *gateway* METRIC *metric* IF *interface*
   Adds a new route to the routing table using the following parameters:

   destination
      The IP address of the host or network, which can be reached by using the gateway.

   netmask
      The subnet mask used for packets going to the previously mentioned destination.

   gateway
      The IP address of the router interface used for routing packets to the previously mentioned destination.

   metric
      The cost metric, usually the number of hops between the local machine and destination, or any arbitrary number to represent the degree of preference of this route when many routes to destination are possible. (The default is 1, and maximum is 9,999.)

   interface
      The interface to add the route to on multihomed machines.

delete [*destination* MASK *netmask* *gateway* METRIC *metric* IF *interface*]
   Removes an entry from the routing table. (Specify enough parameters to make the result unique.)

change [*destination* MASK *netmask* *gateway* METRIC *metric* IF *interface*]
   Modifies an existing route in the routing table. (Specify enough parameters to make the result unique.)

## Examples

Display the routing table on the local machine:

```
route print
===========================================================
Interface List
0x1 ........................ MS TCP Loopback interface
0x1000003 ...00 40 95 d1 29 6c ...... Novell 2000 Adapter.
===========================================================
===========================================================
Active Routes:
Destination      Netmask          Gateway          Interface          Metric
0.0.0.0          0.0.0.0          172.16.11.1      172.16.11.100      1
127.0.0.0        255.0.0.0        127.0.0.1        127.0.0.1          1
172.16.11.0      255.255.255.0    172.16.11.100    172.16.11.100      1
172.16.11.100    255.255.255.255  127.0.0.1        127.0.0.1          1
172.16.255.255   255.255.255.255  172.16.11.100    172.16.11.100      1
224.0.0.0        224.0.0.0        172.16.11.100    172.16.11.100      1
255.255.255.255  255.255.255.255  172.16.11.100    172.16.11.100      1
Default Gateway:        172.16.11.1
===========================================================
Persistent Routes:
  None
```

Add a persistent route to the class B network 133.16.0.0, which is accessible through the local router interface 172.16.11.2:

**route -p add 133.16.0.0 MASK 255.255.0.0 172.16.11.2 METRIC 3**

Verify the result:

```
===========================================================
Interface List
0x1 ........................ MS TCP Loopback interface
0x1000003 ...00 40 95 d1 29 6c ...... Novell 2000 Adapter.
===========================================================
===========================================================
Active Routes:
Destination      Netmask          Gateway          Interface          Metric
0.0.0.0          0.0.0.0          172.16.11.1      172.16.11.100      1
127.0.0.0        255.0.0.0        127.0.0.1        127.0.0.1          1
133.16.0.0       255.255.0.0      172.16.11.2      172.16.11.100      3
172.16.11.0      255.255.255.0    172.16.11.100    172.16.11.100      1
172.16.11.100    255.255.255.255  127.0.0.1        127.0.0.1          1
172.16.255.255   255.255.255.255  172.16.11.100    172.16.11.100      1
224.0.0.0        224.0.0.0        172.16.11.100    172.16.11.100      1
255.255.255.255  255.255.255.255  172.16.11.100    172.16.11.100      1
Default Gateway:        172.16.11.1
===========================================================
Persistent Routes:
Network Address  Netmask          Gateway Address  Metric
133.16.0.0       255.255.0.0      172.16.11.2      3
```

*Commands*

### Notes

- If you use route -f indiscriminately on a server, you could interrupt network communications between the server and other computers on the network, causing users to lose work. However, rebooting the server will restore your default gateways defined in Network in the Control Panel.

- You can use the symbolic names contained in the *Hosts* and *Networks* files instead of IP addresses for destination or gateway parameters in the route command.

- The delete and print commands support wildcards for the destination and gateway parameters.

- The change command is useless; it's easier to delete a route and then add the new one than to modify an existing one.

### See Also

*netstat(7)*

---

## rsh

Runs commands on remote machines running the rsh service.

### Syntax

```
rsh remotehost [-l username] [-n] command
```

### Options

remotehost

The remote machine running the rsh service.

-l username

The credentials used to run the command on the remote host.

-n   Redirection of standard input of **rexec** to NULL. (Try using this for commands that run interactively.)

command

The command to remotely execute (enclose in quotes if there are embedded spaces).

### Examples

Perform a directory listing on the Unix machine *BONGO* as user mitcht by remotely executing the ls command:

```
rsh bongo -l mitcht "ls ~"
doc
fig
read.ps
```

### Notes

- Windows 2000 includes only the client-side **rsh** command, so this command is typically used to remotely execute processes on Unix machines.

- Unlike the **rexec** command discussed earlier, **rsh** does *not* prompt for a password before executing the command remotely. **rsh** uses the same authentication mechanism used by **rcp**, namely the *.rhosts* file on the remote machine.

### See Also

*rcp(7), rexec(7), telnet(7)*

---

## telnet

Runs an interactive shell session on a remote host running the telnet daemon.

### Syntax

```
telnet [hostname [portnumber] ]
```

### Options

telnet [*hostname* [*portnumber*]]

Starts a client-side telnet session by opening a Microsoft Telnet shell within the command shell on the local machine.

*hostname* is the name (DNS or NetBIOS, depending on the network) or IP address of the remote telnet server. If *hostname* is omitted, then the telnet client starts but does not connect to a telnet server. (Use the **open** command in that case to connect.)

*portnumber* is only required if the default port (TCP port 23) is not used by the telnet server.

### Commands

close

Terminates the current telnet session but keeps the telnet shell open on the client

display

Displays the operating parameters (see **set** *option* later in this list)

open

Establishes a connection with a telnet server

quit

Exits the telnet shell and returns to the command prompt

set *option*

Enables different settings, specifically:

NTLM

Authenticates telnet sessions using NTLM (challenge/response) authentication

LOCAL_ECHO

Displays typed keystrokes on the screen

TERM [ANSI | VT100 | VT52 | VTNT]
> Specify the terminal mode to use.

CRLF
> Sends both a carriage return and line feed when Enter is pressed

status
> Displays the status of the connection

unset *option*
> Disables different settings, specifically:

NTLM
> Authenticates telnet sessions using basic authentication (clear text) instead of NTLM (challenge/response) authentication

LOCAL_ECHO
> Causes typed keystrokes not to be displayed on the screen.

CRLF
> Sends only a carriage return (and not a carriage return plus a line feed) when Enter is pressed

## Examples

Start the telnet client on the local machine:

```
C:\>telnet
Microsoft (R) Windows 2000 (TM) Version 5.00 (Build 2195)
Welcome to Microsoft Telnet Client
Telnet Client Build 5.00.99201.1

Escape Character is 'CTRL+]'

Microsoft Telnet>
```

Display the current client settings:

```
Microsoft Telnet> display
Escape Character is 'CTRL+]'
WILL AUTH (NTLM Authentication)
LOCAL_ECHO off
Sending both CR & LF
WILL TERM TYPE

Preferred Term Type is ANSI
```

Open a session with the Windows 2000 telnet server 172.16.11.100:

```
Microsoft Telnet> open 172.16.11.100
*=======================================================
Welcome to Microsoft Telnet Server.
*=======================================================
C:\>
```

Determine the IP address configuration of the remote telnet server:

```
C:\> ipconfig /all
Windows 2000 IP Configuration

Host Name . . . . . . . . . . . . : bach
Primary DNS Suffix  . . . . . . . : mtitworld.com
Node Type . . . . . . . . . . . . : Hybrid
IP Routing Enabled. . . . . . . . : No
WINS Proxy Enabled. . . . . . . . : No
DNS Suffix Search List. . . . . . : mtitworld.com

Ethernet adapter Local Area Connection:

Connection-specific DNS Suffix  . :
Description . . . . . . . . . . . : NE2000 Compatible
Physical Address. . . . . . . . . : 00-40-95-D1-29-6C
DHCP Enabled. . . . . . . . . . . : No
IP Address. . . . . . . . . . . . : 172.16.11.100
Subnet Mask . . . . . . . . . . . : 255.255.255.0
Default Gateway . . . . . . . . . : 172.16.11.1
DNS Servers . . . . . . . . . . . : 172.16.11.100
                                    172.16.11.104
Primary WINS Server . . . . . . . : 172.16.11.50
```

## Notes

- Both Windows NT and Windows 2000 include a telnet client, but there are several significant changes in Windows 2000:

  — Unlike Windows NT Server before it, Windows 2000 Server now includes a telnet service and can function as a telnet server that provides a whole new way of performing remote administration on Windows 2000 servers. See *Telnet Server Administration* in Chapter 5 for more information. Note that the Telnet service must be manually started on the server or have its startup setting changed to Automatic before a telnet client can connect to it.

  — While the telnet client of Windows NT was a GUI utility (*telnet.exe*), the Windows 2000 version runs in console mode instead. This new client also supports NTLM authentication to provide secure authentication between Windows 2000 telnet clients and servers. However, one feature that was provided by the GUI *telnet.exe* of Windows NT, which is not supported in the new command-line Windows 2000 version, is session logging.

- Don't try to remotely start a GUI program such as Solitaire (*sol.exe*) on a remote telnet server using the telnet client, or *Services.exe* will hit 100% CPU usage on the server, and the server will possibly hang. This will probably be fixed in the next service pack.

## See Also

*rexec(7)*, *rsh(7)*

**Commands**

# *tftp*

Stands for trivial file-transfer protocol, which copies files between the client and a host running the TFTP service.

## *Syntax*

```
tftp [-i] hostname [get | put] source [destination]
```

## *Options*

-i   Switches to binary (octet) mode for bytewise transfers of binary files. (Otherwise, the default ASCII mode is used.)

*hostname*
   Indicates the destination host running the TFTP service.

get | put
   Downloads or uploads the file as specified.

*source*
   Specifies the local file you want to transfer. If you use a hyphen, the destination file is printed out on stdout (when getting) or is read from stdin (when putting).

*destination*
   Renames the file after transferring it (destination is optional).

## *Examples*

Transfer the file *C:\pub\smiley.gif* from the local machine to the remote Unix host called *BONGO*:

```
tftp -i bongo put C:\pub\smiley.gif
Transfer successful: 386 bytes in 1 second, 386 bytes/s.
```

## *Notes*

TFTP does not support user authentication, so the user transferring the file must be logged on and must have permission to write to the remote directory. TFTP also uses UDP to transfer files and is therefore not guaranteed as reliable. Use FTP instead for a more reliable method that supports basic authentication.

## *See Also*

*ftp(7)*

---

# *tracert*

Traces the route from the local machine to a remote host.

## *Syntax*

```
tracert [-d] [-h maxhops] [-j hostlist] [-w msec] remotehost
```

## *Options*

-d   Command to not resolve IP addresses into hostnames

-h *maxhops*
   Maximum number of hops for the trace

---

**-j** *hostlist*
> Loose source route along the list of hosts

**-w** *msec*
> Timeout for replies in milliseconds

*remotehost*
> IP address or DNS name of host at remote end of route

## Examples

Trace route from local machine to *www.umanitoba.ca* (my alma mater):

```
tracert www.umanitoba.ca
Tracing route to spica.cc.umanitoba.ca [130.179.16.50] over a maximum of
30 hops:
1   120 ms   281 ms   140 ms   wnpgas01.mts.net [205.200.52.1]
2   121 ms   150 ms   130 ms   wnpgbr00-f00-303.mts.net [205.200.52.7]
3   131 ms   120 ms   200 ms   wnpgbr01-f000-101.mts.net [205.200.28.66]
4   140 ms   110 ms   140 ms   wnpgin-c14out.mts.net [205.200.27.54]
5   120 ms   150 ms   140 ms   207.161.242.34
6   120 ms   141 ms   130 ms   atrouter.cc.umanitoba.ca [207.161.242.18]
7   120 ms   131 ms   140 ms   bbrouter.cc.umanitoba.ca [130.179.0.1]
8   140 ms   140 ms   150 ms   spica.cc.umanitoba.ca [130.179.16.50]
Trace complete.
```

Determine route to Beijing University in China:

```
tracert www.pku.edu.cn -d
Tracing route to sun1000e.pku.edu.cn [202.112.7.12] over a maximum of 30
hops:
1    121 ms    130 ms    100 ms   205.200.52.1
2    110 ms    111 ms    110 ms   205.200.52.7
3    120 ms    110 ms    110 ms   205.200.28.66
4    110 ms    100 ms    120 ms   206.108.110.5
5    100 ms    120 ms    120 ms   206.108.102.81
6    130 ms    131 ms    150 ms   206.108.98.85
7    130 ms    140 ms    141 ms   206.108.98.50
8    130 ms    140 ms    151 ms   206.108.97.21
9    180 ms    180 ms    241 ms   206.108.97.6
10   150 ms    130 ms    170 ms   207.45.208.133
11   290 ms    210 ms    211 ms   207.45.223.89
12   230 ms    220 ms    221 ms   207.45.223.174
13   180 ms    230 ms    211 ms   207.45.223.154
14   250 ms    201 ms    210 ms   207.45.214.190
15   791 ms    881 ms     *       202.112.61.222
16    *        801 ms    851 ms   202.112.36.194
17   781 ms    801 ms    801 ms   202.112.1.62
18    *        761 ms    801 ms   202.112.1.218
19   761 ms     *        802 ms   202.112.1.66
20   761 ms   1061 ms    902 ms   202.112.6.22
21   801 ms    781 ms    741 ms   202.112.6.194
22   821 ms    961 ms    871 ms   202.112.7.12
Trace complete.
```

The asterisks indicate ICMP ECHO packs whose reply was not received in the timeout period (default is one second).

Commands

### Notes

- `tracert` is a troubleshooting tool used to identify failed or congested routers along a route.
- Use the `-d` option to speed the trace by disabling DNS resolution.

### See Also

*pathping(7)*, *ping(7)*

# Miscellaneous Utilities

Listed here are some additional Windows 2000 utilities that can be run from the command line for administrative purposes.

## csvde

Stands for Comma Separated Value Directory Exchange, a utility for bulk import/export of data between comma-delimited (CSV) text files and Active Directory. CSVDE can be used to create multiple user accounts, groups, computers, printers, or other AD objects in a single batch operation.

### Syntax

```
csvde options
```

### Options

CSVDE options are either export-specific, import-specific, or general in nature. There are also options for how credentials are specified for accessing AD.

### General Options

`-c string1 string2`
  Replaces all occurrences of **string1** with **string2** (used to change the distinguished name of objects when importing data from one domain to a different domain).

`-f filename`
  Indicates name of import/export file.

`-i`  Switches to import mode (the default is export mode).

`-j path`
  Specifies location of log file (default is current directory).

`-s servername`
  Specifies the domain controller on which the import/export operation is performed.

`-t portnumber`
  Specifies LDAP port number (the default is 389). The global catalog is port 3,268.

`-u`  Specifies a CSV file is in Unicode format.

`-v`  Specifies verbose mode.

*Options for Export Only*

-d *baseDN*
Specifies the distinguished name of the search base for exporting data.

-g  Disables paged searches.

-l *attributelist*
Lists attributes to export (the default is all attributes). Options for export only.

-m  Omits attributes specific to Active Directory objects. (Examples include Object-GUID, objectSID, pwdLastSet and samAccountType.)

-n  Don't export binary values.

-o *attributelist*
Lists attributes to omit during export.

-p *scope*
Specifies the search scope as either Base, OneLevel, or SubTree.

-r *filter*
Creates an LDAP search filter for exporting data.

*Options for Import Only*

-k  Keep importing even if errors occur.

*Options for Establishing Credentials*

-a *user-distinguished-name password*
Security context (credentials) within which the command runs.

-b *username domain password*
Same as -a but different format for credentials.

## Examples

First create a properly formatted CSV file to create three new user accounts in Active Directory. The file *C:\newusers.txt* contains the following lines of information:

```
DN,objectClass,sAMAccountName,userPrincipalName,displayName,
userAccountControl
"cn=George Smith,ou=Support,dc=mtitcanada,dc=com",user,gsmith,
gsmith@mtitcanada.com,George T. Smith,514
"cn=Barb Smith,ou=Support,dc=mtitcanada,dc=com",user,bsmith,
bsmith@mtitcanada.com,Barbara Lynn Smith,514
"cn=Judy Smith,ou=Support,dc=mtitcanada,dc=com",user,
jsmith,jsmith@mtitcanada.com,Judy Ann Smith,512
```

The meaning of this information is as follows:

DN  This is the distinguished name of object.

objectClass
user specifies user-account object.

sAMAccountName
This is the pre–Windows 2000 user logon name.

userPrincipalName
This is the Windows 2000 user logon name.

displayName
    This is the full name of the user.

userAccountControl
    512 means account is enabled; 514 means disabled.

Now use csvde to import *newusers.txt* and create the three user accounts:

```
csvde -i -f C:\newusers.txt
Connecting to "(null)"
Logging in as current user using SSPI
Importing directory from file "C:\newusers.txt"
Loading entries....
3 entries modified successfully.

The command has completed successfully
```

Use the Active Directory Users and Computers console to verify that the accounts were properly created.

A quick way to list all the possible attributes of user objects is to export all users and look at the first line:

```
csvde -f attribs.txt
Connecting to "(null)"
Logging in as current user using SSPI
Exporting directory to file attribs.txt
Searching for entries...
Writing out entries.................................
.....................................................
...........
Export Completed. Post-processing in progress...
152 entries exported

The command has completed successfully
```

You can also consult the Windows 2000 Server Resource Kit for more information on the attributes of user objects.

*Notes*

* A common use for CSVDE is creating multiple user accounts. To do this, the CSV file you import:

    — Must contain a first line called the attribute line, which specifies the name of each attribute defined in the file.

    — Must contain one additional line for each user account you want to create. The attributes in this line must match the sequence of those in the attribute line (first line). Use quotation marks to include values that have embedded commas.

    — Must contain the path to the user account in AD, the object type, and the user logon name (pre–Windows 2000) for each user.

    — Should contain the user principal name (UPN) for each user.

&mdash; Should specify whether the account is enabled or disabled (the default is `disabled`).

&mdash; Can include any personal information that is an attribute of a user account, such as address or phone number.

Passwords are not included in CSVDE files since these files are text files (*.csv* files) and are thus not secure. CSVDE creates new user accounts and assigns them a blank password. As a result, it is best to have accounts disabled when they are first created, since anyone could log on using the accounts and a blank password.

- CSVDE can only be used to add objects to AD and cannot be used to modify or delete existing objects.

- Microsoft Excel is a good tool for creating CSVDE files since it can export spreadsheet data in CSV format.

### See Also

*ldifde(7)*

---

## dfscmd

Configures an existing Dfs tree.

### Syntax

dfscmd *options*

### Options

? *or* help
Describes these options.

/add \\*dfsname*\*dfsshare*\*path* \\*server*\*share*\*path* [/restore]
Adds a replica to a Dfs volume. With /restore, do not check the destination server.

/map \\*dfsname*\*dfsshare*\*path* \\*server*\*share*\*path* [*comment*]
[/restore]
Creates a new Dfs volume by mapping a Dfs path to a shared folder. The /restore option causes no check to be performed to see if the destination server is available.

/remove \\*dfsname*\*dfsshare*\*path* \\*server*\*share*\*path*
Removes a replica from a Dfs volume.

/unmap \\*dfsname*\*dfsshare*\*path*
Deletes a Dfs volume and removes all of its replicas.

/view \\*dfsname*\*dfsshare* [/partial | /full | /batch || / batchrestore]
Views the volumes in the specified Dfs tree. If no arguments are specified, then only volume names are displayed. The /partial option displays the comments as well, and the /full option lists the full details of the tree. The /batch option is used to output the Dfs tree configuration to a file, which allows the Dfs tree to be recreated using the /batchrestore option if necessary.

*Commands*

## Examples

Add a new Dfs link named SALESREPORTS, which maps to the shared folder *SALES* on the server *TEST* to the existing domain-based Dfs root named \\*mtitcanada. com\public*:

```
dfscmd /map \\mtitcanada.com\public\salesreports \\test\sales
The command completed successfully.
```

Add a second Dfs link named CATALOGS, which maps to the shared folder *CAT* on server *BACH.MTITWORLD.COM*:

```
dfscmd /map \\mtitcanada.com\public\catalogs \\bach.mtitworld.com\cat
The command completed successfully.
```

Add a Dfs replica that maps the existing Dfs link SALESREPORTS to the shared folder *SALES* on server 172.16.11.100:

```
dfscmd /add \\mtitcanada.com\public\salesreports \\172.16.11.100\sales
The command completed successfully.
```

View the full details of the domain-based Dfs tree whose root is \\*mtitcanada.com\ public*:

```
dfscmd /view \\mtitcanada.com\public /full
\\MTITCANADA\public
        \\TEST\pub
\\MTITCANADA\public\salesreports
        \\test\sales
        \\172.16.11.100\sales
\\MTITCANADA\public\catalogs
        \\bach.mtitworld.com\cat
The command completed successfully.
```

## Notes

* The dfscmd command can be used to manage existing Dfs trees (both domain-based and standalone) but cannot be used to create a new Dfs tree. You must use Distributed File System console to create a new Dfs tree by creating a new Dfs root (see *Distributed File System* in Chapter 5 for more information).

* Paths that have embedded spaces must be enclosed in quotes.

## See Also

*Dfs(3,4), Distributed File System(5)*

---

# ldifde

Stands for Lightweight Directory Access Protocol Interchange Format (LDIF) Directory Exchange, a utility for bulk import/export of data between line-delimited (LDIF) text files and Active Directory. ldifde can be used to add, delete, or modify multiple user accounts, groups, computers, printers, or other AD objects in a single batch operation.

---

## Syntax

```
ldifde options
```

## Options

These are the same as for the **csvde** command described previously in this chapter, except for the following additional import-specific option:

**-y**  Use "lazy writes" to improve disk performance for import process

## Examples

Below is a properly formatted LDIF file called *C:\newusers.txt*, which creates three new user accounts. The accounts created are identical to the ones created in the example for the **csvde** command earlier in this chapter:

```
dn: CN=George Smith,OU=Support,DC=mtitcanada,DC=com
objectClass: user
sAMAccountName: gsmith
userPrincipalName: gsmith@mtitcanada.com
displayName: George T. Smith
userAccountControl: 514
# Create user account for Barb Smith

dn: CN=Barb Smith,OU=Support,DC=mtitcanada,DC=com
objectClass: user
sAMAccountName: bsmith
userPrincipalName: bsmith@mtitcanada.com
displayName: Barbara Lynn Smith
userAccountControl: 514
# Create user account for Judy Smith

dn: CN=Judy Smith,OU=Support,DC=mtitcanada,DC=com
objectClass: user
sAMAccountName: jsmith
userPrincipalName: jsmith@mtitcanada.com
displayName: Judy Ann Smith
userAccountControl: 512
```

Use **ldifde** to import the previous file into AD to create the users:

```
ldifde -i -f C:\newusers.txt
Connecting to "test.mtitcanada.com"
Logging in as current user using SSPI
Importing directory from file "C:\newusers.txt"
Loading entries....
3 entries modified successfully.

The command has completed successfully
```

*Commands*

### Notes

- Unlike csvde, which can only be used to add new objects to AD, ldifde can be used to add, delete, or modify them.

- If an attribute is to be left unspecified in an LDIF file, use FILL SEP as the value for the attribute.

- See "Notes" in *csvde* in this chapter for more information.

### See Also

*csvde(7)*

# Index

## Symbols

$ dollar sign, 451, 484
@ symbol, 183
🌐 globe icon, 517
🔨 hammer icon, 516
🧩 puzzle piece icon, 516
🧩🧩 two connecting, 517
↑↓ indicating synchronization, 400

## A

A (Address) records, 105
  updating, 289
  Windows 2000 clients and, 490
aaaa Context command, 684
access control lists (ACLs), command
    for, 627
Accessibility Options utility, 572
accessibility tools
  Magnifier utility, 9, 594
  Narrator utility, 601
  On-Screen Keyboard utility, 9, 604
  Utility Manager for, 619
Accessibility Wizard, 574
account lockout, 40
  settings for, 158
account logon events, 57
account management events, 57

Account Operators, 40, 63
  built-in groups and, 67
account options, 337
account policies, 40, 158
  for Local Security Policies, 180
  (see also Group Policy; Domain
    Security Policy)
account restrictions, 337
account settings, domain user accounts
    and, 337
account templates, benefits of, 334
ACLs (access control lists), cacls
    command for, 627
ACPI standard, 4
Active Directory, 5, 22, 40–52, 264
  administrative tools for (list), 493
  applications, publishing in, 265
  benefits of, 7
  connections, creating, 455
  database, 45
  delegation and, planning/strategies
    for, 73
  DNS, importance of, 100, 102
  global catalog for speeding search
    queries on, 145
  hierarchical structure of, 41, 49–51
  integrated zones in, 110, 327, 488

---

We'd like to hear your suggestions for improving our indexes. Send email to *index@oreilly.com*.

Active Directory (*continued*)
LDIF text files and, 748
location of directories and files, 45
models for, 49–51
objects (see objects, in Active
    Directory)
permissions, 46, 74
planning implementation of, 47–52
resources, publishing in, 265
restoring, 265
shared folders, publishing in, 265, 451
shared printers, publishing in, 265
snap-ins, adding/installing and, 505
Active Directory client software, 53
Active Directory Domains and Trusts, 517
Active Directory Installation Wizard, 45
DNS automatically configured by
    Windows 2000, 102
DNS Server service, installing/
    configuring and, 324
domain controllers, promoting/
    demoting, 331
domains and, 121
mixed modes and, 185
trusts and, 253
what may cause it to fail, 333
Active Directory Schema snap-in, 441
Active Directory Service Interface (see
    ADSI)
Active Directory Sites and Services
    console, 276, 518
Active Directory Users and Computers
    console, 23, 276, 521
active leases, displaying, 285
active paging files, deletions and, 310
Add New Printer Driver Wizard
installing/updating printer drivers, 413
printer drivers and, 423
Add Standard TCP/IP Printer Port
    Wizard, 410
adding
disks, 307
domain user accounts, 334
environment variables, 342
favorites to consoles, 507
Folder snap-ins, 506
hardware, 365
members to a group, 334
remote-access servers, 427

snap-ins, 498–505
Active Directory and, 505
options for, 501–503
tasks to taskpad, 508
(see also entries at installing)
Add/Remove Hardware, 574
Add/Remove Programs, 576
applications shown in, 265
Published option for software
    deployment, 480
Add/Remove Standalone Snap-in dialog
    box, 498, 501
Address bar, adding to taskbar, 9
Address records (see A records)
administrative shares, 52
list of common, 53
administrative templates, 155
administrative tool icon, 517
administrative tools, 17, 492–495
accessing, 516
alphabetical reference to, 516–571
vs. consoles, 493
default (list), 493
installing locally, 495
location of, 503
names of vs. names of snap-ins, 498
for Windows 2000 Professional, 499
(see also utilities)
Administrative Tools utility, 576
Administrator (built-in user account), 54,
    68
renaming, benefit of, 69
when to use, 69
Administrators (built-in group), 54, 61,
    63
Find function for, 352
junior, creating custom consoles
    for, 507
ADSI (Active Directory Service
    Interface), 41
benefits of, 8
Advanced menu option (Network and
    Dial-up Connections
    window), 294
Advanced published or assigned option
    for software deployment, 480
Advanced Startup Options, 55, 89
"AGDLP" mantra, 150
"AGLP" mantra, 150

AGP strategy, 146
"AGUNP" mantra, 152
aliases
    for computers, net name command
        for, 658
    for hosts, resource record contained
        in, 105
Allow access if dial-in permission is
        enabled policy, 222
Allow unsecured password option, 293
allowing/denying
    NTFS permissions, 203
    shared-folder permissions, 205
Alternates button for assigning multiple
        phone numbers, 291
anonymous access, 177
answer files, 169
    for automated Windows 2000
        installation, 376
    caution with, 30
APIPA (Automatic Private IP
        Addressing), 245
    disabling, 25
    drawbacks of, 15
    support for in Windows 2000, 243
    TCP/IP and, 244
Append Data permission, 199
AppleTalk network protocol, 189
    remote access and, 216
AppleTalk Remote Access Protocol, 217
Application Data folder, folder redirection
        and, 142
Application log, 137
application server mode (Terminal
        Services), 464
applications
    publishing in Active Directory, 265
    runas command for, 641
    start command for, 643
ARAP protocol, remote access and, 217
Archive attribute, 55
arp command, 708
Assigned option for software
        deployment, 479
assigning
    drive letters, 307
    drive paths, 307
    NTFS standard/special permissions
        for files, 394–396
        for folders, 395
    printer permissions, 419
    shared-folder permissions, 453

software categories, 481
software, how it works, 160
at command, 32, 624
at symbol (@) in user logon name, 183
attrib command, 626
attributes
    adding
        to classes, 442
        to global catalog, 355
    creating, 442
    for files/folders, 55
    supported by Active Directory, 44
audit events (audit entries), 56
    Event Viewer and, 268
audit policies, 57
    configuring, 267
    tips for, 267
    (see also Group Policy)
auditing, 56, 266
Authenticated Users, 58, 66
Authenticated Users have Full Control
        permission, 202
authentication
    vs. authorization, 221
    creating remote-access policies
        and, 431
    domain user account and, 128
    local user accounts and, 181
    remote-access servers and, 427
    users and, 125
authentication protocols
    preconfigured security settings for, 293
    remote access and, 218
    security option for, 293
    table of, 219
author mode (MMC consoles), 510
authoritativeness, DNS servers and, 105,
        107, 110, 115
authority, delegating (see delegation,
        delegating authority)
authorization vs. authentication, 221
autodial feature, 295
automatic caching, offline files and, 192
Automatic Private IP Addressing (see
        APIPA)
automatic startup type, 228

B

backup domain controllers (see domain
        controllers)
backup jobs, 89

backup logs, 89
Backup Operators, 58, 61, 63
backup sets, 89
backups, 58
  disks and, 310
  performing, 269
  types of, 88
  Windows Backup tools for (see
      Windows Backup tools)
  (see also disaster recovery)
Bandwidth Allocation Protocol (BAP
      protocol), remote access and, 218
Basic authentication, 177
basic disk storage, 95
basic disks, 58, 95
  dynamic storage, converting to, 315
  minimum free space for converting to
      dynamic, 98
  reverting to from dynamic, 314
basic storage, 59
.bat files, 184
BDCs (see domain controllers)
Berkeley Internet Name Domain (BIND
      software), 106
  Windows 2000 and, 108
bindings, 59
  for DHCP servers, modifying, 289
  modifying, 271
  order of, rearranging, 271
  (see also network protocols)
bitmap files, compression and, 70
blocking, 162
.bmp files, compression and, 70
boot menu, 29
  startup options for, 458
boot method, specifying, 327
boot partition/volume, 60
  deletions and, 310
bridgehead servers, 238
  designating preferred, 456
Briefcase, offline files and, 192
browsers (see web browsers)
bug in Windows 2000, Defragment
      Now, 312
built-in domain local groups, 60
  vs. built-in local groups, 178
  in domain setting, 63
  initial membership of (list), 64
  location of, 356
built-in global groups, 60
  in domain setting, 64

initial membership of (list), 65
  location of, 356
built-in groups, 60–68
  on domain controllers, location of in
      Active Directory, 66
  Guests, desktop settings and, 66
  implemented as
    domain, 61
    workgroup, 60
  scope and, 66
built-in local groups, 68
  in domain setting, 62
  initial membership of
    in domain setting (list), 62
    in workgroup setting (list), 61
  vs. built-in domain local groups, 178
  in workgroup setting, 60
built-in system groups, 68
  assigning permissions and, 67
  in domain setting, 65
built-in universal groups, 65
built-in user accounts, 68
Builtin container, groups located in, 67
Builtin folder, delegation and, 278
business model, basing Active Directory
      structure upon, 50

## C

cache.dns file, 113
caching, offline files and, 192
caching-only name servers, 107
  configuring, 325
cacls command, 627
CAL (Client Access License), 249
callback feature, 295
calling station id, 430
canonical name, 43
Canonical Name record (CNAME
      record), 105
catalog, 89
Cert Publishers, 65
Challenge Handshake Authentication
      Protocol (CHAP protocol), remote
      access and, 218
Change permission (Windows NT), 11,
      199, 204
  (see also Modify permission)
CHAP protocol, remote access and, 218
character sets, Windows NT vs.
      Windows 2000, 104
Check Disk utility, 311

child domains, 124, 331
child windows, creating, 507
chkdsk command, 629
chkntfs command, 631
Chopper.exe utility, 143
cipher command, 632
Citrix MetaFrame (Terminal Services
    Client), 248
class-level option (scopes), 287
classes
    adding attributes to, 442
    creating, 442
    specifying
        user-defined, 287
        vendor-defined, 288
Client Access License (CAL), 249
Client installation disks, creating, 463
Client Services, 6
clients, configuring for printing, 411
clock
    Date/Time utility for, 582
    net time command for, 670
clustering, 7
cmd command, 634
.cmd files, logon scripts and, 184
CN (common name), 43
CNAME (Canonical Name) record, 105
COM ports, enabling for direct computer
        connections, 301
Command Interpreter utility, 579
command line, 9
    commands run from, 622–744
    MMC consoles, running from, 513
    security configuration and analysis
        and, 386
    shell, cmd command for, 634
    utilities run from, 23, 572, 622,
        744–750
Command Prompt, location of in
        Windows 2000, 14
commands
    alphabetical reference of, 623–744
    Net, 644–679
    Netshell, 623, 679–707
    start command for, 643
    TCP/IP, 707–744
    Windows NT and, 622
common name (CN), 43
Compatws.inf template file, 180
complete trust model, 124

Compress contents to save disk space
        attribute, 56
compressing
    files/folders, 69, 345
    replication information, 240
computer accounts
    creating/configuring, 272
    Group Policy and, 272
    moving, 272
    net computer command for, 648
computer configuration settings, 154
Computer Management console, 23,
        523–526
    benefits of, 9
    disks, connecting to remotely, 308
    launching, 496
computer names, 24, 70
    displaying/modifying, 274
    (see also DNS; NetBIOS names)
computers
    desktop, benefits of upgrading to
        Windows 2000 Professional, 35
    joining to domain/workgroup, 273
    net view command for, 677
    searching for, 352, 443
    standalone, local security policies
        and, 179
conditions (remote-access attributes), 221
configuration database file, 385
configuration partition, 44
configuration, recommended, 45
Configure DNS Server Wizard, 112
Configure Your Server Wizard, 173, 526
configuring
    audit policies, 267
    autodial feature, 295
    caching-only name servers, 325
    callback feature, 295
    computer accounts, 272
    deployment settings for software
        packages, 481
    DHCP relay agent, 290
    dial-up connections, 291–294
    direct computer connections, 299
    DNS clients, 321
    DNS Server service, 323
    event logs, 343
    forwarders, 325
    frame types, 398
    GPOs, 360

configuring (*continued*)
  hardware, 365
  home folders, 369
  incoming connections, 371
  local-area connections, 382
  Local Security Policy on computer, 385
  local user accounts, 386
  logging options for remote-access
    servers, 428
  loopback, 364
  modems, redial attempts for, 292
  network number, 398
  network protocols, 392
  NWLink network protocol, 397
  offline files, on client and server, 399
  print servers, 421–424
  printer permissions, 411
  printer properties, 412
  printers, 411–414
  redirected folders, 354
  remote-access servers, 427–429
    removing configuration, 431
  rights, 436
  scavenging, 326
  script settings, 360
  security policies, 445
  services, 446
  site links, 455
  sites, 455
  standby settings, 457
  static IP-address pool for remote-access
    clients, 428
  subnets, 455
  TCP/IP, 459
    filtering, 461
    for WINS, 485
  Terminal Services, 462
  user-defined scope options, 288
  VPN connections, 472
  web site (virtual server), 475
  Windows 2000 Server, networking
    components for, 375
  WINS, 484
  zone transfers, 486
connection icon, 292
  offline files and, 401
connections, 24, 71
  Active Directory, creating, 455
  connection icon for, 292

direct computer connections,
  using, 300
  disabling, 292
  disconnecting from, 298
  inbound, 72, 215
  multilink, 218
  outbound, 71, 215
  to print server, 410
  sharing, 298
  status of, displaying, 292
  Windows NT and, 216
Connections node (Terminal
  Services), 462
Console menu, 510
console messages, sending to users, 32
console modes, 510
console trees
  customizing, 506
  drawbacks of, 12
console window, 496
  keyboard shortcuts for navigating, 515
consoles (see MMC consoles)
contacts, searching for, 352
containers, delegation and, 76
Control Panel, 581
convert command, 635
converting disks, 98, 315
copying
  domain user accounts, 334
  files/folders, 346
cost (site link component), 237
Create Files permission, 199
Create Folders permission, 199
Create Partition Wizard, 309
Create Volume Wizard, 309
creating
  Active Directory connections, 455
  attributes, 442
  child windows, 507
  classes, 442
  Client installation disks, 463
  computer accounts, 272
  dial-up connections, 296
  direct computer connections, 301
  domain user accounts, 334–336
  Emergency Repair Disk (ERD), 341
  forward-lookup zones, 488
  global catalog, 355
  GPOs, 361

groups, 356
hardware profiles, 367
home folders, 369
incoming connections, 372
local groups, 383
local user accounts, 387
local user profiles, 387
logical drives, 309
MMC consoles, 497–505
multicast scopes, 285
OUs, 402
partitions, 309
power schemes, 407
remote-access policies, 429
resource records, manually, 486
reverse-lookup zones, 488
roaming user profiles, 438
scopes, 283
security templates, custom, 385
shared folders, 449–451
site links, 456
sites, 456
software categories, 481
static mapping, 485
subdomains, 489
subnets, 456
superscopes, 285
taskpad views, 508
trusts, 467
user principal name (UPN), 389
virtual directories, 476
volumes, 309
VPN connections, 474
web site (virtual server), 477
zones, 487–489
Creator Owner, 66, 72
CSNW utility, 582
.csv files
    multiple domain user accounts
        and, 335
    saving event logs as, 138
csvde command-line utility, 35, 744
current directory, pushd command
        for, 640
custom consoles (see MMC consoles,
        custom)
customizing
    console trees, 506
    MMC consoles, 505–514

**D**

daemons, 228
data encryption
    authentication protocols and, 219
    Host/Guest connections and, 300
    schemes, preconfigured security
        settings for, 293
Data Sources (ODBC), 14, 527
data table, 45
database (Active Directory), 45
datastore, 45
date and time
    Date/Time utility for, 582
    importance of synchronizing when
        scheduling tasks, 32
    importance of when promoting server
        to domain controller, 375
    net time command for, 670
DC (domain component), 43
DDNS (Dynamic DNS), 6
Debugging mode startup option, 91
Default-First-Site, 240
    renaming, 457
default gateways, 244
    assigning additional to network
        connection, 460
defaults
    administrative tools (list), 493
    Default-First-Site, 456
    deployment settings for software
        packages, 480
    event logs, 136
    gateways (see default gateways)
    power schemes, 208
        list of, 606
    printer permissions, 212
    printing, selecting settings for, 413
    remote-access policy, 222
        deleting, 430
    root-zone file, 113
    schema, 224
    security policies, 227
    security settings, restoring on
        computer, 386
    site, 240
    startup types for services, 228
    unsecured passwords setting,
        changing, 293

defaults (*continued*)
    user profiles, creating/deploying, 275
    web site (virtual server), 478
Defragment Now, bug in, 312
defragmenting hard disks (see Disk
    Defragmenter utility)
delegation, 25, 52, 73–76, 116
    delegating authority
      to delegate, 74
      over DHCP servers, 283
      over domains, 276
      over GPOs, 361
      over Inter-Site Transports, 457
      over OUs, 277
      over site objects, 277
      over sites/subnets, 457
    inheritance and, 75
    strategies for, 74
    types of, 74
Delegation of Control Wizard, 276
    domains and, 122
Delete permission, 199
Delete Subfolders and Files
    permission, 199
deleting
    Dfs roots, 280
    domain user accounts, 336
    environment variables, 342
    GPOs, 362
    groups, 357
    local groups, 383
    local user profiles, 387
    partitions, 310
    sites, 456
    volumes, 310
demoting domain controllers, 331
dependencies between services, 233
deploying
    software, 479–484
    .zap files, 482
desktop computers, benefits of upgrading
    to Windows 2000 Professional, 35
Desktop folder, folder redirection
    and, 142
desktops
    administrative templates for managing
      environments of, 155
    consistent, user profiles for, 257–259
    mandatory user profiles and, 391

sending files/folders to, 350
settings for, Guests built-in group
    and, 66
Detail view, 505
Details Pane, 497
    changing display for, 505
    switching to taskpad view, 510
device icons, hardware troubleshooting
    and, 366
Device Manager, 528–531
    caution with, 530
    drawbacks of, 15
devices (see hardware)
Dfs clients, 79
Dfs (Distributed File System), 6, 76–80,
    535
    client cache time, modifying, 280
    implementing, 80
      methods for, 77
    links, 77
      adding to Dfs roots, 278
    planning, 80
    replication policy for, setting, 281
    root replicas, adding, 279
    roots, 77
      adding, 279
      deleting, 280
    shared folders, 78
      adding, 280
    sites and, 240
    software deployment and, 484
    status of, monitoring, 280
    trees (see Dfs trees)
    users and, 79
    working with, 278–281
Dfs topology (see Dfs tree)
Dfs trees, 77
    dfscmd command-line utility for, 747
    Distributed File System for, 535
    example of, 78
dfscmd command-line utility, 747
dhcp Context command, 685
DHCP database, 286
DHCP (Dynamic Host Configuration
    Protocol), 6, 25, 80–86
    console, accessing, 282
    database, 286
    packets, 81
    relay agent (see DHCP relay agent)

Server service, 286
servers (see DHCP servers)
statistics, displaying, 285
TCP/IP management and, 244
terminology, 82
traffic, 81
working with, 282–289
DHCP relay agent, 86, 290
configuring, 290
enabling/disabling on router
interface, 290
DHCP servers, 81
adding, 282
authorizing/unauthorizing, 282
bindings, modifying, 289
commands available in DHCP server
subcontext, 686–689
configuring DNS clients and, 322
delegation and, 283
dhcp Context command for, 685
implementing, 84
records, updating on, 289
stopped unexpectedly, 289
stopping/pausing, 286
DHCP Users group, 63
DHCP server settings and, 289
DHCPACK packet, 82
DHCPDISCOVER packet, 81
DHCPOFFER packet, 82
DHCPREQUEST packet, 82
DhcpSrvLog.xxx audit log, 288
Dial all devices option, 292
Dial devices only as needed option, 292
dial-in inbound connections, 72
setting for, 339
dial-in permissions, granting to users, 372
Dial only the first available device
option, 292
dial-up connections, 71, 291–299
advanced settings for, 294
configuring, 291–294
TCP/IP for, 459
creating, 296
disconnecting from, 298
setting for, 339
status of, monitoring, 298
Dial-up Preferences option, 295
dialing, options for, 295
Digest authentication, 177

direct computer connections, 299–302
configuring, 299
creating, 301
monitoring, 302
directories (see folders)
directory database file, 45
directory replication, 34
directory service access events, 57
Directory Service log, 137
Directory Services Restore Mode startup
option, 91
disabled startup type, 228
disabling (see enabling/disabling)
disaster recovery, 88–92
failed mirrored volumes and, 312
recovery options for, 425
utilities for, best order of use, 91
disconnecting from a connection, 298
Disk Cleanup utility, 311, 584
disk cloning (see disk imaging)
disk configuration, restoring, 314
Disk Defragmenter utility, 584
for defragmenting hard disks, 531
running, 312
disk duplication (see disk imaging)
disk imaging, 170, 377
software for, 171
Disk Management, 533
disks, connecting to remotely, 308
partitions and, vs. Setup, 172
sharing partitions/volumes over the
network and, 318
disk partitioning, preparing for
Windows 2000 Server
installations, 171
disk quotas, 8, 25, 92, 302
enabling/disabling, 303
entries for, monitoring, 303
limits on, 93
setting, 304
per-user basis, 92
usage
generating report on, 306
strategies for, 93
warning levels for, 304
working with, 302–306
disk space, managing, 92
disk storage, 94–98
diskperf command, 636

disks, 25, 94–99, 306
  adding, 307
  backups and, 310
  connecting to remotely, 308
  converting, 98
  defragmenting, 311
  Disk Management for (see Disk
      Management)
  error checking of, 311
  Foreign, 307
  information about, updating, 315
  maintaining, 311
  reactivating, 312
  removing, 307
  rescanning, 314
  reverting, 314
  status of
    displaying, 316
    indicators (list), 312
  terminology in Windows 2000 vs.
      Windows NT, 97
  upgrading, 98, 315
  working with, 306–320
Display utility, 585
displaying
  active leases, 285
  authorization status of DHCP
      servers, 283
  compressed files/folders with alternate
      color, 346
  connection, status of, 292
  DHCP statistics, 285
  disks, status of, 316
  drive path assignments, 318
  Group Policy Container, 154
  links for GPOs, 362
  members of a group, 359
  OUs in Active Directory, 110
  partitions, status of, 316
  properties of files/folders, 351
  remote-access clients, information
      about, 435
  resolver cache information, 324
  resource settings for hardware, 366
  rights assignments, 437
  second site/second domain
      controller, 457
  volumes, status of, 316
  zones in Active Directory, 110
  zones, type of, 489

distinguished name (DN), 43
distributed DNS database, 104
Distributed File System (see Dfs)
distribution groups, 100, 146
distribution lists (Microsoft Exchange 2000
      Server), using distribution groups
      instead of, 147
DN (distinguished name), 43
DNS clients, configuring, 321
  TCP/IP and, 460
DNS console, opening, 325, 486
DNS database, distributed, 104
DNS (Domain Name System), 25,
      100–121
  administrative tools for (list), 493
  clients (see DNS clients)
  computer name compatibility and, 24
  domains, 100
  how it works, 101–116
  IIS and, 176
  implementation, planning, 117–120
  importance of for Active
      Directory, 100, 102
  name queries, support for in
      Windows 2000, 243
  other features of, 116
  servers (see DNS servers)
  working with, 320–325
DNS namespace, planning, 48
DNS Notify, 113
DNS queries, 114
DNS root name, 48
DNS Server log, 137
DNS Server service, 323
DNS servers, 106, 325–328
  administering, 320
  authoritativeness and, 105, 107, 110,
      115
  datafiles on, updating, 327
  DNS tool for, 536
  monitoring, 326
  nslookup command for, 726
  records on, updating with DHCP
      servers, 289
  resource records, modifying
      manually, 26
DNS tool, 536
DnsAdmins (built-in domain local
      group), 63
DnsUpdateProxy, 65

documents
   clearing from print queues, 417
   Indexing Service for, 543
dollar sign ($)
   folders and, 451
   hidden shared folders and, 484
Domain Admins, 64, 124
   limiting membership in, 67
domain-based Dfs, 77, 278
domain-based remote-access servers, 216
domain component (DC), 43
Domain Computers, 64
domain-controller roles, 26
Domain Controller Security Policy, 227,
   538
domain controllers, 26, 42, 64, 124–127
   Active Directory Users and Computers
      for, 521
   auditing and, 268
   demoting, 331
   direct computer connections
      configuring on, 300
      creating on, 301
   Domain Controller Security Policy
      for, 538
   managing, 331
   minimum recommended, 125
   multimaster replication and (see
      multimaster replication)
   promoting, 331
   properties of, changing, 330
   result of installing Windows 2000
      Server and, 173
   roles of, 26
      changing, 330
   sites and, 240
   upgrading, 470
      Windows 2000 Server to, importance
         of date and time for, 375
   working with, 330–333
Domain Guests, 64, 128
domain local groups, 10, 28, 128, 147
domain modes, 123
   changing, 329
domain name, registering, 103
domain naming master role, 330
domain naming masters, 126
domain partition, 44
Domain Security Policy, 121, 227, 539

domain user accounts, 128, 256,
   333–340
   adding, 334
   copying, 334
   creating, 334–336
   deleting, 336
   disabling, 336
      during user's absence, 341
   finding, 336
   moving, 339
   multiple, creating, 335
   naming conventions and, 340
   passwords
      managing, 405
      resetting, 339
   properties of, modifying, 336–339
   renaming, 339
   sending email to, 340
   unlocking, 340
   where to locate, 334
Domain Users, 65, 129
domains, 27, 41, 49, 121–124
   Active Directory Domains and Trusts
      for, 517
   computers, joining to, 273
   delegating authority over, 276
      importance of planning for, 73
   Domain Security Policy for, 539
   drawbacks of, 12
   empty root, 252
   flattening, 124
      Kerberos v5 authentication and, 144
   hierarchical structure of, 49–51
   how many to use, 122, 251
   logging on to, 182, 273
   managing, 329
   meaning in Windows NT vs.
      Windows 2000, 103
   migrating from Windows NT, 123, 127
   mixed mode and, 185
   modes run in, 123
      changing, 329
   name of, 122
   native mode and, 187
   net view command for, 677
   vs. sites, 52, 122, 237
   specifying which to log on to, 389
   upgrading, 469
   working with, 329

downlevel logon name, 182
dragging and dropping, MMC consoles
    and, 13
Drive Image Pro disk-imaging
    software, 171
drive letters, 98
    assigning, 307
drive paths
    assigning, 307
    displaying assignments, 318
    editing and, 318
drivers
    print servers and, 423
    updating for hardware, 29, 366
drives
    identifying, 98
    managing with Logical Drives, 548
    taking ownership of, 403
DriveSpace/DoubleSpace, compressed
        partitions, Windows 2000 Server
        installation and, 173
dual-boot configurations, 27
    upgrading disks and, 316
    Windows 2000 installation and, 175
dynamic disks, 96, 129
    reverting to basic disks, 314
Dynamic DNS (DDNS), 6
Dynamic Host Configuration Protocol (see
    DHCP)
dynamic storage, 129
    basic disks, converting from, 315
dynamic updates, 117
    enabling, 489
    Windows 2000 clients and, 490

E

EAP protocol, remote access and, 218
effective permissions
    NTFS, 203
    shared-folders, 205
EFS (Encrypting File System), 8, 129–132
    accidental deletion of encrypted files/
        folders, 27
    files/folders and, 348
email addresses
    vs. user principal name, 183
    of zone administrator, updating, 491
email, sending to domain user
        accounts, 340

Emergency Repair Disk (ERD), 5, 27, 89,
    136
    creating/using, 341
empty root domains, 252
Enable boot logging startup option, 90
Enable VGA mode startup option, 90
enabling/disabling
    autodial feature, 295
    bindings, 271
    callback feature, 295
    connection, 292
    DHCP relay agent, 290
    disk quotas, 303
    dynamic updates, 489
    GPOs, 362
    hardware, 365
        in hardware profiles, 367
    hibernation, 368
    Internet Connection Sharing (ICS), 294
    local-area connections, 382
    multilink connections on remote-access
        servers, 429
    remote-access servers, 428
    remote access for specific devices, 429
    Routing and Remote Access
        Service, 431–433
    Start menu, personalized, 16
    zone transfers, 486
Encrypt contents to secure data
        attribute, 56
Encrypting File System (see EFS)
encryption
    creating remote-access policies
        and, 431
    files/folders
        copying/moving and, 347
        EFS for, 129–132
    protocols for, remote access and, 219
    recovery and, 131
    remote, 349
    strategies for, 131
energy-saving features, Power Options
        utility for, 606
Enterprise Admins, 65, 132
enterprise networks, Internet Connection
        Sharing and, 294
environment variables, 133–135, 342
    order set in by Windows 2000, 134
    system, used in logon scripts, 184

ERD (see Emergency Repair Disk)
error checking disks, 311
error events, 136
error messages
    "Failure of dependency service to
        start", 381
    "insufficient disk space", 305
    net-command, net helpmsg command
        for, 656
event logs, 28, 136–138, 343
    Event Viewer for, 539
    location of, 138
    settings for, 158
    working with, 137
Event Viewer, 539
    drawbacks of, 15
    event logs, monitoring with, 343
events (auditing), 56
Everyone (built-in system group), 138
Everyone (built-in user group), 66
Everyone has Full Control
        permission, 202, 205
.evt files, saving events logs as, 138
exclusive mode (forwarders), 116
.exe files, logon scripts and, 184
Execute File permission, 199
Executive Software, 312
Extend Volume Wizard, 310
extended partitions, 309
    deletions and, 310
Extensible Authentication Protocol (EAP
        protocol), 218
extension snap-ins/extensions, 504
    (see also snap-ins)
external network number, 190
external trusts (see trusts, external)

F

F5 function key, 283
F8 function key, 89
failed mirrored volumes, recovering, 312
Failed partition/volume status, 314
Failed Redundancy partition/volume
        status, 314
failure events, 137
"Failure of dependency service to start"
        error message, 381
failures, recovering from (see disaster
        recovery)

FAT volumes
    convert command for, 635
    permissions and vs. NTFS
        volumes, 206
favorites, 507
Fax utility, 586
faxes, incoming connections and, 373
file associations, modifying, 349
file attributes, attrib command for, 626
file-encryption key, 130
file-extension priorities for software
        deployment, 482
File is ready for archiving attribute, 55
file permissions, 199
File Replication Service log, 137
File Transfer Protocol (see FTP)
files, 138, 345–352
    associations with default programs,
        modifying, 349
    attributes of, modifying, 349
    auditing and, 268
    compressing, 345
    copying, 346
        permissions and, 203, 205
        rcp command for, 734
    deleting, Full Control to Creator Owner
        permission and, 207
    encrypting, 347
    making available offline, 400
    moving, 346
        permissions and, 203
    new, permission inheritance and, 202
    offline, 191
    opening, 350
    properties of, displaying, 351
    recover command for, 640
    searching for, 443
        in folders, 350
    securing, 350
    sending, 350
    sharing (see shared folders)
    taking ownership of, 403
filesystems
    attributes available for (list), 55
    chkdsk command for, 629
    chkntfs command for, 631
    settings for, 159
    Windows 2000 Server installation
        and, 172

filtering, 162
Find function, 352
  groups and, 357
  (see also Search function)
finger command, 709
flattening domains, 124
  Kerberos v5 authentication and, 144
floppy disks
  creating to install Terminal Services
    Client software, 567
  recreating Windows 2000 Server
    with, 374
  sending files/folders to, 350
flushing resolver cache, 322
Folder Options, location in
    Windows 2000, 14
Folder Options utility, 588
folder permissions, 199
folder redirection, 30, 141, 354
  benefits of, 141
  planning, 141
Folder snap-ins, 506
folders, 138, 345–352
  attributes of, modifying, 349
  auditing and, 268
  compressing, 345
  copying, 346
    permissions and, 203, 205
  customizing, 347
  encrypting, 347
  exploring, 348
  files, searching for in, 350
  Folder Options utility for, 588
  making available offline, 400
  moving, 346
    permissions and, 203
  new, permission inheritance and, 202
  opening, 350
  properties of, displaying, 351
  redirecting (see folder redirection)
  searching for, 443
  securing, 350
  sending, 350
  sharing (see shared folders)
  taking ownership of, 403
  which to encrypt, 131
Fonts utility, 589
For fast searching, allow Indexing Service
    to index this file attribute, 56

forcing
  GPO inheritance, 162
  replication over a connection, 456
Foreign disks, 307
  status of, 312
forests, 41, 142–143
  Kerberos v5 authentication within, 144
formatting
  partitions, 311
  volumes, 311
forms (paper sizes), assigning to paper
    trays, 414
forward-lookup queries, 111
forward-lookup zones, 111
  creating, 488
forwarders, 115
  configuring, 325
Found New Hardware Wizard, 411
FQDNs (fully qualified domain
    names), 103
frame formats, 190
frame types, 190
  configuring, 398
ftp command, 711
FTP (File Transfer Protocol)
  ftp command for, 711
  IIS for, 176
Full Control permission, 204
  ordinary users and, 207
Full Control to Creator Owner
    permission, 207
full zone transfers (Windows NT), 113
fully qualified domain names (see
    FQDNs)
function, basing Active Directory structure
    upon, 50
functional top-level domains, 103

### G

Game Controllers utility, 590
Gateway Services, 6
GCO (Group Policy Container), 154
geographical top-level domains, 103
global catalog, 145, 355
  group replication and, 151
global catalog server, 145
Global Context commands, 682
global groups, 10, 28, 146, 147
  net group command for, 654

global user accounts (see domain user accounts)
globally unique identifier (GUID), 44
🌐 globe icon, 517
GPO inheritance, blocking, 360
GPOs (see Group Policy Objects)
GPT (Group Policy Template), 154
group names, 357
Group Policies
  logon scripts and, 184
  MMC consoles, restricting with, 514
  system policies and, 34
Group Policy, 6, 28, 153–165, 541
  in Active Directory design, 52
  applying, rules governing, 161–163
  benefits of, 8
  computer accounts and, 272
  folder redirection for, 141
  implementing, 161
  inheritance and, 162
  planning for use of, 163–165
  settings for, 155–160
  using to manage offline files centrally, 402
Group Policy Container (GCO), 154
Group Policy Creator Owners, 65
Group Policy Objects (GPOs), 154, 359–363
  Active Directory Users and Computer for creating/configuring, 23
  Active Directory Users and Computers for, 521
  blocking inheritance, 360
  configuring, 360
  creating, 161, 361
  delegating authority over, 76, 361
  deleting, 362
  disabling, 362
  filtering, 362
  forcing, 363
  Group Policy for, 541
  linking, 161, 363
  links for, displaying, 362
  multiple, 162
  opening, 363
Group Policy Template (GPT), 154
group scopes (see scopes)
groups, 28, 146–153
  adding members to, 334, 356
  creating, 356
  delegating authority to, 75, 276

deleting, 357
finding, 357
Local Users and Groups for, 547
membership of, 147
moving, 358
names of, 357
nesting of, 148
properties of, modifying, 357
renaming, 358
rights, configuring for, 436
scopes of, 147
searching for, 352
sending mail to, 358
setting for members of, 338
types of, 146
working with, 356–359
(see also domain local groups; global groups; universal groups)
GSNW utility, 590
guest access, Domain Guests for, 128
Guest (built-in user account), 68, 166
Guest connections, direct computer connections and
  configuring, 299
  creating, 301
Guests, 61, 63, 166
GUID (globally unique identifier), 44

H
🔨 hammer icon, 516
hard quotas, 93
hardware, 29, 166, 365–367
  adding, 365
  compatibility list for devices supported by Windows 2000 Server, 166
  configuring, 365
  Device Manager for, 528–531
  enabling/disabling, 365
    in hardware profiles, 367
  failures with, recovering from (see disaster recovery)
  information about, rescanning disks and, 314
  planning Windows 2000 Server installation and, 170
  reinstalling, 365
  resource settings for, modifying/displaying, 366
  scanning for changes in, 366
  troubleshooting, 366
  uninstalling, 366

hardware profiles, 167
  working with, 367
HCL (hardware compatibility list) for
      devices supported by
      Windows 2000 Server, 166
Healthy partition/volume status, 314
Help balloons, 399, 400, 401
help files, IIS, 177
hibernation, 167, 368
Hidden attribute
  for files, 55, 351
  for folders, 55
hidden folders, 451
hierarchical structure
  Active Directory and, 41, 49–51
  domains and, 49–51
  OUs and, 49–51
Hisecdc.inf template file, 181
Hisecws.inf template file, 181
home folders, 167, 369
  restricting access to by
      Administrators, 207
  setting for network location of, 338
home page, opening, 339
Host connections, direct computer
      connections and
  configuring, 299
  creating, 301
host ID, 243
host servers, 77
hostname command, 714
hostnames, 103
hosts, 103
Hosts file, 120
hot swapping, 307
HTTP (Hypertext Transfer Protocol), IIS
      for, 176
HyperTerminal, 591

*I*

IANA (Internet Assigned Numbers
      Authority), 246
IAS (Internet Authentication Services)
  aaaa Context command for, 684
IAS servers, 64
ICMP Router Discovery, support for in
      Windows 2000, 243
icons illustrating MMC consoles, 516
ICS (see Internet Connection Sharing)
identifying partitions/drives/volumes, 98

IE (Internet Explorer), 592
  Terminal Services Advanced Client
      and, 34
IIS (Internet Information Services), 6,
      176, 545
  built-in user accounts and, 66
  console, opening, 475
IIS permissions for web site, 478
Image Color Management 2.0, 4
ImageCast IC3 disk-imaging software, 171
Improved Troubleshooters, 5
inbound connections, 72, 215
incoming connections, 371
incremental zone transfers, 113
Indexing Service, 543
  attribute for, 56
information events, 136
infrastructure masters, 126, 330
inheritance
  Active Directory permissions and, 47
  delegation and, 75
  permissions and, 201
Initializing partition/volume status, 314
installing
  administrative tools locally, 495
  DHCP Server service, 286
  DNS Server service, 323
  network protocols, 392, 393
  printer drivers, 413
  printers (software interface) for print
      devices, 409
  Recovery Console, 424
  services, 447
  snap-ins, 498–505
    Active Directory and, 505
    options for, 501–503
  Terminal Services, 464
  Terminal Services Client, 465
  vs. upgrading, 255
  Windows 2000 Server, 373–381
    automated installation, 375–378
    from CD, 373–375
    over network, 375
    optional components for, 494
    planning for, 168–175
    post-installation issues, 173
    setup options for, 379
  Windows 2000
    integrated installation, 33
    Recovery Console feature for, 29
  WINS, 485

"insufficient disk space" error
    message, 305
integrated installation, 33
Integrated Windows authentication, 177
IntelliMirror, 30
Interactive (built-in group), 66, 176
interface Context command, 691
internal network numbers, 190
    assigning, 398
International Standards Organization
    (ISO), OIDs and, 225
Internet
    dial-up connection to
        creating, 297
        options for, 297
    presence on, DNS implementation
        and, 48
    searching on, 444
Internet account, options for, 297
Internet Assigned Numbers Authority
    (IANA), 246
Internet Authentication Services (IAS)
    aaaa Context command for, 684
Internet Connection Server, 432
Internet Connection Sharing (ICS)
    enabling, 294
    setting up, 432
    sharing, VPN connections and, 473
Internet Connection Wizard, 297, 591
    computers on LAN, configuring for
        Internet connection, 294
Internet Explorer (IE), 592
    Terminal Services Advanced Client
        and, 34
Internet Information Services (see IIS)
Internet printing, 9, 31, 210
Internet Printing Protocol (IPP), 4
Internet Protocol Security (IPSec), 4
    remote access and, 219
Internet protocols, IIS for, 545
Internet Services Manager, 176
intersite/intrasite replication, 239
inverse-lookup queries, 112
IP addresses, 243
    arp command for, 708
    assigning additional to network
        connection, 460
    DHCP for, 80–86
    excluding, 284

private, 246
reserving, 283
IP Security policies
    on Active Directory, 159
    for Local Security Policies, 180
ipconfig command, 715
IPP (Internet Printing Protocol), 4
IPSec (see Internet Protocol Security)
IPX/SPX protocol, 189
    remote access and, 216
ISO (International Standards
    Organization), OIDs and, 225
items commonly administered, utilities for
    (table), 20–22
iterative queries, 114
IXFR requests, incremental zone transfers
    and, 113

J

js files, logon scripts and, 184

K

KDC (Key Distribution Center), 144
Kerberos policies, 158
Kerberos v5 authentication protocol, 125
    within forests, 144
Key Distribution Center (KDC), 144
keyboard
    Keyboard utility for, 593
    On-Screen Keyboard utility for, 604
keyboard shortcuts
    for MMC consoles, 514–516
    for opening New Object–User dialog
        box, 341
Keyboard utility, 593

L

L2TP protocol, 221
LANs (local-area networks)
    connections to, 71
    Internet connection, setting up
        through, 297
    protocols for, remote access and, 216
Last Known Good Configuration, 5, 29
    option for, 91
Layer 2 Tunneling Protocol (L2TP
    protocol), 221
LDIF text files, ldifde command-line utility
    for, 748

lease time, deleting scopes and, 286
leases, 81
  active, displaying, 285
  renewal of, 82
legacy devices, 365
Legacy Windows clients, updating
    A records, 289
licensing mode, Windows 2000 Server
    installation and, 172
Licensing utility, 546, 594
Lifetime tab, scope expiration date, 285
line printer daemon (LPD) service, 423
line printer remote (LPR) service, 423
link table, 45
List Folder permission, 199
load-balancing, 117
loading sharing, 117
local-area connections, 382
  configuring TCP/IP for, 459
local-area networks (see LANs)
local backup, 88
local groups, 10, 147, 178, 383
  net localgroup command for, 657
local policies, 158
  for Local Security Policies, 180
local print devices
  installing printer for, 409
  terminology and, 209, 409
local security policies, 179
Local Security Policy, 227, 384, 546
  configuring on computer, 385
Local Security Settings console,
    opening, 384
local user accounts, 181, 256, 386
  logon and, 182
local user profiles, 182, 257, 387
Local Users and Groups snap-in, 383,
    547
location
  of administrative tools, 503
  basing Active Directory structure
    upon, 49
  of built-in domain local groups, 356
  of built-in global groups, 356
  of pagefiles, managing, 404
  of saved MMC consoles, 503
locking workstations, 388
log files (Active Directory), 45
log off/logging off, 388
Log On As setting (services), 233

Log On To Windows dialog box, 273,
    389
log on/logging on, 389
logging options, configuring for remote-
    access servers, 428
logical drives
  creating, 309
  Logical Drives snap-in for, 548
  terminology and, 548
logical printers, 209
  pooling and, 412
  terminology and, 409
logical structure, 41
logoff scripts, 157
  configuring, 360
logoff, slowed by offline files, 193
logon, 182
  slowed by offline files, 193
logon events, 57
logon names, 182
  naming conventions and, 340
logon scripts, 157, 183, 391
  assigning to user account, 391
  configuring, 360
logon settings, domain user accounts
    and, 337
logon traffic, sites and, 239
loopback feature, 364
LPD service, 423
LPDSVC service, 423
lpq command, 718
lpr command, 719
LPR service, 423
LPRMON service, 423

**M**

MAC addresses, 283
  arp command for, 708
Magnifier utility, 9, 594
Mail Exchange record (MX record), 105
mail recipients, sending files/folders
    to, 350
Makeboot.exe/Makebt32.exe, recreating
    Windows 2000 floppy disks
    using, 374
Manage Documents printer
    permission, 211, 421
Manage Printers permission, 211, 404
  selecting printing defaults and, 413
Management Saved Consoles, 503

managing
  pagefiles, size and location of, 404
  passwords for domain user
    accounts, 405
  RAS servers, downlevel, 434
  terminal sessions, 465
mandatory user profiles, 185, 258, 391
manual caching, offline files and, 192
manual startup type, 228
"Manually configured server" role, 431,
  433
Map Network Drive wizard, 235
master domain controller, 26
master domains, 124
master name servers, 107
  forcing to notify secondary name
    servers, 489
member servers, 173, 185
  configuring direct computer
    connections on, 300, 301
member sites, 238
members, adding
  to groups, 356
  to local groups, 383
membership of groups, 147
  rules for local groups, 178
Message Queuing utility, 595
messages
  console, 32
  net send command for, 661
metric, assigning, 460
Microsoft Challenge Handshake
  Authentication Protocol (MS-CHAP
  protocol), 218
Microsoft Common Console
  Documents, 503
Microsoft Exchange 2000 Server
  distribution lists, using distribution
    groups instead of, 147
  sites and, 240
Microsoft Management Consoles (see
  MMC consoles)
Microsoft Point-to-Point Encryption (MPPE
  protocol), 219
Microsoft RAS protocol, remote access
  and, 217
mini-Setup program, 378
mirror sets (Windows NT), 185
mirrored volumes, 97, 185
  creating, 309
  recovering failed, 312

mixed mode, 123, 148, 185
  converting scopes and, 150
  nesting groups and, 149
mixed-mode networking, 5
MMC consoles, 4, 31, 492–516
  vs. administrative tools, 493
  alphabetical reference to, 516–571
  benefits of, 7
  creating, 497–505
  custom
    distributing to Administrators, 513
    opening, 503
    reasons for creating, 497
    restricting with Group Policies, 514
  customizing, 505–514
  dragging and dropping, 13
  favorites, adding to, 507
  GPOs and, 359
  icons illustrating, 516
  keyboard shortcuts for, 514–516
  opening in author mode, 510
  options for, setting, 510
  running, 511, 513
  saving, 503, 512
  window (interface), 496
models for Active Directory, 49–51
modems
  options for outbound connections, 292
  Phone and Modem Options utility
    for, 605
Modify permission, 11
  using instead of Read & Execute and
    Write permissions, 207
modifying
  local groups, 384
  local user profiles, 387
  multicast scopes, 285
  NTFS permissions, 393–396
  password options, 406
  power schemes, 407
  printer permissions, 419
  resource records, 491
  scopes, 283, 284
  shared-folder permissions, 453
  shared folders, 450
  taskpad views, 509
monitoring
  direct computer connections, 302
  DNS servers, 326
  incoming connections, 373
  local-area connections, 382

monitoring (*continued*)
  remote-access clients, connected, 434
  remote-access servers, 434
  terminal sessions, 465
  VPN connections, status of, 474
monitors, support for multiple, 587
mountvol command, 637
Mouse utility, 596
Move the contents of Application Data to
    the new location option, 355
moving
  domain user accounts, 339
  files/folders, 346
  Folder snap-ins, 506
  groups, 358
  OUs, 403
  server to different site, 457
MPPE protocol, remote access and, 219
.msc files
  preconfigured for Windows 2000 Server
      (list), 511
  running MMC consoles from command
      line and, 513
  saving consoles as, 503
MS-CHAP, remote access and, 218
.msi files, 159
.mst files, 160
multicast scopes, 85
  creating, 285
  modifying, 285
multihomed computers
  local-area connections and, 383
  NWLink network protocol and, 398
  sites and, 241
multilink connections, 218
  creating remote-access policies
      and, 431
  enabling/disabling on remote-access
      servers, 429
  PPP Multilink dial-up connections, 292
multilink protocols
  remote access and, 218
  table of, 219
multimaster replication, 43, 125
multimedia, Sounds and Multimedia utility
    for, 612
multiple-master domain model, 124
MX (Mail Exchange) record, 105
My Computer, 596

My Documents folder, 186, 597
  folder redirection and, 142
  home folders and, 167
  sending files/folders to, 350
My Network Places, 14, 599
  browsing for printers, 414

**N**

Name Server record (NS record), 105
name servers (see DNS servers)
namespaces, 103
  forests and, 143
  trees and, 250
naming conventions
  domain user accounts and, 340
  for objects, 43
Narrator utility, 601
NAT (Network Address Translation), 246
  setting up server for, 432
native mode, 123, 148, 187
  nesting groups and, 149
  Windows NT member servers running
      in, 35
native scope, converting scopes and, 152
nbtstat command, 720
nesting of groups, 148
net accounts command, 646
net command, 644
Net commands, 644–679
  net help command for, 655
net computer command, 648
net config command, 649
net config server command, 649
net config workstation command, 651
net continue command, 652
net file command, 653
net group command, 654
net help command, 655
net helpmsg command, 656
net localgroup command, 657
net name command, 658
net pause command, 659
net print command, 660
net send command, 661
net session command, 662
net share command, 664
net start command, 666
net statistics command, 668
net stop command, 669

net time command, 670
net use command, 673
net user command, 675
net view command, 677
NetBEUI network protocol, 188, 189
  remote access and, 217
NetBIOS names
  compatibility and, 24
  Windows NT and, 100, 102
NetBIOS over IPX API, 190
NetBIOS over TCP/IP (NetBT), 25
  disabling for specific network
    connections, 243
  nbtstat command for, 720
NetBIOS, Windows 2000 and, 337
NetBT (see NetBIOS over TCP/IP)
NETLOGON, 46
netsh command, 9, 681
Netshell commands, 623, 679–707
Netshell context, Global Context
    commands and, 682
Netshell (netsh.exe), 679
netstat command-line utility, 461, 724
Network Address Translation (see NAT)
Network and Dial-up Connections
    utility, 602
Network and Dial-up Connections
    window, opening, 291, 382
network backup, 88
Network (built-in group), 66, 188
network components enabled for
    outbound dial-up
    connections, 293
Network Connection Wizard, 291
  creating dial-up connection to private
    networks, 296
  VPN connections and, 474
network gateway, configuring remote-
    access server as, 427
network ID, 243
Network Identification Wizard, joining
    computers to domain/
    workgroup, 273
network load balancing, 7
network, logging on and off, 388
Network Neighborhood
    (Windows NT), 14
Network News Transfer Protocol (NNTP),
    IIS for, 176
network number, 190
  configuring, 398

network print devices, 409
network printers (software interface),
    terminology and, 409
network protocols, 189
  installing/configuring, 392
  (see also protocols)
network router, remote-access server
    configured as, 433
Network Solutions, 103
networking
  mixed-mode, 5
  services, 6
    commands for, 644–679
    netsh command for, 681
network-interface print device, 209
New Connection Wizard, Host direct
    computer connections and, 301
New Multicast Scope Wizard, 285
New Object–User dialog box, keyboard
    shortcut for, 341
New Scope Wizard, 284
New Task Wizard, 508
New Taskpad View Wizard, 508
New Zone Wizard, 488
NNTP (Network News Transfer Protocol),
    IIS for, 176
No Media disk status, 312
nonexclusive mode (forwarders), 116
Norton Ghost disk-imaging software, 171
Notepad, creating logon scripts and, 184
Novell, IPX/SPX, 189
NS (Name Server) record, 105
nslookup command, 726
NT File System (NTFS), 4
NTDS (Windows NT Directory Service), 5
Ntdsutil.exe utility, 45
NTFS (NT File System), 4
NTFS permissions, 11, 31, 198–203,
    393–397
  allowing/denying, 203
  copying/moving files/folders and, 346
  EFS and, 129
  standard/special, 199
    assigning to files, 394–396
    assigning to folders, 395
    modifying on files/folders, 396
  using, 201–203
NTFS volumes
  cipher command for, 632
  compressing files/folders on, 69
  directories on, cacls command for, 627

NTFS volumes (*continued*)
  mountvol command for, 637
  permissions and vs. FAT volumes, 206
  setting to Authenticated Users have Full
    Control permission, 202
NTLM (Challenge/Response)
    authentication protocol, 125
Ntuser.dat file, user profiles and, 392
NWLink network protocol, 189
  configuring, 397

## O

object access events, 57
object identifiers (OIDs), 225
object-based delegation, 74
objects
  in Active Directory, 41
    creating, 264
    enabling for auditing, 267
    moving to different container, 264
    searching for with Find
      function, 352
    searching for with Search
      function, 443
    taking ownership of, 404
  Active Directory Users and Computers
    for, 521
  filesystem, enabling auditing for, 268
  moving
    to different container within Active
      Directory, 264
    to different OU, 403
  naming conventions for, 43
ODBC configuration utility, location of in
    Windows 2000, 14
ODBC database connectivity, Data
    Sources for, 527
Offline disk status, 312
offline files, 191, 398, 398–402
  configuring on client and server, 399
  enabling on client or server, 399
  how they work, 192
  implementing, 193
  managed centrally using Group
    Policy, 402
  synchronizing, 400
  working with, 401
Offline Files Wizard, 400
offline folders, 4, 30
OIDs (object identifiers), 225
OnDemand Software, Inc, 479

one-way external trusts, 254
Online (Errors) disk status, 312
On-Screen Keyboard utility, 9, 604
opening
  custom consoles, 503
  files/folders, 350
operations master roles, 26, 126
Operator-Assisted Dialing option, 295
ordinary scope (see scopes)
OUs (organizational units), 41, 49, 193,
    402
  Active Directory Users and Computers
    for, 521
  delegating authority over, 277
    importance of planning for, 73
  hierarchical structure of, 49–51, 195
  moving objects to, 403
  nesting, how deep to go, 195
  publishing shared folders and, 451
  searching for, 352
  using, 194
outbound connections, 71, 215, 291
Outlook Express, sending mail to
    groups, 358
ownership, 196, 403
  permissions and, 196

## P

pagefiles, 196, 404
pagefile.sys file, 196
paging file, 196
panes of console window, 496
PAP protocol
  remote access and, 218
  security option for, 293
paper sizes, assigning to trays, 414
partitions, 44
  compressed, Windows 2000 Server
    installation and, 173
  creating, 309
    (see also disk partitioning)
  deleting, 310
  extended, 309
  formatting, 311
  identifying, 98
  names for, 98
  repairing, 313
  status of
    displaying, 316
    indicators (list), 314

Password Authentication Protocol (see PAP protocol)
"Password never expires" option vs. "User must change password at next logon" option, 406
passwords, 405
  account restrictions and, 338
  options for (list), 406
  policies for, user passwords and, 158
  resetting for domain user accounts, 339
  tips on using, 197
  unsecured, security option for, 293
  Users and Passwords utility for, 618
pathping command, 730
pathping utility, 461
PDC emulator role, 330
PDC emulators, 126
PDC (primary domain controller), 26, 43
  upgrading from Windows NT to Windows 2000, 127
people, searching for, 444
Performance console, 549
  diskperf command for, 636
Performance Logs and Alerts snap-in, 551
permissions, 198–207
  Active Directory, 46, 74
  assigning, strategies for, 205
  changing, caution with, 46
  configuring for printer, 411
  delegating authority to delegate, 74
  effective, 203, 205
  files/folders, 203
  inheritance and, 201
  keeping simple, 75
  modifying/removing, 277
  preventing inheritance of, 201
  printer, 211–213
  vs. rights, 224
  shared-folder (see shared-folder permissions)
  (see also NTFS permissions)
personalized menus, disabling, 16
per-volume basis, 92
Phone and Modem Options utility, 605
phone numbers, Alternates button for assigning multiple, 291
physical memory, pagefile and, 196
physical structure, 42
ping command, 732
  pathping command and, 730

planning
  Active Directory implementation, 47–52
  delegation and, 52
  Dfs, 80
  DNS implementation, 117–120
  DNS namespace, 48
  folder redirection, 141
  Group Policy, use of, 163–165
  printer permissions, 213
  root name, 48
  shared folders, 234
  sites, 240
  Windows 2000 Server installation post-installation issues, 173
  Windows 2000 Server installation, 168–175
  (see also strategies)
platform compatibility, computer names and, 24
Plug and Play devices, 365
Pointer record (PTR record), 105
Point-to-Point Protocol (PPP protocol), 217
Point-to-Point Tunneling Protocol (PPTP protocol), 220
policy change events, 57
popd command, 639
ports
  configuring printer properties and, 412
  print servers and, 421
  remote access and, 429
power button, standby and, 458
Power Options utility, 606
power schemes, 208, 407
  default, list of, 606
  list of, 208
Power Users (built-in group), 61, 208
PPP Multilink (PPMP protocol)
  dial-up connections, configuring, 292
  remote access and, 218
PPP protocol, 217
PPTP protocol, 220
Pre–Windows 2000 Compatible Access, 62
primary domain controller (see PDC)
primary name servers, 106
print devices (see printers [hardware])
print jobs
  clearing from print queues, 417
  managing in queues, 420

print jobs (*continued*)
  net print command for, 660
  print priority of, 413
  spooling, 413, 423
  stuck in print spooler, 418
Print Operators, 63, 213
Print permission, 211
print queues
  clearing documents from, 417
  lpq command for, 718
  managing jobs in, 420
  net print command for, 660
print servers, 209, 214
  configuring, 421–424
  connecting to, 410
Print Services for Unix component, 423
print spooler, 418
printer drivers, 209, 210
  installing/updating, 413
printer icon, 421
  right-clicking on, 417
printer permissions, 211–213
  advanced, 212
  assigning, 419
  configuring, 411
  modifying, 419
  planning, 213
printer pooling, 412
  printer speeds and, 417
printers (hardware), 209, 407–418
  auditing, enabling for, 268
  configuring, 411–414
    properties of, 412
  detected by Windows 2000, 411
  finding, 414
  managing remotely from web
    browsers, 13, 31, 414
  pausing, 415
  Plug and Play, detected by
    Windows 2000, 31
  pooling, 412
  print job priority, 413
  Printers utility for, 607
  queues for
    managing jobs in, 420
    net print command for, 660
  redirecting, 415
  searching for, 352, 444

sharing, 415
  taking ownership of, 404
  terminology and, 209, 409
  using offline, 416
  (see also Internet printing; local print
    devices; network print devices)
printers (software interface), 209
  pooling and, 412
Printers virtual directory, 414
printing
  advanced feature for, 413
  cross-platform, 423
  defaults settings for, selecting, 413
  over the Internet (see Internet printing)
  separator pagefiles for, 413
  Windows terminology for, 409
Printing Defaults button, 413
private IP addresses, 246
private networks, 296
privilege use events, 57
process tracking events, 57
profile (remote access settings), 221
promoting domain controllers, 331
properties
  files/folders, 140
  of printers, configuring, 412
protocols
  authentication, 218
  encryption, 219
  LAN, 216
  multilink, 218
  WAN, 217
PTR (Pointer) record, 105
public key policies, 159
  for Local Security Policies, 180
Published option for software
  deployment, 480
publishing software, 160
pushd command, 640
push/pull partner (WINS), 261
puzzle piece icon, 516
  two connecting, 517

## Q

quick start for transitioning from
  Windows NT to
  Windows 2000, 17–35
quota entries, monitoring, 303
quota limits, enforcing, 303

## R

RADIUS protocol, 219
  creating remote-access policies and, 431
  remote-access servers and, 427
RAID-5 volumes, 98, 214
  creating, 310
RAM, pagefile and, 196
RapiDeploy disk imaging software, 171
RAS Context command, 695
RAS servers, 31, 64
  downlevel, managing, 434
  RAS Context command for, 695
  upgrading domain controllers and, 469
  VPN connections and, 475
rcp command, 734
RCPs over IP, 238
rdisk command, 27
RDN (relative distinguished name), 44
RDP (Remote Desktop Protocol), 248
Read & Execute and Write permissions, using instead of Modify permission, 207
Read Attributes permission, 199
Read Data permission, 199
Read Extended Attributes permission, 199
Read-only attribute, 55
Read permission, 199, 204
readme files, 175
reboots, avoiding endless, 426
reconnection settings, 339
records (see resource records)
recover command, 640
Recovery Console, 5, 8, 29, 91, 214
  installing/using, 424
recovery options, specifying, 425
Recovery setting, 233
recursive queries, 114
Recycle Bin, 607
redial attempts (modems), configuring, 292
redirection (see folder redirection)
referrals, 114
Regenerating partition/volume status, 314
Regional Options utility, 608
registry, administrative templates and, 156
registry keys
  dynamic updates, editing for, 490
  schemas and, 441
registry settings, 159

Registry.pol files, 156
reinstalling
  hardware, 365
  printer drivers, 423
relative distinguished name (RDN), 44
relative ID master roles, 126, 330
remote access, 31, 214–223
  enabling/disabling for specific devices, 429
  how it works, 214
  implementing, 215
  policies for (see remote-access policies)
  server-side, implementing, 215
Remote Access Admin tool, 434
remote-access clients
  configuring static IP-address pool for, 428
  connected, 434
remote-access permission, 221
  granting to users, 433
remote-access policies, 221
  creating, 429
  editing, 431
  how they work, 222
remote-access protocols (WAN protocols), 217
Remote Access Server Setup Wizard, 431
remote-access servers, 426–436
  adding, 427
  configuring, 427–429
    removing configuration, 431
  enabling, 428
  monitoring, 434
  RAS Context command for, 695
  Routing and Remote Access Service for, 554
  starting/stopping, 435
remote administration mode (Terminal Services), 464
Remote Authentication Dial-in User Service (see RADIUS protocol)
remote control, domain user accounts and, 338
Remote Desktop Protocol (RDP), 248
remote encryption, 349
Remote Installation Services (see RIS)
remote management
  configuring recovery options and, 426
  disk quotas and, 304
  disks, connecting to, 308
  remote-access clients and, 434
  rexec command for, 735

remote management (*continued*)
  rsh command for, 738
  tracert command for, 742
Removable Storage, 6
removing
  deployed software, 483
  disks, 307
  global catalog from original domain
    controller, 355
  View menu, 505
renaming
  Administrator, benefit of, 69
  Default-First-Site, 457
  domain user accounts, 339
  Folder snap-ins, 506
  groups, 358
repairing
  partitions/volumes, 313
  system with Recovery Console, 425
replaceable variables used in logon
    scripts, 184
replicas/replica sets, 78, 280
  (see also shared folders)
replication
  Dfs, 78, 80
  domain controllers and, 125
  forcing over a connection, 456
  local user accounts and, 182
  multimaster (see multimaster
    replication)
  policy, setting for Dfs, 281
Replication Policy box, 281
replication topology, checking, 454
replication traffic, sites and, 239
Replicator, 61, 63
Require secured password option, 293
rescanning disks, 314
reservations (IP addresses), creating, 283
reserved client-level option (scopes), 287
resolver cache
  flushing, 322
  information in, displaying, 324
resolvers, 114
  automatic update and, 117
resource records, 105
  adding to zones, 486
  dynamic update and, 117
  modifying, 491
    manually on DNS server, 26
resource settings for hardware, 366
resource usage, auditing and, 56

resources
  publishing in Active Directory, 265
  shared (see shared resources)
resources for further reading
  configuring and synchronizing
    time, 673
  DNS, 101
  IIS, 176
  Remote Access Admin, 434
  TCP/IP network protocol, 242
  web sites, configuring on IIS, 476
  Windows 2000 Active Directory, 5
  Windows 2000 Server Resource Kit, 15
restoring, 89, 223
  Active Directory, 265
  disk configuration, 314
  performing, 270
restricted group settings, 158
Resynching partition/volume status, 314
retention settings for event logs, 343
reverse-lookup queries, 111
reverse-lookup zones, 111
  creating, 488
reverting disks, 314
rexec command, 735
rights, 32, 224
  assigning/withholding, 436
  vs. permissions, 224
RIS (Remote Installation Services), 4, 31
  Windows 2000 Server and, 175
roaming user profiles, 224, 257, 438–441
  customizing, 439
  making mandatory, 391
roaming users, folder redirection as
    alternative for, 141
root domains, 103, 112, 122
root hints file, 112
root name, 48
root name servers, 112
root shares, 77
round-robin, 117
route command, 736
router Context command, 699
router interfaces
  enabling/disabling DHCP relay agent
    on, 290
  interface Context command for, 691
routers
  router Context command for, 699
  Routing and Remote Access Service
    for, 554

Routing and Remote Access Service, 6, 554
    enabling, 431–433
routing table, route command for, 736
RRAS servers, 31
rsh command, 738
rules for copying and moving files/folders, 346
Run box, running utilities from, 572
runas command, 641

## S

Safe Mode, 29
    options for, 90
saving
    .csv files/.txt files as event logs, 138
    MMC consoles, 503, 512
    .msc files as consoles, 503
    search results, 445
ScanDisk tool, replaced with Check Disk utility, 311
Scanners and Cameras utility, 609
scanning for hardware changes, 366
scavenging, 326
schedule (site link component), 238
Scheduled Synchronization Wizard, 401
Scheduled Tasks utility, 609
Schema Admins, 65
schema master roles, 126, 330
schema objects, 225
schema partition, 44
schema table, 45
schemas, 49, 224–226, 441
    modifying, 225
scope-level option, 287
scopes, 81, 83
    activating/deactivating, 282
    configuration, double-checking, 284
    converting, 149–153
    creating, 283
    declining activation of, 284
    deleting, lease time and, 286
    of groups, 147, 358
    modifying, 283, 284
    multicast
        creating, 285
        modifying, 285
    options for, 83
        specifying, 287
        user-defined, configuring, 288

reconciling, 286
    superscopes, creating, 285
    types of, 85
scripts, 157
    multiple, order of execution, 157
    settings for, configuring, 360
.sdb file, 385
Search Assistant
    accessing, 445
    searches by administrators, 353
    searches by users, 443
Search function, 443
    (see also Find function)
search results, saving, 445
secedit command, 28
secedit.exe file, 386
second-level domains, 103
second-level name servers, 112
secondary name servers, 106
    forcing to update secondary zone, 489
Securedc.inf template file, 180
Securews.inf template file, 180
security
    account lockout, 40
    Active Directory for (see Active Directory)
    audit policies and (see audit policies)
    auditing and, 56
    configuring on remote-access server, 427
    net command for, 644
    outbound connections and, 293
    Security Configuration and Analysis for, 556
    VPN connections and, 472
Security Configuration and Analysis, 556
security-configuration database, creating, 384
security groups, 63, 146, 227
security identifiers (see SIDs)
Security log, 137
    setting to shut down when full, 344
security model, Windows 2000 Server installation and, 172
security policies, 227
    configuring, 445
    implementing, 228
security principals, 44
security settings, 158
    administrative tools for (list), 493
    Local Security Policy for, 180, 546

security templates
  for Local Security Policies, 180
  applying to computers, 384
  creating, 446
    custom, 385
  importing, 446
Security Templates snap-in, 558
Send To options, 350
sending mail to groups, 358
separator pages/pagefiles, 413
Serial Line Internet Protocol (SLIP protocol), 217
server cache (DNS servers), clearing, 325
server datafiles, updating, 327
Server Image disk-imaging utility, 171
server-level option (scopes), 287
Server Magic disk-imaging software, 171
Server Operators, 63, 228
Server service, net config server command for, 649
Server Settings node (Terminal Services), 463
Service Pack 1 (SP1), 33
Service record (see SRV record)
services, 228–234, 446
  Active Directory Sites and Services for, 518
  dependencies between, 233
  net start command for, 666
  paused/resuming, 447
    net continue command for, 652
    net pause command for, 659
  Server/Workstation
    net config command for, 649
    net statistics command for, 668
  Services tool/snap-in, 559
  settings for, 233
  stopping, 448
    net stop command for, 669
  Windows 2000 Server (list), 229–232
sessions between server and clients, net session command for, 662
Setup Manager Wizard, 3, 373–381
  other uses for, 381
  partitions and, vs. Disk Management, 172
  setup options for installing Windows 2000 Server, 379
  unattended installations and, 30

Setupmgr.exe, 376
  setup options for installing Windows 2000 Server, 379
share names, 234
  folder names and, 451
shared-disk resources, Dfs for managing, 76–80
shared-folder permissions, 11, 31, 203–205, 452
  allowing/denying, 205
  multiple, 205
  setting to Users have Full Control permission, 205
  using, 204
shared folders, 234–236, 449–452
  Active Directory Users and Computers for, 521
  connecting to, 235
  copying/moving, permissions and, 205
  creating, 449–451
  drawbacks of, 15
  hidden, 484
  locating shared resources for, 33
  modifying, 450
  net file command for, 653
  permissions for, 234
  publishing in Active Directory, 265, 451
  searching for, 352
  Shared Folders snap-in for, 560
  sharing, 234
  taking offline, 281
Shared Folders snap-in, 560
shared printers, publishing in Active Directory, 265
shared resources
  net share command for, 664
  net use command for, 673
  net view command for, 677
shares, folder redirection and, 354
sharing
  connections, 298
  Internet connections, 294
  printers, 415
  roaming user profiles, 440
Shiva Password Authentication Protocol (SPAP protocol), 218
shortcut trusts, 253
shutdown scripts, 157
  configuring, 360

shutting down system, 454
SIDs (security identifiers)
  disk imaging and, 170
  domain user accounts, disabling vs.
    deleting, 336
Simple Mail Transfer Protocol (see SMTP)
simple volumes, 97, 237
  creating, 309
single domain model, 123
single-master domain model, 123
single master replication, 126
site-enabled applications, 240
site links, 237, 238, 240
  configuring, 455
  creating, 456
site objects, delegating authority
    over, 277
sites, 42, 52, 237–241
  Active Directory Sites and Services
    for, 518
  boundaries of, 240
  vs. domains, 52, 122, 237
  moving server to different, 457
  planning, 240
  slow WAN links and, 33
  using, 239
  working with, 454–457
slave domains, 124
SLIP protocol, remote access and, 217
Small Office/Home Office (SOHO)
  Internet Connection Sharing for, 294
  NAT routing protocol and, 432
smart cards, security option for, 293
SMP (symmetric multiprocessing), 7
SMTP (Simple Mail Transfer Protocol)
  IIS for, 176
  over IP, 238
  sites and, 457
snap-ins, 492
  Active Directory Schema, 441
  adding/installing, 498–505
    Active Directory and, 505
    options for, 501–503
  alphabetical reference to, 516–571
  included with Windows 2000 Server
    (list), 500
  Local Users and Groups, 383
  names of vs. names of administrative
    tools, 498
  troubleshooting damaged, 505
  types of, 504

SOA (Start of Authority) record, 105
soft quotas, 93
software
  categories, creating/assigning, 481
  deployment of (see software
    deployment)
  failures, recovering from (see disaster
    recovery)
  grouped into categories, 160
  installation, 159
  redeploying, 483
software deployment, 479–484
  file-extension priorities for, 482
  upgrading/removing deployed
    software, 483
Software Installation and Maintenance
    (see Windows Installer)
software modifications, 160
SOHO businesses (see Small Office/Home
    Office)
Sounds and Multimedia utility, 612
SP1 (Service Pack 1), 33
spanned volumes, 97, 241, 310
  creating, 309
SPAP protocol, remote access and, 218
special identities (see built-in system
    groups)
special permissions, 199
spooler service, 413, 423
SRV (Service) record, 105, 106
standalone computers, 179
standalone Dfs, 77, 278
standalone remote-access servers, 216
standalone servers, 173, 241
  direct computer connections on
    configuring, 299
    creating, 301
standalone snap-ins (see snap-ins)
standard primary zones, standard
    secondary zones, 110, 488
standby mode, 242
  entering, 457
standby settings, configuring
    automatically, 457
start command, 643
Start menu, disabling personalization
    of, 16
Start menu folder, folder redirection
    and, 142
Start menu items, right-clicking to access
    Properties, 9

Start of Authority record (SOA record), 105
starting/stopping
   print spooler, 418
   remote-access servers, 435
   services, 448
startup environment for users, setting for, 339
startup options, 458
startup scripts, 157
   configuring, 360
Startup type setting (services), 233
static IP-address pool, configuring for remote-access clients, 428
static mapping (WINS), 261
   creating, 485
Status setting (services), 233
stopping (see starting/stopping)
strategies
   for assigning permissions, 205
   for disk quotas, 93
   for encryption, 131
   (see also planning)
striped volumes, 97, 242
   creating, 310
structure, 41–43
subdomains, 103
   creating, 489
subfolders, deleting
   Full Control to Creator Owner permission and, 207
   permission for, 199
subnet masks, 243
   assigning additional to network connection, 460
subnets, 42, 238, 240
   Active Directory Sites and Services for, 518
   configuring, 455
   creating, 456
success events, 137
superscopes, 85
   creating, 285
symmetric multiprocessing (SMP), 7
Synchronization Manager, 399
Synchronize permission, 199
synchronizing offline files, 400
   Synchronize utility for, 613
Sysprep.exe utility, 170, 377
Sysprep.inf file, 170

system environment variables used in logon scripts, 184
system events, 57, 136
System Information utility, 563, 615
System log, 136
system partition, 242
   deletions and, 310
system policies, 34
System Policy Editor, 5
System Preparation Tool, 4, 170, 377
system rights (see rights)
system services settings, 159
system, shutting down, 454
system-state data, 90
System utility, 614
system variables, 133
system volume, 242
%systemroot%sysvolscripts, 46
Sysvol, 45

T
Take Ownership permission, 196, 199, 404
Task Scheduler, 32
taskbar
   right-clicking to add Address bar, 9
   Taskbar utility for, 616
task-based delegation, 74
taskpad views, 508
   switching to Details Pane, 510
tasks, 508
   importance of date and time synchronization when scheduling, 32
   Scheduled Tasks utility for, 609
   Task Manager utility for, 617
TCP, support for in Windows 2000, 243
TCP/IP commands, 707–744
TCP/IP filtering, 461
TCP/IP network protocol, 189, 242–246
   configuring, 459
      for WINS, 485
   DHCP for, 80–86
   enhancements to included in Windows 2000, 243
   managing, 244
   netstat command for, 724
   ping command for, 732
   remote access and, 217

settings, ipconfig command for, 715
troubleshooting, 244
TCP/IP print server, lpr command
    for, 719
TCP/IP services, enhanced, 6
Telnet
    as alternative to HyperTerminal, 591
    client/server, 16
    telnet command for, 739
Telnet Server Administration tool, 565
terminal servers, 247
    connecting to, 463
    Terminal Services Configuration
        console for, 567
    Terminal Services Manager console
        for, 569
Terminal Services, 6, 246–249
    benefits of, 7, 247
    built-in user accounts and, 66
    clients, memory requirements to run
        operating systems as, 248
    configuring, 462
    how they work, 247
    implementing, 248
    installing, 464
    working with, 462–467
Terminal Services Advanced Client
    (TSAC), 34
Terminal Services CAL, 249
Terminal Services Client, 248
    installing, 465
Terminal Services Client Creator
    console, 462, 465, 567
Terminal Services Configuration
    console, 462, 567
Terminal Services Configuration Manager
    console, 465
Terminal Services Licensing console, 462,
    465, 568
Terminal Services Manager console, 462,
    465, 569
terminal sessions
    establishing, 463
    managing/monitoring, 465
    terminating, 466
testing, Active Directory implementation
    and, 47
tftp command, 742
third-level domains, 103
time (see date and time)
timeout settings, 339

timeout value for scripts, 157
tips for audit policies, 267
toolbar, in console window, 497
tools (see administrative tools; utilities)
top-level domains, 103
top-level name servers, 112
topological structure, 42
tracert command, 742
    pathping command and, 730
tracert utility, 461
transform files, 160
transitive trusts (see trusts)
transport (site link component), 238
Traverse Folder permission, 199
trees, 41, 249
    empty root domains and, 252
    forests and, 142
    using, 250
troubleshooting, 5
    damaged snap-ins, 505
    Dfs roots, creating, 279
    DHCP servers stopped
        unexpectedly, 289
    DNS servers, 327
    hardware, 366
    Improved Troubleshooters for, 5
    TCP/IP, 244
    VPN client connections, 436
    Windows 2000 startup options and, 89
trust relationships (see trusts)
trusts, 27, 34, 253
    Active Directory Domains and Trusts
        for, 517
    creating, 467
    external, 254
        revoking, 468
    shortcut, 253
    transitive, 34, 253
    verifying, 468
TSAC (Terminal Services Advanced
    Client), 34
two-way arrow (↑↓) indicating
    synchronization, 400
two-way external trusts, 254
two-way transitive trusts (see trusts,
    transitive)
.txt files, saving event logs as, 138

**U**

UDF (uniqueness database file), 169
unattend.doc file, 377

unattend.txt file, 376
uninstalling hardware, 366
uniqueness database file (UDF), 169
universal groups, 10, 28, 147, 254
    using, 151
Unix
    cross-printing to Windows 2000, 423
    daemons, 228
Unreadable disk status, 312
Unrecognized disk status, 312
Update Device Driver Wizard, 366
Update Server Data Files option, 327
updating
    disk information, 315
    printer drivers, 413
upgrading
    deployed software, 483
    disks, 98, 315
    domain controllers, 470
        steps preliminary to, 470
    domains, 469
    vs. installing, 255
    Windows NT systems/domains to
        Windows 2000, 254
    Windows NT domain controllers, 127
UPN suffixes
    Active Directory Domains and Trusts
        for, 517
    adding for domains, 329
UPN (user principal name), 44, 183
    creating, 389
URLs
    Citrix MetaFrame, 248
    Codework, 171
    hardware compatibility list for devices
        supported by Windows 2000
        Server, 166
    IIS help files, 177
    Innovative Software, 171
    Microsoft, readme files, 175
    Network Solutions, 103
    PowerQuest, 171
    Symantec, 171
    Terminal Services deployment, 249
    WinINSTALL software, 479
Use smart card option, 293
user accounts, 35, 256
    assigning logon scripts to, 391
    grouped (see groups)

net accounts command for, 646
net user command for, 675
(see also domain user accounts; local
    user accounts)
user configuration settings (GPOs), 154
user data management, 30
user-defined classes, specifying, 287
user-defined scope options,
    configuring, 288
user logon name (see user principal
    name)
User Manager for Domains, 517
user modes (MMC consoles), 510
"User must change password at next
    logon" password option vs.
    "Password never expires"
    option, 406
user principal name (UPN), 44, 183
    creating, 389
user profiles, 257–259
    default, creating/deploying, 275
    how they work, 258
    local, 257
    mandatory, 185, 258, 391
    roaming, 257
    setting for network location of, 338
    types of, 257
    using instead of logon scripts, 184
user settings management (see roaming
    user profiles)
user variables, 133
%username% replaceable variable, home
    folders and, 370
users, 61, 63, 259
    account policies and, 158
    acting as Account Operators, 40
    Active Directory Users and Computers
        for, 521
    administrative templates for managing
        environments of, 155
    Authenticated Users, 58
    authenticating domain controllers
        and, 125
    delegating authority to, 276
        over GPOs, 361
    domain user accounts for, 128
        disabling during absence of, 341
    Domain Users for, 129
    enabling to use COM ports for direct
        computer connections, 301

finger command for, 709
folder redirection and, 354
granting remote-access permission
    to, 433
home folders for (see home folders)
home page of, opening, 339
local user accounts for, 181
Local Users and Groups for, 547
offline files, logging off and, 193
overriding default print settings, 413
Power Users (see Power Users)
rights, configuring for, 436
roaming user profiles for, 438–441
Search function for, 443
searching for, 352
sending console messages to, 32
setting for membership in groups, 338
startup environment, specifying
    for, 339
storing information about, 337
time-out and reconnection settings
    for, 339
user accounts for, 256
user profiles for (see user profiles)
Users and Passwords utility, 618
Users container, groups located in, 67
Users have Full Control permission, 205
utilities
    alphabetical reference to, 572–621
    best order of use for disaster
        recovery, 91
    Check Disk, 311
    Disk Cleanup, 311
    Disk Defragmenter, 312
    Remote Access Admin, 434
    running from command line, 23, 572
    Sysprep.exe, 4, 170, 377
    for testing TCP/IP configuration, 461
    in Windows 2000 vs. Windows NT
        (tables), 17–22
    (see also administrative tools)
Utility Manager, 619

**V**

.vbs files, logon scripts and, 184
vendor-defined classes, specifying, 288
video adapters, multiple-monitor support
    and, 587
View menu, using, 505
viewing (see displaying)

virtual directories, 177
    creating, 476
virtual memory, 196
virtual private networks (see VPNs)
volume mount points, mountvol
    command for, 637
volume sets, 241
volumes, 97, 260
    creating, 309
    deleting, 310
    extending, 310
    formatting, 311
    mirrored, recovering failed, 312
    mounting, 25
    names for, 98
        problem changing, 310
    repairing, 313
    status of
        displaying, 316
        indicators (list), 314
VPN clients, troubleshooting
    connections, 436
VPN connections, 72
    configuring, 472
        TCP/IP for, 459
    connecting with, 473
    creating, 474
    incoming, remote-access servers
        and, 433
    monitoring status of, 474
    working with, 471–475
VPNs (virtual private networks), 4
    remote access and, 220
    remote-access servers and, 429

**W**

WAN connections, 71
WAN links, slow, 518
WAN protocols, remote access and, 217
WAN traffic
    reducing, caching-only name servers
        and, 107
    slow, forwarders and, 116
warning events, 136
warnings for disk quotas, 304
web browsers, managing printers
    remotely from, 13, 31, 414
web content, searching for, 444
web sharing, creating virtual directories
    with, 477

web site (virtual server), 176, 475–478
  configuring, 475
  creating, 477
  IIS permissions for, 478
Whistler, NetBEUI discontinued with, 188
Windows
  operating systems, acceptable share
    names for, 234
  printing terminology and, 409
Windows 2000, 3–16, 243
  benefits of, 7–9
  BIND software and, 108
  cross-printing to Unix, 423
  Defragment Now, bug in, 312
  disaster recovery (see disaster recovery)
  domains, 100
  drawbacks of, 9–16
  installing
    integrated installation, 33
    Recovery Console feature for, 29
  monitors, support for multiple on, 587
  NetBIOS and, 337
  printers (hardware), detected by, 411
  quick start for transitioning from
    Windows NT, 17–35
  starting up, troubleshooting options
    for, 89
  starting via Advanced Startup
    Options, 55
  upgrading systems/domains from
    Windows NT, 254
  utilities in vs. Windows NT
    (tables), 17–22
Windows 2000 Administration Tools, 4
Windows 2000 Advanced Server, 7
Windows 2000 Backup and Recovery
    Tools (see Windows Backup tools)
Windows 2000 CD, running Recovery
    Console from, 425
Windows 2000 clients
  A records and, 490
  dynamic updates and, 490
Windows 2000 Datacenter Server, 7
Windows 2000 domains, vs. DNS
    domains, 100
Windows 2000 Professional, 3–5
  administrative tools for, 499
  benefits of upgrading desktop
    computers to, 35
  clients, updating A records
    automatically, 289

Windows 2000 Server, 5
  installing, 373–381
    automated installation, 375–378
    from CD, 373–375
    over network, 375
    setup options for, 379
  .msc files preconfigured for (list), 511
  optional components, installing, 494
  planning installation of, 168–175
    post-installation issues, 173
  rebuilding, 270
  Resource Kit for, 15
  services (list), 229–232
  snap-ins included with (list), 500
  upgrading to domain controller,
    importance of date and time
    for, 375
Windows 2000 Server Client Access
    License (CAL), 249
Windows 2000 Server license, 249
Windows 2000 Server Resource Kit,
    Chopper.exe utility and, 143
Windows 2000 Terminal Services Client
    Access License, 249
Windows 9x computers, Active Directory
    client software for, 53
Windows Backup tools, 88
  opening, 269
  running backups, 311
  terminology and, 89
Windows CE (Terminal Services
    Client), 248
Windows clustering, 7
Windows Explorer, 619
Windows Installer, 31, 159, 478–484
  software deployment, steps preliminary
    to, 479
  software packages, adding/configuring
    with, 479–483
Windows Internet Name Service (see
    WINS)
Windows NT
  aspects of changed in Windows
    2000, 14
  backward compatibility and, 148
  commands and, 622
  Computer Management tool and, 524
  connections and, 216
  domain controllers, upgrading, 127,
    470

domains
  migrating from, 123, 127
  upgrading, 254, 469
folders, counterparts of in
    Windows 2000 (tables), 19
global groups and, 147
local groups and, 147
nesting groups and, 149
NetBIOS names and, 100, 102
quick start for transitioning to
    Windows 2000, 17–35
rights and, 436
trusts and, 254
upgrading to Windows 2000
    Server, 374
utilities in vs. Windows 2000
    (tables), 17–22
volume sets, 241
Windows NT 4.0 Server, restoring disk
    configuration and, 314
Windows NT Directory Service (NTDS), 5
Windows NT Explorer, location of in
    Windows 2000, 14
Windows Script Host files used as logon
    scripts, 184
Windows Scripting Host (WSH), 623
Windows System Policy Editor, 5
Windows Terminal (Terminal Services
    Client), 248
Windows Update, 620
  updating printer drivers, 413
WinINSTALL software, 479
Winnt folder, maintaining default
    permissions, 202
WINS clients
  configuring, 484
  TCP/IP and, 460
WINS Context command, 704
WINS proxy, 261
  configuring, 484
WINS record, 106
WINS replication, configuring, 484
WINS server
  subcontext, commands available
      in, 704–706
  WINS Context command for, 704
WINS Users (built-in domain local
    group), 64

WINS (Windows Internet Name
    Service), 6, 260
  clients (see WINS clients)
  installing, 485
  WINS console for, 570
Winsock API, 190
WinZip files, compression and, 70
Wireless Link utility, 621
wizards
  Accessibility, 574
  Active Directory Installation (see Active
      Directory Installation Wizard)
  Add New Printer Driver, 423
    installing/updating printer
        drivers, 413
  Add Standard TCP/IP Printer Port, 410
  Configure DNS Server, 112
  Configure Your Server, 173, 526
  Create Partition, 309
  Create Volume, 309
  Delegation of Control, 276
    domains and, 122
  Extend Volume, 310
  Found New Hardware, 411
  Internet Connection, 297, 591
    computers on LAN, configuring for
        Internet connection, 294
  Map Network Drive, 235
  Network Connection, 291
    creating dial-up connection to
        private networks, 296
    VPN connections and, 474
  Network Identification, joining
      computers to domain/
      workgroup, 273
  New Connection, Host direct computer
      connections and, 301
  New Multicast Scope, 285
  New Scope, 284
  New Task, 508
  New Taskpad View, 508
  New Zone, 488
  Offline Files, 400
  Remote Access Server Setup, 431
  Scheduled Synchronization, 401
  Setup Manager (see Setup Manager
      Wizard)
  Update Device Driver, 366

workgroups, 261
  joining computers to, 273
  small, NetBEUI network protocol
    for, 188
Workstation service, net config
  workstation command for, 651
workstations, locking, 388
Write Attributes permission, 199
Write Data permission, 199
Write Extended Attributes
  permission, 199
WSH (Windows Scripting Host), 623

## Z

.zap files (Zero Administration for
  Windows files), deploying, 482
.zip files, compression and, 70

zone administrator, updating email
  address of, 491
zone files, 109, 111
  default root-zone files, 113
  vs. zones, 112
zone transfers, 113
  configuring, 486
  forcing, 489
zones, 109–112
  converting from one type to
    another, 487
  creating, 487–489
  types of, 488
    displaying, 489
  vs. zone files, 112
  working with, 485–491

# About the Author

Mitch Tulloch is an independent trainer, consultant, and author living in Winnipeg, Canada. He is a Microsoft Certified Trainer (MCT) and Microsoft Certified Systems Engineer (MCSE) with almost 20 years of experience in teaching scientific and technical subjects. Mitch has written a number of books on computer networking and Microsoft BackOffice products and has also written various magazine articles. He is the Windows 2000/NT section lead on *www.swynk.com*, a web site for system administrators who work with BackOffice products.

# Colophon

Our look is the result of reader comments, our own experimentation, and feedback from distribution channels. Distinctive covers complement our distinctive approach to technical topics, breathing personality and life into potentially dry subjects.

The animal on the cover of *Windows 2000 Administration in a Nutshell* is a Guiana crested eagle (*Morphnus guianensis*). This large, slender bird is 31 to 35 inches in length and has broad, rounded wings and a long, black tail marked with 3 wide, gray bands. The plumage of the adult includes a gray-black head, gray neck, brown-gray throat and breast, brown-black mantle, and white-tipped wings, back, and tail. Features also include gray or yellow eyes, black markings around the eyes, black beak, and yellow, featherless legs.

The Guiana crested eagle inhabits the lowland tropical forests of Central and South America—usually well away from human settlement. Ornithologists know little about the behavior of this eagle. It is found in the warmest, most humid parts of the jungle, and it tends to stay near the coastline or river edges. It can be spotted during its frequent soaring, though it is usually only visible when it passes over rivers or other breaks in the forest canopy. While perching atop the highest trees, it will stay nearly motionless for hours at a time, only occasionally moving its head. Like its close relative the Harpy eagle (*Harpia harpyja*), the Guiana crested eagle is large enough to feed on live prey such as smaller birds, opossums, and reptiles. The Harpy eagle, though, is still larger and stronger, feeding on monkeys, sloths, and other arboreal and terrestrial mammals. Eagles of this size are too large to kill prey in the air; so they surprise their prey on the ground, often decapitating their victims.

The most noticeable feature of the Guiana crested eagle is the projecting occipital crest on its head. Unlike the Harpy eagle, which has a bifurcated or double crest, the Guiana crested eagle has a single, undivided crest. The crest consists of feathers uniquely colored with a white base, black center, and white tip. As with other birds' display behaviors, the crest—which can be raised and lowered—is thought to be used as a form of communication. Birds often communicate with vocal or visual displays, including colored plumage during breeding season or elaborate movement routines designed to attract potential mates. With birds such as the Guiana crested eagle, however, behavioral displays usually communicate greeting, threat, submission, or distraction. The crest's graded or variable display (it does not have to be completely raised or lowered, but can be somewhere in between) conveys the intensity of the eagle's impending actions. Even though the display of the occipital crest may be difficult to decipher for those studying this bird, the signals it communicates are likely to be unambiguous to others of its species.

Jeffrey Holcomb was the production editor and copyeditor for *Windows 2000 Administration in a Nutshell*. Rachel Wheeler, Madeleine Newell, Claire Cloutier, and Mary Sheehan provided quality control. Gabe Weiss, Deborah Smith, Matt Hutchinson, Mary Sheehan, Linley Dolby, and Molly Shangraw provided production support. Brenda Miller wrote the index.

Ellie Volckhausen designed the cover of this book, based on a series design by Edie Freedman. The cover image is a 19th-century engraving from the Dover Pictorial Archive. Emma Colby produced the cover layout with QuarkXPress 4.1, using Adobe's ITC Garamond font.

Melanie Wang designed the interior layout based on a series design by Nancy Priest. Mike Sierra implemented the design in FrameMaker 5.5.6. The text and heading fonts are ITC Garamond Light and Garamond Book. The illustrations that appear in the book were produced by Robert Romano using Macromedia FreeHand 8 and Adobe Photoshop 5. This colophon was written by Jeffrey Holcomb.

Whenever possible, our books use a durable and flexible lay-flat binding. If the page count exceeds this binding's limit, perfect binding is used.

# Other Titles Available from O'Reilly

## Microsoft Windows

### Windows XP in a Nutshell

*By David A. Karp, Tim O'Reilly &*
*Troy Mott*
*1st Edition April 2002*
*640 pages, ISBN 0-596-00249-1*

Here is a book for the power user
who is familiar with a previous
version of Microsoft Windows
and wants to go deeper into the
system than the average Windows user does. Rather
than a beginner's guide or tutorial, this straightforward reference delivers more than 500 pages of
concentrated information. For those who are ready
to customize the system or take on daily troubleshooting, *Windows XP in a Nutshell* will unlock
the hidden power of Windows XP.

### Windows XP Annoyances

*By David A. Karp*
*1st Edition October 2002*
*586 pages, ISBN 0-596-00416-8*

This book is not here to complain or to criticize. Rather, the
mission of *Windows XP Annoyances* is to acknowledge the problems and shortcomings of the
latest Windows operating system-and the software
that runs on it-in an effort to overcome them.
Complete with a collection of tools and tech-
niques, this book allows users to improve their
experience with Windows XP and establish control
of the machine-rather than the other way around.

### Windows XP The Home Edition: The Missing Manual

*By David Pogue*
*1st Edition May 2002*
*584 pages, ISBN 0-596-00260-2*

Our latest from the Missing
Manual series begins with a tour
of the Desktop and the new two-
column Start menu, and tips for customizing the
Taskbar and toolbars. Later chapters explore each
control panel and built-in application, walk
through every conceivable configuration, and
show how to set up a small network and share a
single Internet connection among several PCs.
Finally, special chapters celebrate the standard rit-
uals of Windows life: troubleshooting, installation,
and upgrading.

### Windows XP Pro: The Missing Manual

*By Craig Zacker, Linda Zacker &*
*David Pogue*
*1st Edition January 2003*
*672 pages, ISBN 0-596-00348-X*

Windows XP is the latest, most
reliable, and best-looking version
of the world's most widely used
operating system, combining the extremely stable
engine of Windows 2000 with the far superior
compatibility of Windows Me. But one major fail-
ing of Windows remains unaddressed in the XP
edition: It comes without a single page of printed
instructions.

### Windows Me: The Missing Manual

*By David Pogue*
*1st Edition September 2000*
*423 pages, ISBN 0-596-00009-X*

In *Windows Me: The Missing
Manual*, author David Pogue
provides the friendly, authoritative book that should have been
in the box. It's the ideal user's guide for the world's
most popular operating system.

### Windows Me Annoyances

*By David A. Karp*
*1st Edition March 2001*
*472 pages, ISBN 0-596-00060-X*

Based on the author's popular
Annoyances.org web sites, *Windows Me Annoyances* is an
authoritative collection of tech-
niques for customizing Windows Me. Packed with
creative and seldom-documented ways to quickly
identify and fix a particular annoyance or customize Windows for individual needs, it's the
definitive resource for dealing with crashes, unin-
telligible error messages, unwanted icons, and
much more.

# How to stay in touch with O'Reilly

## 1. Visit our award-winning web site

*http://www.oreilly.com/*

★ "Top 100 Sites on the Web"—PC Magazine
★ CIO Magazine's Web Business 50 Awards

Our web site contains a library of comprehensive product information (including book excerpts and tables of contents), downloadable software, background articles, interviews with technology leaders, links to relevant sites, book cover art, and more. File us in your bookmarks or favorites!

## 2. Join our email mailing lists

Sign up to get email announcements of new books and conferences, special offers, and O'Reilly Network technology newsletters at:

*http://elists.oreilly.com*

It's easy to customize your free elists subscription so you'll get exactly the O'Reilly news you want.

## 3. Get examples from our books

To find example files for a book, go to:

*http://www.oreilly.com/catalog*

select the book, and follow the "Examples" link.

## 4. Work with us

Check out our web site for current employment opportunites:

*http://jobs.oreilly.com/*

## 5. Register your book

Register your book at:

*http://register.oreilly.com*

## 6. Contact us

**O'Reilly & Associates, Inc.**
1005 Gravenstein Hwy North
Sebastopol, CA 95472 USA
TEL: 707-827-7000 or 800-998-9938
        (6am to 5pm PST)
FAX: 707-829-0104

**order@oreilly.com**
For answers to problems regarding your order or our products. To place a book order online visit:

*http://www.oreilly.com/order_new/*

**catalog@oreilly.com**
To request a copy of our latest catalog.

**booktech@oreilly.com**
For book content technical questions or corrections.

**corporate@oreilly.com**
For educational, library, government, and corporate sales.

**proposals@oreilly.com**
To submit new book proposals to our editors and product managers.

**international@oreilly.com**
For information about our international distributors or translation queries. For a list of our distributors outside of North America check out:

*http://international.oreilly.com/distributors.html*

**adoption@oreilly.com**
For information about academic use of O'Reilly books, visit:

*http://academic.oreilly.com*

# O'REILLY®

To order: 800-998-9938 • *order@oreilly.com* • *www.oreilly.com*
Online editions of most O'Reilly titles are available by subscription at *safari.oreilly.com*
Also available at most retail and online bookstores.